BARRON'S

HOW TO PREPARE FOR THE

CALIFORNIA REAL ESTATE LICENSING EXAMINATIONS

SALESPERSON, BROKER, APPRAISER

2ND EDITION

J. Bruce Lindeman, Ph.D.
Professor of Real Estate
University of Arkansas
at Little Rock

Jack P. Friedman, Ph.D., CPA, MAI
Author and Real Estate Economist, Dallas, Texas
Former Laguarta Professor of Real Estate
Department of Finance/Real Estate Research Center
Texas A&M University

BARRON'S

All inquiries should be addressed to:
Barron's Educational Series, Inc.
250 Wireless Boulevard
Hauppauge, New York 11788
http://www.barronseduc.com

ISBN-13: 978-0-7641-3124-0
ISBN-10: 0-7641-3124-9

Library of Congress Catalog Card No. 2005048087

Library of Congress Cataloging-in-Publication Data
Lindeman, J. Bruce (John Bruce)
    How to prepare for the California real estate licensing examinations :
salesperson, broker, appraiser / J. Bruce Lindeman, Jack P. Friedman. — 2nd ed.
        p.   cm.
    Rev. ed.: How to prepare for California real estate examinations. c1995.
    Includes index.
    ISBN-13: 978-0-7641-3124-0
    ISBN-10: 0-7641-3124-9
    1. Real property—California. 2. Real estate business—Law and legislation—
California. 3. Real estate business—Licenses—California. I. Friedman, Jack P.
II. Lindeman, J. Bruce (John Bruce) How to prepare for California real estate
examinations. III. Title.

KFC140.Z9L56   2005
346.79404'3'076—dc22   2005048087

PRINTED IN THE UNITED STATES OF AMERICA

9

**10%
POST-CONSUMER
WASTE**
Paper contains a minimum
of 10% post-consumer
waste (PCW). Paper used
in this book was derived
from certified, sustainable
forestlands.

CONTENTS

Figures

Tables

PREFACE

In recent years, legal, social, economic, and financial matters affecting real estate have become more complex, creating greater educational needs for those who are engaged in the real estate business. In California today, a salesperson, broker, or appraiser cannot survive solely on a pleasant disposition and a neat appearance. Real estate workers must be aware of and obey federal, state, and local regulations. They need in-depth knowledge of each property being brokered, including its physical surroundings and its economic, legal, social, and political environment.

Since 1992, California law has required that real estate appraisers be state certified. Appraisers (both experienced workers and new entrants) now must take qualifying examinations that can lead to three levels: licensed, certified residential, and certified general. Therefore, we have included two appraisal chapters in this book, as well as some 500 study questions and three model appraisal examinations. The appraisal section of the book can serve the needs of those desiring preparation for appraiser certification or licensing as well as those who seek sales or broker licenses.

This book was written as an introduction to real estate, taking into consideration real estate complexities and the need for more knowledge among those seeking to meet licensure requirements. It also can satisfy the needs of persons wanting to know more about real property law, contracts, finance, brokerage, ethics, leasing, appraisal, mathematics, fair housing, truth in lending, and other such topics. For the person just wanting to buy or sell a home, the glossary may serve as a reference for greater understanding of the transaction. It alone can prevent misunderstandings that are costly in terms of time and money.

A careful reading of any document is crucial to understanding it. Many people have unfortunately lost money by failing to read and understand contracts before signing them. Similarly, a careful reading of this book will be helpful toward understanding the complex subject—real estate—that it concerns. Questions have been included at the end of each chapter and comprehensive exams at the end of the book so that you can test your understanding of the material presented, both chapter by chapter and at the end. Though your instructor can be of valuable assistance, the knowledge that you gain will approximate the effort that you expend.

Should you become actively engaged in the real estate business, we wish you success. We hope that all your dealings will be honest and fair. Only in this way can the real estate business become recognized as a profession.

We wish to thank the California Association of REALTORS® for their kind permission to reproduce throughout this book several of the forms they publish. Please note that their permission does not imply any endorsement by CAR.

We are grateful to the many people who have aided us in preparing this book, including Suzanne Barnhill, Anna Damaskos, Sara Black, and Max Reed. We thank our families for their patience and dedicate this book to them.

J. Bruce Lindeman
Jack P. Friedman

PART I: INTRODUCTION TO REAL ESTATE

Chapter 1/*How to Use This Book*

If you are reading this book, you are probably interested in employment in the real estate field. Real estate is a fast-growing, exciting field that offers almost unlimited income potential to a person who is willing to work hard and to learn the special features of this very interesting business.

If you want to enter the real estate business as a salesperson, broker, or appraiser, then, among other requirements, you will have to take and pass an examination. Potential real estate salespeople and real estate brokers take *licensing* examinations in order to get sales or brokerage licenses. A person whose ambition is real estate appraisal takes a *licensing* or a *certification* examination. In either case, taking the exam is only one step (you also need educational preparation, for example), but it is a very important one. This book is designed to help you to succeed in taking that important step. To fulfill this purpose, the book has a number of important features that enhance its usefulness to you:

1. This book can be used to study for any licensing or certification examination offered in the real estate field by California.
2. Special emphasis is given to the topics that license applicants find most troublesome on examinations:
   a. Arithmetic and real estate math
   b. Contracts
   c. Closing statements (for broker applicants)
3. Hundreds of sample questions are included at the ends of chapters, covering all the materials discussed.
4. There are *seven* complete model examinations for you to practice on: three for the salesperson exam, one broker's exam, and one each of the three appraiser exams.
5. A full and complete glossary is included, along with instructions as to the best study strategy for getting the most out of it.
6. Chapter 24, the final chapter before the model tests, describes the *strategy* and *techniques* of taking examinations so that you can be sure to get every point possible.

TOPICS

This book is divided into 23 chapters of text, the sample examinations (Chapter 24), and a final chapter of answers and explanations. Each chapter covers a specific topic. Some are long, others short. Remember that the material in most of the chapters complements the material in the others. This is especially true in Part III, "Real Estate Contracts." The first chapter of Part III (Chapter 6, "Introduction to Contracts") is a long one; it discusses all the things you should know that apply to all of the separate contracts you need to know about. Each of the other chapters in Part III is devoted to one or more types or parts of real estate contracts. For each of these chapters, all the general material in Chapter 6 applies to what you are learning. Chapter 7 discusses land description. Chapters 8 through 12 point out the specific characteristics of each type of real estate contract; these characteristics are in addition to all those mentioned in Chapter 6. Chapters 14 and 15 cover appraisal. No matter what exam you're studying for, you should study Chapter 14, but if you aren't preparing for the general appraisal certification exam, you can skip Chapter 15.

SAMPLE QUESTIONS AND EXAMINATIONS

Most chapters are followed by sample questions covering the material contained in the chapter and written in the format most frequently encountered on licensing examinations. You can use these questions to test yourself on what you have read.

When you have finished studying the material in the book, you can take the model examinations that follow Chapter 24. These will allow you to check your retention of the material you have read and will give you some experience in taking real estate examinations in a format similar to the licensing examination. The model examinations have time limits as indicated.

You should not take all the examinations at once. Rather, take one, and then correct it, using the key in Chapter 26. The questions you got wrong will pinpoint the areas in which you need further study. Do this additional studying, and then take the second examination. Once again, use the questions you missed to guide you to still further study. For questions involving mathematics, the answer explanations in Chapter 26 should help you to understand why you missed each question you got wrong and to avoid making the same mistake again. Then take the third examination, once again using the few questions you miss as guides for final study before taking the licensing examination itself.

If you are applying for a broker's license, you will also find the supplemental examinations on closing statements (settlement statements) and on contracts helpful. Because California uses the rectangular survey, there is also an applicable practice exam.

TAKING EXAMINATIONS

Chapter 23 has been specially prepared to give you all the knowledge available concerning the *techniques* of taking examinations. This chapter will tell you all you must know about how to prepare for an examination, how to approach it, and how to get the highest score possible. *Be sure to read Chapter 23!* It provides valuable guidelines for taking the licensing examination and will introduce you to the kind of examination you can expect to encounter.

The salesperson's examination is given at the Department of Real Estate (DRE) locations listed below. It is 3 hours and 15 minutes long and has 150 multiple-choice questions. A passing grade is 70 percent (105 correct answers minimum).

The broker's exam is given at the same DRE locations. It has 200 questions and a passing grade is 75 percent (150 correct answers minimum). The exam takes five hours: 100 questions in a 2½-hour morning session and, after an hour for lunch, 100 more questions in a 2½-hour afternoon session.

All of the appraisal exams are 100 questions, with a 3-hour time limit. They are given at various locations around the state; contact the Office of Real Estate Appraisers (address and phone below) for dates and locations.

STUDY STRATEGY

You should approach your study of the materials you must know in a systematic and sensible way in order to get the most out of it. The following study strategy will be helpful:

1. Get information about the examination you want to take. The California Department of Real Estate will send you information about salesperson and broker's licenses. The Office of Real Estate Appraisers will send you information about appraiser licensing and certification. These are listed below:

For Sales and Broker Licenses:

Sacramento—Principal Office
2201 Broadway
Sacramento, CA 95818-2500
916-227-0931 TDD 916-227-0929
Licensing information:
Broker qualifications: 916-227-0899
Exam scheduling: 916-227-0900
www.dre.ca.gov

Oakland
> *1515 Clay Street, Suite 702*
> *Oakland, CA 94612-1462*
> *510-622-2522*

Los Angeles
> *320 West 4th Street, Suite 350*
> *Los Angeles, CA 90013-1105*
> *213-620-2072*

San Diego
> *1350 Front Street, Suite 3064*
> *San Diego, CA 92101-3687*
> *619-525-4192*

Fresno
> *2250 Mariposa Mall, Room 3070*
> *Fresno, CA 93721-2273*
> *209-445-5009*

For Appraisal Certification:

> *Office of Real Estate Appraisers*
> *1102 Q Street, Suite 4100*
> *Sacramento, CA 95814*
> *916-552-9000*
> *www.orea.ca.gov*

You can call or write to any of these offices (or use the DRE Web site) to get the information. They will send you a packet which briefly describes the examination you want to take, and an application form for the exam.

2. Have you had the required education? All of these examinations require that you have a certain amount of real estate education before you can take the examination. You will be sent a list of approved schools which offer the courses you need.

(a) *Salespeople* must have a total of *three* 3 semester-hour or 4 quarter-hour college-level courses (total of 9 semester-hours or 12 quarter-hours). One of these courses must be in *Real Estate Principles;* the other two may be of your choice from any of the following:

> *Real Estate Practice*
> *Legal Aspects of Real Estate*
> *Real Estate Appraisal*
> *Property Management*
> *Real Estate Finance*
> *Real Estate Economics*
> *Real Estate Office Administration*
> *Accounting*
> *Business Law*
> *Escrows*
> *Mortgage Loan Brokering and Lending*

Salespeople only need complete the Real Estate Principles course *before* taking the examination. However, any successful salesperson examinee who hasn't completed all three of the required courses when first licensed will receive an 18-month *conditional license.* The full education requirement must be completed within this 18-month period or the license will be suspended; if the education isn't completed within four years of initial licensing, the license cannot be renewed.

(b) *Brokers* must complete a total of *eight* college-level courses (24 semester-hours or 32 quarter-hours) *before* taking the examination.

All of the following courses are required:

Real Estate Practice
Legal Aspects of Real Estate
Real Estate Appraisal
Real Estate Finance
Real Estate Economics or Accounting

Any three of the following courses are acceptable electives for completing the eight-course requirement. (If the applicant took both *Real Estate Economics* and *Business Accounting*, only two of the following are required):

Real Estate Principles
Property Management
Real Estate Office Administration
Business Law
Escrows
Mortgage Loan Brokering and Lending
Advanced Legal Aspects of Real Estate
Advanced Real Estate Finance
Advanced Real Estate Appraisal

(c) *Appraisers:* for the residential appraisal license, 90 classroom hours in approved appraisal-related topics; for general appraiser certification, 180 classroom hours; for residential certification, 120 classroom hours.

Applicants for the appraisal license only may receive a *provisional license*, good for two years, if they have not met either education or experience requirements. The missing education and/or experience must be completed during the two-year provisional licensing period. Provisional status cannot be renewed.

3. Have you had the required experience?

(a) Salesperson: no experience required.

(b) Broker: at least two years' full-time licensed salesperson experience (or equivalent) within the last five years.

(c) Appraiser: (As a matter of reference, 2,000 hours of work is generally considered to be the equivalent of one year of full-time work experience.)

For *residential licensed appraiser*, 2,000 hours of acceptable appraisal experience. For certified residential real estate appraiser, 2,500 hours of appraisal experience, of which at least 1,000 hours must be in major residential appraisal work. For certified general real estate appraiser, 3,000 hours of appraisal work, with at least 1,500 hours of nonresidential appraisal work.

4. Get any state study materials that are offered for your exam. For example, we strongly urge salesperson and broker applicants to get *Real Estate Law* ($25 plus tax) from the California Department of Real Estate. (An order form will be in the materials you receive with your examination application, and you also can buy one at any of the DRE offices listed above.) This book contains the entire California Real Estate License Law, as well as other law relevant to sales and brokerage licensees. It is very long, and very dry to read, but you can expect a fair amount of the exam will come out of it. We hit the important points of it in Chapter 5, but it won't hurt to look over the whole thing.

Download *Instructions to License Applicants.* This 60-page pamphlet offers information on:

(a) Eligibility requirements to become licensed

(b) Forms and fees for applications and renewals

(c) DRE office and examination locations, exam scheduling and rescheduling

(d) Exam content list

(e) Other information

You also can download most of *Real Estate Law* from the DRE Web site (http://www.dre.ca.gov). On the DRE home page, click "Real Estate Law" on the tab at the left of the window. This links you to a page that has the downloads available as PDF

(Portable Document Format) files, which can be read with Adobe Reader (if you don't have Adobe Reader, it is a free download from http://www.adobe.com/products/acrobat/readstep2.html). If you don't live near a DRE office, you also can download an order form for *Real Estate Law*.

5. Now begin studying. Start with Chapter 2 in this book, "Definitions of Real Estate Terms." Read it carefully, making sure you take note of all the terms. Don't try to understand them all at this point; just become slightly familiar with them.

6. Proceed through the chapters in the order they appear in the book.

7. When you have read through Chapter 24 and have answered all the questions at the end of each chapter, take the sample examinations in your field of interest. Note your weak areas, to be concentrated upon in later study.

Now you should be ready to take, and PASS, your chosen real estate examination. Be sure to schedule your studying so that you finish up only a day or two before the actual examination; in this way, all the material you have learned will be fresh in your mind.

Chapter 2/*Definitions of Real Estate Terms*

On the following pages is a glossary of real estate terminology. It is quite extensive and probably covers all the terms you might be expected to be familiar with when you take a licensing examination. We suggest that you begin your preparation for the examination by carefully reading over this glossary. This may seem a boring and tedious thing to do, but it will have many advantages. The main benefit is that it will acquaint you with some important terminology used in the real estate business. Once you have studied these terms, the remaining material in this book will be much easier for you to absorb; you will already have some familiarity with most of what you read. In fact, the purpose of the rest of the book is to show you how all the many items defined in the glossary relate to one another in the real estate business.

The best way to study the glossary is to go over it once fairly quickly. Don't skip anything, but don't study it intensely, either. A while later, begin to go over the terms much more carefully, absorbing each definition as it is given. Make sure not to skip over anything: many real estate terms may look familiar because they are composed of familiar words. More likely than not, however, you will find that the *real estate meaning* is *not* the one you are used to. This is one of the more serious problems that many people have with the real estate licensing examinations: you must learn *terminology* and be able to understand and use the special meanings that many words have in a real estate context.

Once you have spent a good amount of time on the terminology, go on through the rest of the book, using the glossary for reference whenever you need to. Later, as the time for the examination approaches, you will find it very helpful to go over the glossary again. It will be a sort of thumbnail review for you to read the terms once again, after you have studied the rest of the book. This will be of considerable help in your final preparation for the examination, especially since you will often encounter strictly definitional questions such as "The term *fee simple* means most nearly——."

Note that italic type within a definition calls attention to important terms that are defined elsewhere as separate entries. Small caps also denote cross references.

Glossary

AAA TENANT / *See* TRIPLE-A TENANT.

ABSTRACT OF TITLE / A summary of all of the recorded instruments and proceedings that affect the title to property.

Importance: A person going to buy real estate or lend money on it wants assurance of ownership. Usually an attorney or title insurance company prepares an abstract of title, based on documents in the county courthouse, to be certain of ownership; and only if title is good or marketable does that person buy or make the loan. Typically, *title insurance* is also acquired.

ABUTTING / Adjoining or meeting. *See also* ADJACENT.

ACCELERATED DEPRECIATION / Depreciation methods, chosen for income tax or accounting purposes, that offer greater deductions in the early years. The straight-line method, rather than accelerated depreciation, generally applies to buildings bought after 1986.

ACCELERATION CLAUSE / A provision in a loan giving the lender the right to declare the entire amount immediately due and payable upon the violation of a different loan provision, such as failure to make payments on time.

Importance: Without an acceleration clause, a missed payment is just that—one overdue payment.

The acceleration clause means the entire loan is due, and the real estate may be foreclosed on.

ACCEPTANCE / The act of agreeing to accept an offer.

Importance: To have a valid contract there must be an offer and an acceptance. The acceptance may be from either party to the other: for example, buyer/seller; landlord/tenant.

ACCESSION / Man-made or natural addition to or improvement of real estate.

ACCESS RIGHT / The right of an owner to get to and from his/her property.

Importance: Property may be or may become encircled by other property. The access right gives an easement by necessity, which allows the owner of landlocked property to cross over adjacent property to reach a street.

ACCRETION / Addition to or improvement of real estate by natural means.

Example: Tides or river flows add land at the shore, *see* ALLUVIUM.

ACRE / A measure of land: 43,560 square feet.

ACTION TO QUIET TITLE / *See* QUIET TITLE SUIT.

ACTUAL EVICTION / Expulsion of a tenant from the property.

ADA / Americans with Disabilities Act.

ADJACENT / Lying near but not necessarily in actual contact with.

Importance: When describing the physical proximity of property, the word includes touching property and other nearby parcels, for example, property across the street.

ADJOINING / Contiguous; attaching; in actual contact with.

Importance: In describing the proximity of land, adjoining property is actually touching.

ADJUSTABLE-RATE MORTGAGE (ARM) / A mortgage loan with an interest rate that is allowed to vary during the life of the loan; usually there are *caps* on the amounts by which the interest rate can change annually and over the life of the loan.

Importance: ARMs are often a viable alternative to fixed rate mortgages, and are especially desirable to the borrower who expects that rates will decline. Often the initial rate is lower than that on a fixed-rate mortgage, and there are caps on the ceiling rate that can be charged if interest rates rise.

ADMINISTRATOR / A person appointed by a court to administer the estate of a deceased individual who left no will.

Importance: If a person dies leaving a will, an executor is usually named to carry out the provisions of the will. When there is no *executor*, an administrator is appointed by the court. The administrator receives a fee.

ADMINISTRATOR'S DEED / A deed conveying the property of a person who died without a will (intestate).

Importance: If a person owned real estate and died without leaving a will, the administrator will give a deed. However, the administrator does not want the potential liability associated with a general warranty deed, so an administrator's deed is used.

ADULT / A person who has attained the age of majority.

Importance: In California, a person who is 18 years of age is considered an adult. Also, some persons who are married or are in military service may be considered adults though not yet 18. A contract with a minor can be *disaffirmed* by the minor or by that person shortly after he/she becomes an adult.

AD VALOREM / According to valuation.

Importance: Used in describing a property tax rate. *See also* AD VALOREM TAX.

AD VALOREM TAX / A tax based on the value of the thing being taxed. **Example:** If the effective tax rate is 1 percent, the tax will be $1 per $100 of property value.

Importance: In California, several taxing jurisdictions levy ad valorem taxes. Tax districts include the city, county, and school district.

ADVERSE POSSESSION / A means of acquiring title to real estate when an occupant has been in actual, open, notorious, exclusive, and continuous occupancy of the property for a minimum of five years in California.

Importance: A person can gain title to real estate (or lose title) by acting in a certain way for long enough. In California this process may take 5 or more years, depending on the circumstances.

AFFIDAVIT / A statement or declaration in writing, sworn to or affirmed before some officer who is authorized to administer an oath or affirmation.

Importance: Some statements must be in the form of an affidavit before they can be recorded. For example, a contractor's lien must be in affidavit form to be perfected.

AFFIRM / To confirm; to ratify; to verify.

AGENCY / The legal relationship between a principal and his/her *agent* arising from a contract in which the principal employs the agent to perform certain acts on the principal's behalf.

Importance: The law of agency governs the rights and obligations of a broker to the principal and of a licensed real estate salesperson to the broker.

AGENCY DISCLOSURE / A written explanation, to be signed by a prospective buyer or seller of real estate, explaining to the client the role that the broker plays in the transaction. The purpose of disclosure is to explain whether the broker represents the buyer or seller or is a dual agent (representing both) or a subagent (an agent of the seller's broker). This allows the customer to understand to which party the broker owes loyalty.

AGENT / A person who undertakes to transact some business or to manage some affair for another, with the authority of the latter. **Example:** An owner employs a broker to act as his agent in selling real property; the broker in turn employs salespersons to act as her agents to sell the same property.

Importance: An agent has certain duties to the principal, including loyalty. The agent is to act in the best interest of the principal, even when such action is not in the agent's best interest.

AIR RIGHTS / The right to use, control, or occupy the space above a designated property. **Example:** The MetLife building in New York City is built on air rights above the Grand Central Railroad Station.

Importance: Most property ownership rights include air rights up to the skies; however, air rights may be limited to a certain height, or, conversely, air rights may be the only property owned, having a floor that begins a stated number of feet above the ground.

ALIENATION / Transferring property to another, as the transfer of property and possession of lands, by gift or by sale, from one person to another.

Importance: In California, property may be transferred by voluntary alienation, as in a sale for cash, or involuntarily, as in a condemnation.

ALL-INCLUSIVE DEED OF TRUST / A second mortgage that includes an underlying first mortgage in its principal balance.

Importance: This may be a way for a lender to gain a high interest rate on a second mortgage, while possibly circumventing certain regulations that apply to second mortgages.

ALLUVIUM (ALLUVION) / Soil deposited by accretion; usually considered to belong to the owner of the land to which it is added.

AMENITIES / In appraising, the nonmonetary benefits derived from property ownership. **Examples:** pride of home ownership; accessibility to good public schools, parks, and cultural facilities.

Importance: Ownership of real estate may add to one's self-esteem and community involvement.

AMORTIZATION / A gradual paying off of a debt by periodic installments.

Importance: Most mortgages require the payment of interest plus at least some amortization of principal, so that the loan is eventually retired by the amortization payments.

AMORTIZATION TERM / The time required to retire a debt through periodic payments; also known as the *full amortization term*. Many mortgage loans have an amortization term of 15, 20, 25, or 30 years. Some have an amortization schedule as a 30-year loan, but require a *balloon payment* in 5, 10, or 15 years.

Importance: Both the lender and the borrower are assured that the loan will be retired through regular payments without the need to refinance.

ANCHOR TENANT / The main tenant in a shopping center, usually a department store in a regional shopping center or a grocery store in a neighborhood shopping center. Large shopping centers may have more than one anchor tenant. The anchor tenant attracts both customers and other tenants.

ANNUAL PERCENTAGE RATE (APR) / The cost of credit, expressed as an annual interest rate, which must be shown in consumer loan documents, as specified by the Federal Reserve's *Regulation Z*, which implements the Federal Truth In Lending Act.

ANNUITY / A series of equal or nearly equal periodic payments or receipts. **Example:** The receipt of $100 per year for the next five years constitutes a $100 five-year annuity.

ANTICIPATION, PRINCIPLE OF / In real estate appraisal, the principle that the value of a property today is the present value of the sum of anticipated future benefits.

Importance: The anticipation principle serves as the basis for the *income approach* to appraisal.

ANTITRUST LAWS / Federal and state acts to protect trade and commerce from monopolies and restrictions.

APPORTIONMENT / (1) *Prorating* property expenses, such as taxes and insurance, between buyer and seller. (2) The partitioning of property into individual parcels by tenants in common.

APPRAISAL / An opinion or estimate of the value of a property.

Importance: If a buyer is unfamiliar with the value of real estate in an area, it is prudent to require that, as a condition of the agreement of sale, the property be appraised for an amount at least equal to the price being paid. Also, lenders require an appraisal of property as a requirement for making a loan. The borrower will pay the appraisal fee.

APPRAISAL APPROACH / One of three methods used in estimating the value of property: *income* *approach, sales comparison approach,* and *cost approach.* See each.

Importance: Having three separate methods to estimate the value of property will add confidence to an appraiser's value estimate. However, not all approaches are applicable for all properties.

APPRAISAL BY SUMMATION / *See* COST APPROACH.

APPRAISAL DATE / In an *appraisal report,* the date to which the value applies; distinguished from *report date.*

Importance: Because market conditions change, the appraisal date establishes the conditions for which the value is estimated.

APPRAISAL FOUNDATION / An organization that came into existence in 1987 in an effort to encourage uniform requirements for appraisal qualifications and reporting standards. *See also* UNIFORM STANDARDS OF PROFESSIONAL APPRAISAL PRACTICE.

APPRAISAL INSTITUTE / An organization of professional appraisers that was formed in 1991 by the merger of the American Institute of Real Estate Appraisers and the Society of Real Estate Appraisers. It offers *MAI* and *SRA* designations.

APPRAISAL REPORT / A document that describes the findings of an appraisal engagement. Reports may be presented in the following formats: oral, letter, form, or narrative, and may be self-contained, summary, or restricted. *See* UNIFORM STANDARDS OF PROFESSIONAL APPRAISAL PRACTICE.

APPRAISER / A person qualified to estimate the value of real property.

Importance: In California, one may be a trainee, licensed appraiser, certified residential appraiser, or certified general appraiser.

APPRECIATION / An increase in the value of property.

Importance: Appreciation is one of the most significant benefits from real estate ownership. Gains from inflation as well as real income are included.

APPURTENANCE / Something that is outside the property itself but is considered a part of the property and adds to its greater enjoyment, such as the right to cross another's land (i.e., a *right-of-way* or *easement*).

Importance: The right to use another's land for a special purpose can materially affect the value of the subject property.

APR / ANNUAL PERCENTAGE RATE.

ARM / *See* ADJUSTABLE RATE MORTGAGE.

ARM'S LENGTH TRANSACTION / The "typical, normal transaction," in which all parties have reasonable knowledge of the facts pertinent to the transaction, are under no pressure or duress to transact, and are ready, willing, and able, to transact.

ASA / A senior professional designation offered by the American Society of Appraisers. The ASA designation is awarded upon meeting rigorous requirements that include extensive experience, education, and approved sample reports.

AS IS / Without guarantees as to condition, as in a sale.

ASSESSED VALUATION / A valuation placed upon property by a public officer or a board, as a basis for taxation.

Importance: The assessed value of a property is typically a reasonable estimate by the tax assessor, who must periodically review all property in the jurisdiction. By contrast, an appraisal of a single property is more likely to approximate its market value.

ASSESSMENT / A charge against real estate made by a government to cover the cost of an improvement, such as a street or sewer line. *See also* ASSESSED VALUATION.

Importance: Property buyers and owners need to recognize that they may have to pay assessments for municipal improvements that affect their property. Frequently, the owner has little or no influence on the decision.

ASSESSMENT RATIO / The ratio of assessed value to market value. **Example:** A county requires a 40 percent assessment ratio on all property to be taxed. Property with a $100,000 value is therefore assessed at $40,000 (40 percent of $100,000), and the tax rate is applied to $40,000.

ASSESSOR / An official who has the responsibility of placing an assessed value on property.

Importance: The assessor estimates the value of each piece of real estate in the tax jurisdiction, but does not fix the tax rate or amount.

ASSIGNEE / The person to whom an agreement or contract is sold or transferred.

Importance: This legal term refers to the person who receives the contract.

ASSIGNMENT / The method or manner by which a right or contract is transferred from one person to another.

Importance: Contracts for the sale of real estate are generally assignable, except when financing must be arranged or certain conditions are imposed on a party. In a lease, an assignment gives all the rights of the original tenant to the new tenant.

ASSIGNOR / A party who assigns or transfers an agreement or contract to another.

Importance: Although many contracts can be assigned, the assignor is not necessarily relieved of the obligation. For example, debts cannot be assigned. Another party can assume a debt, but the original borrower remains liable.

ASSUMABLE LOAN / An existing mortgage loan that allows a subsequent property purchaser to undertake the obligation of the existing loan with no change in loan terms. Loans without *due-on-sale clauses,* including most FHA and VA mortgages, are generally assumable.

ASSUMPTION OF MORTGAGE / The purchase of mortgaged property whereby the buyer accepts liability for the debt that continues to exist. The seller remains liable to the lender unless the lender agrees to release him/her.

Importance: When entering an agreement for the purchase or sale of real estate, the financing should be checked to determine whether the mortgage is assumable. If the mortgage carries favorable terms and is assumable, this fact will add value to the transaction.

ATTACHMENT / Legal seizure of property to force payment of a debt.

Importance: Property can be taken as security for a debt provided that such action has court approval.

ATTEST / To witness to; to witness by observation and signature.

Importance: Certain documents must be attested to as a condition for recording at the county courthouse.

ATTORNEY-IN-FACT / A person who is authorized to act for another under a power of attorney, which may be general or limited in scope.

Importance: A person may give another the right to act for him/her in some or all matters (*power of attorney*). The designated person, called an attorney-in-fact, need not be an attorney at law.

AUTOMATED VALUATION MODEL (AVM) / Computerized method for estimating the value of a property. Often used for mass *appraisal* purposes, such as reassessment of a city's property tax base. **Example:** An appraisal firm collected extensive data on home sales and the distinguishing characteristics of each home. By applying an automated valuation model to the data, the firm could quickly estimate a preliminary value of any home in the local market.

AVULSION / The sudden removal of land from one owner to another that occurs when a river abruptly changes its channel.

Importance: If a stream or river is a boundary line, the boundary may change with the addition or removal of land.

BALANCE, PRINCIPLE OF / In real estate appraisal, the principle that there is an optimal mix of inputs that, when combined with land, will result in the greatest land value. Inputs, or *factors of production,* include labor, capital, and entrepreneurship.

BALLOON PAYMENT / The final payment on a loan, when that payment is greater than the preceding installment payments and satisfies the note in full. **Example:** A debt requires interest-only payments annually for 5 years, at the end of which time the balance of the principal (a balloon payment) is due.

Importance: In arranging financing for real estate, if a balloon is involved the borrower will need to plan for the large balance that will come due.

BAND OF INVESTMENT / A weighted average of debt and equity rates of return.

BARGAIN AND SALE DEED / A deed that conveys real estate, generally lacking a warranty. The *grantor* will thus claim to have ownership but will not defend against all claims.

Importance: Sometimes a property owner does not wish to offer a *warranty deed*, but will give more assurance than is offered by a *quitclaim deed*. A bargain and sale deed is a compromise between those two.

BASE AND MERIDIAN / Imaginary lines used by surveyors to find and describe the location of land.

Importance: In states that use a rectangular or government survey method, these lines are similar to latitude and longitude.

BASE LINE / Part of the *government rectangular survey* method of land description. The base line is the major east-west line to which all north-south measurements refer.

BASIC INDUSTRY MULTIPLIER / In economic base analysis, the ratio of total population in a local area to employment in basic industry. *Basic industry* is considered to be any concern that attracts income from outside the local area. The jobs added in basic industry may also contribute to the need for local service jobs (telephone operator, nurse, supermarket clerk, etc.); and, if the workers have families, additional new people may be brought to the area.

BEFORE-AND-AFTER RULE / In an *eminent domain* award, practice followed by many jurisdictions of appraising the property value both before and after the taking, considering enhancement or injury to the property that was the result of *condemnation.*

BENEFICIARY / The person who receives or is to receive the benefits resulting from certain acts.

BEQUEATH / To give or hand down personal property by a will.

BEQUEST / Personal property that is given by the terms of a will.

BILATERAL CONTRACT / A contract under which each party promises performance. *Contrast* UNILATERAL CONTRACT.

BILL OF ASSURANCE / Recorded restrictions affecting a subdivision and a part of all deeds to lots therein.

BILL OF SALE / A written instrument that passes title of personal property from a seller to a buyer.

Importance: A real estate sales agreement is prepared on an agreement of sale. A bill of sale is used when furniture and portable appliances are sold.

BINDER / An agreement, accompanied by a deposit, for the purchase of real estate, as evidence of good faith on the part of the purchaser.

Importance: Binders are seldom used in California because of general agreement and requirements on brokers to use forms specially promulgated for use in the state.

BIWEEKLY LOAN / A mortgage that requires principal and interest payments at two-week intervals. The payment is exactly half of what a monthly payment would be. Over a year's time, the 26 payments are equivalent to 13 monthly payments on a comparable monthly-payment mortgage. As a result, the loan will be amortized much faster than a loan with monthly payments.

BLANKET MORTGAGE / A single *mortgage* that includes more than one parcel of real estate as security.

Importance: When one piece of property is insufficient collateral for a loan, the borrower may be able to satisfy the requirement by putting up more property as security. It is a good idea to negotiate release clauses whereby each parcel can be released from the mortgage when a portion of the loan is paid off, without having to pay off the entire loan.

BOARD OF DIRECTORS / People selected by stockholders to control the business of the corporation.

BONA FIDE / In good faith; without fraud. **Example:** A purchaser pays for property without knowledge of any title defects. In a bona fide sale the seller accepts consideration without notice of any reason against the sale.

Importance: An act in good faith is open, sincere, and honest.

BOND / A certificate that serves as evidence of a debt. *See also* MORTGAGE.

Importance: There are many types of bonds that may be used in real estate. A *mortgage bond* is secured by a mortgage on property. A *completion bond* (also called *performance bond*) is usually issued by a bonding company to assure completion of construction if a contractor fails.

BOOT / In an exchange principally involving like property (i.e., real estate for real estate), cash or other unlike property to balance the property exchange.

BOY / Abbreviation for "beginning of year."

Importance: In most leases, rent is due in the beginning of each period. If a commercial lease requires annual payments, rent is due in the beginning of the year (BOY).

BROKER / A person who is licensed by California to act for property owners in real estate transactions, within the scope of state law.

Importance: In California, a person must be licensed as a broker to act in a real estate transaction for another. A licensed real estate salesperson must be sponsored by a broker who accepts responsibility for the salesperson's acts. A broker is regulated by the law of agency, which requires the broker to act in the best interest of the principal.

BROKERAGE / The business of being a *broker*.

Importance: Parties are brought together in a real estate transaction, such as a sale, lease, rental, or exchange.

BUILDING CAPITALIZATION RATE / In appraisal, the *capitalization rate* is used to convert an *income stream* into one lump-sum value. The rate for the building may differ from that for the land because the building is a wasting asset.

BUILDING CODES / Regulations established by local governments and describing the minimum structural requirements for buildings, including foundation, roofing, plumbing, electrical, and other specifications for safety and sanitation.

Importance: Work on real estate must be in compliance with the building codes, or it will not pass the required inspections.

BUILDING INSPECTION / Inspection of property as it proceeds under construction to ensure that it meets building codes: foundation, plumbing, electrical wiring, roofing, materials. Also, periodic inspection of existing public buildings for health and safety considerations.

BUILDING LINE / A line fixed at a certain distance from the front and/or sides of a lot, beyond which the building may not project.

Importance: When situating improvements on a lot, it is important to observe the building line. Often, one must check with the city to ascertain exactly where this line is.

BUILDING LOAN AGREEMENT / *See* CONSTRUCTION LOAN.

BUILDING PERMIT / Permission granted by a local government to build a specific structure at a particular site.

BULLET LOAN / Typically a loan with a 5- to 10-year *term* and no *amortization*. At the end of the term, the full amount is due.

BUNDLE OF RIGHTS THEORY / The theory that ownership of realty implies rights, such as occupancy, use and enjoyment, and the right to sell, bequeath, give, or lease all or part of these rights.

Importance: In a real estate transaction, knowing what one has or is acquiring is vital, because some of the bundle of rights may be missing.

BUYDOWN / Payment of discount points at loan origination in order to secure a lower interest rate; the rate may be bought down for only a few years or for the life of the loan.

Importance: When offered low rate financing on property being bought, one should determine whether the buydown applies to just the first few years or the full term of the loan.

BUYER'S BROKER / An agent explicitly representing the buyer. The broker may locate appropriate properties and assist in making an offer and negotiating a contract. The buyer may or may not pay a fee for this service.

CALIFORNIA FAIR HOUSING LAW / "All persons . . . are free and equal, and no matter what their sex, race, color, religion, ancestry, or national origin, are entitled to full and equal accommodations, advantages, facilities, privileges, or services in all business establishments of every kind whatsoever." Originally known as Rumford Fair Housing Act of 1963.

CAL VET LOAN / Home, farm or manufactured home loan to a qualified veteran, with money supplied through the California Veterans' Farm and Home Purchase program.

CANCELLATION CLAUSE / A provision in a contract that gives the right to terminate obligations upon the occurrence of certain specified conditions or events.

Importance: A cancellation clause in a lease may allow the landlord to break the lease upon sale of the building. A lessor may need a cancellation clause if he/she plans to sell the building; the buyer may have another use for it.

CAP / A limit on the amount by which the interest rate on an *adjustable rate mortgage* may be changed; usually there are annual caps and lifetime caps.

Importance: Without caps, interest rates of adjustable rate mortgages can increase without limit.

Also, abbreviation for income *capitalization*.

CAPITALIZATION / A process whereby anticipated future income is converted to one lump sum capital value.

Importance: Rental property evaluation is enhanced by the capitalization process. Income is divided by a *capitalization rate* to estimate value, using the following formula:

$$\text{Property Value} = \frac{\text{Rental Income less Operating Expenses}}{\text{Capitalization Rate}}$$

CAPITALIZATION RATE / A rate of return used to convert anticipated future income into a capital value. The capitalization rate includes interest and principal recovery.

Importance: *See also* CAPITALIZATION.

CAPITALIZED INCOME / The value estimated by the process of converting an *income stream* into a lump-sum amount; also called *capitalized value*.

CAPTURE RATE / The portion of total sales in the real estate market that are sold by one entity or one project.

CARRYING CHARGES / Expenses necessary for holding property, such as taxes and interest on idle property or property under construction.

Importance: When considering nonrental real estate as an investment, carrying charges should be taken into account.

CASH FLOW / Periodic amounts accruing from an investment after all cash expenses, payments, and taxes have been deducted.

CASH-ON-CASH / *See* EQUITY DIVIDEND.

CAVEAT EMPTOR / "Let the buyer beware." The buyer must examine the goods or property and buy at his/her own risk.

Importance: This was once an accepted condition of sale. Home buyers in some states have much more protection now, as sellers and brokers are required to disclose problems or face possible penalties.

CAVEATS / Warnings, often in writing to a potential buyer, to be careful.

CCIM / *See* CERTIFIED COMMERCIAL INVESTMENT MEMBER.

CC&Rs / Covenants, conditions, and restrictions. These are limitations on land use, usually in a deed, imposed in a subdivision. Protects homeowners by preventing certain uses and assuring uniformity.

CEASE AND DESIST / Order by a court or administrative agency prohibiting a person or business from continuing an activity.

Used in real estate brokerage to prevent antitrust behavior among firms, or in illegal discrimination.

CENSUS TRACT / Geographical area mapped by the U.S. government for which demographic information is available. This information may be used by retailers, real estate developers, and brokers to estimate consumer purchasing power in a market area.

CERCLA / Comprehensive Environmental Response Compensation and Liability Act. *See also* SUPER-FUND.

CERTIFICATE OF NO DEFENSE / *See* ESTOPPEL CERTIFICATE.

CERTIFICATE OF OCCUPANCY / A document issued by a local government to a developer permitting the structure to be occupied by members of the public. Issuance of the certificate generally indicates that the building is in compliance with public health and *building codes*.

CERTIFICATE OF REASONABLE VALUE (CRV) / Required for a VA-guaranteed home loan, the CRV is based on an appraiser's estimate of value of the property to be purchased. Because the loan amount may not exceed the CRV, the first step in getting a VA loan is to request an appraisal. Although anyone can request a VA appraisal, it is customary for the lender or the real estate agent to do so. The form used is VA Form 26-1805, Request for Determination of Reasonable Value.

CERTIFICATE OF REDEMPTION / Document provided by county tax collectors showing that all past due property taxes have been paid.

CERTIFIED COMMERCIAL INVESTMENT MEMBER (CCIM) / A designation awarded by the Realtors National Marketing Institute, which is affiliated with the *National Association of Realtors®*.

CERTIFIED GENERAL APPRAISER / A person qualified to appraise any property, under appraiser certification laws adopted by all states.

CERTIFIED PROPERTY MANAGER (CPM) / A member of the Institute of Real Estate Management, an organization affiliated with the *National Association of Realtors®*.

CERTIFIED RESIDENTIAL APPRAISER / A person qualified to appraise residences and up to four units of housing, under appraiser certification law. Standards call for less education, less experience, and a less comprehensive examination than are required for a certified general appraiser.

CERTIFIED RESIDENTIAL BROKER (CRB) / A designation awarded by the Realtors National Marketing Institute, which is affiliated with the *National Association of Realtors®*.

CHAIN / A unit of land measurement, 66 feet in length.

Importance: In surveying, land descriptions sometimes use the chain.

CHAIN OF TITLE / A history of *conveyances* and *encumbrances* affecting a title from the time the original patent was granted, or as far back as records are available. *See also* ABSTRACT OF TITLE.

CHATTEL / Personal property, including autos and household goods and fixtures.

Importance: Many laws have different applications, depending on whether a property is real estate or chattels. It can be important to know the type of property.

CHATTEL MORTGAGE / A pledge of personal property as security for a debt.

CLEAR TITLE / A title free and clear of all *encumbrances*.

Importance: When buying or selling real estate, it is essential to know whether the title is encumbered or clear. If it is not clear, the effect of the encumbrances on the value or use of the real estate must be checked.

CLIENT / The person who employs a broker, lawyer, accountant, appraiser, and so on.

Importance: The law describes certain relationships that a professional has with a client. In a real estate transaction it is essential to know exactly what that relationship is. *See also* AGENCY.

CLOSING / (1) The act of transferring ownership of a property from seller to buyer in accordance with a sales contract. (2) The time when a closing takes place.

CLOSING DATE / The date on which the seller delivers the deed and the buyer pays for the property; also called *settlement date*.

Importance: The *agreement of sale* will reflect when closing is to take place. A buyer or seller may be considered to have defaulted on a contract if unable to close by the agreed upon date.

CLOSING STATEMENT / An accounting of funds from a real estate sale, made to both the seller and the buyer separately. California requires the broker to furnish accurate closing statements to all parties to any transaction in which he/she is an agent.

Importance: This statement shows the accounting, which should be consistent with the agreement of sale. If an error is suspected in the closing statement, the closing should not take place.

CLOUD ON THE TITLE / An outstanding claim or *encumbrance* that, if valid, will affect or impair the owner's title.

Importance: A cloud on title can restrict use and affect ownership. This should be cleared before closing. An attorney or title company should be consulted for assurance of title.

COASTAL ZONE / An area the length of California (about 1,800 miles) inland from the sea line by 1,000 or more yards that must meet local conservation and resource preservation requirements, as authorized by the Coastal Zone Conservation Act.

COLLATERAL / Property pledged as security for a debt.

COLOR OF TITLE / That which appears to be good title but is not.

Importance: A person can be fooled by believing he/she is receiving good title. An attorney or title company's input is essential.

COMMERCIAL PROPERTY / Property designed for use by retail, wholesale, office, hotel, and service users.

Importance: Nearly all cities and towns have zoning that restricts the location of commercial property.

COMMINGLE / To mingle or mix, as by the deposit of another's money in a broker's personal account.

Importance: Brokers generally must maintain all *earnest money* in an account that is separate from their personal funds.

COMMISSION / (1) The amount earned by real estate brokers for their services; (2) the official body that enforces real estate license laws.

Importance: (1) Commissions are the way real estate brokers earn money. (2) The Real Estate Commission in California licenses brokers and salespersons and may suspend a license for certain behavior.

COMMITMENT / A pledge or promise; a firm agreement.

Importance: When financing is needed to buy property, a commitment from a lender must be obtained. The loan terms are noted in the commitment, which may include an interest rate lock-in.

COMMON ELEMENTS / Generally, in a *condominium* development, land or a tract of land considered to be the property of the development in which all owners can enjoy use.

Importance: Owners of condominiums share in the use of and payment for common areas, such as walkways, recreational facilities, and ponds. A homeowner's association typically manages the common area.

COMMON LAW / The body of law that has grown out of legal customs and practices that developed in England. Common law prevails unless superseded by other law.

COMMUNITY PROPERTY / Property accumulated through joint efforts of husband and wife and owned by them in equal shares. The doctrine now exists in Arizona, California, Idaho, Louisiana, Nevada, New Mexico, Texas, Wisconsin, and the state of Washington.

Importance: Husband and wife must agree to all real estate transactions involving community property.

COMPARATIVE MARKET ANALYSIS (CMA) / An estimate of the value of property using only a few indicators taken from sales of comparable properties, such as price per square foot.

Importance: Real estate brokers and agents, because they are not state-certified appraisers, may not perform appraisals. So they estimate the value of a subject property using a CMA in order to serve their clients.

COMPARATIVE SALES APPROACH / *See* SALES COMPARISON APPROACH.

COMPARATIVE UNIT METHOD / An appraisal technique to establish relevant units as a guide to appraising the subject property. **Examples:** (1) Parking garages are compared per space. (2) Bowling centers are compared per lane. (3) Land may be sold per square foot or per front foot.

COMPLETION BOND / A legal instrument used to guarantee the completion of a development according to specifications. More encompassing than a performance bond, which assures that one party will perform under a contract under condition that the other party performs. The completion bond assures production of the development without reference to any contract and without the requirement of payment to the contractor.

COMPOUND INTEREST / Interest paid on the original principal and also on the unpaid interest that has accumulated. **Example:** $100 deposited in a 5 percent savings account earns $5 interest the first year. If this interest is not withdrawn, the account's second-year earnings are 5 percent of $105, or $5.25.

Importance: Compound interest is the cornerstone of all financial computations, including monthly mortgage payments and remaining balances.

COMPREHENSIVE ENVIRONMENTAL RESPONSE COMPENSATION AND LIABILITY ACT (CERCLA) / Federal law, known as *Superfund,* passed in 1980 and reauthorized by *SARA* in 1986. The law imposes strict joint and several liability for cleaning up environmentally contaminated land. Potentially responsible parties include any current or previous owner, generator, transporter, disposer, or party who treated hazardous waste at the site. Strict liability means that each and every party is liable for the full cost of remediation, even parties who were not contaminators.

COMPS / An appraisal term, short for "comparables," that is, comparable properties.

COMPUTERIZED LOAN ORIGINATION (CLO) / Origination of a mortgage loan, usually by someone who is not a loan officer, with the assistance of specialized computer software that ties the originator to one or more mortgage lenders. CLO systems allow real estate brokers to provide a wider array of services.

CONDEMNATION / (1) The taking of private property for public use, with just compensation to the owner, under *eminent domain*; used by governments to acquire land for streets, parks, schools, and by utilities to acquire necessary property; (2) declaring a structure unfit for use.

Importance: All property is subject to condemnation, though the government must show need. The amount of compensation can be disputed.

CONDITION(S) / Provision(s) in a contract that some or all terms of the contract must be met or the contract need not be consummated. **Examples:**
- Buyer must obtain certain financing.
- House must be appraised at a certain amount.
- City must give occupancy permit.
- Seller must pay for certain repairs.

CONDITIONAL SALES CONTRACT / A contract for the sale of property stating that the seller retains title until the conditions of the contract have been fulfilled.

Importance: Generally, buyers have less of an interest under this type of contract than is conveyed by the receipt of a deed at closing.

CONDOMINIUM / A system of ownership of individual units in a multiunit structure, combined with joint ownership of commonly used property (sidewalks, hallways, stairs). *See also* COMMON ELEMENTS.

Importance: A condominium can be mortgaged by its individual owner, who must pay assessments for common area maintenance.

CONFORMING LOAN / A home mortgage loan in which both borrower and property conform to the guidelines of FNMA and FHLMC. A conforming loan will carry a lower interest rate than a nonconforming loan because of its quality and marketability.

CONFORMITY PRINCIPLE / An appraisal principle that holds that property values tend to be maximized when the neighborhood is reasonably homogeneous in social and economic activity.

CONSENT DECREE / A judgment whereby the defendant agrees to stop the activity that was asserted to be illegal, without admitting wrongdoing or guilt.

CONSIDERATION / Anything of value given to induce entering into a contract; it may be money, personal services, love and affection.

Importance: A contract must have some consideration to be legally binding.

CONSTANT / *See* CONSTANT PAYMENT LOAN.

CONSTANT PAYMENT LOAN / A loan on which equal payments are made periodically so that the debt is paid off when the last payment is made.

Importance: Although each periodic payment is the same, the portion that is interest declines over time, whereas the principal portion increases.

CONSTRUCTION LOAN / A loan used to build on real estate.

Importance: Many construction lenders require, among other things, that the builder obtain a commitment for a permanent loan before they will issue a construction loan. Commercial banks are the most common source of construction loans. The rate is often the prime rate plus 2 percent plus 1 or more discount points. The loan is advanced in stages as the project is completed.

CONSTRUCTIVE EVICTION / An eviction existing when, through the fault of the landlord, physical conditions of the property render it unfit for the purpose for which it was leased.

CONSTRUCTIVE NOTICE / The legal presumption that everyone has knowledge of a fact when that fact is a matter of public record. **Example:** A buys land from B, believing that B is the owner. However, B was a huckster; C owned the property. Because C's deed had been properly recorded, A had constructive notice of C's ownership and cannot claim ownership against C.

CONTIGUOUS / Actually touching; contiguous properties have a common boundary. *See also* ADJOINING.

CONTINGENCY CLAUSE / *See* CONDITION(s).

CONTRACT / An agreement between competent parties to do or not to do certain things for a consideration.

Importance: A valid contract is enforceable in a court of law. All contracts for real estate must be in writing to be enforceable, except leases for less than 1 year.

CONTRACT FOR DEED / *See* LAND CONTRACT.

CONTRACT OF SALE / *See* PURCHASE CONTRACT.

CONVENTIONAL LOAN / A mortgage loan other than one guaranteed by the *Veterans Administration* or insured by the *Federal Housing Administration.*

Importance: Conventional loans generally require a larger down payment than others, although the required down payment for conventional loans can be decreased with private mortgage insurance.

CONVERTIBLE ARM / An *adjustable-rate mortgage* that offers the borrower the option to convert payments to a fixed-rate schedule at a specified point within the term of the loan. Conversion is made for a nominal fee, and the interest rate on the fixed-rate loan is determined by a rule specified in the ARM loan agreement.

CONVEY / To deed or transfer title to another.

Importance: This term is used to imply a sale or transfer of ownership.

CONVEYANCE / (1) The transfer of the title of real estate from one to another; (2) the means or medium by which title of real estate is transferred.

Importance: This term usually refers to use of a deed, but can also be used for a lease, mortgage, assignment, encumbrance.

COOPERATIVE / A type of corporate ownership of real property whereby stockholders of the corporation are entitled to use a certain dwelling unit or other units of space.

Importance: Special income tax laws allow the tenant stockholders to deduct on their tax returns the housing interest and property taxes paid by the corporation.

CORPOREAL / Visible or tangible. Corporeal rights in real estate include such things as the right of occupancy under a lease.

COST APPROACH / One of the three appraisal methods of estimating value. The estimated current cost of reproducing the existing improvements, less the estimated depreciation, added to the value of the land, gives the appraised value; also called *appraisal by summation.*

Importance: Most properties sell for market value. The cost approach is useful for proposed construction or for estimating the amount of insurance needed.

COUNTEROFFER / Rejection of an offer to buy or sell, with a simultaneous substitute offer.

COVENANTS / Promises written into deeds and other instruments and agreeing to do or not to do certain acts, or requiring or preventing certain uses of the property.

Importance: When buying real estate, it is prudent to determine whether any of the covenants would inhibit or prevent a proposed use of the property.

CPM / *See* CERTIFIED PROPERTY MANAGER.

CRB / *See* CERTIFIED RESIDENTIAL BROKER.

CUL-DE-SAC / A street with an intersection at one end and a closed turning area at the other. Often appreciated in the design of residential subdivisions for the privacy provided to homes on the street.

CURABLE DEPRECIATION / *Depreciation* or deterioration that can be corrected at a cost less than the value that will be added.

Importance: It is economically profitable to correct curable depreciation.

DAMAGES / The amount recoverable by a person who has been injured in any manner, including physical harm, property damage, or violated rights, through the act or default of another.

Importance: Damages may be awarded for compensation and as a punitive measure, to punish someone for certain acts.

DATE OF APPRAISAL / *See* APPRAISAL DATE.

DEBT/EQUITY RATIO / The relationship of these two components of *purchase capital.* **Example:** Mortgage = $75,000; equity = 25,000. Therefore, the debt/equity ratio is 3:1. This is equivalent to a 75 percent *loan-to-value ratio* loan.

DECREE / An order issued by a person in authority; a court order or decision.

Importance: A decree may be final or interlocutory (preliminary).

DEDICATION / The gift of land by its owner for a public use and the acceptance of it by a unit of government. **Example:** Streets in a subdivision, land for a park, or a site for a school.

DEED / A written document, properly signed and delivered, that conveys title to real property. *See also* BARGAIN AND SALE DEED, GENERAL WARRANTY DEED, QUITCLAIM DEED, SPECIAL WARRANTY DEED.

DEED IN LIEU OF FORECLOSURE / A deed that conveys a defaulting borrower's realty to a lender, thus avoiding foreclosure proceedings.

DEED OF TRUST / *See* TRUST DEED.

DEED RESTRICTION / A clause in a deed that limits the use of land. **Example:** A deed may stipulate that alcoholic beverages are not to be sold on the land for 20 years.

Importance: A buyer should check that deed restrictions will not inhibit an intended use of property; a seller should consider whether he/she wants to restrict the use of land.

DEFAULT / (1) Failure to fulfill a duty or promise, or to discharge an obligation; (2) omission or failure to perform any acts.

Importance: Upon default, the defaulting party may be liable to the other party(ies).

DEFEASANCE / A clause in a mortgage that gives the borrower the right to redeem his/her property after he/she has defaulted, usually by paying the full indebtedness and fees incurred. **Example:** A late payment on a mortgage or other *default* doesn't necessarily cause the borrower to lose the property. Defeasance may allow redemption, though the loan and fees may have to be paid.

DEFENDANT / The party sued in an action at law.

DEFERRED GAIN / Any gain not subject to tax in the year realized but postponed until a later year.

DEFERRED PAYMENTS / Money payments to be made at some future date.

DEFICIENCY JUDGMENT / A court order stating that the borrower still owes money when the security for a loan does not entirely satisfy a defaulted debt.

Importance: When property is foreclosed on, the amount realized by the sale of the collateral may not satisfy the debt. The lender may be able to get a deficiency judgment to recover the balance owed.

DELAYED EXCHANGE / *See* SECTION 1031.

DELIVERY / Transfer of the possession of a thing from one person to another.

Importance: In a real estate transaction there should be delivery of a deed. For example, if an owner dies without giving a deed to a relative while alive, a verbal promise to give the property is inadequate.

DEMOGRAPHY / The study of population characteristics of people in an area, including age, sex, and income.

DEPARTMENT OF REAL ESTATE (DRE) / The California State agency that administers the Real Estate Law, including licensing of brokers and salespersons.

DEPRECIATION / (1) In appraisal, a loss of value in real property due to age, physical deterioration, or functional or economic obsolescence; (2) in accounting, the allocation of the cost of an asset over its economic useful life.

Importance: It should be recognized that the value of real estate may decline; also, that one can reduce income taxes by claiming depreciation as a tax expense.

DEPRESSION / Economic conditions causing a severe decline in business activity, reflecting high unemployment, excess supply, and public fear.

DEVISE / A gift of real estate by will or last testament.

DEVISEE / A person who inherits real estate through a will.

DIRECT CAPITALIZATION / The value estimated by dividing *net operating income* by an overall *capitalization rate* to estimate value. *See also* CAPITALIZATION. **Example:**

Gross income	$100,000
Operating expenses	−40,000
Net operating income	$ 60,000
Capitalization rate	0.12
Value estimate	$500,000

DIRECT SALES COMPARISON APPROACH / *See* SALES COMPARISON APPROACH.

DIRECTIONAL GROWTH / The location or direction toward which a city is growing.

Importance: An investor can often make a profit by purchasing land in the path of a city's growth.

DISCHARGE IN BANKRUPTCY / The release of a bankrupt party from the obligation to repay debts that were, or might have been, proved in bankruptcy proceedings.

DISCOUNTED LOAN / One that is offered or traded for less than its face value. *See* DISCOUNT POINTS.

DISCOUNTED PRESENT VALUE / *See* DISCOUNTING.

DISCOUNTING / The process of estimating the present value of an *income stream* by reducing expected *cash flow* to reflect the *time value of money*. Discounting is the opposite of compounding; mathematically they are reciprocals.

DISCOUNT POINTS / Amounts paid to the lender (usually by the seller) at the time of origination of a loan, to account for the difference between the market interest rate and the lower face rate of the note (often required when FHA or VA financing is used).

Importance: Discount points must be paid in cash at closing. Buyer and seller should agree, at the time they prepare an agreement of sale, as to who is to pay the points, or what the limits are on the number of points to be paid.

DISPOSSESS PROCEEDINGS / The legal process by a landlord to remove a tenant and regain possession of property.

Importance: If a tenant breaches a lease, the landlord will want to regain possession of the property.

DISTINGUISHED REAL ESTATE INSTRUCTOR (DREI) / A *real estate* teacher, typically of licensing preparation courses, who has been designated by the *Real Estate Educators Association*. **Example:** To qualify as a DREI, Don had to demonstrate classroom teaching techniques to a panel of teachers, who judged his effectiveness. Don also offered experience and expertise in real estate law.

DISTRIBUTEE / A person receiving or entitled to receive land as the representative of the former owner; an heir.

DOCUMENTARY EVIDENCE / Evidence in the form of written or printed papers.

Importance: Documentary evidence generally carries more weight than oral evidence.

DRE / *See* DEPARTMENT REAL ESTATE.

DUAL AGENT / An agent who represents more than one party to a transaction.

DUE DILIGENCE / (1) Making a reasonable effort to perform under a contract. (2) Making a reasonable effort to provide accurate, complete information. A study that often precedes the purchase of property or the underwriting of a loan or investment; considers the physical, financial, legal, and social characteristics of the property and expected investment performance.

DURESS / Unlawful constraint exercised upon a person whereby he/she is forced to do some act against his/her will. **Example:** "Your signature or your brains will be on this contract."

Importance: A person who signs a contract or performs another act under duress need not go through with the agreement.

EARNEST MONEY / A deposit made by a purchaser of real estate as evidence of his/her good faith.

Importance: Earnest money should accompany an offer to buy property. Generally, a broker, attorney, or title company deposits the money in a separate account, beyond the control of the principals, until the contract is completed.

EASEMENT / The right, privilege, or interest that one party has in the land of another. **Example:** The right of public utility companies to lay their lines across others' property.

Importance: Easements allow utility service without requiring the public utility to buy the land. However, a potential real estate purchaser should determine exact locations of all easements to be sure they won't interfere with planned land uses.

ECONOMIC DEPRECIATION / Loss of value from all causes outside the property itself. **Example:** An expensive private home may drop in value when a sanitary landfill is placed nearby.

ECONOMIC LIFE / The remaining period for which real estate improvements are expected to generate more income than operating expenses cost.

Importance: As land improvements age, they tend to command less rent (in real terms) while maintenance costs rise. The economic life is the expected life of positive contributions to value by buildings or other land improvements.

ECONOMIC OBSOLESCENCE / *See* ECONOMIC DEPRECIATION.

EFFECTIVE GROSS INCOME / For income-producing property, *potential gross income*, less a vacancy and collection allowance, plus miscellaneous income. *See also* GROSS INCOME. **Example:** An office building rents for $12 per square foot and contains 100,000 leasable square feet. A 5 percent vacancy and collection allowance is expected. A small concession stand provides $1,000 of annual revenue.

Potential gross income:	
$12 × 100,000	= $1,200,000
Less: Vacancy and collection allowance @ 5%	−60,000
Add: Miscellaneous income	+1,000
Effective gross income	$1,141,000

EJECTMENT / An action to regain possession of *real property*, and to obtain damages for unlawful possession.

Importance: Ejectment allows a rightful owner to remove a squatter or trespasser.

EMINENT DOMAIN / The right of the government or a public utility to acquire property for necessary public use by *condemnation*; the owner must be fairly compensated.

Importance: Governments or those with governmental authority can acquire property they need under the Federal Fifth Amendment and state constitutions. As to the amount paid, the parties are entitled to a "day in court."

ENCROACHMENT / A building, a part of a building, or an obstruction that physically intrudes upon, overlaps, or trespasses upon the property of another.

Importance: A *survey* is often required as part of a real estate contract, to determine whether there are any encroachments on the property.

ENCUMBRANCE / Any right to or interest in land that diminishes its value. Included are outstanding mortgage loans, unpaid taxes, easements, deed restrictions, mechanics' liens, leases, and deed restrictions.

ENDORSEMENT / The act of signing one's name on the back of a check or note, with or without further qualification; also, the signature itself.

ENVIRONMENTAL ASSESSMENT / A study of the property and area to determine health hazards:

Phase I. To identify the presence of hazards (e.g., asbestos, radon, PCBs, leaking underground storage tanks).

Phase II. To estimate the cost of remediation or cleanup.

Phase III. To remediate the environmental contamination.

ENVIRONMENTAL IMPACT REPORT (OR STATEMENT) / describes effects on the environment of a proposed development; may be required by a local government to assure the absence of damage to the environment.

EOY / Abbreviation for "end of year."

Importance: Most mortgage loans call for payments at the end of each period. If the loan requires annual payments, a payment would be due at the end of the year (EOY).

EQUITABLE TITLE / The interest held by one who has agreed to purchase but has not yet closed the transaction.

EQUITY / The interest or value that the owner has in real estate over and above the liens against it.
Example: If a property has a market value of $10,000, but there is a $7,500 mortgage loan on it, the owner's equity is $2,500.

EQUITY DIVIDEND / The annual *cash flow* that an equity investor receives; same as *cash-on-cash* return.

EQUITY OF REDEMPTION / The right of a real estate owner to reclaim property after default, but before foreclosure proceedings, by payment of the debt, interest, and costs. *See also* DEFEASANCE.

EQUITY YIELD RATE / The rate of return on the *equity* portion of an investment, taking into account periodic *cash flow* and the proceeds from resale. The timing and amounts of *cash flow* after debt service are considered, but not income taxes.

EROSION / The gradual wearing away of land through process of nature, as by streams and winds.

Importance: Planting vegetation can often prevent soil erosion.

ESCALATOR MORTGAGE / *See* ADJUSTABLE-RATE MORTGAGE.

ESCAPE CLAUSE / A provision in a contract that allows one or more of the parties to cancel all or part of the contract if certain events or situations do or do not occur.

ESCHEAT / The reversion of property to California in the event that the owner dies without leaving a will and has no legal heirs.

Importance: In the absence of a will, the assets of a person who has no legal heirs will escheat to California in five years.

ESCROW / An agreement between two or more parties providing that certain instruments or property be placed with a third party for safekeeping, pending the fulfillment or performance of some act or condition.

Importance: It is prudent to place money or property in escrow rather than to give it to the other principal of a pending transaction.

ESCROW ACCOUNT / *See* TRUST ACCOUNT.

ESCROW AGENT / A neutral third party (such as a lawyer, broker, or title company) who is trusted by buyer and seller to close a transaction. The buyer and seller give instructions with conditions that must be met in order to close.

ESTATE / The degree, quantity, nature, and extent of interest a person has in real or personal property.

ESTATE AT SUFFERANCE / The wrongful occupancy of property by a tenant after his/her lease has expired.

ESTATE AT WILL / The occupation of real estate by a tenant for an indefinite period, terminable by one or both parties at will.

ESTATE FOR LIFE / An interest in property that terminates upon the death of a specified person. *See also* LIFE ESTATE.

ESTATE FOR YEARS / An interest in land that allows possession for a definite and limited time.

ESTATE IN REVERSION / An estate left by a *grantor* for him/herself, to begin after the termination of some particular estate granted by him/her.
Example: A landlord's estate in reversion becomes his/hers to possess when the lease expires.

ESTOPPEL CERTIFICATE / A document by which, for example, the mortgagor (borrower) certifies that the mortgage debt is a lien for the amount stated. He/she is thereafter prevented from claiming that the balance due differed from the amount stated. Estoppels apply also to leases.

Importance: The buyer of property on which there is a mortgage or lease should get estoppels to be sure the terms of those agreements are as expected. The right to get estoppel certificates may be written into the lease or mortgage.

ET AL. / Abbreviation of *et alii* ("and others").

ET UX. / Abbreviation of *et uxor* ("and wife").

EVALUATION / A study of the potential uses of a property, but not to determine its present value.

Importance: Evaluations include studies as to the market for and the marketability of a property, feasibility, *highest and best use*, land use, and supply and demand.

EVICTION / A legal proceeding by a lessor (landlord) to recover possession of property.

Importance: Eviction allows a landlord to regain property when a tenant does not uphold the lease. A legal process must be followed.

EVICTION, PARTIAL / A legal proceeding whereby the possessor of the property is deprived of a portion thereof.

EXCESS (ACCELERATED) DEPRECIATION / The accumulated difference between *accelerated depreciation* claimed for tax purposes and what *straight-line depreciation* would have been. Generally, excess accelerated depreciation is recaptured (taxed) as ordinary income upon a sale, instead of receiving more favorable capital gains treatment. *See* DEPRECIATION RECAPTURE.

EXCESS RENT / The amount by which the *rent* under an existing *lease* exceeds the rental rate on comparable existing space.

Importance: Should the lease expire or the tenant break the lease, the new rental rate will probably be at (lower) market rates.

EXCHANGE / Under Section 1031 of the Internal Revenue Code, like-kind property used in a trade or business or held as an investment can be exchanged tax free. *See also* BOOT.

EXCLUSIONARY ZONING / Zoning laws of a community that would serve to prohibit low and moderate income housing; considered to be illegal.

EXCLUSIVE AGENCY LISTING / An employment contract giving only one broker the right to sell the property for a specified time and also allowing the owner to sell the property him/herself without paying a commission.

Importance: This is sometimes arranged when an owner wants to continue personal selling efforts while employing a broker. Acceptable to some brokers for some properties.

EXCLUSIVE RIGHT TO SELL LISTING / An employment contract giving the broker the right to collect a commission if the property is sold by anyone, including the owner, during the term of the agreement, and often beyond the term to someone the broker introduced. *Compare* EXCLUSIVE AGENCY LISTING; *contrast with* OPEN LISTING.

EXECUTE / (1) To make out a contract; (2) to perform a contract fully.

Importance: In real estate, unsigned contracts are generally meaningless.

EXECUTED CONTRACT / A contract all terms and conditions of which have been fulfilled.

Importance: When executed, a contract is enforceable.

EXECUTOR / A person designated in a will to carry out its provisions concerning the disposition of the estate.

Importance: The person making a will should name an executor or co-executor who is trustworthy and capable of carrying out the terms of the will. If there is no will and no executor, the court appoints an *administrator*.

EXECUTRIX / A woman who performs the duties of an executor.

EXPENSE RATIO / A comparison of *operating expenses* to *potential gross income*. This ratio can be compared over time and with that of other properties to determine the relative operating efficiency of the property considered. **Example:** An apartment complex generates potential gross income of $1,000,000 annually, and incurs operating expenses of $400,000 over the same time period. The expense ratio of 40 percent can be compared to its historical rate and the same ratios competitive properties. The comparison may disclose reasons for differences that can be used to bolster the property's efficiency.

FACTORS OF PRODUCTION / In economics, land, labor, capital, and entrepreneurship.

FAIR HOUSING LAW / A federal law that forbids discrimination on the basis of race, color, sex, religion, handicap, familial status, or national origin in the selling or renting of homes and apartments. *See* RUMFORD FAIR HOUSING ACT.

FAMILY LIMITED PARTNERSHIP / A *limited partnership* whose interests are owned by members of the same family. By this arrangement, gift and estate taxes may be reduced. However, owners will not enjoy the freedom of complete ownership or free transferability of interest provided by other ownership vehicles. *See* MINORITY DISCOUNT.

FARMER MAC / *See* FEDERAL AGRICULTURAL MORTGAGE CORPORATION.

FDIC / *See* FEDERAL DEPOSIT INSURANCE CORPORATION.

FEDERAL AGRICULTURAL MORTGAGE CORPORATION / Federal agency established in 1988 to provide a secondary market for farm mortgage loans. Informally called *Farmer Mac*.

FEDERAL DEPOSIT INSURANCE CORPORATION (FDIC) / A U.S. government agency that insures depositors' accounts in commercial banks and savings and loan associations.

Importance: Federal insurance, up to $100,000 per account, provides depositor confidence in the banking system and in the individual bank. Banks and savings and loan associations add liquidity to the real estate market.

FEDERAL HOUSING ADMINISTRATION (FHA) / A U.S. government agency that insures to lenders the repayment of real estate loans.

Importance: The FHA is instrumental in assuring that financing is available for housing for low and moderate income levels. Programs include single-family homes, condos, apartments, nursing homes, even new towns.

FEDERAL NATIONAL MORTGAGE ASSOCIATION (FNMA) / A U.S. government-sponsored corporation that buys and sells existing residential mortgages; known as Fanny Mae.

Importance: FNMA significantly increases liquidity in the mortgage market. Without FNMA, it might be difficult for lenders who originate loans to find buyers for those loans. FNMA has standardized the loan submission and approval process, and has brought the mortgage finance business on a par with other national credit markets.

FEDERALLY RELATED TRANSACTION / A real estate transaction that is overseen by a federal agency including: Federal Reserve Board; Federal Deposit Insurance Corporation; Office of Comptroller of Currency; Office of Thrift Supervision; National Credit Union Association; and Resolution Trust Corporation.

Importance: A real estate appraiser used in a federally related transaction must be state licensed or certified.

FEE SIMPLE OR FEE ABSOLUTE / Absolute ownership of real property; the owner is entitled to the entire property with unconditional power of disposition during his/her life, and the property descends to his/her heirs and legal representatives upon his/her death intestate.

Importance: When buying real estate, the seller can give only the rights he/she has. A buyer should determine whether complete ownership in fee simple will be received.

FF&E / FURNITURE, FIXTURES, AND EQUIPMENT.

FHA / *See* FEDERAL HOUSING ADMINISTRATION.

FHA LOAN / A mortgage loan insured by the FHA.

Importance: FHA loans generally reduce the required down payment to 3 percent (sometimes less) but require FHA mortgage insurance, in addition to interest, at 0.5 percent annually.

FIDUCIARY / (1) A person who, on behalf of or for the benefit of another, transacts business or handles money or property not his/her own. (2) Founded on trust; the nature of trust.

Importance: A fiduciary, or a person in such capacity, must act in the best interest of the party who has placed trust.

FILTERING DOWN / The process whereby, over time, a housing unit or neighborhood is occupied by progressively lower-income residents.

FINAL SUBDIVISION MAP / *See* SUBDIVISION MAP ACT.

FINAL VALUE ESTIMATE / In an *appraisal* of *real estate*, the appraiser's value conclusion. **Example:** An appraiser has determined these three amounts of value based on each appraisal approach:

Cost approach	$600,000
Sales comparison approach	575,000
Income approach	560,000

She then reconciles these amounts, decides which is most relevant, and offers a final value estimate. If the income approach is considered most indicative of purchaser behavior, the amount may be $560,000 to $570,000, depending on the relative weight assigned to each approach.

FINANCIAL FEASIBILITY / The ability of a proposed land use or change of land use to justify itself from an economic point of view.

Importance: Financial feasibility is one test of the *highest and best use* of land, but not the only test. Nor does the financial feasibility of a project necessarily make it the most rewarding use of land.

FINANCING LEASE / A lease wherein lessee becomes lessor to the operating tenant.

FIRREA / Financial Institutions Reform, Recovery, and Enforcement Act.

FIRST MORTGAGE / A mortgage that has priority as a *lien* over all other mortgages.

Importance: Generally, the first mortgage is the one recorded first. When a first mortgage is retired, existing mortgages of lower priority will move up. In case of foreclosure, the first mortgage will be satisfied before other mortgages.

FIXED EXPENSES / In the operation of *real estate*, expenses that remain the same regardless of occupancy. *Contrast* VARIABLE EXPENSES. **Examples:** Insurance and interest expenses are expected to be the same, whether or not a building is occupied, so they are fixed expenses. By contrast, the costs of utilities and office cleaning will vary with occupancy.

FIXTURES / Personal property attached to the land or improvements so as to become part of the real estate.

Importance: When buying or selling real estate, it is best to specifically identify which appliances remain and which do not. Otherwise, fixtures remain with the property.

FLOOR LOAN / The minimum that a lender is willing to advance on a *permanent mortgage*. An additional principal amount will be loaned upon attainment of a certain occupancy rate.

FNMA / *See* FEDERAL NATIONAL MORTGAGE ASSOCIATION.

FORBEARANCE / A policy of restraint in taking legal action to remedy a *default* or other breach of contract, generally in the hope that the default will be cured, given additional time.

FORCE MAJEURE / An unavoidable cause of delay or of failure to perform a *contract* obligation on time.

FORECLOSURE / A legal procedure whereby property pledged as security for a debt is sold to pay a defaulted debt.

Importance: Foreclosure gives a lender the right to sell property that was pledged for a debt. All parties to a mortgage contract should recognize its consequences.

FORFEITURE / Loss of money or anything else of value because of failure to perform under contract.

FRACTIONAL INTEREST / Ownership of some but not all of the rights in *real estate*. Examples are *easement*, hunting rights, and *leasehold estate*.

FRAUD / The intentional use of deception to purposely cheat or deceive another person, causing him/her to suffer loss.

Importance: Fraud, intentionally deceiving another, is far worse than misrepresentation, which is an incorrect or untrue statement. Consequently, punishment for fraud is more severe.

FREEHOLD / An interest in real estate without a predetermined time span. **Example:** A fee simple or a life estate.

FRONT FOOT / A standard measurement of land, applied at the frontage of its street line.

Importance: This measure is used for city lots of generally uniform depth. Prices are often quoted as the number of dollars per front foot.

FULL AMORTIZATION TERM / *See* AMORTIZATION TERM.

FULLY AMORTIZED LOAN / A loan having payments of *interest* and *principal* that are suffi-

cient to liquidate the loan over its term; self-liquidating. *See also* AMORTIZATION TERM.

FUNCTIONAL DEPRECIATION / Loss of value from all causes within the property, except those due to physical deterioration. **Example:** A poor floor plan or outdated plumbing fixtures.

FUNCTIONAL OBSOLESCENCE / *See* FUNCTIONAL DEPRECIATION.

FUNDS FROM OPERATIONS (FFO) / A measure of the profitability of a *real estate investment trust (REIT)*. FFO begins with net income as derived using *GAAP (generally accepted accounting principles)*. To that it adds depreciation deductions and deductions for amortization of deferred charges, which are noncash deductions. FFO does not consider extraordinary items and gains (losses) on the sale of real estate.

FURNITURE, FIXTURES, AND EQUIPMENT (FF&E) / A term frequently found in the ownership of a hotel or motel. This type of property wears out much more rapidly than other components of a hotel or motel, so an owner or prospective buyer needs to establish the condition, cost, and frequency of replacement of FF&E.

FUTURE VALUE OF ONE / *See* COMPOUND INTEREST.

GAAP / Generally accepted accounting principles. The set of rules considered standard and acceptable by certified public accountants. Accounting deductions are required for real estate depreciation, even for assets that appreciate in value.

GABLE ROOF / A pitched roof with sloping sides.

GAMBREL ROOF / A double pitched roof having a steep lower slope with a flatter slope above.

GAP MORTGAGE / A loan that fills the difference between the *floor loan* and the full amount of the *permanent mortgage*.

GENERAL WARRANTY DEED / A deed in which the *grantor* agrees to protect the *grantee* against any other claim to title of the property and also provides other promises. *See also* WARRANTY DEED.

Importance: This is the best type of deed to receive.

GEOGRAPHIC INFORMATION SYSTEMS (GIS) / A computer mapping program whereby land characteristics and/or *demographic* information are color-coded and often overlaid. The purpose is to determine locations of various business activities and demographics.

GIFT DEED / A deed for which the consideration is love and affection, and no material consideration is involved.

Importance: A gift deed is frequently used to transfer real estate to a relative.

GI LOAN / *See* VA LOAN.

GLA / *See* GROSS LEASABLE AREA.

GNMA / Government National Mortgage Association (Ginnie Mae).

GOVERNMENT RECTANGULAR SURVEY / A rectangular system of land survey that divides a district into 24-mile-square tracts from the *meridian* (north-south line) and the *base line* (east-west line). The tracts are divided into 6-mile-square parts called townships, which are in turn divided into 36 tracts, each 1 mile square, called sections.

Importance: This system is still used in several western states. For urban or suburban purposes the *lot and block number* and/or *metes and bounds* methods predominate.

GRACE PERIOD / Additional time allowed to perform an act or make a payment before a *default* occurs.

Importance: Many mortgage contracts have a grace period before a late payment is considered a default. It is usually wise to solve the problem before the grace period expires.

GRADE / (1) Ground level at the foundation of a building; (2) the degree of slope on land (e.g., a 2 percent grade means that the elevation rises 2 feet for every 100 linear feet).

Importance: The grade of land should be checked to determine whether it suits a planned use of the land.

GRADED LEASE / *See* GRADUATED LEASE.

GRADIENT / The slope, or rate of increase or decrease in elevation, of a surface; usually expressed as a percentage. *See also* GRADE.

GRADUATED LEASE / A lease that provides for graduated changes in the amount of rent at stated intervals; seldom used in short-term leases.

Importance: Graduated leases allow rent changes automatically, so that there is no need to revise the entire lease just to change the rent. These are often long-term leases that suit both landlord and tenant.

GRANT / A technical term used in deeds of conveyance of property to indicate a transfer.

GRANT DEED / A type of special warranty deed whereby the seller grants that he or she has not encumbered the property and transferred such encumbrance in the sale, and has not deeded the property to another. This is the form of deed most commonly used in California.

GRANTEE / The party to whom the title to real property is conveyed; the buyer.

GRANTOR / The person who conveys real estate by deed; the seller or donor.

GRI / A graduate of the REALTORS® Institute, which is affiliated with the *National Association of REALTORS®*.

Importance: The GRI designation indicates that a real estate salesperson or broker has gone beyond the minimum educational requirements.

GRM / *See* GROSS RENT MULTIPLIER.

GROSS INCOME / Total income from property before any expenses are deducted. Gross income may be further described as *potential*, which assumes neither vacancy nor collection losses, or *effective*, which is net of vacancy and collection losses.

GROSS LEASABLE AREA (GLA) / The floor area that can be used by a *tenant*; generally measured from the center of joint partitions to outside wall surfaces. *Contrast* NET LEASABLE AREA.

GROSS LEASE / A lease of property whereby the landlord (lessor) is responsible for paying all property expenses, such as taxes, insurance, utilities, and repairs. *Contrast* NET LEASE.

Importance: Landlord and tenant agree in writing as to who pays each operating expense. Otherwise there is strong likelihood for disagreement and litigation.

GROSS POSSIBLE RENT / *See* POTENTIAL GROSS INCOME.

GROSS RENT MULTIPLIER (GRM) / The sales price divided by the rental rate. **Example:** The sales price is $40,000; the gross monthly rent is $400; the GRM = $40,000/$400 = 100. It may also be expressed as an annual figure (8.333), that is, the number of years of rent equaling the purchase price.

Importance: In many investment situations the price is set based on a multiple of the rent level.

GROUND LEASE / An agreement for the rent of land only, often for a long term, at the expiration of which all of the real estate belongs to the landowner.

Importance: Sometimes land can be purchased or leased separately from buildings, thus splitting ownership into components that are more desirable. A property buyer or lessee must be mindful of the lease terms and the effect of such a lease on using or financing the property.

GROUND RENT / The rent earned by leased land.

Importance: Ground leases may be net or gross. In a net lease the *tenant* pays expenses, such as insurance and real estate taxes.

GUARANTEE OF TITLE / Document resulting from examination of public records, in which the examiner guarantees the title to be as described. A precursor of *title insurance*; rarely used today.

GUARDIAN / A person appointed by a court to administer the affairs of an individual who is not capable of administering his/her own affairs.

Importance: An *incompetent* cannot enter a valid contract. It is important to deal with the person's guardian.

HABENDUM CLAUSE / The "to have and to hold" clause that defines or limits the quantity of the estate granted in the deed. **Example:** "To have and to hold for one's lifetime" creates a life estate.

HANDYMAN SPECIAL / In real estate brokerage jargon, a property that is in need of repair, a fixer-upper. The implication is that the property is a bargain for someone who can accomplish the repairs economically.

HEIRS AND ASSIGNS / Terminology used in deeds and wills to provide that the recipient receive a *fee simple* estate in lands rather than a lesser interest.

Importance: These words give the recipient complete ownership, not just an estate for a limited duration of time.

HEREDITAMENTS / Any property that may be inherited, whether real or personal, tangible or intangible.

HIGHEST AND BEST USE / The legally and physically possible use that, at the time of *appraisal*, is most likely to produce the greatest net return to the land and/or buildings over a given time period.

Importance: To realize the full value of land, the improvements built on it must represent its highest and best use.

HIP ROOF / A pitched roof formed by four walls sloped in different directions. The two longer sides of the roof form a ridge at the top.

HISTORIC DISTRICT / A designated area where the buildings are considered to have some significant historic character. Such designation makes the area eligible for certain federal assistance programs and protects the area from clearance in conjunction with federally sponsored programs.

HOLDER IN DUE COURSE / A person who has taken a note, check, or similar asset (1) before it was overdue, (2) in good faith and for value, and (3) without knowledge that it had been previously dis-

honored and without notice of any defect at the time it was negotiated to him/her.

Importance: A holder in due course is an innocent buyer of paper (a debt).

HOLDOVER TENANT / A tenant who remains in possession of leased property after the expiration of the lease term.

Importance: A holdover tenant has a *tenancy at sufferance*. The landlord may dictate the terms of occupancy.

HOME EQUITY LOAN / A loan secured by a second mortgage on one's principal residence, generally to be used for some nonhousing expenditure.

HOMESTEAD / The status provided to a homeowner's principal residence by California statutes; protects the home against judgments up to specified amounts.

Importance: In California, the owner can continue possession and enjoyment of a home against the wishes of creditors.

HOMESTEAD EXEMPTION / In California, a $7,000 reduction in the assessed value allowed for a person's principal residence.

Importance: In California, the homestead exemption reduces assessed values for owners.

HUD / U.S. Department of Housing and Urban Development.

HVAC / An acronym that refers to the climate control system in buildings (Heating, Ventilation, and Air Conditioning).

HYPOTHECATE / To pledge a thing as security without having to give up possession of it.

Importance: The word *hypothecate* comes (through Late Latin and French) from a Greek word meaning "to put down as a deposit" and has the same meaning as the French-derived word *mortgage*.

ILLIQUIDITY / Inadequate cash to meet obligations. Real estate is considered an illiquid investment because of the time and effort required to convert it to cash.

IMPLIED AGENCY / Occurs when the words and actions of the parties indicate that there is an agency relationship.

IMPROVEMENT RATIO / The value of *improvements* relative to the value of unimproved land. **Example:** Land worth $250,000 was improved with a $750,000 building. The improvement ratio is $750,000/$250,000 or 3:1.

IMPROVEMENTS / Additions to raw land that tend to increase value, such as buildings, streets, sewers.

Importance: An improvement is anything except the raw land. *See also* HIGHEST AND BEST USE.

INCHOATE / (1) Recently or just begun; (2) unfinished, begun but not completed. **Examples:** In real estate, this term can apply to *dower* or *curtesy* rights prior to the death of a spouse, instruments that are supposed to be recorded, and interests that can ripen into a vested estate.

INCOME / The money or other benefit coming from the use of something. Gross sales or income is the full amount received; net income is the remainder after subtracting expenses. Many persons in real estate prefer to use *cash flow* as the measure of income, whereas those in accounting prefer *net income*.

INCOME APPROACH / One of the three appraisal methods used in arriving at an estimate of the market value of property; the value of the property is the present worth of the income it is expected to produce during its remaining life.

Importance: Annual income for rental property can be capitalized into value to estimate the property's worth.

INCOME MULTIPLIER / The relationship of price to income. *See also* GROSS RENT MULTIPLIER.

INCOME PROPERTY / Property whose ownership appeal is that it produces income. **Examples:** Office buildings, shopping centers, rental apartments, hotels.

INCOME STREAM / A regular flow of money generated by a business or investment.

INCOMPETENT / A person who is unable to manage his/her own affairs by reason of insanity, imbecility, or feeblemindedness.

Importance: When conducting business with an incompetent, his/her guardian's consent is required.

INCURABLE DEPRECIATION / (1) A defect that cannot be cured or is not financially practical to cure; (2) a defect in the "bone structure" of a building.

Importance: When appraising real estate using the *cost approach*, incurable depreciation is separated from curable to indicate the actual loss in value sustained by the property.

INDENTURE / A written agreement made between two or more persons having different interests.

Importance: Indentures are used in mortgages, deeds, and bonds. They describe the terms of the agreement.

INDEPENDENT CONTRACTOR / A contractor who is self-employed for tax purposes. When real estate salespeople are self-employed, the broker is not required to withhold taxes.

INDEPENDENT FEE APPRAISER / A person who estimates the value of property but has no interest in the property and is not associated with a lending association or other investor.

INDEX / (1) A statistic that indicates some current economic or financial condition. Indexes are often used to make adjustments in wage rates, rental rates, loan interest rates, and pension benefits set by long-term contracts. (2) To adjust contract terms according to an index.

INDEX LEASE / A lease in which rentals are tied to an agreed upon index of costs. **Example:** Rentals are to increase along with the Consumer Price Index.

Importance: An index lease can provide fairness to both parties in a long-term leasing arrangement.

INDUSTRIAL PROPERTY / Property used for industrial purposes, such as factories and power plants.

Importance: Land to be used for industrial purposes must be zoned for that purpose.

INFLATION / A loss in the purchasing power of money; an increase in the general price level. Inflation is generally measured by the Consumer Price Index, published by the Bureau of Labor Statistics.

Importance: Real estate is considered a hedge against inflation because it tends to be long lasting and holds its value in real terms. As the value of the dollar drops, real estate tends to command more dollars. For example, a home purchased in 1967 for $50,000 was resold in 1976 for $100,000 and in 2006 for $400,000. The home did nothing to cause its price to change; inflation caused the house to command more dollars.

INFRASTRUCTURE / The basic public works of a city or subdivision, including roads, bridges, sewer and water systems, drainage systems, and essential public utilities.

INJUNCTION / A writ or order issued by a court to restrain one or more parties to a suit or a proceeding from performing an act that is deemed inequitable or unjust in regard to the rights of some other party or parties in the suit or proceeding.

Importance: An injunction can prevent a wrong-doing while the legal process continues, that is, before a final judgment is made about the rights of the parties.

INNOCENT PURCHASER / One who buys an asset without knowing of a flaw in the title or property. *See* BONA FIDE purchaser.

IN REM / Latin for "against the thing." A proceeding against *realty* directly, as distinguished from a proceeding against a person (used in taking land for nonpayment of taxes, and so on). By contrast, *in Personam* means "against the person."

INSTALLMENTS / Parts of the same debt, payable at successive periods as agreed; payments made to reduce a mortgage.

Importance: Many debts are paid in installments that include interest for a recent period plus some amount for *amortization*.

INSTALLMENT TO AMORTIZE ONE DOLLAR / A mathematically computed factor, derived from *compound interest* functions, that offers the level periodic payment required to retire a $1.00 loan within a certain time frame. The periodic installment must exceed the periodic interest rate. *See also* AMORTIZATION; AMORTIZATION TERM.

INSTRUMENT / A written legal document, created to effect the rights and liabilities of the parties to it. **Examples:** Deed, will, lease.

INSURABLE TITLE / A title that can be insured by a title insurance company.

Importance: When acquiring real estate, a buyer should determine whether the title is insurable. If not, there are probably valid claims that will affect his/her use or ownership.

INSURANCE COVERAGE / Total amount and type of insurance carried.

Importance: It is conservative to retain insurance coverage based on the replacement value or cost of one's valuables.

INTANGIBLE VALUE / Value that cannot be seen or touched. **Example:** The goodwill of an established business.

INTEREST / (1) Money paid for the use of money; (2) the type and extent of ownership.

INTEREST RATE / (1) The percentage of a sum of money charged for its use; (2) the rate of return on an investment.

Importance: The loan interest rate is an important ingredient in determining the periodic installment payment.

INTERPLEADER / A proceeding initiated by a neutral third party to determine the rights of rival claimants to property or a transaction.

Importance: An escrow agent in California may call for an interpleader when there is a dispute between the buyer and seller.

INTER VIVOS TRUST / A trust set up during one's lifetime.

INTESTACY / *See* INTESTATE.

INTESTATE / A person who dies leaving no will or a defective will. His/her property goes to his/her legal heirs.

Importance: California law determines inheritance rules for intestates. If there are no heirs, the property *escheats* to the state.

INVESTMENT ANALYSIS / A study of the likely return from a proposed investment with the objective of evaluating the amount an investor may pay for it, the investment's suitability to that investor, or the feasibility of a proposed real estate development.

INVESTMENT PROPERTY / Property that is owned for its income generating capacity or expected resale value. **Example:** Apartments, office buildings, undeveloped land.

INVESTMENT VALUE / The estimated value of a certain real estate investment to a particular individual or institutional investor; may be greater or less than *market value*, depending on the investor's particular situation.

INVOLUNTARY ALIENATION / A loss of property for nonpayment of debts such as taxes or mortgage foreclosure.

INVOLUNTARY LIEN / A lien imposed against property without the consent of the owner (unpaid taxes, special assessments).

Importance: A lien can be created without any action by the landowner.

IRREVOCABLE / Incapable of being recalled or revoked; unchangeable, unalterable.

JEOPARDY / Peril, danger, risk. **Example:** Property pledged as security for a delinquent loan is in jeopardy of *foreclosure*.

JOINT TENANCY / Ownership of realty by two or more persons, each of whom has an undivided interest with *right of survivorship*. **Example:** A and B own land in joint tenancy. Each owns half of the entire (undivided) property. Upon A's death, B will own the entire property, or vice versa.

JOINT VENTURE / An agreement between two or more parties who invest in a single business or property.

JUDGMENT / A court decree stating that one individual is indebted to another and fixing the amount of the indebtedness.

Importance: A judgment is a final determination of the matter, decided by a court.

JUDGMENT CREDITOR / A person who has received a court decree or judgment for money due to him/her.

JUDGMENT DEBTOR / A person against whom a judgment has been issued by a court for money owed.

JUDGMENT LIEN / The claim upon the property of a debtor resulting from a judgment. **Example:** A won't pay his debt to B. After establishing the debt in court, B may be allowed by the court to put a lien on A's real estate.

JUDICIAL FORECLOSURE / When a trustee or mortgagee requests court supervision of a foreclosure action.

JUNIOR LIEN / See JUNIOR MORTGAGE.

JUNIOR MORTGAGE / A *mortgage* whose claim against the property will be satisfied only after prior mortgages have been sold; also called *junior lien*.

Importance: A junior (second, third) mortgage has value as long as the borrower continues payments or the property's value is in excess of the mortgage debts.

LACHES / Delay or negligence in asserting one's legal rights.

Importance: If a person does not act in a reasonable time to assert his/her rights, he/she may be barred from doing so because of the delay.

LAND / The surface of the earth; any part of the surface of the earth. (Note: Legal definitions often distinguish land from water.)

LAND CONTRACT / A real estate installment selling arrangement whereby the buyer may use, occupy, and enjoy land, but no *deed* is given by the seller (so no title passes) until all or a specified part of the sale price has been paid.

Importance: In comparison to a deed, a land contract is easier to foreclose should the buyer fail to make the payments.

LAND LEASE / Only the ground is covered by the lease. *See also* GROUND LEASE.

LANDLORD / A person who rents property to another; a *lessor*.

LANDMARK / A fixed object serving as a boundary mark for a tract of land.

Importance: In surveying, a landmark serves as a reference point.

LAND PATENT / See PATENT.

LAND, TENEMENTS, AND HEREDITAMENTS / A phrase used in early English law to express all sorts of *real estate*.

Importance: This is the most comprehensive description of real estate.

LEAD-BASED PAINT / Considered a hazardous material, principally because children may eat the chips. It is potentially poisonous, and its existence in property is to be disclosed. Its presence is often difficult to determine because applications of lead-based paint may have been covered over by more recent applications of paint that is free of lead.

LEASE / A contract in which, for a consideration called *rent*, one who is entitled to the possession of real property (the *lessor*) transfers those rights to another (the *lessee*) for a specified period of time.

Importance: A lease is an essential agreement, allowing an owner to transfer possession to a user for a limited amount of time.

LEASED FEE / The landlord's ownership interest in a *property* that is under *lease*. *Contrast* LEASEHOLD.

LEASEHOLD OR LEASEHOLD ESTATE / The interest or estate on which a *lessee* (tenant) of real estate has his/her lease.

Importance: A leasehold can be quite valuable when the tenant's rent is below the market rate and the lease is for a long term.

LEASEHOLD IMPROVEMENTS / Fixtures, attached to *real estate*, that are generally acquired or installed by the tenant. Upon expiration of the *lease*, the tenant can generally remove them, provided that removal does not damage the property and is not in conflict with the lease. **Examples:** Cabinets, light fixtures, window treatments of a retail store in a leased building.

LEASEHOLD VALUE / The value of a tenant's interest in a *lease*, especially when the *rent* is below market level and the lease has a long remaining term.

LEASE WITH OPTION TO PURCHASE / A lease that gives the lessee (tenant) the right to purchase the property at an agreed upon price under certain conditions.

Importance: Because the option allows but does not compel the purchase, it gives the tenant time to consider acquisition.

LEGAL DESCRIPTION / Legally acceptable identification of real estate by the (1) *government rectangular survey*, (2) *metes and bounds*, or (3) *lot and block number* method.

LESSEE / A person to whom property is rented under a *lease*; a tenant.

LESSOR / A person who rents property to another under a *lease*; a landlord.

LEVEL ANNUITY / See ANNUITY.

LEVERAGE / The use of borrowed funds to increase purchasing power and, ideally, to increase the profitability of an investment.

Importance: If the property increases in value or yields financial benefits at a rate above the borrowed money interest rate, leverage is favorable, also called positive. But if the rate of property benefits is less than the interest rate, the investor's losses are increased.

LICENSE / (1) Permission; (2) a privilege or right granted by California to an individual to operate as a real estate broker or salesperson.

Importance: (1) License allows a person to use property for a limited time. (2) In California, a person must be licensed as a broker (or salesperson) to receive payment for a sale, lease, or other transaction.

LICENSED APPRAISER / Generally, an *appraiser* who meets certain state requirements, but lacks the experience or expertise of a certified appraiser. *See also* CERTIFIED GENERAL APPRAISER; CERTIFIED RESIDENTIAL APPRAISER.

LICENSEE / A person who holds a real estate license.

Importance: In California, only licensees are entitled to receive compensation for assisting with a real estate transaction. Education and the passing of examinations are requirements of licensing.

LIEN / A charge against property making it security for the payment of a debt, judgment, mortgage, or taxes; a lien is a type of *encumbrance*.

Importance: A lien makes the property collateral for a debt. Some liens may allow the property to be sold to satisfy the debt.

LIFE ESTATE / A freehold interest in land that expires upon the death of the owner or some other specified person.

Importance: A person with a life estate may use the property, but not abuse it, for as long as he/she lives. Then it reverts to the *remainderman*.

LIFE TENANT / A person who is allowed to use property for his/her lifetime or for the lifetime of another designated person. *See also* LIFE ESTATE.

LIKE-KIND PROPERTY / Property having the same nature. *See* SECTION 1031.

LIMITED LIABILITY COMPANY (LLC) / Organization form recognized in many states that may be treated as a partnership for federal tax purposes and has limited liability protection for the owners at the state level. The entity may be subject to the state franchise tax as a corporation. Many states also recognized *limited liability partnerships,* in which the individual partners are protected from the liabilities of the other partners. These entities are considered *partnerships* for both federal and state tax purposes. **Example:** A limited liability company may be an excellent way to own real estate because it may provide many of the legal advantages of a corporation and the tax advantages of a partnership. States may impose restrictions, for example by limiting the number of owners.

LIMITED PARTNERSHIP / *Partnership* in which there is at least one partner who is passive and whose liability is limited to the amount invested and at least one partner whose liability extends beyond monetary investment. *See* FAMILY LIMITED PARTNERSHIP. **Example:** Abel, a syndicator, forms a *limited partnership* with Price, Stone, and Wise. Abel invests his time and talent, is the general partner, and owns 10% of the partnership. Price, Stone, and Wise have each invested $30,000 cash and are limited partners. They buy property with a $90,000 down payment and a $500,000 mortgage. The property drops in value by $250,000. Price, Stone, and Wise lose their equity, and Abel, the general partner, is responsible for additional losses.

LIQUIDATED DAMAGES / An amount agreed upon in a contract that one party will pay the other in the event of a breach of the contract.

LIS PENDENS / Latin for "suit pending"; recorded notice that a suit has been filed, the outcome of which may affect title to a certain land.

Importance: Title to the property under consideration may be in jeopardy.

LISTING / (1) A written employment contract between a *principal* and an *agent* authorizing the agent to perform services for the principal involving the latter's property; (2) a record of property for sale by a broker who has been authorized by the owner to sell; (3) the property so listed. *See also* EXCLUSIVE AGENCY LISTING, EXCLUSIVE RIGHT TO SELL LISTING, NET LISTING, OPEN LISTING.

LITIGATION / The act of carrying on a lawsuit.

LITTORAL / Part of the shore zone of a large body of water.

Importance: Littoral rights differ from *riparian rights,* which pertain to a river or stream.

LOAN CLOSING / *See* CLOSING.

LOAN CONSTANT / *See* MORTGAGE CONSTANT.

LOAN-TO-VALUE RATIO (LTV) / The ratio obtained by dividing the mortgage principal by the property value.

Importance: Lenders typically provide loans with a stated maximum loan-to-value ratio. For conventional home loans it is typically 80 percent. In many cases it can be increased to 95 percent if mortgage insurance is purchased. VA and FHA loans may offer higher ratios.

LOCK-IN / An agreement to maintain a certain price or rate for a certain period of time.

Importance: In many *mortgage* commitments the lender agrees to lock-in the interest rate for a certain period, such as 60 days. Sometimes a lock-in is provided only upon payment of a *commitment* fee.

LOT AND BLOCK NUMBER / A land description method that refers to a recorded plat. **Exam-**

ple: Lot 6, Block F of the Sunnybrook Estates, District 2 of Rover County, Rhode Island.

LOT LINE / A line bounding a lot as described in a survey of the property.

Importance: Lot lines mark boundaries. There may also be building *setback* requirements, or *building lines*, within a lot.

LTV / *See* LOAN-TO-VALUE RATIO.

MAI / A professional designation offered by the *Appraisal Institute*

Importance: The MAI designation is one of the most coveted in real estate. Many appraisals of large commercial properties are done by MAIs.

MAJORITY / The age at which a person is no longer a minor and is fully able to conduct his/her own affairs; in California, majority is 18.

Importance: A contract with a minor is voidable by the minor.

MARGIN / A constant amount added to the value of the *index* for the purpose of adjusting the interest rate on an *adjustable-rate mortgage*.

MARGINAL PROPERTY / Property that is barely profitable to use. **Example:** The sale of cotton that has been efficiently raised yields $100, but the cotton cost $99.99 to raise. The land is therefore considered marginal land.

MARKETABILITY STUDY / An analysis, for a specific client, of the probable sales of a specific type of real estate product.

MARKETABLE TITLE / A title that a court will consider so free from defect that it will enforce its acceptance by a purchaser; similar to *insurable title*.

MARKET ANALYSIS / A study of the supply and demand conditions in a specific area for a specific type of property or service. A market analysis report is generally prepared by someone with experience in real estate, economics, or marketing. It serves to help decide what type of project to develop and is also helpful in arranging permanent and construction financing for a proposed development.

MARKET APPROACH / *See* SALES COMPARISON APPROACH.

MARKET DATA APPROACH / *See* SALES COMPARISON APPROACH.

MARKET PRICE / The actual price paid in a market transaction; a historical fact.

Importance: *Market value* is a theoretical concept, whereas market price has actually occurred.

MARKET STUDY / *See* MARKET ANALYSIS.

MARKET VALUE / The highest price a buyer, willing but not compelled to buy, will pay, and the lowest price a seller, willing but not compelled to sell, will accept. Many conditions are assumed to exist.

Importance: In theory, property would sell for its market value.

MASS APPRAISING / An effort, typically used by tax *assessors*, to determine the salient characteristics of properties in a given submarket, to allow an approximation of value for each. Sophisticated statistical techniques are used frequently in mass appraising.

MATERIAL FACT / A fact that is germane to a particular situation; one that participants in the situation may reasonably be expected to consider.

Importance: In a contract, a material fact is one without which the contract would not have been made.

MECHANIC'S LIEN / A lien given by law upon a building or other improvement upon land, and upon the land itself, as security for the payment for labor done upon, and materials furnished for, the improvement.

Importance: A mechanic's lien protects persons who helped build or supply materials.

MEETING OF THE MINDS / Agreement by all parties to a contract to its terms and substance.

Importance: When there is a meeting of the minds, the contract is not based on secret intentions of one party that were withheld from another.

MELLO-ROOS BONDS AND TAXES / Bonds issued and taxes levied under the authority of the Mello-Roos Community Facilities Act of 1982, which authorizes the formation of community facilities districts, the issuance of bonds, and the levying of special taxes to finance designated public facilities and services. Effective July 1, 1993, the seller of a property consisting of one to four dwelling units subject to the lien of a Mello-Roos community facilities district must make a good-faith effort to obtain from the district a disclosure notice concerning the special tax and give the notice to a prospective buyer.

MERIDIAN / North-south line used in government rectangular survey.

METES AND BOUNDS / A land description method that relates the boundary lines of land, setting forth all the boundary lines together with their terminal points and angles.

Importance: A person can follow a metes and bounds description on a plat or on the ground.

MILL / One tenth of a cent; used in expressing tax rates on a per dollar basis. **Example:** A tax rate of 60 mills means that taxes are 6 cents per dollar of assessed valuation.

MINERAL LEASE / An agreement that provides the lessee the right to excavate and sell minerals on the property of the lessor or to remove and sell petroleum and natural gas from the pool underlying the property of the lessor. In return, the lessor receives a royalty payment based on the value of the minerals removed.

MINERAL RIGHTS / The privilege of gaining income from the sale of oil, gas, and other valuable resources found on land.

MINOR / A person under an age specified by law (18 in California).

Importance: Real estate contracts entered into with minors are voidable by the minor.

MINORITY DISCOUNT / A reduction from the *market value* of an asset because the minority interest owner(s) cannot direct the business operations and the interest lacks marketability.

MISREPRESENTATION / An untrue statement, whether deliberate or unintentional. It may be a form of nondisclosure where there is a duty to disclose or the planned creation of a false appearance. Where there is misrepresentation of *material fact,* the person injured may sue for *damages* or rescind the contract.

MONUMENT / A fixed object and point designated by surveyors to establish land locations. **Examples:** Posts, pillars, stone markers, unique trees, stones, pipes, watercourses.

MORATORIUM / A time period during which a certain activity is not allowed.

MORTGAGE / A written instrument that creates a lien upon real estate as security for the payment of a specified debt.

Importance: The mortgage allows a defaulted debt to be satisfied by forcing a sale of the property.

MORTGAGE BANKER / One who originates, sells, and services *mortgage* loans. Most loans are insured or guaranteed by a government agency or private mortgage insurer.

MORTGAGE BROKER / One who, for a fee, places loans with investors but does not service such loans.

MORTGAGE COMMITMENT / An agreement between a lender and a borrower to lend money at a future date, subject to the conditions described in the agreement.

Importance: The terms of the commitment are important, especially the interest rate *lock-in,* if there is one.

MORTGAGE CONSTANT / The percentage ratio between the annual mortgage payment and the original amount of the debt.

MORTGAGEE / A person who holds a *lien* on or *title* to property as security for a debt.

Importance: The mortgagee receives the lien; the *mortgagor* receives the loan.

MORTGAGE LOAN DISCLOSURE STATEMENT / A statement that discloses to a prospective borrower the terms and conditions of a mortgage loan; it is required by law to be furnished by mortgage brokers before the borrower becomes obligated under the loan, and must be on a form approved by the California Real Estate Commissioner.

MORTGAGOR / A person who pledges his/her property as security for a loan. *See also* MORTGAGEE.

MOST PROBABLE SELLING PRICE / A property's most likely selling price when not all the conditions required for a *market value* estimate are relevant. **Example:** An appraiser estimated a property's most likely sales price at $100,000, assuming a sale within 20 days, whereas its market value of $120,000 might require up to 6 months to realize.

MULTIPLE LISTING / An arrangement among a group of real estate *brokers*; they agree in advance to provide information about some or all of their listings to the others and also agree that commissions on sales of such listings will be split between listing and selling brokers.

MULTIPLIER / A factor, used as a guide, applied by multiplication to derive or estimate an important value. **Examples:** (1) A *gross rent multiplier* of 6 means that property renting for $12,000 per year can be sold for six times that amount, or $72,000. (2) A population multiplier of 2 means that, for each job added, two people will be added to a city's population.

NAR / *See* NATIONAL ASSOCIATION OF REALTORS®.

NATIONAL ASSOCIATION OF REALTORS® (NAR) / An organization devoted to encouraging professionalism in real estate activities.

Importance: The NAR has strong lobbyists that protect the interest of the real estate community, especially of homeowners. It also has affiliates related to appraising, counseling, and managing real estate.

NEGATIVE AMORTIZATION / An increase in the outstanding balance of a loan resulting from the inadequacy of periodic debt service payments to cover required interest charged on the loan. Generally occurs under indexed loans for which the applicable interest rate may be increased without increasing the monthly payments. Negative amortization will occur if the indexed interest rate is increased.

NET INCOME / In real estate this term is now *net operating income.* In accounting, net income is the actual earnings, after deducting all expenses, including interest and depreciation, from gross sales.

NET LEASABLE AREA (NLA) / For office and retail properties, the portion used exclusively by the tenant; generally excludes hallways, restrooms, and other common areas.

Importance: The rent per square foot may be judged consistently between buildings when it is based on this space measurement.

NET LEASE / A lease whereby, in addition to the rent stipulated, the lessee (tenant) pays such things as taxes, insurance, and maintenance. The landlord's rent receipt is thereby net of those expenses.

Importance: The responsibility for maintenance costs is shifted to the lessee; the lessor is a passive investor.

NET LISTING / A listing in which the broker's *commission* is the excess of the sale price over an agreed upon (net) price to the seller; discouraged in California. **Example:** A house is listed for sale at $100,000 net. The broker's commission is $1 if it sells for $100,001. But if it sells for $150,000, the broker receives $50,000.

NET OPERATING INCOME (NOI) / Income from property or business after operating expenses have been deducted, but before deducting income taxes and financing expenses (interest and principal payments).

NLA / *See* NET LEASABLE AREA.

NOI / *See* NET OPERATING INCOME.

NONCONFORMING LOAN / Home mortgage loan that does not meet the standards of, or is too large to be purchased by, FNMA or FHLMC. Typically, the *interest rate* is at least half a percentage point higher than for a conforming loan.

NONCONFORMING USE / A use that violates *zoning ordinances* or codes but is allowed to continue because it began before the zoning restriction was enacted.

Importance: This allows a prior use to continue, but puts restrictions on future uses of the property.

NONRECOURSE / Carrying no personal liability. Lenders may take the property pledged as collateral to satisfy a debt, but they have no *recourse* to other assets of the borrower.

NOTARY PUBLIC / An officer who is authorized to take acknowledgments to certain types of documents, such as *deeds*, *contracts*, and *mortgages*, and before whom affidavits may be sworn.

Importance: Most documents must be notarized as a condition of being recorded.

NOTE / A written instrument that acknowledges a debt and promises to pay.

Importance: A note is enforceable in a court of law. Collateral for the note may be sold to satisfy the debt.

NOTICE TO QUIT / A notice to a tenant to vacate rented property.

Importance: The tenant is permitted to complete the term of the lease, except in cases of *tenancy at will* or *tenancy at sufferance*.

NOVATION / Substitution of a revised agreement for an existing one, with the consent of all parties involved. Technically, any time parties to an existing contract agree to change it, the revised document is a novation.

NULL AND VOID / Having no legal validity.

OBLIGEE / The person in whose favor an obligation is entered into.

OBLIGOR / The person who binds him/herself to another; one who has engaged to perform some obligation; one who makes a bond.

OBSOLESCENCE / (1) A loss in value due to reduced desirability and usefulness of a structure because its design and construction have become obsolete; (2) loss due to a structure's becoming old-fashioned, not in keeping with modern needs, with consequent loss of income; and (3) changes outside the property.

Importance: Obsolescence can cause a loss in value just as *physical deterioration* does.

OFFEROR / One who extends an offer to another.

OFFICE BUILDING / A structure primarily used for the conduct of business, such as administration, clerical services, and consultation with clients and associates. Such buildings can be large or small and may house one or more business concerns.

OPEN-END MORTGAGE / A mortgage under which the mortgagor (borrower) may secure additional funds from the mortgagee (lender), usually stipulating a ceiling amount that can be borrowed.

Importance: A development in real estate finance is a line-of-credit home equity loan. This works the same as an open-end mortgage.

OPEN LISTING / A listing given to any number of brokers without liability to compensate any except the one who first secures a buyer ready, willing, and able to meet the terms of the listing or secures the seller's acceptance of another offer. The sale of the property automatically terminates all open listings.

OPEN MORTGAGE / A mortgage that has matured or is overdue and is therefore open to foreclosure at any time.

OPERATING EXPENSE RATIO / A mathematical relationship derived by dividing *operating expenses* by *potential gross income*.

Importance: A comparison of rents for properties would be incomplete without also comparing operating expenses. Apartments generally have operating expense ratios between 30 and 50 percent; this may be exceeded when the lessor pays utilities or the apartments are in low-rent areas. Office buildings often have higher operating expense ratios (40 and 60 percent) because more intensive management and maintenance, such as cleaning services, are provided.

OPERATING EXPENSES / Amounts paid to maintain property, such as repairs, insurance, property taxes, but not including financing costs or depreciation.

OPERATING LEASE / A lease between the lessee and a sublessee who actually occupies and uses the property.

Importance: In an operating lease the lessee runs the property; by contrast, in a *financing lease* the lessee becomes lessor to the operating tenant.

OPERATING STATEMENTS / Financial reports on the cash flow of a business or property. *See* CASH FLOW, RENT ROLL.

OPTION / The right, but not the obligation, to purchase or lease a property upon specified terms within a specified period. **Example:** The right to buy certain land within 90 days at $5,000 per acre. The property becomes reserved for that time period.

OPTIONEE / One who receives or purchases an option.

OPTIONOR / One who gives or sells an option.

OPTION TO PURCHASE / A contract that gives one the right (but *not* the obligation) to buy a property within a certain time, for a specified amount, and subject to specified conditions.

ORAL CONTRACT / An unwritten agreement. With few exceptions, oral agreements for the sale or use of real estate are unenforceable. However, an oral lease for less than 1 year could be valid in California.

Importance: When dealing with real estate, agreements should be in writing.

ORIGINAL EQUITY / The amount of cash initially invested by the underlying *real estate* owner; distinguished from sweat equity or payments made after loan is made.

OVERAGE / *See* PERCENTAGE RENT.

OVERALL CAPITALIZATION RATE (OVERALL RATE OF RETURN) / The rate obtained by dividing *net operating income* by the purchase price of the property.

Importance: Rates of return from properties may be compared to each other; or the rate may be divided into income to estimate property value.

OWNERSHIP RIGHTS TO REALTY / Possession, enjoyment, control, and disposition.

PACKAGE MORTGAGE / A mortgage arrangement whereby the principal amount loaned is increased to include *personalty* (e.g., appliances) as well as *realty*; both realty and personalty serve as collateral.

P&I / Principal and interest (payment).

PARCEL / A piece of property under one ownership; a lot in a subdivision.

PARTIALLY AMORTIZED LOAN / A loan that requires some payments toward *principal* but does not fully retire the debt, thereby requiring a *balloon payment*. *See also* AMORTIZATION.

PARTIAL OR FRACTIONAL INTEREST / The ownership of some, but not all, the rights in *real estate*. **Examples:** (1) *Leasehold;* (2) *easement;* (3) *hunting rights*.

PARTITION / The division of real property between those who own it in undivided shares. **Example:** A and B own land as tenants in common until they partition it. Thereafter, each owns a particular tract of land.

PARTNERSHIP / An agreement between two or more entities to go into business or invest. Either partner may bind the other, within the scope of the partnership. Each partner is liable for all the partnership's debts. A partnership normally pays no taxes but merely files an information return. The individual partners pay personal income tax on their share of income.

PARTY WALL / A wall built along the line separating two properties, lying partly on each. Either owner has the right to use the wall and has an *easement* over that part of the adjoining owner's land covered by the wall.

PATENT / Conveyance of title to government land; also called a *land patent*.

PAYMENT CAP / A contractual limit on the amount of adjustment allowed in the monthly payment for an *adjustable-rate mortgage* at any one adjustment period. Generally it does not affect the interest rate charged. If the allowable payment does not cover interest due on the principal at the adjusted rate of interest, *negative amortization* will occur.

PERCENTAGE LEASE / A lease of property in which the rental is based on a percentage of the volume of sales made upon the leased premises. It usually provides for minimum rental and is regularly used for retailers who are tenants.

Importance: The retailer pays additional rent only if sales are high; the shopping center owner has an incentive to make an attractive shopping area.

PERCENTAGE RENT / The rent payable under a *percentage lease*; also called *overage*. Typically, the percentage applies to sales in excess of a pre-established base amount of the dollar sales volume.

Importance: Percentage rent provides incentive to a landlord for making a store or shopping area appeal to the market.

PERIODIC ESTATE / A lease, such as from month to month or year to year. Also known as periodic tenancy.

PERMANENT MORTGAGE / A mortgage for a long period of time (more than 10 years).

Importance: A permanent mortgage usually replaces construction or interim financing, and provides steady interest income plus *amortization* payments to the lender, For the borrower it means that there is no need to seek new financing.

PERSONAL LIABILITY / An individual's responsibility for a debt. Most mortgage loans on real estate are *recourse* (i.e., the lender can look to the property and the borrower for repayment). *Contrast* NONRECOURSE.

PERSONALTY / Personal property, that is, all property that is not *realty*.

Importance: Many laws and terms that apply to real property are not the same as those for personalty. When dealing with both types, appropriate law and terminology must be applied.

PHYSICAL DEPRECIATION (DETERIORATION) / The loss of value from all causes of age and action of the elements. **Examples:** Faded paint, broken window, hole in plaster, collapsed porch railing, sagging frame.

PLANNED UNIT DEVELOPMENT (PUD) / A zoning or land-use category for large tracts which allows several different intensities and forms of land use, planned as a single, well-integrated unit.

PLAT / A plan or map of a certain piece or certain pieces of land. **Examples:** A subdivision plat or a plat of one lot.

PLAT BOOK / A public record containing maps of land showing the division of the land into streets, blocks, and lots and indicating the measurements of the individual parcels.

Importance: The tax assessors office, usually in a city or county, maintains a plat book that is open for public inspection.

PLOTTAGE / Increment in the value of a plot of land that has been enlarged by assembling smaller plots into one ownership.

Importance: Combining several small tracts into one ownership can provide a large enough land area for a more profitable use than would be possible otherwise. However, it is often difficult to get several owners to sell, as some hold out for a high price.

PMI / Abbreviation for private mortgage insurance.

POCKET CARD / Identification required for *salespersons* and *brokers* in California.

Importance: Issued by the state licensing agency, it identifies its holder as a licensee and must be carried at all times.

POINTS / Fees paid to induce lenders to make a *mortgage* loan. Each point equals 1 percent of the loan principal. Points have the effect of reducing the amount of money advanced by the lender, thus increasing the effective interest rate.

POLICE POWER / The right of any political body to enact laws and enforce them for the order, safety, health, morals, and general welfare of the public.

Importance: Government authorities get the power of *eminent domain* through their police power.

POTENTIAL GROSS INCOME / The theoretical amount of money that would be collected in a year if all units in a rental building were fully occupied all year; also called *gross possible rent*.

POWER CENTER / a shopping center with few TENANTS, most of them ANCHOR TENANTS. Generally, a power center's anchor tenants are "category killers," that is, the dominant retailers in the markets they serve.

POWER OF ATTORNEY / An instrument authorizing a person to act as the agent of the person granting it.

Importance: By using a power of attorney, one can designate a specific person to do everything or just certain limited activities.

PREMISES / Land and tenements; an estate: the subject matter of a *conveyance*.

PREPAYMENT CLAUSE / A clause in a mortgage that gives a mortgagor (borrower) the privilege of paying the mortgage indebtedness before it becomes due.

Importance: Sometimes a penalty must be paid if prepayment is made, but payment of *interest* that is not yet due is waived.

PRESERVATION DISTRICT / A zoning designation to protect and maintain wildlife, park land, scenic areas, or historic districts.

PRICE FIXING / Illegal effort by competing businesses to maintain the same price, such as the commission rate on the sale of real estate.

PRIMARY LEASE / A lease between the owner and a tenant who, in turn, has sublet all or part of his/her interest.

Importance: The tenant in the primary lease is still responsible to the landlord, even though the subtenant(s) occupy the space.

PRINCIPAL / (1) The employer of an *agent* or *broker*; the broker's or agent's client; (2) the amount of money raised by a mortgage or other loan, as distinct from the interest paid on it.

PROBATE (PROVE) / To establish the validity of the will of a deceased person.

Importance: Probate relates not only to the validity of a will but also to matters and proceedings of estate administration.

PROBATE COURT / *See* SURROGATE'S COURT.

PROCURING CAUSE / A legal term that means the cause resulting in accomplishing a goal. Used in real estate to determine whether a broker is entitled to a commission.

PROJECTION PERIOD / The time duration for estimating future *cash flows* and the resale proceeds from a proposed real estate investment.

PROMISSORY NOTE / A promise to pay a specified sum to a specified person under specified terms.

PROPERTY / (1) The rights that one individual has in lands or goods to the exclusion of all others; (2) rights gained from the ownership of wealth. *See also* PERSONALTY; REAL PROPERTY.

PROPERTY LINE / The recorded boundary of a plot of land.

Importance: A *survey* is performed in order to establish property lines and describe them on a *plat*.

PROPERTY MANAGEMENT / The operation of property as a business, including rental, rent collection, maintenance.

Importance: Property managers remove the daily burden from real estate investors, thus allowing them to be free from daily business operations.

PROPOSITION 13 (Prop 13) / Law in California pertaining to ad valorem tax assessments. Rolls back assessments to 1975 base values; reassessments may occur at market value upon a sale. Limits taxes to one percent of the value amount, and limits annual increases to a maximum of two percent per year.

PROPRIETORSHIP / Ownership of a business, including income-producing real estate, by an individual, as contrasted with a partnership or corporation.

PRORATE / To allocate between seller and buyer their proportionate shares of an obligation paid or due; for example, to prorate real property taxes or insurance.

Importance: Many items of expense are prorated between buyer and seller, to the date of closing.

PUD PLANNED UNIT DEVELOPMENT.

PUR AUTRE VIE / For the life of another. A life estate pur autre vie grants a life estate to one person that expires on the death of another person.

PURCHASE CAPITAL / The amount of money used to purchase real estate, regardless of the source.

PURCHASE CONTRACT / A written contract between purchaser and seller, in which the purchaser agrees to buy, and the seller agrees to sell, certain real estate upon the terms and conditions of the agreement.

Importance: When you are buying or selling property, your rights and obligations are described in this document. Offer this document, or accept it, only when you are satisfied that it contains exactly what you will agree to (no more, no less) in a final transaction.

PURCHASE MONEY MORTGAGE / A mortgage given by a grantee (buyer) to a grantor (seller) in part payment of the purchase price of real estate.

Importance: Institutional lenders are often unable or unwilling to finance certain types of property, so the seller must accept a purchase money mortgage to facilitate a sale.

QUIET ENJOYMENT / The right of an owner, or any other person legally entitled to possession, to the use of property without interference.

Importance: No interference should be caused by a landlord to a tenant who is in compliance with a lease.

QUIET TITLE SUIT / A suit in court to remove a defect, cloud, or suspicion regarding the legal rights of an owner to a certain parcel of *real property*.

Importance: A potential claimant is told to bring forward his/her claim so its validity can be judged. If it is not valid, the claimant must stop interference with the owner.

QUITCLAIM DEED / A deed that conveys only the *grantor's* rights or interest in real estate, without stating their nature and with no warranties of ownership.

Importance: This deed is often used to remove a possible cloud from the title.

RANGE LINES / In the *government rectangular survey* method of land description, lines parallel to the principal *meridian*, marking off the land into 6-mile strips known as ranges; they are numbered east or west of the principal meridian. *See also* BASE AND MERIDIAN.

RATE OF INTEREST / *See* INTEREST RATE.

REAL ESTATE / Land and all attachments that are of a permanent nature.

Importance: Real estate is distinguished from personal property. At one time real estate was the sole source of wealth and achieved a special place in the law because of its importance.

REAL ESTATE ADVISORY COMMISSION / A group of ten members that makes recommendations to the Real Estate Commissioner on relevant matters.

REAL ESTATE AGENT / *See* AGENT.

REAL ESTATE COMMISSIONER / The head of the *California Department of Real Estate*; appointed by the governor, he or she also appoints and presides over the *Real Estate Advisory Commission*.

REAL ESTATE EDUCATION AND RESEARCH FUND / A fund supported by a portion of real estate license fees, to be used to encourage research in real estate-related areas of interest in California.

REAL ESTATE EDUCATORS ASSOCIATION / A professional organization composed primarily of persons who teach *real estate* in junior colleges and proprietary license preparation schools.

REAL ESTATE INVESTMENT TRUST (REIT) / A *real estate* mutual fund, allowed by income tax laws to avoid the corporate tax if 95 percent of its income is distributed. It sells shares of ownership and must invest in real estate or mortgages.

Importance: A REIT allows small investors to participate in the ownership of large, potentially profitable, real estate projects.

REAL ESTATE SETTLEMENT PROCEDURES ACT (RESPA) / A law that states how *mortgage* lenders must treat those who apply for federally related real estate loans on property with one to four dwelling units. Intended to provide borrowers with more knowledge when they comparison shop for mortgage money.

REAL PROPERTY / The right to use real estate, as (1) *fee simple* estate, (2) *life estate*, or (3) *leasehold* estate; sometimes also defined as *real estate*.

REALTOR® / A professional in real estate who subscribes to a strict code of ethics as a member of the local and California boards and of the *National Association of REALTORS®*.

Importance: Fewer than half of those licensed to sell real estate are REALTORS®. In many areas a person must be a REALTOR® to participate in the predominant *multiple listing* service.

REALTY / The property rights to real estate.

REAPPRAISAL LEASE / A lease whereby the rental level is periodically reviewed and reset by independent appraisers.

Importance: Landlord and tenant can agree on a long-term lease knowing that the rent will be fair throughout the term because of the reappraisal clauses in the lease.

RECAPTURE CLAUSE / In a contract, a clause permitting the party who grants an *interest* or right to take it back under certain conditions.

RECESSION / Economic slowdown; officially declared after two consecutive quarters of reduced gross domestic product.

RECISION / *See* RESCISSION.

RECORDING / The act of entering *instruments* affecting the title to real property in a book of public record.

Importance: Recording in this manner gives public notice of the facts recorded.

RECOURSE / The ability of a lender to claim money from a borrower in *default*, in addition to the property pledged as *collateral*.

REDLINING / An illegal practice of a lender refusing to make home loans in certain areas. The term is derived from a lender circling with a red pencil on a map, areas where the institution will not lend.

Importance: If home loans will not be made in a certain area, property values will plummet and neighborhoods deteriorate rapidly. Redlining is an illegal discriminatory practice.

REDUCTION CERTIFICATE / A document in which the mortgagee (lender) acknowledges the sum due on the mortgage loan.

Importance: This is used when mortgaged property is sold and the buyer assumes the debt.

REGULATION Z / Implementation by the Federal Reserve of the Federal Truth In Lending Act; it specifies how the *annual percentage rate* of a loan is calculated and expressed in consumer loan documents.

REGULATORY TAKING / A series of government limits to property use that constitutes a condemnation of property.

REIT / *See* REAL ESTATE INVESTMENT TRUST.

RELEASE / The act by which some claim or interest is surrendered.

RELEASE CLAUSE / A clause in a mortgage that gives the owner of the property the privilege of paying off a portion of the indebtedness, thus freeing a part of the property from the mortgage.

Importance: Release clauses are frequently used when a mortgage covers more than one property (*blanket mortgage*), so that a particular parcel can be released upon some payment.

RELICTION / Gradual subsidence of waters, leaving dry land.

Importance: Ownership of land beneath a lake, for example, can become more important as reliction occurs.

RELOCATION SERVICE / A company that contracts with other firms to arrange the relocation of employees from one city to another. The service generally handles the sale of the employee's home and purchase of a new home. Furniture-moving services may also be included.

REMAINDER / An estate that takes effect after the termination of a prior estate, such as a *life estate*.

Importance: The *remainderman* owns the property outright upon the death of the *life tenant*.

REMAINDERMAN / The person who is to receive possession of a property after the death of a *life tenant*.

Importance: Many people wish to allow a surviving spouse to occupy property for the rest of his/her life, with a child as the remainderman.

REMEDIATION / The cleanup of an environmentally contaminated site. *See* CERCLA.

RENT / The compensation paid for the use of real estate.

Importance: Rent is the most important portion of a lease and may be paid in money, services, or other valuables.

RENT MULTIPLIER / *See* GROSS RENT MULTIPLIER.

RENT ROLL / A list of tenants, generally with the lease rent and expiration date for each tenant.

REPLACEMENT COST / The cost of erecting a building to take the place of or serve the functions of a previous structure.

Importance: Replacement cost often sets the upper limit on value; it is often used for insurance purposes.

REPORT DATE / In an appraisal, usually the date of the last property inspection.

REPRODUCTION COST / The normal cost of exact duplication of a property as of a certain date. Note: Replacement requires the same functional utility for a property, whereas a reproduction is an exact duplicate, using the same materials and craftsmanship.

RESALE PRICE / In a projection of real estate investment performance, the selling price that it is assumed a property could fetch at the end of the projection period. *See also* RESALE PROCEEDS.

RESALE PROCEEDS / Net cash remaining to investor after sale of investment property and paying mortgage payoff and selling costs.

RESCISSION / The act of canceling or terminating a contract. Rescission is allowed when the contract was induced by fraud, duress, misrepresentation, or mistake. *Regulation Z* allows one to rescind certain credit transactions within three business days (not applicable to first mortgages on a home); purchasers of certain land that must be registered by the Department of Housing and Urban Development may rescind within three business days.

RESIDENTIAL SALES COUNCIL / An affiliate of the Realtors National Marketing Institute of the *National Association of Realtors®* that provides educational and promotional materials for members, most of whom are involved in residential real estate sales or brokerage.

RESTRAINT ON ALIENATION / A legal situation that would, if allowed to be enforced, prevent property from being sold easily. Restraints on alienation are against public policy so they cannot be enforced by law.

RESTRICTION / A limitation placed upon the use of property, contained in the deed or other written *instrument* in the chain of title.

Importance: If buying property with restrictions, the buyer should determine its suitability for the uses he/she requires.

RESTRICTIVE COVENANT / *See* RESTRICTION.

REVERSION / The right of a lessor to possess leased property upon the termination of a lease.

Importance: A lease is valid for an established term, after which the lessor receives the reversion.

REVERSIONARY INTEREST / The interest a person has in property upon the termination of the preceding estate.

Importance: A lessor's interest in leased property is a reversionary interest.

REVOCATION / The recalling of a power of authority conferred, as a revocation of a power of attorney, a license, an agency.

Importance: A person with the authority to convey may also have authority to revoke, with reason.

RIDER / An amendment or attachment to a contract.

RIGHT OF SURVIVORSHIP / The right of a surviving joint tenant to acquire the interest of a deceased joint owner; the distinguishing feature of *joint tenancy* and *tenancy by the entireties*.

Importance: The right of survivorship is often used where the joint tenants are closely related.

RIGHT-OF-WAY / (1) The right to use a particular path for access or passage; a type of easement; (2) the areas of subdivisions dedicated to government for use as streets, roads, and other public access to lots.

RIPARIAN OWNER / A person who owns land bounding upon a lake, river, or other body of water.

RIPARIAN RIGHTS / Rights pertaining to the use of water on, under, or adjacent to one's land.

Importance: In most states, riparian rights do not permit property owners to alter the flow of water to their downstream neighbors. Riparian rights give the right to reasonable use of water.

RUMFORD FAIR HOUSING ACT OF 1963 / Known as *California Fair Housing Law,* banned discrimination in housing.

SALE-LEASEBACK / The simultaneous purchase of property and lease back to the seller. The lease portion of the transaction is generally long-term. The seller-lessee in the transaction is converted from an owner to a tenant.

SALES COMPARISON APPROACH / One of three appraisal approaches; also called *market approach* and *market data approach.* Value is estimated by analyzing sales prices of similar properties (comparables) recently sold.

Importance: Virtually all appraisals of homes, and many appraisals of other properties rely most heavily on the sales comparison approach. Two other approaches are *cost* and *income.*

SALES CONTRACT / *See* LAND CONTRACT.

SALESPERSON / A person who is licensed to deal in real estate or perform any other act enumerated by California real estate license law, while in the employ of a *broker* licensed by the state.

Importance: A salesperson's license is required for anyone to sell another's property. The salesperson must have a sponsoring broker.

SALES PRICE / The amount of money required to be paid for real estate according to a contract, or previously paid.

SALVAGE VALUE / The estimated value that an asset will have at the end of its useful life.

Importance: Real estate improvements, though long lasting, have a limited useful life at the end of which there may be salvage or scrap value.

SANDWICH LEASE / A lease held by a lessee who sublets all or part of his/her interest, thereby becoming a lessor. Typically, the sandwich lease-holder is neither the owner nor the user of the property.

Importance: The sandwich lessee tries to profit from income tax advantages or the rent differential between the other leases.

SARA / *See* SUPERFUND AMENDMENTS AND REAUTHORIZATION ACT.

SATISFACTION OF MORTGAGE / *See* SATISFACTION PIECE.

SATISFACTION PIECE / An *instrument* for recording and acknowledging final payment of a mortgage loan.

Importance: After a loan has been paid off, the borrower should record a satisfaction of mortgage or satisfaction piece.

SECTION (of Land) / One square mile in the *government rectangular survey.* There are 36 sections in a 6-mile-square township.

SECTION 1031 / The section of the Internal Revenue Code that deals with tax-deferred exchanges of certain property. General rules for a tax-deferred exchange of real estate are that the properties must be (1) exchanged or qualify as a delayed tax-free exchange, (2) like-kind property (real estate for real estate), and (3) held for use in a trade or business or held as an investment.

SECURITY INSTRUMENT / An interest in real estate that allows the property to be sold upon a default on the obligation for which the security interest was created. The security interest is more specifically described as a mortgage or a trust deed.

SEIZIN / The possession of realty by a person who claims to own a *fee simple estate* or a *life estate* or other salable interest.

Importance: Seizin is a covenant needed to transfer ownership to another.

SENIOR RESIDENTIAL APPRAISER (SRA) / A designation awarded by the Appraisal Institute.

Importance: Many of the most qualified residential appraisers have this designation.

SEPARATE PROPERTY / Property acquired by either spouse prior to marriage or by gift or devise after marriage, as distinct from *community property.*

Importance: In community property states, property that is separate before marriage can remain that way; property acquired during marriage by joint effort is community property.

SETBACK / The distance from the curb or other established line within which no buildings may be erected. *Compare* BUILDING LINE.

Importance: Setbacks must be observed; if they are violated during construction, the property may have to be razed.

SETTLEMENT DATE / *See* CLOSING DATE.

SETTLEMENT STATEMENT / *See* CLOSING STATEMENT.

SEVERALTY / *See* TENANCY IN SEVERALTY.

SPECIAL ASSESSMENT / An *assessment* made against a property to pay for a public improvement by which the assessed property is supposed to be especially benefited.

Importance: A municipality may install a new sewer line or sidewalk; each owner along the path may be charged a special assessment, in addition to a regular tax.

SPECIAL-PURPOSE PROPERTY / A building with limited uses and marketability, such as a church, theater, school, public utility.

SPECIAL WARRANTY DEED / A deed in which the *grantor* limits the title warranty given to the *grantee* to anyone claiming by, from, through, or under him/her; the grantor. The grantor does not warrant against title defects arising from conditions that existed before he/she owned the property.

Importance: The seller does not guarantee title against all claims—just those while he/she was the owner.

SPECIFIC PERFORMANCE / A legal action in which the court requires a party to a contract to perform the terms of the contract when he/she has refused to fulfill his/her obligations.

Importance: This action is used in real estate because each parcel of land is unique; consequently a contract concerning one parcel cannot be transferred or applied to another.

SPOT ZONING / The act of rezoning a parcel of land for a different use from all surrounding parcels, in particular where the rezoning creates a use that is incompatible with surrounding land uses.

SRA / *See* SENIOR RESIDENTIAL APPRAISER.

STATE-CERTIFIED APPRAISER / *See* CERTIFIED GENERAL APPRAISER; CERTIFIED RESIDENTIAL APPRAISER.

STATUTE / A law established by an act of a legislature.

Importance: Statutes are written laws; laws are also made through judicial interpretation and government administration.

STATUTE OF FRAUDS / Part of the California Civil Code that provides that certain contracts must be in writing in order to be enforceable; applies to deeds, mortgages, and other real estate contracts, with the exception of agreements to be performed within one year, such as a lease.

Importance: The statute of frauds requires that contracts involving real estate be in writing.

STATUTE OF LIMITATIONS / A certain statutory period after which a claimant is barred from enforcing his/her claim by suit.

Importance: If a practice continues beyond the statute of limitations the person who is adversely affected may be barred from trying to prevent it.

STATUTORY DEDICATION / The owners of a subdivision or other property file a plat that results in a grant of public property, such as the streets in a development.

STEP-UP LEASE / *See* GRADUATED LEASE.

STIPULATIONS / The terms within a written *contract*.

STRAIGHT-LINE DEPRECIATION / Equal annual reductions in the book value of property; used in accounting for replacement and tax purposes.

Importance: Straight-line provides less depreciation in the early years of an asset than does an accelerated method. Most taxpayers prefer accelerated depreciation because it minimizes current taxes. However, for financial reporting purposes, most companies prefer straight-line because it provides a higher net income.

SUBAGENCY / The relationship under which a sales agent tries to sell a property listed with another agent. This situation is common under a *multiple listing* service (MLS). A listing contract is taken by a listing broker and entered into the MLS, from which any member broker may sell the property. The listing broker and the selling broker split the commission.

SUBDIVIDED LANDS LAW / Statewide law regulating the sale of subdivided land; requires that the subdivision meet state standards, and that the *Real Estate Commissioner* issue a *Subdivision Public Report* before any sales occur; prospective purchasers must be given a copy of the report.

SUBDIVIDING / The division of a tract of land into smaller tracts.

Importance: Subdividing allows raw acreage to be developed with streets, utilities, and other amenities added, resulting in lots ready for houses to be built.

SUBDIVISION / A tract of land divided into lots or plots suitable for home building purposes. Subdivisions must meet the California *Subdivided Lands Law* before the *Real Estate Commissioner* will issue a public report.

SUBDIVISION MAP ACT / State law authorizing local governments to require that, before any subdivision of land is approved, a tentative subdivision map showing the subdivision, utilities, improvements, etc., be submitted to the local planning commission. When the subdivision is approved, a final subdivision map is prepared which describes the subdivision as approved, including modifications required.

SUBDIVISION PUBLIC REPORT / A document providing details of a subdivision, its financing, its obligations, and showing that it meets the requirements of the *Subdivided Lands Law*; sales in a subdivision cannot be closed until the *Real Estate Commissioner* has issued the report.

SUBJECT TO MORTGAGE / A method of taking title to mortgaged real property without being personally responsible for the payment of any portion of the amount due. The buyer must make payments in order to keep the property; however, if he/she fails to do so, only his/her equity in that property is lost.

SUBLEASE / A lease from a lessee to another lessee. The new lessee is a sublessee or subtenant. *See also* SANDWICH LEASE.

SUBLET / *See* SUBLEASE.

SUBORDINATED GROUND LEASE / A lease used when the *mortgage* has priority over the *ground lease*.

Importance: In case of a *default*, the unsubordinated interest has a prior claim to the subordinated interest.

SUBORDINATE MORTGAGE / One having a lower priority to another; the subordinate mortgage has a claim in foreclosure only after satisfaction of mortgage(s) with priority.

SUBORDINATION CLAUSE / A clause or document that permits a mortgage recorded at a later date to take priority over an existing mortgage.

Importance: Ordinarily a second mortgage automatically moves up to become a first *lien* when the first mortgage is retired. If the second mortgage has a subordination clause, it will remain a second mortgage when a first mortgage is refinanced.

SUBSURFACE RIGHTS / *Same as* MINERAL RIGHTS.

SUPERFUND / The commonly used name for CERCLA, the federal environmental cleanup law. If a site is on the Superfund list, it is required to be cleaned up by any and all previous owners, operators, transporters, and disposers of waste to the site. The federal governemnt will clean such sites, requiring the responsible parties to pay the cleanup costs. Imposes strict liability.

SUPERFUND AMENDMENTS AND REAUTHORIZATION ACT (SARA) / Law that confirmed the continued existence of SUPERFUND. SARA put more teeth into CERCLA, though SARA provides an innocent landowner defense for a buyer who conducted a Phase I environmental study, with negative results, before the aquisition.

SURETY / A person who guarantees the performance of another; a guarantor.

Importance: The surety becomes liable for the contract, just like the original principal. The surety is called when the principal fails to perform some duty.

SURRENDER / The cancellation of a lease before its expiration by mutual consent of the lessor and the lessee.

Importance: Surrender occurs only when both parties agree to it.

SURROGATE'S COURT (PROBATE COURT) / A court having jurisdiction over the proof of wills and the settling of estates and of citations.

SURVEY / (1) The process by which a parcel of land is measured and its area ascertained; (2) the blueprint showing the measurements, boundaries, and area.

Importance: A survey is needed to determine exact boundaries and any *easements* or *encroachments*.

TAX / A charge levied upon persons or things by a government.

Importance: Many different types of taxes affect real estate. Most local governments levy an *ad valorem tax* based on the property value. The federal government and California have an income tax, but rental property owners may deduct operating expense, interest, and depreciation expense, thereby reducing their taxable income.

TAX SALE / The sale of property after a period of nonpayment of taxes.

Importance: Unpaid taxes become a *lien*. Property may be sold for the nonpayment of taxes.

TEASER RATE / An unusually low interest rate offered for the first few months or year of a mortgage loan; used as an enticement to potential borrowers.

Importance: When comparing interest rates on loans offered, a buyer should determine future rate adjustments, as the initial rate may be discovered to be a teaser.

TENANCY AT SUFFERANCE / Tenancy established when a lawful tenant remains in possession of property after expiration of a lease.

Importance: The tenant at sufferance has no estate or title; the landlord may oust the tenant at any time.

TENANCY AT WILL / A license to use or occupy lands and tenements at the will of the owner.

Importance: There is no fixed length of possession. The tenant may leave or may be put out at any time.

TENANCY BY THE ENTIRETIES / An estate that exists only between husband and wife, with equal right of possession and enjoyment during their joint lives and with the *right of survivorship;* that is, when one dies, the property goes to the surviving tenant.

TENANCY IN COMMON / An ownership of realty by two or more persons, each of whom has an undivided interest, without the *right of survivorship*. Upon the death of one of the owners, his/her ownership share is inherited by the party or parties designated in his/her will.

TENANCY IN SEVERALTY / Ownership of real property by an individual as an individual; ownership by one person or by a legal entity.

Importance: Tenancy in severalty is distinguished from joint ownership and/or community property, whereby two or more persons are owners.

TENANT / A person who is given possession of real estate for a fixed period or at will. *See also* LEASE.

TENANT IMPROVEMENTS (TIs) / Those changes, typically to office, retail, or industrial property, to accommodate specific needs of a tenant. TIs include installation or relocation of interior walls or partitions, carpeting or other floor covering, shelves, windows, and toilets. The cost of these is negotiated in the lease.

TENEMENTS / (1) Everything of a permanent nature; (2) anything attached to the soil. In common usage a tenement is a run-down apartment building.

TERMITES / Insects that bore into wood and destroy it.

Importance: Termite inspections by reputable pest control companies are often required in a real estate transaction. In some places it is customary to require a seller to post a termite bond as assurance that the foundation has been properly treated.

TERMS / Conditions and arrangements specified in a contract.

Importance: Anything lawful may be included in a contract and becomes part of its terms.

TESTAMENT / A will.

TESTAMENTARY TRUST / Trust, created by a will, which comes into effect only after the testator's death.

TESTATE / Having made a valid will. *Contrast* INTESTATE.

TESTATOR / A man who makes a will.

TESTATRIX / A woman who makes a will.

"TIME IS OF THE ESSENCE" / A phrase that, when inserted in a contract, requires that all references to specific dates and times of day concerning performance be interpreted exactly.

TIME VALUE OF MONEY / The concept that money available now is worth more than the same amount in the future because of its potential earning capacity.

TITLE / Evidence that the owner of land is in lawful possession thereof; evidence of ownership. The word is often clarified or qualified by an adjective, such as *absolute, good, clear, marketable, defective, legal.*

TITLE ABSTRACT / *See* ABSTRACT OF TITLE.

TITLE INSURANCE / An insurance policy that protects the holder from any loss sustained by reason of defects in the title.

Importance: The premium is paid once and is good only until ownership changes.

TITLE SEARCH / An examination of the public records to determine the ownership and *encumbrances* affecting real property.

Importance: A title search is typically performed before *title insurance* is issued. If the search shows a title risk, the policy may contain an exception or may not be issued.

TOPOGRAPHY / The state of the surface of the land; may be rolling, rough, flat.

Importance: The topography may affect the way land can be developed, including potential uses.

TORT / A wrongful act that is not a crime but that renders the perpetrator liable to the victim for damages.

TOWNSHIP / A 6-mile-square tract delineated by *government rectangular survey.*

TRACT / A *parcel* of land, generally held for *subdividing;* a *subdivision.*

TRADE FIXTURES / Articles placed in rented buildings by the tenant to help carry out trade or business. The tenant may remove the fixtures before the expiration of the lease, but, if the tenant fails to do so shortly after the lease expires, the fixtures become the landlord's property.

TRADING UP / Buying a larger, more expensive property.

TRANSFER DEVELOPMENT RIGHTS / A type of *zoning ordinance* that allows owners of property zoned for low-density development or conservation use to sell development rights to other property owners. The development rights purchased permit the landowners to develop their parcels at higher density than otherwise. The system is designed to provide for low-density uses, such as historic preservation, without unduly penalizing some landowners.

TRIPLE-A TENANT / A tenant with an excellent credit record; also called *AAA tenant.* **Example:** The U.S. Postal Service and the American Telephone and Telegraph Company are examples of triple-A tenants because they are unlikely to *default* on a lease.

TRIPLE-NET LEASE / A lease whereby the tenant pays all expenses of operations, including property taxes, insurance, utilities, maintenance, and repair.

TRUST DEED / A *conveyance* of real estate to a third person to be held for the benefit of another;

commonly used in California in place of mortgages that conditionally convey title to the lender.

TRUSTEE / A person who holds property in trust for another to secure performance of an obligation; the neutral party in a *trust deed* transaction.

TRUSTEE'S DEED / The deed received by the purchaser at a foreclosure sale; issued by the *trustee* acting under a *trust deed.*

TRUSTOR / The person who conveys property to a trustee, to be held in behalf of a beneficiary; in a trust deed arrangement, the trustor is the owner of real estate and the beneficiary is the lender.

UNDIVIDED INTEREST / An ownership right to use and possession of a property that is shared among co-owners, with no one co-owner having exclusive rights to any portion of the property. *Contrast with* PARTITION.

UNEARNED INCREMENT / An increase in the value of real estate due to no effort on the part of the owner; often due to an increase in population.

Importance: *Appreciation* of land in the path of growth is considered an unearned increment because the landowners did nothing to cause it.

UNIFORM COMMERCIAL CODE (UCC) / A group of laws to standardize the state laws that are applicable to commercial transactions. Few of the laws have relevance to real estate.

UNIFORM RESIDENTIAL APPRAISAL REPORT (URAR) / A standard form for reporting the *appraisal* of a dwelling.

Importance: This form is required for use by the major secondary mortgage purchasers. It provides numerous checklists and appropriate definitions and certifications that are preprinted on the form.

UNIFORM RESIDENTIAL LANDLORD AND TENANT ACT (URLTA) / A model law governing residential leasing practice and leases, adopted wholly or in part by about 15 states.

UNIFORM STANDARDS OF PROFESSIONAL APPRAISAL PRACTICE (USPAP) / Standards promulgated by the *Appraisal Foundation* that set forth the requirements for research and reporting with which a professional appraiser is to comply.

UNILATERAL CONTRACT / An obligation given by one party contingent on the performance of another party, but without obligating the second party to perform. *Contrast with* BILATERAL CONTRACT.

UNITY / Four unities are required to create a joint tenancy: interest, possession, time, and title. In other words, the joint tenants must have an equal interest arising from the same conveyance, the same undivided possession, and the same use over the same time.

UNRUH ACT / California civil law that covers goods and services. Provides that real estate borrowers be given explicit notices of default on a mortgage in order to protect a homeowner from loss of a home due to default on a retail installment purchase.

UNRUH CIVIL RIGHTS ACT / Act that bans discrimination by business establishments.

URAR / *See* UNIFORM RESIDENTIAL APPRAISAL REPORT.

URBAN PROPERTY / City property; closely settled property.

Importance: Urban property is more valuable than rural or suburban land because of its greater business activity.

URLTA / *See* UNIFORM RESIDENTIAL LANDLORD AND TENANT ACT.

USPAP / *See* UNIFORM STANDARDS OF PROFESSIONAL APPRAISAL PRACTICE.

USURY / A rate of interest higher than that permitted by law.

Importance: California usury laws have different ceiling interest rates applying to each type of loan. Penalties are severe for usury rates.

VALID / (1) Having force, or binding force; (2) legally sufficient and authorized by law.

Importance: A valid contract can be enforced in court.

VA LOAN / Home loan guaranteed by the U.S. Veterans Administration (VA) under the Servicemen's Readjustment Act of 1944 and later.

Importance: The VA guarantees restitution to the lender in the event of default, up to a stated amount.

VALUATION / (1) Estimated worth or price; (2) valuing by appraisal.

Importance: Valuation is the process of estimating the worth of an object.

VALUE / (1) The worth of all the rights arising from ownership; (2) the quantity of one thing that will be given in exchange for another.

Importance: Price is the historic amount that was paid; value is an estimate of what something is worth. Often value is qualified as to a specific type: market, user, assessed, insurable, speculative.

VARIABLE EXPENSES / Property operating costs that increase with occupancy.

VENDEE / A purchaser; a buyer.

VENDEE'S LIEN / A *lien* against property under a *contract of sale*, to secure the deposit paid by a purchaser.

VENDOR / A seller.

VERIFICATION / Sworn statements before a duly qualified officer as to the correctness of the contents of an *instrument*.

VICARIOUS LIABILITY / The responsibility of one person for the acts of another.

VIOLATION / An act, a deed, or conditions contrary to law or the permissible use of real property.

Importance: When there is a violation of a law or contract, the perpetrator may be liable for damages and/or penalties.

VOID / Having no force or effect; unenforceable.

VOIDABLE / Capable of being voided, but not void unless action is taken to void. **Example:** Contracts to real estate entered into by minors are voidable only by the minors.

VOLUNTARY ALIENATION / Legal term describing a sale or gift made by the seller or donor of his/her own free will.

WAIVER / The voluntary renunciation, abandonment, or surrender of some claim, right, or privilege.

Importance: A person may waive a right when that right is not especially important to him/her in the overall transaction.

WARRANTY / A promise or representation contained in a *contract*.

Importance: Usually a seller's warranty pertains to the quality, character, or title of goods that are sold.

WARRANTY DEED / A deed that contains a covenant that the *grantor* will protect the *grantee* against any and all claims; usually contains covenants assuring good title, freedom from *encumbrances*, and *quiet enjoyment*. *See also* GENERAL WARRANTY DEED; SPECIAL WARRANTY DEED.

WASTE / Often found in a mortgage or lease contract, this term refers to property abuse, destruction, or damage, (beyond normal wear and tear). The possessor causes unreasonable injury to the holders of other interests in the land, house, garden, or other property. The injured party may attempt to terminate the contract or sue for damages.

WATER TABLE / The distance from the surface of the ground to a depth at which natural groundwater is found.

Importance: The water table may affect the type of buildings that are possible on a parcel of land, and the ability to get well water.

WETLANDS / Land, such as swamps, marshes, and bogs, normally saturated with water. Development may be prohibited because it could disturb the environment. The U.S. Army Corps of Engineers (COE) and the U.S. Environmental Protection Agency (EPA) have adopted a regulatory definition for administering the Section 404 permit program of the Clean Water Act (CWA) as follows: "those areas that are inundated or saturated by surface or groundwater at a frequency and duration sufficient to support, and that under normal circumstances do support, a prevalence of vegetation typically adapted for life in saturated soil conditions."

WILL / The disposition of one's property to take effect after death.

Importance: If a person dies without a will (*intestate*), the property goes to his/her heirs at law. If a person dies intestate without heirs, the property *escheats* to California.

WITHOUT RECOURSE / Words used in endorsing a note or bill to denote that the future holder is not to look to the debtor personally in the event of nonpayment: the creditor has recourse only to the property and the borrower is held harmless after foreclosure.

Importance: In *default*, the borrower can lose the property mortgaged, but no other property. There can be no *deficiency judgment*.

WRAPAROUND MORTGAGE / A mortgage that includes in its balance an underlying mortgage. Instead of having distinct and separate first and second mortgages, a wraparound mortgage includes both. For example, suppose that there is an existing first mortgage of $100,000 at 8 percent interest. A second mortgage can be arranged for $50,000 at 12 percent interest. Instead of getting that second mortgage, the borrower arranges a wraparound for $150,000 at 10 percent. The first mortgage of $100,000 is included in the $150,000. The borrower pays the wraparound lender one payment on the $150,000 wraparound, and the wrap lender remits the payment on the first mortgage to the first mortgage lender.

ZONE / An area set off by the proper authorities for specific use, subject to certain restrictions or restraints. Changing the zoning of property usually requires approval by the city council.

ZONING ORDINANCE / An act of city, county, or other authorities specifying the type of use to which property may be put in specific areas. **Examples:** residential, commercial, industrial.

Chapter 3/*Fundamentals of Real Estate Law*

Introduction

This is the first chapter of subject matter material. Much of what is mentioned in this chapter will be discussed in greater detail in future chapters. Here, however, we are going to summarize California real estate law in its entirety, with the exception of license and contract law.

The subject matter of this chapter is a very fertile source of license examination questions, particularly because it concerns things that the average layperson knows little or nothing about. In this manner the examining authorities can make sure that successful licensing applicants have, indeed, studied the laws and customs of the real estate business and know enough about it to be worthy of public trust.

Property

Property refers to the legal rights to use and enjoy any thing. Strictly speaking, the term *property* does not refer to the things themselves, but to the legal rights that a society allows someone with regard to the use of and enjoyment of these things. In practice, however, we tend to use the word *property* to mean the things themselves, so we don't think it odd for someone to say, "That car is my property." To be absolutely proper, however, he should be saying, "The *rights* to use and enjoy that car are my property."

That may sound like nitpicking, and perhaps it is. When you are speaking of legal matters, though, it is essential to be precise and clear, or you can land in serious trouble. If a contract is drawn up vaguely, or if the description of a piece of land is inexact, the preparer can be held responsible for problems caused by the ambiguity.

Property is divided into two kinds: *real property* and *personal property*. Respectively, these are also known as *realty* and *personalty*. Realty is the property rights to real estate; personalty is the property rights to everything else.

Both realty and personalty can divided into the *tangible* and *intangible*. When we speak of realty, these things are referred to as *corporeal* and *incorporeal*. Corporeal property is the right to use, own, and enjoy real estate directly. The term *incorporeal* concerns the right to use property that actually belongs to another; examples are easements, rights-of-way, or mere permission to use someone else's property.

Real estate is defined as *land and everything permanently attached to it*. A "permanent attachment" is (a) anything that grows on the land, (b) anything that is built upon the land (including roads, fences, etc., as well as buildings), and (c) fixtures.

Fixtures are items that may appear to be personal property but are considered to be part of the land also. Fixtures may include window air conditioners, major appliances, draperies, and other items of that nature. There is no cut-and-dried definition of a fixture, so many of the court disputes concerning real estate contracts involve misunderstandings concerning what are and aren't fixtures.

Many objects can be either realty or personalty, depending on how they are used. A brick is personalty until it is mortared into place on the wall of a building, at which time it becomes realty. A tree is realty when it is growing, but it becomes personalty when it is cut down. Fixtures are the "gray area," where an argument can be made either way as to the nature of the item. California courts decide such a problem based upon the following.

1. The *intent* of the person(s) who put it there. This is the most important criterion; if the court can determine what the intent was (was it *meant* to remain as a part of the real estate?), then usually there is no need to inquire further.

   Often, however, it is difficult or impossible to determine for sure just what the original intent was, because whoever put it there is long gone, dead, or can't be found. Then the court will consider the following tests:

2. How it is *attached* to the property. The more "permanently" it is attached, the more likely it is to be a fixture. A window air conditioner inserted in a hole put into the wall for the purpose of containing it is more likely to be a fixture than if it just sits in a window and is easily removed.

3. Relationship to the land's expected use. The more it is *adapted* to the use of the land, the more likely it is to be a fixture.

4. Agreement of the parties: if buyer and seller agree that it is a fixture, then it is—no matter what it may be. This is the way to avoid dispute: write into the purchase contract the nature (fixture or personal property) of anything that may be at all doubtful.

Corporeal property involving real estate is almost always real property as well. Incorporeal real estate property can be either real or personal property. Easements usually are real property; short-term leases (in most states, leases of one year or less) also are personal property.

Estates in Land

The collection of rights that someone may have in real estate can be called an *estate* if it is large enough. Estates are divided into two groups: *freehold* and *nonfreehold*. The basic difference is that a freehold estate is of uncertain duration because it extends until the owner chooses to dispose of it or, if he doesn't, until he dies, and we never know just how long that will be. The divisions of freehold estates are *inheritable* and *noninheritable*. Nonfreehold estates involve various kinds of leases. Leases are contracted for specific periods of time, so it is known exactly when these kinds of estates will cease to exist.

Inheritable estates are called *fee simple* estates. Basically these give their owners absolute rights to do whatever they want with the land involved, subject only to the general law, such as zoning and building codes. Most important, as far as the law is concerned, is the right to *dispose* of the estate in any legal manner: by selling it, by giving it away, or by willing it to someone.

Noninheritable estates are called *life estates*. In a life estate arrangement the owner, called the *life tenant*, has the right to use, occupy, and enjoy the property so long as he lives, but upon his death the ownership of the property goes to a predetermined person (or persons) referred to as the *remainderman*. When the life tenant dies, if the remainderman is not the original grantor, it is called an "estate in remainder." Since the life tenant has rights to the property only so long as he lives, he can transfer to others only those rights. Consequently he may sell his interest to someone, but that person will have to relinquish the property upon the original life tenant's death. The same would happen if the life tenant leased the property to someone and died before the lease expired. Furthermore, the life tenant is considered to be the custodian of the property for the remainderman: he cannot allow the property to deteriorate beyond ordinary wear and tear, because he must protect the remainderman's interest in it.

There is a special form of life estate that is *pur autre vie*. This term is French, meaning "for another life." In such a life estate, the duration is not for the tenant's life, but for that of another person. For example, I purchase a specially built home to accommodate my severely disabled daughter. The purpose is to provide her with a place to reside, with a caretaker, for the rest of her life, after which time I want the home to become the property of a charity. My daughter is legally incompetent and cannot own real estate in her own name. One option that I have would be to grant the home to my son pur autre vie; the "other life" would be that of my disabled daughter. The charity would be the remainderman. My son would be the life tenant so long as my daughter lives; upon her death, the property would revert to the charity.

Nonfreehold estates are leases for specific terms. The lessee, or tenant, has the right (unless she contracts to give it up) to assign or otherwise dispose of her leasehold rights if she has a *leasehold estate*. Furthermore, she has the right to use, occupy, and enjoy the real estate during the period of her lease.

An estate in land requires that its owner have the following rights: the right to *possess* the land, the right to *use* the land, and the right to *dispose* of his estate to someone else. Possession means, basically, just that: the right to occupy the land and make use of it, and to exclude everyone else from the land. A person who has *some* rights to use land, but not all possessory rights, is said to have an *interest* in land. An interest occurs when a person has a month-to-month lease that either party can terminate at any time (*tenancy at will*) because no specific duration is mentioned. An interest also occurs when *license to use* is involved; here there is mere permission, and not even a contractual arrangement. This might occur if someone asked permission to come onto your land one afternoon to go fishing.

Creation of Estates in Land

Estates in land are created in the following ways: by *will, descent, voluntary alienation, involuntary alienation*, and *adverse possession*. (*Alienation* is a legal term that means "passing property to another.") One receives an estate *by will* if he inherits it by being *so designated in someone's will*. One receives an estate *by descent* if he is *designated by law* as the recipient of some property of a deceased person. This occurs if the person dies *intestate* (with no will); every state has laws governing the disposition of such property.

Voluntary alienation is the most common means whereby a person receives estates in land. This term refers to voluntary exchanges, sales, and gifts, wherein the one who gives up the property does so willingly. *Involuntary alienation* occurs where the owner of an estate is forced, in a legal manner, to give up some or all of her rights by the action of law. This most commonly occurs in the case of bankruptcy or of having some other kind of legal judgment entered against one, such as a foreclosure or failure to pay property taxes. Involuntary alienation also occurs by eminent domain (see page 48) and by adverse possession.

Adverse possession is a special means of acquiring ownership. All states have statutes permitting adverse possession, which is the right of a person who has used another's land actually to receive a legal claim to that land, in fee simple. The ancient idea behind this is that, if the true owner is so uninterested in his land that he does nothing during this period of time to prevent someone else from putting it to use, the community is better off by letting this other person actually have the full rights to the land. Adverse possession cannot be acquired overnight; in California, it takes five years to establish these rights. The adverse possession must be *open, notorious, continuous,* and *hostile*. This means that the claimant, during the required time period, must have acted completely as if the property were his own, including defending his "rights" against encroachment by others and being perfectly open in his actions. He must also have paid the property taxes for at least five years. The adverse possession must continue throughout the statutory period; a person can't use someone else's land for the summer of 1975 and later for the summer of 2006 and then claim that he has been using it for 31 years. Further, no tenant can claim against his landlord, because every time a tenant pays rent he legally acknowledges that the person receiving payment is the true owner. Nor may one claim against the government, on the theory that one is already the nominal "owner" of public property. *Easements* (see page 46) also can be acquired by adverse possession; they are called *easements by prescription*.

Tenancies

In California, estates in land may be owned in a variety of ways, depending on the number of people involved and their relationship. These various forms of ownership are called *tenancies*. *Tenancy in severalty* is ownership by one person. *Tenancy in common* is a form of ownership by two or more persons. Each one owns an *undivided interest*, which means that he owns a fraction of each part of the realty. In this arrangement, each is entitled to his share of the profits and is responsible to the other owners for his share of the costs and expenses. No part of the land may be disposed of without the consent of all, unless they have a specific arrangement whereby less than unanimity can force a decision. Tenants in common need not own equal shares. They may dispose of their shares in any way they choose, unless they have specifically agreed upon some limitation; this means that A and B may buy real estate as tenants in common and later on B may sell his share to C, making A and C tenants in common. Further, a tenant in common may will his share to someone else or give it away.

Joint tenancy is similar to tenancy in common except for one important difference: joint tenants have the *right of survivorship*. This means that if a joint tenant dies her share is divided proportionally among the surviving joint tenants. Consequently, a joint tenant cannot will her share to someone else. However, she can sell or give her interest away; the new owners will then have the status of tenants in common.

Tenancy by the entireties is a special form of joint ownership allowed only to married couples. In states where it is used, it protects the rights of the family to jointly owned property by providing the same basic rights and responsibilities as joint tenancy while also protecting the property against any foreclosure due to judgment or debt against one of the parties.

All of the forms of tenancy just discussed have to do with freehold estates. There are two major types of tenancies that refer to nonfreehold estates:

Tenancy at will occurs when there is a lease arrangement, but no specific time period is agreed upon. Essentially, then, either party can terminate the arrangement whenever he wants (i.e., at will), so its duration is uncertain.

Tenancy at sufferance occurs when a tenant remains on the property after the expiration of a lease. This differs from tenancy at will in that often some aspects of the original lease contract may be considered to be in force (such as those requiring notice before termination or prohibitions against certain kinds of uses or activities by the tenant). Many states have enacted laws requiring that, even in cases of tenancy at sufferance or tenancy at will, the parties give one another certain minimum notice before termination of the arrangement.

Community Property

In many states there are special forms of tenancy (*by the entirety*) for married couples, as well as laws (*dower laws, curtesy laws*) mandating that a surviving spouse receive a certain minimum portion of a deceased spouse's estate. California does not have such laws because it is one of nine *community property* states.* Under community property law, any property acquired by either spouse during a marriage is considered to be owned *equally* by *both*. There are some exceptions to community property; these are called *separate property*. Separate property includes (a) anything owned as separate property before the marriage, (b) anything acquired with the proceeds of the sale of, or from the income of separate property, and (c) anything acquired by one of the spouses by gift or inheritance.

Spouses may agree, by contract, either before or during a marriage, to specify particular property as community or separate property. When a married couple takes title to property, unless the conveyance (deed for real property, bill of sale for personal property) specifies otherwise, it is assumed that they will hold the property as community property.

Limitations on Estates and Interests

Very few estates or interests are completely free of restrictions or encumbrances; one or more of the following will affect most of them: easements, restrictive covenants, or liens.

EASEMENTS

An *easement* is the right of one landowner to use land belonging to another for a specific purpose. The most common kinds of easements are access easements, utility easements, and drainage easements. All of these allow someone who is *not* an owner of the affected property to make use of that property for some reason. An *access easement* allows someone to cross a

---

*The others are Arizona, Idaho, Louisiana, Nevada, New Mexico, Texas, Washington, and Wisconsin.

property to reach (i.e., obtain access to) another property. These rights exist where one parcel of land is completely blocked by others from access to a public right-of-way. A *utility easement* is a right held by a utility company to put its utility lines on private property, usually for the purpose of providing service to that property. A *drainage easement* requires that a property owner not disturb a natural or manmade drainage pattern that crosses his land.

Easements are created in all the ways that estates are; most commonly, however, they are created by voluntary alienation or adverse possession. In some states, a person who sells a part of his land that does not have direct access to a public right-of-way is legally bound to provide the purchaser with an access easement.

RESTRICTIVE COVENANTS

A *restrictive covenant* is a contract whereby a group of neighboring landowners agree to do (or *not* to do) a certain thing or things so as to mutually benefit all. Covenants most commonly occur in residential subdivisions and are created by the developer as a means of assuring prospective buyers that the neighborhood will be required to meet certain standards. Examples of covenants are prohibitions against using a lot for more than one single-family dwelling, limitations on the minimum size of structures to be built, and specification of architectural style. In California, the entire collection of restrictions applying to a subdivision is called the *Declaration of Restrictions*.

LIENS

Liens are claims against the owner of a property, with that property being usable as security for the claim. Claims for unpaid property taxes are liens, as, in many states, are mortgages. Also, anyone who has done work or provided materials so as to enhance the value of a property may, if not paid on time, secure a *mechanic's lien* against the property. If liens are not paid in the legal manner, the holder of the lien can foreclose against the property. *Foreclosure* is a legal process whereby a person holding a legal claim against a property may have the court order the property to be sold so as to provide funds to pay the claim.

Liens, restrictive covenants, and easements are, legally speaking, *a part of the property* and cannot be separated from it without the consent of all parties involved. A person who is considering buying property must be aware that all encumbrances on the property will remain with it after she acquires title, unless something is done to remove them.

Condominium

All states have passed laws that permit the establishment of *condominium* interests in land. *Condominium* is a legal term, describing a certain kind of ownership of land; it does *not* refer to any particular architectural style. In theory, any kind of property, serving any use, can be owned in condominium. Condominium is the only ownership form that includes a fee simple and an in-common interest at the same time. In this form of ownership, one has title to a part of a larger piece of property, with the right to use his part exclusively and the right to share some of the rest with the other owners. Typically, in a residential condominium one would have the right to use one's own dwelling unit, and no right to enter the units owned by others. However, one would share the right, with the others, to use the "common property," which might include private drives within the project, recreational facilities, common hallways, and elevators. Most important, the law allows an owner of a condominium unit to mortgage and otherwise encumber his unit; if he defaults, a lienholder may force the sale of his unit, but the other owners in the condominium project cannot be held responsible for anything.

A residential condominium development usually has a "homeowners' association" or some similar group that is elected by the owners of the units in the project. The function of the association is to ensure that the common property in the development is taken care of and also to make and enforce whatever rules the owners as a group want to enforce within their private community. Many people who have bought condominium units have found later that the rules and regulations of the association do not permit them to do everything they want to. For example, the association may have a rule limiting overnight guests to no more than two per unit, or requiring that only certain kinds of flowers be planted in the front yards. An owner who may wish to have more guests, or to plant different flowers, can find herself in conflict with the association and will be required to conform to the rules.

Many condominium projects have quite a lot of common property; swimming pools, park areas, parking lots, bicycle paths, tennis courts, clubhouses, and gatehouses are examples. The owners of units in the project own these common elements together, as a group. Their association looks after the common property and assesses each unit owner a fee (called a *condominium fee*), usually monthly, to get the funds necessary to maintain it. An owner who does not pay this fee will usually find that the association has the legal power to file a lien on his unit in order to collect the money.

Title and Recordation

A person who owns real estate is said to hold *title* to the land. There is no such thing as "title papers" to real estate, as there are with automobiles and certain other chattels. The term *title* refers to the validity of the available evidence that backs up one's claim to land. Normally, all deeds, liens, restrictions, and easements affecting land are recorded, usually in the courthouse of the county in which the land is located. Some leases, contracts of sale, and other documents may be recorded as well. The object of *recordation* is to provide a means whereby anyone may check the validity of any claim to land. In a legal sense, therefore, the ownership of all land and all rights to land should be a matter of record. These records are public, which means that anyone may examine them. It also means that anything that is recorded gives everyone *constructive notice* of the information recorded; therefore, in a court of law one is assumed to be aware of all information in the public records.

The total of the evidence in the records will be the validity of the *title* an owner holds. *Good title* is title that cannot be impeached by the records. Title that appears to be good but is not is said to be *color of title*.

Eminent Domain and Escheat

There are two special ways in which the government may acquire title to real estate. The most important is *eminent domain*; this is the right of the government to acquire privately owned property to be put to a public use, even if the private owner is unwilling to dispose of it. Government needs this power in order to operate efficiently for the benefit of everyone. Imagine the problems if, when the government decided to build a road, it had to look all over to find willing sellers for land needed for the project—the road might wander all around, and quite possibly it couldn't be built at all.

In an eminent domain situation the government can't just seize the land; it must pay the owner the "fair market value" of the land. However, once the government has established that it needs the land for a legitimate public use, there is no way to stop it. All a landowner can do is to dispute the price being offered; if he thinks it is unfair, he may sue for a higher award and have the court make the final decision. Usually the government will approach the landowner to work out an amicable arrangement, and quite often the landowner agrees to the offered price and there is no dispute. If, however, the landowner is reluctant or refuses to negotiate, the government will *condemn* the affected land. Condemnation is a legal process whereby the owner is dispossessed of the property and must leave. He retains the right to dispute the price being offered; but once condemnation has begun, a time will come when he must leave the land, which will be transferred to the government whether or not the payment question has been settled. All levels of government have power of eminent domain; also, many states have granted limited eminent domain power to private enterprises such as railroads, and utility companies.

Escheat is a process whereby land for which no legal owner exists reverts to government, which then can dispose of it or use it as it sees fit. Escheat most commonly occurs when someone dies intestate and no legal heirs can be found.

Questions on Chapter 3 _____

1. Which of the following is most accurately described as personal property?
   - (A) A fixture
   - (B) A chattel
   - (C) An improvement
   - (D) Realty

2. Which of the following is *not* corporeal property?
   - (A) A fee simple estate
   - (B) A leasehold
   - (C) An easement
   - (D) A fixture

Questions 3–5 concern the following situation:

Mr. Jones died; his will left to Mrs. Jones the right to use, occupy, and enjoy Mr. Jones's real estate until her death. At that time the real estate was to become the property of their son Willis.

3. Mrs. Jones is a
   - (A) remainderman
   - (B) life tenant
   - (C) joint tenant
   - (D) tenant in common

4. Willis is a
   - (A) remainderman
   - (B) life tenant
   - (C) joint tenant
   - (D) tenant in common

5. Mrs. Jones has a
   - (A) fee simple estate in joint tenancy with Willis
   - (B) fee simple estate as tenant in common with Willis
   - (C) life estate
   - (D) life estate in joint tenancy with Willis

6. Which of the following is *not* realty?
   - (A) A fee simple estate
   - (B) A leasehold for indefinite duration
   - (C) Lumber
   - (D) A life estate

7. Real estate is defined as
   - (A) land and buildings
   - (B) land and all permanent attachments
   - (C) land and everything growing on it
   - (D) land only

8. An item of personalty that is affixed to realty so as to be used as a part of it is
   - (A) a fixture
   - (B) a chattel
   - (C) personal property
   - (D) an encumbrance

9. A freehold estate is
   - (A) one acquired without paying anything
   - (B) any leasehold
   - (C) any estate wherein one may use the property as he wishes
   - (D) an estate of uncertain duration

10. Which is *not* considered a permanent attachment to land?
    - (A) Anything growing on it
    - (B) Fixtures
    - (C) Chattels
    - (D) Anything built upon the land

11. A person who has some rights to use land, but not all possessory rights, is said to have
    - (A) an interest in land
    - (B) an estate in land
    - (C) a life estate in land
    - (D) a tenancy in common

12. A person who has permission to use land, but has no other rights, has
    - (A) tenancy at sufferance
    - (B) tenancy in common
    - (C) license to use
    - (D) a fee simple estate

13. A person who receives title to land by virtue of having used and occupied it for a certain period of time, without actually paying the previous owner for it, receives title by
    - (A) will
    - (B) descent
    - (C) alienation
    - (D) adverse possession

14. A person who dies leaving no will is said to have died
    - (A) intestate
    - (B) without heirs
    - (C) unbequeathed
    - (D) unwillingly

15. A person who owns an undivided interest in land with at least one other, and has the right of survivorship, is said to be a
    - (A) tenant in common
    - (B) tenant at will
    - (C) joint tenant
    - (D) tenant at sufferance

16. Tenancy in severalty refers to
    - (A) ownership by one person only
    - (B) ownership by two persons only
    - (C) ownership by at least three persons
    - (D) a special form of joint ownership available only to married couples

17. Community property includes
    - (A) property owned by either spouse during the marriage
    - (B) property acquired during a marriage with the husband's earnings from his job
    - (C) property inherited by the wife during the marriage
    - (D) property given to either spouse by a parent

18. An easement is
    - (A) the right to use the property of another for any purpose
    - (B) the right to use the property of another for a specific purpose
    - (C) a private contract and does not permanently affect the realty
    - (D) the right to keep another from using one's land illegally

19. The process whereby a person holding a claim against property can have the property sold to pay the claim is
    - (A) a lien
    - (B) a covenant
    - (C) a mechanic's lien
    - (D) foreclosure

20. A person who appears to own property, but does not, is said to have
    - (A) good title
    - (B) recorded evidence of title
    - (C) constructive notice
    - (D) color of title

21. Two people who own undivided interests in the same realty, with right of survivorship, have
    - (A) tenancy in severalty
    - (B) tenancy in common
    - (C) tenancy at sufferance
    - (D) joint tenancy

22. A fee simple estate is
    - (A) a freehold estate
    - (B) a life estate
    - (C) an estate for years
    - (D) an estate in abeyance

23. Which of the following is considered a permanent attachment to land?
    (A) Improvements to land
    (B) A fixture
    (C) Trees growing on the land
    (D) All of the above

24. A person who has some rights to land, but not all the possessory rights, has
    (A) a life estate
    (B) an interest in land
    (C) an estate at will
    (D) a fixture

25. A person who has color of title to land has
    (A) the appearance of title
    (B) forgeries of state title papers
    (C) a right to one-half the income from the land
    (D) foreign ownership

26. A life estate *pur autre vie* is one in which
    (A) the life tenant must occupy the premises and may not lease them to anyone else
    (B) the duration of the life estate is based on the duration of the life of someone other than the life tenant
    (C) the life tenant has died
    (D) the life tenant may not occupy the property himself/herself

27. Which of the following would not be real property?
    (A) A lease for one month
    (B) An easement
    (C) Permanent ownership of mineral rights on someone else's land
    (D) A life estate

28. *Adverse possession* may establish
    (A) use of property
    (B) a claim to title
    (C) who owes back taxes
    (D) homestead rights

29. An *easement by prescription* may establish
    (A) use of property
    (B) a claim to title
    (C) who owes back taxes
    (D) homestead rights

30. Fifty feet of land was added to Apple's farm because a river changed its course. This is an example of
    (A) accretion
    (B) avulsion
    (C) riparian rights
    (D) usufructory

31. Fifty feet of beachfront land was removed by a flood. This is an example of
    (A) riparian rights
    (B) estovers
    (C) avulsion
    (D) emblements

32. If someone dies without a will, a(n) _____ is appointed to settle the estate.
    (A) executor
    (B) administrator
    (C) notary public
    (D) attorney-in-fact

33. If someone dies leaving a will, he or she died in this legal state.
    (A) Testate
    (B) Intestate
    (C) Executory
    (D) *Pur autre vie*

34. As used in real estate practices, the land of a *riparian* owner borders on
    (A) a river
    (B) a stream
    (C) a watercourse
    (D) any of the above

35. *Community property* is property owned by
    (A) churches
    (B) husband and wife
    (C) the municipality
    (D) the community

36. A person holding title to real property in severalty would most likely have
    (A) a life estate
    (B) an estate for years
    (C) ownership in common with others
    (D) sole ownership

37. Joint ownership of real property by two or more persons, each of whom has an undivided interest (not necessarily equal) without right of survivorship, is
    (A) a tenancy in partnership
    (B) a tenancy by the entireties
    (C) a tenancy in common
    (D) a leasehold tenancy

38. Generally, the taking of private land by governmental bodies for public use is governed by due process of law and is accomplished through
    (A) exercise of the police power
    (B) eminent domain
    (C) reverter
    (D) escheat

39. Governmental land use planning and zoning are important examples of
    (A) exercise of eminent domain
    (B) use of police power
    (C) deed restrictions
    (D) encumbrance

40. The covenant of *quiet enjoyment* most directly relates to
    (A) nuisances maintained on adjoining property
    (B) possession of real property
    (C) title to real property
    (D) all of the above

41. An interest in real property may be acquired either by prescription or by adverse possession. The interest resulting from prescription is
    (A) the right to use another's land
    (B) a possessory title
    (C) an equitable interest
    (D) a private grant

ANSWERS

1. **B**	10. **C**	19. **D**	28. **B**	37. **C**
2. **C**	11. **A**	20. **D**	29. **A**	38. **B**
3. **B**	12. **C**	21. **D**	30. **A**	39. **B**
4. **A**	13. **D**	22. **A**	31. **C**	40. **B**
5. **C**	14. **A**	23. **D**	32. **B**	41. **A**
6. **C**	15. **C**	24. **B**	33. **A**	
7. **B**	16. **A**	25. **A**	34. **D**	
8. **A**	17. **B**	26. **B**	35. **B**	
9. **D**	18. **B**	27. **A**	36. **D**	

Chapter 4/*Agency Law*

A licensed real estate broker or salesperson is an *agent*; therefore his practice comes under the *laws of agency*. He is also affected by the real estate license law of his state, a topic that will be discussed in Chapter 5.

An agency relationship involves two parties: the *principal* and the *agent*. The agency relationship is contractual, but it also is covered by the general requirements of agency law. In the real estate business, a broker acts as an agent for his *employer*, or principal, who is the owner of the property for which the broker is seeking a buyer or tenant. A licensed salesperson usually is treated as the agent of the *broker*, because license law does not permit salespersons to act without the supervision of a broker.

A real estate broker is a *special agent*. He is called this because his powers are limited, usually to finding someone with whom his principal can deal. A *general agent* is a person whose powers are broader and may extend so far as to commit her employer to action. Note that a real estate broker usually has little or no power actually to commit her principal to anything; the principal may refuse to deal with anyone the broker brings to him, although he still may be liable to pay the broker a commission.

Broker Defined

Under California law, a real estate broker is:

a person who, for a compensation or in expectation of a compensation, regardless of the form or time of payment, does or negotiates to do one or more of the following acts for another or others:

(a) Sells or offers to sell, buys or offers to buy, solicits prospective sellers or purchasers of, solicits or obtains listings of, or negotiates the purchase, sale, or exchange of real property or a business opportunity.

(b) Leases or rents or offers to lease or rent, or places for rent, or solicits listings of places for rent, or solicits for prospective tenants, or negotiates the sale, purchase or exchanges of leases on real property, or on a business opportunity, or collects rents from real property, or improvements thereon, or from business opportunities.

(c) Assists or offers to assist in filing an application for the purchase or lease of, or in locating or entering upon, lands owned by the state or federal government.

(d) Solicits borrowers or lenders for or negotiates loans or collects payments or performs services for borrowers or lenders or note owners in connection with loans secured directly or collaterally by liens on real property or on a business opportunity.

(e) Sells or offers to sell, buys or offers to buy, or exchanges or offers to exchange a real property sales contract, or a promissory note secured directly or collaterally by a lien on real property or on a business opportunity, and performs services for the holders thereof.[*]

There are some exemptions under this definition. Exempt persons include (1) resident managers of hotels, motels, trailer parks, and apartment buildings; (2) employees of owners or brokers who are resident managers; and (3) other employees who perform these tasks under

---

[*]"Real Estate Law and Subdivided Lands Law," from *Business and Professions Code*, in effect January 1, 2005, Division 4, Part 1, Chapter 1, p. 25.

appropriate supervision of a licensed broker or owner. Tasks that may be engaged in by such persons include:

(A) Showing rental units and common areas to prospective tenants.

(B) Providing or accepting preprinted rental applications, or responding to inquiries from a prospective tenant concerning the completion of the application.

(C) Accepting deposits or fees for credit checks or administrative costs and accepting security deposits and rents.

(D) Providing information about rental rates and other terms and provisions of a lease or rental agreement, as set out in a schedule provided by the employer.

(E) Accepting signed leases and rental agreements from prospective tenants.†

The penalty for acting as a broker or salesperson without a license or holding oneself out by advertising as a broker or salesperson is a fine of up to $10,000 or six months in jail or both. A corporation may be fined up to $50,000.‡

Duties of Parties

An agent is employed to deal with third parties on behalf of his principal. The agent is an employee of the principal and must follow his principal's instructions implicitly. Furthermore, he has a duty to act in his employer's best interests, even when doing so means that he cannot act in his own favor. More specifically, agency law requires that the agent abide by the following obligations to his principal:

- He must *obey* his principal's instructions (except, of course, when he is instructed to do something illegal).
- He must be *loyal* to his principal's interests.
- He must act in *good faith*.
- He is expected to use *professional judgment, skill,* and *ability* in his actions. This is particularly true in the case of licensed agents such as real estate brokers, who are assumed to have met certain standards by virtue of having to be licensed.
- He must be able to *account* for all money belonging to others that comes into his possession. Real estate brokers often collect rents, earnest money payments, and other money on behalf of their principals.
- He must perform his duties *in person*. Normally, this would mean that he could not delegate his duties to anyone else unless the principal approved of the arrangement. Because of the nature of the real estate brokerage business and the establishment of the broker-salesperson relationship by all state licensing laws, however, a real estate broker has the implied right to delegate his function to duly licensed salespersons and brokers in his employ.
- He must keep his principal *fully informed* of developments affecting their relationship. A real estate broker should report all offers made on the principal's property, as well as all other information he acquires that may affect the principal's property, price, or other relevant factors.

The principal has obligations to the agent as well. Most of these have to do with money: the principal is obliged to *compensate* the agent for her services, to *reimburse* the agent for expenses paid on behalf of the principal, and to *secure* the agent against any loss due to proper performance of her duties. The principal also has the implied duty to make the agent fully aware of her duties and to inform her fully about anything that will affect her performance.

Real Estate Agency Contracts

In real estate, an agency contract is called a *listing*. The details of drawing up these contracts are discussed in Chapter 11. The Statute of Frauds requires most listings to be written. Here, however, we can briefly distinguish among the various kinds of listings. Among listings of property for *sale* are the following:

---

†Ibid., p. 26.
‡Ibid., p. 36.

In an *open* listing the principal agrees to compensate the agent only if the agent actually finds the buyer with whom the principal finally deals. A single owner may have open listings with many brokers, since she is obliging herself to pay only upon performance, and the broker makes his effort at his own risk.

In an *exclusive agency* listing the principal agrees to employ no other broker, and if the property is sold by any licensed agent a commission will be paid to the listing broker. State license law usually requires that any other agent must work *through* a broker having an exclusive listing; the participating brokers must then agree on a means by which they will share in the commission. However, the commission always will be paid to the listing broker, who then may pay a share to the other broker(s) who cooperated in the deal.

An *exclusive-right-to-sell* listing guarantees that the principal will pay the broker a commission regardless of who actually sells the property. This applies even if the principal herself finds the buyer, with no aid at all from the broker. (Note that under an exclusive agency listing the principal does not have to pay a commission if she herself finds the buyer.)

Usage of the term *exclusive listing* varies from one place to another. In some localities the term refers to an exclusive agency; in others it refers to the exclusive right to sell; in still others it refers to both types interchangeably.

A *net* listing is one in which the principal agrees to receive a given net amount. The excess by which the sale price exceeds the net amount goes to the broker as his commission. In many states net listings are illegal; in California they are not illegal but are "frowned upon" or otherwise disapproved of in some quasi-official manner. The big problem with net listings is that the agent is strongly tempted to act in his own interest rather than that of his employer. To illustrate, suppose a net listing contract with a proposed net to the seller of $250,000 is agreed upon. By law, anytime the broker solicits an offer he must report it to the principal. However, let us assume that an offer of exactly $250,000 is made; if the broker transmits it, the seller probably will accept and the broker will receive no compensation. Clearly, there is the temptation to illegally "hide" the offer, and any subsequent offers, until one yielding a satisfactory excess over the listed price is received; obviously such action is contrary to the agent's legal responsibilities to his employer. A further source of trouble with net listings arises when a knowledgeable agent deals with a naive seller; there may exist an opportunity for the agent to convince the seller to sign a net listing at a low price, thereby guaranteeing the agent a large commission when he finds a buyer who will pay true market value.

The Agency Relationship in Real Estate Brokerage

In a *listing contract* (see Chapter 11), the agency relationship is between the owner of the listed real estate and the broker whom the owner hires to sell or lease the real estate. This makes sense; however, in the real estate brokerage business it is very common for other brokers to be involved in the transaction. Brokers very often *cooperate* with one another: they agree to allow one another to seek buyers (or tenants) for each others' listings. If another broker finds a buyer (tenant), then the listing broker agrees to share with that other broker the commission paid by the property owner. This situation leads to the question of whom all these agents actually represent. In *traditional agency*, all agents involved in a cooperated transaction represent *only the seller:* buyers have no agent looking out for their interests. It's called traditional agency because that's the way it was always done until about 20 years ago. At that time the states began to allow *buyer agency*. Buyer agency occurs when the licensee specifically represents the buyer(s), and a contract to that effect is signed. This way, buyers get agency representation: a professional who is looking out for *their* interests. (Buyer agents are compensated with a share of the commission paid by the seller, just as in traditional agency.)

California requires *agency disclosure* by real estate brokers; upon first contact with a prospective buyer, the broker must provide notification that he actually represents the seller, and does not look out for the specific needs and interests of the buyer. The law specifies a certain form that must be given to the buyer, and the broker cannot proceed with any dealings with that buyer until the broker has received from the buyer a signed form acknowledging that the buyer understands the agency relationship the broker has with the seller.

The brokerage business itself has developed the *direct buyer-broker agency*. Here the broker and the buyer have their own contract in which the broker agrees to represent the buyer's interests, and not the seller's. Since this arrangement, although not illegal, is not the traditional one of exclusive seller agency by all brokers, the seller and the seller's broker must be notified that the buyer's broker is not representing the seller in the transaction. A key point is that everyone involved in a transaction must be aware of what the agency relationships are before the negotiations for a transaction begin. Figure 4-1 shows an *agency disclosure form*, which must be presented by real estate salespeople to anyone they deal with (prospective buyers or sellers) upon first contact with them. An agent taking a listing normally would be the seller's agent. One showing property to a prospective buyer could be either the buyer's or the seller's agent. In times past, *all* salespeople were considered agents of the seller, because they all shared in the commission paid by the seller. Nowadays, however, it is very common in California for salespeople showing property to prospective buyers to agree to be the buyer's agent. It is customary that a buyer's agent will be compensated out of the commission paid by the seller to the listing agent. So long as everyone is aware of the compensation arrangement, there is no problem. (Note that the disclosure form mentions that the buyer's agent may be compensated out of funds paid by the seller.)

When a buying prospect prepares to make an offer on a property, the *agency confirmation form* (Figure 4-2) is prepared. This form, when executed, assures that everyone involved in the transaction is aware of all of the agency relationships.

Here is something very important: Illustrations of contracts and other forms are not included in this book just to take up space; they are here for you to study! Look them over carefully, and *read* them! Note also that California contracts typically have the relevant law printed on them, in some cases on the reverse of the form itself, which is not reproduced here.

In many transactions there is little problem identifying the agents and their principals. However, there can arise the problem of *dual agency*. A salesperson lists a home for sale and, in the contract and disclosure agreement, is named as the seller's agent. So far so good; when other agents arrive with buying prospects, no problem arises. But suppose the listing agent finds a buying prospect herself? Whose agent is she? Can she represent *both* buyer and seller? Usually yes, so long as both buyer and seller are aware of the dual agency, and both realize that the agent represents *neither* of them exclusively. This can be a very dicey situation, though, and agents are well advised to avoid it unless they are absolutely certain that no problems will arise. A 21st-century innovation that is beginning to appear in some states is *designated agency*. Although it is not yet in use in California, it is possible that it will be incorporated into California law in the not-so-distant future. Designated agency is supposed to solve a problem brought on by buyer agency: suppose a licensee has a buyer agency with someone who is looking for a house. The licensee thinks that the prospect will be interested in a certain home for which this same licensee also has a listing contract. Now the agent is under agency contract to both parties. One solution is to have both buyer and seller agree to a dual agency with the licensee, but, as we have seen, dual agency has its drawbacks. With designated agency, the licensee's principal broker appoints another licensee (the *designated agent*) in the same office to represent one of the parties (usually the buyer), while the original licensee represents *only* the other party in this one situation. One thing must always be remembered: in California, it is illegal for a *selling agent* in a transaction to represent *only* the buyer. This would violate the agency relationship already established with the seller.

CALIFORNIA ASSOCIATION OF REALTORS®

DISCLOSURE REGARDING REAL ESTATE AGENCY RELATIONSHIPS
(As required by the Civil Code)
(C.A.R. Form AD, Revised 10/04)

When you enter into a discussion with a real estate agent regarding a real estate transaction, you should from the outset understand what type of agency relationship or representation you wish to have with the agent in the transaction.

SELLER'S AGENT
A Seller's agent under a listing agreement with the Seller acts as the agent for the Seller only. A Seller's agent or a subagent of that agent has the following affirmative obligations:
To the Seller:
    A Fiduciary duty of utmost care, integrity, honesty, and loyalty in dealings with the Seller.
To the Buyer and the Seller:
    (a) Diligent exercise of reasonable skill and care in performance of the agent's duties.
    (b) A duty of honest and fair dealing and good faith.
    (c) A duty to disclose all facts known to the agent materially affecting the value or desirability of the property that are not known to, or within the diligent attention and observation of, the parties.

An agent is not obligated to reveal to either party any confidential information obtained from the other party that does not involve the affirmative duties set forth above.

BUYER'S AGENT
A selling agent can, with a Buyer's consent, agree to act as agent for the Buyer only. In these situations, the agent is not the Seller's agent, even if by agreement the agent may receive compensation for services rendered, either in full or in part from the Seller. An agent acting only for a Buyer has the following affirmative obligations:
To the Buyer:
    A fiduciary duty of utmost care, integrity, honesty, and loyalty in dealings with the Buyer.
To the Buyer and the Seller:
    (a) Diligent exercise of reasonable skill and care in performance of the agent's duties.
    (b) A duty of honest and fair dealing and good faith.
    (c) A duty to disclose all facts known to the agent materially affecting the value or desirability of the property that are not known to, or within the diligent attention and observation of, the parties.

An agent is not obligated to reveal to either party any confidential information obtained from the other party that does not involve the affirmative duties set forth above.

AGENT REPRESENTING BOTH SELLER AND BUYER
A real estate agent, either acting directly or through one or more associate licensees, can legally be the agent of both the Seller and the Buyer in a transaction, but only with the knowledge and consent of both the Seller and the Buyer.

In a dual agency situation, the agent has the following affirmative obligations to both the Seller and the Buyer:
    (a) A fiduciary duty of utmost care, integrity, honesty and loyalty in the dealings with either the Seller or the Buyer.
    (b) Other duties to the Seller and the Buyer as stated above in their respective sections.

In representing both Seller and Buyer, the agent may not, without the express permission of the respective party, disclose to the other party that the Seller will accept a price less than the listing price or that the Buyer will pay a price greater than the price offered.

The above duties of the agent in a real estate transaction do not relieve a Seller or Buyer from the responsibility to protect his or her own interests. You should carefully read all agreements to assure that they adequately express your understanding of the transaction. A real estate agent is a person qualified to advise about real estate. If legal or tax advice is desired, consult a competent professional.

Throughout your real property transaction you may receive more than one disclosure form, depending upon the number of agents assisting in the transaction. The law requires each agent with whom you have more than a casual relationship to present you with this disclosure form. You should read its contents each time it is presented to you, considering the relationship between you and the real estate agent in your specific transaction.

This disclosure form includes the provisions of Sections 2079.13 to 2079.24, inclusive, of the Civil Code set forth on the reverse hereof. Read it carefully.

I/WE ACKNOWLEDGE RECEIPT OF A COPY OF THIS DISCLOSURE AND THE PORTIONS OF THE CIVIL CODE PRINTED ON THE BACK (OR A SEPARATE PAGE).

BUYER/SELLER _____ Date _____ Time _____ AM/PM

BUYER/SELLER _____ Date _____ Time _____ AM/PM

AGENT _____ By _____ Date _____
      (Please Print)   (Associate-Licensee or Broker Signature)

THIS FORM SHALL BE PROVIDED AND ACKNOWLEDGED AS FOLLOWS (Civil Code § 2079.14):
• When the listing brokerage company also represents Buyer, the Listing Agent shall have one AD form signed by Seller and one signed by Buyer.
• When Buyer and Seller are represented by different brokerage companies, the Listing Agent shall have one AD form signed by Seller and the Buyer's Agent shall have one AD form signed by Buyer and one AD form signed by Seller.

The System for Success®

Published and Distributed by:
REAL ESTATE BUSINESS SERVICES, INC.
a subsidiary of the California Association of REALTORS®
525 South Virgil Avenue, Los Angeles, California 90020

Reviewed by _____ Date _____

EQUAL HOUSING OPPORTUNITY

AD REVISED 10/04 (PAGE 1 OF 1) PRINT DATE

DISCLOSURE REGARDING REAL ESTATE AGENCY RELATIONSHIPS (AD PAGE 1 OF 1)

Figure 4-1. California Agency Disclosure Form

CONFIRMATION REAL ESTATE AGENCY RELATIONSHIPS
(As required by the Civil Code)
(C.A.R. Form AC-6, Revised 1987)

Subject Property Address _____
The following agency relationship(s) is/are hereby confirmed for this transaction:

LISTING AGENT: _____

is the agent of (check one):
❏ the Seller exclusively; or
❏ both the Buyer and Seller

SELLING AGENT: _____

(if not the same as Listing Agent)
is the agent of (check one):
❏ the Buyer exclusively; or
❏ the Seller exclusively; or
❏ both the Buyer and Seller

I/WE ACKNOWLEDGE RECEIPT OF A COPY OF THIS CONFIRMATION.

Seller _____ Date _____   Buyer _____ Date _____

Seller _____ Date _____   Buyer _____ Date _____

Listing Agent _____ By _____ Date _____
(Please Print)   (Associate Licensee or Broker-Signature)

Selling Agent _____ By _____ Date _____
(Please Print)   (Associate Licensee or Broker-Signature)

A REAL ESTATE BROKER IS QUALIFIED TO ADVISE ON REAL ESTATE. IF YOU DESIRE LEGAL ADVICE, CONSULT YOUR ATTORNEY.

This form is available for use by the entire real estate industry. It is not intended to identify the user as a REALTOR®. REALTOR® is a registered collective membership mark which may be used only by members of the NATIONAL ASSOCIATION OF REALTORS® who subscribe to its Code of Ethics.

The copyright laws of the United States (17 U.S. Code) forbid the unauthorized reproduction of this form by any means, including facsimile or computerized formats.
Copyright © 1987-1997, CALIFORNIA ASSOCIATION OF REALTORS®

Published and Distributed by:
REAL ESTATE BUSINESS SERVICES, INC.
a subsidiary of the California Association of REALTORS®
525 South Virgil Avenue, Los Angeles, California 90020

Reviewed by _____ Date _____

CONFIRMATION REAL ESTATE AGENCY RELATIONSHIPS (AC-6 PAGE 1 OF 1) REVISED 1987

Figure 4-2.   California Agency Confirmation Form

Earning the Commission

Under common law, a broker earns his commission when he produces a buyer (or tenant) with whom the principal is willing to deal. From then on, whether the deal actually will go through rests with the principal. However, many listing contracts today put the risk back on the broker by specifying that the commission is not payable until the sale closes.

As mentioned previously, the principal is not obliged to deal with anyone whom the broker brings; that is, the principal, by hiring the broker, incurs no legal responsibility to the *third party*. Consequently, a buyer who is willing to pay the asking price and meet all the conditions set down by the principal in the listing agreement normally will have no legal recourse if the principal refuses to deal with him, unless the buyer's civil rights have been violated.

Nevertheless, the principal's obligations to the broker remain. In the listing agreement an acceptable price and terms of sale are specified. If the broker produces a bona fide offer that meets all these conditions, then the principal is liable to pay the broker a commission even if she chooses not to accept the offer. This is required, because the broker has satisfied the terms of his employment contract, and there *is* a contract between him and the principal. There is *no* contract however, between the principal and third parties (such as potential buyers), so she is not liable to them.

If the broker's principal refuses to pay him a commission that the broker feels he has earned, he may sue in court to receive it. To be successful, he must prove three things:

1. that he was *licensed* throughout the time, beginning with the solicitation of the listing until the closing of the deal and the passing of title (or the notification by the principal that she will not accept an offer that meets the terms of the listing agreement);

2. that he had a contract of employment with the principal (the best evidence here is a written contract); and

3. that he was the "efficient and procuring cause" of the sale; that is, that he actually brought about the sale within the terms of the listing contract. In an open listing this would mean that he actually found the eventual buyer. In an exclusive agency listing, he must have found the buyer or the buyer must have been found by a licensed agent. An exclusive-right-to-sell listing effectively defines the broker as having earned a commission when and if the property is sold.

The rate of commission is not fixed by law. The rate or amount may be negotiated by the broker and seller or buyer.

Termination of an Agency Contract

Agency contracts can be terminated by a variety of events, though some of them are relatively uncommon. In a broad sense, contracts can be terminated in two ways: by the *actions of the parties* to them, or *by law* when certain events occur.

Termination by the actions of the parties includes the following:

The contract is terminated by *performance* when both parties perform their duties as prescribed and the event for which the agency is created ends. In the real estate business, a listing agency contract is terminated by performance when there is a "meeting of the minds" between the principal and the third party found by the agent. Sometimes, however, the contract will specify some other event (usually title closing, in the event of a listing for sale) as the actual termination of the contractual relationship.

The parties may *mutually agree* to terminate the relationship before it has been terminated by performance.

The agent may *resign*. In this case, the agent may be liable to the principal for damages due to his breach of the contract, but he cannot be held to perform under the contract.

The principal may *discharge* the agent. Once again, the principal, too, can be liable for damages due to her breach of the contract, but she cannot be forced to continue the employment of the agent.

The agent may resign, or the principal may discharge the agent, without penalty if it can be proved that the other party was not properly discharging his or her duties under the contract. An agent would be justified in resigning if, for example, his principal did not provide him with enough information to do his job well or required that he perform some illegal act in the execution of his duties. An agent could be discharged justifiably if it could be shown that he was not faithful to his duties or was acting contrary to the interests of the principal.

Termination of the contractual relationship also occurs automatically, *by law*, with the occurrence of certain events, such as the following:

The *death of either party* terminates an agency relationship.

If either party becomes *legally incompetent*, the agency relationship ceases.

Bankruptcy of either party, so as to make continuation of the relationship impossible, terminates the relationship.

Destruction of the subject matter terminates any agency relationship. In real estate this would include such events as the burning down of a house or the discovery of another claim on the title that would make it impossible for the owner of the property to pass good and marketable title.

Questions on Chapter 4

1. A real estate broker is a
   (A) general agent
   (B) special agent
   (C) secret agent
   (D) travel agent

2. Which of the following is *not* required of an agent with respect to his principal?
   (A) To be loyal
   (B) To act in person
   (C) To account for his own personal finances
   (D) To act in the principal's best interests

3. A listing contract that says that the broker will receive a commission no matter who sells the property is called
   (A) an open listing
   (B) a net listing
   (C) an exclusive agency listing
   (D) an exclusive-right-to-sell listing

4. Which of the following does *not* terminate an agency relationship?
   (A) Making an offer
   (B) The death of either party
   (C) The resignation of the agent
   (D) The destruction of the subject matter

5. To prove her right to a commission a broker must show
   (A) that she was licensed throughout the transaction
   (B) that she had a contract of employment
   (C) that she was the "efficient and procuring cause" of the sale
   (D) all of the above

6. A net listing is one
   (A) that requires the broker to seek a net price for the property
   (B) that is legal in all states
   (C) that most ethical brokers would prefer to use
   (D) in which the broker's commission is the amount by which the sale price exceeds the agreed-upon net price the seller desires

7. Among other things, the principal is obligated to
   (A) compensate the agent for his services
   (B) give the agent full authority to accept or turn down offers
   (C) give the agency the principal's financial statement
   (D) none of the above

8. A real estate agent
   (A) must always represent the seller
   (B) may represent the buyer if the buyer-broker agency is disclosed to all parties
   (C) may not take listings if she represents buyers
   (D) need not disclose a buyer-broker agency relationship

9. A special agent is one
   (A) whose powers are limited to certain specific functions
   (B) who must report to a licensing agency
   (C) who has less then a certain amount of experience as an agent
   (D) who is not a licensed agent

10. Among other things, an agent is obligated to
   (A) act in the principal's best interests unless these conflict with the agent's own interests
   (B) keep an accurate account of all money he receives on behalf of the principal
   (C) never disclose the agency relationship to anyone
   (D) represent only one principal at a time

11. In California, which of the following is illegal?
   (A) Selling agent represents only the buyer
   (B) Selling agent represents both buyer and seller
   (C) Buyer's agent represents both buyer and seller
   (D) All of the above are illegal

12. The agency disclosure form must be executed
   (A) when the sale closes escrow
   (B) only if there is dual agency
   (C) when a salesperson agrees to work for a broker
   (D) upon first contact with a potential seller or buyer

13. The rate of commission on a real estate sale in California is
   (A) typically 6% of the selling price
   (B) mandated at various rates by California law
   (C) paid to the salesperson, who gives 50% to the broker
   (D) negotiable between the broker and (typically) seller

14. As a general rule, escrow money received by the broker pending a closing
   (A) is given to the seller on signing the contract
   (B) may be spent by the broker for repairs to the property
   (C) is deposited immediately in the broker's trust account
   (D) shared equally by the broker and salesperson

15. An unlicensed employee of a broker who prepares an advertisement to sell a house
   (A) is free to do so
   (B) must have the broker's prior written approval
   (C) must become licensed
   (D) must accurately describe the house

16. Copies of all listings, deposit receipts, canceled checks, and trust records must be retained by a licensed real estate broker for
   (A) one year
   (B) two years
   (C) three years
   (D) five years

17. If the broker, while acting as agent in a sale of real property, misrepresents the principal's property to a buyer, the broker may cause the principal to be subjected to
   (A) rescission of the sale by the buyer
   (B) a court action for damages by the buyer
   (C) tort liability
   (D) any of the above

18. A broker selling a property on which he holds an option should notify the purchaser that he is acting as
   (A) an optionor
   (B) a mortgagor
   (C) a beneficiary
   (D) a principal

19. The maximum commission a broker may charge a seller for the sale of residential income property is
    (A) set forth in the Real Estate Law
    (B) negotiable
    (C) no more than 10 percent of the total sales price
    (D) determined by local custom

20. The position of trust assumed by the broker as an agent for a principal is described most accurately as
    (A) a gratuitous relationship
    (B) a trustor relationship
    (C) a fiduciary relationship
    (D) an employment relationship

21. The Agency Relationship Disclosure Law became effective in
    (A) 1960
    (B) 1975
    (C) 1988
    (D) 1998

ANSWERS

1. **B**	7. **A**	13. **D**	19. **B**
2. **C**	8. **B**	14. **C**	20. **C**
3. **D**	9. **A**	15. **B**	21. **C**
4. **A**	10. **B**	16. **C**	
5. **D**	11. **A**	17. **D**	
6. **D**	12. **D**	18. **D**	

Chapter 5/*Real Estate License Law*

In 1919, California became the first state to successfully require licensure of real estate brokers and salespeople. Real estate licensing is an exercise of the state's *police power,* granted to government by the U.S. Constitution. You are encouraged to get a copy of the book *Real Estate Law* from the California Department of Real Estate. It costs about $25, plus tax, and can be purchased at any DRE office (see list in Chapter 1), or ordered by mail. It is 700 pages long and contains all of the California laws and regulations which could have anything whatever to do with real estate licensees. The real estate licensing laws, which are in the *California Business and Professions Code*, take up about 150 of those pages; much of the rest is covered elsewhere in this book. *Real Estate Law* is kind of dry reading, but we encourage you to look it over closely. We can't possibly cover everything that is stuffed into a 700-page book, but we will hit the important parts that are most likely to appear on the exam.

You also can download most of *Real Estate Law* from the DRE Web site at http://www.dre.ca.gov (see Chapter 1). About 12 percent of both the salesperson exam and the broker exam is devoted to questions about California license law and agency law. An additional 24 percent of the salesperson exam and 27 percent of the broker exam is on "The Practice of Real Estate" and "Mandated Disclosures."

Brokerage, Broker, and Salesperson

A *real estate brokerage* business is one which, in an agency relationship and for compensation, sells, leases, or solicits buyers, sellers, tenants, or lessors for real estate owned by others. A real estate brokerage business may be a sole proprietorship (owned and operated by an individual), a corporation, or a partnership. With a few exceptions (see below), anyone who performs any of these brokerage-related activities must be licensed as either a broker or a salesperson.

A *real estate broker* is one who is licensed to independently operate a real estate brokerage business. A *real estate salesperson* performs brokerage functions, but must be employed by a licensed broker and may not operate independently. A real estate broker is not required to operate independently; a broker licensee may be employed by another broker just as a salesperson licensee would. A licensed salesperson may not operate or manage a brokerage business, may not hold or control a majority of the stock in a corporate brokerage, and may not be a director or officer in a corporate brokerage. A corporate brokerage must be operated by a licensed broker, who is called the *broker-officer.* In a brokerage partnership, all partners must be licensed brokers.

A licensed salesperson may not operate independently and may not be an owner (full or part) of a real estate brokerage business. California requires licensed salespeople to work for and be under the supervision of a licensed broker. Usually this is referred to as the broker's "holding" the salesperson's license. The license is not actually issued to the salesperson; rather, it is issued to that salesperson's broker. The supervisory responsibility of the broker is a serious matter because the broker is liable for anything and everything the salesperson does in the course of the brokerage business. In fact, all agency contracts negotiated by a salesperson are actually contracts between the seller (or buyer) and the *broker,* and not just between the salesperson and the principal.

To become a broker in California, one must have gained two years' full-time experience as a salesperson (or equivalent) in the past five years. The employing broker must submit a form to verify a salesperson's full-time employment.

A salesperson may not receive *any* form of compensation for brokerage-related activity except *directly from* his/her employing broker. The salesperson's employment agreement with the broker must be in writing. However, the manner in which the salesperson is paid (salary, commission, and how much) is subject to negotiation between the salesperson and broker. These rules also apply to a broker licensee who is employed by another broker.

In any brokerage business, the licenses of all licensees (brokers and salespersons) associated with the business must be available to the public for inspection. They don't have to be posted in public view, but they have to be readily available upon request.

Real estate brokers also may deal in businesses as well as real estate. For example, a building that houses a shoe store is real estate (the building and land) and the business that occupies the real estate is the shoe retailing business. Business brokerage, in California, is called *business opportunity brokerage*.

Exemption from Licensing

Some people who perform what seems to be real estate brokerage activity do not have to be licensed. The main ones include:

1. Anyone buying or selling his or her own real estate.
2. An attorney-at-law, in the course of his or her duties to clients.
3. Anyone who has a properly executed power of attorney allowing him or her to act for a party to a transaction.
4. A trustee selling under a deed of trust.
5. Anyone acting under an order of any court.
6. A trustee, or receiver, in bankruptcy.
7. An officer of a corporation performing such functions for the corporation without receiving special compensation (that is, a commission) for doing so.

Other exemptions from licensure include resident managers of apartment buildings and complexes or their employees; short-term (vacation) rental agents; employees of certain lending institutions; employees of real estate brokers for specific, limited functions; lenders making loans guaranteed or insured by an agency of the federal government; certain agricultural associations; licensed personal property brokers; cemetery authorities; certain collectors of payments for lenders or on notes for owners in connection with loans secured directly or collaterally by liens on real property, provided such collectors annually meet exemption criteria; and clerical help.

Obtaining the License

Review Chapter 1 for the education and experience necessary to qualify to take the licensing examination. An information packet about applying for the examination is available by calling or visiting a DRE office or Web site (see Chapter 1 for DRE offices). The packet includes the application for the examination. Applicants must prove that they have had the required education by having transcripts submitted by the educational institution(s) they attended for the required instruction. In addition to the specified real estate–related instruction that is required, applicants for real estate licenses must be at least 18 years of age and have the equivalent of a high school education.

Applicants who pass the examination will receive an application for the license itself. When it is submitted to DRE, it must be accompanied by the required fingerprint card and the processing fee required. Real estate licenses are good for four years. They may be renewed for additional four-year periods by paying a renewal fee, provided that the licensee has completed the required continuing education (described in the next paragraph) during the four-year license period. If a license is not renewed, it expires, and the holder is no longer allowed to engage in any activity for which the license is required. However, for the first two years after a license expires it can still be renewed by paying a (higher) late renewal fee. Anyone whose license still has not been renewed once this two-year period has passed must go through the entire licensing process all over again, including the examination, to become licensed anew.

Even after the license is received, and the education requirements for initial licensure have been met, the law requires licensees to receive *continuing education*. During the first four-year licensing period, a licensee must complete 45 *classroom hours* of continuing education, including at least three hours in each of four required areas: (1) ethics, (2) agency relationships and duties, (3) trust fund handling, and (4) fair housing. License renewals after the first one will require only two of these four topics to be covered in continuing education. One important thing about the continuing education credit: it may *not* include courses that are taken to qualify for licensure. So, provisionally licensed salespersons (see Chapter 1) who have to take courses to fulfill their education requirement may not use those courses to fulfill continuing education requirements as well. Also, licensed salespeople who are taking the required courses needed to qualify to take the broker's license examination cannot use those courses to simultaneously satisfy continuing education requirements.

The California Department of Real Estate

The *California Department of Real Estate* (usually called *DRE*) administers and enforces the real estate licensing laws. The *Real Estate Commissioner* is its administrative officer; he or she is appointed by the governor and serves at the governor's discretion. The commissioner appoints *ten* members to the *Real Estate Advisory Commission*; *six* of the members must be licensed brokers in California and the other *four* must be *unlicensed*. The Advisory Commission is supposed to "express views" and "make recommendations" to the commissioner. The Real Estate Commissioner must either have been a practicing California real estate broker for five years or have been in other real estate activity for at least five of the ten years preceding his or her appointment. The commissioner must call meetings of the Advisory Commission at least four times a year, and he or she presides at those meetings.

DRE administers the real estate licensing laws, prepares and administers examinations for licensure, and screens licensure candidates. It takes disciplinary action against licensees who violate license law or the commissioner's regulations. It also enforces licensing laws by investigating real estate brokerage activity (for which a real estate license is required) being done by unlicensed people. It also is charged with enforcing some California subdivision laws (see Chapter 23), and regulating certain franchises and real estate securities.

DRE enforces real estate license law because it has the power to restrict, suspend, or revoke licenses of those who violate the law. The commissioner must investigate a complaint against a licensee, provided that the complainant submits it in writing. The commissioner can take statements from anyone involved, including the licensee, and can examine records such as bank, escrow, title records, etc., that are relevant to the complaint. If warranted, a formal hearing presided over by an administrative law judge will be held; evidence is presented and sworn testimony taken. The licensee may have an attorney, if desired. If the charges are proven, then the commissioner can restrict, suspend, or revoke the license. The penalty depends upon the severity of the licensee's offense.

You should read and become familiar with the California Real Estate License Law and the *Regulations of the Real Estate Commissioner*. Both are in the *Real Estate Law* book that you can get from the DRE. You can also read them online and download them. The license law is at www.dre.cahwnet.gov/relaw_pdf/Relaw.pdf, and the regulations are at www.dre.ca.gov/relaw_pdf/Regs.pdf. Both can also be accessed from the DRE home page, www.dre.ca.gov.

In sale, lease, and exchange transactions, conduct that would subject the licensee to adverse action, penalty, or discipline under Sections 10176 and 10177 of the Business and Professions code include, but are not limited to, the following acts and omissions:

(1) Knowingly making a substantial misrepresentation of the likely value of real property to:

    (A) Its owner either for the purpose of securing a listing or for the purpose of acquiring an interest in the property for the licensee's own account.

    (B) A prospective buyer for the purpose of inducing the buyer to make an offer to purchase the real property.

(2) Representing to an owner of real property when seeking a listing that the licensee has obtained a bona fide written offer to purchase the property, unless at the time of the representation the licensee has possession of a bona fide written offer to purchase.

(3) Stating or implying to an owner of real property during listing negotiations that the licensee is precluded by law, by regulation, or by the rules of any organization, other than the broker firm seeking the listing, from charging less than the commission or fee quoted to the owner by the licensee.

(4) Knowingly making substantial misrepresentations regarding the licensee's relationship with an individual broker, corporate broker, or franchise brokerage company or that entity's/person's responsibility for the licensee's activities.

(5) Knowingly underestimating the probable closing costs in a communication to the prospective buyer or seller of real property in order to induce that person to make or to accept an offer to purchase the property.

(6) Knowingly making a false or misleading representation to the seller of the real property as to the form, amount, and/or treatment of a deposit toward the purchase of the property made by an offeror.

(7) Knowingly making a false or misleading representation to the seller of real property, who has agreed to finance all or part of a purchase price by carrying back a loan, about a buyer's ability to repay the loan in accordance with its terms and conditions.

(8) Making an addition to or modification of the terms of an instrument previously signed or initialed by a party to a transaction without the knowledge and consent of the party.

(9) A representation made as a principal or agent to a prospective purchaser of a promissory note secured by real property about the market value of the securing property without a reasonable basis for believing the truth and accuracy of the representation.

(10) Knowingly making a false or misleading representation or representing without a reasonable basis for believing its truth, the nature and/or condition of the interior or exterior features of a property when soliciting an offer.

(11) Knowingly making a false or misleading representation or representing, without a reasonable basis for believing its truth, the size of a parcel, square footage of improvements, or the location of the boundary lines of real property being offered for sale, lease, or exchange.

(12) Knowingly making a false or misleading representation or representing to a prospective buyer or lessee of real property, without a reasonable basis to believe its truth, that the property can be used for certain purposes with the intent of inducing the prospective buyer or lessee to acquire an interest in the real property.

(13) When acting in the capacity of an agent in a transaction for the sale, lease, or exchange of real property, failing to disclose to a prospective purchaser or lessee facts known to the licensee materially affecting the value or desirability of the property, when the licensee has reason to believe that such facts are not known to nor readily observable by a prospective purchaser or lessee.

(14) Willfully failing, when acting as a listing agent, to present or cause to be presented to the owner of the property any written offer to purchase received prior to the closing of a sale, unless expressly instructed by the owner not to present such an offer, or unless the offer is patently frivolous.

(15) When acting as the listing agent, presenting competing written offers to purchase real property to the owner in such a manner as to induce the owner to accept the offer which will provide the greatest compensation to the listing broker without regard to the benefits, advantages, and/or disadvantages to the owner.

(16) Failing to explain to the parties or prospective parties to a real estate transaction for whom the licensee is acting as an agent the meaning and probable significance of a contingency in an offer or contract that the licensee knows or reasonably believes may affect the closing date of the transaction, or the timing of the vacating of the property by the seller or its occupancy by the buyer.

(17) Failing to disclose to the seller of real property in a transaction in which the licensee is an agent for the seller the nature and extent of any direct or indirect interests that the licensee expects to acquire as a result of the sale. The prospective purchase of the property by a person related to the licensee by blood or marriage, purchase by an entity in which the licensee has an ownership interest, or purchase by any other person with whom the licensee occupies a special relationship where there is a reasonable

probability that the licensee could be indirectly acquiring an interest in the property shall be disclosed to the seller.

(18) Failing to disclose to the buyer of real property, in a transaction in which the licensee is an agent for the buyer, the nature and extent of a licensee's direct or indirect ownership interest in such real property. The direct or indirect ownership interest in the property by a person related to the licensee by blood or marriage, by an entity in which the licensee has an ownership interest, or by any other person with whom the licensee occupies a special relationship shall be disclosed to the buyer.

(19) Failing to disclose to a principal for whom the licensee is acting as an agent any significant interest the licensee has in a particular entity when the licensee recommends the use of the services or products of such entity.*

Trust Funds

Most brokerage firms have occasion to be entrusted with other people's money. Common examples are deposits made by buyers when a purchase contract is executed, or rents received by brokers who are managing and leasing property. Any trust monies received by a broker (or other broker or salesperson employed by the broker) must, *by the next business day*, be (a) given to the principal on whose behalf they were received, (b) placed into a neutral escrow depository, or (c) deposited in the broker's trust money account which the broker must keep at a financial institution. This trust money does not belong to the broker although, for convenience, he/she often "keeps" it; the trust money account allows the broker to keep the trust money safely. Because the broker is merely the trustee of the account, the law recognizes that the funds in the account don't belong to the broker and can never be taken by anyone who may have a claim against the broker. Interest-bearing accounts are permitted, with some restrictions, but the accounting involved is such a nightmare that most brokers do not use them.

Under certain circumstances, the broker does not have to put the money in safekeeping immediately. With the knowledge of the broker's principal, the broker can hold a post-dated check, or a promissory note, or some such device until an agreed-upon time. Also, during negotiation of a purchase contract, the prospective buyer may instruct the broker, in writing, not to deposit the check unless and until a purchase contract has been agreed upon.

There are two grievous sins that brokers can commit with respect to trust accounts. First, they can fail to keep meticulous trust account records. The law requires the records to be accurate and up to date; inspectors from DRE have the right to enter a broker's place of business, unannounced, anytime during reasonable business hours to inspect the records. The second deadly sin is *commingling*. This refers to mixing the broker's own business and/or personal funds with trust account funds. Because the whole idea of the trust account is to keep trust monies safely segregated from the broker's own funds, it is obvious why commingling is such a serious offense. There is one minor exception: the broker can keep up to $100 of the broker's own funds in the trust account for the express purpose of paying the bank charges associated with the account (because the broker may *not* assess the service charges against the people to whom the trust money itself belongs).

The broker must keep records of all trust fund activity for three years.

The Real Estate Fund

California has a *Real Estate Fund* that is funded by DRE with a portion of license fees collected. There are two aspects to the fund: (1) the *Education and Research Account*, and (2) the *Recovery Account*. Up to 8 percent of fees collected may be credited to the Education and Research Account, and up to 12 percent to the Recovery Account.

---

*California Department of Real Estate, *Information Relating to Real Estate Practice, Licensing and Examinations*, pp. 20–22.

These accounts serve quite different purposes. The Education and Research Account is used for approved real estate education and research projects at universities and colleges throughout California. The Recovery Account is used to recompense members of the public who, after appropriate application and presentation of their case, can show that they have been defrauded or have otherwise unjustifiably suffered loss by or at the hands of a real estate licensee. Normally the Recovery Account is supported by a portion of the regular license fees collected by DRE; however, the law does allow that whenever the balance in the Recovery Account falls below $200,000, DRE may, for the next four years, assess an additional fee to renewing licensees (above the basic $7 from broker renewals, $4 from salesperson renewals).

To claim against the Recovery Account, a victim must have been awarded a judgment by a court, arbitrator, referee, etc., against a licensee, and the judgment must arise from something the licensee did in the course of business. Furthermore, the victim can claim, from the Recovery Account, only that portion of the judgment which cannot be collected directly from the offending licensee. The victim has to file a written claim with DRE describing the judgment, and showing that reasonable attempts have been made to collect from the licensee, and that the claimant has notified the licensee that a claim against the Recovery Account is being filed. DRE has 90 days to act on the application. There is a limit of $20,000 payable by the fund as a result of any single transaction, and $100,000 total for all transactions against any licensee. This means that, if the licensee defrauded many people, there may have to be some proration of the sums available from the Recovery Account. Once the Recovery Account has paid out money on a claim against a licensee, that person's license is suspended and cannot be renewed until he/she has repaid the entire amount, plus interest, to the Recovery Account.

Notification of DRE

DRE must be kept up-to-date with the business addresses of all licensed brokers and with the broker affiliation of all licensed salespeople. A broker must notify DRE of any change of business address. When a salesperson is first licensed, the salesperson and broker apply to have the salesperson's new license issued to the broker. (Note that salespeople are not issued their own licenses; the licenses are held by their brokers.) If the broker discharges a salesperson, DRE must be notified immediately. If a salesperson leaves one broker and affiliates with another, the first broker gives the salesperson his/her license; the salesperson notes the change on it and gives it to the new broker. The salesperson and new broker must notify DRE of the change within five days of the new employment.

If a broker or salesperson surrenders his license, or her license is suspended or revoked, then he or she must immediately cease all real estate brokerage activity. All salespeople employed by a broker whose brokerage license is surrendered, suspended, or revoked must also cease all real estate brokerage activity until they can affiliate with a different broker, and DRE is notified of the new association.

Record Keeping

Brokers must keep records of all business for at least three years after the business is concluded. For all real estate transactions, this means keeping records for three years after escrow settlement. For trust accounts it means that records of each transaction must be kept for three years after the transaction is concluded. Salesperson's contracts, copies of DRE forms, and notifications, etc., must be kept for three years as well. So must the business's bank statements, other employee records, etc.

Violations of License Law

Following, in outline form, are the most common violations of license law. Or, to put it in a more realistic fashion, here are the many ways in which you can *lose your license!* Note that a licensee may appeal any adverse decision by the commissioner to the court system.

A. MISHANDLING MONEY BELONGING TO OTHERS

1. Commingling trust (or escrow) money with one's own funds.

2. Not remitting funds quickly, once they are received; that is, depositing in trust account or with an escrow agent by next business day.

3. Salesperson's not remitting funds quickly to broker.

4. Accepting noncash payments on behalf of principal without principal's agreement. (Checks are considered to be cash.)

B. MISREPRESENTATION AND FRAUD
All of these practices are *misrepresentation or fraud.* Some state laws list a number of such practices; others simply say, ". . . for any misrepresentation or fraud . . . ," or some words to that effect.

1. False advertising.

2. Intentionally misleading someone.

3. Acting for more than one party to a transaction without the knowledge of all parties.

4. Using a trademark or other identifying insignia of a firm or organization (such as the National Association of REALTORS®) of which one is not a member.

5. Salesperson's pretending to be a broker or to be employed by a broker not his own.

6. Not identifying oneself as a licensee in any transaction in which one is also a party.

7. Taking kickbacks, referral fees, commissions, placement fees, and so on in association with one's duties from persons who are not one's principal, and without the principal's knowledge.

8. Guaranteeing future profits.

9. Offering property on terms other than those authorized by the principal.

10. Pretending to represent a principal by whom one is not actually employed.

11. Failing to identify the broker in all advertising.

C. IMPROPER BUSINESS PRACTICE

1. Failing to submit all offers to the principal.

2. Attempting to thwart another broker's exclusive listing.

3. Inducing someone to break a contract.

4. Failing to put an expiration date in a listing.

5. Putting one's sign on a property without the owner's permission.

6. Failing to post a required bond; failing to keep the bond up to date.

7. Blockbusting.

8. Discriminating.

D. FAILURE TO IMPART REQUIRED INFORMATION

1. Failure to leave copies of contracts with all parties involved.

2. Failure to deliver a closing statement to all parties entitled to one (if broker is also settlement agent).

3. Failure to inform some or all parties of closing costs.

E. IMPROPER HANDLING OR PAYMENT OF COMMISSIONS

1. Paying a commission to an unlicensed person.

2. Paying a commission to a licensee not in one's employ.

3. Salesperson's receiving a commission from anyone other than her employing broker.

F. AGENCY DISCLOSURE

1. Failing to disclose to prospective buyers that broker is agent of the seller.

2. Failing to disclose buyer-broker agency to seller or seller's broker (including when to do so).

G. OTHER

1. Being convicted of certain crimes (felonies, some misdemeanors involving misrepresentation):

2. Violating any part of the license law.

3. Making false statements on the license application.

4. Showing any evidence of "incompetence," "unworthiness," "poor character," and so on. (This is a "catch-all" provision.)

Questions on Chapter 5 _____

1. A licensee's license must be
   (A) carried in his wallet at all times
   (B) kept on the wall in his home
   (C) available for examination in the broker's office
   (D) kept on the wall at the Real Estate Commission

2. A person must be licensed if she is to sell
   (A) her own home
   (B) property belonging to an estate for which she is executor
   (C) property belonging to clients who pay her a commission
   (D) property she has inherited

3. A broker must place funds belonging to others in
   (A) his office safe, to which only he knows the combination
   (B) a safety deposit box
   (C) an account maintained by the Real Estate Commission
   (D) a trust, or escrow, account, or with an escrow agent

4. License laws forbid
   (A) collecting a commission from more than one party to a transaction
   (B) soliciting for listings before one is licensed
   (C) both A and B
   (D) neither A nor B

5. A licensee's license can be revoked for
   (A) closing a deal
   (B) intentionally misleading someone into signing a contract that she ordinarily would not sign
   (C) both A and B
   (D) neither A nor B

6. Real estate licenses, once received,
   (A) remain in effect indefinitely
   (B) are good for four years unless renewed
   (C) must be filed in the county records
   (D) may be inherited by the licensee's spouse

7. A broker's unlicensed secretary may
   (A) sell property provided that he does it under the broker's direct supervision
   (B) sell or negotiate deals so long as he does not leave the office
   (C) refer interested clients to the broker or her employed licensees
   (D) all of the above

8. A broker may use escrow moneys held on behalf of others
   (A) for collateral for business loans
   (B) for collateral for personal loans
   (C) to make salary advances to licensees in his employ
   (D) none of the above

9. In order to do business, a licensee must
   (A) make proper application for a license
   (B) pass a licensing examination
   (C) have a license issued by the appropriate state agency
   (D) all of the above

10. A licensee can lose his license for which of the following?
    (A) Paying a commission to a nonlicensed person
    (B) Using moneys received as commissions to pay office help
    (C) both A and B
    (D) neither A nor B

11. A licensee can lose her license for
    (A) selling properties quickly, at low prices
    (B) buying property for her own use from her principal
    (C) both A and B
    (D) neither A nor B

12. Which of the following is not required to have a real estate license?
    (A) A resident manager of an apartment project
    (B) A resident manager of an apartment project who, for a fee, sells a house across the street
    (C) A student who sells houses as part of a research project
    (D) All of the above

13. A licensed salesperson
    (A) must be under the supervision of a broker
    (B) can collect commission payments only from his broker
    (C) must have his license held by his employing broker
    (D) all of the above

14. In order to sell property belonging to a trust for which he is trustee, the trustee must have a
(A) broker's license
(B) salesperson's license
(C) trustee's license
(D) none of the above

15. A person who is employed to lease property, but not to sell it,
(A) must be licensed
(B) is an agent
(C) may be paid a salary or commission
(D) all of the above

16. California license renewal fees are paid
(A) every 4 years
(B) every 2 years
(C) every year
(D) every 3 years

17. In California
(A) buyer-broker agency must be disclosed
(B) disclosure of the broker-seller agency must be made to buyers
(C) no agency disclosure is required
(D) A and B both are true

18. Licensees must pay fees for the following:
(A) transferring employ to another broker
(B) fingerprinting
(C) reactivating an inactive license
(D) all of the above

19. The California real estate licensing laws are part of the
(A) Business and Professions Code
(B) Code of Licenses
(C) Civil Real Estate Code
(D) Health and Public Safety Code

20. Licensed salesperson Fleming is independently wealthy. She feels that real estate brokerage is potentially a very lucrative business. However, she has tried and failed to pass the broker's examination numerous times. She forms a corporation, XYZ Realty, Inc., of which she owns 75 percent of the shares. The other 25 percent are owned by Broker Hansen, who has agreed to be the broker-officer of the company.
(A) They must have at least two more stockholders to satisfy the Corporations Code.
(B) This arrangement violates the law.
(C) Broker Hansen can't be broker-officer and own shares at the same time.
(D) All of the above are correct.

21. Broker Johnson receives a cash deposit from Jones, who has signed a purchase contract to buy real estate from Smith. Which of the following may Broker Johnson *not* do?
(A) Give the money to Smith.
(B) Deposit the money with a neutral escrow depository.
(C) Put the money in the brokerage office safe for safekeeping.
(D) Deposit the money in the brokerage's trust money account.

22. Morgan is treasurer of ABC, Inc. ABC wished to buy land for a new plant and Morgan negotiated the entire deal at a price and terms very favorable to ABC. As a result, ABC paid Morgan a commission of 10 percent of the purchase price of the land. Morgan does not have a real estate license.
(A) The law limits Morgan's payment to no more than 5 percent, since he has no license.
(B) This practice is within the law.
(C) Morgan should have had a real estate license in order to collect the commission.
(D) By making this deal, Morgan automatically becomes licensed under the "grandfather clause" of the license law.

23. Payment from the Recovery Account for any single transaction is limited to a total of
    (A) $10,000
    (C) $50,000
    (B) $20,000
    (D) $100,000

24. A California Real Estate license is good for negotiating
    (A) anywhere in the state of California
    (B) the sale of any kind of real property
    (C) the sale of property outside California, if negotiation occurs inside California
    (D) all of the above

25. A licensed salesperson may act independently (that is, not in the employ of a broker)
    (A) in any transaction valued at less than $10,000
    (B) to sell her own house, provided all parties know she holds a license
    (C) if he owns at least 51 percent of the stock in the brokerage firm that employs him
    (D) if all other parties involved in the transaction are also licensed

26. Including the real estate commissioner, there are _____ members of the advisory commission.
    (A) 9
    (C) 11
    (B) 10
    (D) 12

27. Salesperson Sherry leaves the employ of Broker Bob, and is employed by Broker Louise.
    (A) Sherry and Louise must notify DRE within 5 days of the change.
    (B) Sherry cannot do this without prior permission from DRE.
    (C) Sherry cannot do this unless Broker Bob agrees to it in writing.
    (D) Broker Louise must compensate Broker Bob, and register the compensation with DRE.

28. Total Recovery Account payment for one licensee (multiple transactions) is limited to
    (A) $10,000
    (C) $50,000
    (B) $20,000
    (D) $100,000

29. For how long after a transaction is concluded must a broker keep his or her records of the transaction?
    (A) Two years
    (C) Four years
    (B) Three years
    (D) Five years

30. A real estate salesperson's compensation is
    (A) 50% of the broker's share
    (B) whatever the seller agreed to
    (C) paid by the broker
    (D) set by California law

31. A qualified license applicant's name appears on a delinquent child support list. The applicant
    (A) cannot be licensed at all
    (B) must clear up the deficiency before licensing
    (C) may receive a temporary 150-day license
    (D) must be granted a license based on meeting educational and testing requirements

32. Of the following, which is the most important reason for a broker to maintain a trust fund account in addition to a regular business account?
    (A) To provide a means of control over the destiny of transactions being negotiated.
    (B) It is easier from an accounting point of view.
    (C) The bank is responsible for any loss to the trust fund account resulting from embezzlement.
    (D) The possible consequences should a legal action be taken against the broker.

33. A California real estate license is good only in
    (A) the city where it was obtained
    (B) the county where it was obtained
    (C) the state of California
    (D) the 50 U.S. states

34. When a salesperson transfers a license, the new broker must advise the DRE within
    (A) three days   (C) ten days
    (B) five days   (D) thirty days

35. If the California Real Estate Commissioner needs legal advice, he would go to the
    (A) Real Estate Board
    (B) California Association of REALTORS®
    (C) state attorney general
    (D) in-house counsel

36. After one becomes a broker, the most appropriate term for that person is
    (A) REALTOR®   (C) associate
    (B) Realtist®   (D) broker

37. After one's real estate license expires, there is a grace period of _____ to renew, upon paying fees, without a reexamination requirement.
    (A) one year   (C) five years
    (B) two years   (D) There is no grace period.

38. A broker must keep records for _____ year(s).
    (A) one   (C) three
    (B) two   (D) four

39. An unlicensed person who practices real estate may be
    (A) required to return all commissions earned to the state
    (B) fined up to $10,000 and subject to other possible legal action
    (C) prohibited from ever becoming licensed
    (D) all of the above

40. The maximum the DRE will pay to a victim from the recovery fund for one transaction is
    (A) $10,000   (C) $50,000
    (B) $20,000   (D) $100,000

41. The maximum DRE recovery fund disbursement on behalf of one real estate licensee is
    (A) $10,000   (C) $50,000
    (B) $20,000   (D) $100,000

ANSWERS

1. **C**	10. **A**	19. **A**	28. **D**	37. **B**
2. **C**	11. **D**	20. **B**	29. **B**	38. **C**
3. **D**	12. **A**	21. **C**	30. **C**	39. **B**
4. **B**	13. **D**	22. **C**	31. **C**	40. **B**
5. **B**	14. **D**	23. **B**	32. **D**	41. **D**
6. **B**	15. **D**	24. **D**	33. **C**	
7. **C**	16. **A**	25. **B**	34. **B**	
8. **D**	17. **D**	26. **C**	35. **C**	
9. **D**	18. **D**	27. **A**	36. **D**	

PART III: REAL ESTATE CONTRACTS

Chapter 6/*Introduction to Contracts*

Most people have a little familiarity with contracts. A popular misconception is that a contract must be filled with obscure, legalistic language and printed in nearly invisible type. Some contracts do appear this way, but these days more and more contracts that consumers encounter are in print that you can see and are written so that they can be understood.

While it is true, as we shall see, that contracts must conform to certain standards, usually the only requirement of the *language* is that it *say clearly what it is supposed to say*. These days there is an admirable trend to simplify and clarify the language of most contracts, eliminating elaborate language that serves no useful purpose.

We can approach the study of contracts with confidence; a little familiarity with them will reveal the basic logic behind the laws and customs that surround them and will eliminate the mystery that usually clouds the layperson's view of these documents.

Contracts and Real Estate

The real estate business is dominated by contracts. Buying, selling, mortgaging, leasing, and listing real estate all involve particular kinds of contracts. To become familiar with the real estate business, we must devote a considerable part of our study to contracts *in general*, as well as to the *specific kinds* that concern real estate.

For convenience we divide real estate contracts into two rather loosely defined groups. Our *major* contracts are associated with the kinds of real estate dealings that most frequently occur: these are *listings, purchase contracts, deeds, mortgages* (or *deeds of trust),* and *leases.* Other contractual arrangements, which involve particular kinds of circumstances and so are less frequently encountered, constitute our *minor* contracts. Note that this division into major and minor is a grouping we are making for our own convenience. The law and the courts do not make this distinction: to them a contract is a contract, and the parties to all contracts have the same rights of access to the courts and to legal enforcement of their contractual promises.

REAL ESTATE CONTRACTS

Figure 6-1 arranges the major contracts in the order in which they might be encountered in a typical series of transactions. First an owner (a seller) enters into a *listing contract* with a broker; in this contract the seller agrees to pay a commission when the broker has found an acceptable buyer for the listed property. In California, when a buyer is contacted, the law requires that an *agency disclosure* be made to the buyer by the seller's broker at that time (see Chapter 4 for discussion of agency disclosure). When a buyer becomes interested in the listed property, negotiations begin; if there is a buyer-broker agency relationship (see Chapter 4), disclosure of it must be made to the seller and/or his broker during the negotiations. If the buyer and the seller agree to transact, they will sign a *purchase agreement*, in which they agree that at some time in the future the seller will convey the property to the buyer; this conveyance will occur when the *deed* is executed by the seller and delivered to the buyer. The buyer may then seek to borrow part of the cost of the property, so he offers a lender a *mortgage* or *deed of trust* as collateral for the *note*, which serves as evidence of the debt he owes. Also, he decides to rent part of the premises to someone else, with whom he enters into a *lease* contract.

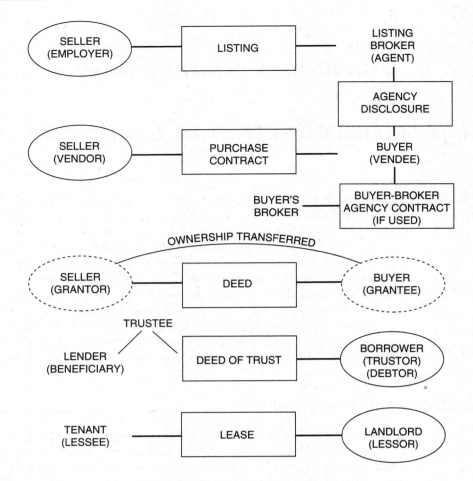

Figure 6-1.   Major Contracts. Note: Owners of real estate are circled.

PARTIES TO CONTRACTS

In each of these contracts, the parties have specific names. In a listing contract, the seller is the *employer* and the broker is the *agent*. In the contract of sale, the seller becomes the *vendor* and the buyer is the *vendee*. The parties to the deed are the *grantor* and the *grantee*; the mortgage contract is between the *mortgagor* (owner) and *mortgagee* (lender); the deed of trust involves the *trustor* (borrower), *trustee* (impartial third party) and *beneficiary* (lender). The *lessor's* real estate is made available to the *lessee* in a lease contract. Generally, the suffix *-or* refers to the person who conveys rights, privileges, or something else of value to the person whose title has the suffix *-ee*. In subsequent chapters each of the real estate contracts will be discussed in detail, but first we examine the basic principles that apply to all contracts.

WHAT IS A CONTRACT?

A contract is an agreement between two or more *parties*, in which each of the parties pledges to do, or is shown to have done, *something* that will benefit the others. (A contract can also oblige someone *not* to do a certain thing.) This "something" can take a multitude of forms. A common one is a payment of money, though contracts involving no money payment can be perfectly valid. Each of the parties must be shown to benefit, so contracts must involve *exchanges* of benefits. A gives something to B, in return for which B gives something to A. A common example is a purchase: I give money to you, and you give me the thing I am buying from you. However, a valid contract need not involve money: I can swap my automobile for your lawn mower, or we can agree that neither of us will build on our land an ugly structure that will be in the line of sight of the other.

Although there are other requirements that must be met, the critical test of the validity of a contract is the issue of whether or not the parties can be shown to benefit from it. The amount of benefit doesn't really matter; but if benefit to one or both parties is totally lacking, then usually there is no contract, for it is an ancient precept of law that no one should give something for nothing. If *any* measurable or identifiable benefit is mentioned in the contract, that will be enough. If you and I sign an agreement that says simply that I will give you my automobile next Tuesday, no court will require me to live up to this promise, because no benefit *to me* is mentioned. However, if our agreement says that I will give you my car next Tuesday in return for one dollar paid by you to me, the courts *will* enforce the agreement against me: it will be a contract because I am receiving some benefit. The fact that my car may be worth much more than one dollar is immaterial here; all that matters is that *both* parties receive *some* benefit: you get my car and I get your dollar.

ENFORCEMENT OF CONTRACTS

A valid contract has the "force of law" among the parties to it. It is as if they had agreed to "pass" a law among themselves and promised to abide by it. However, when a person violates the provisions of a contract, the police, or a flock of judges and bailiffs, do not descend upon him and demand that he keep his bargain. In fact, the law will do nothing about private contractual disputes unless one of the injured parties petitions the court to intervene. At that point, the law requires the affected parties to appear and to present their arguments. Then the court (i.e., a judge or a jury) makes a decision as to what is to be done, and by whom. (This description, of course, is somewhat oversimplified; resolving a contractual dispute—or any other—in court often consumes considerable time and expense.) It is likely that many violated contracts never reach court because the offended parties do not want the bother of a court case. Even so, there is always that possibility; all parties to a contract have the inherent right to request the court to render judgment if they feel that other parties to the agreement are not living up to it.

Generally, a person who brings a contract to court has two remedies available. First, she can ask that the court require *specific performance* of the offending party, that is, that the court order the other party to live up to the agreement. Often, however, by the time a contract dispute reaches court it is too late for mere performance to do any (or enough) good. In such a case, the injured party may seek *damages*. Here she would claim that she had suffered some loss because of the other party's violation of the contract and would ask that the court order the violator to make the loss good. Note the use of the words *court order* here. Once the court has reached a decision, the parties to the dispute are *required by law* to abide by it.* If they do not, they are in contempt of court and can be jailed or fined if need be. In this manner, behind every contractual arrangement there lies the threat of court action, which can be backed up by potentially severe penalties.

Most contract cases that come to court are not cut and dried. Rarely does a person enter into a contract with the intention to violate it; furthermore, one who *knows* that he is in violation of a contract rarely has the stubbornness (or foolishness) to go ahead with a court showdown he knows he will lose. What usually happens is that *all* parties to a dispute think they are right and the other(s) wrong. The parties *interpret* their agreement differently and are unable to resolve their differences. By taking the matter to court, they ask the court to render a judgment as to who is right and what is to be done.

Requirements of Valid Contracts

A contract cannot be considered by a court unless it is valid. While certain kinds of contracts may have additional requirements for validity, *all* contracts must have the following attributes:

1. Mutual agreement
2. Consideration
3. Legally competent parties

---

*This assumes that the decision is not appealed. But an appeal only delays an eventual unappealed, or unappealable, decision, which must be respected.

4. Lawful purpose
5. Legal form

1. MUTUAL AGREEMENT

Mutual agreement (often referred to as *offer and acceptance, reality of consent, mutual assent, meeting of the minds*, and similar phrases) means that all parties recognize that an offer has been made and has been accepted by the other parties. All are agreed as to what each party has done, with respect to the contract, as well as to what each party is still required to do in the future. Generally, the parties will agree to do, or not to do, some thing or things, in return for some kind of obligation from the others.

Provided that the other essentials of a contract are present, once an offer has been accepted, a contract exists. The one making the offer is the *offeror*, and the one to whom it is made is the *offeree*. The actions of both of them in creating the contract must be shown to be intentional and deliberate: generally their signatures to a written contract are evidence of this, provided that no fraud, misrepresentation, duress, or mistake is present. However, many binding contracts need not be written; in such cases it is the testimony of the affected parties that provides the evidence that an agreement exists. (Duress, misrepresentation, and fraud are discussed later in this chapter.)

2. CONSIDERATION

Legal consideration refers to the "benefit" received by the parties. Each party must be shown to be obligated to do (or not to do) something, in return for some action or nonaction by the other parties to the contract. The benefit can take many forms; all that must be shown is that the party receiving the benefit agreed that it was of use to him and that he was willing to obligate himself in some way in order to get it. Payment of money is always consideration, as is the transfer of ownership of anything that can be shown to have a market value. In addition, the transfer of many *rights* is consideration; for example, a lease transfers rights to use property, but not ownership of the property.

Examples. Here are some examples of consideration in a contract:
1. A pays $500,000 to B. B transfers ownership of a house to A.
2. A pays B $1,200 per month. B gives A the right to use an apartment for each month for which A pays.
3. A pays B $7.50. B lets A watch a movie in B's theater.
4. A agrees not to hang her laundry outside where B and C can see it. B agrees not to hang his laundry where A and C can see it. C agrees not to hang her laundry where A and B can see it.
5. A agrees to use his best efforts to try to find a buyer for B's house. B agrees to pay A a commission of 6 percent of the sale price if A finds a suitable buyer.
6. A agrees to pay B $392,000 in 60 days, at which time B will transfer to A ownership of a particular house.
7. A pays B $1,000. B gives A the right to purchase B's land for $25,000 at any time of A's choosing during the next six months.
8. A transfers ownership of her house to B. B transfers to A the ownership of his parking lot, four albums of rare stamps, two sets of dishes, and a mongrel dog.
9. A pays B $10,000. B transfers to A the ownership of a producing diamond mine in South Africa.
10. A transfers to his son, A, Jr., the ownership of the family estate in return for the "love and affection" that A, Jr. has given to A in the past.
11. A pays B $10,000. B agrees to pay A $126.70 per month for the next 10 years.
12. A pays B $10,000. B gives A the right to have B's house sold if B defaults on her debt to A.

In all of these instances there exists legal consideration; these examples show but a few of the many forms it can take. In many cases it includes the payment of money; in (4), (8), and (10), however, no money changes hands. In most, the consideration involves the parties doing something or performing some act; in (4), however, the parties agree *not* to do something. Examples (2), (3), (4), (7), and (12) include the exchange of rights; (5) includes the exchange of services; and the others involve the exchange of ownership of things.

These are examples of real estate contracts we will examine in more detail later. Example (2) is a *lease*; (4) is a *restrictive covenant*; (5) is a *listing*; (6) is a *contract of sale*; (7) is an *option*; (12) is a *mortgage*; and (1), (8), (9), and (10) are *deeds*. Many of these contracts are purchases of one kind or another; examine (11) closely and you will discover that it is a *loan* or a *note*: A lends B $10,000, which B agrees to repay (at a 9 percent interest rate) in equal monthly installments of $126.70 for the next 10 years. Example (5) is a *listing*; it is also an *employment contract*, wherein the services of one of the parties are purchased by the other party.

Good Consideration, Valuable Consideration

In all except (10) we have *"valuable"* consideration. Valuable consideration is anything that is of value to practically everyone and thus can be sold for money. Money, of course is "valuable," as is ownership of things, the receipt of someone's services, receipt of various kinds of rights, and the like. However, things such as friendship, love, and affection are not valuable consideration, because their value is entirely subjective. You may set a very high value upon the attention and friendship you receive from your best friend, but to most of the rest of us the attention is valueless, since we don't even know him. Furthermore, a person's affection is not a transferable benefit. Rights, ownership, money, services, and such things can be passed on (or sold) to practically anyone, but you can't sell your best friend's affection to someone else. Consequently, such things as friendship and love are called *"good"* consideration. They are of value to the one who receives them, and if she agrees to transfer benefit in return for them she can be held to her bargain.

The law does *not* require that *equal* consideration accrue to all parties. So long as consideration is there, the law is satisfied, provided of course that there no fraud or duress is involved. There is only one exception: the courts will not enforce a contract requiring the simultaneous exchange of different sums of money.

In some cases a contract doesn't have to spell out the exact amount of consideration. Of course, a deed contract ought to describe the real estate very carefully, but often, in deeds, the price paid may be described as, for example, "ten dollars and other good and valuable consideration." Because deeds are recorded, and therefore available to the public to see, many buyers don't want nosy people to find out exactly what they paid for their real estate. This kind of wording, especially for money consideration, is perfectly all right. It says that one has received consideration, and that is all that is necessary.

3. LEGALLY COMPETENT PARTIES

Competent parties are persons who have the legal right to enter into contractual arrangements. Not all legal persons are human beings: corporations, partnerships, trusts, and some other organizations can also be parties to a contract. You can contract to purchase an automobile from ABZ Auto Sales, Inc., even though this company is not a living, breathing being. Furthermore, not all humans are competent to contract; many are legally unable to do so, and many more may contract only under carefully defined circumstances.

Nonhuman Parties

Usually each party to a contract must assure himself of the other's legal competence. Although the law places few restrictions upon the possible contracting ability of nonhuman parties, often these organizations will operate under self-imposed restrictions. A corporation's charter, for example, can permit or prevent certain kinds of contractual agreements on the part of the organization; in addition, it can provide that some or all of the permitted functions be carried out in certain ways. For this reason a person who contracts with an organization must assure himself, first, that the outfit is permitted to engage in such a contract, and, second, that the contract is executed and carried out in consistency with the organization's permitted limitations and prescribed methods.

People

Among people, there are two major categories of incompetent parties: infants and insane persons, along with several minor ones: drunkards, convicts, and others.

a. *Infants* (or *minors*).   These are people who have not yet attained the age of majority (18 years old in California). While you may not think that a hulking 17-year-old football star could be incompetent at *anything*, the law says he is. Furthermore, a person who may be immature, ignorant, or naive in business judgment still may be considered by the law to be perfectly competent to take responsibility for her actions if she has attained the age of majority. Minors are not prohibited from contracting, so no law is broken if a minor signs a contract. However, the contract is viewed in a special way by the law: the minor can *void* the contract later on, if he wishes, but adult parties to the contract do *not* have that privilege. The minor may not, however, void (or *disaffirm*) only *part* of the contract; he must abandon it entirely. If he contracts to buy property from an adult, he will have the right to declare the contract void, if he wishes, any time before it is carried out. The adult, however, must honor the contract unless and until the minor actually disaffirms it. If the adult does not keep his bargain, the minor can sue. The adult will receive no help from the courts if the minor disaffirms. However, the minor cannot, say, disaffirm the part of the contract that specifies he must pay for the property, while at the same time requiring the adult to transfer it to him anyway; he must abandon the *entire* contract. Furthermore, if he disaffirms it after the adult has provided him some benefit under it, he may have to pay for (or return) that which he had already received by the time he decided to void the contract.

The whole idea behind the legal specification of some people as incompetent is a matter of protection. An *infant* is considered too young to bind herself to agreements; the law gives her protection by allowing her to void most agreements that she gets herself into. Once an infant attains the age of majority she becomes an adult and loses this protection, but she *is* given a "reasonable" time beyond the attainment of majority to decide whether she will disaffirm any contracts that she entered into as a minor.

b. *Insane Persons.*   The law also extends this "protection" to other categories of people, the largest being *insane persons*. Unlike infancy, however, insanity is a state that can come and go. One who is sane can become insane, and one who is insane can become cured and so become sane again. Also, it is possible for a person who is under severe stress or suffering from some other transitory disturbance to become so disoriented that the law may extend the protection of incompetence to him during that episode.

Legal protection of an insane person takes two forms. First, if he has had a guardian appointed by the court, then all contracts he enters into are *void*, and he has no capacity to contract at all. Notice that an infant's contracts are *voidable*, whereas the contracts of an insane person under guardianship are *void*. If the insane person has no guardian, his contracts, too, are voidable rather than void. He has the choice to require that his bargains with others be carried out or to disaffirm the contracts.

Neither the infant nor the insane person may disaffirm *all* kinds of contracts; generally, courts will enforce against them contracts for *necessaries*. Examples of necessaries are food, clothing, and shelter; sometimes other things are included as well. For example, in some cases contracts for employment or for education may be considered necessaries. Once again, the law is extending another form of protection: an adult usually will not care to contract with an infant or someone else she knows may later plead incompetence and void the contract. Consequently, a truthful incompetent may be at a serious disadvantage if his personal circumstances *require* him to contract. Therefore, the law allows some incompetents what amounts to a limited competency. For things that are "necessary" to them they are allowed to create binding contracts, which they cannot disaffirm and which a court can enforce against them. As a result, competent parties receive the protection *they* seek in a contractual arrangement and any reluctance they may have to deal with an incompetent is eliminated.

c. Other Incompetency. Certain other forms of incapacity "earn" one the legal protection of incompetency. A contract made by a person who is severely intoxicated with alcohol or is under the dominating influence of drugs known to affect judgment may later be considered voidable. Many states consider felon prisoners to be without the right to contract; this situation is described by the rather grim term of *civilly dead*. Usually, when the sentence has been served, and sometimes at the time parole is secured, most rights will be restored.

4. LAWFUL PURPOSE

A contract that requires any of its parties to violate the law usually is void. However, if it is possible to do so without impairing the contract's basic purpose, a court will uphold the contract but strike out that part requiring an illegal act. A very good example concerns the Federal Fair Housing Act of 1968. Among other things, this law declared illegal language in some deeds that required buyers of some real estate to agree they would resell only to people of certain racial or cultural backgrounds. At the time the law was enacted, vast numbers of deeds to homes contained such clauses, but that fact did not void those deeds in their entirety. The outlawing of these clauses had no great effect upon the main purpose of the deeds, which was to transfer title to realty in return for consideration. However, if someone had created a special agreement for the sole purpose of restricting the racial or cultural background of purchasers of certain real estate, then that entire contract would have been voided by the enactment of the law. If this kind of agreement came into being after the law was passed, it would be illegal from the beginning and would *never* be a contract.

The essential rule of lawful purpose, then, is that a contract that exists substantially for the purpose of requiring an illegal act is void. So also is a contract in which an illegal act is required, the elimination of which would materially alter the purpose or effect of the contract. When, however, an illegal act is included in a contract but is not essential to the basic intent or purpose of the agreement, a court often will void only the illegal part while letting the rest stand.

5. LEGAL FORM

Some contracts are required to follow a certain form or to be drawn in a certain manner. For example, deeds and contracts of sale require that "legal" descriptions of the property be included; if they are missing or are defective, the entire contract may be invalid. It should be pointed out, though, that much of the wordy, archaic language that frequently appears in contracts is *not* required by any law and appears only as a result of tradition.

Statute of Frauds: Real Estate Contracts Must Be Written

Every state including California has enacted a body of law called the *Statute of Frauds*; in California it is part of the California Civil Code. The Statute of Frauds requires certain contracts to be in writing, including all contracts that cannot be performed within one year, and all contracts in which land or an interest in land is transferred. Brokers' listing contracts for any of these also are required to be in writing. So are most other real estate contracts including purchase agreements, deeds, mortgages, deeds of trust, leases for more than one year, and brokers' listing contracts for any of these, which must be in writing.

The definition of "land or an interest in land" is very specific and also quite broad. It includes future interests, so, in addition to deeds, contracts of sale must be written. It includes partial interests, so mortgages must be written. It includes improvements to land and attachments to it, so contracts involving purchase of buildings or growing plants must be written, even if the actual land beneath them is not part of the transaction. However, once an attachment to land is severed from it (e.g., trees are cut down or crops are reaped), the attachment becomes personal property and is no longer subject to the part of the Statute of Frauds that covers realty. This law usually covers much more than just realty contracts, though, so it is quite possible that many other nonrealty contracts can be required to be written.

Duress, Misrepresentation, and Fraud _____

All parties to a valid contract must have entered into it willingly and without having been misled as to pertinent facts concerning the arrangement. Consequently, you cannot expect a court to enforce a contract against someone if you pointed a gun at his head to force him to sign, or if you deliberately or unintentionally misled him so that he agreed to its terms, on the basis of this false information. The former kind of situation is described as one of *duress*; the latter is either *misrepresentation* or *fraud*.

DURESS

Duress can take any number of forms. When circumstances force a person to do something against her will, one could say that duress exists, but the law does not always see the situation in that way. If the duress is caused by a party who benefits under the contract, then a court usually will recognize it as such; this covers situations such as forcing someone's assent by threatening her illegally. But other circumstance can also create duress: Jones discovers that he has a rare, expensive disease and must sell his home in order to raise money to pay for the cure. A person who buys from him at this time might make an advantageous deal legally, if Jones is in a hurry to sell. If the duress is caused by one's own action, the court is reluctant to recognize it. If you buy a new house and therefore are desperate to sell your old home, that situation is pretty much your own fault. If you create your own duress, you usually have to suffer with it.

MISREPRESENTATION AND FRAUD

Misrepresentation and fraud go a few steps further: here someone is led into a bad bargain on the basis of false information. Misrepresentation is loosely defined as the *unintentional* giving of false information, whereas fraud is *deliberate*. There is another difference, too: fraud is a *crime* as well as a civil wrong. This means that, whereas a victim of either fraud or misrepresentation is entitled to compensation for what he was misled into losing, a victim of fraud may sue also for punitive damages, which are a form of extra payment required of the culprit as a kind of punishment. Finally, the perpetrator of a fraud may also be prosecuted in criminal court and may end up being convicted and imprisoned.

Proving Misrepresentation or Fraud

A victim must prove three things to show that misrepresentation or fraud exists: (1) that the incorrect information was relevant to the contract she is disputing—that is, it was *material*; (2) that it was reasonable for her to rely on this false information; and (3) that this reliance led her to suffer some loss as a result.

Let's consider an example. Brown considers buying Green's house. Brown asks Green whether the house is free of termites, and Green says that it is. Actually the house is infested. If Brown later buys the house based, in part, upon Green's information and subsequently discovers termite infestation, he may have a case. The point at issue is material: it is reasonable for Brown to base his decision to buy at least partly upon the assurance that no termites inhabit the premises. When he finds them, it is obvious that he has suffered a loss; therefore the first and third conditions are met. Now he must show that it was reasonable to rely upon Green (the owner at the time) to give him accurate information on this matter. If the court agrees with Brown, he has proved his case. If Green knew about the termites and deliberately lied, then he committed fraud. If he truly thought there were no termites, then he misrepresented.

If one or more of the three conditions are missing, fraud or misrepresentation cannot be claimed successfully. If Brown had not bought Green's house, he could not claim relief because he suffered no loss due to the falsehood. Also, if he had asked a neighbor a few houses away about the termite problem in Green's house and had depended on the neighbor's incorrect information, it is unlikely that he could get help from the court, because he would have great difficulty showing that it was reasonable to rely on a neighbor for this kind of information.

Some Information Must Be Divulged

For some kinds of contracts, the law requires that certain information be divulged by at least some of the parties. If it is not, then misrepresentation or fraud may exist. For example, most licensing laws require that brokers inform other parties if the brokers are acting as principals in the contract, as well as agents. Also, California requires a broker to disclose which party she is acting for, especially if more than one party to a transaction is paying her a commission.

Discharge and Breach of Contracts

Contractual arrangements can be terminated in two general ways. *Discharge* of a contract occurs when no one is required to perform under it anymore. *Breach of contract* occurs when one party makes performance impossible, even though other parties are willing, by refusing to do his part or by otherwise preventing discharge of the contract.

DISCHARGE

Discharge can be considered the "amicable" situation in which the parties to a contract agree that the arrangement is terminated. Most often, discharge occurs by *performance*; that is, everyone has done what he has promised to do and nothing more is required of anyone. Other forms of discharge include agreement to terminate a contract, for one reason or another, before it would have been discharged by performance. Such a reason might be the substitution of a new party for one of the original parties; this original party, then, would have had her duties discharged. Sometimes the parties may decide to terminate one agreement by substituting another one for it. Discharge can also occur when the parties simply agree to abandon the contract without substituting a new party or another agreement for it.

Statute of Limitations

The law limits the time during which contracting parties can take a dispute concerning a contract to court. In California contract law, the Statute of Limitations limits how long one has to file suit concerning a dispute over a contract. The time limit varies according to the type of contract and the nature of the complaint:

> *two years for any oral contract*
> *fraud: three years after the fraud is discovered*
> *four years for any written agreement*
> *five years to recover title to real property*
> *judgment: ten years after the judgment is awarded*

Once the limit has passed, a dispute will not be heard in court, so, in that sense, the contract may be said to be discharged, because it can no longer be enforced. It is greatly advisable that any agreement discharging a contract for reasons other than performance or limitation be in writing. Under some situations (particularly when some, but not all, parties have performed or begun to perform under the contract) an agreement discharging an existing contract *must* be in writing.

BREACH

Breach occurs when a party violates the provisions of a contract; often this action can be serious enough to terminate the contract by making it impossible to continue the arrangement. The injured parties must seek remedy from the court; usually it takes the form of a judgment for *damages* against the party causing the breach. Sometimes, however, it may be feasible to secure a judgment for *specific performance*, which requires the breaching party to perform as he had agreed. To be successful in court, the injured parties must be able to show that a breach has indeed occurred. Failure by a party to perform entirely as specified in the contract constitutes a breach, as does a declaration that he does not intend to perform. Finally, there is a breach if a party creates a situation wherein it is impossible for every party to the contract to perform as specified. Once any of these events has occurred, there is a breach, and one attribute of a breaching of a contract is that it terminates the obligations of the other parties as well. The person who has breached a contract cannot have that agreement held good against any of the other parties.

INJUSTICE

The court will not enforce a contract if doing so will result in an obvious injustice. While the law is precise, its enforcement is allowed to be compassionate. Consider a case where Smith and Jones come to an *oral* agreement, wherein Smith pays money to Jones, and Jones transfers title to a piece of land to Smith. Smith then builds a house upon the land, whereupon Jones claims title to the land (and to the attachments, including the house) on the grounds that the contract transferring title was oral and therefore invalid. In a case as cut and dried as this, the court would award title to Smith, despite the absence of a written contract, for two reasons. First, there is a principle of law that recognizes an oral contract of this nature provided that the purchaser has "substantially" improved the property; otherwise he clearly would suffer unjustly. Second, if Jones had engineered the entire scheme specifically in order to take advantage of Smith, then Jones's case would be dismissed; a person can't use the law to obtain an unfair advantage over someone else who is acting in good faith.

OUTSIDE CIRCUMSTANCES

Finally, a contract can be terminated because of some outside circumstance. For example, new legislation may invalidate some kinds of contracts. The death of one of the parties usually will void a contract; also, if a party becomes ill or injured to the point where she cannot perform, she often can void a contract without penalty. If it turns out that the parties have made a mistake as to what their agreement constitutes, then the contract can be nullified. For example, if Emmett thinks a contract of sale involves his purchase of Jane's property on *First Street* and Jane thinks she has agreed to sell Emmett the property she owns on *Twenty-first Street*, there is no contract, because there hasn't been a meeting of the minds. Finally, if the subject matter of the contract is destroyed, the contract ceases to exist.

Questions on Chapter 6

1. A contract in which an owner of real estate employs a broker for the purpose of finding a buyer for the real estate is a
   (A) deed
   (B) contract of sale
   (C) listing
   (D) lease

2. A contract in which property is transferred from one person to another is a
   (A) deed
   (B) contract of sale
   (C) listing
   (D) lease

3. The two parties to a lease contract are the
   (A) landlord and the serf
   (B) rentor and the rentee
   (C) lessor and the lessee
   (D) grantor and the grantee

4. The requirement that all parties to the contract have an understanding of the conditions and stipulations of the agreement is
   (A) reality of consent
   (B) meeting of the minds
   (C) offer and acceptance
   (D) all of the above

5. Consideration that has value only to the person receiving it is
   (A) illegal in any transaction
   (B) good consideration
   (C) valuable consideration
   (D) contingent consideration

6. A person who is too young to be held to a contractual arrangement is called
   (A) youthful
   (B) incompetent
   (C) an emancipated minor
   (D) civilly dead

7. One who is otherwise incompetent to make a contract may be bound to contracts for
   (A) anything but real estate
   (B) real estate only
   (C) necessaries
   (D) food, clothing, and shelter not to exceed $100 per week

8. Which of the following contractual arrangements would be unenforceable?
   (A) A agrees to buy B's house.
   (B) A agrees with B that B shall steal money from C.
   (C) A agrees to find a buyer for B's car.
   (D) A agrees with B that B shall make restitution to C for money stolen by B. ✓

9. The law that requires that most real estate contracts be written to be enforceable is the
   (A) Statute of Limitations
   (B) Statute of Frauds
   (C) Statute of Written Real Estate Agreements
   (D) Statute of Liberty

10. A contract in which A agrees to allow B to use A's real estate in return for periodic payments of money by B is a
    (A) deed
    (B) contract of sale
    (C) lease
    (D) mortgage

11. When a person deliberately lies in order to mislead a fellow party to a contract, this action is
    (A) fraud
    (B) misrepresentation
    (C) legal if no third parties are hurt
    (D) all right if it is not written into the contract

12. Holding a gun to someone's head to force him to sign a contract is
    (A) attempted murder
    (B) permissible only in exceptional circumstances
    (C) duress
    (D) rude and inconsiderate but not illegal so long as the gun doesn't go off

13. When a party to a contract makes performance under it impossible, the result is
    (A) breach of contract   X A
    (B) discharge of contract
    (C) performance of contract
    (D) abandonment of contract

when a party to a contract makes performance under it impossible, the result is breach of contract.

14. A contract in which A agrees to purchase B's real estate at a later date is
    (A) a deed
    (B) an option   X C
    (C) a contract of sale
    (D) a lease

A contract which A agrees to purchase B's real estate @ a later date is a contract of sale.

15. Contracts made by a minor are
    (A) enforceable at all times
    (B) void
    (C) voidable by either party
    (D) voidable only by the minor

16. Incompetent parties include
    (A) minors
    (B) insane persons
    (C) people with court-appointed guardians
    (D) all of the above

17. The parties to a deed are the
    (A) vendor and vendee
    (B) grantor and grantee
    (C) offeror and offeree
    (D) acceptor and acceptee

18. If A and B have a contractual arrangement and B violates the contract, A may
    (A) do nothing but suffer the consequences
    (B) sue in court for damages and/or specific performance
    (C) call the police and have B arrested unless B agrees to cooperate
    (D) damage B to the extent that she has damaged A

19. A agrees to sell his brand new limousine to B in return for one dollar. Later A wishes to back out of the deal.
    (A) He may not do so.
    (B) He may do so because he is not getting the true value of the limousine.
    (C) He may only require that B pay a fair price for the limousine.
    (D) Both actions are clear evidence of insanity, so the contract is void.

20. A agrees to trade her car to B in exchange for a vacant lot that B owns.
    (A) This is a valid contractual arrangement.
    (B) This is not a contract, because no money changes hands.
    (C) This is not a contract, because unlike items can't he traded.
    (D) This is not a valid contract, because the car is titled in A's name.

21. Two offers are received by the broker at the same time. The broker must
    (A) present both offers
    (B) present only the higher offer
    (C) present only the offer that provides a greater commission
    (D) use his or her best judgment as to which offer to present

22. In a legal purchase contract, the seller is often referred to as the
    (A) trustor
    (B) divisor
    (C) donor
    (D) vendor

23. A contract based on an illegal consideration is
    (A) valid
    (B) void
    (C) legal
    (D) enforceable

ANSWERS

1. **C**	6. **B**	11. **A**	16. **D**	21. **A**
2. **A**	7. **C**	12. **C**	17. **B**	22. **D**
3. **C**	8. **B**	13. **A**	18. **B**	23. **B**
4. **D**	9. **B**	14. **C**	19. **A**	
5. **B**	10. **C**	15. **D**	20. **A**	

Chapter 7/ *Description of Land*

Recognized, uniform methods of land description are essential to proper contractual transactions involving land. If the land in a transaction cannot be identified, our legal system will not recognize the transaction as binding. Therefore, proper description of the land involved is an essential part of contracts of sale, deeds, leases, options, mortgages, listings, and virtually all other kinds of real estate contracts.

There are four generally accepted methods of land description in the United States:

1. Rectangular survey
2. Metes and bounds
3. Lot and block number
4. Monument or occupancy

The purpose of all of these is to *identify* real estate. Often, in the terminology of the real estate business, descriptions are called "legal descriptions," giving the impression that there is some particular formula that must be followed. Actually, the only legal point of any importance is that the description be *sufficient to identify the property*. If the property can be identified from the description given, then the description is good. Otherwise, no matter how elaborate it may appear, it is faulty.

Most description methods are designed to demonstrate to a surveyor a means of marking the outline of the land on the ground. Most descriptions do not include buildings; remember that real estate is land *and all attachments to it*, so a description of the land automatically includes all improvements, unless they are *specifically excluded*.

Rectangular Survey Descriptions

The U.S. government rectangular survey is used in California, and in the states indicated in Figure 7-1. The government rectangular survey divides the land into squares 6 miles on a side; these are called *townships*. Each township is identified with respect to its distance from the *base line* and the *principal meridian*. There are several sets of principal meridians and base lines throughout the country, so each principal meridian carries a name or number to distinguish it from all the others; each one has a single base line paired with it.

Principal meridians are imaginary lines that run north-south. Base lines are imaginary lines that run east-west. Parallel to the principal meridians and 6 miles apart from each other are other *meridians*. Parallel to the base line are other lines called *parallels*; these are also 6 miles apart. Altogether, this system of north-south meridians and east-west parallels cuts the map up into a grid of 6-mile squares, as in Figure 7-2.

The vertical (north-south) rows of townships are called *ranges*, and the horizontal (east-west) rows of townships are *tiers*. Each township can be identified by labeling the range and tier in which it is found. The ranges and tiers are numbered according to their distances and directions from the principal meridian, or the base line. For example, the principal meridian will have a row of townships on each side of it. The one to the east is called *Range 1 East*, while the one to the west is *Range 1 West*. Similarly, the tier immediately north of the base line is called *Tier 1 North*, while the one below it is *Tier 1 South*.

To specify a particular township, a description must state both the tier and the range in which the township appears. These specifications usually are given in the form of abbreviations, such as T3N ((Tier 3 North) or R4W (Range 4 West). Figure 7-2 identifies a number of

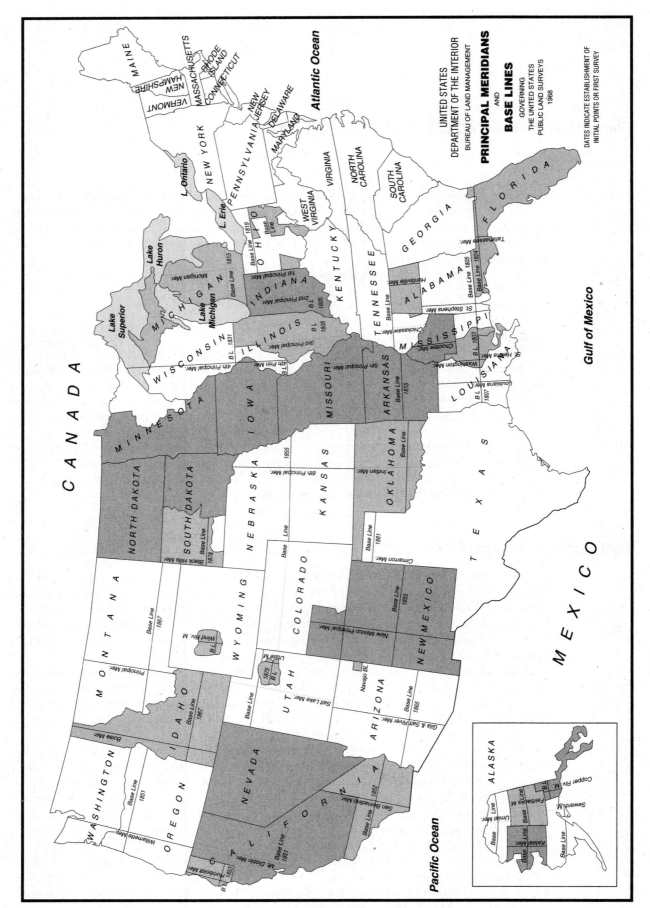

Figure 7-1. Government Rectangular Survey

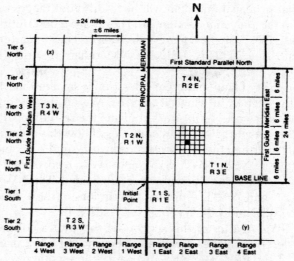

Figure 7-2.   Six-Mile Square Grid

townships by this kind of description; note that you simply count the number of ranges (or tiers) from the principal meridian (or the base line) to the particular township, and specify the direction taken. For practice, try to identify all the unmarked townships in Figure 7-2.

Of course, most tracts of land are less than 6 square miles, so it becomes necessary to identify which *part* of the township is the specific piece of land under consideration. This is done by dividing the township into smaller and smaller parcels until the one of interest is all that is left.

All townships are divided into 1-mile squares, as shown in Figure 7-3. Since each township is 6 miles square, it will contain 36 square miles. Each of these is always numbered, as shown in Figure 7-3. Each square-mile tract is called a *section*. Section 1 in any township, then, is the square mile at the very northeast corner of the township; Section 2 is immediately west of Section 1, and so on. Section 21 will be in the fourth row from the top of the township and in the third column from the west. In other words, the north border of Section 21 is 3 miles south of the north boundary of the township; the east border of Section 21 is 3 miles west of the east boundary of the township.

As an example, let us assume that the township illustrated in Figure 7-3 is the one in Figure 7-2 with the sections drawn in; that is, it is T2N, R2E. If, then, we wanted to describe Section 21 of this township, we would write, "Sec. 21, T2N, R2E." We would also have to specify which principal meridian we were using, although in states with only one principal meridian it is not strictly necessary to identify the meridian in a valid description.

Notice that for each principal meridian there is only *one* T2N, R2E. All other townships

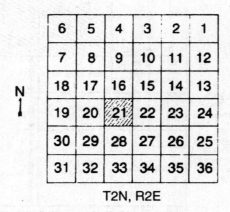

T2N, R2E

Figure 7-3.   Numbering for Township Grids

using that principal meridian will be in different ranges or tiers, or both. Furthermore, each township has only *one* Section 21. Therefore, a description such as "Sec. 21, T2N, R2E, 5th PM" describes a single square-mile tract of land in eastern Arkansas, on the Fifth Principal Meridian. "Sec. 21, T2N, R2E, Boise Meridian" describes a square-mile tract in southwestern Idaho.

If the tract of land under consideration is smaller than 1 square mile, we must further subdivide the section in which it appears. We do this by dividing the section into quarters or halves; if necessary, we further subdivide the resulting parts until we arrive at the tract we are considering. Figure 7-4 shows examples of how this is done. The entire section can be divided into four quarters: the northeast, northwest, southeast, and southwest quarters. These would be written as NE¼, NW¼, SE¼, and SW¼, respectively. In Figure 7-4 the SE¼ quarter is shown; the others have been further subdivided. The NW¼ quarter has been divided into two halves, E½ and W½. The proper descriptions of these subdivisions would be E½, NW¼, Sec. 21, T2N, R2E and W½, NW¼, Sec. 21, T2N, R2E.

The SW¼ quarter of this section has been divided into a number of smaller parcels; the proper description of each is given. The smallest is the shaded tract NW¼, SW¼, NW¼, SW¼, Sec. 21, T2N, R2E. The NE¼ quarter of the section has been divided slightly differently: the N½ is divided by the distance from the boundaries of N½, NE¼.

Each square mile contains 640 acres. The quarters, then, contain 160 acres each. Further subdivision yields smaller tracts that can be easily measured in terms of acreage; all the tracts subdivided in Figure 7-4 have the acreage indicated. In any case, it is a simple matter to determine acreage from most rectangular survey descriptions: multiply the series of fractions given in the description; then multiply the result by the 640 acres contained in the section. For example, the NW¼ quarter contains 160 acres: ¼ × 640 = 160. The very small tract cited in the preceding paragraph is NW¼, SW¼, NW¼, SW¼, so its acreage is ¼ × ¼ × ¼ × ¼ × 640 = 2½ acres.

Tracts such as those described in the N½, NE¼ subdivision aren't quite as easy to determine, since they aren't described entirely in fractions of the full section. For these, however, it is a relatively simple matter to determine the lengths of the sides in feet; then the total number of square feet can be determined. An acre contains 43,560 square feet; therefore by di-

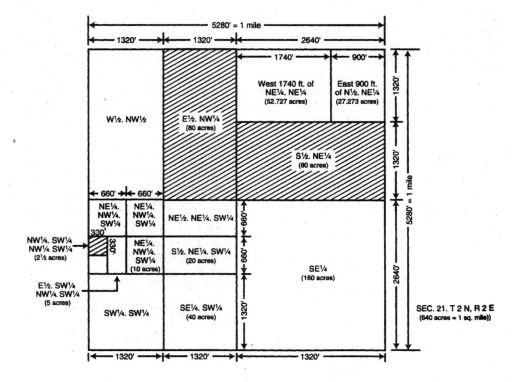

Figure 7-4. Subdivision of a Section

viding the square footage of the entire tract by 43,560, we can obtain the acreage of the tract in question.

Sometimes a specific tract cannot be described using a single rectangular survey description; in such cases it is perfectly all right to use several descriptions, each for part of the tract, making sure that all the descriptions together will describe the entire tract. For example, the large L-shaped shaded tract in Figure 7-4 would be described as "E½, NW¼ and S½, NE¼; Sec. 21, T2N, R2E." Note, however, that it is almost always necessary that rectangular survey descriptions be of fairly regular tracts with straight sides. The boundaries almost always must run north-south or east-west. Usually the survey is not a good system for describing irregular tracts, tracts with curved or wandering boundaries, and very small tracts; these are better described using other methods.

One final feature of the rectangular survey description system must be noted: north-south lines on our planet are not parallel because they all meet at the poles. Therefore, the meridians must be adjusted every so often to keep them from getting too close together. This is done by shifting every *fourth* meridian, each 24 miles away from the base line. These meridians, called *guide meridians*, are shown in Figure 7-2. The parallels at which the adjustments take place, that is, every fourth parallel, are called *standard parallels*. Standard parallels and guide meridians are named to indicate their numbers and distance from the respective base line or principal meridian.

A detailed illustration of the three meridians used in California is shown in Figure 7-5.

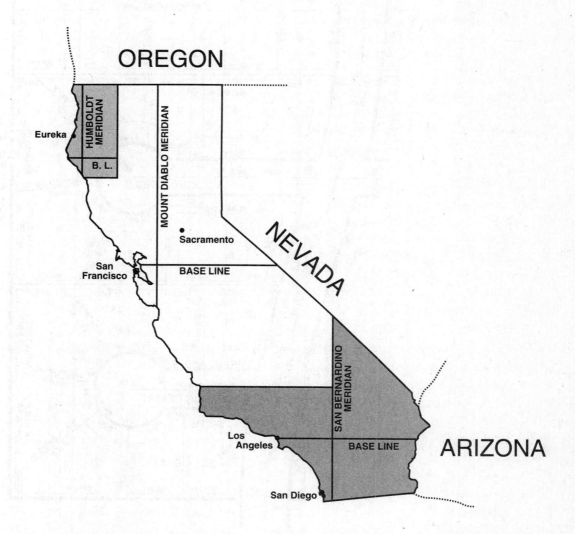

Figure 7-5.   The Three California Meridians

Metes and Bounds Descriptions

Metes and bounds descriptions indicate to the surveyor how to locate the corners of a tract. By locating the corners, one also locates the sides, since they run from corner to corner. Following is a metes and bounds description of Lot 15 in Figure 7-6. This lot is shown enlarged in Figure 7-7.

> "BEGINNING at a point being the southeast corner of the intersection of Vicious Circle and Alongthe Avenue, thence one hundred and six and forty-hundredths feet (106.40') north 90°0'0" east, thence one hundred and twenty feet (120.00') south 0°0'0" east, thence seventy-three and fourteen-hundredths feet (73.14') south 90°0'0" west, thence one hundred and twenty-four and fifty-three hundredths feet (124.53') north 15°29'26" west to the point of beginning; said tract lying and being in Gotham City, Copperwire County, California."

Note that a metes and bounds description must have the following components:

1. A properly identified *point of beginning*.
2. *Distance* and *direction* given for each side.

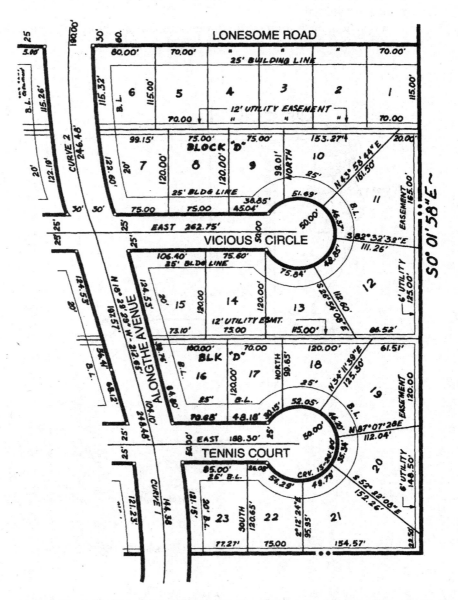

Figure 7-6. Block D, Stripmine Estates, Gotham City, Copperwire County, California

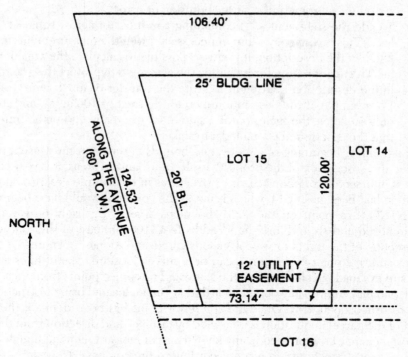

Figure 7-7. Lot 15, Block D, Stripmine Estates

The preceding description contains all these. The point of beginning is identified as the intersection of two public streets; this is permissible, since a person may always consult the public records to find out exactly where these streets are. From that point, the surveyor is directed to proceed a certain distance, and in a certain direction. By following this description, he can arrive *only* at the specific points described, and these points are the corners of the lot. He will have outlined the particular plot of land in question by following this description; thus it is a good description.

The accuracy of the description is the only point of any consequence in a court of law. The description can progress clockwise or counterclockwise. Directions (north, south, etc.) may be capitalized or not. The description should include, of course, the name of the city (or county) and the state in which the real estate is located.

Often a metes and bounds description may include more language than in the fairly minimal example provided here. Common additional elements are as follows:

1. To define the street rights-of-way, lot lines of adjacent lots, and so on, along which directed lines travel. Example: ". . . thence one hundred feet (100.00') north 63°30'0" west along the southern right-of-way boundary of Thirtieth Street, thence one hundred feet (100.00') north 88°0'0" west along the southern boundary of Lot 44, ..."

2. To end each direction with the words ". . . to an iron pin . . ." or ". . . to a point . . ." or some other language suggesting that there is a mark on the ground to refer to. More often than not, there is no marker now in existence, though at the time the lot originally was laid out, many years ago, there indeed was. However, over the years these things disappear, erode, and otherwise become invisible.

3. To refer to actual things on the ground that can be found. If these things are relatively permanent and obvious, they are referred to as *monuments*. Examples: large, identifiable trees, visible streambeds, milestones, stone walls or other constructions, and occasionally genuine monuments placed at a location by the original surveyors for the very purpose of serving as references for descriptions. One serious point to keep in mind is that, if monuments are mentioned in a metes and bounds description, and the directed lines and monuments conflict, then the monuments rule. This means that, if the distance and measurement given say to go 200 feet due north to a certain milestone and

the milestone actually is 193 feet, 6 degrees west of north, the latter measurement will rule in the description. For this reason, the inclusion of too many monuments in a description can sometimes cause confusion or error.

4. To add the statement ". . . containing *x* number of acres (square feet, etc.), more or less." This is convenient, but unnecessary; given the measurements and directions supplied by the description, it is always possible to calculate the area of the parcel if need be. The major reason for including the acreage is to protect the grantor against an error in the description that might indicate the transfer of much more (or much less) land. For example, if the description mentions a tract of 100 acres, and the tract actually is only 10 acres, the inclusion of a statement of area would be an immediate indication that the description contained a mistake.

The point of beginning of a metes and bounds description must use a point of reference outside the description of the property itself. In urbanized areas, it is very common to use the nearest intersection of public roads or streets, as in the sample description given. [If that description had been of Lot 14, which is not at the corner, it would have begun as follows: "BEGINNING at a point on the south boundary line of the right-of-way of Vicious Circle, one-hundred-and-six and forty-hundredths feet (106.40') east of the southeast corner of the intersection of the rights-of-way of Vicious Circle and Alongthe Avenue. . . ."] In government survey states, a point of reference can be a survey location. Many states also have had their own surveys made in all or part of the state, and reference points from these may be used. Indeed, one may refer to any point on earth that can be located using instructions from any publicly recorded document. Once the reference point has been defined, the actual beginning point of the parcel in question is identified by distance and direction from the reference point.

Distance may be expressed in any known unit of measurement, although the most common by far is feet. Directions are given according to the compass. However, in most parts of the United States there are two "sets" of compass directions: magnetic bearings and true bearings. Magnetic bearings refer to the magnetic poles; true bearings, to the geographic poles. If magnetic bearings are used, then, in order to achieve true bearings, they must be corrected for the location at which the survey was made and the date. The reason is that the magnetic pole is not at the same location as the true pole; furthermore, the magnetic pole "drifts" and so is located slightly differently at different times.

By convention, compass bearings are described as numbers of degrees east or west (or south). There are 360 degrees in a full circle, 90 degrees in a right (square) angle. The symbol for *degree* is °, so 90° means 90 degrees. Each degree is divided into 60 *minutes* (symbol:') and each minute is composed of 60 *seconds* (symbol:"). The statement N 44°31'56" E is read as "North 44 degrees, 31 minutes, 56 seconds east."

Due east is exactly 90° away from north, toward the east; it is written as N 90° E. "Due" northeast is half that distance from true north, written as N 45° E. If directions are south of due east or west, they are measured by their deviations from true south. A direction slightly north of due west would be N 89° W; if it were slightly *south* of due west, it would be S 89° W. These and several other examples of various directions are shown in Figure 7-8.

Lot and Block Number

Lot and block number descriptions are common in urban areas where *plats* of subdivisions must be recorded. A plat is a map of the manner in which land is divided into lots; Figure 7-6 is an example of a plat. If the plat is a matter of public record (i.e., has been recorded), it is quite sufficient to refer to it for the legal description of property it illustrates. For example, it would be enough to describe Lot 15 on that plat as "Lot 15, Block D, Stripmine Estates, Gotham City, Copperwire County, California." Given this description, a surveyor could look up this subdivision in the records, find the plat of Block D, and from it get all the information he needed to do an accurate survey of the lot.

Lot and block number descriptions are very simple to do and take little space. Therefore, in areas where the records are such that they can be used, they are very popular. It should be pointed out also that reference can be made to *any* recorded document in the preparation of a description. Thus, if lot and block descriptions are impossible, it may be possible simply to

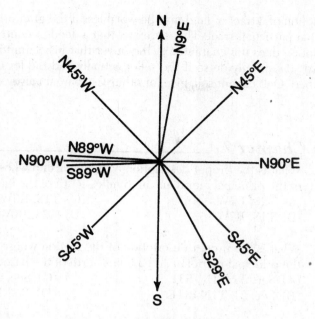

Figure 7-8. Compass Bearings

refer to a previous deed or other recorded instrument in which a description of the property appears. This should be done however, only if the previous description is exactly the same as the one to be used at present; even so, it is potentially inconvenient in that, whereas copies of plats are easily obtained, and often can be received directly from developers and dealers, old deeds and other documents have to be dug out of the records.

Monument and Occupancy Descriptions

Monument descriptions are similar superficially to metes and bounds descriptions. The difference is that monument descriptions rely entirely upon monuments and specify no distance or direction, except from the monuments themselves to important points of the survey. A monument description might read: "Beginning at the intersection of Highway 9 and County Road 445, thence along the right-of-way of County Road 445 to the end of a stone wall; thence from the end of the stone wall through the center of a large, freestanding oak tree to the center of a streambed; thence along the streambed to the point where the streambed intersects Highway 9; thence along Highway 9 to the point of beginning." Since this description can be followed in order to outline the property, it is a valid description, but there is always the risk that the monuments may move or disappear. These descriptions are used mainly for large rural tracts of relatively inexpensive land, where a full survey may entail much greater expense than is warranted by the usefulness of the land.

Occupancy descriptions are very vague: "All that land known as the Miller Farm"; "All that land bordered by the Grant Farm, Happy Acres Home for the Elderly, the Ellis Farm, and State Highway 42." With this kind of description one must rely on the community's general impression of what constitutes the Miller Farm, the Grant Farm, and so on. Occupancy descriptions are very weak because they indicate no specific boundaries at all. A similar situation arises when street addresses are used as descriptions. Although houses and other buildings usually have address numbers visibly displayed on them, these give no indication at all of the actual extent of the property.

Limits of Descriptions

It is important to understand that descriptions, while they may accurately describe land, do not provide any guarantee of *title* to that land. A deed that contains a perfectly usable description of a tract of land may be worthless if the grantor has little or no right to convey title to that particular tract. The mere fact that a deed or contract of sale contains a particular description does not guarantee to the buyer that his claim to the described land will hold up in court. It can only do so if the seller actually had the legal right to transfer the land she described. One cannot sell, give, or otherwise bargain away what one does not own.

Questions on Chapter 7

1. What is the proper description of the township whose *northeast* corner is 36 miles west of the principal meridian and 6 miles south of the base line?
   (A) T2S, R7W
   (B) T1S, R7W
   (C) T1S, R6W
   (D) T2S, R6W

2. What is the proper description of the section whose *northwest* corner is 5 miles east of the principal meridian and 2 miles north of the base line?
   (A) Sec. 23, T1N, R1E
   (B) Sec. 24, T1N, R1E
   (C) Sec. 29, T1N, R1E
   (D) Sec. 25, T1N, R1E

3. How many miles apart are the guide meridians?
   (A) 12
   (B) 4
   (C) 24
   (D) 18

4. The east-west lines at which guide meridians are adjusted are
   (A) adjustment lines
   (B) base line extensions
   (C) parallels of adjustment
   (D) standard parallels

5. The number of acres in 1 square mile is
   (A) 640
   (B) 5280
   (C) 1000
   (D) 160

Questions 6–13 concern Figure A, shown at right.

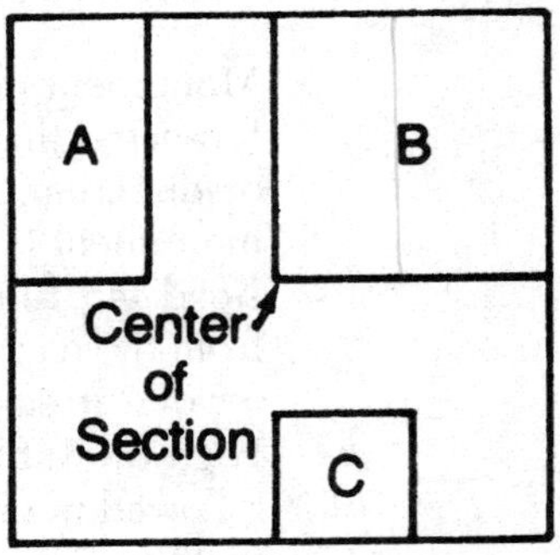

6. How many acres does the tract marked A contain?
   (A) 640
   (B) 160
   (C) 80
   (D) 40

7. How many acres does the tract marked B contain?
   (A) 640
   (B) 160
   (C) 80
   (D) 40

8. How many acres does the tract marked C contain?
   (A) 640
   (B) 160
   (C) 80
   (D) 40

9. The description of Tract A is
   (A) NW¼, NW¼
   (B) N½, NE¼
   (C) W½, NW¼
   (D) W½, N½

10. The description of Tract B is
    (A) NE¼
    (B) NE½
    (C) NE¼, NE¼
    (D) NE¼, NE¼, N½

11. The description of Tract C is
    (A) SE¼, SE¼
    (B) SW¼, SW¼
    (C) SE¼, SW¼
    (D) SW¼, SE¼

Figure A.
Diagram of a Section

12. Assume that the illustrated section is Section 8 of a particular township. What section would you be in if you traveled exactly 2¾ miles due *south* from the *center* of Section 8?
    (A) Sec. 11   (C) Sec. 20
    (B) Sec. 12   (D) Sec. 29

13. Assume that the southeast corner of the section is exactly 28 miles south of the base line and 11 miles west of the principal meridian. In what township is it located?
    (A) T2W, R5S   (C) T6S, R2W
    (B) T5S, R2W   (D) T6S, R3W

14. The line behind which all buildings on a lot must be placed is called the
    (A) set line   (C) construction limit
    (B) setback, or building line   (D) backup, or setdown line

15. Which of the following is most nearly due west?
    (A) N 88° W   (C) S 89°58′3″ W
    (B) N 79°66′43″ W   (D) W 0°4′ N

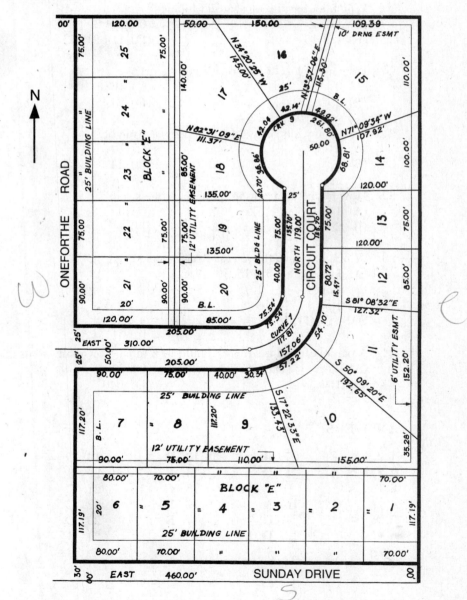

Figure *B.*   Block E Quagmire Village, Metropolis, Snakebite County, California

16. Which of the following would *not* be a proper way to begin a metes and bounds description of Lot 10?
    (A) "Beginning at the southwest corner of Lot 10 . . ."
    (B) "Beginning at the street intersection nearest Lot 10 . . ."
    (C) "Beginning at a point 110 feet northwest of Lot 10 . . ."
    (D) All of the above

17. "All that land known as the Jones Farm" is which kind of description?
    (A) Invalid   (C) Metes only
    (B) Occupancy   (D) Rural

Questions 18–23 refer to the plat shown in Figure B.

18. Which lot has the most footage on Circuit Court?
    (A) Lot 10   (C) Lot 20
    (B) Lot 18   (D) Lot 21

19. Which lot has the most street footage?
    (A) Lot 7   (C) Lot 20
    (B) Lot 18   (D) Lot 21

20. How many lots border on Circuit Court?
    (A) 9   (C) 16
    (B) 15   (D) 21

21. How many lots have sides that are *not* straight?
    (A) 8   (C) 10
    (B) 9   (D) 11

22. How many lots front on more than one street?
    (A) 1   (C) 3
    (B) 2   (D) 4

23. Which lots have the *fewest* straight sides?
    (A) Lots 10, 11, 14, 15, 16, 17, 20
    (B) Lots 10, 11, 14, 16
    (C) Lots 11, 14, 16
    (D) Lots 11, 16

24. A parcel of land is square, ½ mile by ½ mile. How many acres does it contain?
    (A) 40   (C) 320
    (B) 160   (D) 640

ANSWERS

1. **A**	7. **B**	13. **B**	19. **D**
2. **D**	8. **D**	14. **B**	20. **B**
3. **C**	9. **C**	15. **C**	21. **C**
4. **D**	10. **A**	16. **D**	22. **C**
5. **A**	11. **D**	17. **B**	23. **D**
6. **C**	12. **D**	18. **C**	24. **B**

Chapter 8/*Purchase Contracts*

A purchase contract for real estate describes the rights and obligations of the purchaser(s) and seller(s) of real estate. Days, weeks, or months later, at an *escrow closing*, the seller(s) will deliver a deed that transfers legal title to the property; the purchaser(s) will provide payment for the property as described in the purchase contract.

A purchase contract is *"the deal."* This means that all the provisions that the parties want, all the "ifs, ands, or buts," must be set forth in this contract; all the negotiation, "wheeling and dealing," "give and take," and such have to occur and be settled *before* the purchase contract exists. Once there is a purchase contract, it is too late for any more negotiation; all the parties to the agreement must abide by it, and none of them can change anything in it unless all other parties agree to the change. Therefore, it is vitally important that the parties to this contract make sure that all the conditions and requirements that they want with regard to the sale and purchase of the real estate are contained in the purchase contract.

It is possible to sell property merely by delivery of a deed in exchange for payment and thus bypass the purchase contract. However, the parties, especially the buyer, face a lot of risk. A title search must be performed to satisfy the buyer that the seller can give ownership, and time is required for such a search. The buyer may also need time to arrange financing. Most lenders will consider real estate loans only after they have studied the purchase contract. In short, it is rare for a transfer of real estate to be completed without such a contract. Furthermore, it is of paramount importance that all parties involved in a transaction understand their contractual obligations and privileges.

Upon completion of the purchase contract, the purchaser (*vendee*) receives an "equitable" title. Equity, in law, attempts to treat things as they should be to be fair and considers the purchaser to have "equitable title," although legal title remains with the seller (*vendor*) until closing. Therefore, if there is a casualty loss—a fire, for example—before closing, the risk may be upon the purchaser. However, considering that equity is intended to be fair, the risk of loss before closing should not pass automatically to the purchaser in all instances. There are situations in which the seller should be responsible and courts will hold him to be so. To avoid potential problems concerning risk of loss, the purchase contract should specify who has the burden of loss prior to closing and which party is obligated to complete the transaction and to receive the proceeds from insurance.

The Statute of Frauds requires that contracts for the sale of real estate be in writing to be enforceable. The *parol evidence* rule prevents oral testimony from being introduced when it conflicts with better (written) evidence. Consequently, care should be exercised in the preparation of a purchase contract.

A purchase contract should contain any *contingency clauses*, or *contingencies*, that the parties want. These "what if?" provisions often allow a buyer or seller to cancel the deal without penalty if something does or doesn't happen (the *if* part). For example, the seller may have her home on the market because her employer is transferring her, but wants to be able to cancel the deal *if* the transfer falls through. A buyer may need to sell his own home in order to be able to buy the seller's property, so he wants to be able to cancel the deal *if* he can't make the sale of his own property within a reasonable time. A great many homebuying purchase contracts are *contingent upon financing*; this means that the buyer can cancel the deal *if* he is unable to get a suitable purchase loan. Many preprinted purchase contracts have common contingencies already written into them: The buyer can cancel the deal *if* the seller can't provide clear title, *if* the property is severely damaged before closing, *if* termite infestation is found. The seller can cancel the deal *if* the buyer doesn't get financing approval within a certain time.

CALIFORNIA
RESIDENTIAL PURCHASE AGREEMENT
AND JOINT ESCROW INSTRUCTIONS
For Use With Single Family Residential Property — Attached or Detached
(C.A.R. Form RPA-CA, Revised 10/02)

CALIFORNIA
ASSOCIATION
OF REALTORS®

Date _____, at _____, California.
1. **OFFER:**
   A. **THIS IS AN OFFER FROM** _____ ("Buyer").
   B. **THE REAL PROPERTY TO BE ACQUIRED** is described as _____
      _____, Assessor's Parcel No. _____, situated in
      _____, County of _____*, California, ("Property").
   C. **THE PURCHASE PRICE** offered is _____
      _____ Dollars $ _____.
   D. **CLOSE OF ESCROW** shall occur on _____ (date)(or ☐ _____ **Days** After Acceptance).
2. **FINANCE TERMS:** Obtaining the loans below **is a contingency** of this Agreement unless: **(i)** either 2K or 2L is checked below; or **(ii)** otherwise agreed in writing. Buyer shall act diligently and in good faith to obtain the designated loans. Obtaining deposit, down payment and closing costs **is not a contingency.** Buyer represents that funds will be good when deposited with Escrow Holder.
   A. **INITIAL DEPOSIT:** Buyer has given a deposit in the amount of . . . .$ _____
      to the agent submitting the offer (or to ☐ _____), by personal check
      (or ☐ _____), made payable to _____,
      which shall be held uncashed until Acceptance and then deposited within **3 business days** after
      Acceptance (or ☐ _____), with
      Escrow Holder, (or ☐ into Broker's trust account.)
   B. **INCREASED DEPOSIT:** Buyer shall deposit with Escrow Holder an increased deposit in the amount of . . .$ _____
      within _____ **Days** After Acceptance, or ☐ _____.
   C. **FIRST LOAN IN THE AMOUNT OF** . . . .$ _____
      (1) NEW First Deed of Trust in favor of lender, encumbering the Property, securing a note payable at
      maximum interest of _____% fixed rate, or _____% initial adjustable rate with a maximum
      interest rate of _____%, balance due in _____ years, amortized over _____ years. Buyer
      shall pay loan fees/points not to exceed _____. (These terms apply whether the designated loan
      is conventional, FHA or VA.)
      (2) ☐ FHA ☐ VA: (The following terms only apply to the FHA or VA loan that is checked.)
      Seller shall pay _____% discount points. Seller shall pay other fees not allowed to be paid by Buyer,
      ☐ not to exceed $_____. Seller shall pay the cost of lender required Repairs (including
      those for wood destroying pest) not otherwise provided for in this Agreement, ☐ not to exceed $
      _____. (Actual loan amount may increase if mortgage insurance premiums, funding fees or
      closing costs are financed.)
   D. **ADDITIONAL FINANCING TERMS:** ☐ Seller financing, (C.A.R. Form SFA); ☐ secondary financing, ...$ _____
      (C.A.R. Form PAA, paragraph 4A); ☐ assumed financing (C.A.R. Form PAA, paragraph 4B)
      _____
      _____
   E. **BALANCE OF PURCHASE PRICE** (not including costs of obtaining loans and other closing costs) in the amount of . . .$ _____
      to be deposited with Escrow Holder within sufficient time to close escrow.
   F. **PURCHASE PRICE (TOTAL):** . . . .$ _____
   G. **LOAN APPLICATIONS:** Within **7** (or ☐ _____) **Days** After Acceptance, Buyer shall provide Seller a letter from lender or mortgage loan broker stating that, based on a review of Buyer's written application and credit report, Buyer is prequalified or preapproved for the NEW loan specified in 2C above.
   H. **VERIFICATION OF DOWN PAYMENT AND CLOSING COSTS:** Buyer (or Buyer's lender or loan broker pursuant to 2G) shall, within **7** (or ☐ _____) **Days** After Acceptance, provide Seller written verification of Buyer's down payment and closing costs.
   I. **LOAN CONTINGENCY REMOVAL: (i)** Within **17** (or ☐ _____) **Days** After Acceptance, Buyer shall, as specified in paragraph 14, remove the loan contingency or cancel this Agreement; **OR (ii)** (if checked) ☐ the loan contingency shall remain in effect until the designated loans are funded.
   J. **APPRAISAL CONTINGENCY AND REMOVAL:** This Agreement is (**OR,** if checked, ☐ is **NOT**) contingent upon the Property appraising at no less than the specified purchase price. If there is a loan contingency, at the time the loan contingency is removed (or, if checked, ☐ within **17** (or ____) **Days** After Acceptance), Buyer shall, as specified in paragraph 14B(3), remove the appraisal contingency or cancel this Agreement. If there is no loan contingency, Buyer shall, as specified in paragraph 14B(3), remove the appraisal contingency within **17** (or ____) **Days** After Acceptance.
   K. ☐ **NO LOAN CONTINGENCY** (If checked): Obtaining any loan in paragraphs 2C, 2D or elsewhere in this Agreement is NOT a contingency of this Agreement. If Buyer does not obtain the loan and as a result Buyer does not purchase the Property, Seller may be entitled to Buyer's deposit or other legal remedies.
   L. ☐ **ALL CASH OFFER** (If checked): No loan is needed to purchase the Property. Buyer shall, within **7** (or ☐ _____) **Days** After Acceptance, provide Seller written verification of sufficient funds to close this transaction.
3. **CLOSING AND OCCUPANCY:**
   A. Buyer intends (or ☐ does not intend) to occupy the Property as Buyer's primary residence.
   B. **Seller-occupied or vacant property:** Occupancy shall be delivered to Buyer at _____ AM/PM, ☐ on the date of Close Of Escrow; ☐ on _____; or ☐ no later than _____ **Days** After Close Of Escrow. (C.A.R. Form PAA, paragraph 2.) If transfer of title and occupancy do not occur at the same time, Buyer and Seller are advised to: **(i)** enter into a written occupancy agreement; and **(ii)** consult with their insurance and legal advisors.

RPA-CA REVISED 10/02 (PAGE 1 OF 8) Print Date

Buyer's Initials (_____)(_____)
Seller's Initials (_____)(_____)

Reviewed by _____ Date _____

EQUAL HOUSING
OPPORTUNITY

CALIFORNIA RESIDENTIAL PURCHASE AGREEMENT (RPA-CA PAGE 1 OF 8)

Figure 8-1. Real Estate Purchase Contract and Receipt for Deposit

Property Address: _____ Date: _____

C. **Tenant-occupied property: (i) Property shall be vacant** at least **5 (or ☐ _____) Days** Prior to Close Of Escrow, unless otherwise agreed in writing. **Note to Seller: If you are unable to deliver Property vacant in accordance with rent control and other applicable Law, you may be in breach of this Agreement.**

OR **(ii)** (if checked) ☐ **Tenant to remain in possession.** The attached addendum is incorporated into this Agreement (C.A.R. Form PAA, paragraph 3.);

OR **(iii)** (if checked) ☐ **This Agreement is contingent** upon Buyer and Seller entering into a written agreement regarding occupancy of the Property within the time specified in paragraph 14B(1). If no written agreement is reached within this time, either Buyer or Seller may cancel this Agreement in writing.

D. At Close Of Escrow, Seller assigns to Buyer any assignable warranty rights for items included in the sale and shall provide any available Copies of such warranties. Brokers cannot and will not determine the assignability of any warranties.

E. At Close Of Escrow, unless otherwise agreed in writing, Seller shall provide keys and/or means to operate all locks, mailboxes, security systems, alarms and garage door openers. If Property is a condominium or located in a common interest subdivision, Buyer may be required to pay a deposit to the Homeowners' Association ("HOA") to obtain keys to accessible HOA facilities.

4. **ALLOCATION OF COSTS** (If checked): Unless otherwise specified here, this paragraph only determines who is to pay for the report, inspection, test or service mentioned. If not specified here or elsewhere in this Agreement, the determination of who is to pay for any work recommended or identified by any such report, inspection, test or service shall be by the method specified in paragraph 14B(2).

A. **WOOD DESTROYING PEST INSPECTION:**

(1) ☐ Buyer ☐ Seller shall pay for an inspection and report for wood destroying pests and organisms ("Report") which shall be prepared by _____, a registered structural pest control company. The Report shall cover the accessible areas of the main building and attached structures and, if checked: ☐ detached garages and carports, ☐ detached decks, ☐ the following other structures or areas _____. The Report shall not include roof coverings. If Property is a condominium or located in a common interest subdivision, the Report shall include only the separate interest and any exclusive-use areas being transferred and shall not include common areas, unless otherwise agreed. Water tests of shower pans on upper level units may not be performed without consent of the owners of property below the shower.

OR (2) ☐ (If checked) The attached addendum (C.A.R. Form WPA) regarding wood destroying pest inspection and allocation of cost is incorporated into this Agreement.

B. **OTHER INSPECTIONS AND REPORTS:**

(1) ☐ Buyer ☐ Seller shall pay to have septic or private sewage disposal systems inspected _____.

(2) ☐ Buyer ☐ Seller shall pay to have domestic wells tested for water potability and productivity _____.

(3) ☐ Buyer ☐ Seller shall pay for a natural hazard zone disclosure report prepared by _____.

(4) ☐ Buyer ☐ Seller shall pay for the following inspection or report _____.

(5) ☐ Buyer ☐ Seller shall pay for the following inspection or report _____.

C. **GOVERNMENT REQUIREMENTS AND RETROFIT:**

(1) ☐ Buyer ☐ Seller shall pay for smoke detector installation and/or water heater bracing, if required by Law. Prior to Close Of Escrow, Seller shall provide Buyer a written statement of compliance in accordance with state and local Law, unless exempt.

(2) ☐ Buyer ☐ Seller shall pay the cost of compliance with any other minimum mandatory government retrofit standards, inspections and reports if required as a condition of closing escrow under any Law. _____.

D. **ESCROW AND TITLE:**

(1) ☐ Buyer ☐ Seller shall pay escrow fee _____. Escrow Holder shall be _____.

(2) ☐ Buyer ☐ Seller shall pay for **owner's** title insurance policy specified in paragraph 12E _____. Owner's title policy to be issued by _____. (Buyer shall pay for any title insurance policy insuring Buyer's **lender**, unless otherwise agreed in writing.)

E. **OTHER COSTS:**

(1) ☐ Buyer ☐ Seller shall pay County transfer tax or transfer fee _____.

(2) ☐ Buyer ☐ Seller shall pay City transfer tax or transfer fee _____.

(3) ☐ Buyer ☐ Seller shall pay HOA transfer fee _____.

(4) ☐ Buyer ☐ Seller shall pay HOA document preparation fees _____.

(5) ☐ Buyer ☐ Seller shall pay the cost, not to exceed $ _____, of a one-year home warranty plan, issued by _____ with the following optional coverage: _____.

(6) ☐ Buyer ☐ Seller shall pay for _____.

(7) ☐ Buyer ☐ Seller shall pay for _____.

5. **STATUTORY DISCLOSURES (INCLUDING LEAD-BASED PAINT HAZARD DISCLOSURES) AND CANCELLATION RIGHTS:**

A. **(1)** Seller shall, within the time specified in paragraph 14A, deliver to Buyer, if required by Law: **(i)** Federal Lead-Based Paint Disclosures and pamphlet ("Lead Disclosures"); and **(ii)** disclosures or notices required by sections 1102 et. seq. and 1103 et. seq. of the California Civil Code ("Statutory Disclosures"). Statutory Disclosures include, but are not limited to, a Real Estate Transfer Disclosure Statement ("TDS"), Natural Hazard Disclosure Statement ("NHD"), notice or actual knowledge of release of illegal controlled substance, notice of special tax and/or assessments (or, if allowed, substantially equivalent notice regarding the Mello-Roos Community Facilities Act and Improvement Bond Act of 1915) and, if Seller has actual knowledge, an industrial use and military ordnance location disclosure (C.A.R. Form SSD).

(2) Buyer shall, within the time specified in paragraph 14B(1), return Signed Copies of the Statutory and Lead Disclosures to Seller.

(3) In the event Seller, prior to Close Of Escrow, becomes aware of adverse conditions materially affecting the Property, or any material inaccuracy in disclosures, information or representations previously provided to Buyer of which Buyer is otherwise unaware, Seller shall promptly provide a subsequent or amended disclosure or notice, in writing, covering those items. **However, a subsequent or amended disclosure shall not be required for conditions and material inaccuracies disclosed in reports ordered and paid for by Buyer.**

Buyer's Initials (_____)(_____)
Seller's Initials (_____)(_____)

RPA-CA REVISED 10/02 (PAGE 2 OF 8)

Reviewed by _____ Date _____

CALIFORNIA RESIDENTIAL PURCHASE AGREEMENT (RPA-CA PAGE 2 OF 8)

Figure 8-1.   Real Estate Purchase Contract and Receipt for Deposit (*continued*)

Property Address: _____ Date: _____

(4) If any disclosure or notice specified in 5A(1), or subsequent or amended disclosure or notice is delivered to Buyer after the offer is Signed, Buyer shall have the right to cancel this Agreement within **3 Days** After delivery in person, or **5 Days** After delivery by deposit in the mail, by giving written notice of cancellation to Seller or Seller's agent. (Lead Disclosures sent by mail must be sent certified mail or better.)

(5) Note to Buyer and Seller: Waiver of Statutory and Lead Disclosures is prohibited by Law.

  B. **NATURAL AND ENVIRONMENTAL HAZARDS:** Within the time specified in paragraph 14A, Seller shall, if required by Law: **(i)** deliver to Buyer earthquake guides (and questionnaire) and environmental hazards booklet; **(ii)** even if exempt from the obligation to provide a NHD, disclose if the Property is located in a Special Flood Hazard Area; Potential Flooding (Inundation) Area; Very High Fire Hazard Zone; State Fire Responsibility Area; Earthquake Fault Zone; Seismic Hazard Zone; and **(iii)** disclose any other zone as required by Law and provide any other information required for those zones.

  C. **DATA BASE DISCLOSURE:** NOTICE: The California Department of Justice, sheriff's departments, police departments serving jurisdictions of 200,000 or more and many other local law enforcement authorities maintain for public access a data base of the locations of persons required to register pursuant to paragraph (1) of subdivision (a) of Section 290.4 of the Penal Code. The data base is updated on a quarterly basis and a source of information about the presence of these individuals in any neighborhood. The Department of Justice also maintains a Sex Offender Identification Line through which inquiries about individuals may be made. This is a "900" telephone service. Callers must have specific information about individuals they are checking. Information regarding neighborhoods is not available through the "900" telephone service.

6. **CONDOMINIUM/PLANNED UNIT DEVELOPMENT DISCLOSURES:**

  A. **SELLER HAS: 7 (or ☐ _____) Days** After Acceptance to disclose to Buyer whether the Property is a condominium, or is located in a planned unit development or other common interest subdivision (C.A.R. Form SSD).

  B. If the Property is a condominium or is located in a planned unit development or other common interest subdivision, Seller has **3 (or ☐ _____) Days** After Acceptance to request from the HOA (C.A.R. Form HOA): **(i)** Copies of any documents required by Law; **(ii)** disclosure of any pending or anticipated claim or litigation by or against the HOA; **(iii)** a statement containing the location and number of designated parking and storage spaces; **(iv)** Copies of the most recent 12 months of HOA minutes for regular and special meetings; and **(v)** the names and contact information of all HOAs governing the Property (collectively, "CI Disclosures"). Seller shall itemize and deliver to Buyer all CI Disclosures received from the HOA and any CI Disclosures in Seller's possession. Buyer's approval of CI Disclosures is a contingency of this Agreement as specified in paragraph 14B(3).

7. **CONDITIONS AFFECTING PROPERTY:**

  A. Unless otherwise agreed: **(i) the Property is sold (a) in its PRESENT physical condition as of the date of Acceptance and (b) subject to Buyer's Investigation rights; (ii)** the Property, including pool, spa, landscaping and grounds, is to be maintained in substantially the same condition as on the date of Acceptance; and **(iii)** all debris and personal property not included in the sale shall be removed by Close Of Escrow.

  B. **SELLER SHALL, within the time specified in paragraph 14A, DISCLOSE KNOWN MATERIAL FACTS AND DEFECTS affecting the Property, including known insurance claims within the past five years, AND MAKE OTHER DISCLOSURES REQUIRED BY LAW (C.A.R. Form SSD).**

  C. **NOTE TO BUYER: You are strongly advised to conduct investigations of the entire Property in order to determine its present condition since Seller may not be aware of all defects affecting the Property or other factors that you consider important. Property improvements may not be built according to code, in compliance with current Law, or have had permits issued.**

  D. **NOTE TO SELLER: Buyer has the right to inspect the Property and, as specified in paragraph 14B, based upon information discovered in those inspections: (i) cancel this Agreement; or (ii) request that you make Repairs or take other action.**

8. **ITEMS INCLUDED AND EXCLUDED:**

  A. **NOTE TO BUYER AND SELLER:** Items listed as included or excluded in the MLS, flyers or marketing materials are **not** included in the purchase price or excluded from the sale unless specified in 8B or C.

  B. **ITEMS INCLUDED IN SALE:**

    (1) All EXISTING fixtures and fittings that are attached to the Property;

    (2) Existing electrical, mechanical, lighting, plumbing and heating fixtures, ceiling fans, fireplace inserts, gas logs and grates, solar systems, built-in appliances, window and door screens, awnings, shutters, window coverings, attached floor coverings, television antennas, satellite dishes, private integrated telephone systems, air coolers/conditioners, pool/spa equipment, garage door openers/remote controls, mailbox, in-ground landscaping, trees/shrubs, water softeners, water purifiers, security systems/alarms; and

    (3) The following items: _____

    _____

    (4) Seller represents that all items included in the purchase price, unless otherwise specified, are owned by Seller.

    (5) All items included shall be transferred free of liens and without Seller warranty.

  C. **ITEMS EXCLUDED FROM SALE:** _____

    _____

9. **BUYER'S INVESTIGATION OF PROPERTY AND MATTERS AFFECTING PROPERTY:**

  A. Buyer's acceptance of the condition of, and any other matter affecting the Property, is a contingency of this Agreement as specified in this paragraph and paragraph 14B. Within the time specified in paragraph 14B(1), Buyer shall have the right, at Buyer's expense unless otherwise agreed, to conduct inspections, investigations, tests, surveys and other studies ("Buyer Investigations"), including, but not limited to, the right to: **(i)** inspect for lead-based paint and other lead-based paint hazards; **(ii)** inspect for wood destroying pests and organisms; **(iii)** review the registered sex offender database; **(iv)** confirm the insurability of Buyer and the Property; and **(v)** satisfy Buyer as to any matter specified in the attached Buyer's Inspection Advisory (C.A.R. Form BIA). Without Seller's prior written consent, Buyer shall neither make nor cause to be made: **(i)** invasive or destructive Buyer Investigations; or **(ii)** inspections by any governmental building or zoning inspector or government employee, unless required by Law.

  B. Buyer shall complete Buyer Investigations and, as specified in paragraph 14B, remove the contingency or cancel this Agreement. Buyer shall give Seller, at no cost, complete Copies of all Buyer Investigation reports obtained by Buyer. Seller shall make the Property available for all Buyer Investigations. Seller shall have water, gas, electricity and all operable pilot lights on for Buyer's Investigations and through the date possession is made available to Buyer.

Buyer's Initials (_____)(_____)
Seller's Initials (_____)(_____)

Reviewed by _____ Date _____

CALIFORNIA RESIDENTIAL PURCHASE AGREEMENT (RPA-CA PAGE 3 OF 8)

Figure 8-1. Real Estate Purchase Contract and Receipt for Deposit (*continued*)

Property Address: _____   Date: _____

10. REPAIRS: Repairs shall be completed prior to final verification of condition unless otherwise agreed in writing. Repairs to be performed at Seller's expense may be performed by Seller or through others, provided that the work complies with applicable Law, including governmental permit, inspection and approval requirements. Repairs shall be performed in a good, skillful manner with materials of quality and appearance comparable to existing materials. It is understood that exact restoration of appearance or cosmetic items following all Repairs may not be possible. Seller shall: **(i)** obtain receipts for Repairs performed by others; **(ii)** prepare a written statement indicating the Repairs performed by Seller and the date of such Repairs; and **(iii)** provide Copies of receipts and statements to Buyer prior to final verification of condition.

11. BUYER INDEMNITY AND SELLER PROTECTION FOR ENTRY UPON PROPERTY: Buyer shall: **(i)** keep the Property free and clear of liens; **(ii)** Repair all damage arising from Buyer Investigations; and **(iii)** indemnify and hold Seller harmless from all resulting liability, claims, demands, damages and costs. Buyer shall carry, or Buyer shall require anyone acting on Buyer's behalf to carry, policies of liability, workers' compensation and other applicable insurance, defending and protecting Seller from liability for any injuries to persons or property occurring during any Buyer Investigations or work done on the Property at Buyer's direction prior to Close Of Escrow. Seller is advised that certain protections may be afforded Seller by recording a "Notice of Non-responsibility" (C.A.R. Form NNR) for Buyer Investigations and work done on the Property at Buyer's direction. Buyer's obligations under this paragraph shall survive the termination of this Agreement.

12. TITLE AND VESTING:
   A. Within the time specified in paragraph 14, Buyer shall be provided a current preliminary (title) report, which is only an offer by the title insurer to issue a policy of title insurance and may not contain every item affecting title. Buyer's review of the preliminary report and any other matters which may affect title are a contingency of this Agreement as specified in paragraph 14B.
   B. Title is taken in its present condition subject to all encumbrances, easements, covenants, conditions, restrictions, rights and other matters, whether of record or not, as of the date of Acceptance except: **(i)** monetary liens of record unless Buyer is assuming those obligations or taking the Property subject to those obligations; and **(ii)** those matters which Seller has agreed to remove in writing.
   C. Within the time specified in paragraph 14A, Seller has a duty to disclose to Buyer all matters known to Seller affecting title, whether of record or not.
   D. At Close Of Escrow, Buyer shall receive a grant deed conveying title (or, for stock cooperative or long-term lease, an assignment of stock certificate or of Seller's leasehold interest), including oil, mineral and water rights if currently owned by Seller. Title shall vest as designated in Buyer's supplemental escrow instructions. THE MANNER OF TAKING TITLE MAY HAVE SIGNIFICANT LEGAL AND TAX CONSEQUENCES. CONSULT AN APPROPRIATE PROFESSIONAL.
   E. Buyer shall receive a CLTA/ALTA Homeowner's Policy of Title Insurance. A title company, at Buyer's request, can provide information about the availability, desirability, coverage, and cost of various title insurance coverages and endorsements. If Buyer desires title coverage other than that required by this paragraph, Buyer shall instruct Escrow Holder in writing and pay any increase in cost.

13. SALE OF BUYER'S PROPERTY:
   A. This Agreement is NOT contingent upon the sale of any property owned by Buyer.
   OR B. ☐ (If checked): The attached addendum (C.A.R. Form COP) regarding the contingency for the sale of property owned by Buyer is incorporated into this Agreement.

14. TIME PERIODS; REMOVAL OF CONTINGENCIES; CANCELLATION RIGHTS: The following time periods may only be extended, altered, modified or changed by mutual written agreement. Any removal of contingencies or cancellation under this paragraph must be in writing (C.A.R. Form CR).
   A. SELLER HAS: 7 (or ☐ _____) Days After Acceptance to deliver to Buyer all reports, disclosures and information for which Seller is responsible under paragraphs 4, 5A and B, 6A, 7B and 12.
   B. (1) BUYER HAS: 17 (or ☐ _____) Days After Acceptance, unless otherwise agreed in writing, to:
      (i) complete all Buyer Investigations; approve all disclosures, reports and other applicable information, which Buyer receives from Seller; and approve all matters affecting the Property (including lead-based paint and lead-based paint hazards as well as other information specified in paragraph 5 and insurability of Buyer and the Property); and
      (ii) return to Seller Signed Copies of Statutory and Lead Disclosures delivered by Seller in accordance with paragraph 5A.
      (2) Within the time specified in 14B(1), Buyer may request that Seller make repairs or take any other action regarding the Property (C.A.R. Form RR). Seller has no obligation to agree to or respond to Buyer's requests.
      (3) By the end of the time specified in 14B(1) (or 2I for loan contingency or 2J for appraisal contingency), Buyer shall, in writing, remove the applicable contingency (C.A.R. Form CR) or cancel this Agreement. However, if **(i)** government-mandated inspections/ reports required as a condition of closing; or **(ii)** Common Interest Disclosures pursuant to paragraph 6B are not made within the time specified in 14A, then Buyer has **5 (or ☐ _____) Days** After receipt of any such items, or the time specified in 14B(1), whichever is later, to remove the applicable contingency or cancel this Agreement in writing.
   C. CONTINUATION OF CONTINGENCY OR CONTRACTUAL OBLIGATION; SELLER RIGHT TO CANCEL:
      (1) Seller right to Cancel; Buyer Contingencies: Seller, after first giving Buyer a Notice to Buyer to Perform (as specified below), may cancel this Agreement in writing and authorize return of Buyer's deposit if, by the time specified in this Agreement, Buyer does not remove in writing the applicable contingency or cancel this Agreement. Once all contingencies have been removed, failure of either Buyer or Seller to close escrow on time may be a breach of this Agreement.
      (2) Continuation of Contingency: Even after the expiration of the time specified in 14B, Buyer retains the right to make requests to Seller, remove in writing the applicable contingency or cancel this Agreement until Seller cancels pursuant to 14C(1). Once Seller receives Buyer's written removal of all contingencies, Seller may not cancel this Agreement pursuant to 14C(1).
      (3) Seller right to Cancel; Buyer Contract Obligations: Seller, after first giving Buyer a Notice to Buyer to Perform (as specified below), may cancel this Agreement in writing and authorize return of Buyer's deposit for any of the following reasons: **(i)** if Buyer fails to deposit funds as required by 2A or 2B; **(ii)** if the funds deposited pursuant to 2A or 2B are not good when deposited; **(iii)** if Buyer fails to provide a letter as required by 2G; **(iv)** if Buyer fails to provide verification as required by 2H or 2L; **(v)** if Seller reasonably disapproves of the verification provided by 2H or 2L; **(vi)** if Buyer fails to return Statutory and Lead Disclosures as required by paragraph 5A(2); or **(vii)** if Buyer fails to sign or initial a separate liquidated damage form for an increased deposit as required by paragraph 16. **Seller is not required to give Buyer a Notice to Perform regarding Close of Escrow.**
      (4) Notice To Buyer To Perform: The Notice to Buyer to Perform (C.A.R. Form NBP) shall: **(i)** be in writing; **(ii)** be signed by Seller; and **(iii)** give Buyer at least **24 (or ☐ _____)** hours (or until the time specified in the applicable paragraph, whichever occurs last) to take the applicable action. A Notice to Buyer to Perform may not be given any earlier than **2 Days** Prior to the expiration of the applicable time for Buyer to remove a contingency or cancel this Agreement or meet a 14C(3) obligation.

Buyer's Initials (_____)(_____)
Seller's Initials (_____)(_____)

RPA-CA REVISED 10/02 (PAGE 4 OF 8)

Reviewed by _____ Date _____

CALIFORNIA RESIDENTIAL PURCHASE AGREEMENT (RPA-CA PAGE 4 OF 8)

Figure 8-1.   Real Estate Purchase Contract and Receipt for Deposit (*continued*)

Property Address: _____   Date: _____

D. EFFECT OF BUYER'S REMOVAL OF CONTINGENCIES : If Buyer removes, in writing, any contingency or cancellation rights, unless otherwise specified in a separate written agreement between Buyer and Seller, Buyer shall conclusively be deemed to have: **(i)** completed all Buyer Investigations, and review of reports and other applicable information and disclosures pertaining to that contingency or cancellation right; **(ii)** elected to proceed with the transaction; and **(iii)** assumed all liability, responsibility and expense for Repairs or corrections pertaining to that contingency or cancellation right, or for inability to obtain financing.

E. EFFECT OF CANCELLATION ON DEPOSITS: If Buyer or Seller gives written notice of cancellation pursuant to rights duly exercised under the terms of this Agreement, Buyer and Seller agree to Sign mutual instructions to cancel the sale and escrow and release deposits to the party entitled to the funds, less fees and costs incurred by that party. Fees and costs may be payable to service providers and vendors for services and products provided during escrow. **Release of funds will require mutual Signed release instructions from Buyer and Seller, judicial decision or arbitration award. A party may be subject to a civil penalty of up to $1,000 for refusal to sign such instructions if no good faith dispute exists as to who is entitled to the deposited funds (Civil Code §1057.3).**

15. FINAL VERIFICATION OF CONDITION: Buyer shall have the right to make a final inspection of the Property within **5 (or** _____**) Days** Prior to Close Of Escrow, NOT AS A CONTINGENCY OF THE SALE, but solely to confirm: **(i)** the Property is maintained pursuant to paragraph 7A; **(ii)** Repairs have been completed as agreed; and **(iii)** Seller has complied with Seller's other obligations under this Agreement.

16. LIQUIDATED DAMAGES: If Buyer fails to complete this purchase because of Buyer's default, Seller shall retain, as liquidated damages, the deposit actually paid. If the Property is a dwelling with no more than four units, one of which Buyer intends to occupy, then the amount retained shall be no more than 3% of the purchase price. Any excess shall be returned to Buyer. Release of funds will require mutual, Signed release instructions from both Buyer and Seller, judicial decision or arbitration award.
BUYER AND SELLER SHALL SIGN A SEPARATE LIQUIDATED DAMAGES PROVISION FOR ANY INCREASED DEPOSIT. (C.A.R. FORM RID)

Buyer's Initials _____/_____	Seller's Initials _____/_____

17. DISPUTE RESOLUTION:

A. MEDIATION: Buyer and Seller agree to mediate any dispute or claim arising between them out of this Agreement, or any resulting transaction, before resorting to arbitration or court action. Paragraphs 17B(2) and (3) below apply whether or not the Arbitration provision is initialed. Mediation fees, if any, shall be divided equally among the parties involved. If, for any dispute or claim to which this paragraph applies, any party commences an action without first attempting to resolve the matter through mediation, or refuses to mediate after a request has been made, then that party shall not be entitled to recover attorney fees, even if they would otherwise be available to that party in any such action. THIS MEDIATION PROVISION APPLIES WHETHER OR NOT THE ARBITRATION PROVISION IS INITIALED.

B. ARBITRATION OF DISPUTES: (1) Buyer and Seller agree that any dispute or claim in Law or equity arising between them out of this Agreement or any resulting transaction, which is not settled through mediation, shall be decided by neutral, binding arbitration, including and subject to paragraphs 17B(2) and (3) below. The arbitrator shall be a retired judge or justice, or an attorney with at least 5 years of residential real estate Law experience, unless the parties mutually agree to a different arbitrator, who shall render an award in accordance with substantive California Law. The parties shall have the right to discovery in accordance with California Code of Civil Procedure §1283.05. In all other respects, the arbitration shall be conducted in accordance with Title 9 of Part III of the California Code of Civil Procedure. Judgment upon the award of the arbitrator(s) may be entered into any court having jurisdiction. Interpretation of this agreement to arbitrate shall be governed by the Federal Arbitration Act.
(2) EXCLUSIONS FROM MEDIATION AND ARBITRATION: The following matters are excluded from mediation and arbitration: (i) a judicial or non-judicial foreclosure or other action or proceeding to enforce a deed of trust, mortgage or installment land sale contract as defined in California Civil Code §2985; (ii) an unlawful detainer action; (iii) the filing or enforcement of a mechanic's lien; and (iv) any matter that is within the jurisdiction of a probate, small claims or bankruptcy court. The filing of a court action to enable the recording of a notice of pending action, for order of attachment, receivership, injunction, or other provisional remedies, shall not constitute a waiver of the mediation and arbitration provisions.
(3) BROKERS: Buyer and Seller agree to mediate and arbitrate disputes or claims involving either or both Brokers, consistent with 17A and B, provided either or both Brokers shall have agreed to such mediation or arbitration prior to, or within a reasonable time after, the dispute or claim is presented to Brokers. Any election by either or both Brokers to participate in mediation or arbitration shall not result in Brokers being deemed parties to the Agreement.
"NOTICE: BY INITIALING IN THE SPACE BELOW YOU ARE AGREEING TO HAVE ANY DISPUTE ARISING OUT OF THE MATTERS INCLUDED IN THE 'ARBITRATION OF DISPUTES' PROVISION DECIDED BY NEUTRAL ARBITRATION AS PROVIDED BY CALIFORNIA LAW AND YOU ARE GIVING UP ANY RIGHTS YOU MIGHT POSSESS TO HAVE THE DISPUTE LITIGATED IN A COURT OR JURY TRIAL. BY INITIALING IN THE SPACE BELOW YOU ARE GIVING UP YOUR JUDICIAL RIGHTS TO DISCOVERY AND APPEAL, UNLESS THOSE RIGHTS ARE SPECIFICALLY INCLUDED IN THE 'ARBITRATION OF DISPUTES' PROVISION. IF YOU REFUSE TO SUBMIT TO ARBITRATION AFTER AGREEING TO THIS PROVISION, YOU MAY BE COMPELLED TO ARBITRATE UNDER THE AUTHORITY OF THE CALIFORNIA CODE OF CIVIL PROCEDURE. YOUR AGREEMENT TO THIS ARBITRATION PROVISION IS VOLUNTARY."
"WE HAVE READ AND UNDERSTAND THE FOREGOING AND AGREE TO SUBMIT DISPUTES ARISING OUT OF THE MATTERS INCLUDED IN THE 'ARBITRATION OF DISPUTES' PROVISION TO NEUTRAL ARBITRATION."

Buyer's Initials _____/_____	Seller's Initials _____/_____

Buyer's Initials (_____)(_____)
Seller's Initials (_____)(_____)

Reviewed by _____ Date _____

CALIFORNIA RESIDENTIAL PURCHASE AGREEMENT (RPA-CA PAGE 5 OF 8)

Figure 8-1.   Real Estate Purchase Contract and Receipt for Deposit (*continued*)

Property Address: _____   Date: _____

18. PRORATIONS OF PROPERTY TAXES AND OTHER ITEMS: Unless otherwise agreed in writing, the following items shall be PAID CURRENT and prorated between Buyer and Seller as of Close Of Escrow: real property taxes and assessments, interest, rents, HOA regular, special, and emergency dues and assessments imposed prior to Close Of Escrow, premiums on insurance assumed by Buyer, payments on bonds and assessments assumed by Buyer, and payments on Mello-Roos and other Special Assessment District bonds and assessments that are now a lien. The following items shall be assumed by Buyer WITHOUT CREDIT toward the purchase price: prorated payments on Mello-Roos and other Special Assessment District bonds and assessments and HOA special assessments that are now a lien but not yet due. Property will be reassessed upon change of ownership. Any supplemental tax bills shall be paid as follows: **(i)** for periods after Close Of Escrow, by Buyer; and **(ii)** for periods prior to Close Of Escrow, by Seller. TAX BILLS ISSUED AFTER CLOSE OF ESCROW SHALL BE HANDLED DIRECTLY BETWEEN BUYER AND SELLER. Prorations shall be made based on a 30-day month.

19. WITHHOLDING TAXES: Seller and Buyer agree to execute any instrument, affidavit, statement or instruction reasonably necessary to comply with federal (FIRPTA) and California withholding Law, if required (C.A.R. Forms AS and AB).

20. MULTIPLE LISTING SERVICE ("MLS"): Brokers are authorized to report to the MLS a pending sale and, upon Close Of Escrow, the terms of this transaction to be published and disseminated to persons and entities authorized to use the information on terms approved by the MLS.

21. EQUAL HOUSING OPPORTUNITY: The Property is sold in compliance with federal, state and local anti-discrimination Laws.

22. ATTORNEY FEES: In any action, proceeding, or arbitration between Buyer and Seller arising out of this Agreement, the prevailing Buyer or Seller shall be entitled to reasonable attorney fees and costs from the non-prevailing Buyer or Seller, except as provided in paragraph 17A.

23. SELECTION OF SERVICE PROVIDERS: If Brokers refer Buyer or Seller to persons, vendors, or service or product providers ("Providers"), Brokers do not guarantee the performance of any Providers. Buyer and Seller may select ANY Providers of their own choosing.

24. TIME OF ESSENCE; ENTIRE CONTRACT; CHANGES: Time is of the essence. All understandings between the parties are incorporated in this Agreement. Its terms are intended by the parties as a final, complete and exclusive expression of their Agreement with respect to its subject matter, and may not be contradicted by evidence of any prior agreement or contemporaneous oral agreement. If any provision of this Agreement is held to be ineffective or invalid, the remaining provisions will nevertheless be given full force and effect. **Neither this Agreement nor any provision in it may be extended, amended, modified, altered or changed, except in writing Signed by Buyer and Seller.**

25. OTHER TERMS AND CONDITIONS, including attached supplements:
  A. ☑ Buyer's Inspection Advisory (C.A.R. Form BIA)
  B. ☐ Purchase Agreement Addendum (C.A.R. Form PAA paragraph numbers: _____)
  C. ☐ Statewide Buyer and Seller Advisory (C.A.R. Form SBSA)
  D. _____
     _____

26. DEFINITIONS: As used in this Agreement:
  A. **"Acceptance"** means the time the offer or final counter offer is accepted in writing by a party and is delivered to and personally received by the other party or that party's authorized agent in accordance with the terms of this offer or a final counter offer.
  B. **"Agreement"** means the terms and conditions of this accepted California Residential Purchase Agreement and any accepted counter offers and addenda.
  C. **"C.A.R. Form"** means the specific form referenced or another comparable form agreed to by the parties.
  D. **"Close Of Escrow"** means the date the grant deed, or other evidence of transfer of title, is recorded. If the scheduled close of escrow falls on a Saturday, Sunday or legal holiday, then close of escrow shall be the next business day after the scheduled close of escrow date.
  E. **"Copy"** means copy by any means including photocopy, NCR, facsimile and electronic.
  F. **"Days"** means calendar days, unless otherwise required by Law.
  G. **"Days After"** means the specified number of calendar days after the occurrence of the event specified, not counting the calendar date on which the specified event occurs, and ending at 11:59PM on the final day.
  H. **"Days Prior"** means the specified number of calendar days before the occurrence of the event specified, not counting the calendar date on which the specified event is scheduled to occur.
  I. **"Electronic Copy"** or **"Electronic Signature"** means, as applicable, an electronic copy or signature complying with California Law. Buyer and Seller agree that electronic means will not be used by either party to modify or alter the content or integrity of this Agreement without the knowledge and consent of the other.
  J. **"Law"** means any law, code, statute, ordinance, regulation, rule or order, which is adopted by a controlling city, county, state or federal legislative, judicial or executive body or agency.
  K. **"Notice to Buyer to Perform"** means a document (C.A.R. Form NBP), which shall be in writing and Signed by Seller and shall give Buyer at least 24 hours **(or as otherwise specified in paragraph 14C(4))** to remove a contingency or perform as applicable.
  L. **"Repairs"** means any repairs (including pest control), alterations, replacements, modifications or retrofitting of the Property provided for under this Agreement.
  M. **"Signed"** means either a handwritten or electronic signature on an original document, Copy or any counterpart.
  N. **Singular and Plural** terms each include the other, when appropriate.

Buyer's Initials (_____)(_____)
Seller's Initials (_____)(_____)

Copyright © 1991-2004, CALIFORNIA ASSOCIATION OF REALTORS®, INC.
RPA-CA REVISED 10/02 (PAGE 6 OF 8)

Reviewed by _____ Date _____

EQUAL HOUSING OPPORTUNITY

CALIFORNIA RESIDENTIAL PURCHASE AGREEMENT (RPA-CA PAGE 6 OF 8)

Figure 8-1.   Real Estate Purchase Contract and Receipt for Deposit (*continued*)

Property Address: _____ Date: _____

27. AGENCY:
    A. DISCLOSURE: Buyer and Seller each acknowledge prior receipt of C.A.R. Form AD "Disclosure Regarding Real Estate Agency Relationships."
    B. POTENTIALLY COMPETING BUYERS AND SELLERS: Buyer and Seller each acknowledge receipt of a disclosure of the possibility of multiple representation by the Broker representing that principal. This disclosure may be part of a listing agreement, buyer-broker agreement or separate document (C.A.R. Form DA). Buyer understands that Broker representing Buyer may also represent other potential buyers, who may consider, make offers on or ultimately acquire the Property. Seller understands that Broker representing Seller may also represent other sellers with competing properties of interest to this Buyer.
    C. CONFIRMATION: The following agency relationships are hereby confirmed for this transaction:
    Listing Agent _____ (Print Firm Name) is the agent
    of (check one): ☐ the Seller exclusively; or ☐ both the Buyer and Seller.
    Selling Agent _____ (Print Firm Name) (if not same as Listing Agent) is the agent of (check one): ☐ the Buyer exclusively; or ☐ the Seller exclusively; or ☐ both the Buyer and Seller. Real Estate Brokers are not parties to the Agreement between Buyer and Seller.

28. JOINT ESCROW INSTRUCTIONS TO ESCROW HOLDER:
    A. The following paragraphs, or applicable portions thereof, of this Agreement constitute the joint escrow instructions of Buyer and Seller to Escrow Holder, which Escrow Holder is to use along with any related counter offers and addenda, and any additional mutual instructions to close the escrow: 1, 2, 4, 12, 13B, 14E, 18, 19, 24, 25B and C, 26, 28, 29, 32A, 33 and paragraph D of the section titled Real Estate Brokers on page 8. If a Copy of the separate compensation agreement(s) provided for in paragraph 29 or 32A, or paragraph D of the section titled Real Estate Brokers on page 8 is deposited with Escrow Holder by Broker, Escrow Holder shall accept such agreement(s) and pay out from Buyer's or Seller's funds, or both, as applicable, the Broker's compensation provided for in such agreement(s). The terms and conditions of this Agreement not set forth in the specified paragraphs are additional matters for the information of Escrow Holder, but about which Escrow Holder need not be concerned. Buyer and Seller will receive Escrow Holder's general provisions directly from Escrow Holder and will execute such provisions upon Escrow Holder's request. To the extent the general provisions are inconsistent or conflict with this Agreement, the general provisions will control as to the duties and obligations of Escrow Holder only. Buyer and Seller will execute additional instructions, documents and forms provided by Escrow Holder that are reasonably necessary to close the escrow.
    B. A Copy of this Agreement shall be delivered to Escrow Holder within **3** business days after Acceptance (or ☐ _____). Buyer and Seller authorize Escrow Holder to accept and rely on Copies and Signatures as defined in this Agreement as originals, to open escrow and for other purposes of escrow. The validity of this Agreement as between Buyer and Seller is not affected by whether or when Escrow Holder Signs this Agreement.
    C. Brokers are a party to the escrow for the sole purpose of compensation pursuant to paragraphs 29, 32A and paragraph D of the section titled Real Estate Brokers on page 8. Buyer and Seller irrevocably assign to Brokers compensation specified in paragraphs 29 and 32A, respectively, and irrevocably instruct Escrow Holder to disburse those funds to Brokers at Close Of Escrow or pursuant to any other mutually executed cancellation agreement. Compensation instructions can be amended or revoked only with the written consent of Brokers. Escrow Holder shall immediately notify Brokers: **(i)** if Buyer's initial or any additional deposit is not made pursuant to this Agreement, or is not good at time of deposit with Escrow Holder; or **(ii)** if Buyer and Seller instruct Escrow Holder to cancel escrow.
    D. A Copy of any amendment that affects any paragraph of this Agreement for which Escrow Holder is responsible shall be delivered to Escrow Holder within **2** business days after mutual execution of the amendment.

29. BROKER COMPENSATION FROM BUYER: If applicable, upon Close Of Escrow, **Buyer** agrees to pay compensation to Broker as specified in a separate written agreement between Buyer and Broker.

30. TERMS AND CONDITIONS OF OFFER:
This is an offer to purchase the Property on the above terms and conditions. All paragraphs with spaces for initials by Buyer and Seller are incorporated in this Agreement only if initialed by all parties. If at least one but not all parties initial, a counter offer is required until agreement is reached. Seller has the right to continue to offer the Property for sale and to accept any other offer at any time prior to notification of Acceptance. Buyer has read and acknowledges receipt of a Copy of the offer and agrees to the above confirmation of agency relationships. If this offer is accepted and Buyer subsequently defaults, Buyer may be responsible for payment of Brokers' compensation. This Agreement and any supplement, addendum or modification, including any Copy, may be Signed in two or more counterparts, all of which shall constitute one and the same writing.

Buyer's Initials (_____)(_____)
Seller's Initials (_____)(_____)

RPA-CA REVISED 10/02 (PAGE 7 OF 8)

Reviewed by _____ Date _____

EQUAL HOUSING OPPORTUNITY

CALIFORNIA RESIDENTIAL PURCHASE AGREEMENT (RPA-CA PAGE 7 OF 8)

Figure 8-1. Real Estate Purchase Contract and Receipt for Deposit (*continued*)

Property Address: _____ Date: _____

31. EXPIRATION OF OFFER: This offer shall be deemed revoked and the deposit shall be returned unless the offer is Signed by Seller and a Copy of the Signed offer is personally received by Buyer, or by _____, who is authorized to receive it by 5:00 PM on the third calendar day after this offer is signed by Buyer (or, if checked, ☐ by _____ (date), at _____ AM/PM).

Date _____ Date _____

BUYER _____ BUYER _____

(Print name) _____ **(Print name)** _____

(Address) _____

32. BROKER COMPENSATION FROM SELLER:
    A. Upon Close Of Escrow, **Seller** agrees to pay compensation to Broker as specified in a separate written agreement between Seller and Broker.
    B. If escrow does not close, compensation is payable as specified in that separate written agreement.
33. ACCEPTANCE OF OFFER: Seller warrants that Seller is the owner of the Property, or has the authority to execute this Agreement. Seller accepts the above offer, agrees to sell the Property on the above terms and conditions, and agrees to the above confirmation of agency relationships. Seller has read and acknowledges receipt of a Copy of this Agreement, and authorizes Broker to deliver a Signed Copy to Buyer.
    ☐ (If checked) **SUBJECT TO ATTACHED COUNTER OFFER, DATED** _____.

Date _____ Date _____

SELLER _____ SELLER _____

(Print name) _____ **(Print name)** _____

(Address) _____

(___/___)   **CONFIRMATION OF ACCEPTANCE:** A Copy of Signed Acceptance was personally received by Buyer or Buyer's authorized
(Initials)   agent on (date) _____ at _____ AM/PM. **A binding Agreement is created when a Copy of Signed Acceptance is personally received by Buyer or Buyer's authorized agent whether or not confirmed in this document.** Completion of this confirmation is not legally required in order to create a binding Agreement; it is solely intended to evidence the date that Confirmation of Acceptance has occurred.

REAL ESTATE BROKERS:
A. **Real Estate Brokers are not parties to the Agreement between Buyer and Seller.**
B. Agency relationships are confirmed as stated in paragraph 27.
C. If specified in paragraph 2A, Agent who submitted the offer for Buyer acknowledges receipt of deposit.
D. **COOPERATING BROKER COMPENSATION:** Listing Broker agrees to pay Cooperating Broker **(Selling Firm)** and Cooperating Broker agrees to accept, out of Listing Broker's proceeds in escrow: **(i)** the amount specified in the MLS, provided Cooperating Broker is a Participant of the MLS in which the Property is offered for sale or a reciprocal MLS; or **(ii)** ☐ (if checked) the amount specified in a separate written agreement (C.A.R. Form CBC) between Listing Broker and Cooperating Broker.

Real Estate Broker (Selling Firm) _____
By _____ Date _____
Address _____ City _____ State _____ Zip _____
Telephone _____ Fax _____ E-mail _____

Real Estate Broker (Listing Firm) _____
By _____ Date _____
Address _____ City _____ State _____ Zip _____
Telephone _____ Fax _____ E-mail _____

ESCROW HOLDER ACKNOWLEDGMENT:
Escrow Holder acknowledges receipt of a Copy of this Agreement, (if checked, ☐ a deposit in the amount of $ _____),
counter offer numbers _____ and _____, and agrees to act as Escrow Holder subject to paragraph 28 of this Agreement, any supplemental escrow instructions and the terms of Escrow Holder's general provisions.

Escrow Holder is advised that the date of Confirmation of Acceptance of the Agreement as between Buyer and Seller is _____

Escrow Holder _____ Escrow # _____
By _____ Date _____
Address _____
Phone/Fax/E-mail _____
Escrow Holder is licensed by the California Department of ☐ Corporations, ☐ Insurance, ☐ Real Estate. License # _____

(___/___)   **REJECTION OF OFFER:** No counter offer is being made. This offer was reviewed and rejected by Seller on
(Seller's Initials)   _____ (Date)

SURE TRAC
The System for Success®

Published by the
California Association of REALTORS®

EQUAL HOUSING OPPORTUNITY

RPA-CA REVISED 10/02 (PAGE 8 OF 8)

Reviewed by _____ Date _____

CALIFORNIA RESIDENTIAL PURCHASE AGREEMENT (RPA-CA PAGE 8 OF 8)

Figure 8-1.   Real Estate Purchase Contract and Receipt for Deposit (*continued*)

If residential property is sold "as is," California law states that such a stipulation applies only to "patent defects"; these are *obvious* defects. The seller, therefore, should disclose any hidden problems of which he or she is aware, as well as state in the purchase contract that there may be other defects that he or she isn't aware of. Note that the rights of buyers of "as is" commercial properties are not nearly so rigorously protected.

Figure 8-1 shows a California *Residential Purchase Agreement and Joint Escrow Instructions* that is commonly used. Readers from other states will note that it is quite long-winded— a total of eight pages. But then it leaves little unsaid; note that adequate provision is made for all parts discussed in the next two sections. *Read this contract carefully!* Note the provisions for various kinds of notices, disclosures, and so forth. They won't all be used in every transaction, but many of these items could show up in examination questions.

A deposit is not necessarily a legal requirement of a purchase contract (the parties' promises to perform in the future usually are sufficient as the required consideration), but it is very common that the buyer put down a cash deposit at the time the purchase contract is agreed upon. It serves as evidence of his good-faith intentions to perform under the contract.

Requirements of a Valid Purchase Contract

Like any contract, a purchase contract must conform to the general requirements of contracts as described in Chapter 6. Within purchase contracts themselves, there are six essentials that also must be observed:

1. The interests and identities of the parties
2. Legal description of the real estate
3. The price and how it is to be paid
4. Contingencies and other terms of the sale
5. Settlement date
6. Signatures of the parties

1. INTERESTS AND IDENTITIES OF THE PARTIES

Who is (are) the buyer(s)? Who is (are) the seller(s)? These are the parties to the contract. The name(s) of the seller(s) should be as they are on their recorded deed for the property. The name(s) of the buyer(s) should be as they will be on the new deed.

2. LEGAL DESCRIPTION OF THE REAL ESTATE

The real estate has to be described; methods of describing real estate were presented in Chapter 7. Simple descriptions (lot and block number descriptions; uncomplicated rectangular survey descriptions) should be written into the contract, but whoever is writing it should take special care to make sure the description is *accurate*.

If the description is complicated, the chances of error are high, especially with metes and bounds descriptions with all their numbers, directions, and so on. A complicated description often won't be written into the contract, but will be *incorporated by reference* to an exhibit; the location of an *existing* accurate version may be attached as an exhibit. Most commonly, the referred document will be one that already is in the public records; the obvious one is the existing recorded deed of the sellers. (If theirs also incorporates a description by reference, then you refer to whatever document that deed refers to.) Because the public records are open to anyone, it is easy to find the referred document and get the description from it. An example of a reference description could be "all that land described in deed from X to Y, dated June 17, 1941, page 133, book 122 of the Coppermine County, California, public records." This tells anyone who reads the contract exactly where to find the description. The description by reference can be used only if the real estate currently being transferred is *exactly the same* as described in the referenced description. If any changes have been made to boundaries of the land, then a new description must be written.

Note that land descriptions don't contain any information about improvements to the land (house, drive, etc.). That's okay; remember, real estate is *land and all permanent attachments to it*, so if you acquire the described land you're also getting whatever is on it.

3. THE PRICE AND HOW IT IS TO BE PAID

The exact price must be described. Usually a buyer doesn't have all the cash to pay for the property and must secure a mortgage loan to be able to complete the purchase. The purchase contract should describe the actual cash amount to be provided by the buyer(s) and the amount of borrowed money that they will provide. If the seller is willing to accept an IOU for all or part of the purchase price (a *purchase money mortgage,* or what we call *seller financing*), that should be included, too. It would be wise for the buyer(s) to insist on including the desired terms of the mortgage loan they need: the maximum interest rate they will pay, the term (15 years, 30 years, etc.) and any other loan terms they consider important—as well as a stipulation that if they can't find the desired loan within a reasonable time, they have the right to cancel the purchase with no penalty.

4. CONTINGENCIES AND OTHER TERMS OF THE SALE

These are the "what-ifs" and other specific requirements that the parties agree to. We described one contingency above: "what if" the buyer(s) can't get the mortgage loan they want? Then they can back out of the deal without losing anything. Many of these are written into standard contract forms: the seller must provide "good and marketable" title; the buyer must apply for a loan within ___ days. What if the buyer wants to move in *before* the settlement date (or the seller wants to stay on for a while *after* the settlement date)? Should rent be paid? How much? There should be an interim lease agreement.

5. SETTLEMENT DATE

A *settlement date* (in some places it's called the *closing date*) must be in a purchase contract. This is the deadline by which the contract requirements should be completed, the deadline by which the buyer must pay for the property and the seller must provide the deed. Without a settlement date, there isn't a requirement that the contract be completed; either party could dawdle all they wanted. If it turns out that the date in the contract is too optimistic (the parties don't have time to complete everything they have to do), the settlement date can always be amended to a later one, with agreement of all parties.

6. SIGNATURES OF THE PARTIES

As with any contract, all parties to it must sign it; this is the legal way of showing that they all agree to it. Signatures to a purchase contract don't have to be notarized.

If you look at a purchase contract provided by a brokerage firm, you also will see a section in which the commission to the broker, and when it is to be paid, is described. (Some generic forms from stationery stores include this part, too.) This section actually is a separate contract between seller(s) and broker. It isn't really necessary because their listing contract already obligates the seller to pay the broker, but most brokerage firms include it in their purchase contract forms anyway.

Parts of a Real Estate Purchase Contract _____

A real estate purchase contract will normally contain certain parts. These parts and their purposes are as follows:

Part	*Purpose*
Parties	States the names of the seller (vendor) and buyer (vendee).
Property description	Provides a legal or an adequate description of the subject property and the fixtures included.
Sales price	States the amount to be paid at closing in cash and from the proceeds of financing.

Part	*Purpose*
Financing conditions	Purchaser stipulates acceptable conditions of financing, including the type of loan, loan-to-value ratio, interest rate, monthly payments.
Earnest money	Notes the amount of the good-faith deposit presented to the seller or his agent. Also called *hand money* or *escrow money*.
Type of deed	Describes the type of deed to be given at closing.
Title evidence	Describes the type of evidence to be considered satisfactory assurance that the seller can give title.
Title approval	Describes the rights of purchaser and seller in the event that the purchaser objects to a flaw in the title.
Property condition	States whatever changes (if any) are required to be made to the property.
Prorations	Calls for the proration of prepaid or unpaid taxes, insurance, rents, etc., between buyer and seller.
Loss	Affixes responsibility for casualty losses until closing.
Possession	Establishes a date for possession.
Closing	Establishes a date for closing.
Broker	Acknowledges the existence of a real estate broker, specifies the commission rate, and identifies the principal who will pay the commission.
Default	Describes the obligations of parties in the event one fails to perform.
Contingencies	Describes any "what if" provisions of the contract, and the conditions under which the parties may cancel the contract without penalty.
Miscellaneous provisions	States whatever other provisions buyer and seller agree upon.
Signatures	Principals, brokers, escrow agents.

Negotiation (Offer, Counteroffer, Acceptance)

Purchase contracts (or any other kind) don't just pop out of the air, ready to go. They are the result of *negotiation.* Negotiation of a purchase contract for real estate usually begins with an *offer* from an interested potential buyer. (The person making the offer is the *offeror;* the person receiving it is the *offeree.*) The buyer probably knows what the seller wants (price, terms, etc.), but very often the buyer won't agree to everything, so the offer will be somewhat different from the seller's desires. The seller will consider the buyer's offer and can either accept it, turn it down, or turn it down and make a *counteroffer* back to the buyer. Now it's the buyer's turn; she may accept the seller's offer, turn it down, or make another offer back to the seller. This can go on for several cycles; eventually either the parties will agree on a final deal, and a contract will be made, or they may decide that it's hopeless and will stop negotiating and go their own ways.

A key element of the negotiation process is that *no one involved is obligated to anyone until a contract exists.* No one is *required* to negotiate; no one is *required* to keep on negotiating once the process has begun. Anyone involved may terminate the process simply by refusing to go on with it. The law lays down some simple rules for the negotiation process.

Once an offer is *accepted,* it isn't an offer any more: it has become a *contract.* Once a contract exists, the negotiation process ends; because the parties have finally come to an agreement, there's nothing more to discuss. If a party later on decides that he wants some more conditions, it's too late. The contract already exists, and he must abide by it. Of course, he can always approach the other parties and ask to amend the existing contract, but the other parties have no obligation to reopen negotiations.

During negotiation, only one offer can exist at any given moment in time. If A makes an offer to buy B's real estate, an offer exists. It is up to B to decide what to do.

1. She can accept A's offer, and thus create a contract.
2. She can reject A's offer, in which case no offer exists any more.
3. She can make a counteroffer back to A, in which case A's offer doesn't exist any more. Now there is *another* offer on the table, from B to A. Making a counteroffer therefore means that two things are being done simultaneously: the offer that was "on the table" is *rejected,* and a new offer is made "the other way."

There's one other thing going on. An offer may be withdrawn *at any time, so long as it has not been accepted.* While B is pondering A's offer, A can, at any time, notify B that the offer is withdrawn. If that happens, that's the end of the offer: it no longer exists. But if, before then, B notifies A that she accepts the offer, the offer doesn't exist any more *because it has become a contract.* You can't "withdraw" a contract.

If an offer is rejected, it doesn't exist any more and can't be "resurrected" later on. Consider the following conversation:

Jane: Mike, I'll give you $150,000 for your house.
Mike: No, I need at least $175,000.
Jane: Forget it. That's too much.
Mike: Okay, I'll take the $150,000.

Is there now a contract for Jane to buy Mike's house for $150,000?

NO! Let's take it step by step. First, Jane made an offer to buy Mike's house for $150,000. Mike then counteroffered the house to Jane for $175,000. By doing this, he *rejected* Jane's offer for $150,000 and then replaced her offer to him with *his offer to her* for $175,000. Jane then rejected Mike's offer to her. But she didn't make any other offer back to him. At that point, there was no offer on the table at all. When Mike said he'd "take the $150,000," no contract came into being because there wasn't an offer from Jane any more for him to accept. He had already *rejected* Jane's original offer, so it didn't exist any more. His statement "Okay, I'll take the $150,000" actually creates a *new* offer *from him to Jane* to sell her the house for $150,000. She doesn't have to accept it. If she does, then Mike and Jane will have a contract. If she says something like "I've changed my mind, I don't want your house," then she has, in turn, rejected Mike's new offer, and there's no offer on the table.

This is a very important aspect of the law of offer and acceptance: *until a contract exists, no one has any obligation to anyone else!* If you look at a preprinted purchase contract, you will probably see language on the order of "this offer will remain open until _____." You're supposed to put a date, or a time of day and a date, in the blank space. What does this mean? Must whoever made the offer sit and wait until the deadline to see if the other party accepts the offer? Is that other party guaranteed that length of time to ponder the offer? *NO!* Because this is an offer, no one is obligated to anything. The offeror can withdraw the offer at any time until the offeree accepts it. The only way this language can be interpreted is to mean that if the deadline arrives and the offeree hasn't responded to the offer, then the offer will automatically be *withdrawn* at that time. In effect, this provision is putting a limited lifetime on the offer, and nothing more.

Many real estate agents are apparently unaware of this part of the law. Both your authors have heard of situations where someone wanted to withdraw an offer (maybe he got a better one in the meantime) and the licensee told him, "You can't do that; you've agreed to leave the offer open until that time." This is wrong and could expose the licensee to a lawsuit.

If an offer is accepted by the offeree, it doesn't become a contract until the offeror (or the offeror's agent) has been *notified* of the acceptance. The law says you can't be held to a contract if you don't know that it exists. Because notifying an agent is the same as notifying that agent's principal, if a buyer tells the listing agent that he or she will accept a counteroffer from the seller, the contract exists at that point. Or, if a buyer's agent is notified that the seller accepts an offer from the buyer, there is a contract. (In either case, a professional licensee will immediately call his or her principals to notify them of the acceptance.) Notification doesn't have to be in writing; it can be oral, such as by phone.

Finally, it is common practice, especially in brokered transactions, for offers between potential buyer and seller to be made using purchase contract forms. Typically, a buyer wants to make an offer on a home. The buyer (or agent involved) will fill out a purchase contract form, with all the terms that the buyer wants written into it. The buyer signs it, and it is submitted to the seller. If the seller accepts the offer, he signs it, and a contract exists once the buyer is notified. The seller presumably is happy because he got an offer he was willing to accept. The buyer is happy because the seller has agreed to all the terms, conditions, price, and so on, that she wanted. Most of the time, though, the offeree does *not* agree with all the terms of the offer. If a counteroffer is made, it is common practice to cross out the parts the offeree doesn't like, write the desired changes in the margins of the form, and add anything else that is desired the same way. The offeree initials or signs by all those changes, signs the document, and submits it to the offeror. (Because the counteroffer rejects the original offer, the original offeror and offeree now have changed places.) In California, however, it is more common to use a *Counteroffer* form, such as the one in Figure 8-4. Note that the form provides only generic (blank) space for "changes"; this means that the changes in the counteroffer must be described very specifically and in detail!

One may also prepare a counteroffer on a new purchase contract form. However, in California this entails preparing an eight-page form, so it isn't done that way unless the counteroffer has so many changes that the Counteroffer form doesn't have enough room to describe them in the necessary detail.

Transfer Disclosure Form

Figure 8-5 illustrates a *transfer disclosure form*. This disclosure must be made to the buyer before the closing of the sale. Note, also, that the broker cannot fill out Part II (Seller's Information). That *must* be done by the seller. Look this illustration over carefully, as you have been warned to do for contracts and forms introduced earlier in this book.

DISCLOSURES THAT MUST BE MADE

California offers a 53-page brochure, *Disclosure in Real Property Transactions,* at its Web site (www.dre.ca.gov/disclosures.htm). This booklet describes most of the disclosures to be made in a resale of property. There are disclosures concerning the property and its characteristics that must be made (1) by the seller and/or real estate agent, (2) by real estate agents in the transfer of residential real estate, (3) in financing property, and (4) related to subdivisions and for the transfer of a business opportunity.

The *Easton v. Strassburger* case confirms that both the seller and the agent must make full disclosure of material facts to a potential buyer. A variety of disclosures are required of agents and sellers, except in certain exempt transactions. Some prominent areas of disclosure for residential property are

- Age, condition, and any defects or malfunctions of the structural components and/or plumbing, electrical, heating, or other mechanical systems
- Easements, common driveways, or fences
- Room additions, structural alterations, repairs, replacements, or other changes, especially those made without required building permits
- Flood, drainage, settling, or soil problems on or near the property
- Zoning violations, such as nonconforming uses or insufficient setbacks
- Homeowners' association obligations and deed restrictions or "common area" problems
- Citations against the property or lawsuits against the owner or affecting the property
- Neighborhood noise or nuisance problems
- Location of the property within a known earthquake zone

The required disclosure must be delivered to the prospective buyer as soon as practicable before transfer of title, or before the execution of the contract in the case of a lease option, sales contract, or ground lease coupled with improvements. If any disclosure or amended disclosure is delivered after execution of the offer by the buyer, the buyer has three days after delivery in person or five days after delivery by deposit in the United States mail to terminate the offer or agreement to purchase by delivering a written notice of termination to the seller or to the seller's agent.

CALIFORNIA
ASSOCIATION
OF REALTORS®

BUYER'S INSPECTION ADVISORY
(C.A.R. Form BIA, Revised 10/02)

Property Address: _____ ("Property").

A. IMPORTANCE OF PROPERTY INVESTIGATION: The physical condition of the land and improvements being purchased is not guaranteed by either Seller or Brokers. For this reason, you should conduct thorough investigations of the Property personally and with professionals who should provide written reports of their investigations. A general physical inspection typically does not cover all aspects of the Property nor items affecting the Property that are not physically located on the Property. If the professionals recommend further investigations, including a recommendation by a pest control operator to inspect inaccessible areas of the Property, you should contact qualified experts to conduct such additional investigations.

B. BUYER RIGHTS AND DUTIES: You have an affirmative duty to exercise reasonable care to protect yourself, including discovery of the legal, practical and technical implications of disclosed facts, and the investigation and verification of information and facts that you know or that are within your diligent attention and observation. The purchase agreement gives you the right to investigate the Property. If you exercise this right, and you should, you must do so in accordance with the terms of that agreement. This is the best way for you to protect yourself. It is extremely important for you to read all written reports provided by professionals and to discuss the results of inspections with the professional who conducted the inspection. You have the right to request that Seller make repairs, corrections or take other action based upon items discovered in your investigations or disclosed by Seller. If Seller is unwilling or unable to satisfy your requests, or you do not want to purchase the Property in its disclosed and discovered condition, you have the right to cancel the agreement if you act within specific time periods. If you do not cancel the agreement in a timely and proper manner, you may be in breach of contract.

C. SELLER RIGHTS AND DUTIES: Seller is required to disclose to you material facts known to him/her that affect the value or desirability of the Property. However, Seller may not be aware of some Property defects or conditions. Seller does not have an obligation to inspect the Property for your benefit nor is Seller obligated to repair, correct or otherwise cure known defects that are disclosed to you or previously unknown defects that are discovered by you or your inspectors during escrow. The purchase agreement obligates Seller to make the Property available to you for investigations.

D. BROKER OBLIGATIONS: Brokers do not have expertise in all areas and therefore cannot advise you on many items, such as soil stability, geologic or environmental conditions, hazardous or illegal controlled substances, structural conditions of the foundation or other improvements, or the condition of the roof, plumbing, heating, air conditioning, electrical, sewer, septic, waste disposal, or other system. The only way to accurately determine the condition of the Property is through an inspection by an appropriate professional selected by you. If Broker gives you referrals to such professionals, Broker does not guarantee their performance. You may select any professional of your choosing. In sales involving residential dwellings with no more than four units, Brokers have a duty to make a diligent visual inspection of the accessible areas of the Property and to disclose the results of that inspection. However, as some Property defects or conditions may not be discoverable from a visual inspection, it is possible Brokers are not aware of them. If you have entered into a written agreement with a Broker, the specific terms of that agreement will determine the nature and extent of that Broker's duty to you. **YOU ARE STRONGLY ADVISED TO INVESTIGATE THE CONDITION AND SUITABILITY OF ALL ASPECTS OF THE PROPERTY. IF YOU DO NOT DO SO, YOU ARE ACTING AGAINST THE ADVICE OF BROKERS.**

E. YOU ARE ADVISED TO CONDUCT INVESTIGATIONS OF THE ENTIRE PROPERTY, INCLUDING, BUT NOT LIMITED TO THE FOLLOWING:
1. **GENERAL CONDITION OF THE PROPERTY, ITS SYSTEMS AND COMPONENTS:** Foundation, roof, plumbing, heating, air conditioning, electrical, mechanical, security, pool/spa, other structural and non-structural systems and components, fixtures, built-in appliances, any personal property included in the sale, and energy efficiency of the Property. (Structural engineers are best suited to determine possible design or construction defects, and whether improvements are structurally sound.)
2. **SQUARE FOOTAGE, AGE, BOUNDARIES:** Square footage, room dimensions, lot size, age of improvements and boundaries. Any numerical statements regarding these items are APPROXIMATIONS ONLY and have not been verified by Seller and cannot be verified by Brokers. Fences, hedges, walls, retaining walls and other natural or constructed barriers or markers do not necessarily identify true Property boundaries. (Professionals such as appraisers, architects, surveyors and civil engineers are best suited to determine square footage, dimensions and boundaries of the Property.)
3. **WOOD DESTROYING PESTS:** Presence of, or conditions likely to lead to the presence of wood destroying pests and organisms and other infestation or infection. Inspection reports covering these items can be separated into two sections: Section 1 identifies areas where infestation or infection is evident. Section 2 identifies areas where there are conditions likely to lead to infestation or infection. A registered structural pest control company is best suited to perform these inspections.
4. **SOIL STABILITY:** Existence of fill or compacted soil, expansive or contracting soil, susceptibility to slippage, settling or movement, and the adequacy of drainage. (Geotechnical engineers are best suited to determine such conditions, causes and remedies.)

BIA REVISED 10/02 (PAGE 1 OF 2)

Buyer's Initials (_____)(_____)
Seller's Initials (_____)(_____)

| Reviewed by _____ Date _____ |

EQUAL HOUSING OPPORTUNITY

MASTER COPY

BUYER'S INSPECTION ADVISORY (BIA PAGE 1 OF 2)

Figure 8-2. Buyer's Inspection Advisory

Property Address: _____   Date: _____

5. **ROOF:** Present condition, age, leaks, and remaining useful life. (Roofing contractors are best suited to determine these conditions.)
6. **POOL/SPA:** Cracks, leaks or operational problems. (Pool contractors are best suited to determine these conditions.)
7. **WASTE DISPOSAL:** Type, size, adequacy, capacity and condition of sewer and septic systems and components, connection to sewer, and applicable fees.
8. **WATER AND UTILITIES; WELL SYSTEMS AND COMPONENTS:** Water and utility availability, use restrictions and costs. Water quality, adequacy, condition, and performance of well systems and components.
9. **ENVIRONMENTAL HAZARDS:** Potential environmental hazards, including, but not limited to, asbestos, lead-based paint and other lead contamination, radon, methane, other gases, fuel oil or chemical storage tanks, contaminated soil or water, hazardous waste, waste disposal sites, electromagnetic fields, nuclear sources, and other substances, materials, products, or conditions (including mold (airborne, toxic or otherwise), fungus or similar contaminants). (For more in formation on these items, you may consult an appropriate professional or read the booklets "Environmental Hazards: A Guide for Homeowners, Buyers, Landlords and Tenants," "Protect Your Family From Lead in Your Home" or both.)
10. **EARTHQUAKES AND FLOODING:** Susceptibility of the Property to earthquake/seismic hazards and propensity of the Property to flood. (A Geologist or Geotechnical Engineer is best suited to provide information on these conditions.)
11. **FIRE, HAZARD AND OTHER INSURANCE:** The availability and cost of necessary or desired insurance may vary. The location of the Property in a seismic, flood or fire hazard zone, and other conditions, such as the age of the Property and the claims history of the Property and Buyer, may affect the availability and need for certain types of insurance. Buyer should explore insurance options early as this information may affect other decisions, including the removal of loan and inspection contingencies. (An insurance agent is best suited to provide information on these conditions.)
12. **BUILDING PERMITS, ZONING AND GOVERNMENTAL REQUIREMENTS:** Permits, inspections, certificates, zoning, other governmental limitations, restrictions, and requirements affecting the current or future use of the Property, its development or size. (Such information is available from appropriate governmental agencies and private information providers. Brokers are not qualified to review or interpret any such information.)
13. **RENTAL PROPERTY RESTRICTIONS:** Some cities and counties impose restrictions that limit the amount of rent that can be charged, the maximum number of occupants; and the right of a landlord to terminate a tenancy. Deadbolt or other locks and security systems for doors and windows, including window bars, should be examined to determine whether they satisfy legal requirements. (Government agencies can provide information about these restrictions and other requirements.)
14. **SECURITY AND SAFETY:** State and local Law may require the installation of barriers, access alarms, self-latching mechanisms and/or other measures to decrease the risk to children and other persons of existing swimming pools and hot tubs, as well as various fire safety and other measures concerning other features of the Property. Compliance requirements differ from city to city and county to county. Unless specifically agreed, the Property may not be in compliance with these requirements. (Local government agencies can provide information about these restrictions and other requirements.)
15. **NEIGHBORHOOD, AREA, SUBDIVISION CONDITIONS; PERSONAL FACTORS:** Neighborhood or area conditions, including schools, proximity and adequacy of law enforcement, crime statistics, the proximity of registered felons or offenders, fire protection, other government services, availability, adequacy and cost of any speed-wired, wireless internet connections or other telecommunications or other technology services and installations, proximity to commercial, industrial or agricultural activities, existing and proposed transportation, construction and development that may affect noise, view, or traffic, airport noise, noise or odor from any source, wild and domestic animals, other nuisances, hazards, or circumstances, protected species, wetland properties, botanical diseases, historic or other governmentally protected sites or improvements, cemeteries, facilities and condition of common areas of common interest subdivisions, and possible lack of compliance with any governing documents or Homeowners' Association requirements, conditions and influences of significance to certain cultures and/or religions, and personal needs, requirements and preferences of Buyer.

> Buyer and Seller acknowledge and agree that Broker: **(i)** Does not decide what price Buyer should pay or Seller should accept; **(ii)** Does not guarantee the condition of the Property; **(iii)** Does not guarantee the performance, adequacy or completeness of inspections, services, products or repairs provided or made by Seller or others; **(iv)** Does not have an obligation to conduct an inspection of common areas or areas off the site of the Property; **(v)** Shall not be responsible for identifying defects on the Property, in common areas, or offsite unless such defects are visually observable by an inspection of reasonably accessible areas of the Property or are known to Broker; **(vi)** Shall not be responsible for inspecting public records or permits concerning the title or use of Property; **(vii)** Shall not be responsible for identifying the location of boundary lines or other items affecting title; **(viii)** Shall not be responsible for verifying square footage, representations of others or information contained in Investigation reports, Multiple Listing Service, advertisements, flyers or other promotional material; **(ix)** Shall not be responsible for providing legal or tax advice regarding any aspect of a transaction entered into by Buyer or Seller; and **(x)** Shall not be responsible for providing other advice or information that exceeds the knowledge, education and experience required to perform real estate licensed activity. Buyer and Seller agree to seek legal, tax, insurance, title and other desired assistance from appropriate professionals.

By signing below, Buyer and Seller each acknowledge that they have read, understand, accept and have received a Copy of this Advisory. Buyer is encouraged to read it carefully.

_____   _____   _____   _____
Buyer Signature   Date   Buyer Signature   Date

_____   _____   _____   _____
Seller Signature   Date   Seller Signature   Date

Published and Distributed by:
REAL ESTATE BUSINESS SERVICES, INC.
a subsidiary of the California Association of REALTORS®
525 South Virgil Avenue, Los Angeles, California 90020

Reviewed by _____ Date _____

BIA REVISED 10/02 (PAGE 2 OF 2)

MASTER COPY

BUYER'S INSPECTION ADVISORY (BIA PAGE 2 OF 2)

Figure 8-2.   Buyer's Inspection Advisory (*continued*)

FOR YOUR PROTECTION: GET A HOME INSPECTION
(C.A.R. Form HID, Revised 2/04)

Name of Buyer(s) _____

Property Address _____

WHY A BUYER NEEDS A HOME INSPECTION

A home inspection gives the buyer more detailed information about the overall condition of the home prior to purchase. In a home inspection, a qualified inspector takes an in-depth, unbiased look at your potential new home to:
- evaluate the physical condition: structure, construction, and mechanical systems
- identify items that need to be repaired or replaced
- estimate the remaining useful life of the major systems, equipment, structure, and finishes

APPRAISALS ARE DIFFERENT FROM HOME INSPECTIONS

An appraisal is different from a home inspection. Appraisals are for lenders; home inspections are for buyers. An appraisal is required for three reasons:
- to estimate the market value of a house
- to make sure that the house meets FHA minimum property standards/requirements
- to make sure that the house is marketable

FHA DOES NOT GUARANTEE THE VALUE OR CONDITION OF YOUR POTENTIAL NEW HOME

If you find problems with your new home after closing, FHA can not give or lend you money for repairs, and FHA can not buy the home back from you.

RADON GAS TESTING

The United States Environmental Protection Agency and the Surgeon General of the United States have recommended that all houses should be tested for radon. For more information on radon testing, call the National Radon Information Line at 1-800-SOS-Radon (1-800-644-6999). As with a home inspection, if you decide to test for radon, you may do so before signing your contract, or you may do so after signing the contract as long as your contract states the sale of the home depends on your satisfaction with the results of the radon test.

BE AN INFORMED BUYER

It is your responsibility to be an informed buyer. Be sure that what you buy is satisfactory in every respect. You have the right to carefully examine your potential new home with a qualified home inspector. You may arrange to do so before signing your contract, or may do so after signing the contract as long as your contract states that the sale of the home depends on the inspection.

I/we understand the importance of getting an independent home inspection. I/we have considered this before signing a contract with the seller for a home. Furthermore, I/we have carefully read this notice and fully understand that FHA will not perform a home inspection nor guarantee the price or condition of the property.

☐ I/We choose to have a home inspection performed.
☐ I/We choose **not** to have a home inspection performed.

Signature _____   Date _____

Signature _____   Date _____

Published and Distributed by:
REAL ESTATE BUSINESS SERVICES, INC.
a subsidiary of the California Association of REALTORS®
525 South Virgil Avenue, Los Angeles, California 90020

SURE TRAC
The System for Success®

HID REVISED 2/04 (PAGE 1 OF 1)   Print Date

Reviewed by _____ Date _____

EQUAL HOUSING OPPORTUNITY

FOR YOUR PROTECTION: GET A HOME INSPECTION   (HID PAGE 1 OF 1)

Figure 8-3.   For Your Protection: Get a Home Inspection

CALIFORNIA
ASSOCIATION
OF REALTORS®

COUNTER OFFER No. _____
For use by Seller or Buyer. May be used for Multiple Counter Offer.
(C.A.R. Form CO, Revised 10/04)

Date _____, at _____, California.
This is a counter offer to the: ☐ California Residential Purchase Agreement, ☐ Counter Offer, or ☐ Other _____ ("Offer"),
dated _____, on property known as _____ ("Property"),
between _____ ("Buyer") and _____ ("Seller").

1. **TERMS:** The terms and conditions of the above referenced document are **accepted subject to the following:**
    A. Paragraphs in the Offer that require initials by all parties, but are not initialed by all parties, are excluded from the final agreement unless specifically referenced for inclusion in paragraph 1C of this or another Counter Offer.
    B. Unless otherwise agreed in writing, down payment and loan amount(s) will be adjusted in the same proportion as in the original Offer.
    C. _____
        _____
        _____
        _____
        _____
        _____
        _____

    D. The following attached supplements are incorporated into this Counter Offer: ☐ Addendum No. _____
        ☐ _____ ☐ _____

2. **RIGHT TO ACCEPT OTHER OFFERS:** Seller has the right to continue to offer the Property for sale or for other transaction, and to accept any other offer at any time prior to notification of acceptance, as described in paragraph 3. If this is a Seller Counter Offer, Seller's acceptance of another offer prior to Buyer's acceptance and communication of notification of this Counter Offer, shall revoke this Counter Offer.

3. **EXPIRATION:** This Counter Offer shall be deemed revoked and the deposits, if any, shall be returned unless this Counter Offer is signed by the Buyer or Seller to whom it is sent and a Copy of the signed Counter Offer is personally received by the person making this Counter Offer or _____
    who is authorized to receive it, by 5:00PM on the third day after this Counter Offer is made or, (if checked)
    by ☐ _____ (date), at _____ AM/PM. This Counter Offer may be executed in counterparts.

4. ☐ **(If checked:) MULTIPLE COUNTER OFFER:** Seller is making a Counter Offer(s) to another prospective buyer(s) on terms that may or may not be the same as in this Counter Offer. Acceptance of this Counter Offer by Buyer shall **not** be binding unless and until it is subsequently re-Signed by Seller in paragraph 7 below and a Copy of the Counter Offer Signed in paragraph 7 is personally received by Buyer or by _____, who is authorized to receive it, by 5:00 PM on the third Day After this Counter Offer is made or, (if checked) by ☐ _____ (date), at _____ AM/PM. Prior to the completion of all of these events, Buyer and Seller shall have no duties or obligations for the purchase or sale of the Property.

5. **OFFER: BUYER OR SELLER MAKES THIS COUNTER OFFER ON THE TERMS ABOVE AND ACKNOWLEDGES RECEIPT OF A COPY.**
    _____ Date _____
    _____ Date _____

6. **ACCEPTANCE: I/WE** accept the above Counter Offer (If checked ☐ **SUBJECT TO THE ATTACHED COUNTER OFFER**) and acknowledge receipt of a Copy.
    _____ Date _____ Time _____ AM/PM
    _____ Date _____ Time _____ AM/PM

7. **MULTIPLE COUNTER OFFER SIGNATURE LINE:** By signing below, Seller accepts this Multiple Counter Offer. **NOTE TO SELLER: Do NOT sign in this box until after Buyer signs in paragraph 6. (Paragraph 7 applies only if paragraph 4 is checked.)**
    _____ Date _____ Time _____ AM/PM
    _____ Date _____ Time _____ AM/PM

8. (_____/_____) (Initials) **Confirmation of Acceptance:** A Copy of Signed Acceptance was personally received by the maker of the _____ Counter Offer, or that person's authorized agent as specified in paragraph 3 (or, if this is a Multiple Counter Offer, the Buyer or Buyer's authorized agent as specified in paragraph 4) on (date) _____, at _____ AM/PM. **A binding Agreement is created when a Copy of Signed Acceptance is personally received by the the maker of the Counter Offer, or that person's authorized agent (or, if this is a Multiple Counter Offer, the Buyer or Buyer's authorized agent) whether or not confirmed in this document. Completion of this confirmation is not legally required in order to create a binding Agreement; it is solely intended to evidence the date that Confirmation of Acceptance has occurred.**

SURE TRAC
The System for Success®

Published and Distributed by:
REAL ESTATE BUSINESS SERVICES, INC.
a subsidiary of the California Association of REALTORS®
525 South Virgil Avenue, Los Angeles, California 90020

Reviewed by _____ Date _____

EQUAL HOUSING
OPPORTUNITY

CO REVISED 10/04 (PAGE 1 OF 1)   Print Date

COUNTER OFFER (CO PAGE 1 OF 1)

Figure 8-4.   Counteroffer Form

The obligation to prepare and deliver disclosures is imposed upon the seller and the seller's agent and any agent acting in cooperation with such agent. If more than one real estate agent is involved in the transaction, the agent obtaining the offer (unless otherwise instructed by the seller) is required to deliver the disclosures to the prospective buyer. If the disclosure is based on a report or opinion of an expert, such as a contractor or structural pest control operator, the seller and the agent may be protected from liability for any error as to the item covered by the report or opinion.

Mello-Roos Disclosure

The Mello-Roos Community Facilities Act of 1982 authorizes the formation of community facilities districts, the issuance of bonds, and the levying of special taxes thereunder to finance designated public facilities and services. Civil Code Section 1102.6b requires that a seller of a property consisting of one to four dwelling units subject to the lien of a Mello-Roos community facilities district make a good-faith effort to obtain from the district a disclosure notice concerning the special tax and give the notice to a prospective buyer. The same exemptions apply as for delivery of a Real Property Disclosure Statement.

Disclosure Regarding Lead-Based Paint Hazards

Many housing units in California still contain lead-based paint, which was banned for residential use in 1978. Lead-based paint can peel, chip, and deteriorate into contaminated dust, thus becoming a lead-based paint hazard. A child's ingestion of the lead-laced chips or dust may result in learning disabilities, delayed development, or behavior disorders.

The federal Real Estate Disclosure and Notification Rule requires that owners of "residential dwellings" built before 1978 disclose to their agents and to prospective buyers or lessees/renters the presence of lead-based paint and/or lead-based paint hazards and any known information and reports about lead-based paint and lead-based paint hazards (location and condition of the painted surfaces, etc.).

Disclosure of Geological Hazards and Earthquake Fault Zones

Pursuant to the Alquist-Priolo Earthquake Fault Zoning Act, the State Geologist is in the process of identifying areas of the state susceptible to "fault creep" and delineating these areas on maps prepared by the State Division of Mines and Geology.

A seller of real property situated in an earthquake fault zone, or the agent of the seller and any agent acting in cooperation with such agent, must disclose to the buyer that the property is or may be situated in an earthquake fault zone. This disclosure must be made on the Natural Hazard Zone Disclosure Statement.

In addition, the Seismic Safety Commission has developed a *Homeowner's Guide to Earthquake Safety* for distribution to real estate licensees and the general public. The guide includes information on geologic and seismic hazards for all areas, explanations of related structural and nonstructural hazards, recommendations for mitigating the hazards of an earthquake, and a statement that safety or damage prevention cannot be guaranteed with respect to a major earthquake, and that only precautions such as retrofitting can be undertaken to reduce that risk. The Seismic Safety Commission has also developed a *Commercial Property Owner's Guide to Earthquake Safety*.

Delivery of a booklet is required in the following transactions:

1. Transfer of any real property improved with a residential dwelling built prior to January 1, 1960, and consisting of one to four units any of which are of conventional light-frame construction (*Homeowner's Guide*).
2. Transfer of any masonry building with wood-frame floors or roofs built before January 1, 1975 (if residential, both guides; if commercial property, only the *Commercial Guide*).

Buyer Inspections

Buyers are encouraged to inspect the property. Figure 8-2 is called Buyer's Inspection Advisory, and Figure 8-3 is For Your Protection: Get a Home Inspection. These remind the buyer that they need to do an inspection, in addition to disclosusres provided to them.

REAL ESTATE TRANSFER DISCLOSURE STATEMENT
(CALIFORNIA CIVIL CODE §1102, ET SEQ.)
(C.A.R. Form TDS, Revised 10/03)

THIS DISCLOSURE STATEMENT CONCERNS THE REAL PROPERTY SITUATED IN THE CITY OF _____
_____, COUNTY OF _____, STATE OF CALIFORNIA,
DESCRIBED AS _____.

THIS STATEMENT IS A DISCLOSURE OF THE CONDITION OF THE ABOVE DESCRIBED PROPERTY IN COMPLIANCE WITH SECTION 1102 OF THE CIVIL CODE AS OF (date) _____. IT IS NOT A WARRANTY OF ANY KIND BY THE SELLER(S) OR ANY AGENT(S) REPRESENTING ANY PRINCIPAL(S) IN THIS TRANSACTION, AND IS NOT A SUBSTITUTE FOR ANY INSPECTIONS OR WARRANTIES THE PRINCIPAL(S) MAY WISH TO OBTAIN.

I. COORDINATION WITH OTHER DISCLOSURE FORMS

This Real Estate Transfer Disclosure Statement is made pursuant to Section 1102 of the Civil Code. Other statutes require disclosures, depending upon the details of the particular real estate transaction (for example: special study zone and purchase-money liens on residential property).

Substituted Disclosures: The following disclosures and other disclosures required by law, including the Natural Hazard Disclosure Report/Statement that may include airport annoyances, earthquake, fire, flood, or special assessment information, have or will be made in connection with this real estate transfer, and are intended to satisfy the disclosure obligations on this form, where the subject matter is the same:

☐ Inspection reports completed pursuant to the contract of sale or receipt for deposit.
☐ Additional inspection reports or disclosures: _____
_____

II. SELLER'S INFORMATION

The Seller discloses the following information with the knowledge that even though this is not a warranty, prospective Buyers may rely on this information in deciding whether and on what terms to purchase the subject property. Seller hereby authorizes any agent(s) representing any principal(s) in this transaction to provide a copy of this statement to any person or entity in connection with any actual or anticipated sale of the property.

THE FOLLOWING ARE REPRESENTATIONS MADE BY THE SELLER(S) AND ARE NOT THE REPRESENTATIONS OF THE AGENT(S), IF ANY. THIS INFORMATION IS A DISCLOSURE AND IS NOT INTENDED TO BE PART OF ANY CONTRACT BETWEEN THE BUYER AND SELLER.

Seller ☐ is ☐ is not occupying the property.

A. The subject property has the items checked below (read across):

☐ Range	☐ Oven	☐ Microwave
☐ Dishwasher	☐ Trash Compactor	☐ Garbage Disposal
☐ Washer/Dryer Hookups		☐ Rain Gutters
☐ Burglar Alarms	☐ Smoke Detector(s)	☐ Fire Alarm
☐ TV Antenna	☐ Satellite Dish	☐ Intercom
☐ Central Heating	☐ Central Air Conditioning	☐ Evaporator Cooler(s)
☐ Wall/Window Air Conditioning	☐ Sprinklers	☐ Public Sewer System
☐ Septic Tank	☐ Sump Pump	☐ Water Softener
☐ Patio/Decking	☐ Built-in Barbecue	☐ Gazebo
☐ Sauna		
☐ Hot Tub	☐ Pool	☐ Spa
☐ Locking Safety Cover*	☐ Child Resistant Barrier*	☐ Locking Safety Cover*
☐ Security Gate(s)	☐ Automatic Garage Door Opener(s)*	Number Remote Controls _____
Garage: ☐ Attached	☐ Not Attached	☐ Carport
Pool/Spa Heater: ☐ Gas	☐ Solar	☐ Electric
Water Heater: ☐ Gas	☐ Water Heater Anchored, Braced, or Strapped*	
Water Supply: ☐ City	☐ Well	☐ Private Utility or
Gas Supply: ☐ Utility	☐ Bottled	☐ Other _____
☐ Window Screens	☐ Window Security Bars ☐ Quick Release Mechanism on Bedroom Windows*	

Exhaust Fan(s) in _____ 220 Volt Wiring in _____ Fireplace(s) in _____
☐ Gas Starter _____ ☐ Roof(s): Type: _____ Age: _____ (approx.)
☐ Other: _____

Are there, to the best of your (Seller's) knowledge, any of the above that are not in operating condition? ☐ Yes ☐ No. If yes, then describe. (Attach additional sheets if necessary): _____
_____

(*see footnote on page 2)

Buyer's Initials (_____)(_____)
Seller's Initials (_____)(_____)

Reviewed by _____ Date _____

EQUAL HOUSING OPPORTUNITY

TDS REVISED 10/03 (PAGE 1 OF 3) Print Date

REAL ESTATE TRANSFER DISCLOSURE STATEMENT (TDS PAGE 1 OF 3)

Figure 8-5. Transfer Disclosure Form

Property Address: _____ Date: _____

B. Are you (Seller) aware of any significant defects/malfunctions in any of the following? ☐ Yes ☐ No. If yes, check appropriate space(s) below.

☐ Interior Walls ☐ Ceilings ☐ Floors ☐ Exterior Walls ☐ Insulation ☐ Roof(s) ☐ Windows ☐ Doors ☐ Foundation ☐ Slab(s)
☐ Driveways ☐ Sidewalks ☐ Walls/Fences ☐ Electrical Systems ☐ Plumbing/Sewers/Septics ☐ Other Structural Components

(Describe: _____
_____
_____)

If any of the above is checked, explain. (Attach additional sheets if necessary.): _____
_____
_____
_____
_____

*This garage door opener or child resistant pool barrier may not be in compliance with the safety standards relating to automatic reversing devices as set forth in Chapter 12.5 (commencing with Section 19890) of Part 3 of Division 13 of, or with the pool safety standards of Article 2.5 (commencing with Section 115920) of Chapter 5 of Part 10 of Division 104 of, the Health and Safety Code. The water heater may not be anchored, braced, or strapped in accordance with Section 19211 of the Health and Safety Code. Window security bars may not have quick release mechanisms in compliance with the 1995 edition of the California Building Standards Code.

C. Are you (Seller) aware of any of the following:

1. Substances, materials, or products which may be an environmental hazard such as, but not limited to, asbestos, formaldehyde, radon gas, lead-based paint, mold, fuel or chemical storage tanks, and contaminated soil or water on the subject property . . . . ☐ Yes ☐ No
2. Features of the property shared in common with adjoining landowners, such as walls, fences, and driveways, whose use or responsibility for maintenance may have an effect on the subject property . . . . ☐ Yes ☐ No
3. Any encroachments, easements or similar matters that may affect your interest in the subject property . . . . ☐ Yes ☐ No
4. Room additions, structural modifications, or other alterations or repairs made without necessary permits . . . . ☐ Yes ☐ No
5. Room additions, structural modifications, or other alterations or repairs not in compliance with building codes . . . ☐ Yes ☐ No
6. Fill (compacted or otherwise) on the property or any portion thereof . . . . ☐ Yes ☐ No
7. Any settling from any cause, or slippage, sliding, or other soil problems . . . . ☐ Yes ☐ No
8. Flooding, drainage or grading problems . . . . ☐ Yes ☐ No
9. Major damage to the property or any of the structures from fire, earthquake, floods, or landslides . . . . ☐ Yes ☐ No
10. Any zoning violations, nonconforming uses, violations of "setback" requirements . . . . ☐ Yes ☐ No
11. Neighborhood noise problems or other nuisances . . . . ☐ Yes ☐ No
12. CC&R's or other deed restrictions or obligations . . . . ☐ Yes ☐ No
13. Homeowners' Association which has any authority over the subject property . . . . ☐ Yes ☐ No
14. Any "common area" (facilities such as pools, tennis courts, walkways, or other areas co-owned in undivided interest with others) . . . . ☐ Yes ☐ No
15. Any notices of abatement or citations against the property . . . . ☐ Yes ☐ No
16. Any lawsuits by or against the Seller threatening to or affecting this real property, including any lawsuits alleging a defect or deficiency in this real property or "common areas" (facilities such as pools, tennis courts, walkways, or other areas co-owned in undivided interest with others) . . . . ☐ Yes ☐ No

If the answer to any of these is yes, explain. (Attach additional sheets if necessary.): _____
_____
_____
_____

Seller certifies that the information herein is true and correct to the best of the Seller's knowledge as of the date signed by the Seller.

Seller_____ Date _____

Seller_____ Date _____

Buyer's Initials (_____)(_____)
Seller's Initials (_____)(_____)

Copyright © 1991-2003, CALIFORNIA ASSOCIATION OF REALTORS®, INC.
TDS REVISED 10/03 (PAGE 2 OF 3)

Reviewed by _____ Date _____

REAL ESTATE TRANSFER DISCLOSURE STATEMENT (TDS PAGE 2 OF 3)

Figure 8-5.　Transfer Disclosure Form (*continued*)

Property Address: _____ Date: _____

III. AGENT'S INSPECTION DISCLOSURE
(To be completed only if the Seller is represented by an agent in this transaction.)

THE UNDERSIGNED, BASED ON THE ABOVE INQUIRY OF THE SELLER(S) AS TO THE CONDITION OF THE PROPERTY AND BASED ON A REASONABLY COMPETENT AND DILIGENT VISUAL INSPECTION OF THE ACCESSIBLE AREAS OF THE PROPERTY IN CONJUNCTION WITH THAT INQUIRY, STATES THE FOLLOWING:

☐ Agent notes no items for disclosure.

☐ Agent notes the following items: _____
_____
_____
_____
_____

Agent (Broker Representing Seller) _____ By _____ Date _____
(Please Print)   (Associate Licensee or Broker Signature)

IV. AGENT'S INSPECTION DISCLOSURE
(To be completed only if the agent who has obtained the offer is other than the agent above.)

THE UNDERSIGNED, BASED ON A REASONABLY COMPETENT AND DILIGENT VISUAL INSPECTION OF THE ACCESSIBLE AREAS OF THE PROPERTY, STATES THE FOLLOWING:

☐ Agent notes no items for disclosure.

☐ Agent notes the following items: _____
_____
_____
_____
_____

Agent (Broker Obtaining the Offer) _____ By _____ Date _____
(Please Print)   (Associate Licensee or Broker Signature)

V. BUYER(S) AND SELLER(S) MAY WISH TO OBTAIN PROFESSIONAL ADVICE AND/OR INSPECTIONS OF THE PROPERTY AND TO PROVIDE FOR APPROPRIATE PROVISIONS IN A CONTRACT BETWEEN BUYER AND SELLER(S) WITH RESPECT TO ANY ADVICE/INSPECTIONS/DEFECTS.

I/WE ACKNOWLEDGE RECEIPT OF A COPY OF THIS STATEMENT.

Seller _____ Date _____ Buyer _____ Date _____
Seller _____ Date _____ Buyer _____ Date _____

Agent (Broker Representing Seller) _____ By _____ Date _____
(Please Print)   (Associate Licensee or Broker Signature)

Agent (Broker Obtaining the Offer) _____ By _____ Date _____
(Please Print)   (Associate Licensee or Broker Signature)

SECTION 1102.3 OF THE CIVIL CODE PROVIDES A BUYER WITH THE RIGHT TO RESCIND A PURCHASE CONTRACT FOR AT LEAST THREE DAYS AFTER THE DELIVERY OF THIS DISCLOSURE IF DELIVERY OCCURS AFTER THE SIGNING OF AN OFFER TO PURCHASE. IF YOU WISH TO RESCIND THE CONTRACT, YOU MUST ACT WITHIN THE PRESCRIBED PERIOD.

A REAL ESTATE BROKER IS QUALIFIED TO ADVISE ON REAL ESTATE. IF YOU DESIRE LEGAL ADVICE, CONSULT YOUR ATTORNEY.

SURE·TRAC
The System for Success®

Published and Distributed by:
REAL ESTATE BUSINESS SERVICES, INC.
a subsidiary of the California Association of REALTORS®
525 South Virgil Avenue, Los Angeles, California 90020

Reviewed by _____ Date _____

EQUAL HOUSING OPPORTUNITY

TDS REVISED 10/03 (PAGE 3 OF 3)

REAL ESTATE TRANSFER DISCLOSURE STATEMENT (TDS PAGE 3 OF 3)

Figure 8-5. Transfer Disclosure Form (*continued*)

Questions on Chapter 8

1. Whenever all principals agree to the terms of a real estate contract, there has been
   (A) legality of object
   (B) meeting of the minds
   (C) reality of consent
   (D) bilateral consideration

2. The law that requires contracts for the sale of real estate to be in writing to be enforceable is the
   (A) Statute of Frauds
   (B) Statute of Limitations
   (C) Statute of Liberty
   (D) parol evidence rule

3. A person who has the power to sign the name of his principal to a purchase contract is a(n)
   (A) special agent
   (B) optionee
   (C) tenant in common
   (D) attorney-in-fact

4. A valid contract of purchase or sale of real property must be signed by the
   (A) broker
   (B) agent and seller
   (C) seller only
   (D) buyer and seller

5. Hand money paid upon the signing of a purchase contract is called
   (A) an option
   (B) a recognizance
   (C) a deposit
   (D) a freehold estate

6. What is *not* an essential element of a valid contract?
   (A) Offer and acceptance
   (B) Capacity of participants
   (C) Lack of ambiguity
   (D) Lawful purpose

7. A seller of real estate is also known as the
   (A) vendee
   (B) grantor
   (C) vendor
   (D) grantee

8. In any real estate purchase contract there must be
   (A) an offer and acceptance
   (B) a leasing arrangement
   (C) a mortgage loan
   (D) prepayment of taxes

9. If, upon receipt of an offer to purchase under certain terms, the seller makes a counteroffer, the prospective purchaser is
   (A) bound by his original offer
   (B) bound to accept the counteroffer
   (C) bound by the agent's decision
   (D) relieved of his original offer

10. A contract that has no force or effect is said to be
    (A) voidable
    (B) void
    (C) inconsequential
    (D) a contract of uncertain sale

11. A purchase contract, to be enforceable, must have
    (A) the signature of the wife of a married seller
    (B) an earnest money deposit
    (C) competent parties
    (D) witnesses

12. A party to a purchase contract normally has the right to
    (A) change the provisions in the contract if it is convenient to her
    (B) change the provisions in the contract if it will save her money
    (C) back out of the contract if she finds a better deal
    (D) none of the above

13. Which of the following would *not* be a contingency clause in a purchase contract?
    (A) The settlement will be within 90 days.
    (B) The seller can cancel the deal if the buyer cannot get suitable financing.
    (C) The buyer can cancel the deal if Aunt Minnie won't lend him $10,000.
    (D) The deal is off if the property is infested with termites.

14. Which of the following is *not* true?
    (A) A purchase contract must contain a legal description of the land being sold.
    (B) An unwritten purchase contract is not enforceable in court.
    (C) Once a purchase contract is signed, there is no way to avoid going through with the deal.
    (D) A purchase contract should specify a time limit by which the sale will be closed.

15. Sam presents Joe with a real estate purchase contract, signed by Sam, offering Joe $100,000 for Joe's house. Joe agrees with all of Sam's offer, except that Joe wants the price to be $110,000. Joe should
    (A) wait for someone to make a better offer
    (B) wait for Sam to make a better offer
    (C) present Sam with a counteroffer form changing the price to $110,000
    (D) Present Sam with a new real estate purchase contract with the higher price and everything else the same

16. To be valid, a real estate purchase contract must be signed by
    (A) a licensed real estate broker   (C) the buyer's lender
    (B) the seller's attorney   (D) none of the above

17. When a real estate purchase contract is agreed to, the buyer receives
    (A) equitable title
    (B) a new mortgage loan
    (C) the right to occupy the premises
    (D) the right to lease the property until escrow closes

18. A real estate purchase contract should include
    (A) a proper description of the real estate
    (B) the names of the buyer(s) and seller(s)
    (C) the signatures of all parties involved
    (D) all of the above.

19. Joe offers to buy Susie's house for $225,000. Susie examines Joe's offer and then offers to sell her house to Joe for $250,000. Which of the following is true?
    (A) An offer from Susie to Joe now exists.
    (B) No offer exists.
    (C) Two offers exist: one from Joe to Susie, one from Susie to Joe.
    (D) A contract between Joe and Susie now exists.

20. The instrument used to test for radon gas is a
    (A) micrometer   (C) spectrometer
    (B) radonometer   (D) metronome

21. The principal health problem with lead-based paint is
    (A) headaches   (C) asbestosis
    (B) lung cancer   (D) ingestion of paint chips by children

22. A *bill of sale* is used to transfer
    (A) assumed mortgage   (C) trust deed
    (B) subject to mortgage   (D) personal property

23. If title and possession do not occur simultaneously, there should be an interim
    (A) lease (interim occupancy agreement)
    (B) option
    (C) exchange
    (D) novation

24. _____ means something is left to be done to a contract.
    (A) Executed   (C) Unfulfilled
    (B) Executory   (D) Unlisted

25. The date that a mechanic's lien takes is the date
    (A) the project began   (C) the bill was presented
    (B) the project was finished   (D) the bill was past due

26. A notary public
    (A) makes the statement
    (B) requires a graduate-level education
    (C) provides acknowledgment
    (D) assures a genuine deed

27. In real estate parlance, *alienation* means
    (A) walking away from a transaction
    (B) offending the seller
    (C) breaking a lease
    (D) transferring title

28. The booklet *A Homeowner's Guide to Earthquake Safety* must be given to buyers of
    dwellings of one to four units in
    (A) wood-frame buildings built before 1960
    (B) masonry buildings with wood-frame floors or roofs built before 1975
    (C) both A and B
    (D) neither A nor B

29. Lead-based paint disclosure is required for residential properties having one to four
    units that were built before
    (A) 1960   (C) 1978
    (B) 1975   (D) 1992

30. An "as is" sale of one to four dwelling units
    (A) requires a Real Property Transfer Disclosure Statement
    (B) does not require a Real Property Transfer Disclosure Statement
    (C) exempts the seller from mentioning undisclosed defects
    (D) reduces buyer risk

31. An injured party has _____ year(s) to file legal action on the Real Property Trans-
    fer Disclosure Statement.
    (A) one   (C) three
    (B) two   (D) five

32. The *Easton v. Strassburger* case makes it clear that when a seller and agent are in a trans-
    action, material facts about the property must be disclosed to a potential buyer by
    (A) the seller
    (B) the agent
    (C) the seller and the agent
    (D) neither the seller nor the agent except in response to a direct question from the
        buyer

33. If the agent or seller personally delivers the Real Property Transfer Disclosure Statement to the buyer after the offer is accepted, the buyer has _____ day(s) to rescind the contract.
    (A) one
    (B) three
    (C) twelve
    (D) The buyer cannot rescind the contract.

34. Under the Mello-Roos Community Facilities Act of 1982, disclosure of tax liens should be given to the
    (A) agent   (C) seller
    (B) buyer   (D) none of the above

35. The Mello-Roos Community Facilities Act of 1982 may be used to finance part of
    (A) houses   (C) shopping centers
    (B) subdivisions   (D) industrial developments

ANSWERS

1. **B**	8. **A**	15. **C**	22. **D**	29. **C**
2. **A**	9. **D**	16. **D**	23. **A**	30. **A**
3. **D**	10. **B**	17. **A**	24. **B**	31. **B**
4. **D**	11. **C**	18. **D**	25. **A**	32. **C**
5. **C**	12. **D**	19. **A**	26. **C**	33. **B**
6. **C**	13. **A**	20. **C**	27. **D**	34. **B**
7. **C**	14. **C**	21. **D**	28. **C**	35. **B**

Chapter 9/*Deeds and Title Insurance*

To transfer (alienate) an interest in real estate during his lifetime, the owner (*grantor*) surrenders a *deed of conveyance* to another (the *grantee*). The deed of conveyance, also simply called a *deed*, is covered by the Statute of Frauds; consequently, it must be in writing to be enforceable. Title insurance is used to protect an owner's or lender's interest in real estate. Personal property is transferred by a *bill of sale*.

Deeds are contracts, and nothing more. They are *not* "title papers" similar to the official documents you get from the state showing that you are the owner of a particular car. Deeds are not "guaranteed" or "backed up" by any government entity. The deed transfers property rights, but those rights are only as "good" as the public records show that they are. Therefore, a deed should be recorded to give the public constructive notice of its existence. Any document recorded in the public records must be *acknowledged;* for most of us that means it must be *notarized.* Notarization is done by a *notary public,* someone who is licensed by the state to be a witness to the authenticity of signatures. In some counties, a few public officials (mayor, county manager, alderman, etc.) may also be authorized to acknowledge documents. The only guarantee provided by the recording entity (usually a county government) is that the recorded document is a true copy of the original; there is no government guarantee of the contents of the document.

Types of Deeds

There are three basic types of deeds in common use in California: *general warranty deeds*, *special warranty deeds*, and *quit claims* (Figure 9-1). The type of deed usually received by real estate buyers in California is a *grant deed* (Figure 9-2), which is a type of special warranty deed. Note that the illustrated deeds say practically nothing; they have room for the names of the parties and the property description, and some recording and tax business. The key elements are the use of the words "hereby REMISE, RELEASE AND FOREVER QUITCLAIM to" in the quitclaim deed; this language, by California law, defines the deed as a quitclaim deed. The use of the words "hereby GRANT(S) to" in the grant deed similarly define this as a grant deed, as described below.

The general warranty deed contains assurances by the grantor
1. that he has title to the property and the power to convey it (covenant of seizin);
2. that his title is good against claims by others (covenant of quiet enjoyment);
3. that the property is free of encumbrances except as specified (covenant against encumbrances);
4. that he will perform whatever else is necessary to make the title good (covenant of further assurances); and
5. that he will forever defend the rights of the grantee (covenant of warranty forever).

In contrast, the quitclaim deed carries no warranties whatsoever. The grantor gives up all of his rights to the property without even implying that he has or has ever had any such rights. Should the grantor be possessed of the property in fee simple absolute, then a quitclaim deed serves to transfer complete ownership. However, if a grantor owns nothing, that is exactly what a grantee will receive from the quitclaim deed. The quitclaim deed is usually used to clear up an imperfection in the title, called a *cloud on title.*

RECORDING REQUESTED BY

AND WHEN RECORDED MAIL THIS DEED AND, UNLESS OTHERWISE
SHOWN BELOW, MAIL TAX STATEMENT TO:

Name

Street
Address

City &
State
Zip

Title Order No. _____ Escrow No. _____

SPACE ABOVE THIS LINE FOR RECORDER'S USE

T 360 LEGAL (1-94)

Quitclaim Deed

THE UNDERSIGNED GRANTOR(s) DECLARE(s)
DOCUMENTARY TRANSFER TAX IS $ _____
☐ _____ unincorporated area ☐ City of _____
Parcel No. _____
☐ computed on full value of property conveyed, or
☐ computed on full value less value of liens or encumbrances remaining at time of sale, and

FOR A VALUABLE CONSIDERATION, receipt of which is hereby acknowledged,

hereby REMISE, RELEASE AND FOREVER QUITCLAIM to

the following described real property in the
county of   , state of California:

Dated _____

STATE OF CALIFORNIA
COUNTY OF _____ } S.S.

On _____ before me,

a Notary Public in and for said County and State, personally appeared
_____

personally known to me (or proved to me on the basis of satisfactory
evidence) to be the person(s) whose name(s) is/are subscribed to the
within instrument and acknowledged to me that he/she/they executed
the same in his/her/their authorized capacity(ies), and that by his/her/their
signature(s) on the instrument the person(s), or the entity upon behalf
of which the person(s) acted, executed the instrument.

WITNESS my hand and official seal

Signature _____

(This area for official notorial seal)

MAIL TAX STATEMENTS TO PARTY SHOWN ON FOLLOWING LINE; IF NO PARTY SHOWN, MAIL AS DIRECTED ABOVE

_____
Name   Street Address   City & State

Figure 9-1.   Quitclaim Deed
Reprinted with permission, CALIFORNIA ASSOCIATION OF REALTORS®.
Endorsement not implied.

RECORDING REQUESTED BY

AND WHEN RECORDED MAIL THIS DEED AND, UNLESS OTHERWISE
SHOWN BELOW, MAIL TAX STATEMENT TO:

Name

Street
Address

City &
State
Zip

Title Order No. _____ Escrow No. _____

T 355 Legal (2-94)

SPACE ABOVE THIS LINE FOR RECORDER'S USE

Grant Deed

THE UNDERSIGNED GRANTOR(s) DECLARE(s)

DOCUMENTARY TRANSFER TAX IS $ _____
☐ _____ unincorporated area ☐ City of _____
Parcel No. _____
☐ computed on full value of interest or property conveyed, or
☐ computed on full value less value of liens or encumbrances remaining at time of sale, and

FOR A VALUABLE CONSIDERATION, receipt of which is hereby acknowledged,

hereby GRANT(S) to

the following described real property in the
county of _____, state of California:

Dated _____

STATE OF CALIFORNIA
COUNTY OF _____ } S.S.

On _____ before me,

_____
a Notary Public in and for said County and State, personally appeared

_____

personally known to me (or proved to me on the basis of satisfactory
evidence) to be the person(s) whose name(s) is/are subscribed to the
within instrument and acknowledged to me that he/she/they executed
the same in his/her/their authorized capacity(ies), and that by his/her/their
signature(s) on the instrument the person(s), or the entity upon behalf
of which the person(s) acted, executed the instrument.

WITNESS my hand and official seal

Signature _____

(This area for official notarial seal)

MAIL TAX STATEMENTS TO PARTY SHOWN ON FOLLOWING LINE; IF NO PARTY SHOWN, MAIL AS DIRECTED ABOVE

Name   Street Address   City & State

Figure 9-2. Grant Deed
Reprinted with permission, CALIFORNIA ASSOCIATION OF REALTORS®.
Endorsement not implied.

A "cloud on a title" (also called a *title defect*) is a circumstance in which the public records are not perfectly clear about who owns or has rights to certain property rights. For example, Elrod wants to buy Sally Smith's real estate. The public records show that Sally, along with her brothers Melvin and Paul, inherited the property from their father some time ago. Sally insists that she is the sole owner, and there is an executor's deed that names only Sally as the grantee from the estate. So, according to the records, the "cloud" is that there is nothing to show that Melvin and Paul ever gave up their rights to inherit. What actually happened is that when their father died, the three siblings agreed that Sally would get the house, and Sally would give up to them her share of their father's stocks and bonds. But the executor failed to get quitclaim deeds for the house from each of the brothers to Sally. Now Sally must get, and record, quitclaim deeds from them to "clear" the title.

A deed that contains some but not all of the covenants of a warranty deed is a *special* or *limited warranty* deed. Special warranty deeds typically contain assurances only against claims that may have originated while that grantor held title. It does not protect against claims that originated previously. In California, because the use of title insurance is so prevalent, the deed commonly given is a *grant deed*, which is a form of special warranty deed. It has two covenants: (1) the estate transferred is free of any encumbrances (except those in the public records) made by or through the grantor, and (2) the grantor has not previously conveyed any part of the transferred estate to anyone else.

Other forms of special warranty deeds used in California are: *trustee's deed*, from foreclosure sale of a deed of trust; *sheriff's deed*, from foreclosure of a court judgment; and *tax deed*, from tax collector selling property for which property taxes were unpaid. Most of these are grouped in a category called *special warranty deeds*.

Deed Requirements

The following elements must be present in a deed for it to be considered valid:
1. A legally competent grantor
2. A designated grantee
3. Consideration—even though only a token amount is shown
4. Words of conveyance
5. The interest being conveyed
6. A description of the property
7. Grantor's proper signature
8. Delivery of the deed and acceptance

Execution of the Deed

To be considered complete, a deed must be signed by the grantor and delivered to the grantee or delivered in escrow (see below). Occasionally, problems arise when an undelivered deed is found in the grantor's home after his death. The grantee named may claim ownership; but since the grantor never delivered the deed, courts will not agree that transfer was intended.

The requirement for delivery of the deed generally is considered very literally; that is, the grantee actually must have come into physical possession of the document in order for title to be considered transferred to her. The grantee may arrange for her agent to accept delivery for her. A common form of such delivery is *delivery in escrow*. In this situation, the grantor delivers the deed to a trustee or escrow agent, who holds it pending completion of some required action by the grantee (such as payment in full of a note given in payment for all or part of the price). Delivery is considered to have occurred as soon as the escrow agent or trustee received the deed, so title is transferred. However, because the grantee has no deed in her possession, she will have difficulty disposing of the title until she fulfills the necessary requirements to get the deed released to her by the agent.

Public Records and Title Search _____

Records concerning real estate are maintained in the courthouse of each county in California. Whenever someone receives a deed, a deed of trust (or mortgage), or other key document in real estate including a long-term lease, he or she may *record* it in the county courthouse. One need not record a deed to own the property. By recording a deed, a person gives *constructive notice* to the world of his or her ownership interest. Constructive notice means that anyone in the world who would have an interest in a property is assumed to know what is in the recorded documents affecting that property. Anyone thereafter who searches courthouse records concerning this property would see the documents transferring ownership to the grantee and could avert a proposed transaction if good title were not available. If a grantee fails to record a deed, he or she runs the risk that an unscrupulous grantor may sell the property again, and that other buyer, who doesn't know of the first buyer's rights, records his deed. A dispute will arise and it is likely the second buyer's ownership interest will be upheld. The first buyer is unable to establish an earlier date of ownership because his or her deed was not recorded first, (and perhaps is still not recorded) and the second buyer was innocent of wrongdoing and acted in good faith.

When one wants to buy real estate in California, one will sign a real estate purchase agreement (see Chapter 8) which will specify the deed to be given. Because of the potential risk of loss in every transaction, it is prudent for an attorney to be engaged to *search the title*. In any transaction where a trust deed (or mortgage loan) is to be used, the potential lender will insist on a title search. Often, the attorney is associated with a title company (see below) as an agent or employee. The attorney may provide an *abstract of title*, which is a condensed history of the title, a summary of the chain of title, and a list of all liens, charges, and encumbrances affecting the title. Sometimes the attorney's work is simpler. If the property sold recently and the same title company searched the title previously, then an update from the previous title report may be adequate.

Title Insurance _____

The purpose of title insurance is to protect a purchaser's or a lender's interest in property. As a real estate transaction is closed (see Chapter 19 on closing), the seller receives money and the buyer receives a piece of paper, the deed. How can the buyer be certain that the deed is good? Or suppose the seller was thought to be an heir to an estate, but the will naming him was successfully challenged? That is, suppose the seller was a fraud who forged the signature of the real heir? In these cases, the seller could not have given legal title, but there was nothing in the public records to show that fact. Since a buyer cannot get a larger interest than the seller has, a buyer in these circumstances would end up with nothing. Therefore, a buyer is critically interested in getting good title. Because a lender's collateral is the property, the lender also is most interested in assuring the buyer gets good title.

Based on the attorney's research, the title insurer will issue a *preliminary title report*, which is a promise to insure the title. This document may have a list of exceptions against which the title company will not insure. The buyer's and lender's attorneys should determine whether any of the exceptions are likely to have validity, and if one poses a threat to ownership, advise their client to not complete the transaction until this *cloud on the title* is cleared.

In most transactions there is no title problem and a title policy will be issued at closing. Payment for title insurance is made only once for property purchased, and is valid for as long as that party owns the property. Lenders will demand enough title insurance to cover the full amount they lend. Buyers would be well advised to insure the full amount that they paid, so as to cover their equity investment in the property. The additional cost will be very small, and the peace of mind well worth it.

Questions on Chapter 9

1. X hands Y a deed with the intent to pass title and orally requests Y not to record the deed until X dies. When is the deed valid?
   (A) Immediately
   (B) When Y records the deed
   (C) When X dies
   (D) Never

2. A quitclaim deed conveys only the interest of the
   (A) guarantee
   (B) property
   (C) claimant
   (D) grantor

3. Which of the following forms of deeds has one or more guarantees of title?
   (A) Quitclaim deed
   (B) Executor's deed
   (C) General warranty deed
   (D) Special-form deed

4. The deed form most commonly used in California is the
   (A) grant deed
   (B) general warranty deed
   (C) quitclaim deed
   (D) tax deed

5. The Statute of Frauds
   (A) requires certain contracts to be in writing to be enforceable
   (B) requires a license to operate as a broker or a salesperson
   (C) regulates escrow accounts
   (D) regulates fraud conveyance

6. For a deed to be recorded, it must be in writing and must
   (A) be signed by the grantee
   (B) state the actual purchase price
   (C) be acknowledged
   (D) be free of all liens

7. The most comprehensive ownership of land at law is known as
   (A) an estate for years
   (B) a life estate
   (C) a fee simple
   (D) a defeasible title

8. From the standpoint of the grantor, which of the following types of deeds creates the least liability?
   (A) Special warranty
   (B) General warranty
   (C) Grant deed
   (D) Quitclaim

9. The recording of a deed
   (A) passes the title
   (B) insures the title
   (C) guarantees the title
   (D) gives constructive notice of ownership

10. Title to real property may pass by
    (A) deed
    (B) bill of sale
    (C) both A and B
    (D) neither A nor B

11. Real property title may be conveyed by
    (A) adverse possession
    (B) inheritance
    (C) deed
    (D) all of the above

12. A warranty deed protects the grantee against a loss by
    - (A) casualty
    - (B) defective title
    - (C) both A and B
    - (D) neither A nor B

13. Recordation of a deed is the responsibility of the
    - (A) grantor
    - (B) grantee
    - (C) both A and B
    - (D) neither A nor B

14. Deeds should be recorded
    - (A) as soon as possible after delivery
    - (B) within 30 days of delivery
    - (C) within one year
    - (D) none of the above

15. A deed of conveyance must be signed by
    - (A) the grantee and the grantor
    - (B) only the grantor
    - (C) only the grantee
    - (D) none of the above

16. A deed to be valid need not necessarily be
    - (A) signed
    - (B) written
    - (C) sealed
    - (D) delivered

17. The party to whom a deed conveys real estate is the
    - (A) grantee
    - (B) grantor
    - (C) beneficiary
    - (D) recipient

18. Deeds are recorded in the
    - (A) county courthouse
    - (B) city hall
    - (C) Federal Land Book
    - (D) state capital

19. A deed must
    - (A) contain the street address of the property
    - (B) state the nature of the improvement on the land (dwelling)
    - (C) contain an adequate description to identify the property sold
    - (D) state the total area in the tract

20. What is the maximum number of grantees that can be named in a deed?
    - (A) Two
    - (B) Four
    - (C) Ten
    - (D) There is no limit

21. Property is identified in a deed by the
    - (A) habendum
    - (B) consideration
    - (C) description
    - (D) acknowledgment

22. Attestation, by a notary public or other qualified official, of the signature on a deed or mortgage is called an
    - (A) authorization
    - (B) acknowledgment
    - (C) execution
    - (D) authentication

23. For which reason or reasons is a deed recorded?
    - (A) To insure certain title
    - (B) To give notice of a transaction to the world
    - (C) To satisfy a requirement of state law
    - (D) To save title insurance cost

24. Ownership of property is transferred when
    - (A) the grantor signs the deed
    - (B) the grantor's signature has been notarized

(C) delivery of the deed is made

(D) the correct documentary stamps are put on the deed and canceled

25. From the point of view of the grantee, the safest kind of deed that can be received is a
    (A) general warranty deed
    (B) special warranty deed
    (C) quitclaim or release deed
    (D) trustee's deed

26. Which of the following statement(s) is (are) true?
    (A) A quitclaim deed transfers whatever interest a grantee has in property.
    (B) A quitclaim deed carries a warranty of good title.
    (C) Both A and B
    (D) Neither A nor B

27. The reason why the grant deed is most prevalent in California is
    (A) the widespread use of title insurance
    (B) most other kinds of deed are illegal
    (C) the only alternative is the quitclaim, and few grantees want that kind of deed
    (D) it is required for community property

28. What does title insurance insure against?
    (A) Improper property description in a deed of trust
    (B) Unrecorded defects in the title chain
    (C) Assigned leases and assumed mortgages
    (D) Loss of mineral rights

29. *Escheat* is a way for
    (A) the state to receive title upon the death of an owner who leaves no will
    (B) partnerships to get along
    (C) individuals to pass title
    (D) a spouse to receive title by divorce

30. The county recorder maintains
    (A) tax rate data
    (B) index of recordings
    (C) broker license information
    (D) all of the above

31. A quitclaim deed conveys only the present right, title, and interest of the
    (A) grantor
    (B) servient tenement
    (C) grantee
    (D) property

32. For a grant deed to be valid, the land description must be
    (A) perfect
    (B) approximate
    (C) adequate
    (D) within one acre of land

33. A trust deed is a
    (A) security device
    (B) exculpation matter
    (C) novation
    (D) all of the above

34. A *grant deed* is used
    (A) as a security device
    (B) to transfer title
    (C) to transfer Civil War relics
    (D) for the same purpose as a quitclaim deed

35. A grant deed must be signed by
     (A) grantee
     (B) grantor
     (C) both grantee and grantor
     (D) neither grantee nor grantor

36. The California "standard form" policy of title insurance on real property insures against loss occasioned by
     (A) a forgery in the chain of recorded title
     (B) liens or encumbrances not disclosed by official records
     (C) rights of parties in possession of the property
     (D) actions of governmental agencies regulating the use or occupancy of the property

37. A CLTA standard title insurance policy
     (A) is commonly obtained by homeowners
     (B) protects against forgery
     (C) does not require an onsite property inspection
     (D) all of the above

ANSWERS

1. **A**	9. **D**	17. **A**	25. **A**	33. **A**
2. **D**	10. **A**	18. **A**	26. **D**	34. **B**
3. **C**	11. **D**	19. **C**	27. **A**	35. **B**
4. **A**	12. **B**	20. **D**	28. **B**	36. **A**
5. **A**	13. **B**	21. **C**	29. **A**	37. **D**
6. **C**	14. **A**	22. **B**	30. **B**	
7. **C**	15. **B**	23. **B**	31. **A**	
8. **D**	16. **C**	24. **C**	32. **C**	

Chapter 10/*Leases and Property Management*

A lease is a contract that transfers possession of property in exchange for rent.

The real estate owner is known as the *landlord* or *lessor;* the user is the *tenant* or *lessee.* The landlord retains a *reversionary right*; that is, he retains the right to use the property upon expiration of the lease. The tenant holds a *leasehold estate,* that is, a personal property interest that gives the tenant the right to use the property for the lease term and under the conditions stipulated in the lease.

Types of Leasehold Estates

1. Estate for years
2. Estate from year to year
3. Tenancy at will
4. Tenancy at sufferance

In California, the maximum length of time that agricultural land can be put under lease at one time is 51 years. For all other real property, including mineral leases, the maximum lease term is 99 years.

An *estate for years* has a stated expiration date. The period included may be only 1 day or more than 50 years. When the lease term ends, the tenant is to vacate the property.

An *estate from year to year* (also called *periodic estate or estate from period to period*) does not have a fixed expiration date. It is automatically renewed for another period (week, month, year) unless adequate notice for termination is given. One period of notice is generally adequate; less than 1 year is acceptable in the case of a year-to-year lease.

A *tenancy at will* allows the tenant to remain with the consent of the landlord. At any time, either the tenant or the landlord may terminate the agreement. "Emblements" arise by operation of law to give tenants-at-will the right to harvest growing crops.

A tenant who holds property beyond the lease term and without the landlord's consent is a "holdover tenant." The form of estate is called *tenancy at sufferance*. A holdover tenancy has the fewest rights of any leasehold estate.

Requirements of a Valid Real Estate Contract

Since a lease is a contract for the use of real estate, it must meet all the requirements for a valid real estate contract. These requirements include:

1. Offer and acceptance
2. Competent parties
3. Consideration
4. Adequate description of the property
5. Written form

In California, an oral lease for less than one year can be binding. Any provision that is legal can be included in a lease. Some common lease provisions are discussed below.

SOME COMMON LEASE PROVISIONS

Rent

Rent may be payable in any form that the parties agree upon. Typically, rent is payable in money, but it may also be payable in crops, labor, and so on—whatever the landlord and tenant agree upon. *Straight* or *flat* leases call for level amounts of rent. *Step-up* or *step-down*, *graduated*, or *reappraisal* leases provide for fluctuating amounts of rent.

A *percentage lease* requires the tenant to pay, as rent, a percentage of sales. Usually a basic rent is stipulated to guarantee a minimum amount. For example, a lease may require that a retailer-tenant pay $10,000 rent annually, plus 2 percent of gross sales in excess of $500,000. Should sales be under $500,000, the rent is $10,000; for sales of $600,000, the rent is $12,000, that is, $10,000 basic plus 2 percent of the $100,000 excess sales.

Operating Expenses

A lease that requires the landlord to pay operating expenses, such as utilities, repairs, insurance, and property taxes, is called a *gross lease*. The lessor considers the rent to be gross income and receives net operating income after he pays operating expenses out of his own pocket. A *net lease* requires the tenant to pay operating expenses. The landlord receives the rent as a net return.

The terms *net* and *gross*, though often used, may be inadequate to describe a lease. *Hybrid*, *seminet,* and *net-net* are used to describe the degree to which a party may be responsible for operating expenses. Careful reading of a lease by interested parties is necessary to avoid misunderstandings.

Escalation

Escalation or *step* provisions are found in long-term gross leases. Should certain operating expenses exceed a designated amount, the increase is passed on to the tenant.

Assignment and Subletting

Unless specifically prohibited in a lease, a tenant has the right to assign or sublet. In either case, the original lessee remains liable to fulfill the lease contract.

An *assignment* occurs when the tenant transfers all the rights and obligations stipulated in the lease to a third party (the assignee).

Should the original tenant wish to keep a portion of the property for his own use or to rent the premises to a third party for a term shorter than his lease, he may sublet. *Subletting* involves a second lease; the original tenant becomes a lessor for part of the property or for the entire property for part of the lease term.

Sale of the Property

When leased property is sold, the lease survives the sale. The tenant is allowed to continue use under the lease terms.

Termination of a Lease

The normal termination of a lease is the result of *performance*. When both landlord and tenant have fulfilled their lease obligations, there is said to be performance.

Another method of terminating a lease is by *agreement*. Landlord and tenant may agree to terminate the lease before its stated expiration date. Compensation may be included in such an agreement.

A *breach* may also cause termination. When either party fails to perform under a lease, there is said to be a breach. Although a breach can terminate a lease, it does not cancel all provisions. The violating party may be held liable for damages. When a tenant has breached a lease, the landlord's remedy is in court. Using a court order, a landlord may eject or *evict* a tenant.

A tenant who vacates property before the fixed expiration date of a lease is responsible for the remaining rent. If the property is eventually leased, the tenant owes only the difference in rent, plus expenses incurred in obtaining a substitute tenant. However, vacating property fails to terminate a lease except by *constructive eviction.* In this form of breach the landlord makes it very difficult or impossible for the tenant to "enjoy" the leased premises as contracted. In effect, the landlord's actions force the tenant to leave. Examples are very noisy repair work that goes on night after night in an apartment building; turning off utilities for long periods of time; closing the parking lot in a retail shopping center.

A *ground lease* is a long-term lease of land or air space. The tenant usually builds whatever improvements are desired. The landlord receives what is called *triple-net* rent; this means that the tenant pays not only operating expenses, but also property taxes and mortgage payments. Ground leases are for very long periods of time, usually 25 to as many as 99 years.

Lease provisions frequently encountered are described below. (Not all of the provisions will be found in every lease.)

Provision	*Purpose*
Premises	Describes the property being leased
Term	States the term of the lease
Rent	Describes rental amount, date, and place payable
Construction of building and improvements	Describes improvements for proposed property or property to be renovated to suit tenant
Common area	Describes maintenance of common-use areas, such as those in shopping centers
Taxes	States who will pay ad valorem taxes and escalation amounts
Repairs	States which party is responsible for repairs and maintenance
Alterations	States responsibilities and rights of tenant to alter improvements
Liability insurance	Designates party who is responsible to carry liability insurance and the extent
Other insurance	Designates party who is responsible to carry hazard insurance and the extent
Damage by fire and casualty	Describes operation of lease in the event of a fire or other casualty
Payment for utilities	States which party must pay charges for water, heat, gas, electricity, sewage disposal, and other utilities
Subordination	Describes rights between landlord and tenant in the event of mortgage foreclosure
Certificate of lease status	Obligates tenant to inform mortgage lender of occupancy and rent status
Condemnation and eminent domain	Describes operation of lease in the event of a taking or partial taking of the property
Compliance of law	Requires landlord and tenant to comply with laws and ordinances
Access by landlord	Allows landlord to inspect property
Mechanic's liens	Describes the discharge of mechanic's liens
Assignment and subletting	Limits the tenant's rights to assign or sublet
Nonliability of landlord	Frees landlord from liability due to injury or damage within premises
Right to cure defaults	Allows landlord to cure tenant defaults and require reimbursement
Use	Permits tenant the use of property for specific purposes
Notices	Describes method to serve notice to a party
Definitions	Defines terms used in the lease
Partial invalidity	Describes operation of lease when parts of lease are held to be invalid

Provision	Purpose
Waiver of redemption	Permits tenant to waive all rights upon lease expiration
Bankruptcy or insolvency	Describes required notice and operation of lease in the event of bankruptcy
Default	Defines lease default
Surrender	Describes how tenant is to leave property upon expiration of the lease
Arbitration	Provides a method to settle disputes
Brokers	Notes whether a broker was involved in lease negotiation
Encumbrances	Describes rights and obligations of parties to deliver and return property (with respect to liens, easements, etc.)
Quiet enjoyment	Agreement by landlord that tenant, while he performs, may have, hold, and enjoy property without interference
Other restrictions	May limit the leasing of space in a shopping center to a competitor
Entire agreement	States that the written lease is the entire agreement
Percentage clause	Stipulates conditions affecting a percentage lease
Recapture clause	Stipulates that in a percentage lease a lessor may terminate lease if lessee's revenues do not attain a specified level within a certain length of time

Landlord-Tenant Law

Both landlord and tenant have certain rights and responsibilities. By law, landlords provide certain warranties to tenants: habitability (plumbing, heat, and electrical services are safe and work properly; building, stairways, halls, and the like are safe and sound, clean, and free of pests; public areas are properly maintained, with no leaks and no broken windows or doors). Landlords are liable for injuries due to violations of any of the above, or where landlord's due diligence would be expected. If the landlord says the property is secure, then the landlord is liable for violations of security. Because the premises are leased to the tenant, and the lease conveys possession, the landlord's right to enter the leased premises is severely restricted, except in an emergency, unless the tenant consents, the tenant has abandoned the premises, the landlord has a court order allowing entry, or the landlord has given reasonable notice to make necessary or tenant-desired repairs.

Tenant's duties include paying rent when due, keeping premises clean and sanitary, not violating any building codes or permitting occupancy in excess of terms agreed in lease or limited by law, exercising reasonable care in the use of the premises, using the premises for the intended purpose, within the law, and keeping others from damaging the premises. The tenant has the right of "quiet enjoyment," which basically means noninterference by the landlord with the tenant's right to use and occupy the premises in the manner for which they are intended. Also, if after giving reasonable notice of necessary repairs to the landlord, the repairs haven't been made, the tenant may withhold up to one month's rent to spend on such repairs. However, this withholding of rent cannot be done more than twice a year.

Eviction

If the tenant violates the lease agreement (the most common offense is not paying the rent), stays in the premises after the lease expires, or uses the premises in some illegal manner, the landlord may have the tenant *evicted*. This is a legal process, involving officers of the court (the sheriff's office); it is very risky for a landlord to "evict" a tenant himself without going through the required process.

The process is cumbersome. First the landlord must give the tenant a *three-day notice* to "quit, cure, or pay rent." *Quit* means to leave voluntarily. *Cure* means to stop doing whatever is in violation of the lease or the law, and repair any damage it caused. If the tenant doesn't do any of this, then the landlord goes to court and files an *unlawful detainer action* against the tenant; this gives the tenant five days to appear and answer the landlord's charges. If the tenant does appear, the court (judge) will listen to what both tenant and landlord have to say, consider any other relevant evidence and make a decision as to who is to do what. If the tenant doesn't appear, the court issues a *writ of possession* which gives the tenant five days to vacate; if the tenant doesn't leave, he or she can be physically evicted by the sheriff.

Some states allow the landlord to claim against the tenant's possessions for unpaid rent and other damages (this is called *distraint*). California does *not* allow this! Instead, if the tenant leaves property on the premises, an inventory of it must be made by a sheriff's officer, and then the goods must be stored by the landlord for 30 days. The tenant can get them back by paying storage and transfer costs. After 30 days, they can be sold; the landlord can take from the proceeds the costs of storage and sale, but the rest of the money must be given to the tenant, even if the tenant still owes the landlord for unpaid rent or damage to the premises.

Landlords also are prohibited from *retaliatory eviction*, which is eviction, rent increase, or other interference with tenant's legal and contracted rights within 180 days of the tenant exercising a legally protected right, including such things as complaining about the premises to the landlord or a public agency, being involved in a lawful tenants' organization, legally withholding rent for repairs, and so on.

Property Management

Property management is the business of seeking and negotiating with tenants for the use of other people's real estate. It is a real estate brokerage function, and property managers in all states are required to hold real estate sales or brokerage licenses. (*Resident managers* of apartment buildings or projects are allowed by most states to function without a license, provided that they do not manage any other properties and are employed either by the property owner or a properly licensed property manager.)

Some brokers who claim to be "property managers" may do little more than find tenants for vacant properties, and collect payment for doing so. Actually, a *professional* property manager does a lot more. In fact, he is able to do everything associated with the proper management of a property, so that the owner need do nothing at all. Property management functions include leasing, negotiating with potential tenants, advertising, developing leasing plans, arranging maintenance and repairs, and paying all bills (out of rent receipts). Of course, property managers are paid for their services. Normally, their payment is a commission on rent payments collected; however, they may instead (or also) receive a flat fee.

Certain special kinds of lease arrangements often are found in managed properties. Retail property (e.g., shopping centers) often features *percentage leases*. In this type of lease, all or part of the tenant's rent is a percentage of her gross business revenues. The theory here is that a well-managed and popular shopping center will generate good business for tenants, and so they will be willing to pay part of their intake as rent. Also, the property manager is encouraged to promote and advertise the shopping center because by doing so he gets more people to come to it, spend more money, and thus generate more rent.

Many percentage leases contain *recapture clauses*. These allow the property manager to void the lease if the tenant does not do at least a certain volume of business within a certain time. In this way the management avoids getting stuck with a poor tenant or one who does not do much business.

Questions on Chapter 10

1. Which of the following statements is correct?
   (A) The tenant is known as the lessor.
   (B) The owner leasing property is the lessee.
   (C) The tenant is the lessee.
   (D) None of the above

2. Under a net lease, who is liable for payment of insurance and repairs?
   (A) Lessor
   (B) Lessee
   (C) Sublessee
   (D) Both A and B

3. A gross lease requires the tenant to pay rent based on
   (A) gross sales
   (B) net sales
   (C) gross profit
   (D) none of the above

4. A percentage lease requires the tenant to pay a
   (A) percentage of taxes and insurance
   (B) percentage of net income as rent
   (C) percentage of sales as rent
   (D) none of the above

5. A tenant is delinquent in paying rent. The landlord should
   (A) call the sheriff to evict him
   (B) bring a court action
   (C) give him 30 days' notice
   (D) turn off water, lights, etc.

6. A lease that requires the landlord to pay the operating expenses of the property is called
   (A) a gross lease
   (B) an assigned lease
   (C) a percentage lease
   (D) a net lease

7. A lease for less than 1 year
   (A) may be oral
   (B) must be in writing
   (C) may be oral but must be reduced to writing within 1 year
   (D) is always invalid

8. Transfer, by a tenant, of the rights and obligations of an existing lease to another tenant is called
   (A) assignment of lease
   (B) a release
   (C) subletting
   (D) an eviction

9. A contract that transfers possession but not ownership of property is
   (A) a special warranty deed
   (B) an option
   (C) an easement
   (D) a lease

10. When an individual holds property past the expiration of a lease without the landlord's consent, the leasehold estate he has is a
    (A) tenancy at sufferance
    (B) freehold estate
    (C) common of pasturage
    (D) holdover tenant

11. A sublease is a
    (A) lease made by a lessor
    (B) lease made by a lessee and a third party
    (C) lease for basement space
    (D) condition of property

12. A landlord rents a store to a furniture retailer on a percentage lease. On which of the following is the percentage usually based?
    (A) Market value
    (B) Sales price
    (C) Tenant's gross sales
    (D) Tenant's net income

13. Which of the following will *not* terminate a lease?
    (A) Performance
    (B) Breach
    (C) Surrender
    (D) Vacancy

14. When a leased property is sold, what effect does the sale have upon the tenant?
    (A) The tenant must record the lease in the recorder's office.
    (B) The tenant must obtain an assignment from the purchaser.
    (C) The tenant must move out after reasonable notice.
    (D) There is no effect.

15. A lease for more than 1 year *must* be in writing to be enforceable because the
    (A) landlord or tenant might forget the terms
    (B) tenant must sign the agreement to pay rent
    (C) Statute of Frauds requires it
    (D) lease can then be assigned to another person

16. A lease can state that the rent is to be paid in
    (A) labor
    (B) crops
    (C) cash
    (D) any of the above

17. An estate at will is
    (A) a limited partnership
    (B) a tenancy of uncertain duration
    (C) an inheritance by will
    (D) a life tenancy

18. A reversionary interest
    (A) expires when a lease is signed
    (B) allows land to escheat at the termination of a lease
    (C) is a landlord's right to use of property upon expiration of a lease
    (D) constitutes a breach of a lease

19. A leasehold estate is a
    (A) large home built on leased land
    (B) personal property interest in real estate
    (C) landlord's interest in realty
    (D) none of the above

20. Escalation clauses in a lease provide for
    (A) term extensions
    (B) elevator and escalator maintenance
    (C) increased rentals because of higher operating expenses
    (D) purchase options

21. Which of the following statements is true?
    (A) Property managers are required to be licensed in all states.
    (B) Percentage leases are illegal in many states.
    (C) An unlicensed person may solicit tenants for several properties provided that she works for a licensed property manager.
    (D) Property managers do not negotiate leases.

22. Which of the following is true?
    (A) Property management is a real estate brokerage function.
    (B) Resident managers of apartment complexes don't always have to be licensed.
    (C) Property managers usually are paid a percentage of rents collected as their fee.
    (D) All of the above

23. A person who remains on leased property, without the landlord's consent, after the expiration of a lease is
    (A) a tenant at will
    (B) a tenant *par duration*
    (C) a tenant in common
    (D) a tenant at suffrance

24. A lease that requires that all or part of the tenant's rent be based on the tenant's revenues is
    - (A) a lease at will
    - (B) a flat lease
    - (C) a percentage lease
    - (D) a gross lease

25. To begin eviction proceedings against a tenant, a landlord should give the tenant a
    - (A) writ of possession and eviction
    - (B) three-day notice to quit, cure, or pay rent
    - (C) unlawful detainer action from the sheriff
    - (D) a distraint of no cure

26. A landlord may enter the premises without notice
    - (A) whenever he/she wants to
    - (B) only during business hours
    - (C) only when the tenant is at home
    - (D) only in an emergency

27. If a nonpaying tenant leaves personal property behind in the premises, the landlord may
    - (A) claim all of it
    - (B) claim only enough to pay the unpaid rent
    - (C) claim in the value of one month's rent
    - (D) none of the above

28. If after reasonable notice from the tenant the landlord has not made legally required repairs, the tenant may
    - (A) withhold and spend up to one month's rent for the repairs, no more than twice a year
    - (B) withhold and spend up to two months' rent on such repairs, but only once a year
    - (C) not withhold any rent
    - (D) none of the above

29. The maximum term of an agricultural lease in California is _____ years.
    - (A) 10
    - (B) 20
    - (C) 40
    - (D) 51

30. If a landlord files an unlawful detainer action, a tenant has _____ day(s) to appear.
    - (A) one
    - (B) three
    - (C) five
    - (D) thirty

31. The legal action to remove a defaulting tenant is a(n)
    - (A) unlawful detainer action
    - (B) sublease
    - (C) assignment
    - (D) recapture

32. A triple-net lease is one where the tenant pays
    - (A) property taxes
    - (B) insurance
    - (C) maintenance
    - (D) all of the above

33. A strip shopping center is a
    - (A) regional mall
    - (B) neighborhood center
    - (C) nonconforming use
    - (D) string of neighborhood stores

34. A commercial property investor is typically most interested in
    - (A) land value
    - (B) current net income
    - (C) tax shelter
    - (D) appreciation

35. Parallel wooden members used to support floor and ceiling loads are called
    - (A) rafters
    - (B) joists
    - (C) headers
    - (D) studs

36. *HVAC* refers to
    - (A) high vacancy and collection
    - (B) high volume and commissions
    - (C) he vacates as convenient
    - (D) heating, ventilation, and air conditioning

37. In a typical percentage lease, rent is calculated as a percentage of
    - (A) assets of the lessee's business
    - (B) net sales of the lessee's business
    - (C) gross sales of the lessee's business
    - (D) net taxable income of the lessee's business

ANSWERS

1. **C**	9. **D**	17. **B**	25. **B**	33. **D**
2. **B**	10. **A**	18. **C**	26. **D**	34. **B**
3. **D**	11. **B**	19. **B**	27. **D**	35. **B**
4. **C**	12. **C**	20. **C**	28. **A**	36. **D**
5. **B**	13. **D**	21. **A**	29. **D**	37. **C**
6. **A**	14. **D**	22. **D**	30. **C**	
7. **A**	15. **C**	23. **D**	31. **A**	
8. **A**	16. **D**	24. **C**	32. **D**	

Chapter 11/*Listings and Buyer Agency Agreements*

A *listing* is a contract of employment between a principal (property owner) and an agent (broker) to sell or lease real estate. Under the terms of the listing contract, the principal agrees to pay the broker a commission when the broker locates a party who is ready, willing, and able to buy or lease the listed property at its list price. Should an offer be tendered for less than the list price, the broker is entitled to a commission only if the transaction is consummated. A different kind of contract between a real estate broker and his/her client is a *buyer agency agreement*. We usually don't call them listings, though, because the term *listing* always has referred to property for sale.

Normally, the seller pays the commission at closing. It is possible for a buyer to agree to pay a commission in lieu of the seller or in addition to the seller, so long as all parties are aware of the circumstances.

Types of Listings

Listings can be categorized into five broad types as follows:
1.   Open listings
2.   Exclusive agency listings
3.   Exclusive right to sell listings
4.   Net listings
5.   Multiple listings
Each type is described below.

1.   OPEN LISTINGS

Using an open listing, the principal offers the broker a commission provided that the broker secures a purchaser. The owner reserves the right to list the property with other brokers or to sell the property himself. Thus, the open listing is open to other real estate brokers. All open listings are automatically canceled upon a sale of the property, so that the seller pays no more than one commission, to one broker.

2.   EXCLUSIVE AGENCY LISTINGS

In an exclusive agency listing one broker is employed to the exclusion of all other brokers. The owner retains the right to sell the property herself without paying a commission. However, if the property is sold by a broker other than the listing broker, the listing broker is still entitled to a commission.

3.   EXCLUSIVE RIGHT TO SELL LISTINGS

The exclusive right to sell listing allows the employed broker to collect a commission upon the sale, no matter who sells the property. Whether the employed broker, another broker, or the owner procures a purchaser, a broker with an exclusive right to sell gains his fee upon the sale (see Figure 11-1).

At first glance, such a contract may seem to be to a seller's disadvantage. Even if the seller procures a buyer on her own, or another broker finds one, the listing broker earns a commis-

RESIDENTIAL LISTING AGREEMENT - EXCLUSIVE
(Exclusive Authorization and Right to Sell)
(C.A.R. Form RLA, Revised 10/04)

1. **EXCLUSIVE RIGHT TO SELL:** _____ ("Seller")
hereby employs and grants _____ ("Broker")
beginning (date) _____ and ending at 11:59 P.M. on (date) _____ ("Listing Period")
the exclusive and irrevocable right to sell or exchange the real property in the City of _____,
County of_____, California, described as: _____
_____ ("Property").

2. **ITEMS EXCLUDED AND INCLUDED:** Unless otherwise specified in a real estate purchase agreement, all fixtures and fittings that
are attached to the Property are included, and personal property items are excluded, from the purchase price.
ADDITIONAL ITEMS EXCLUDED: _____.
ADDITIONAL ITEMS INCLUDED: _____.
Seller intends that the above items be excluded or included in offering the Property for sale, but understands that: **(i)** the purchase
agreement supersedes any intention expressed above and will ultimately determine which items are excluded and included in the sale;
and **(ii)** Broker is not responsible for and does not guarantee that the above exclusions and/or inclusions will be in the purchase agreement.

3. **LISTING PRICE AND TERMS:**
   A. The listing price shall be: _____
   _____ Dollars ($ _____).
   B. Additional Terms: _____
   _____

4. **COMPENSATION TO BROKER:**
   **Notice: The amount or rate of real estate commissions is not fixed by law. They are set by each Broker
   individually and may be negotiable between Seller and Broker (real estate commissions include all
   compensation and fees to Broker).**
   A. Seller agrees to pay to Broker as compensation for services irrespective of agency relationship(s), either ☐ _____ percent
   of the listing price (or if a purchase agreement is entered into, of the purchase price), or ☐ $ _____,
   AND _____, as follows:
   (1) If Broker, Seller, cooperating broker, or any other person procures a buyer(s) who offers to purchase the Property on the
   above price and terms, or on any price and terms acceptable to Seller during the Listing Period, or any extension.
   OR (2) If Seller, within _____ calendar days **(a)** after the end of the Listing Period or any extension, or **(b)** after any cancellation
   of this Agreement, unless otherwise agreed, enters into a contract to sell, convey, lease or otherwise transfer the Property
   to anyone ("Prospective Buyer") or that person's related entity: **(i)** who physically entered and was shown the Property during
   the Listing Period or any extension by Broker or a cooperating broker; or **(ii)** for whom Broker or any cooperating broker
   submitted to Seller a signed, written offer to acquire, lease, exchange or obtain an option on the Property. Seller, however,
   shall have no obligation to Broker under paragraph 4A(2) unless, not later than **3 calendar days** after the end of the Listing
   Period or any extension or cancellation, Broker has given Seller a written notice of the names of such Prospective Buyers.
   OR (3) If, without Broker's prior written consent, the Property is withdrawn from sale, conveyed, leased, rented, otherwise transferred,
   or made unmarketable by a voluntary act of Seller during the Listing Period, or any extension.
   B. If completion of the sale is prevented by a party to the transaction other than Seller, then compensation due under paragraph
   4A shall be payable only if and when Seller collects damages by suit, arbitration, settlement or otherwise, and then in an amount
   equal to the lesser of one-half of the damages recovered or the above compensation, after first deducting title and escrow
   expenses and the expenses of collection, if any.
   C. In addition, Seller agrees to pay Broker: _____.
   D. Seller has been advised of Broker's policy regarding cooperation with, and the amount of compensation offered to, other
   brokers.
   (1) Broker is authorized to cooperate with and compensate brokers participating through the multiple listing service(s)
   ("MLS"): **(i)** as per Broker's policy; **OR (ii)** (if checked) by offering MLS brokers: either ☐ _____ percent of the
   purchase price, or ☐ $ _____.
   (2) Broker is authorized to cooperate with and compensate brokers operating outside the MLS as per Broker's policy.
   E. Seller hereby irrevocably assigns to Broker the above compensation from Seller's funds and proceeds in escrow. Broker may
   submit this Agreement, as instructions to compensate Broker pursuant to paragraph 4A, to any escrow regarding the Property
   involving Seller and a buyer, Prospective Buyer or other transferee.
   F. (1) Seller represents that Seller has not previously entered into a listing Agreement with another broker regarding the Property,
   unless specified as follows: _____.
   (2) Seller warrants that Seller has no obligation to pay compensation to any other broker regarding the Property unless the
   Property is transferred to any of the following individuals or entities: _____
   _____.
   (3) If the Property is sold to anyone listed above during the time Seller is obligated to compensate another broker: **(i)** Broker is
   not entitled to compensation under this Agreement; and **(ii)** Broker is not obligated to represent Seller in such transaction.

Seller acknowledges receipt of a copy of this page.
Seller's Initials (_____)(_____)

Reviewed by _____ Date _____

RLA REVISED 10/04 (PAGE 1 OF 3)   Print Date

RESIDENTIAL LISTING AGREEMENT - EXCLUSIVE (RLA PAGE 1 OF 3)

Figure 11-1.   Exclusive Right to Sell Listing

Property Address: _____ Date: _____

5. **OWNERSHIP, TITLE AND AUTHORITY:** Seller warrants that: **(i)** Seller is the owner of the Property; **(ii)** no other persons or entities have title to the Property; and **(iii)** Seller has the authority to both execute this Agreement and sell the Property. Exceptions to ownership, title and authority are as follows: _____.

6. **MULTIPLE LISTING SERVICE:** All terms of the transaction, including financing, if applicable, will be provided to the selected MLS for publication, dissemination and use by persons and entities on terms approved by the MLS. Seller authorizes Broker to comply with all applicable MLS rules. MLS rules allow MLS data to be made available by the MLS to additional Internet sites unless Broker gives the MLS instructions to the contrary. MLS rules generally provide that residential real property and vacant lot listings be submitted to the MLS within 48 hours or some other period of time after all necessary signatures have been obtained on the listing agreement. However, Broker will not have to submit this listing to the MLS if, within that time, Broker submits to the MLS a form signed by Seller (C.A.R. Form SEL or the locally required form) instructing Broker to withhold the listing from the MLS. Information about this listing will be provided to the MLS of Broker's selection unless a form instructing Broker to withhold the listing from the MLS is attached to this listing Agreement.

7. **SELLER REPRESENTATIONS:** Seller represents that, unless otherwise specified in writing, Seller is unaware of: **(i)** any Notice of Default recorded against the Property; **(ii)** any delinquent amounts due under any loan secured by, or other obligation affecting, the Property; **(iii)** any bankruptcy, insolvency or similar proceeding affecting the Property; **(iv)** any litigation, arbitration, administrative action, government investigation or other pending or threatened action that affects or may affect the Property or Seller's ability to transfer it; and **(v)** any current, pending or proposed special assessments affecting the Property. Seller shall promptly notify Broker in writing if Seller becomes aware of any of these items during the Listing Period or any extension thereof.

8. **BROKER'S AND SELLER'S DUTIES:** Broker agrees to exercise reasonable effort and due diligence to achieve the purposes of this Agreement. Unless Seller gives Broker written instructions to the contrary, Broker is authorized to order reports and disclosures as appropriate or necessary and advertise and market the Property by any method and in any medium selected by Broker, including MLS and the Internet, and, to the extent permitted by these media, control the dissemination of the information submitted to any medium. Seller agrees to consider offers presented by Broker, and to act in good faith to accomplish the sale of the Property by, among other things, making the Property available for showing at reasonable times and referring to Broker all inquiries of any party interested in the Property. Seller is responsible for determining at what price to list and sell the Property. **Seller further agrees to indemnify, defend and hold Broker harmless from all claims, disputes, litigation, judgments and attorney fees arising from any incorrect information supplied by Seller, or from any material facts that Seller knows but fails to disclose.**

9. **DEPOSIT:** Broker is authorized to accept and hold on Seller's behalf any deposits to be applied toward the purchase price.

10. **AGENCY RELATIONSHIPS:**
    A. **Disclosure:** If the Property includes residential property with one-to-four dwelling units, Seller shall receive a "Disclosure Regarding Agency Relationships" form prior to entering into this Agreement.
    B. **Seller Representation:** Broker shall represent Seller in any resulting transaction, except as specified in paragraph 4F.
    C. **Possible Dual Agency With Buyer:** Depending upon the circumstances, it may be necessary or appropriate for Broker to act as an agent for both Seller and buyer, exchange party, or one or more additional parties ("Buyer"). Broker shall, as soon as practicable, disclose to Seller any election to act as a dual agent representing both Seller and Buyer. If a Buyer is procured directly by Broker or an associate-licensee in Broker's firm, Seller hereby consents to Broker acting as a dual agent for Seller and such Buyer. In the event of an exchange, Seller hereby consents to Broker collecting compensation from additional parties for services rendered, provided there is disclosure to all parties of such agency and compensation. Seller understands and agrees that: **(i)** Broker, without the prior written consent of Seller, will not disclose to Buyer that Seller is willing to sell the Property at a price less than the listing price; **(ii)** Broker, without the prior written consent of Buyer, will not disclose to Seller that Buyer is willing to pay a price greater than the offered price; and **(iii)** except for (i) and (ii) above, a dual agent is obligated to disclose known facts materially affecting the value or desirability of the Property to both parties.
    D. **Other Sellers:** Seller understands that Broker may have or obtain listings on other properties, and that potential buyers may consider, make offers on, or purchase through Broker, property the same as or similar to Seller's Property. Seller consents to Broker's representation of sellers and buyers of other properties before, during and after the end of this Agreement.
    E. **Confirmation:** If the Property includes residential property with one-to-four dwelling units, Broker shall confirm the agency relationship described above, or as modified, in writing, prior to or concurrent with Seller's execution of a purchase agreement.

11. **SECURITY AND INSURANCE:** Broker is not responsible for loss of or damage to personal or real property, or person, whether attributable to use of a keysafe/lockbox, a showing of the Property, or otherwise. Third parties, including, but not limited to, appraisers, inspectors, brokers and prospective buyers, may have access to, and take videos and photographs of, the interior of the Property. Seller agrees: **(i)** to take reasonable precautions to safeguard and protect valuables that might be accessible during showings of the Property; and **(ii)** to obtain insurance to protect against these risks. Broker does not maintain insurance to protect Seller.

12. **KEYSAFE/LOCKBOX:** A keysafe/lockbox is designed to hold a key to the Property to permit access to the Property by Broker, cooperating brokers, MLS participants, their authorized licensees and representatives, authorized inspectors, and accompanied prospective buyers. Broker, cooperating brokers, MLS and Associations/Boards of REALTORS® are **not** insurers against injury, theft, loss, vandalism or damage attributed to the use of a keysafe/lockbox. Seller does (or if checked ☐ does not) authorize Broker to install a keysafe/lockbox. If Seller does not occupy the Property, Seller shall be responsible for obtaining occupant(s)' written permission for use of a keysafe/lockbox.

13. **SIGN:** Seller does (or if checked ☐ does not) authorize Broker to install a FOR SALE/SOLD sign on the Property.

14. **EQUAL HOUSING OPPORTUNITY:** The Property is offered in compliance with federal, state and local anti-discrimination laws.

15. **ATTORNEY FEES:** In any action, proceeding or arbitration between Seller and Broker regarding the obligation to pay compensation under this Agreement, the prevailing Seller or Broker shall be entitled to reasonable attorney fees and costs from the non-prevailing Seller or Broker, except as provided in paragraph 19A.

16. **ADDITIONAL TERMS:** _____
    _____
    _____
    _____

RLA REVISED 10/04 (PAGE 2 OF 3) Print Date

Seller acknowledges receipt of a copy of this page.
Seller's Initials (_____)(_____)

| Reviewed by _____ Date _____ |

EQUAL HOUSING OPPORTUNITY

RESIDENTIAL LISTING AGREEMENT - EXCLUSIVE (RLA PAGE 2 OF 3)

Figure 11-1. Exclusive Right to Sell Listing (*continued*)

Property Address: _____ Date:_____

17. MANAGEMENT APPROVAL: If an associate licensee in Broker's office (salesperson or broker-associate) enters into this Agreement on Broker's behalf, and Broker or Manager does not approve of its terms, Broker or Manager has the right to cancel this Agreement, in writing, within 5 days after its execution.

18. SUCCESSORS AND ASSIGNS: This Agreement shall be binding upon Seller and Seller's successors and assigns.

19. DISPUTE RESOLUTION:

   A. MEDIATION: Seller and Broker agree to mediate any dispute or claim arising between them out of this Agreement, or any resulting transaction, before resorting to arbitration or court action, subject to paragraph 19B(2) below. Paragraph 19B(2) below applies whether or not the arbitration provision is initialed. Mediation fees, if any, shall be divided equally among the parties involved. If, for any dispute or claim to which this paragraph applies, any party commences an action without first attempting to resolve the matter through mediation, or refuses to mediate after a request has been made, then that party shall not be entitled to recover attorney fees, even if they would otherwise be available to that party in any such action. THIS MEDIATION PROVISION APPLIES WHETHER OR NOT THE ARBITRATION PROVISION IS INITIALED.

   B. ARBITRATION OF DISPUTES: (1) Seller and Broker agree that any dispute or claim in Law or equity arising between them regarding the obligation to pay compensation under this Agreement, which is not settled through mediation, shall be decided by neutral, binding arbitration, including and subject to paragraph 19B(2) below. The arbitrator shall be a retired judge or justice, or an attorney with at least 5 years of residential real estate law experience, unless the parties mutually agree to a different arbitrator, who shall render an award in accordance with substantive California Law. The parties shall have the right to discovery in accordance with Code of Civil Procedure §1283.05. In all other respects, the arbitration shall be conducted in accordance with Title 9 of Part III of the California Code of Civil Procedure. Judgment upon the award of the arbitrator(s) may be entered in any court having jurisdiction. Interpretation of this agreement to arbitrate shall be governed by the Federal Arbitration Act.

   (2) EXCLUSIONS FROM MEDIATION AND ARBITRATION: The following matters are excluded from mediation and arbitration hereunder: **(i)** a judicial or non-judicial foreclosure or other action or proceeding to enforce a deed of trust, mortgage, or installment land sale contract as defined in Civil Code §2985; **(ii)** an unlawful detainer action; **(iii)** the filing or enforcement of a mechanic's lien; and **(iv)** any matter that is within the jurisdiction of a probate, small claims, or bankruptcy court. The filing of a court action to enable the recording of a notice of pending action, for order of attachment, receivership, injunction, or other provisional remedies, shall not constitute a waiver of the mediation and arbitration provisions.

   "NOTICE: BY INITIALING IN THE SPACE BELOW YOU ARE AGREEING TO HAVE ANY DISPUTE ARISING OUT OF THE MATTERS INCLUDED IN THE 'ARBITRATION OF DISPUTES' PROVISION DECIDED BY NEUTRAL ARBITRATION AS PROVIDED BY CALIFORNIA LAW AND YOU ARE GIVING UP ANY RIGHTS YOU MIGHT POSSESS TO HAVE THE DISPUTE LITIGATED IN A COURT OR JURY TRIAL. BY INITIALING IN THE SPACE BELOW YOU ARE GIVING UP YOUR JUDICIAL RIGHTS TO DISCOVERY AND APPEAL, UNLESS THOSE RIGHTS ARE SPECIFICALLY INCLUDED IN THE 'ARBITRATION OF DISPUTES' PROVISION. IF YOU REFUSE TO SUBMIT TO ARBITRATION AFTER AGREEING TO THIS PROVISION, YOU MAY BE COMPELLED TO ARBITRATE UNDER THE AUTHORITY OF THE CALIFORNIA CODE OF CIVIL PROCEDURE. YOUR AGREEMENT TO THIS ARBITRATION PROVISION IS VOLUNTARY."

   "WE HAVE READ AND UNDERSTAND THE FOREGOING AND AGREE TO SUBMIT DISPUTES ARISING OUT OF THE MATTERS INCLUDED IN THE 'ARBITRATION OF DISPUTES' PROVISION TO NEUTRAL ARBITRATION."

Seller's Initials _____ / _____	Broker's Initials _____ / _____

20. ENTIRE AGREEMENT: All prior discussions, negotiations and agreements between the parties concerning the subject matter of this Agreement are superseded by this Agreement, which constitutes the entire contract and a complete and exclusive expression of their agreement, and may not be contradicted by evidence of any prior agreement or contemporaneous oral agreement. If any provision of this agreement is held to be ineffective or invalid, the remaining provisions will nevertheless be given full force and effect. This Agreement and any supplement, addendum or modification, including any photocopy or facsimile, may be executed in counterparts.

By signing below, Seller acknowledges that Seller has read, understands, accepts and has received a copy of this Agreement.

Seller _____ Date _____

Address _____ City _____ State _____ Zip _____

Telephone _____ Fax _____ E-mail _____

Seller _____ Date _____

Address _____ City _____ State _____ Zip _____

Telephone _____ Fax _____ E-mail _____

Real Estate Broker (Firm) _____

By (Agent) _____ Date _____

Address _____ City _____ State _____ Zip _____

Telephone _____ Fax _____ E-mail _____

Published and Distributed by:
REAL ESTATE BUSINESS SERVICES, INC.
a subsidiary of the California Association of REALTORS®
525 South Virgil Avenue, Los Angeles, California 90020

RLA REVISED 10/04 (PAGE 3 OF 3) Print Date

Reviewed by _____ Date _____

RESIDENTIAL LISTING AGREEMENT - EXCLUSIVE (RLA PAGE 3 OF 3)

Figure 11-1.   Exclusive Right to Sell Listing (*continued*)

sion. However, this rigid arrangement gives the listing broker the assurance that the property is available for sale by him only. Brokers employed by other types of listings may be dismayed to learn that property has been sold by the owner or another broker. Since this does not occur under an exclusive right to sell, the employed broker has more incentive to devote his efforts and to spend money to promote the sale of the listed property. In recognition of this fact, most real estate boards emphasize the exclusive right to sell listing, particularly for single-family dwellings.

4. NET LISTINGS

In a net listing the property owner fixes the amount that he wishes to receive from a sale. He informs the broker, for example, that he wants a $175,000 check from the sale. The broker may keep any amount as a commission so long as the seller "nets" $175,000. Thus, if the sale price is $175,001, the commission is $1; a sale at $190,000 yields a $15,000 commission.

Generally, net listings are held in poor repute in the real estate brokerage business. In many states they are illegal; but they are legal in California. They offer opportunities for unscrupulous brokers to violate their agency relationships with their principals (the owners who list their properties with them). An owner who isn't knowledgeable about the actual value of her property could be talked into net listing the property at a low price, thereby all but guaranteeing the broker an unusually high payment for selling the property. Even if the listing price is reasonable, brokers may try to "hide" or may illegally turn down offers that the owner probably would accept but that don't provide enough excess for what the broker thinks is an adequate commission. For example, a property is net-listed for $200,000. Obviously, the owner will take any offer of $200,000 or more, since the net listing assures her of receiving the full $200,000 (but no more) from any offer of at least $200,000. A broker who receives an offer of $210,000 may consider his $10,000 share too little, and be tempted to try on his own to negotiate a higher price, turn the offer down, delay transmitting the offer, or otherwise violate his obligation under license law to *immediately* transmit the offer to the owner.

Professional real estate brokerage associations suggest that, when offered a net listing, the broker add her customary charge to the net amount and then inform the seller of the resulting list price. For example, a 6 percent commission rate added to a $160,000 net figure results in a $170,213 offering price. Six percent of $170,213 is $10,213, leaving $160,000 for the seller. The arithmetic works as follows:

$$\frac{\text{Net Amount to Seller}}{\text{Fraction of Sales Price to Seller*}} = \text{List Price with Commission}$$
$$(\text{*}100\% \text{ less commission})$$

When the $160,000 net figure and the 6 percent rate of commission are used, the list price becomes:

$$\frac{\$160,000}{0.94} = \$170,213$$

California law requires that when agents having net listings present offers to their principals, the agents must disclose the dollar amount and percentage amount of the commission to be received.

5. MULTIPLE LISTINGS

In metropolitan areas, most brokers agree to pool all of their listings. They form a *multiple listing association* to coordinate activities. Through that association, brokers agree to share their exclusive right to sell listings; any cooperating broker may sell property that another has listed. Upon the sale of multiple-listed property, the commission is split between the listing and the selling broker in accordance with the agreement established by the multiple listing association. A small fraction of the commission is paid to the association to cover its expenses of operation, which include the periodic publication, in writing and/or by computer, of the features of all listed property of the brokers belonging to that multiple listing association.

Agency Law

A broker is an agent for his principal. The broker's duties, obligations, and responsibilities to his principal are covered by the Law of Agency. Chapter 4 of this book describes this body of law as it pertains to real estate brokerage. In California, details of an agency relationship in a residential transaction must be presented in writing to the buyer and seller as soon as practicable. Specifically, the written disclosure should be made to the buyer before making an offer to purchase, and to the seller before the offer is accepted. Ordinarily, this is accomplished by having the buyer sign and return to the agent a form (usually designed and prescribed by law) that describes the agency relationship, so that the prospect realizes that the agent's loyalty is to the seller. Sometimes brokers represent buyers in negotiations and transactions. In such cases they are agents of the buyer, not the seller, and there has to be an agency contract between broker and buyer. Disclosure is required here, too; when negotiations begin with a seller (or seller's broker) of a property the buyer is interested in, the seller and/or listing broker must be notified of the buyer-broker agency relationship.

Rate of Commission

As a matter of law, commission rates for the sale of real estate are negotiable between the principal and his broker. The rate or amount should be specified in the listing contract to avoid misunderstandings.

Listing Period

Contracts for the listing of real estate should have a fixed expiration date. Most contracts provide 60 to 120 days for the sale of single-family homes and 6 months to a year for commercial property and apartment complexes. The law does not establish limits, so the actual period agreed upon is a matter of negotiation.

Occasionally, after having been shown a particular piece of property through a broker, a prospect and the property owner may arrange a sale "behind the broker's back." Together they wait for the listing to expire, then contract for the sale without advising the broker, in an attempt to elude the payment of a commission. Despite the fact that the listing has expired, courts are likely to require payment to a licensed broker whose listing expired, if she can show that she was the procuring cause of the sale.

Termination of Listings

Listing agreements may be terminated either by the parties or by operation of law.

Termination by the parties can occur through:

1. *Performance.* The broker procures a purchaser; the listing contract is terminated when the sale is completed.
2. *Mutual consent.* Both parties agree to terminate the listing.
3. *Expiration of agreed time.* A listing generally has a definite expiration date. If it doesn't, the listing ends after a reasonable period. In many states a listing must have a fixed expiration date.

4. *Revocation by the principal.* At any time, the principal may revoke authority given to the broker. However, the principal may be liable for damages resulting from the breach of contract, but not if he can show the agent to have been negligent in her duties, as by disloyalty, dishonesty, or incompetence.

5. *Revocation by the broker.* An agent may terminate the listing contract or abandon it. However, he may be held liable for damages to the principal because of failure to complete the object of the listing contract.

Termination by law can occur through:

1. *Death of either party.* The death of either the principal or the broker generally causes termination of a listing contract.

2. *Bankruptcy of either party.* Bankruptcy of a principal or an agent normally terminates an agency.

3. *Insanity of either party.* If either party is judged to be insane, he is considered incapable of completing the contract; therefore, the listing contract will terminate.

4. *Destruction of the property.* If the property upon which the agency had been created is destroyed, the agency is terminated.

Buyer Agency Agreements

As agents, real estate brokers don't just represent sellers (in listing contracts); they can also represent buyers. When they do, the broker and buyer execute a *buyer agency agreement* (Figure 11-2). This contract obligates a broker to represent the buyer and to look out for the buyer's interests. As the buyer's agent, the broker or salesperson can point out other properties that might better suit the buyer's needs, can state that a given property may be overpriced, and can otherwise advise and assist the buyer to get the best possible property to suit the buyer's needs, and at the best possible price. A listing broker or salesperson shouldn't offer this kind of assistance to a potential buyer because it would violate the agency obligation to the seller created by the listing contract.

Most buyer agency agreements are exclusive; that is, the buyer agrees not to employ another broker during the term of the buyer agency contract. Of particular concern is how the buyer's agent will be paid. In "traditional" real estate brokerage, all agents are paid out of the proceeds of the commission paid by the seller to his/her listing broker. Almost everywhere in the United States, buyer agency works the same way. Today's listing contracts typically stipulate that the seller will allow a buyer's agent to be paid from the proceeds of the commission that the seller will pay, and the buyer agency contract usually says that this is how the buyer's broker will be paid. However, the buyer agency contract also describes payment that the buyer must make if the buyer receives out-of-the-ordinary kinds of services from the broker, or if the buyer decides to buy a property that is under a listing contract that does *not* allow commission-sharing with a buyer's broker.

Buyer agency agreements are very popular; the reason is obvious. They give the buyer access to the same level of advice and expertise that sellers have traditionally always had from their brokers.

Buyer agency agreements are subject to the same agency law provisions as listing contracts and may be terminated the same ways as described above for listing contracts. Buyer agency agreements also have limited terms (60–120 days is typical).

BUYER BROKER AGREEMENT - EXCLUSIVE
Right to Represent
(C.A.R. Form BBE, Revised 10/04)

1. **EXCLUSIVE RIGHT TO REPRESENT:** _____ ("Buyer")
grants _____ ("Broker")
beginning on (date) _____ and ending at: (i) 11:59 p.m. on (date) _____, or (ii) completion of
a resulting transaction, whichever occurs first ("Representation Period"), the exclusive and irrevocable right, on the terms
specified in this Agreement, to represent Buyer in acquiring real property or a manufactured home. Broker agrees to exercise
due diligence and reasonable efforts to fulfill the following authorizations and obligations. Broker will perform its obligations
under this Agreement through the individual signing for Broker below, who is either Broker individually or an associate-licensee
(an individual licensed as a real estate salesperson or broker who works under Broker's real estate license). Buyer agrees that
Broker's duties are limited by the terms of this Agreement, including those limitations set forth in paragraphs 5 and 6.

2. **AGENCY RELATIONSHIPS:**
   A. DISCLOSURE: If the property described in paragraph 4 includes residential property with one-to-four dwelling units,
   Buyer acknowledges receipt of the "Disclosure Regarding Real Estate Agency Relationships" form prior to entering into
   this Agreement.
   B. BUYER REPRESENTATION: Broker will represent, as described in this Agreement, Buyer in any resulting transaction.
   C. (1) POSSIBLE DUAL AGENCY WITH SELLER: (C(1) APPLIES UNLESS C(2)(i) or (ii) is checked below.)
   Depending on the circumstances, it may be necessary or appropriate for Broker to act as an agent for both Buyer and a seller,
   exchange party, or one or more additional parties ("Seller"). Broker shall, as soon as practicable, disclose to Buyer any
   election to act as a dual agent representing both Buyer and Seller. If Buyer is shown property listed with Broker, Buyer
   consents to Broker becoming a dual agent representing both Buyer and Seller with respect to those properties. In event of
   dual agency, Buyer agrees that: (a) Broker, without the prior written consent of Buyer, will not disclose to Seller that the Buyer
   is willing to pay a price greater than the price offered; (b) Broker, without the prior written consent of Seller, will not disclose
   to Buyer that Seller is willing to sell property at a price less than the listing price; and (c) other than as set forth in (a) and
   (b) above, a dual agent is obligated to disclose known facts materially affecting the value or desirability of the Property to
   both parties.
   OR (2) SINGLE AGENCY ONLY: (APPLIES ONLY IF (i) or (ii) is checked below.)
   ☐ **(i)** Broker's firm lists properties for sale: Buyer understands that this election will prevent Broker from showing Buyer
   those properties that are listed with Broker's firm or from representing Buyer in connection with those properties. Buyer's
   acquisition of a property listed with Broker's firm shall not affect Broker's right to be compensated under paragraph 3. In any
   resulting transaction in which Seller's property is not listed with Broker's firm, Broker will be the exclusive agent of Buyer and not
   a dual agent also representing Seller.
   OR ☐ **(ii)** Broker's firm DOES NOT list property: Entire brokerage firm only represents buyers and does not list property. In any
   resulting transaction, Broker will be the exclusive agent of Buyer and not a dual agent also representing Seller.
   D. OTHER POTENTIAL BUYERS: Buyer understands that other potential buyers may, through Broker, consider, make offers on
   or acquire the same or similar properties as those Buyer is seeking to acquire. Buyer consents to Broker's representation of
   such other potential buyers before, during and after the Representation Period, or any extension thereof.
   E. CONFIRMATION: If the Property includes residential property with one-to-four dwelling units, Broker shall confirm the agency
   relationship described above, or as modified, in writing, prior to or coincident with Buyer's execution of a Property Contract.

3. **COMPENSATION TO BROKER:**
   **NOTICE: The amount or rate of real estate commissions is not fixed by law. They are set by each Broker
   individually and may be negotiable between Buyer and Broker (real estate commissions include all
   compensation and fees to Broker).**
   Buyer agrees to pay to Broker, irrespective of agency relationship(s), as follows:
   A. AMOUNT OF COMPENSATION: (Check (1), (2) or (3). Check only one.)
   ☐ **(1)** _____ percent of the acquisition price AND (if checked ☐) $ _____
   OR ☐ **(2)** $_____
   OR ☐ **(3)** Pursuant to the compensation schedule attached as an addendum _____.
   B. BROKER RIGHT TO COMPENSATION: Broker shall be entitled to the compensation provided for in paragraph 3A:
   (1) If Buyer enters into an agreement to acquire property described in paragraph 4, on those terms or any other terms
   acceptable to Buyer during the Representation Period, or any extension thereof.
   (2) If, within ____ calendar days after expiration of the Representation Period or any extension thereof, Buyer enters into an
   agreement to acquire property described in paragraph 4, which property Broker introduced to Buyer, or for which Broker
   acted on Buyer's behalf. The obligation to pay compensation pursuant to this paragraph shall arise only if, prior to or within
   3 (or ☐ _____) calendar days after expiration of this Agreement or any extension thereof, Broker gives Buyer a written
   notice of those properties which Broker introduced to Buyer, or for which Broker acted on Buyer's behalf.

Buyer and Broker acknowledge receipt of a copy of this page.

Buyer's Initials (_____)(_____)
Broker's Initials (_____)(_____)

| Reviewed by _____ Date _____ |

BBE REVISED 10/04 (PAGE 1 OF 4)

BUYER BROKER AGREEMENT – EXCLUSIVE (BBE PAGE 1 OF 4)

Figure 11-2. Buyer Agency Agreement

Buyer: _____ Date: _____

C. **PAYMENT OF COMPENSATION:** Compensation is payable:
  (1) Upon completion of any resulting transaction, and if an escrow is used, through escrow.
  (2) If acquisition is prevented by default of Buyer, upon Buyer's default.
  (3) If acquisition is prevented by a party to the transaction other than Buyer, when Buyer collects damages by suit, settlement or otherwise. Compensation shall equal one-half of the damages recovered, not to exceed the compensation provided for in paragraph 3A, after first deducting the unreimbursed expenses of collection, if any.

D. **BUYER OBLIGATION TO PAY COMPENSATION:** Buyer is responsible for payment of compensation provided for in this Agreement. However, if anyone other than Buyer compensates Broker for services covered by this Agreement, that amount shall be credited toward Buyer's obligation to pay compensation. If the amount of compensation Broker receives from anyone other than Buyer exceeds Buyer's obligation, the excess amount shall be disclosed to Buyer and if allowed by law paid to Broker, or (if checked) ☐ credited to Buyer, or ☐ other _____.

E. Buyer hereby irrevocably assigns to Broker the compensation provided for in paragraph 3A from Buyer's funds and proceeds in escrow. Buyer agrees to submit to escrow any funds needed to compensate Broker under this Agreement. Broker may submit this Agreement, as instructions to compensate Broker, to any escrow regarding property involving Buyer and a seller or other transferor.

F. "**BUYER**" includes any person or entity, other than Broker, related to Buyer or who in any manner acts on Buyer's behalf to acquire property described in paragraph 4.

G. (1) Buyer has not previously entered into a representation agreement with another broker regarding property described in paragraph 4, unless specified as follows (name other broker here): _____
  (2) Buyer warrants that Buyer has no obligation to pay compensation to any other broker regarding property described in paragraph 4, unless Buyer acquires the following property(ies):_____,
  (3) If Buyer acquires a property specified in G(2) above during the time Buyer is obligated to compensate another broker, Broker is neither: (i) entitled to compensation under this Agreement, nor (ii) obligated to represent Buyer in such transaction.

4. **PROPERTY TO BE ACQUIRED:**
Any purchase, lease or other acquisition of any real property or manufactured home described as follows:
_____
_____
Price range: $_____ to $_____

5. **BROKER AUTHORIZATIONS AND OBLIGATIONS:**
A. Buyer authorizes Broker to: (i) locate and present selected properties to Buyer, present offers authorized by Buyer, and assist Buyer in negotiating for acceptance of such offers; (ii) assist Buyer with the financing process, including obtaining loan pre-qualification; (iii) upon request, provide Buyer with a list of professionals or vendors who perform the services described in the attached Buyer's Inspection Advisory; (iv) order reports, and schedule and attend meetings and appointments with professionals chosen by Buyer; (v) provide guidance to help Buyer with the acquisition of property; and (vi) obtain a credit report on Buyer.

B. For property transactions of which Broker is aware and not precluded from participating in by Buyer, Broker shall provide and review forms to create a property contract ("Property Contract") for the acquisition of a specific property ("Property"). With respect to such Property, Broker shall: (i) if the Property contains residential property with one-to-four dwelling units, conduct a reasonably competent and diligent on-site visual inspection of the accessible areas of the Property (excluding any common areas), and disclose to Buyer all facts materially affecting the value or desirability of such Property that are revealed by this inspection; (ii) deliver or communicate to Buyer any disclosures, materials or information received by, in the personal possession of or personally known to the individual signing for Broker below during the Representation Period; and (iii) facilitate the escrow process, including assisting Buyer in negotiating with Seller. Unless otherwise specified in writing, any information provided through Broker in the course of representing Buyer has not been and will not be verified by Broker. Broker's services are performed in compliance with federal, state and local anti-discrimination laws.

6. **SCOPE OF BROKER DUTY:**
A. While Broker will perform the duties described in paragraph 5B, Broker recommends that Buyer select other professionals, as described in the attached Buyer's Inspection Advisory, to investigate the Property through inspections, investigations, tests, surveys, reports, studies and other available information ("Inspections") during the transaction. Buyer agrees that these Inspections, to the extent they exceed the obligations described in paragraph 5B, are not within the scope of Broker's agency duties. Broker informs Buyer that it is in Buyer's best interest to obtain such Inspections.

B. Buyer acknowledges and agrees that Broker: (i) Does not decide what price Buyer should pay or Seller should accept; (ii) Does not guarantee the condition of the Property; (iii) Does not guarantee the performance, adequacy or completeness of inspections, services, products or repairs provided or made by Seller or others; (iv) Does not have an obligation to conduct an inspection of common areas, or offsite areas of the Property; (v) Shall not be responsible for identifying defects on the Property, in common areas or offsite unless such defects are visually observable by an inspection of reasonably accessible areas of the Property or are known to Broker; (vi) Shall not be responsible for inspecting public records or permits concerning the title or use of Property; (vii) Shall not be responsible for identifying the location of boundary lines or other items affecting title; (viii) Shall not be responsible for verifying square footage, representations of others or information contained in Investigation reports, Multiple Listing Service, advertisements, flyers or other promotional material; (ix) Shall not be responsible for providing legal or tax advice regarding any aspect of a transaction entered into by Buyer or Seller; and (x) Shall not be responsible for providing other advice or information that exceeds the knowledge, education and experience required to perform real estate licensed activity. Buyer agrees to seek legal, tax, insurance, title and other desired assistance from appropriate professionals.

Buyer and Broker acknowledge receipt of a copy of this page.
Buyer's Initials (_____)(_____)
Broker's Initials (_____)(_____)
Reviewed by _____ Date _____

BUYER BROKER AGREEMENT – EXCLUSIVE (BBE PAGE 2 OF 4)

Figure 11-2. Buyer Agency Agreement (*continued*)

Buyer: _____ Date: _____

C. Broker owes no duty to inspect for common environmental hazards, earthquake weaknesses, or geologic and seismic hazards. If Buyer receives the booklets titled "Environmental Hazards: A Guide for Homeowners, Buyers, Landlords and Tenants," "The Homeowner's Guide to Earthquake Safety," or "The Commercial Property Owner's Guide to Earthquake Safety," the booklets are deemed adequate to inform Buyer regarding the information contained in the booklets and, other than as specified in 5B above, Broker is not required to provide Buyer with additional information about the matters described in the booklets.

7. **BUYER OBLIGATIONS:**
A. Buyer agrees to timely view and consider properties selected by Broker and to negotiate in good faith to acquire a property. Buyer further agrees to act in good faith toward the completion of any Property Contract entered into in furtherance of this Agreement. Within 5 (or ☐ _____) calendar days from the execution of this Agreement, Buyer shall provide relevant personal and financial information to Broker to assure Buyer's ability to acquire property described in paragraph 4. If Buyer fails to provide such information, or if Buyer does not qualify financially to acquire property described in paragraph 4, then Broker may cancel this Agreement in writing. Buyer has an affirmative duty to take steps to protect him/herself, including discovery of the legal, practical and technical implications of discovered or disclosed facts, and investigation of information and facts which are known to Buyer or are within the diligent attention and observation of Buyer. Buyer is obligated to and agrees to read all documents provided to Buyer. Buyer agrees to seek desired assistance from appropriate professionals, selected by Buyer, such as those referenced in the attached Buyer's Inspection Advisory.
B. Buyer shall notify Broker in writing (C.A.R. Form BMI) of any material issue to Buyer, such as, but not limited to, Buyer requests for information on, or concerns regarding, any particular area of interest or importance to Buyer ("Material Issues").
C. Buyer agrees to: (i) indemnify, defend and hold Broker harmless from all claims, disputes, litigation, judgments, costs and attorney fees arising from any incorrect information supplied by Buyer, or from any Material Issues that Buyer fails to disclose in writing to Broker, and (ii) pay for reports, Inspections and meetings arranged by Broker on Buyer's behalf.
D. Buyer is advised to read the attached Buyer's Inspection Advisory for a list of items and other concerns that typically warrant Inspections or investigation by Buyer or other professionals.

8. **DISPUTE RESOLUTION:**
A. **MEDIATION:** Buyer and Broker agree to mediate any dispute or claim arising between them out of this Agreement, or any resulting transaction, before resorting to arbitration or court action, subject to paragraph 8B(2) below. Paragraph 8B(2) below applies whether or not the arbitration provision is initialed. Mediation fees, if any, shall be divided equally among the parties involved. If, for any dispute or claim to which this paragraph applies, any party commences an action without first attempting to resolve the matter through mediation, or refuses to mediate after a request has been made, then that party shall not be entitled to recover attorney fees, even if they would otherwise be available to that party in any such action. THIS MEDIATION PROVISION APPLIES WHETHER OR NOT THE ARBITRATION PROVISION IS INITIALED.
B. **ARBITRATION OF DISPUTES:** (1) Buyer and Broker agree that any dispute or claim in law or equity arising between them regarding the obligation to pay compensation under this Agreement, which is not settled through mediation, shall be decided by neutral, binding arbitration, including and subject to paragraph 8B(2) below. The arbitrator shall be a retired judge or justice, or an attorney with at least five years of residential real estate law experience, unless the parties mutually agree to a different arbitrator, who shall render an award in accordance with substantive California law. The parties shall have the right to discovery in accordance with Code of Civil Procedure §1283.05. In all other respects, the arbitration shall be conducted in accordance with Title 9 of Part III, of the California Code of Civil Procedure. Judgment upon the award of the arbitrator(s) may be entered in any court having jurisdiction. Interpretation of this agreement to arbitrate shall be governed by the Federal Arbitration Act.
(2) EXCLUSIONS FROM MEDIATION AND ARBITRATION: The following matters are excluded from mediation and arbitration hereunder: (i) a judicial or non-judicial foreclosure or other action or proceeding to enforce a deed of trust, mortgage, or installment land sale contract as defined in Civil Code §2985; (ii) an unlawful detainer action; (iii) the filing or enforcement of a mechanic's lien; (iv) any matter that is within the jurisdiction of a probate, small claims, or bankruptcy court; and (v) an action for bodily injury or wrongful death, or for any right of action to which Code of Civil Procedure §337.1 or §337.15 applies. The filing of a court action to enable the recording of a notice of pending action, for order of attachment, receivership, injunction, or other provisional remedies, shall not constitute a waiver of the mediation and arbitration provisions.

"NOTICE: BY INITIALING IN THE SPACE BELOW YOU ARE AGREEING TO HAVE ANY DISPUTE ARISING OUT OF THE MATTERS INCLUDED IN THE 'ARBITRATION OF DISPUTES' PROVISION DECIDED BY NEUTRAL ARBITRATION AS PROVIDED BY CALIFORNIA LAW AND YOU ARE GIVING UP ANY RIGHTS YOU MIGHT POSSESS TO HAVE THE DISPUTE LITIGATED IN A COURT OR JURY TRIAL. BY INITIALING IN THE SPACE BELOW YOU ARE GIVING UP YOUR JUDICIAL RIGHTS TO DISCOVERY AND APPEAL, UNLESS THOSE RIGHTS ARE SPECIFICALLY INCLUDED IN THE 'ARBITRATION OF DISPUTES' PROVISION. IF YOU REFUSE TO SUBMIT TO ARBITRATION AFTER AGREEING TO THIS PROVISION, YOU MAY BE COMPELLED TO ARBITRATE UNDER THE AUTHORITY OF THE CALIFORNIA CODE OF CIVIL PROCEDURE. YOUR AGREEMENT TO THIS ARBITRATION PROVISION IS VOLUNTARY."

"WE HAVE READ AND UNDERSTAND THE FOREGOING AND AGREE TO SUBMIT DISPUTES ARISING OUT OF THE MATTERS INCLUDED IN THE 'ARBITRATION OF DISPUTES' PROVISION TO NEUTRAL ARBITRATION."

Buyer's Initials _____/_____   Broker's Initials _____/_____

Buyer and Broker acknowledge receipt of a copy of this page.
Buyer's Initials (_____X_____)
Broker's Initials (_____X_____)

Reviewed by _____ Date _____

BUYER BROKER AGREEMENT – EXCLUSIVE (BBE PAGE 3 OF 4)

Figure 11-2.   Buyer Agency Agreement (*continued*)

Buyer: _____ Date: _____

9. **TIME TO BRING LEGAL ACTION:** Legal action for breach of this Agreement, or any obligation arising therefrom, shall be brought no more than two years from the expiration of the Representation Period or from the date such cause of action may arise, whichever occurs first.

10. **OTHER TERMS AND CONDITIONS,** including ATTACHED SUPPLEMENTS: ☑ Buyer's Inspection Advisory (C.A.R. Form BIA)
_____
_____
_____
_____
_____
_____

11. **ATTORNEY FEES:** In any action, proceeding or arbitration between Buyer and Broker regarding the obligation to pay compensation under this Agreement, the prevailing Buyer or Broker shall be entitled to reasonable attorney fees and costs, except as provided in paragraph 8A.

12. **ENTIRE AGREEMENT:** All understandings between the parties are incorporated in this Agreement. Its terms are intended by the parties as a final, complete and exclusive expression of their agreement with respect to its subject matter, and may not be contradicted by evidence of any prior agreement or contemporaneous oral agreement. This Agreement may not be extended, amended, modified, altered or changed, except in writing signed by Buyer and Broker. In the event that any provision of this Agreement is held to be ineffective or invalid, the remaining provisions will nevertheless be given full force and effect. This Agreement and any supplement, addendum or modification, including any copy, whether by copier, facsimile, NCR or electronic, may be signed in two or more counterparts, all of which shall constitute one and the same writing.

Buyer acknowledges that Buyer has read, understands, accepts and has received a copy of this Agreement.

Buyer _____ Date _____
Address _____ City _____ State _____ Zip _____
Telephone _____ Fax _____ E-mail _____

Buyer _____ Date _____
Address _____ City _____ State _____ Zip _____
Telephone _____ Fax _____ E-mail _____

Real Estate Broker (Firm) _____
By (Agent) _____ Date _____
Address _____ City _____ State _____ Zip _____
Telephone _____ Fax _____ E-mail _____

Published and Distributed by:
REAL ESTATE BUSINESS SERVICES, INC.
a subsidiary of the California Association of REALTORS®
525 South Virgil Avenue, Los Angeles, California 90020

The System for Success®

BBE REVISED 10/04 (PAGE 4 OF 4)

Reviewed by _____ Date _____

BUYER BROKER AGREEMENT – EXCLUSIVE (BBE PAGE 4 OF 4)

Figure 11-2. Buyer Agency Agreement (*continued*)

Dual Agency

In *dual agency*, the licensee represents both buyer and seller at the same time. Dual agency creates potential conflict because it is impossible for a dual agent to provide full agency responsibility to both parties at the same time. Therefore, the agency disclosure (see Figure 4-1) severely restricts the actual agency responsibility that the dual agent has. Typically the dual agent cannot tell the seller the maximum price the buyer is willing to pay and cannot tell the buyer the minimum price the seller would accept. Nor can the dual agent tell either party about any particular urgency to transact (or lack of it) that the other party may have. Essentially, the dual agent is pretty much prohibited from giving either party any of the information they would be most eager to get.

In California, a dual agency can exist even if more than one agent is involved. If other agents in a transaction are "associated" with either the buyer's or the seller's agent, it is dual agency. Association usually means that the agents are members of the same brokerage firm. For example, it would be a dual agency if a buyer wanted to look at (or make an offer on) a property listed by a salesperson in the same firm as the buyer's agent. Both buyer and seller must be given agency disclosure forms by every agent involved.

Questions on Chapter 11

1. When more than one broker is employed by an owner to sell real estate, there exists
   (A) an exclusive agency listing
   (B) an open listing
   (C) an exclusive right to sell
   (D) a unilateral listing

2. To collect a commission in court, a broker must show that
   (A) he is licensed
   (B) he had a contract of employment
   (C) he is the cause of the sale
   (D) all of the above

3. The broker's responsibility to the owner of realty is regulated by
   (A) the law of agency
   (B) the law of equity
   (C) rendition superior
   (D) investiture

4. What is a real estate listing?
   (A) A list of brokers and salespersons
   (B) A list of property held by an owner
   (C) The employment of a broker by an owner to sell or lease
   (D) A written list of improvements on land

5. Under an open listing
   (A) the seller is not legally required to notify other agents in the case of sale by one of the listing brokers
   (B) the owner may sell the property without paying a commission
   (C) both A and B
   (D) neither A nor B

6. If the listing owner sells her property while the listing agreement is valid, she is liable for a commission under a(n) _____ listing agreement.
   (A) net
   (B) exclusive right to sell
   (C) exclusive agency listing
   (D) open

7. Under an exclusive agency listing,
   (A) the seller may sell by his own effort without obligation to pay a commission ✓
   (B) the broker receives a commission regardless of whether the property is sold
   (C) both A and B
   (D) neither A nor B

8. The listing agreement may not be terminated
   (A) without compensation if the broker has found a prospect ready, able, and willing to buy on the seller's terms
   (B) because of incompetence of the prospect
   (C) if the seller files for bankruptcy
   (D) if the listing agreement is for a definite time

9. A dual agent   ✗ B
   (A) may perform the same duties for both buyer and seller that she would if she were agent for only one of them
   (B) is severely restricted in the agency duties that she can perform for either party
   (C) may represent either party, but only one of them at a time
   (D) is someone who has more that one property listed

10. Under which type of listing are brokers reluctant to actively pursue a sale, because of the risk of losing a sale to competing brokers?
   (A) An exclusive right to sell listing   (C) An open listing
   (B) A net listing   (D) A multiple listing ← MLS-

11. A principal may sell her property without paying a commission under
   (A) an open listing ✓   (C) both A and B   ✗ C
   (B) an exclusive agency listing ✓   (D) neither A nor B

12. The rate of commission is normally fixed under   never fixed always between buyer & seller
   (A) a net listing   (C) both A and B
   (B) an open listing   (D) neither A nor B   ✗ B

13. Buyer and seller both may pay a commission so long as
   (A) all parties are aware of the situation
   (B) payments are made to the same broker
   (C) both A and B   ✗ A
   (D) neither A nor B

14. It is possible to terminate a listing by
   (A) revocation by the principal   (C) both A and B
   (B) revocation by the agent   (D) neither A nor B   ✗ C

15. An exclusive right to sell listing enables
   (A) the seller to sell the property himself without paying a commission
   (B) cooperating brokers to sell and earn a commission
   (C) both A and B
   (D) neither A nor B

16. In-house sales could result in an undisclosed   always have to disclose dual agency
   (A) listing   (C) double commission
   (B) conflict of brokers   (D) dual agency

17. Failure to disclose a dual agency can lead to
    (A) loss of commission
    (B) license suspension or revocation
    (C) civil action by the injured party
    (D) all of the above

18. To be enforceable, a listing agreement for the sale of real estate must be
    (A) written on a special form
    (B) in written form
    (C) oral or in writing
    (D) for a term of at least twelve days

19. To be enforceable, a listing to sell personal property or a business opportunity must be
    (A) written on a special form
    (B) in written form
    (C) oral or in writing
    (D) for a term of at least twelve days

20. In order to plant a FOR SALE sign in the front yard, a broker must
    (A) be licensed
    (B) get the owner's permission
    (C) place the property in the multiple listing system
    (D) pay rent to the owner

Completing Listing Contracts

Questions 21 through 33 are based upon the following narrative:

You are a salesperson for Able Realty. On May 10, 2006, you list a 10-year-old house owned by Mr. and Mrs. Nebulous under an exclusive right to sell listing for 120 days. The property is a one-story brick house with four bedrooms and two baths. It has a full basement, which measures 35 ft. × 40 ft. The lot measures 120 ft. × 70 ft.; it is fenced. It is described as Lot 9, Block F, of the Lake Alpine Subdivision, Marin County, California. It is also known as 1314 Geneva Drive.

The house has central air conditioning and an entrance foyer. The living room measures 15 ft. × 12 ft. Bedrooms are about average size for this type of house, in your opinion. The house has an eat-in kitchen with a built-in oven and range. The owners state that the dishwasher and refrigerator will remain, but they plan to take the clothes washer and dryer.

The house is heated by natural gas. Water is heated the same way. Water is supplied by the county. The house is on a sewer line.

Bunn is the elementary school; Gunter, the junior high; Washington, the high school.

The tax rate is 1 percent; the latest tax appraisal is $170,000.

You list the house for $298,500. The commission rate is 6 percent. There is an existing, assumable 8.5 percent mortgage on the property. The current balance is $204,687.36, with equal monthly payments of $1,649.99. The owners will accept a second mortgage for up to $30,000 at a 9 percent interest rate for 7 years.

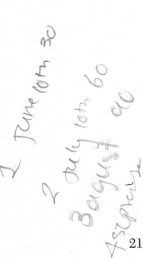

21. Which of the following is correct?
    (A) The washer and dryer remain.
    (B) The refrigerator and dishwasher remain.
    (C) There is no refrigerator.
    (D) Only the washer remains.

22. The listing expires on
    (A) May 10, 2006
    (B) July 10, 2006
    (C) July 9, 2006
    (D) none of the above

23. Which of the following is correct?
    (A) Natural gas heats the house.
    (B) The house is on a sewer line.
    (C) Both A and B
    (D) Neither A nor B

24. Taxes for the year are
    (A) $1,530
    (B) $1,700
    (C) $15,300
    (D) $17,000

25. If the house is sold at the listed price, the commission will be
    (A) $13,467
    (B) $16,323
    (C) $17,910
    (D) none of the above

26. Which of the following is *not* correct?
    (A) The house is at 1413 Geneva Drive.
    (B) The house has a fenced yard.
    (C) The basement contains 1,400 square feet.
    (D) The listing contract date is May 10, 2006.

27. Which of the following is correct concerning schools?
    (A) Gunter—junior high
    (B) Bunn—high
    (C) Washington—elementary
    (D) None of the above

28. Which features does the house have?
    (A) Central air conditioning
    (B) A fireplace
    (C) Five bedrooms
    (D) Only one bath

29. The basement measurements are
    (A) 30 ft. × 40 ft.
    (B) 40 ft. × 40 ft.
    (C) 35 ft. × 40 ft.
    (D) none of the above

30. The lot is in Block _____ of the Lake Alpine Subdivision.
    (A) A
    (B) B
    (C) C
    (D) none of the above

31. Which of the following is correct?
    (A) There is an eat-in kitchen.
    (B) The dining room is 15 ft. × 12 ft.
    (C) The home has two stories.
    (D) Both A and B are correct.

32. The listing is for a period of
    (A) 90 days
    (B) 3 months
    (C) 120 days
    (D) six months

33. The house has
    (A) a ½ acre lot
    (B) a wood exterior
    (C) three baths
    (D) four bedrooms

ANSWERS

1. **B**	8. **A**	15. **D**	22. **D**	29. **C**
2. **D**	9. **B**	16. **D**	23. **C**	30. **D**
3. **A**	10. **C**	17. **D**	24. **B**	31. **A**
4. **C**	11. **C**	18. **B**	25. **C**	32. **C**
5. **C**	12. **B**	19. **C**	26. **A**	33. **D**
6. **B**	13. **A**	20. **B**	27. **A**	
7. **A**	14. **C**	21. **B**	28. **A**	

The properly filled-out contract follows:

EXCLUSIVE AUTHORIZATION TO SELL

SALES PRICE: $298,500 **TYPE HOME** One-story **TOTAL BEDROOMS** 4 **TOTAL BATHS** 2

ADDRESS: 1314 Geneva Drive **JURISDICTION OF:** San Rafael, Marin County, CA

AMT. OF LOAN TO BE ASSUMED $ 204,687.36 **AS OF WHAT DATE:** 5/10/06 **TAXES & INS. INCLUDED:** no **YEARS TO GO** ___ **AMOUNT PAYABLE MONTHLY $** 1,649.79 @ 8.5 % **TYPE LOAN** ___

MORTGAGE COMPANY ___ **2nd TRUST $** ___

ESTIMATED EXPECTED RENT MONTHLY $ ___ **TYPE OF APPRAISAL REQUESTED:** ___

OWNER'S NAME Mr. & Mrs. Nebulous **PHONES: (HOME)** ___ **(BUSINESS)** ___

TENANTS NAME ___ **PHONES: (HOME)** ___ **(BUSINESS)** ___

POSSESSION ___ **DATE LISTED:** 5/10/06 **EXCLUSIVE FOR** 4 months **DATE OF EXPIRATION** 9/9/06

LISTING BROKER Able Realty **PHONE** ___ **KEY AVAILABLE AT** ___

LISTING SALESMAN You **HOME PHONE:** ___ **HOW TO BE SHOWN** ___

(1) ENTRANCE FOYER ☒ CENTER HALL ☐	(18) AGE 10 Cent. AIR CONDITIONING ☒	(32) TYPE KITCHEN CABINETS
(2) LIVING ROOM SIZE 15'x12' FIREPLACE ☐	(19) ROOFING TOOL HOUSE ☒	(33) TYPE COUNTER TOPS
(3) DINING ROOM SIZE	(20) GARAGE SIZE PATIO ☐	(34) EAT-IN SIZE KITCHEN ☒
(4) BEDROOM TOTAL: 4 DOWN UP	(21) SIDE DRIVE ☐ CIRCULAR DRIVE ☐	(35) BREAKFAST ROOM ☐
(5) BATHS TOTAL: 2 DOWN UP	(22) PORCH ☐ SIDE ☐ REAR ☐ SCREENED ☐	(36) BUILT-IN OVEN & RANGE ☒
(6) DEN SIZE FIREPLACE ☐	(23) FENCED YARD yes OUTDOOR GRILL ☐	(37) SEPARATE STOVE INCLUDED ☐
(7) FAMILY ROOM SIZE FIREPLACE ☐	(24) STORM WINDOWS ☐ STORM DOORS ☐	(38) REFRIGERATOR INCLUDED ☒
(8) RECREATION ROOM SIZE FIREPLACE ☐	(25) CURBS & GUTTERS ☐ SIDEWALKS ☐	(39) DISHWASHER INCLUDED ☒
(9) BASEMENT SIZE 35'x40'	(26) STORM SEWERS ☐ ALLEY ☐	(40) DISPOSAL INCLUDED ☐
NONE ☐ 1/4 ☐ 1/3 ☐ 1/2 ☐ 3/4 ☐ FULL ☒	(27) WATER SUPPLY County	(41) DOUBLE SINK ☐ SINGLE SINK ☐
(10) UTILITY ROOM SIZE	(28) SEWER ☒ SEPTIC ☐	STAINLESS STEEL ☐ PORCELAIN ☐
TYPE HOT WATER SYSTEM: Nat'l Gas (	(29) TYPE GAS: NATURAL ☒ BOTTLED ☐	(42) WASHER INCLUDED no DRYER INCLUDED no
(11) TYPE HEAT Natural Gas	(30) WHY SELLING	(43) PANTRY ☐ EXHAUST FAN ☐
(12) EST. FUEL COST		(44) LAND ASSESSMENT $
(13) ATTIC ☐	(31) DIRECTIONS TO PROPERTY	(45) IMPROVEMENTS $
PULL DOWN STAIRWAY ☐ REGULAR STAIRWAY ☐ TRAP DOOR ☐		(46) TOTAL ASSESSMENT $ 170,000
(14) MAIDS ROOM ☐ TYPE BATH		(47) TAX RATE 1%
LOCATION		(48) TOTAL ANNUAL TAXES $ 1,700
(15) NAME OF BUILDER		(49) LOT SIZE 120'x70'
(16) SQUARE FOOTAGE		(50) LOT NO 9 BLOCK F SECTION
(17) EXTERIOR OF HOUSE Brick		Lake Alpine Subdivision

NAME OF SCHOOLS: **ELEMENTARY** Bunn **JR. HIGH** Gunter

HIGH Washington **PAROCHIAL** ___

PUBLIC TRANSPORTATION: ___

NEAREST SHOPPING AREA: ___

REMARKS: Seller will accept 2nd Mtg. for up to $30,000 at 7% interest rate for 7 years.

Date: May 10, 2006

In consideration of the services of _____ Able Realty _____ (herein called "Broker") to be rendered to the undersigned (herein called "Owner"), and of the promise of Broker to make reasonable efforts to obtain a Purchaser therefor, Owner hereby lists with Broker the real estate and all improvements thereon which are described above (all herein called "the property"), and Owner hereby grants to Broker the exclusive and irrevocable right to sell such property from 12:00 Noon on _____ May 10 _____, 20 06 until 12:00 Midnight on _____ Sept 7 _____, 20 06 (herein called "period of time"), for the price of Two Hundred Ninety-Eight Thousand Five Hundred Dollars ($ 298,500) or for such other price and upon such other terms (including exchange) as Owner may subsequently authorize during the period of time.

It is understood by Owner that the above sum or any other price subsequently authorized by Owner shall include a cash fee of _____ 6% _____ per cent of such price or other price which shall be payable by Owner to Broker upon consummation by any Purchaser or Purchasers of a valid contract of sale of the property during the period of time and whether or not Broker was a procuring cause of any such contract of sale.

If the property is sold or exchanged by Owner, or by Broker or by any other person to whom the property was shown by Broker or any representative of Broker within sixty (60) days after the expiration of the period of time mentioned above, Owner agrees to pay to Broker a cash fee which shall be the same percentage of the purchase price as the percentage mentioned above.

Broker is hereby authorized by Owner to place a "For Sale" sign on the property and to remove all signs of other brokers or salesmen during the period of time, and Owner hereby agrees to make the property available to Broker at all reasonable hours for the purpose of showing it to prospective Purchasers.

Owner agrees to convey the property to the Purchaser by warranty deed with the usual covenants of title and free and clear from all encumbrances, tenancies, liens (for taxes or otherwise), but subject to applicable restrictive covenants of record. Owner acknowledges receipt of a copy of this agreement.

WITNESS the following signature(s) and seal(s):

Date Signed: _____ _____ (SEAL)
(Owner)

Listing Broker _____

Address _____ **Telephone** _____ _____ (SEAL)
(Owner)

Chapter 12/*Other Real Estate Contracts*

People dealing in real estate may want to accomplish transactions that do not involve the categories of contracts discussed in Chapters 8 through 11. Contracts not included in those categories are:

1. Contracts for the exchange of real estate
2. Real property sales contract
3. Options
4. Assignments
5. Novations

Each of these contracts is discussed below.

Contracts for Exchange

A *contract for exchange* is used when principals want to exchange property. You may wonder why people would want to swap their real estate, but there are peculiarities in the U.S. Internal Revenue Code that confer tax advantages on some kinds of exchanges. However, these advantages are available only for investment property (property held for rental and income) and property used in one's business. Therefore, people who exchange homes that they live in (their residences) can't use these tax breaks (those who sell their own homes are offered different tax breaks), so a residential broker or salesperson is unlikely to encounter an exchange transaction. If both properties are agreed by the owners to be of equal value and both are unencumbered, they may be swapped without additional consideration. This transaction may be beneficial to the principals. For example, one person may own land and want income-producing property, whereas the other party may have the opposite holdings and needs. A swap accomplishes the objectives of both parties. Further, if it is an even swap of real estate used in trade or business or held as an investment, and no additional consideration is given, the transaction may possibly be tax-free for both parties, even though the properties exchanged are worth much more now than they cost originally.

More often than not, the properties exchanged are of different values. Then the party who gives up the lower-valued property must also give other consideration so that the trade becomes a fair one, acceptable to both parties. Personal property (cash, cars, diamonds, etc.) put into an exchange to equalize the total value of all property exchanged is called *boot*. The party who receives boot may be taxed to the extent of the unlike property received or, if less, to the gain realized. *Unlike property* in a real estate exchange transaction is anything that isn't real estate. *Like-kind property* is real estate. The tax advantage only applies to the value of like-kind property that is exchanged.

Mortgaged property can be exchanged. Suppose Mr. Jones owns a $10,000 vacant lot free and clear; Mr. Smith owns a $50,000 building with a $40,000 mortgage against it. Since the equity of both is $10,000, the exchange is a fair trade. Smith's boot received is relief from a $40,000 debt.

Deferred exchanges are now commonplace; see page 297. Two-way exchanges may be more or less difficult to accomplish than three-way trades, or trades involving four parties. There is no limit to the number of parties involved in an exchange. So far as the broker is concerned, he usually represents both parties in a dual agency capacity.

Real Property Sales Contract

In a *real property sales contract*, the property seller finances the sale but does not surrender the deed until all payments have been made. This type of contract typically allows the purchaser to gain possession, but not ownership, of the land while paying for it. Since the seller retains the deed until the final payment, he is well protected in the event of default. Because the land is still legally his, he doesn't have to go through foreclosure; he can have the defaulting buyer evicted quickly and regain full possession and ownership of the land.

A real property sales contract is also known as a *land contract* and an *installment land sale contract*. It is sometimes used for the sale of subdivided land, especially in resort communities.

Options

An *option* gives its holder the right, but *not* the obligation, to buy specific property within a certain time at a specified price. The option need not be exercised. An *optionee* can elect not to purchase the property, in which case amounts paid to acquire the option belong to the property owner, who is the *optionor*.

Consideration must be paid with an option. Upon exercise of the option, the amount paid for the option may or may not apply to the sales price, depending upon the agreement.

An option may be used by a speculator who is uncertain whether a significant increase in the value of the property is forthcoming. Through purchasing an option, she can be assured of a fixed price for the property in a set time span. If the value increase materializes, she exercises the option. Otherwise, she lets it lapse and loses only the cost of the option. The holder of an option may sell the option itself (at a gain or a loss) if she wishes to do so.

Assignments

Assignments refer to the transfer of contracts. Through an assignment, a person may convey to someone else his rights under a contract. A lease may be assigned, as may a contract of sale, a deed, an option, and so on. The person who gives or assigns the contract is the assignor, the receiver the assignee. It should be noted that the assignor is not automatically relieved of his duties to other parties under the earlier contract. If a lease contract exists and is assigned, for example, the original lessee is still bound to pay rent if the assignee fails to do so.

Novations

A *novation* is a contract used to substitute a new contract for an existing contract between the same parties. It may also be used to substitute or replace one party to a contract with a different party. Thus, a novation is used to amend an agreement or substitute the parties involved.

A novation must be bilateral: both parties must agree to it. Suppose a home is to be sold, with the buyer assuming the seller's mortgage. Since the seller made a contract to repay the debt, she cannot automatically substitute the new buyer for herself on the debt. Acceptance of the substitution must come from the lender. The process used for this substitution is called a *novation*. In such a case, the original contract has been assigned, while at the same time the assignor has been relieved of her obligations to other parties to the contract.

Questions on Chapter 12

1. Property, unlike real estate, that is used to equalize the value of all property exchanged is called
   (A) listing
   (B) gain
   (C) boot
   (D) equalizers

   ex of pork & beans

2. Mr. Hill has a 6-month option on 10 acres at $1,000 per acre. Mr. Hill may
   (A) buy the property for $10,000 ✓
   (B) sell the option to another
   (C) not buy the land ✓
   (D) all of the above

3. A contract that gives someone the right but not the obligation to buy at a specified price within a specified time is
   (A) a contract for sale
   (B) an option
   (C) an agreement of sale
   (D) none of the above

4. A real property sales contract also is known as
   (A) an installment land sales contract ✓
   (B) a mortgage
   (C) land contract ✓
   (D) both A and C

5. Which of the following best describes an installment or real property sales contract?
   (A) A contract to buy land only
   (B) A mortgage on land
   (C) A means of conveying title immediately, while the purchaser pays for the property
   (D) A method of selling real estate whereby the purchaser pays for the property in regular installments, while the seller retains title to the property

6. Mr. Beans owns land worth $50,000; Mr. Pork owns a house worth $300,000, subject to a $200,000 mortgage that Beans will assume. For a fair trade,
   (A) Pork should pay $50,000 cash in addition
   (B) Beans should pay $50,000 cash (or other boot) in addition
   (C) Beans and Pork may trade properties evenly
   (D) none of the above

   Beans 50,00   Pork 300,00   200,00   100,000

7. A speculator can tie up land to await value enhancement, without obligating himself, through the use of
   (A) an installment land contract
   (B) an option
   (C) a contract for deed
   (D) A and C only

8. Ms. Smith wants to buy Jones's house and assume the 6 percent mortgage. Jones should
   (A) assign the debt
   (B) grant an option on the debt
   (C) ask the lender for a novation to substitute Smith
   (D) none of the above

9. Larry assigned his rights to use leased property to Allen. Allen stopped paying rent. Larry may
   (A) sue Allen for the rent
   (B) not pay the property owner since he hasn't received payment from Allen
   (C) both A and B
   (D) neither A nor B

   X A   *Larry sublettted*

10. Treasure Homes sold a lot to Mr. Kay under a real property land sales contract. Upon making the down payment, Kay is entitled to
    (A) a warranty deed
    (B) use of the property
    (C) a fee simple estate
    (D) all of the above

11. A like-kind exchange or deferred like-kind exchange is allowed under Section _____ of the Internal Revenue Code.
    (A) 8
    (B) 1031
    (C) 1231
    (D) 1250

12. A *land contract* is also known as a(n)
    (A) installment land sale contract
    (B) real property sales contract
    (C) contract for deed
    (D) all of the above

13. In a typical land contract, the seller transfers the deed
    (A) at closing
    (B) upon receipt of disclosures
    (C) after the rescission period expires
    (D) when final payment is made

14. Like-kind exchanges of mortgaged property are based on
    (A) appraised property value
    (B) equity value
    (C) book value
    (D) adjusted tax basis

15. Before the expiration of an option, the optionee may
    (A) buy the property
    (B) choose to do nothing
    (C) sell the option
    (D) do any of the above

ANSWERS

1. **C**	4. **D**	7. **B**	10. **B**	13. **D**
2. **D**	5. **D**	8. **C**	11. **B**	14. **B**
3. **B**	6. **B**	9. **A**	12. **D**	15. **D**

PART IV: REAL ESTATE ANALYSIS

Chapter 13/*Mortgages and Finance*

California real estate professionals learn very early in their careers that borrowed money is the lifeblood of the real estate business, because nearly all real estate purchases are made with borrowed funds. In addition, most real estate development and construction use borrowed money. Without access to such funds, these aspects of the real estate business dry up quickly; such cessation of activity has occurred several times during periods of "tight" money, when interest rates are high and loanable funds scarce.

There are several reasons for this dependence on borrowed money in the real estate business. Perhaps the most significant reason is that real estate is *expensive*. Even a modest home costs tens of thousands of dollars; apartment projects, office buildings, shopping complexes, and the like often cost in the millions. Very few of the more than 59 percent of California families that own their own homes could do so if they had not been able to borrow a significant portion of the price at the time of purchase. Quite simply, very few families have the kind of ready cash necessary to buy a home without borrowing, especially in California, with the high price of housing. Similarly, very few real estate developers or builders have enough cash on hand to finance completely the ventures they engage in.

Another fact that contributes to the importance of borrowed money in the real estate business is that real estate is *very good collateral* for loans. It lasts a long time and so can be used to back up loans that have very long repayment terms, such as the 20 to 30 years typical of most home mortgage loans. This enables real estate owners to spread the cost of an asset over a long payment term, so that they can afford more expensive units, as well as to spread the payment over the time they expect to use the asset.

Real estate is *stable in value*. Of course, some real estate values are more stable than others, but generally a lender can expect that real estate collateral will not depreciate quickly and may indeed rise in value.

Real estate investors like to borrow money to buy real estate because it gives them *leverage*. As a simple example, suppose someone buys an apartment complex costing $5 million by putting up $1 million of his own money and getting a mortgage loan for the other $4 million. In effect, he has gained "control" of a $5 million property but has used only $1 million to do it. By borrowing he is able to buy considerably more than if he used only his own money; if he is wise in his choices of the real estate to buy, he may improve his investment profits considerably by borrowing.

Mortgages and Notes

In the financing of real estate in California, two important documents are employed: the *loan*, the evidence for which is a *promissory note* or *bond*, and the security instrument (*mortgage*),

PROMISSORY NOTE	**SECURITY INSTRUMENT (MORTGAGE)**
Date I owe you $100,000, payable at the rate of $900 per month for 20 years, beginning next month. Signed, T. Borrower	Date If I don't pay on the attached note, you can take 34 Spring Street, Hometown, California. Signed, T. Borrower

which is a pledge of property as security for a debt. A simplified sample of a promissory note and of a security instrument (mortgage) is shown on page 163.

Since the borrower gives the promissory note and security instrument to the lender, the borrower is the *mortgagor*. The lender is the *mortgagee*. (The suffix *-or* always signifies the giver, whereas *-ee* describes the receiver.)

A security instrument (mortgage) and a promissory note are both contracts. Any provisions that are agreed upon may be written into either contract, so long as such provisions are legal. The essential elements of a note are (a) a promise to pay at (b) a fixed or determinable time (c) a certain sum of money (d) to a payee or to bearer, (e) signed by the borrower.

Title and Lien Theory

California is a lien theory state. Trust deeds or mortgages are viewed either as transfers of property (title theory) or as the creation of a lien (lien theory). Title theory holds that the property is transferred to the lender subject to an automatic return of the property to the borrower upon payment of the loan. Lien theory holds that a mortgage gives the lender a lien on the property, but not title to it.

Types of California Security Instruments

In California, the preferred security instrument is a *deed of trust*, which is also called a *trust deed*. A mortgage can be used in lieu of a trust deed, though the mortgage is seldom encountered in California because it has lost popularity over the past few decades.

A popular but erroneous concept is that the borrower gets a mortgage (or deed of trust). The borrower really *gives* the mortgage (or deed of trust), which is the document that pledges property as security for a loan. The borrower gets a *loan*. Some people use popular terminology, such as "I got a mortgage on my new house" though readers should be aware of the legal reality. The borrower gave a mortgage and got a loan. Accordingly, a strict definition question, for example, "Who gets the mortgage when real estate is purchased?" would be answered, *the lender*.

Mortgages Compared with Trust Deeds

Mortgages and trust deeds are both *security instruments*. The similarity of these documents is that both serve as a pledge of property to secure a loan. With either, if there is a default on the loan, the lender may claim the property and sell it to satisfy the debt. If the property is sold for more than the debt plus expenses of sale (an event that is unlikely) the excess belongs to the borrower. The principal difference between the two instruments is the foreclosure process and the borrower's right to regain the property after foreclosure, which is called the *right of redemption*.

MORTGAGE

In a mortgage there are two parties, the borrower (mortgagor) and lender (mortgagee). The lender gets the right to foreclose upon certain default, and can step in directly to do so, acting within the foreclosure laws of California.

TRUST DEED

In a trust deed there are usually three parties. The borrower, who is the trustor, transfers title to the property to a trustee. The trustee holds title, quietly, on behalf of the beneficiary (the lender) until and unless there is a default on the debt. If that occurs, the trustee may then sell the property at foreclosure and transfer the money to the lender.

Unlike most other states, California allows the trustee and the beneficiary to be one and the same party. Having both roles is not considered an automatic conflict of interest. However, in most situations in California, a title company acts as trustee.

Mortgage vs. Trust Deed Foreclosure Compared _____

It may seem to an observer that the mortgage gives the lender more authority and a quicker resolution to foreclose after a default. However, a mortgage also would give an unscrupulous lender an opportunity to refuse payment from the borrower in order to claim that there was a default on valuable property, in an effort to get the full principal amount immediately. This is especially tempting for a lender who has provided a contract that he now wishes to get out of, such as a low-interest-rate loan, or when he badly needs the money back.

So, to protect a borrower against an unscrupulous lender, California provides redemption rights for borrowers. The *equity of redemption* is a right given to borrowers to reclaim ownership after default on a loan, before foreclosure. In addition, there is a period set by California law, called a *statutory redemption period*, of up to a year after foreclosure, when the sale does not pay off the mortgage debt. The redemption period is three months when the mortgage is fully paid off at foreclosure. During this period, the prior owner, the one whose ownership was foreclosed, can redeem the property, regaining ownership. This is done by paying the principal, back interest and foreclosure expenses.

This creates risk for a potential buyer at foreclosure. Picture the buyer at foreclosure who provided the highest bid, became the owner, and spent substantial amounts to improve the property. Then, within a year of foreclosure, the prior owner announces that he will buy the property back for the mortgage plus interest in arrears and expenses. (Statutory redemption also provides rights to a junior mortgage lender, who may have received little or nothing at foreclosure).

When a trust deed is used, there is no right of redemption following the trustee's sale. The sale is final and absolute. The absence of a redemption period following a foreclosure sale is the compelling reason that the trust deed is favored in California.

The trustee is trusted by both parties to observe all laws. Consequently, the need for redemption is minimized, and California accordingly prevents redemption for someone foreclosed when a deed of trust is used.

Suppose that the trust deed provides that ninety days after default on a payment, foreclosure proceedings may begin. The trustee is trusted by the borrower to wait the full ninety days and, if there is a foreclosure sale, that all required rules of a foreclosure sale will be followed. This will prevent a lender from giving a bargain sale to a friend and demanding an unwarranted deficiency from the borrower. The lender trusts the trustee to file for foreclosure on the 91st day, and not be persuaded by the borrower to wait longer or to accept a token payment when the full amount is due.

California Mortgage Foreclosure _____

To foreclose in California, notice of the sale must be posted in the courthouse 20 days before the sale and advertised weekly in the legal newspaper of general circulation for at least three weeks. The property is then auctioned off on the courthouse steps to the highest cash bidder, though the mortgage lender may bid it in for the mortgage amount, without using cash.

In California, liens that predated the mortgage generally have a prior claim. This includes tax liens, judgment liens, and mechanic's liens. In fact, if a contract with a contractor predates the mortgage, it has priority, even though work was performed after the mechanic's lien was placed. For example, suppose an owner reaches an agreement with a contractor on January 1. The mortgage is placed on the property on February 1. The contractor begins work March 1. The mechanic's lien has priority over the mortgage.

As noted earlier, the right of redemption gives the borrower of a mortgage one year to reclaim the property by paying back the full principal, interest, and expenses. If the foreclosure sale provided full payment to lenders, the redemption period is shortened to three months.

Should the foreclosure sale bring less than the amount of debt, the mortgage lender can apply for a *deficiency judgment*. In California, deficiency judgments are prohibited for most real estate situations. These include all purchase money mortgages and any foreclosure under a power of sale. In addition, the lender may generally not bid less than the amount of lien.

In California, a debtor may use bankruptcy to delay foreclosure. Filing a bankruptcy petition stops the enforcement of a lien against the bankrupt person's property.

California Trust Deed Foreclosure

Trust deed foreclosure in California is relatively quick and at a low cost because a third party holds title, with the power of sale. The trustee records a notice of default and, at least 20 days prior to the sale, sends a copy by registered mail to all persons who requested notice. The letter states the time and place of sale. Notice of the sale must be posted in the courthouse and published in the newspaper for at least 20 days before the sale. Essentially the sale must be advertised once a week for three weeks.

Generally at public sale, the trustee bids in the amount of debt to claim the property. Other bidders must pay with cash or a certified check. There is not much point in a lender bidding in a smaller amount because deficiency judgments are not possible when a trust deed is used. A smaller amount may be bid by a lender if a suit against the borrower for *waste* is contemplated.

After the trustee's sale, the trustor has no redemption rights. Again, that explains why a trust deed is favored over a mortgage.

A trust deed may be foreclosed by court action (judicial foreclosure) and the lender could possibly gain a deficiency judgment, but the process is much longer and would give the borrower redemption rights, just as he would have under a mortgage.

Sue on the Note

A creditor may sue on the promissory note in California. That is, he or she may decide not to foreclose, but simply to demand payment for the amount borrowed. This would be preferred if the borrower is wealthy and the property is no longer valuable and not desired. However, by suing on the note, the lender may give up any opportunity for foreclosure. In other words, in California a lender may be allowed to demand payment for the debt or take the property to satisfy the debt, but not both.

Mortgage Loan Classification

Mortgages are often classified or described according to particular provisions. Several types of mortgages and their provisions are described below. (The term *mortgage* is used here for simplicity; the actual document is a *deed of trust*.)

VA MORTGAGES (ALSO KNOWN AS GI MORTGAGES)

Department of Veteran's Affairs (VA) loans are made by private lenders. The VA guaranty on the loan protects the lender against loss if the payments are not made. The amount of guaranty on the loan is calculated as follows:

Loan Amount	Guaranty
Up to $45,000	50% of loan amount
$45,000 to $56,250	$22,500
$56,251 to $144,000	40% of loan amount, subject to maximum of $36,000
Over $144,000	25% of Freddie Mac conforming loan limit

The VA provides each eligible veteran with a maximum guaranty, called an "entitlement." Each veteran's current (2004) entitlement is $36,000; an entitlement of up to 25 percent of Freddie Mac's conforming loan limit may be obtained for loans over $144,000 used to buy or construct a home. The maximum guaranty for 2005 would be $89,912. This is 25 percent of Freddie Mac's conforming loan limit of $359,650 for a single-family residence.

A particular advantage of the VA loan program is that no down payment on the home is required: the VA loan can be for 100 percent of the purchase price. Most lenders limit the amount of a VA loan over $144,000 to four times the available entitlement plus any down payment the veteran makes. Therefore, a no-down-payment loan has an effective maximum (2004) of $359,650.

Only eligible veterans may originate a new VA loan, but anyone may assume a VA loan from a veteran. So long as a VA loan exists, the guaranty on the loan is "charged" against the entitlement of the veteran who originated it. Nonetheless, a veteran who still has a VA loan charged against his or her entitlement may have "remaining entitlement" to use for another VA loan.

The main advantage of the VA loan is its no-down-payment features. Lenders have greater security because they may look to the borrower, the VA, and/or the property in the event of default. For example, suppose that a veteran borrows $144,000 on a VA mortgage, reduces it to $140,000, and then defaults. The property is foreclosed and sold for $100,000. The VA will repay the lender $40,000 (the outstanding balance less the amount realized at foreclosure) plus expenses of foreclosure.

FHA MORTGAGES

The Federal Housing Administration (FHA), which is now part of the Department of Housing and Urban Development (HUD), has many programs that help to provide housing. They insure single-family and multifamily housing loans, nursing home mortgage loans, and loans on mobile homes and other properties. Some FHA loans provide subsidies to eligible borrowers. An FHA-insured loan requires only a small down payment, which is the principal advantage to borrowers. Borrowers need their own cash only for the down payment and closing costs. The required down payment is 3 percent of the first $50,000 of price plus closing costs, and 5 percent of the amount over $50,000. There also are maximum limits on the amount of an FHA-insured single-family loan, from (as of 2005) as little as $160,176 in some low-cost areas to $290,319 in designated high-cost areas (up to $312,895 in many parts of California; see https://entp.hud.gov/idapp/html/hicost1.cfm).

The fee for FHA mortgage loan insurance is paid partly at origination (2¼ percent of the loan amount) and partly by a fee of ½ (0.50) percent per year paid monthly. The insurance is supposed to be paid for by the borrower, although it is possible to bargain with the seller of the property to have him pay some or all of the fee due at origination. Even with the insurance premium, however, the cash requirement for an FHA loan is relatively small. This feature and the fact that borrower qualification standards are somewhat less stringent than for conventional loans are the main attractions of FHA loans to borrowers. The main attraction for lenders is the insurance of the loan balance. Note that property, lender, and borrower must all meet FHA qualifications.

CONVENTIONAL MORTGAGES: CONFORMING AND JUMBO

Conventional mortgages are loans that are neither guaranteed by the VA nor insured by the FHA. Generally, they are the fixed-rate, fixed-principal-and-interest-payment type. In 2005, the maximum amount for a single-family house to conform to Federal Home Loan Mortgage Corporation (FHLMC) or Federal National Mortgage Association (FNMA) guidelines was $359,650. Loans above that amount are called "jumbo." Jumbo mortgages may be insured privately, with *private mortgage insurance* (called PMI in the mortgage business). Normally, on conventional loans with 80 percent loan-to-value ratio or less, no PMI is required. However, if the loan is for more than 80 percent of the lower of (a) the appraised value of the mortgaged property or (b) its sale price, lenders will require PMI, which is paid for by the borrower. Conventional loans may be for as much as 100 percent of the purchase price, provided that PMI covering the loan amount in excess of 80 percent loan-to-value can be purchased. As a practical matter, however, the cost of PMI makes loans of much more than 90 percent loan-to-value so expensive as not to be worthwhile.

SUBPRIME MORTGAGES

Loans that do not conform to FHLMC or FNMA guidelines may still be available, though typically at higher interest rates. For example, many people without an adequate historical credit record may arrange a loan, called "subprime." One case applies to those who have recently become self-employed and cannot meet FNMA or FHLMC for historical self-employment earnings. Lenders may offer a loan, but because it is not a conforming loan, and consequently is not marketable to FNMA or FHLMC, and therefore carries higher risk, it will have a higher interest rate.

FICO SCORE

Fair Isaac Company has developed a credit rating system that most lenders weigh heavily in deciding whether to offer a loan. The system is called FICO. You can get a better understanding of it from www.fico.com. It scores one's creditworthiness on a scale of 300 (the worst) to 850 (the best). Major credit bureaus (TransUnion, Experian, and Equifax) apply FICO. Some lenders will exceed typical underwriting criteria for those with high FICO scores.

TERM LOANS, AMORTIZING LOANS, AND BALLOON PAYMENT LOANS

A *term loan* requires only interest payments until maturity. At the end of the maturity term, the *entire* principal balance is due.

Amortizing loans require regular, periodic payments. Each payment is greater than the interest charged for that period, so that the principal amount of the loan is reduced at least slightly with each payment. The amount of the monthly payment for an amortizing loan is calculated to be adequate to retire the *entire* debt over the amortization period.

A *balloon payment loan* requires interest and some principal to be repaid during its term, but the debt is not fully liquidated. Upon its maturity, there is still a balance to be repaid.

FIRST AND JUNIOR MORTGAGES

Mortgages may be recorded at county courthouses to give notice of their existence. The mortgage loan that is recorded first in the courthouse against a property remains a *first mortgage* until it is fully paid off. In the event of default and foreclosure, the lender who holds the first mortgage receives payment in full *before* other mortgage lenders receive anything.

Any mortgage recorded after the first mortgage is called a *junior mortgage*. Junior mortgages are further described as *second, third, fourth*, and so on, depending upon the time they were recorded in relation to other mortgage loans on the same property. The earlier a mortgage is recorded, the earlier the mortgagee's claim in a foreclosure action.

HOME EQUITY LINES OF CREDIT

The *home equity line of credit* is like a second mortgage loan, but the borrower does not have to take possession of all of the money at one time. This type of loan is well suited for borrowers who anticipate that they will need more money in the near future, but do not need it immediately.

Setting up a home equity line can be like applying for a credit card. However, because a second mortgage is involved, there is processing, including an appraisal of the property. The application fee may be up to 2 percent of the line of credit, though some lenders may reduce or even waive this fee. Some plans also charge an annual fee to encourage the borrower to use the line once it has been granted. In addition, many plans require the borrower to take out a minimum amount when the loan is granted.

Home equity lines of credit offer a flexible way to access home equity, thereby financing periodic needs with tax-deductible interest. (Up to $100,000 of home equity loans generate tax-deductible housing interest, whereas personal interest is no longer deductible.) Borrowers may tailor the plan to the way they want to handle the payments and can draw upon the line with checks (good for infrequent, large withdrawals) or credit cards (for frequent, smaller withdrawals).

BUDGET MORTGAGES

Budget mortgages require a homeowner to pay, in addition to monthly interest and principal payments, one-twelfth of the estimated taxes and insurance into an escrow account. These mortgages reduce a lender's risk, for the lender is thus assured that adequate cash will be available when an annual tax or insurance bill comes due.

PACKAGE MORTGAGE

Package mortgages include appliances, drapes, and other items of personal property in the amount loaned. The lender tends to exercise more control over a borrower's monthly obligations, and the borrower is able to spread the payment for such items over a lengthy period.

CHATTEL MORTGAGE

A *chattel mortgage* is a mortgage on personal property. The property may be a car, boat, furniture, or the like.

BLANKET MORTGAGE

A *blanket mortgage* covers more than one parcel of real estate. *Release provisions* are usually included to allow individual parcels to be released from the mortgage upon payment of part of the mortgage principal.

OPEN-END MORTGAGE

In an *open-end mortgage*, the balance is initially increased; that is, the funding remains open for an additional amount. A homeowner may buy a house needing extensive repair work, so he or she will initially pay, say, $125,000 and get a $100,000 loan, with the provision that the balance of the loan can be increased to, say, $200,000 as repair work progresses.

FLEXIBLE-PAYMENT MORTGAGE

As will be seen in the next section, in an adjustable-rate mortgage (ARM), the adjusted payment directly follows the change in interest rates. In a *flexible-payment loan*, in contrast, changes in the interest rate may not be directly felt in the payment; there may be payment caps that limit the change in payments. Instead of the payment rising to pay for the higher interest requirement, the principal balance increases.

WRAPAROUND LOAN

The *wraparound loan* is really a second mortgage that includes the existing first mortgage in its balance. Suppose property is worth $1 million and has a $600,000 first mortgage at a low interest rate, say 6 percent. A lender might be willing to advance $150,000 at 10 percent in the form of a second mortgage, but there are negative legal or image characteristics associated with the second mortgage. So the potential second mortgagee advances $150,000 in cash and calls the loan a $750,000 wraparound ($600,000 + $150,000 = $750,000). The interest rate on the wraparound is 8 percent. The borrower pays the wraparound lender the payment on $750,000, and the wraparound lender makes the payments on the first mortgage. The first mortgage remains intact. The 8 percent return on the wraparound is a blended rate.

SWING LOAN

A *swing loan* allows a borrower to "swing a deal." Suppose a homeowner is buying a new house but hasn't sold the old one. A swing loan is provided by a bank for a short term to use as equity in the new house; the loan must be repaid when the old house is sold.

CONSTRUCTION LOAN

A *construction loan* is a loan that funds construction by advancing money in steps as the project is developed. Generally, it is considered to be a high risk and is accompanied by a high interest rate, discount points, and fees. Underwriting is more difficult for a proposed project than for one that exists in the market. The construction lender does not want to advance more than is put in the project, so the loan is made in increments: when the land is purchased, when streets and utilities are installed, when foundations are poured, when framing and roofing are begun, and so on. Before providing a construction loan, a lender generally requires a commitment for permanent financing when an income property is built.

For a *subdivision loan,* release provisions allow parcels to be removed as collateral so the lots may be sold. To release a lot requires a payment against the loan.

BRIDGE LOAN

A *bridge loan* is a short-term loan to cover the period between the construction loan and the permanent loan. There may be a time lag during which a short-term loan is needed.

GAP LOAN

A *gap loan* is used to fill in for a shortfall until certain conditions have been met, such as an occupancy percentage rate for an office building. The permanent financing may have a floor amount, payable when construction is complete, and a higher amount when occupancy reaches a certain level. A gap loan funds the difference until occupancy reaches the specified level.

HOME EQUITY LOAN

For a household that is house rich and cash poor, a *home equity loan* may be a tempting way to finance a child's college education, pay medical bills, or serve another purpose. A home equity loan is likely to be simply a second mortgage. It typically carries a lower rate than other types of consumer finance.

LAND CONTRACT

In a *land contract,* also called a *contract for deed,* an *installment sales contract,* or an *agreement for sale,* title does not pass until the final payment is made. This is often used to finance recreational or resort property or for buyers with poor credit ratings.

SALE-LEASEBACK

A lease and a loan share many of the same characteristics, so a lease can be structured to be like a loan. Instead of borrowing to raise money and then repay the loan, an owner can sell property and lease it back for a long term (25 or 30 years). The sale generates cash (like borrowing a mortgage), and the rental payments are like mortgage payments. At the end of the lease term there may be a purchase option at a small amount for the property user. This is sometimes a method of arranging 100 percent financing and controlling property without a legal purchase.

Mortgage Repayment

For decades only one mortgage repayment method was available for home loans: *fixed-interest, fixed-payment amortization.* On these loans, the interest rate was always the same, the monthly payment was always the same, and when all the scheduled payments had been made, the loan balance was paid in full. Beginning in the 1970s, however, a variety of other methods entered the mortgage market. Today, the most popular loans are fixed-rate mortgages (FRMs) and adjustable-rate mortgages (ARMs), each of which has several variations.

FIXED-RATE MORTGAGES

The *fixed-rate mortgage (FRM)* is the most popular modern mortgage instrument. It features an interest rate that does not change; it is "fixed" over the life of the loan. Fixed-rate loans can have any term up to 30 years (even longer in certain restricted government-subsidized programs). The most popular term, however, is 30 years, followed by 15 years and 20 years. In a typical FRM the monthly payment remains the same throughout the loan term; by the end of the term the loan has been completely repaid to the lender. However, there are some plans in which the monthly payment is not always the same; the most common of these are graduated payment mortgages and balloon mortgages.

Graduated Payment Mortgage (GPM)

The GPM is designed to allow a relatively low monthly payment in the first years of the loan; the payment is increased by some amount (or percentage) every year until it becomes high enough to fully amortize (pay off) the loan over the remaining term. Typically, this final payment level will be reached after 5 to as many as 10 years. One unpleasant feature of most GPMs is *negative amortization* in the early years. The loan amount actually goes up instead of down at first, because the payments during the first 3 to 5 years aren't even enough to pay the accumulating interest on the loan; the unpaid interest is added to the loan amount, which keeps growing until the payments become high enough to cover the interest.

Balloon Mortgage

The balloon mortgage features reasonable monthly payments, but a term too short to allow for the loan to be fully paid. Therefore, at the end of the term a large final payment the ("balloon" payment) is due. A typical arrangement is for the borrower to make payments as though the loan had a 30-year term; however, after 10 or 15 years the loan comes due and the entire unpaid balance must be paid.

ADJUSTABLE-RATE MORTGAGES

Adjustable-rate mortgages (ARMs) feature interest rates that change every so often. A change in the interest rate, of course, usually means a change in the amount of the monthly payment as well. ARMs were first introduced in the 1970s, but did not become really popular with borrowers until the 1980s, by which time several modifications had been introduced that helped overcome consumer reluctance. When ARMs were first offered, a wide variety of terms and conditions were available. Nowadays the ARM has been fairly well standardized into a few popular versions that have many features in common. All have *periodic adjustment*, an interest rate based upon some *index* of interest rates, and both periodic and lifetime *caps* on interest rates.

The *period* of the loan is the frequency at which adjustments occur; common periods are 6 months and 1 year, but longer periods (3 to 5 years) are gaining in popularity. Today most ARMs have the interest rate adjusted every year. Interest rates aren't adjusted arbitrarily; they are based upon an *index* of interest rates. The ARM contract specifies the index used and the *margin*. Each time the rate is adjusted, this margin will be added to the index rate to get the new rate for the ARM loan for the following period.

The *caps* are limits on changes in the interest rate. The *periodic cap* limits the amount of change for any one period; the *lifetime cap* provides upper and lower interest rate limits that apply for the entire life of the loan. The most popular cap arrangements are "l and 5" (limited largely to FHA and VA loans) and "2 and 6." The first number is the periodic cap; the second, the lifetime cap. An "annual ARM with 2 and 6 caps" will be adjusted every year (annually), by no more than 2 percentage points (the periodic cap) above or below the previous year's rate, and over the life of the loan the interest rate can't rise by more than 6 percentage points (the lifetime cap) above the original rate. ARMs are popular with lenders, who don't want to get stuck with low-interest loans in a period of rising rates, but have been difficult to "sell" to borrowers, most of whom are unwilling risk a rise in interest rates, which would increase their loan payments. The mortgage industry is addressing this concern with a variety of features and concessions tied to ARM loans. The most popular and effective of these are *convertibility* and *teaser rates*.

The convertibility feature, which is not an automatic part of all ARM loans, allows the borrower to convert the ARM loan to an FRM loan at some time in the future, usually 3, 4, or 5 years after the loan is originated. Typically a fee, usually 0.5 to 1 percent of the loan amount, is charged for conversion. The appeal of convertibility is that the loan doesn't have to be an ARM forever, and the borrower feels "safer" with the ARM because of the conversion privilege.

Teaser rates are unusually low *initial* interest rates. They are very common in ARMs with annual (or shorter) adjustment periods. An interest rate that is attractively low for the first year or two of the ARM translates into low initial payments and thus into genuine money savings for the borrower. Teaser rates can have another useful effect: if the lifetime cap applies to the initial loan rate, then the maximum interest rate on the loan will be relatively low as well. Teaser rates are typically 3 or more percentage points below current FRM interest rates. For example, if FRM loans are available at 7 percent interest for 30-year mortgages, the teaser rate for a 30-year annual ARM with 2 and 6 caps probably will be around 4 percent, or maybe even lower. This would result in a lifetime cap of 4 percent + 6 percent, or 10 percent. Even if, a year after origination, the interest rate were to rise by the full 2 percent annual cap, the second year's rate would be 6 percent, still a full point less than the original FRM rate.

To illustrate, for a 30-year FRM for $500,000 at 7 percent interest, the monthly payment would be $3,326.51. An ARM of $500,000, with a 4 percent teaser rate, would require a montly payment of $2,387.08 for the first year, and a maximum possible payment (at 6 percent interest) of $2,981.50 the second year. The ARM borrower would be more than $11,200 ahead the first year and another $4,140 ahead the second year, for total cash savings of $15,400 over the first two years. This "money in the pocket" provides many borrowers with a strong incentive to choose the ARM, particularly if it also has the convertibility feature.

ARMs with longer adjustment periods (3, 5, and even 7 years) are becoming more popular. If they have teaser rates, these rates are much closer to the FRM rate (1 percent to 1.5 percent less, at the most); periodic caps on these loans are higher, although a lifetime cap of about 6 percent is common.

OTHERS

Reverse Annuity Mortgage (RAM)

Here the lender makes the payments to the borrower, gradually advancing money to a (typically elderly) homeowner. The amounts advanced, plus interest, become the principal of the loan. Payments to the lender are deferred until a sale of the property, the death of the homeowner, or a time when the balance owed approaches the market value of the home. RAMs also can be arranged whereby money, borrowed against the home, is used to purchase an annuity contract that will pay the homeowner for life. The homeowner then pays the mortgage interest with income from the annuity.

Biweekly Mortgages

Here the lender figures the monthly payment on a 30-year amortizing loan, then requires half to be paid every 2 weeks. Because there are twenty-six 2-week periods in a year, this is the equivalent of paying for 13 months per year. As a result the loan is retired in 18 to 22 years. For borrowers who are paid every 2 weeks, such a mortgage may fit the budget well. However it may not appeal to those who are paid monthly.

Lenders

SAVINGS AND LOAN ASSOCIATIONS

Savings and loan associations are active originators of residential mortgages in the United States. Most sell the loans in the secondary market.

COMMERCIAL BANKS

Commercial banks originate many residential mortgages; they are more active, however, in the construction loan field and in other types of lending. They have a great deal of latitude in the types of activity in which they engage, but strict limitations are imposed for each type.

MUTUAL SAVINGS BANKS

Mutual savings banks have no stockholders; they operate for the benefit of depositors. Some invest in residential mortgages.

LIFE INSURANCE COMPANIES

Life insurance companies invest a relatively small amount of their total assets in residential mortgage loans. They are quite active in permanent mortgage loans on income-producing property, including apartments, shopping centers, and office buildings.

MORTGAGE COMPANIES

Mortgage companies, also known as *mortgage bankers,* are the most common sources of home mortgages. They originate almost two-thirds of all residential mortgages. However, these businesses do not lend their own money; they are not financial institutions. Rather, they originate and service home mortgage loans on behalf of large investors (insurance companies, banks, pension funds, and the like) in mortgage loans. Mortgage bankers receive a fee for originating loans and fees for servicing them: collecting payments, holding escrows, dunning late payers, and so on.

FEDERAL NATIONAL MORTGAGE ASSOCIATION

The *Federal National Mortgage Association* (also known as *FNMA* or *Fannie Mae*) is a federally chartered, privately owned and managed corporation. It does not make direct loans to homeowners; rather, it purchases first mortgage loans, many originated by mortgage bankers, in the secondary mortgage market. FNMA thereby aids in the liquidity of mortgage investments, making mortgages more attractive investments. FNMA presently owns a significant percentage of all residential mortgages.

FEDERAL HOME LOAN MORTGAGE CORPORATION

The *FHLMC,* or *Freddie Mac,* is a privately owned corporation that, like FNMA, buys mortgages on the secondary market. It buys much of its inventory from savings and loan associations and commercial banks. It also sells participations in pools of mortgages.

GOVERNMENT NATIONAL MORTGAGE ASSOCIATION

The *Government National Mortgage Association* (*GNMA* or *Ginnie Mae*) is a U.S. Government entity that encourages low-income housing. It will guarantee packages consisting of FHA or VA loans.

FARMERS HOME ADMINISTRATION

This agency, *FmHA,* which has regional branches, provides financing for the purchase and operations of farms and rural homes and guarantees loans on such properties made by others.

Lender Criteria

Institutional lenders perform a process called *underwriting.* The purpose of this is to assess the risks of making the loan. They look at the property and the borrower. As to the property, the lender typically arranges for an appraisal (cost is paid by the borrower), which will provide information about the property's value, its location, and market conditions, including comparable sales.

The lender will get a credit report on the borrower, financial statements, and letters from employers concerning salary, term of employment, and prospects for the continuation of employment. Lenders will verify bank accounts and other assets of the borrower, as well as liabilities.

For a conventional loan on a single-family home, the lender will normally require a 20 percent down payment. This would be a *loan-to-value ratio* of 80 percent. If the borrower seeks a greater loan-to-value ratio, he will be required to get private mortgage insurance (PMI). Up to 90 and 95 percent loan-to-value ratios may be obtained. For a duplex or four-unit property, a larger down payment (25 percent) is normally required.

Lenders have certain guidelines to follow if they want to be able to have a truly marketable loan—that is, a loan that can be sold to FNMA or FHLMC. This is called a *conforming loan*. The lender will provide a *qualifying ratio* of housing payments to gross income of 28 percent and of total fixed payments to gross income of 36 percent. For example, suppose the Andersons earn $10,000 per month. The maximum housing payments they would be allowed are $2,800 per month, including principal, interest, taxes, and insurance. When payments on other long-term debt are considered, such as car loans, the maximum allowed would be $3,600. However, these guidelines may be exceeded by borrowers with high FICO scores.

Many lenders will offer *nonconforming loans* to those who don't qualify. These loans won't conform to FNMA/FHLMC guidelines, and a higher rate of interest is therefore charged. But they may allow a marginal borrower to purchase the home desired.

With income-producing property, a lender will also look to the debt coverage ratio and insist that the net operating income from the property exceed debt service by a comfortable margin, that is, by 25 percent or more. So a debt service coverage ratio of 1.25 times net operating income may be required.

When considering a loan on the stock in a cooperative apartment, lenders will consider the risk. If it is an existing, sold-out development, it is less risky than one that is to be built or converted from rental apartments. For those, the developer or sponsor's filings of stock with the attorney general may offer clues to the likelihood of success.

CalVet Program

The California Department of Veteran's Affairs administers a program to assist veterans in financing a farm or home, including a mobile home, at low interest rates, with low or no down payment. As of January 1, 2005, CalVet has funds for all qualified wartime-era veterans, regardless of when they served in the military, and for peacetime veterans who qualify as first-time home buyers or purchase homes in certain target areas. CalVet loans are financed by the sale of bonds. The maximum loan amount as of January 11, 2005, is $359,650. More information on criteria and loan programs available is provided in Figure 13-1.

Mortgage Loan Disclosure

The Mortgage Loan Disclosure Statement (Borrower) (see Figure 8-2) and Seller Financing Addendum and Disclosure (see Figure 8-3) provide information about the financing of the purchase.

Current Loan Terms, Fees & Rates and Funding Source Restrictions (*Effective 4/4/2005*)

Current Rate	Funds Source	Wartime Service Required?	Loan Programs available for
5.15%	**Qualified Veterans Mortgage Bonds** (General Obligation Bonds) 1	Yes – Must have service prior to 1/1/1977 and apply within 30 years of date of release from active duty	CalVet / VA CalVet 97 CalVet 80/20
5.50%	**Unrestricted Funds**	No	

Interest rates and loan terms are subject to change. Contact your local CalVet District Office, check our website at *www.cdva.ca.gov*, or call 800-952-5626 for current information.

Loan Programs

Loan Program ▶	**CalVet / VA**	**CalVet 97**	**CalVet 80/20**
Maximum Loan	$359,650 (including funding fee) (effective 1/1/2005)	$359,650 (effective 1/1/2005)	$359,650 (effective 1/1/2005)
Property / Program Type	New & Existing Homes (including VA approved Condominiums & PUDs)	New or Existing Homes (including VA approved Condominiums & PUDs) Construction Loans Rehabilitation Loans Mobile Homes on Land Mobile Homes in Parks[1]	New or Existing Homes (including VA approved Condominiums & PUDs) Construction Loans Rehabilitation Loans Mobile Homes on Land Mobile Homes in Parks[1]
Down payment	0%	3%	20%
Funding Fee	1.25% - 3.3%[2] (<u>may</u> be financed)	1.25 – 2% (<u>must be paid</u> in escrow)[3]	None
Loan Origination Fee	1%	1%	1%
Other Requirements	VA Certificate of Eligibility for full entitlement		

[1] For Mobile Homes <u>in Parks</u> the maximum loan is $125,000 and the interest rate is 1% higher (6.15% or 6.5%)

[2] The funding fee for CalVet/**VA** loans is waived for veterans with disability ratings of 10% or higher. The fee is not waived on CalVet97 loans

[3] The funding fee for CalVet 97 loans may be financed when the down payment is 5% or greater.

[4] Current Members of the **California National Guard** or the **US Military Reserves** who have never been ordered to active duty are eligible if they qualify as "first time home buyers" or purchase homes in certain "targeted areas", and meet income and purchase price limits. Please contact one of our District Offices for additional information.

Loan Terms (4/4/2005)

Figure 13-1. CalVet Home Loans

MORTGAGE LOAN DISCLOSURE STATEMENT (BORROWER)

CALIFORNIA ASSOCIATION OF REALTORS®

(As required by the Business and Professions Code §10241 and Title 10, California Administrative Code, §2840)

_____
(Name of Broker/Arranger of Credit)

_____
(Business Address of Broker)

I. SUMMARY OF LOAN TERMS
A. PRINCIPAL AMOUNT . . . . $ _____

B. ESTIMATED DEDUCTIONS FROM PRINCIPAL AMOUNT
1. Costs and Expenses (See Paragraph III-A) . . . . $ _____
*2. Broker Commission/Organization Fee (See Paragraph III-B) . . . $ _____
3. Lender Origination Fee/Discounts (See Paragraph III-B) . . . $ _____
4. Additional compensation will/may be received from lender not deducted from loan proceeds.
   □ YES $ _____ (if known) or □ NO
5. Amount to be Paid on Authorization of Borrower (See Paragraph III) . . . $ _____

C. ESTIMATED CASH PAYABLE TO BORROWER (A less B) . . . $ _____

II. GENERAL INFORMATION ABOUT LOAN
A. If this loan is made, Borrower will be required to pay the principal and interest at _____% per year, payable as follows: _____ payments of $ _____
(number of payments) (monthly/quarterly/annually)
and a **FINAL/BALLOON** payment of $ _____ to pay off the loan in full.

NOTICE TO BORROWER: IF YOU DO NOT HAVE THE FUNDS TO PAY THE BALLOON PAYMENT WHEN IT COMES DUE, YOU MAY HAVE TO OBTAIN A NEW LOAN AGAINST YOUR PROPERTY TO MAKE THE BALLOON PAYMENT. IN THAT CASE, YOU MAY AGAIN HAVE TO PAY COMMISSIONS, FEES AND EXPENSES FOR THE ARRANGING OF THE NEW LOAN. IN ADDITION, IF YOU ARE UNABLE TO MAKE THE MONTHLY PAYMENTS OR THE BALLOON PAYMENT, YOU MAY LOSE THE PROPERTY AND ALL OF YOUR EQUITY THROUGH FORECLOSURE. KEEP THIS IN MIND IN DECIDING UPON THE AMOUNT AND TERMS OF THIS LOAN.

B. This loan will be evidenced by a promissory note and secured by a deed of trust on property identified as (street address or legal description):
_____
_____

C. 1. Liens presently against this property (do not include loan being applied for):

Nature of Lien	Priority	Lienholder's Name	Amount Owing

2. Liens that will remain against this property after the loan being applied for is made or arranged (include loan being applied for):

Nature of Lien	Priority	Lienholder's Name	Amount Owing

NOTICE TO BORROWER: Be sure that you state the amount of all liens as accurately as possible. If you contract with the broker to arrange this loan, but it cannot be arranged because you did not state these liens correctly, you may be liable to pay commissions, fees and expenses even though you do not obtain the loan.

MS REVISED 10/2000 (PAGE 1 OF 3) Print Date

Borrower acknowledges receipt of copy of this page.
Borrower's Initials (_____)(_____)

Reviewed by _____ Date _____

EQUAL HOUSING OPPORTUNITY

MORTGAGE LOAN DISCLOSURE STATEMENT (MS PAGE 1 OF 3)

Figure 13-2. Mortgage Loan Disclosure Statement

Property Address: _____ Date: _____

D. If Borrower pays all or part of the loan principal before it is due, a PREPAYMENT PENALTY computed as follows may be charged:
_____
_____
_____

E. Late Charges: ☐ YES, see loan documents   or   ☐ NO

F. The purchase of credit life or credit disability insurance by a borrower is not required as a condition of making this loan.

G. Is the real property which will secure the requested loan an "owner-occupied dwelling?" ☐ YES____ or ☐ NO____
(Borrower initial opposite YES or NO)

An "owner-occupied dwelling" means a single dwelling unit in a condominium or cooperative or residential building of four or fewer separate dwelling units, one of which will be owned and occupied by a signatory to the mortgage or deed of trust for this loan within 90 days of the signing of the mortgage or deed of trust.

III. DEDUCTIONS FROM LOAN PROCEEDS

A. Estimated Maximum Costs and Expenses of Arranging the Loan to be Paid Out of Loan Principal:

PAYABLE TO

	Broker	Others
1. Appraisal fee	_____	_____
2. Escrow fee	_____	_____
3. Title insurance policy	_____	_____
4. Notary fees	_____	_____
5. Recording fees	_____	_____
6. Credit investigation fees	_____	_____
7. Other costs and expenses:	_____	_____

Total Costs and Expenses .... $ _____

*B. Compensation........................ $ _____
1. Brokerage Commission/Origination Fee ..... $ _____
2. Lender Origination Fee/Discounts..... $ _____

C. Estimated Payment to be Made out of Loan Principal on Authorization of Borrower

PAYABLE TO

	Broker	Others
1. Fire or other hazard insurance premiums	_____	_____
2. Credit life or disability insurance premiums (see Paragraph II-F)	_____	_____
3. Beneficiary statement fees	_____	_____
4. Reconveyance and similar fees	_____	_____
5. Discharge of existing liens against property:	_____	_____
6. Other:	_____	_____

Total to be Paid on Authorization of Borrower .... $ _____

If this loan is secured by a first deed of trust on dwellings in a principal amount of less than $30,000 or secured by a junior lien on dwellings in a principal amount of less than $20,000, the undersigned licensee certifies that the loan will be made in compliance with Article 7 of Chapter 3 of the Real Estate Law.

*This loan **may / will / will not** (delete two) be made wholly or in part from broker-controlled funds as defined in Section 10241(j) of the Business and Professions Code.

Borrower acknowledges receipt of copy of this page.
Borrower's Initials (_____)(_____)
Reviewed by _____ Date _____

EQUAL HOUSING OPPORTUNITY

MORTGAGE LOAN DISCLOSURE STATEMENT (MS PAGE 2 OF 3)

Figure 13-2.   Mortgage Loan Disclosure Statement (*continued*)

Property Address: _____ Date: _____

*NOTICE TO BORROWER: This disclosure statement may be used if the Broker is acting as an agent in arranging the loan by a third person or if the loan will be made with funds owned or controlled by the broker. If the Broker indicates in the above statement that the loan "may" be made out of Broker-controlled funds, the Broker must notify the borrower prior to the close of escrow if the funds to be received by the Borrower are in fact Broker-controlled funds.

_____   _____
Name of Broker   Broker Representative

_____   _____
License Number   License Number

_____ OR _____
Signature of Broker   Signature

The Department of Real Estate License Information phone number is _____.

NOTICE TO BORROWER:

DO NOT SIGN THIS STATEMENT UNTIL YOU HAVE READ AND UNDERSTAND ALL OF THE INFORMATION IN IT. ALL PARTS OF THE FORM MUST BE COMPLETED BEFORE YOU SIGN.

Borrower hereby acknowledges the receipt of a copy of this statement.

DATED _____   _____

                                                                    (Borrower)

                                                          _____

                                                                    (Borrower)

<u>Broker Review</u>: Signature of Real Estate Broker after review of this statement.

DATED _____   _____

                                                    Real Estate Broker or Assistant Pursuant to Section 2725

Published and Distributed by:
REAL ESTATE BUSINESS SERVICES, INC.
a subsidiary of the California Association of REALTORS®
525 South Virgil Avenue, Los Angeles, California 90020

MS REVISED 10/2000 (PAGE 3 OF 3) Print Date

Reviewed by _____ Date _____

MORTGAGE LOAN DISCLOSURE STATEMENT (MS PAGE 3 OF 3)

Figure 13-2.   Mortgage Loan Disclosure Statement (*continued*)

CALIFORNIA ASSOCIATION OF REALTORS®

SELLER FINANCING ADDENDUM AND DISCLOSURE
(California Civil Code §§2956-2967)
(C.A.R. Form SFA, Revised 10/02)

This is an addendum to the ☐ California Residential Purchase Agreement, ☐ Counter Offer, or ☐ Other _____
_____, ("Agreement"), dated _____,
On property known as _____ ("Property"),
between _____ ("Buyer"),
and _____ ("Seller").
Seller agrees to extend credit to Buyer as follows:

1. **PRINCIPAL; INTEREST; PAYMENT; MATURITY TERMS:** ☐ Principal amount $ _____, interest at _____%
    per annum, payable at approximately $ _____ per ☐ month, ☐ year, or ☐ other _____,
    remaining principal balance due in _____ years.

2. **LOAN APPLICATION; CREDIT REPORT:** Within **5 (or** ☐ _____**) Days** After Acceptance: **(a)** Buyer shall provide Seller a completed
    loan application on a form acceptable to Seller (such as a FNMA/FHLMC Uniform Residential Loan Application for residential one to four
    unit properties); and **(b)** Buyer authorizes Seller and/or Agent to obtain, at Buyer's expense, a copy of Buyer's credit report. Buyer shall
    provide any supporting documentation reasonably requested by Seller. Seller, after first giving Buyer a Notice to Buyer to Perform, may
    cancel this Agreement in writing and authorize return of Buyer's deposit if Buyer fails to provide such documents within that time, or if
    Seller disapproves any above item within **5 (or** ☐ _____**) Days** After receipt of each item.

3. **CREDIT DOCUMENTS:** This extension of credit by Seller will be evidenced by: ☐ Note and deed of trust; ☐ All-inclusive
    note and deed of trust; ☐ Installment land sale contract; ☐ Lease/option (when parties intend transfer of equitable title);
    OR ☐ Other (specify) _____

**THE FOLLOWING TERMS APPLY ONLY IF CHECKED. SELLER IS ADVISED TO READ ALL TERMS, EVEN THOSE NOT
CHECKED, TO UNDERSTAND WHAT IS OR IS NOT INCLUDED, AND, IF NOT INCLUDED, THE CONSEQUENCES THEREOF.**

4. ☐ **LATE CHARGE:** If any payment is not made within _____ **Days** After it is due, a late charge of either $ _____,
    or _____% of the installment due, may be charged to Buyer. **NOTE:** On single family residences that Buyer intends to occupy,
    California Civil Code §2954.4(a) limits the late charge to no more than 6% of the total installment payment due and requires a
    grace period of no less than 10 days.

5. ☐ **BALLOON PAYMENT:** The extension of credit will provide for a balloon payment, in the amount of $ _____,
    plus any accrued interest, which is due on _____ (date).

6. ☐ **PREPAYMENT:** If all or part of this extension of credit is paid early, Seller may charge a prepayment penalty as follows (if
    applicable): _____. Caution: California Civil Code
    §2954.9 contains limitations on prepayment penalties for residential one-to-four unit properties.

7. ☐ **DUE ON SALE:** If any interest in the Property is sold or otherwise transferred, Seller has the option to require immediate
    payment of the entire unpaid principal balance, plus any accrued interest.

8.* ☐ **REQUEST FOR COPY OF NOTICE OF DEFAULT:** A request for a copy of Notice of Default as defined in California Civil
    Code §2924b will be recorded. **If Not**, Seller is advised to consider recording a Request for Notice of Default.

9.* ☐ **REQUEST FOR NOTICE OF DELINQUENCY:** A request for Notice of Delinquency, as defined in California Civil Code §2924e,
    to be signed and paid for by Buyer, will be made to senior lienholders. **If not**, Seller is advised to consider making a Request for
    Notice of Delinquency. Seller is advised to check with senior lienholders to verify whether they will honor this request.

10.* ☐ **TAX SERVICE:**
    A. If property taxes on the Property become delinquent, tax service will be arranged to report to Seller. **If not**, Seller is
    advised to consider retaining a tax service, or to otherwise determine that property taxes are paid.
    B. ☐ Buyer, ☐ Seller, shall be responsible for the initial and continued retention of, and payment for, such tax service.

11. ☐ **TITLE INSURANCE:** Title insurance coverage will be provided to **both** Seller and Buyer, insuring their respective interests
    in the Property. **If not**, Buyer and Seller are advised to consider securing such title insurance coverage.

12. ☐ **HAZARD INSURANCE:**
    A. The parties' escrow holder or insurance carrier will be directed to include a loss payee endorsement, adding Seller to
    the Property insurance policy. **If not**, Seller is advised to secure such an endorsement, or acquire a separate
    insurance policy.
    B. Property insurance **does not** include earthquake or flood insurance coverage, unless checked:
    ☐ Earthquake insurance will be obtained; ☐ Flood insurance will be obtained.

13. ☐ **PROCEEDS TO BUYER:** Buyer will receive cash proceeds at the close of the sale transaction. The amount received will be
    approximately $ _____, from _____ (indicate source of
    proceeds). Buyer represents that the purpose of such disbursement is as follows: _____.

14. ☐ **NEGATIVE AMORTIZATION; DEFERRED INTEREST:** Negative amortization results when Buyer's periodic payments are
    less than the amount of interest earned on the obligation. Deferred interest also results when the obligation does not
    require periodic payments for a period of time. In either case, interest is not payable as it accrues. This accrued interest
    will have to be paid by Buyer at a later time, and may result in Buyer owing more on the obligation than at its origination.
    The credit being extended to Buyer by Seller will provide for negative amortization or deferred interest as indicated below.
    (Check A, B, or C. CHECK ONE ONLY.)
    ☐ **A.** All negative amortization or deferred interest shall be added to the principal _____
        (e.g., annually, monthly, etc.), and thereafter shall bear interest at the rate specified in the credit documents (compound interest);
    OR ☐ **B.** All deferred interest shall be due and payable, along with principal, at maturity;
    OR ☐ **C.** Other _____.

*(For Paragraphs 8-10) In order to receive timely and continued notification, Seller is advised to record appropriate notices and/or to
notify appropriate parties of any change in Seller's address.

SFA REVISED 10/02 (PAGE 1 OF 3) Print Date

Buyer's Initials (_____)(_____)
Seller's Initials (_____)(_____)

Reviewed by _____ Date _____

EQUAL HOUSING OPPORTUNITY

SELLER FINANCING ADDENDUM AND DISCLOSURE (SFA PAGE 1 OF 3)

Figure 13-3.   Seller Financing Disclosure Statement

Property Address: _____ Date: _____

15. ☐ **ALL-INCLUSIVE DEED OF TRUST; INSTALLMENT LAND SALE CONTRACT:** This transaction involves the use of an all-inclusive (or wraparound) deed of trust or an installment land sale contract. That deed of trust or contract shall provide as follows:

A. In the event of an acceleration of any senior encumbrance, the responsibility for payment, or for legal defense is: _____ ; OR ☐ **Is not** specified in the credit or security documents.

B. In the event of the prepayment of a senior encumbrance, the responsibilities and rights of Buyer and Seller regarding refinancing, prepayment penalties, and any prepayment discounts are: _____ ; OR ☐ **Are not** specified in the documents evidencing credit.

C. Buyer will make periodic payments to _____ (Seller, collection agent, or any neutral third party), who will be responsible for disbursing payments to the payee(s) on the senior encumbrance(s) and to Seller. **NOTE:** The Parties are advised to designate a neutral third party for these purposes.

16. ☐ **TAX IDENTIFICATION NUMBERS:** Buyer and Seller shall each provide to each other their Social Security Numbers or Taxpayer Identification Numbers.

17. ☐ **OTHER CREDIT TERMS** _____

18. ☐ **RECORDING:** The documents evidencing credit (paragraph 3) will be recorded with the county recorder where the Property is located. **If not**, Buyer and Seller are advised that their respective interests in the Property may be jeopardized by intervening liens, judgments, encumbrances, or subsequent transfers.

19. ☐ **JUNIOR FINANCING:** There will be additional financing, secured by the Property, junior to this Seller financing. Explain: _____

20. SENIOR LOANS AND ENCUMBRANCES: The following information is provided on loans and/or encumbrances that will be **senior** to Seller financing. **NOTE:** The following are estimates, unless otherwise marked with an asterisk (*). If checked: ☐ A separate sheet with information on additional senior loans/encumbrances is attached

	1st	2nd
A. Original Balance	$ _____	$ _____
B. Current Balance	$ _____	$ _____
C. Periodic Payment (e.g. $100/month):	$ _____	$ ____ / ____
Including Impounds of:	$ _____	$ ____ / ____
D. Interest Rate (per annum)	_____ %	_____ %
E. Fixed or Variable Rate:	_____	_____
If Variable Rate: Lifetime Cap (Ceiling)	_____	_____
Indicator (Underlying Index)	_____	_____
Margins	_____	_____
F. Maturity Date	_____	_____
G. Amount of Balloon Payment	$ _____	$ _____
H. Date Balloon Payment Due	_____	_____
I. Potential for Negative Amortization? (Yes, No, or Unknown)	_____	_____
J. Due on Sale? (Yes, No, or Unknown)	_____	_____
K. Pre-payment penalty? (Yes, No, or Unknown)	_____	_____
L. Are payments current? (Yes, No, or Unknown)	_____	_____

21. BUYER'S CREDITWORTHINESS: (CHECK EITHER A OR B. Do not check both.) In addition to the loan application, credit report and other information requested under paragraph 2:

A. ☐ No other disclosure concerning Buyer's creditworthiness has been made to Seller;

OR B. ☐ The following representations concerning Buyer's creditworthiness are made by Buyer(s) to Seller:

Borrower _____	**Co-Borrower** _____
1. Occupation _____	1. Occupation _____
2. Employer _____	2. Employer _____
3. Length of Employment _____	3. Length of Employment _____
4. Monthly Gross Income _____	4. Monthly Gross Income _____
5. Other _____	5. Other _____

22. ADDED, DELETED OR SUBSTITUTED BUYERS: The addition, deletion or substitution of any person or entity under this Agreement or to title prior to close of escrow shall require Seller's written consent. Seller may grant or withhold consent in Seller's sole discretion. Any additional or substituted person or entity shall, if requested by Seller, submit to Seller the same documentation as required for the original named Buyer. Seller and/or Brokers may obtain a credit report, at Buyer's expense, on any such person or entity.

Buyer's Initials (_____)(_____)
Seller's Initials (_____)(_____)

Reviewed by _____ Date _____

EQUAL HOUSING OPPORTUNITY

SELLER FINANCING ADDENDUM AND DISCLOSURE (SFA PAGE 2 OF 3)

Figure 13-3. Seller Financing Disclosure Statement (*continued*)

Property Address: _____ Date: _____

23. CAUTION:

    A. If the Seller financing requires a balloon payment, Seller shall give Buyer written notice, according to the terms of Civil Code §2966, at least 90 and not more than 150 days before the balloon payment is due if the transaction is for the purchase of a dwelling for not more than four families.

    B. If **any** obligation secured by the Property calls for a balloon payment, Seller and Buyer are aware that refinancing of the balloon payment at maturity may be difficult or impossible, depending on conditions in the conventional mortgage marketplace at that time. There are no assurances that new financing or a loan extension will be available when the balloon prepayment, or any prepayment, is due.

    C. If **any** of the existing or proposed loans or extensions of credit would require refinancing as a result of a lack of full amortization, such refinancing might be difficult or impossible in the conventional mortgage marketplace.

    D. In the event of default by Buyer: (1) Seller may have to reinstate and/or make monthly payments on any and all senior encumbrances (including real property taxes) in order to protect Seller's secured interest; (2) Seller's rights are generally limited to foreclosure on the Property, pursuant to California Code of Civil Procedure §580b; and (3) the Property may lack sufficient equity to protect Seller's interests if the Property decreases in value.

If this three-page Addendum and Disclosure is used in a transaction for the purchase of a dwelling for not more than four families, it shall be prepared by an Arranger of Credit as defined in California Civil Code §2957(a). (The Arranger of Credit is usually the agent who obtained the offer.)

_____
Arranger of Credit - (Print Firm Name)   By _____   Date _____

Address _____ City _____ State _____ Zip _____

Phone _____ Fax _____

BUYER AND SELLER ACKNOWLEDGE AND AGREE THAT BROKERS: (A) WILL NOT PROVIDE LEGAL OR TAX ADVICE; (B) WILL NOT PROVIDE OTHER ADVICE OR INFORMATION THAT EXCEEDS THE KNOWLEDGE, EDUCATION AND EXPERIENCE REQUIRED TO OBTAIN A REAL ESTATE LICENSE; OR (C) HAVE NOT AND WILL NOT VERIFY ANY INFORMATION PROVIDED BY EITHER BUYER OR SELLER. BUYER AND SELLER AGREE THAT THEY WILL SEEK LEGAL, TAX AND OTHER DESIRED ASSISTANCE FROM APPROPRIATE PROFESSIONALS. BUYER AND SELLER ACKNOWLEDGE THAT THE INFORMATION EACH HAS PROVIDED TO THE ARRANGER OF CREDIT FOR INCLUSION IN THIS DISCLOSURE FORM IS ACCURATE. BUYER AND SELLER FURTHER ACKNOWLEDGE THAT EACH HAS RECEIVED A COMPLETED COPY OF THIS DISCLOSURE FORM.

Buyer _____ Date _____
               (signature)

Address _____ City _____ State _____ Zip _____

Phone _____ Fax _____ E-mail _____

Buyer _____ Date _____
               (signature)

Address _____ City _____ State _____ Zip _____

Phone _____ Fax _____ E-mail _____

Seller _____ Date _____
               (signature)

Address _____ City _____ State _____ Zip _____

Phone _____ Fax _____ E-mail _____

Seller _____ Date _____
               (signature)

Address _____ City _____ State _____ Zip _____

Phone _____ Fax _____ E-mail _____

SURE TRAC The System for Success™

Published by the California Association of REALTORS®

Reviewed by _____ Date _____

SFA REVISED 10/02 (PAGE 3 OF 3)

SELLER FINANCING ADDENDUM AND DISCLOSURE (SFA PAGE 3 OF 3)

Figure 13-3.   Seller Financing Disclosure Statement (*continued*)

*Broker-Arranged Loans*_____

The Real Property Loan Law in California provides a maximum commission for real estate brokers who negotiate real estate loans. The commission ceiling depends on the loan type, amount, and term, as follows:

Table 13-1.
BROKER COMMISSIONS ALLOWED ON VARIOUS TYPES OF LOANS

Type of Loan	Amount of Loan	Term	Maximum Commission
First trust deed	Up to $30,000	Less than 3 years	5% of loan
"	"	3 years and up	10% of loan
"	Over $30,000	Any	No ceiling
Second trust deed	Up to $20,000	Less than 2 years	5% of loan
"	"	2–3 years	10% of loan
"	"	3 years and up	15% of loan
"	Over $20,000	Any	No ceiling

In addition to broker commissions, costs and fees such as for appraisal, credit check, notary, survey, may be charged up to a limit as shown below. Title and recording fees may be added to these amounts.

Table 13-2.
MAXIMUM COSTS AND FEES ON VARIOUS LOAN AMOUNTS

Loan Amount	Maximum Costs and Fees
Up to $7,800	Actual costs, or $390, whichever is less.
$7,800 to $14,000	Actual costs, or 5% of loan amount, whichever is less.
Above $14,000	Actual costs, up to $700.

A Mortgage Loan Disclosure Statement is to be signed by the borrower.

Features of Mortgage Loans _____

POINTS

One *point* is 1 percent of the amount of the loan. Some mortgage loan charges are expressed in terms of points. These charges are either *fees* or *discounts*. Typical fees expressed in points are origination fees, conversion fees (ARM to FRM; see page 172), prepayment penalties, and so on. The actual dollar amount of such a fee depends upon the dollar amount of the loan involved. For example, some new mortgage loans have origination fees. Usually the fee is about one point, or 1 percent of the loan amount. For a loan of $100,000, then, the fee will be $1,000 (1 percent of $100,000); for a loan of $75,000 the fee will be $750, and so on.

Discount points are something else, although they, too are expressed as percentages of the loan amount. Discounts are paid at origination in order to reduce the face interest rate on the loan. (You can think of discounts as somewhat like interest paid in advance.) Depending upon the amount of the discount required, a lender will offer a variety of interest rates on new mortgage loans. For example, a "menu" of interest rates might be: 6.5 + 0, 6.25 + 1.25, 6 + 2.5. These mean that the lender will offer an interest rate of 6.5 percent with no discount (usually called "par"); 6.25 percent in return for a payment of 1.25 percent of the loan amount (a 1.25-point discount); and 6 percent in return for a 2.5-point discount. For a $100,000 loan from this menu, the borrower's face interest rate will be 6.5 percent if no discount is paid, 6.25 percent if $1,250 is paid in advance, and 6 percent for an advance payment of $2,500. Why would anyone pay discounts? Actually, many borrowers don't. However, *sellers* often do for a variety of reasons, usually concerned with making a sale more attractive to a buyer.

Discounts also are used as *buydowns*, often in association with teaser interest rates. Buydowns substitute an initial charge for interest later in the loan. Most often they are used to provide an unusually low interest rate during the early period of a loan. For example, if the "normal" rate of interest is 7 percent, a lender may offer a buydown (for a fee of about 5.5 percent of the loan amount) that will give the loan an interest rate of 4 percent the first year, 5 percent the second, and 6 percent the third. After the third year, the interest rate will be 7 percent for the rest of the loan period.

PREPAYMENT PENALTIES AND PRIVILEGES

Most home mortgage loans allow the borrower to pay off the principal balance at any time. Many commercial mortgages require a penalty, such as 3 percent of the outstanding balance, for early debt retirement. The penalty rate may decline as the loan ages.

ACCELERATION CLAUSES

An *acceleration clause* states that the full principal balance becomes due upon certain default. If one or more payments are past due (depending on the agreement), the entire loan becomes due.

LOAN ASSUMPTION

Property offered for sale may be encumbered by a loan bearing a low interest rate, which makes it attractive to the real estate purchaser. The buyer may pay the seller for his equity (the difference between the property value if free and clear and the amount of debt) and then *assume* the loan. The purchaser then becomes liable for the loan and its required payments. The original borrower, however, is not automatically freed from his obligation. He may ask the lender for a *novation* (see page 160), which serves to release him from responsibility, and then substitute the new property owner as the sole debtor. In the absence of a novation, the lender may look to the property and to both the original borrower and the subsequent purchaser for repayment.

Rather than assume a loan, a purchaser may agree to take the property *subject* to a mortgage loan. In doing so, the buyer acknowledges the debt, but it does not become her personal liability. In the event of default, she stands to lose no more than her investment.

DUE-ON-SALE CLAUSE

The *due-on-sale clause* requires that the full outstanding balance of a mortgage loan must be paid when the property is sold. This would prevent a low interest rate loan from being assumed in a sale because the full loan amount would be accelerated. In a famous California case, *Wellenkamp vs. Bank of America, 1978*, the California court struck down the due-on-sale clause. They held it to be an unreasonable restraint on alienation (sale) and said it was not to be enforced unless the lender could demonstrate an increase in risk due to the loan assumption.

In response, in 1982 the U.S. Supreme Court decided that due-on-sale clauses were fully enforceable by all federally licensed lenders, including federally chartered savings and loan associations. Thereafter, many California state-chartered lending institutions changed their charters to U.S. agencies to become federally chartered, so they could enforce the due-on-sale clause. Since 1985, the due-on-sale clause has been allowed to be enforced by all financial institutions.

IMPOUND ACCOUNTS

Many loans, especially those on single-family homes, require the borrower to include $\frac{1}{12}$ of the estimated annual taxes and insurance with each monthly payment. The deposits are placed into the *impound account* to assure that the money will be available when payment is due for these annual expenses. Generally, lenders pay no interest to borrowers on these accounts. However, California law prohibits excessive amounts from being collected. The amount required in the account is limited to what is allowed by the Real Estate Settlement Procedure Act (RESPA), which is the prorated taxes and insurance plus up to two months' reserves. California law requires any excess to be refunded to the borrower within 30 days.

CALIFORNIA USURY

Usury is defined as the charging of an excessive rate of interest. California has usury laws, though those pertaining to real estate are relatively flexible, and they apply mainly to private lenders.

Banks and savings and loan associations in California are exempt from usury laws. California's Proposition 2, passed by its voters in 1979, exempted from usury any loan secured by real estate and arranged by a real estate broker.

Usury laws do apply to consumer loans (not real estate) at 10 percent. Loans for the purchase of goods used in the construction or improvement of real estate, by lenders who are not exempt as noted above, are at 10 percent, or 5 percent above the Federal Reserve's discount rate, whichever is greater.

Seller-financed real estate (a purchase money mortgage) is treated as an extension of credit, and not a loan for usury purposes. Therefore, usury laws are generally not applicable to seller financing.

All federally related residential first mortgages were exempted from state usury law in 1980 by the Depository Institutions Deregulation and Monetary Control Act of 1980. This exemption would apply to such loans made by federally insured institutions in California. The act includes loans on single family homes and condominiums, mobile homes and cooperative homes. These loans are exempt from California's usury law. Today, private loans on real estate comprise the bulk of real estate loans that are subject to California usury.

USURY PENALTIES

The penalty for usury in California is substantial. If a borrower has paid usurious interest, he or she may collect the full amount of interest paid in the last two years plus treble damages for the last year of the loan.

ESTOPPEL CERTIFICATE

An *estoppel certificate* is a statement that prevents its issuer from asserting different facts at a later date. For example, a mortgage originator may wish to sell the mortgage loan (the right to collect payments) to another. The loan purchaser may ask for an estoppel certificate, whereby the borrower states the amount he owes. Later, the borrower is stopped from asserting that he owed less at the time he signed the estoppel certificate.

RELEASING FROM PROPERTY MORTGAGES

Four methods by which property may be released from mortgages are:
1. *Release deed.* This document from the lender states that the loan is paid off and that the lender releases property from the lien.
2. *Parcel or land release.* This releases part of mortgaged property from the mortgage, usually upon payment of part of the debt.
3. *Postponement of lien.* The lien is not satisfied but is subordinated, meaning that it assumes a lower priority.
4. *Foreclosure.* This is described in detail below.

FORECLOSURE, DEFICIENCY JUDGMENTS, AND EQUITY OF REDEMPTION

Upon certain default, a lender may be allowed to go through an authorized procedure, known as *foreclosure,* to have the property applied to the payment of the debt. Should the property sell at foreclosure for more than the unpaid first mortgage loan plus the expenses of the foreclosure action, the excess belongs to the junior lenders, if any. After all lenders have received full payment, any excess funds go to the borrower.

It is more likely that the proceeds from a foreclosure will be inadequate to pay mortgage indebtedness. In this case, the lender may attempt to get a *deficiency judgment* for the amount of the loan that remains unpaid. This requires the borrower to pay the deficiency personally. Deficiency judgments are difficult to establish in California. Commercial property mortgagors are frequently able to negotiate *exculpatory* clauses in their loans. Exculpatory clauses cause loans to be *nonrecourse*; when such a clause exists, a defaulting borrower may lose the real estate that he has pledged, but he is not personally liable for the debt. The lender may look only to the property as collateral.

Should property be foreclosed, the borrower has the right to redeem the property by repaying in full the principal owed. This California *redemption* must be exercised within the time period prescribed by California law. With a trust deed, there is no redemption after foreclosure. With a mortgage loan, the period in California may be up to one year.

QUESTIONS TO ANSWER ABOUT CALIFORNIA

Distinguish between a trust deed and a mortgage. Which is prevalent in California?

_____

Does California allow redemption offer foreclosure? Please explain the conditions.

_____

Questions on Chapter 13

1. The major source of single-family home mortgage loan funds is
   (A) California Association of Realtors
   (B) commercial banks
   (C) mortgage bankers
   (D) the Federal National Mortgage Association (FNMA)

2. A conventional mortgage is
   (A) amortizing
   (B) guaranteed by the FHA
   (C) not guaranteed by any government agency
   (D) approved by the VA

3. A chattel mortgage is usually given in connection with
   (A) realty
   (B) farms
   (C) personal property
   (D) commercial property

4. The lending of money at a rate of interest above the legal rate is
   (A) speculation
   (B) usury
   (C) both A and B
   (D) neither A nor B

5. One discount point is equal to
   (A) 1 percent of the sales price
   (B) 1 percent of the interest rate
   (C) 1 percent of the loan amount
   (D) none of the above

6. Discount points in FHA and VA loans are generally paid by the
   (A) lender
   (B) purchaser
   (C) seller
   (D) broker

7. The main appeal of VA mortgages to borrowers lies in
   (A) low interest rates
   (B) minimum down payments
   (C) an unlimited mortgage ceiling
   (D) easy availability

8. When a loan is assumed on property that is sold,
   (A) the original borrower is relieved of further responsibility
   (B) the purchaser becomes liable for the debt
   (C) the purchaser must obtain a certificate of eligibility
   (D) all of the above

9. An estoppel certificate is required when the
   (A) mortgage is sold to an investor
   (B) property is sold
   (C) property is being foreclosed
   (D) mortgage is assumed

10. An owner who seeks a mortgage loan and offers three properties as security will give
    (A) a blanket mortgage
    (B) an FHA mortgage
    (C) a conventional mortgage
    (D) a chattel mortgage

11. A clause in a mortgage or accompanying note that permits the creditor to declare the entire principal balance due upon certain default of the debtor is
    (A) an acceleration clause
    (B) an escalation clause
    (C) a forfeiture clause
    (D) an excelerator clause

12. Which of the following statements is (are) false?
    (A) VA loans are insured loans.
    (B) FHA loans are guaranteed loans.
    (C) Both A and B
    (D) Neither A nor B

13. A second mortgage is
    (A) a lien on real estate that has a prior mortgage on it
    (B) the first mortgage recorded
    (C) always made by the seller
    (D) smaller in amount than a first mortgage

14. A large final payment on a mortgage loan is
    (A) an escalator
    (B) a balloon
    (C) an amortization
    (D) a package

15. A requirement for a borrower under an FHA-insured loan is that he
    (A) not be eligible for a VA or conventional loan
    (B) have cash for the down payment and closing costs
    (C) have his wife sign as coborrower
    (D) certify that he is receiving welfare payments

16. A mortgaged property can
    (A) be sold without the consent of the mortgagee
    (B) be conveyed by the grantor's making a deed to the grantee
    (C) both A and B
    (D) neither A nor B

17. In the absence of an agreement to the contrary, the mortgage normally having priority will be the one
    (A) for the greatest amount
    (B) that is a permanent mortgage
    (C) that was recorded first
    (D) that is a construction loan mortgage

18. The mortgagor's right to reestablish ownership after delinquency is known as
    (A) reestablishment
    (B) satisfaction
    (C) equity of redemption
    (D) acceleration

19. The Federal National Mortgage Association is active in the
    (A) principal mortgage market
    (B) secondary mortgage market
    (C) term mortgage market
    (D) second mortgage market

20. The money for making FHA loans is provided by
    (A) qualified lending institutions
    (B) the Department of Housing and Urban Development
    (C) the Federal Housing Administration
    (D) the Federal Savings and Loan Insurance Corporation

21. Amortization is best defined as
    (A) liquidation of a debt
    (B) depreciation of a tangible asset
    (C) winding up a business
    (D) payment of interest

22. A mortgage is usually released of record by a
    (A) general warranty deed
    (B) quitclaim deed
    (C) satisfaction piece
    (D) court decree

23. Loans from savings and loan associations may be secured by mortgages on
    (A) real estate
    (B) mobile homes
    (C) both A and B
    (D) neither A nor B

24. The borrower is the
    (A) mortgagee
    (B) creditor
    (C) mortgagor
    (D) both A and B

25. In an amortizing mortgage, the
    (A) principal is reduced periodically along with the payment of interest for that period
    (B) principal is paid at the end of the term
    (C) lenders have greater security than in an unamortizing mortgage
    (D) loan-to-value ratio does not exceed 30 percent

26. A term mortgage is characterized by
    (A) level payments toward principal
    (B) interest-only payments until maturity
    (C) variable payments
    (D) fixed payments including both principal and interest

27. Mortgage bankers
    (A) are subject to regulations of the Federal Reserve System
    (B) are regulated by federal, not state, corporation laws
    (C) act as primary lenders
    (D) earn fees paid by new borrowers and lenders

28. The seller of realty takes, as partial payment, a mortgage called
    (A) sales financing
    (B) note toting
    (C) primary mortgage
    (D) purchase money mortgage

29. In California, a mortgage and a trust deed are both
    (A) security instruments
    (B) title policies
    (C) novations
    (D) estoppels

30. The Federal Housing Administration's role in financing the purchase of real property is to
    (A) act as the lender of funds
    (B) insure loans made by approved lenders
    (C) purchase specific trust deeds
    (D) do all of the above

31. The instrument used to remove the lien of a trust deed from record is called a
    (A) satisfaction
    (B) release deed
    (C) deed of conveyance
    (D) certificate of redemption

32. The type of mortgage loan that permits borrowing additional funds at a later date is called
    (A) an equitable mortgage
    (B) a junior mortgage
    (C) an open-end mortgage
    (D) an extensible mortgage

33. A loan to be completely repaid, principal and interest, by a series of regular, equal installment payments is a
    (A) straight loan
    (B) balloon-payment loan
    (C) fully amortized loan
    (D) variable-rate mortgage loan

34. The instrument used to secure a loan on personal property is called a
    (A) bill of sale
    (B) trust deed
    (C) security agreement
    (D) bill of exchange

35. A secured real property loan usually consists of
    (A) financing statement and trust deed
    (B) the debt (note) and the lien (deed of trust)
    (C) FHA or PMI insurance
    (D) security agreement and financing statement

36. When a loan is fully amortized by equal monthly payments of principal and interest, the amount applied to principal
    (A) and interest remains constant
    (B) decreases while the interest payment increases
    (C) increases while the interest payment decreases
    (D) increases by a constant amount

37. A *subordination clause* in a trust deed may
    (A) permit the obligation to be paid off ahead of schedule
    (B) prohibit the trustor from making an additional loan against the property before the trust deed is paid off
    (C) allow for periodic renegotiation and adjustment in the terms of the obligation
    (D) give priority to liens subsequently recorded against the property

38. PMI stands for
    (A) public money interest
    (B) payments made on investments
    (C) principal and mortgage interest
    (D) private mortgage insurance

39. High loan-to-value ratio loans generally are accompanied by
    (A) FHA insurance
    (B) VA guarantees
    (C) PMI
    (D) any of the above

40. Low interest rates cause
    (A) higher inflation rates
    (B) housing to be more affordable
    (C) higher loan-to-value ratios
    (D) owner financing to be more readily available

41. Rental income received appears on
    (A) balance sheet
    (B) cash flow statement
    (C) both of the above
    (D) neither of the above

42. A prepayment penalty is allowed on
    (A) FHA loans
    (B) VA loans
    (C) CalVet loans
    (D) all of the above

43. CalVet loans are financed by the sale of
    (A) bonds
    (B) mortgages
    (C) deeds
    (D) tax liens

44. A trust deed will always have a(n)
    (A) acceleration clause
    (B) assumability clause
    (C) prepayment penalty
    (D) lis pendens

45. Capital markets refers to
    (A) mortgages
    (B) bonds
    (C) stocks
    (D) all of the above

46. Mortgage bankers typically
    (A) originate loans
    (B) sell loans
    (C) borrow from banks under a line of credit
    (D) all of the above

47. Fannie Mae
    (A) buys loans
    (B) acquires loans in the secondary market
    (C) is the largest owner of mortgages in the United States
    (D) all of the above

48. When a buyer takes property *subject to* a loan, the seller
    (A) is relieved of debt
    (B) remains liable on the loan
    (C) both A and B
    (D) is no longer obligated on the loan

49. Mortgage bankers sell the loans they originate on the
    (A) bank market
    (B) FHLB market
    (C) secondary market
    (D) capital market

50. A *due on sale clause*
    (A) means the loan is due when the property is sold
    (B) benefits the lender
    (C) is a form of acceleration
    (D) all of the above

51. Virtually all deeds of trust will have a clause that states that the full principal is due upon certain default. This is called a(n)
    (A) release clause
    (B) acceleration clause
    (C) novation clause
    (D) assignability clause

52. A VA loan amount is based on
    (A) Certificate of Reasonable Value
    (B) term of military service
    (C) secondary mortgage market
    (D) FNMA loan limits

ANSWERS

1. C	10. A	19. B	28. D	37. D	46. D
2. C	11. A	20. A	29. A	38. D	47. D
3. C	12. C	21. A	30. B	39. D	48. B
4. B	13. A	22. C	31. B	40. B	49. C
5. C	14. B	23. C	32. C	41. B	50. D
6. C	15. B	24. C	33. C	42. C	51. B
7. B	16. C	25. A	34. C	43. A	52. A
8. B	17. C	26. B	35. B	44. A	
9. A	18. C	27. D	36. C	45. D	

Chapter 14/**Appraisals**

Examination Content Outline _____

An appraiser is a professionally qualified person who, for a fee, estimates the value of real estate. The Appraisal Foundation sets requirements for all states to follow, although states can have more extensive requirements. Real Property Appraisal Qualifications will increase significantly as of January 1, 2008. The present requirements for California licensees are listed below.

Category	Scope of Practice/Education/Experience
Trainee License	• Appraisal of property that the supervising appraiser is permitted to appraise. • Requires 90 hours of education, including 15 hours on the Uniform Standards of Professional Appraisal Practice (USPAP). • No experience required.
Residential License	• Appraisal of a 1- to 4-unit residential property up to a transaction value of $1 million if noncomplex, or $250,000, if complex in nature. • Appraisal of non-residential property up to a transaction value of $250,000. This includes the appraisal of vacant land where the highest and best use is for 1- to 4-family purposes. • Requires 90 hours of acceptable education, and at least 2,000 hours of experience.
Certified Residential License	• Appraisal of 1- to 4-unit residential property without regard to transaction value or complexity. Appraisal of nonresidential property up to a transaction value of $250,000. This includes the appraisal of vacant or unimproved land where the highest and best use is for 1- to 4-family purposes. • Appraisal of small apartment buildings of five or more units is not permitted. • Requires 120 hours of acceptable education. • Requires at least 2,500 hours of appraisal experience covering at least 2½ years.
Certified General License	• Appraisal of all real estate without regard to transaction value or complexity. • Requires 180 hours of acceptable education. • Requires at least 3,000 hours of experience covering at least 2½ years; at least 1,500 hours of experience must be in nonresidential property.

Examinatio
Certified General, Cer
Real Propert

Part IV: Real Estate Analysis

F. Lea

192 /

Percentages represent the estimated p

I. **INFLUENCES ON REAI**
   Certified general exami
   Certified residential e
   Licensure examinatic
   A. Physical and envi
   B. Economic
   C. Governmental
   D. Social

II. **LEGAL CONSIDER**
    Certified general examin
    Certified residential examina
    Licensure examination 6–8%
    A. Real estate vs. real property
    B. Real property vs. personal property
       1. Fixtures
       2. Trade fixtures[†]
       3. Machinery and equipment[†]
    C. Limitations on real estate ownership
       1. Private
          a. Deed restrictions
          b. Leases
          c. Mortgages
          d. Easements
          e. Liens
          f. Encroachments
       2. Public
          a. Police power
             (1) Zoning
             (2) Building and fire codes
             (3) Environmental regulations
          b. Taxation
             (1) Property tax
             (2) Special assessments
          c. Eminent domain
          d. Escheat
    D. Legal rights and interests
       1. Fee simple estate
       2. Life estate
       3. Leasehold interest
       4. Leased fee interest
       5. Other legal interests
          a. Easement
          b. Encroachment
    E. Forms of property ownership
       1. Individual
       2. Tenancies and undivided interest
       3. Special ownership forms
          a. Condominiums

[†]Certified general exam only

Cooperative

Timesharing*

gal descriptions

1. Metes and bounds

2. Government survey

3. Lot and block

G. Transfer of title

1. Basic types of deeds

2. Recordation

III. **TYPES OF VALUE** (page 201)
Certified general examination 2–3%
Certified residential examination 3–5%
Licensure examination 3–5%

A. Market value or value in exchange

B. Price

C. Cost

D. Investment value

E. Value in use

F. Assessed value

G. Insurable value

H. Going-concern value†

IV. **ECONOMIC PRINCIPLES** (page 204)
Certified general examination 3–5%
Certified residential examination 7–9%
Licensure examination 7–9%

A. Anticipation

B. Balance

C. Change

D. Competition

E. Conformity

F. Contribution

G. Increasing and decreasing returns

H. Opportunity cost†

I. Substitution

J. Supply and demand

K. Surplus productivity

V. **REAL ESTATE MARKETS AND ANALYSIS** (page 206)
Certified general examination 5–7%
Certified residential examination 5–7%
Licensure examination 5–7%

A. Characteristics of real estate market

1. Availability of information

2. Changes in supply vs. demand

3. Immobility of real estate

4. Segmented markets

5. Regulations

B. Absorption analysis

1. Demographic data

2. Competition

3. Absorption

4. Forecasts

5. Existing space inventory†

6. Current and projected space surplus†

7. New space†

---

†Certified general exam only
*Licensure and certified residential exam only

      C.   Role of money and capital markets
          1.   Competing investments
          2.   Sources of capital
      D.   Real estate financing
          1.   Mortgage terms and concepts
              a.   Mortgagor
              b.   Mortgagee
              c.   Principal and interest
          2.   Mortgage payment plan
              a.   Fixed rate, level payment
              b.   Adjustable rate
              c.   Buy down
              d.   Other
          3.   Types of mortgages
              a.   Conventional
              b.   Insured

VI. VALUATION PROCESS (page 209)
     Certified general examination 2–4%
     Certified residential examination 4–6%
     Licensure examination 4–6%
      A.   Definition of problem
          1.   Purpose and use of appraisal
          2.   Interests to be appraised
          3.   Type of value to be estimated
          4.   Date of value estimate
          5.   Limiting conditions
      B.   Collection and analysis of data
          1.   National and regional trends
          2.   Economic base
          3.   Local area and neighborhood
              a.   Employment
              b.   Income
              c.   Trends
              d.   Access
              e.   Locational convenience
          4.   Site and improvements
      C.   Analysis of highest and best use
      D.   Application and limitations of each approach to value
          1.   Sales comparison
          2.   Cost
          3.   Income capitalization
      E.   Reconciliation and final value estimate
      F.   Appraisal report

VII. PROPERTY DESCRIPTION (page 212)
     Certified general examination 2–4%
     Certified residential examination 2–4%
     Licensure examination 2–4%
      A.   Site description
          1.   Utilities
          2.   Access
          3.   Topography
          4.   Size
      B.   Improvement description
          1.   Size
          2.   Condition
          3.   Utility
      C.   Basic construction and design

  1. Techniques and materials
    a. Foundations
    b. Framing
    c. Finish (exterior and interior)
    d. Mechanical
  2. Functional utility

VIII. HIGHEST AND BEST USE ANALYSIS (page 212)
  Certified general examination 5–7%
  Certified residential examination 5–7%
  Licensure examination 5–7%
  A. Four tests
    1. Physically possible
    2. Legally permitted
    3. Economically feasible
    4. Maximally productive
  B. Vacant site or as if vacant
  C. As improved
  D. Interim use

IX. APPRAISAL MATHEMATICS AND STATISTICS (page 214)
  Certified general examination 3–5%
  Certified residential examination 1–3%
  Licensure examination 1–3%
  A. Compound interest concepts[†]
    1. Future value of $1[†]
    2. Present value of $1[†]
    3. Future value of an annuity of $1 per period[†]
    4. Present value of an annuity of $1 per period[†]
    5. Sinking fund factor[†]
    6. Installment to amortize $1 (loan constant)[†]
  B. Statistical concepts used in appraisal
    1. Mean
    2. Median
    3. Mode
    4. Range
    5. Standard deviation

X. SALES COMPARISON APPROACH (page 215)
  Certified general examination 10–12%
  Certified residential examination 21–24%
  Licensure examination 21–24%
  A. Research and selection of comparables
    1. Data sources
    2. Verification
    3. Units of comparison
      a. Income[†]
        (1) Potential gross income multiplier[†]
        (2) Effective gross income multiplier[†]
        (3) Overall rate[†]
      b. Size
        (1) Square feet
        (2) Acres
        (3) Other
      c. Utility (examples only)
        (1) Motel and apartment units[†]
        (2) Theater seats[†]

[†]Certified general exam only

                    (3)   Rooms*
                    (4)   Beds*
                    (5)   Other
              d.   Data sources*
        B.   Elements of comparison
              1.   Property rights conveyed
                    a.   Easements
                    b.   Leased fee/leasehold
                    c.   Mineral rights†
                    d.   Others
              2.   Financing terms and cash equivalency
                    a.   Loan payment
                    b.   Loan balance
              3.   Conditions of sale
                    a.   Arm's length sale
                    b.   Personalty
              4.   Market conditions at time of contract and closing
              5.   Location
              6.   Physical characteristics
              7.   Tenant improvements†
        C.   Adjustment process
              1.   Sequence of adjustments
              2.   Dollar adjustments
              3.   Percentage adjustments
              4.   Paired-sales analysis
        D.   Application of sales comparison approach
XI.   **SITE VALUE** (page 218)
      Certified general examination 3–5%
      Certified residential examination 4–6%
      Licensure examination 4–6%
      A.   Sales comparison
      B.   Land residual
      C.   Allocation
      D.   Extraction
      E.   Ground rent capitalization†
      F.   Subdivision analysis†
              1.   Development cost: direct and indirect†
              2.   Contractor's overhead and profit†
              3.   Forecast absorption and gross sales†
              4.   Entrepreneurial profit†
              5.   Discounted value conclusion†
      G.   Plottage and assemblage
XII. **COST APPROACH** (page 219)
      Certified general examination 9–12%
      Certified residential examination 8–10%
      Licensure examination 8–10%
      A.   Steps in cost approach
              1.   Reproduction vs. replacement cost
                    a.   Comparative unit method
                    b.   Unit-in-place method
                    c.   Quantity survey method
                    d.   Cost service index
              2.   Accrued depreciation

---

*Licensure and certified residential exam only
†Certified general exam only

---

†Certified general exam only

Appraisal

An *appraisal* is an expert's opinion of value. Appraisals are used in real estate when a professional's opinion of value is needed. Because each property is unique and is not traded in a centralized, organized market, value estimates require the collection and analysis of market data.

To understand what appraisals are, please examine the preceding definition more closely.

[†]Certified general exam only

By an *expert*, we mean a person with the competence and experience to do the type of analysis required. You can get opinions of value from the sales agent, the owner, the tenant, or anyone else familiar with the property. However, these opinions may not be very useful and probably won't be convincing as evidence of value. Usually, an appraisal expert has attained some type of designation through formal study and examination by a recognized body such as the state or a professional organization.

An *opinion* is a judgment supported by facts and logical analysis. The appraiser considers all available information that reflects on the value of the property and then follows a logical process to arrive at an opinion. The result is not merely a guess but is a careful reading of the facts in the case.

The appraisal process is a sequence of steps that an appraiser uses in a systematic fashion to derive an estimate of value.

THE APPRAISAL OR VALUATION PROCESS

The preparation of an appraisal report is an eight-step problem-solving exercise that begins with *defining the problem*, for example, "to estimate market value." The second step is to *plan the appraisal*. The third is *data collection and verification*. Fourth, the *highest and best use* of the site is considered, and fifth, the *land value* is estimated. Three *approaches to appraisal: cost, market data* (or direct sales comparison), and *income* (or capitalization) are applied as a sixth step. Each approach provides an independent value estimate. The seventh step is *reconciliation*, in which the value estimates from the three approaches are considered and a *final value conclusion* is reached. The last step is to provide a written *report*. See Figure 14-1 The Appraisal Process.

GOVERNMENT REGULATION

At one time, anyone could claim to be an appraiser, since there was no mandatory test of the skills required to estimate property value. The higher qualifications of some individuals were (and still are) recognized by professional designations conferred by appraisal associations, but such designation was not a requirement for practice as an appraiser. Since 1992, however, a real estate appraiser must be licensed or certified in order to appraise property in a federally related transaction. Since federally related transactions include any in which an FDIC-insured bank, or FSLIC, FNMA, FHLMC, or GNMA, is involved, probably 90 percent or more of real estate appraisals are now prepared by a state-licensed or -certified appraiser.

Government regulation was imposed as a result of the savings and loan association débacle of the 1980s, when numerous savings institutions collapsed, largely as a result of defective or nonexistent real estate appraisals. An appraisal serves as evidence that a loan is properly supported by collateral and thus serves to protect our nation's financial institutions.

NEED FOR APPRAISAL

An appraisal may be sought for any of a number of purposes, including the following:
1. To help buyers and/or sellers determine how much to offer or accept.
2. To assist lenders in determining the maximum prudent amount to lend on real estate.
3. To arrive at fair compensation when private property is taken for public use.
4. To determine the amount to insure, or the value loss caused by a natural disaster.
5. To determine the viability of a proposed building, renovation, or rehabilitation program.
6. To assist in corporate mergers, reorganizations, and liquidations.
7. To determine taxes due, including income, gift, estate, and ad valorem taxes.

STEP ONE: DEFINITION OF THE PROBLEM

    a. Purpose of assignment
    b. Type of value sought
    c. Identification of property and legal interests
    d. Date of appraisal

STEP TWO: PLAN OF APPRAISAL

    a. Determine data requirements
    b. Identify appropriate methodology
    c. Estimate time and personnel needs
    d. Provide fee and assignment proposal

STEP THREE: COLLECTION AND VERIFICATION OF DATA

    a. Area and neighborhood
    b. Site and off-site
    c. Improvement analysis
    d. Law and government
    e. Economic activity data—income, costs, sales

STEP FOUR: ANALYSIS OF HIGHEST AND BEST USE OF LAND

    a. As if vacant
    b. As improved

STEP FIVE: ESTIMATE LAND VALUE

STEP SIX: APPLICATION OF RELEVANT VALUATION APPROACHES

    a. Income approach
    b. Market approach
    c. Cost approach
    d. Analysis

STEP SEVEN: RECONCILIATION

    a. Review of facts as related to valuation principles
    b. Statistical and probability indications
    c. Logic and judgment
    d. Final indicated value conclusions

STEP EIGHT: REPORT OF FINAL VALUE ESTIMATE

Restricted • Summary • Self-contained

Figure 14-1. The Appraisal Process

Source: Adapted from *Income Property Appraisal and Analysis*, by Jack P. Friedman and Nicholas Ordway (Englewood Cliffs, NJ: Prentice-Hall, 1987).

I. Influences on Real Estate Value

Forces affecting real estate values operate on the international and national, regional, and local community levels. These forces can be categorized as follows:
1. Physical and environmental
2. Economic-financial
3. Political-governmental-legal
4. Sociological

PHYSICAL AND ENVIRONMENTAL

Physical and environmental forces include such factors as dimensions, shape, area, topography, drainage, and soil conditions, as well as utilities, streets, curbs, gutters, sidewalks, landscaping, and the effect of legal restraints (zoning, deed restrictions) on physical development.

Nuisances and hazards are also to be considered, including contaminated air and water and environmentally hazardous building materials such as asbestos, PCBs, certain types of mold, and urea formaldehyde.

ECONOMIC-FINANCIAL

The fixed location of land and its immobility distinguish land from other assets. Land is dependent on where it is and what surrounds it. Urban land derives its value from its location. The most significant determinants of value are the type of industry in the area, employment and unemployment rates and types, interest rates, per capita and household income, and stability. These matters also affect the individual property, including real estate prices and mortgage payments.

POLITICAL-GOVERNMENTAL-LEGAL

Political-governmental-legal factors focus on the services provided, such as utilities, spending and taxation policies, police and fire protection, recreation, schools, garbage collection, and on planning, zoning, and subdivision regulations. Building codes and the level of taxes and assessments are also important considerations.

SOCIOLOGICAL

Sociological factors are concerned with the characteristics of people living in the area, the population density and homogeneity, and compatibility of the land uses with the needs of residents.

II. Legal Considerations in Appraisal

Appraisers are expected to know and consider legal matters affecting real estate in making their appraisals. These matters are covered elsewhere in this book. Specific topics and coverage follow:
A. Real estate vs. real property (Chapters 2 and 3)
B. Real property vs. personal property (Chapters 2 and 3)
   1. Fixtures
   2. Trade fixtures
   3. Machinery and equipment
C. Limitations on real estate ownership (Chapters 2 and 3)
   1. Private
      a. Deed restrictions
      b. Leases
      c. Mortgages

d. Easements
e. Liens
f. Encroachments
2. Public
  a. Police power
    (1) Zoning
    (2) Building and fire codes
    (3) Environmental regulations
  b. Taxation
    (1) Property tax
    (2) Special assessments
  c. Eminent domain
  d. Escheat
D. Legal rights and interests (Chapters 3 and 9)
1. Fee simple estate
2. Life estate
3. Leasehold interest
4. Leased fee interest
5. Other legal interests
  a. Easement
  b. Encroachment
E. Forms of property ownership (Chapter 3)
1. Individual
2. Tenancies and undivided interest
3. Special ownership forms
  a. Condominiums
  b. Cooperative
  c. Timesharing
F. Legal descriptions (Chapter 7)
1. Metes and bounds
2. Government survey
3. Lot and block
G. Transfer of title (Chapter 9)
1. Basic types of deeds
2. Recordation

III. Types of Value

There are numerous types of value that the appraiser may be asked to estimate.

MARKET VALUE

The most common type is *market value*, which is defined below.

The most probable price which a property should bring in a competitive and open market under all conditions requisite to a fair sale, the buyer and seller each acting prudently and knowledgeably, and assuming the price is not affected by undue stimulus. Implicit in this definition is the consummation of a sale as of a specified date and the passing of title from seller to buyer under conditions whereby:

1. *buyer and seller are typically motivated;*
2. *both parties are well informed or well advised, and acting in what they consider their best interests;*
3. *a reasonable time is allowed for exposure in the open market;*
4. *payment is made in terms of cash in United States dollars or in terms of financial arrangements comparable thereto; and*

5. *the price represents the normal consideration for the property sold unaffected by special or creative financing or sales concessions granted by anyone associated with the sale.*[*]

Persons performing appraisal services on property that may be subject to condemnation are cautioned to seek the exact definition of market value applicable in the jurisdiction where the services are being performed.

COMPARATIVE MARKET ANALYSIS

Very often, property owners want to get an idea of what their real estate is worth, without paying for a full appraisal. For example, a homeowner may contact a broker or salesperson to list her house, and will accept the broker's or salesperson's judgment of its value or the asking price to be listed when it is put on the market. A broker may not wish to spend the time to prepare a full-blown appraisal just to solicit a listing, even if she is perfectly qualified to do so. Further, unless the broker is licensed or certified by the state as an appraiser and has no conflict of interest, the appraisal could not be used to support a loan made by a federally chartered bank or savings association.

The broker or salesperson will prepare a *comparative market analysis* (CMA) for this purpose. Unlike the standard preprinted forms required for Fannie Mae/Freddie Mac residential appraisals, there is no standard form for a CMA. Brokers are free to include whatever information they wish to use, and to present it in any manner.

A CMA is likely to show recent sales of other houses in the neighborhood and their salient characteristics. It may also show properties currently for sale on the market. Consider the data in Table 14-1.

Table 14-1.

COMPARATIVE MARKET ANALYSIS

Property	Price	Date	Sq. Ft.	No. Bedrooms	No. Baths	Stories	Per Sq. Ft.
Subject	?	Now	2,000	4	2	1	?
Comp 1	$420,000	Last year	2,100	4	2	2	$280.00
Comp 2	$380,000	Last year	1,950	3	1.5	1	$194.88
Comp 3	$470,000	Six months	2,250	4	2.5	1	$202.88
Asking 1	$430,000	Now	2,050	3	2	2	$209.74
Asking 2	$450,000	Now	2,100	3	2	1	$214.28

This particular CMA might be used to judge a market range (highest and lowest prices per square foot). However, it offers no information on special features, the age or condition of the houses, how long it took to sell them, or how long the existing listings have been on the market. So a CMA is not as detailed or thorough as an appraisal, though it may provide a reasonable indication of market value.

RESIDENTIAL MARKET ANALYSIS

A *residential market analysis* (RMA) provides information on the current situation of the housing market. It tries to answer the question, "How is the market?" A response might be, "There are currently 102 homes for sale in northeast Rochester. Twenty homes were newly listed last month, and 27 sold last month. The average time on the market for those that sold was 62 days. Of those that sold, 67 percent were in the $200,000–$250,000 price range, with 10 percent in the $250,000–$300,000 range and 5 percent above $300,000. Eight percent were below $150,000, and 10 percent were between $150,000 and $200,000. Houses with fewer than two full bathrooms are not doing well. About half of the buyers are local 'move-ups,' with the other half transferees. Prices seem to be rising slightly."

[*]*Dictionary of Real Estate Appraisal,* 4th ed. (Chicago: Appraisal Institute, 2002), p.177; definition 3.

As is apparent, the purpose of an RMA is to describe the current condition of the real estate market. This may help answer the question of whether this is a good time to buy or sell and whether prices are rising or falling.

AUTOMATED VALUATION MODELS

Automated Valuation Models (AVMs) apply complex statistical techniques to data on comparable sales to offer an estimate of value. AVMs are often used by those offering home equity loans who don't want to incur a $350–$400 appraisal fee. For a typical fee of $50, a value estimate is provided, which may consider the size, age, location, and number of rooms in the house. If a lender wants greater assurance of value than an AVM offers, he may ask for a site visit or a full appraisal.

EVALUATIONS

An *evaluation* of real estate is a study that does not lead to an estimate of market value. An evaluation may be performed to consider the feasibility of a proposed use (the feasibility study), the highest and best use of the property, or a market study that considers the supply and demand in the current market for a certain type of land use.

CONTRASTING VALUE WITH COST AND PRICE

Value, cost, and price are not the same. *Value* is a measure of how much a purchaser would likely be willing to pay for the property being appraised. *Cost* is a measure of the expenditures necessary to produce a similar property. Depending on several factors, this cost could be higher or lower than the current value. *Price* is the historic fact of how much was spent on similar properties in past transactions. Neither past prices nor cost will necessarily represent a fair measure of current value.

OTHER KINDS OF VALUE

Different kinds of value are necessary because of different needs and functions. Included are such values as *loan value, insurable value, market value, book value, rental value, fair value, salvage value, investment value,* and many others. Certain of the more common types are described below.

LOAN VALUE OR MORTGAGE VALUE

Loan or *mortgage value* is the same as market value. Property serving as collateral for a loan or mortgage is normally valued at market value.

INVESTMENT VALUE

Investment value is the estimated value of a certain real estate investment to a particular individual or institutional investor. It may be greater or less than market value, depending on the investor's particular situation. For example, the investment value of vacant land in the path of growth would be greater for a young, aggressive investor who has time to wait for fruition than for an elderly widow who needs available cash for living expenses. Similarly, the investment value of a tax shelter is greater for a high-tax-bracket investor than for a tax-exempt pension plan.

VALUE IN USE AND VALUE IN EXCHANGE

Value in use, which tends to be subjective because it is not set in the market, is the worth of a property to a specific user or set of users. It considers the value of the property when put to a specific use as part of a going concern. For example, the use of a factory where automobiles are assembled may have a high value to the manufacturer, even though the market value of the property is difficult to measure and may be low because there are few interested buyers. Value in use is distinguished from *value in exchange*, which is the value of a commodity, in terms of money, to people in general rather than to a specific person. Value in exchange is a more objective measure and is commonly identified with market value.

ASSESSED VALUE

The *assessed value* (or *assessed valuation*) is the value of property established for tax purposes. Although tax assessors try to value most property at market value (or some specified fraction of market value), the fact that they must assess a great number of properties periodically on a limited budget often means that assessed values are quite different from market values.

INSURABLE VALUE

The *insurable value* of a property is the cost of total replacement of its destructible improvements. For example, suppose a home that sold for $100,000 ten years ago would cost $200,000 to rebuild today, not including land cost. Its insurable value would be $200,000 even if its current market value, including the land, was only $175,000.

GOING-CONCERN VALUE

Going-concern value is the worth of a business, such as a hotel, based on its operations. The replacement cost of the property may be much more or much less than the business is worth.

IV. Economic Principles

Economics involves combining the *factors of production* to result in a product that is worth more than the cost of the individual factors. The factors of production are land, labor, capital, and entrepreneurship. For example, to produce a bushel of wheat may require $1 for land rent, $1 for labor, $1 for equipment, and $1 for the business management and risk-taking entrepreneur. This is a total of $4, so the farming operation would not occur unless the expected selling price was $4.01 or more per bushel. Many economists recognize only three factors of production, regarding profit as the owners' compensation for their risk taking and inputs of management and entrepreneurship. Certain economic principles are associated with real estate valuation. The major principles are explained below.

ANTICIPATION

Anticipation is determination of the present worth of income or other benefits one expects to receive in the future from the ownership of property. For income-producing properties, value is based on the anticipated net receipts from the operation of the assets plus any amounts to be received upon resale.

BALANCE (PROPORTIONALITY)

For any type of land use, there are optimal amounts of different factors of production that can be combined to create maximum land values. Land, labor, capital, and entrepreneurship can be combined in different proportions, as is demonstrated by the number of houses that may be erected on a parcel of land. Values are maximized when factors are in proportion, or *balance* is achieved.

CHANGE

Real estate values tend not to remain constant, but to vary over time. New technology and social patterns create new demands for real estate. Demographic *changes* create needs for different kinds of housing. People's desires and tastes undergo transitions. Neighborhoods go through a life cycle of growth, maturity, decline, and renewal. Any of these factors and many others can change the utility of real estate at a given location.

Objects wear out. New businesses are started, and others end. The land use pattern is modified by private and public actions. Money supply and interest rates fluctuate. Economic conditions create opportunities or stifle growth.

COMPETITION

When profits exceed the income necessary to pay for the factor of production, *competition* will tend to enter the market, causing average net incomes to fall. This principle is important to an analyst attempting to estimate the value of property that is selling above the cost of its replacement. Its high cost attracts builders and developers, who can earn a large profit from new construction.

CONFORMITY

Conformity is a measure of how well the architectural style and levels of amenities and services offered by a real estate development meet market needs and expectations. A project that fails to conform to market standards is likely to suffer a financial penalty. This does not mean, for example, that all buildings in a particular location must be of the same architectural style. However, the architectural styles and the land use must be compatible. Consider the consequences of building a brightly painted Victorian house replete with architectural gingerbread in a neighborhood of split-level houses. Consider also what would happen if a municipal incinerator were constructed next to a nursing home. The nursing home might have to close because of the health hazard posed by the smoke and other pollution.

CONTRIBUTION

Contribution is the amount by which the value or net income of an economic good is increased or decreased by the presence or absence of some additional factor of production. Contribution is the value increment or detriment to an economic good by the addition of some new factor, rather than the actual cost of the new factor itself. In real estate, some things add more than their cost of production, whereas others may actually detract from value. For example, a new exterior paint job may improve the appearance of a house and make it more salable. On the other hand, a potential buyer may regard a swimming pool as a liability rather than an asset.

An example of the principle of contribution would be a builder's deliberation over whether to add a tennis court to an apartment complex. The cost of this feature is $25,000. With the added tennis court, the complex is worth $1,100,000. Without it, it is worth only $1,000,000. Thus, the tennis court would add $75,000 to the overall value. Since the cost of adding this amenity is less than its contribution, a prudent builder would construct the tennis court.

INCREASING AND DECREASING RETURNS

As resources are added to fixed agents in production, net returns will tend to increase at an increasing rate up to a certain point. Thereafter, total returns will increase at a decreasing rate until the increment to value is less than the cost of resource unit input. A common problem faced by the owners of land is the determination of how intensively their land should be developed. Development should become more intensive as long as profit increases. For example, the profit on a downtown office building, to be sold above cost, may increase with the height of the building, up to a point. Above that height, the profit may decline.

OPPORTUNITY COST

Opportunity cost is the return forfeited by not choosing an alternative. A person with $25,000 to invest may choose to buy equity in a rental residence rather than to purchase a certificate of deposit. The opportunity cost is the interest not received on the CD.

SUBSTITUTION

The maximum value of a property is set by the lowest price or cost at which another property of equivalent utility may be acquired. This *substitution* principle underlies each of the three traditional approaches to value used in the appraisal process: (1) direct sales comparison, (2) income, and (3) cost. A rational purchaser will pay no more for a property than the lowest price being charged for another property of equivalent utility. Likewise, it is not prudent to pay more for an existing project if another one of equivalent utility can be produced, without unreasonable delay, for a lower cost. If an investor is analyzing an income stream, the maximum price is set by examining the prices at which other income streams of similar risk and quality can be purchased.

SUPPLY AND DEMAND

Supply is the quantity of goods, such as real estate, available at a given price schedule; *demand* is the quantity of goods desired at this price schedule. Demand is based on the desire of potential purchasers to acquire real estate, provided that they also have sufficient sources of financing to act on their desires. Together, supply and demand interact to establish prices.

In the long run, supply and demand are relatively effective forces in determining the direction of price changes. An excessive supply or lack of demand will tend to depress price levels. A contrary pressure, which serves to raise prices, occurs when there is either an inadequate supply or a high demand.

SURPLUS PRODUCTIVITY

Surplus productivity is the net income attributed to land after the costs of labor, capital, and entrepreneurship have been paid. Because land is physically immobile, the factors of labor, capital, and entrepreneurship must be attracted to it; therefore, these factors are compensated first. If any money is left over, this residual amount is paid as rent to the owner. In economic theory, land is said to have "residual value" and has worth only if a surplus remains after paying for the other factors of production.

V. Real Estate Markets and Analysis

This topic is concerned with the characteristics of the real estate market, the analysis of use of additional space (absorption), the role of money and capital markets, and the financing terms available for a property. Market analysis and absorption are discussed below. Mortgages and finance were considered in Chapter 13.

REAL ESTATE MARKETS

Real estate is not a single market but consists rather of a series of submarkets with different desires and needs that can change independently of one another. Consequently, real estate markets are said to be *segmented*. The market for retail space in north Atlanta may be quite different from that in east, west, or south Atlanta. Even within the directional quadrants there are significant differences, depending on the distance from downtown and from the nearest major artery or intersection. Within a narrow geographic area there may be a saturation of one type of retail space but not enough of another. For example, neighborhood shopping centers, which typically have a supermarket and a drugstore as anchor tenants, may be abundant, whereas there is no convenient regional mall.

AVAILABILITY OF INFORMATION

One key to successful appraisal is the ability to locate reliable, consistent data. Sources of market data for rental income and expense are described below.

Nationally Disseminated Rental and Operating Expense Data

Certain national organizations collect information from owners and managers in major cities regarding local rents and operating expenses. Such information can be used judiciously to determine whether the data for a particular property appears consistent with experience reported nationally. Because the real estate market is fragmented, a data source appropriate for the specific property must be used.

Office Buildings. The Building Owners and Managers Association (BOMA) International provides information on office building rental rates and operating expenses experienced by its members in major U.S. cities. BOMA's address is

Building Owners and Managers Association International
1201 New York Avenue NW, Suite 300
Washington, DC 20005
www.boma.org

Shopping Centers. The Urban Land Institute (ULI) releases a new edition of *Dollars and Cents of Shopping Centers* every two years. ULI's address is

Urban Land Institute
1025 Thomas Jefferson Street, Suite 500W
Washington, DC 20007
www.uli.org

Apartments, Condominiums, and Cooperatives. The Institute of Real Estate Management (IREM) of the National Association of REALTORS® periodically provides the *Income/Expense Analysis* for various types of buildings (elevator, walk-up, others) in different cities. IREM's address is

Institute of Real Estate Management
430 N. Michigan Avenue
Chicago, IL 60611
www.irem.org

Hotels and Motels. One source of information on national and local trends is Smith Travel Research. Its address is

Smith's Travel Research
735 E. Main Street
Hendersonville, TN 37075
Phone: (615) 824-8664
Fax: (615) 824-3848
www.smithtravelresearch.com

Local Sources of Real Estate Data

Local organizations often collect real estate data, usually for membership use or sale to interested parties. These include the following:

Local Boards of REALTORS. Most metropolitan areas have a Board of REALTORS, or other broker group, that sponsors a multiple listing service (MLS). Upon the sale of property listed through the MLS, the broker must supply information about the completed transaction. Each property sold and its terms of sale are therefore available on computer or in a published book. Some REALTOR boards provide information to members only; some share with other real estate organizations.

Local Tax Assessing Offices. Assessing offices usually keep a file card on every property in the jurisdiction, noting property characteristics, value estimate, and data from which the estimate was derived. Many jurisdictions are notified of every sale or building permit, for immediate update of affected properties.

Local Credit Bureaus and Tax Map Companies. These may have data on certain parcels; since their main business is not evaluation, however, they are not regular sources.

University Research Centers.   University research centers, many of which are supported by state broker and salesperson license fees, may have aggregated data on real estate transactions collected from other sources throughout the state. These data are often helpful in identifying trends established over time and by city for various types of property. Additional research and educational information may also be available from such centers.

Private Data Sources.   Many real estate investors retain files on their property. They will often share information, usually for reciprocity rather than payment.

Property Owners.   Property owners' records include permanent records such as deeds, leases, and copies of mortgages (lenders have the original mortgage documents), as well as periodic accounting and tax return information about a property's recent past. An owner's report may be of limited immediate use, however, because it may be disorganized, contain extraneous information, or be arranged poorly for appraisal purposes. Also, data from a single property cannot offer a broad perspective on the market.

DEMAND FOR PROPERTY

An appraiser must always be concerned about the demand for a property. People must want to use the property enough to pay the rent asked. If the demand to use the property is high, the demand to buy the property will also be high. High demand means top rents, low vacancies, and good resale prospects. Poor demand means rent reductions, high vacancies, and a property that is hard to sell.

The following are the key items that produce demand for real estate:

Economic growth in the local area increases demand for all properties. New jobs and more residents increase the need for developed real estate. Rising incomes mean higher rents and prices, as well as more retail sales.

Good-quality property raises demand. A property should have all the standard features expected in the market, plus something extra that the competition doesn't have. Appearance, features, size, and services are valued in the market.

A *good location* improves demand. Location can make a poor-quality property profitable, while a good property in the wrong place can suffer.

A *competitive price* can increase demand. If a property is less than ideal, it may be able to compete on the basis of price. It is important to know what segment of the market the property is intended to serve and to price accordingly.

The *cost of alternatives* also determines demand. Apartments are more popular when house prices are high. Houses sell better when interest rates are low.

The demand for a type of property can be estimated by a market analysis. This will indicate whether there is room for more of that type of property in the market. The demand for a specific property can be determined by comparing its features, location, and price to those of similar properties.

Market Analysis

Market analysis is the identification and study of current supply and demand conditions in a particular area for a specific type of property. Such a study is used to indicate how well a particular piece of real estate will be supported by the market. It identifies the most likely users of the project and determines how well they are being served by the existing supply of properties. In essence, the study shows whether there is a need for a new project, or whether an existing project has a good future.

For example, suppose a developer is considering construction of new luxury apartments in a certain town. A market study will first examine the sources of demand for the units. It will identify a *target market*: the type of tenants most likely to be attracted to the property. Description of the target market may include family income, typical family structure, and the features that potential buyers will desire in a residence. The analysis will then survey the market area and use all relevant available data sources to see how many people of this type exist and where they live. A good study will project growth trends in the target market, since a likely source of tenants will be new arrivals.

Next, the study will examine supply conditions. The number and the location of similar properties are identified. A survey of vacancies indicates how well supply matches demand. Features and characteristics of competing properties should be described, and some indication of market rents found. In addition, any new projects that will come along should be identified.

An appraiser should determine whether the market is unbalanced. When the supply of a certain type of real estate is short, rents and prices may be high, but only temporarily. New competition will add to the supply and drive prices down. By contrast, when a market is over-supplied, the price must be low enough to offer an attractive investment.

Market analysis is used to estimate the pace of rent-up or sales for a new project. This *absorption rate* may be expressed as an overall rate ("The market needs 1,000 new apartment units per year") or as a specific rate for the project ("Given current competition, the project should capture 200 new rentals per year"). An absorption rate estimate is important in projecting the revenue production of a property.

A market analysis may indicate that there is little demand for the type of project envisioned. Then a change in plans is needed; the project can be redirected to a different target market. The study may also be used to help in the design of the project. It may identify some feature lacking in the existing supply that, if included in the proposed project, will offer a competitive advantage. At the same time, it will probably be necessary to offer the standard features of the competition. The market study will also help in pricing the product for the indicated target market.

Feasibility Analysis

A *feasibility study* tests not only market conditions but also the financial viability of a proposed project. It is not enough to describe the market for rental units; one must also explore whether the cost of production can be maintained at a price that allows a profit or meets some investment objective.

VI. The Valuation Process

As noted earlier in this chapter, the steps in the appraisal or valuation process are as follows:
1. Define the problem to be solved.
2. Plan the appraisal.
3. Collect and verify data.
4. Analyze the highest and best use of the land.
5. Estimate the land value.
6. Apply relevant valuation approaches.
7. Reconcile the value indications and make a final value estimate.
8. Report the final value estimate.

DEFINE THE PROBLEM

In defining the problem to be solved, the appraiser must ascertain a number of items. A definition of value should be formulated at the outset of the valuation process. The property to be valued and the property rights to be appraised must be identified. Also, the date of the estimate of value must be determined. The use of the appraisal should be addressed, in order to determine the needs and requirements of the client. Finally, the appraiser must consider and set forth any special limiting conditions that will be part of the appraisal.

PLAN THE APPRAISAL

The second step is planning the appraisal. This includes determining the data needed and identifying potential data sources, identifying the methodology to be applied, estimating the time and personnel needed, estimating the fee, and scheduling the work to be performed.

COLLECT AND VERIFY DATA

Part three of the valuation process involves gathering data related to the subject property and its environs (region and immediate neighborhood), and comparable market data. A narrative report often starts with national trends, then proceeds to the region and local area. General data gathering relates to the region in which the property is located and the interaction of social, economic, governmental, and environmental forces. A neighborhood description is included. A *neighborhood* is an area of complementary land uses that may be delineated by natural barriers, political boundaries, income levels of inhabitants, or streets.

The appraiser, in gathering specific data and completing research into general data, should seek to identify any factors that directly or indirectly influence the subject property, so that these factors can be considered in the appraisal. Specific data are those related directly to the subject property. These include site data, improvement data, zoning data, ad valorem tax data, and market data. *Market data* is a broad term referring to all real estate sales, listings, leases, and offers that are used in developing the three approaches to value (see below). Thus, data requirements are set by the appraisal problem to be addressed. Not only must data be collected, but also the accuracy of the collected information must be verified.

ANALYZE THE HIGHEST AND BEST USE

After describing and analyzing the subject environs, site, and improvements, the appraiser analyzes the *highest and best use* of the property. The highest and best use analysis for improved properties has a twofold purpose: (1) to determine the highest and best use of the site as if vacant, and (2) to analyze the highest and best use of the property as improved. The highest and best use of the site as if vacant is required so that land with similar highest and best uses can be used for comparison purposes in the land value estimate section of the appraisal. Also, the existing improvements are evaluated in regard to the highest and best use of the site as if vacant. If the existing improvements do not conform to this use of the site, changes or modifications should be considered. The highest and best use of a property is a very crucial conclusion, as the three approaches to value are developed on the basis of this determination.

ESTIMATE THE LAND VALUE

The next step in the valuation process involves estimating the value of the site as if vacant. In determining this value, consideration must be given to the highest and best use of the site. One or more of the following methods can be used to arrive at an indication of the value of the site as if vacant:

1. Sales comparison
2. Allocation
3. Extraction
4. Subdivision development
5. Land residual technique
6. Ground rent capitalization

APPLY VALUATION APPROACHES

After the site value estimate, the three approaches to value: the cost approach, the direct sales comparison (market data) approach, and the income approach are developed. Sometimes, one or more of the three approaches is not applicable to a given property and is not developed in the appraisal. In this case, the appraiser should state why the approach is not applicable. This can be determined, however, only by careful analysis of the property being appraised in relation to the analytical tools available to the appraiser. A short explanation of each approach follows; the three approaches are considered in detail later in this chapter.

Cost Approach

The cost approach is based on the principle of substitution. It recognizes that buyers often judge the value of an existing structure by comparing it with the cost to construct a new structure of the same type. In developing the cost approach, the appraiser estimates the cost to replace or reproduce the improvements, deducts depreciation (if any), and then adds to this figure the estimated value of the site or land as if vacant. The major limitation of this approach is the difficulty in estimating accrued depreciation, particularly when depreciation is present in more than one form.

Direct Sales Comparison Approach

The direct sales comparison approach recognizes that no informed and prudent person will pay more for a property than it would cost to purchase an equally desirable substitute property (the principle of substitution). In developing this approach, the appraiser locates sales of properties similar to the property being appraised (called *comparable sales*) and provides details describing them in the appraisal report. These sale properties are then compared to the property being appraised, and adjustments are made for differences between each such property and the property under appraisal. The reliability of this approach is directly related to the quality and quantity of the sales data.

Income Capitalizaiton Approach

The income capitalization approach is based on the principle of anticipation, which states that value is created by the anticipation of future benefits to be derived from ownership of a given property. The appraiser is primarily concerned with the future benefits to be derived from operation of the subject property—the net operating income (NOI), or cash flow. The steps in this approach include estimating potential gross income by comparison with competing properties, deducting a market derived vacancy and collection loss allowance, and estimating expenses (derived from historical and/or market experience) to determine a projected stream of net operating income. The income stream is then capitalized into an indication of value by using capitalization rates extracted from competitive properties in the market, or by using other techniques when applicable.

RECONCILIATION

It should be noted that all three approaches are closely interrelated, and that all three use market data: the cost approach utilizes data from the market on labor and materials costs, the direct sales comparison approach analyzes sales of similar properties, and the income capitalization approach determines the market investment return rates. Also, data and conclusions from one approach are often used in one or more of the other approaches. If good data are available for application of all three approaches, the resulting indications should fall within a narrow range.

Among the factors considered in the final estimate of value are the accuracy, reliability, and pertinence of the information available for each approach. Major considerations in the *reconciliation* of value indications are which approach has the best data, which is the most likely to be free of error, and which is the most reliable for the type of property being appraised. A final value estimate should be rounded so as not to give a false impression of the precision associated with an opinion.

REPORT

The final step in the appraisal process is the report of defined value. Three types of written reports for real estate appraisals prepared under the *Uniform Standards of Professional Appraisal Practice* (USPAP) are:

1. Self-contained
2. Summary
3. Restricted use

A *self-contained report* provides all details about the property and the data used to appraise it. A *summary report* can summarize many of the details, which are included in work papers. A *restricted use report* is abbreviated so much that its use is usually restricted to one party such as the property owner, who knows all about the property (but not its value) and doesn't need extensive explanations in a report.

A *form report* is a summary report placed on a preprinted form, generally used for one- to four-family dwellings. An *oral report* may be provided to a client; however, all the research must have been performed before providing the oral report and must be retained in the appraiser's files.

COMPLETE AND LIMITED APPRAISALS

A *complete appraisal,* under USPAP, must have all the relevant approaches: cost, market, and income. An appraisal may be *complete* with just one approach if the others are not relevant. For example, a tract of land may require only the market approach to be complete. The income and cost approaches are not likely to be relevant.

A *limited appraisal* omits one or more approaches that may be relevant. Appraising an apartment complex by using only the market approach is likely to result in a limited appraisal because the income and/or cost approach may be relevant. A limited appraisal is permitted under USPAP as long as it is so described and the resulting appraisal is credible.

VII. Property Description

The site, improvements, and construction design must be described in an appraisal to allow the reader to understand the physical qualities of the property.

SITE DESCRIPTION

The size and shape of the site are described, and any impediment to development or any superior qualities are noted. If a parcel is narrow or awkwardly shaped, this fact is mentioned. Road frontage (or lack of access) and topography are noted. Zoning is described, detailing allowable uses and the current use. The appraiser should note, with reference to maps, whether the property is in a flood-prone area. The availability of utilities at the site, including water supply and sewers, gas and electricity, and, if appropriate, cable television, is noted.

IMPROVEMENTS DESCRIPTION

The size, condition, and utility of the improvements must be described in the appraisal report, accompanied by photographs of the property, both inside and out. Photographs give the reader a visual impression in addition to the written description of the information to be conveyed. Anything relevant about the usefulness (or lack thereof) and condition of the property is described.

BASIC CONSTRUCTION AND DESIGN

When plans and specifications are available, the appraiser can refer to them in describing the design and construction. Otherwise, he must rely on visual impressions and answers to questions provided by owners, lessees, or neighbors. At the least, the report should describe the foundation (concrete slab, pier and beam), framing, finish (inside and out), and electrical and mechanical systems.

The usefulness of the building is important. Functionality is affected by such factors as ceiling height for warehouse space, pedestrian traffic flow for retail locations, and layout of office space for office buildings.

VIII. Highest and Best Use Analysis

Highest and best use is defined as follows:

The reasonably probable and legal use of vacant land or an improved property, which is physically possible, appropriately supported, financially feasible, and that results in the highest value. The four criteria the highest and best *use must meet are legal permissibility, physical possibility, financial feasibility, and maximum profitability.* [*]

The four criteria are applied in sequential order. Potential uses are narrowed through the consideration of each criterion so that, by the time the last criterion is applied, only a single use is indicated. A property often will have numerous uses that are physically possible; a lesser number that are both physically possible and legally permissible; fewer still that are physically possible, legally permissible, and financially feasible; and only a single use that meets all four criteria.

As the definition implies, there are two types of highest and best use: the highest and best use of land or a site as if vacant, and the highest and best use of property as improved. The highest and best use of land or a site as if vacant can be specifically defined as follows:

Among all reasonable, alternative uses, the use that yields the highest present land value, after payments are made for labor, capital, and coordination. The use of a property based on the assumption that the parcel of land is vacant or can be made vacant by demolishing any improvements [†]

In valuing an improved parcel, consideration should be given to the additional value, if any, of the improvements. The highest and best use of property as improved is defined as follows:

The use that should be made of a property as it exists. An existing property should be renovated or retained as is so long as it continues to contribute to the total market value of the property, or until the return from a new improvement would more than offset the cost of demolishing the existing building and constructing a new one. [‡]

HIGHEST AND BEST USE OF THE LAND AS IF VACANT

This type of use forms the basis of land value in the cost approach. Four tests are employed in the effort to determine the highest and best use of land. The first three are physical, legal, and financial. Uses that meet the first three tests are then considered to determine which is the maximally productive. Highest and best use analysis assumes that any existing building can be demolished.

PHYSICALLY POSSIBLE

The appraiser describes the uses surrounding the site and in the neighborhood, along with the traffic flow on the subject's street and nearby thoroughfares. Visibility and access are described as they affect potential uses. The size and shape are considered, and the question of whether these attributes lend themselves to certain uses or are impediments is discussed. Nearby transportation systems (bus, subway, rail) are also considered. Availability of utilities is a physical factor that can limit or impede development.

LEGALLY PERMISSIBLE

Legal restrictions include private restrictions and existing public land use regulations—in most cities, zoning. Often, only a title search by a competent attorney will uncover deed restrictions. It is therefore recommended that a title search be made if any question regarding deed restrictions arises. If common restrictions (e.g., utility and drainage easements) exist, the appraiser can state whether they appear to adversely affect the site's development potential. The appraiser should specify what is allowed within the zoning classification.

---

[*]*The Dictionary of Real Estate Appraisal*, 4th ed. (Chicago: Appraisal Institute, 2002), p. 135.

[†]Ibid.

[‡]Ibid.

FINANCIALLY FEASIBLE

The financial feasibility of the physically possible and legally permissible uses of the site is considered. In this analysis, consideration is given to the supply and demand levels for residential, retail, and industrial properties within the area.

MAXIMALLY PRODUCTIVE

On the basis of surrounding existing uses, most probable type of use and, within this range, possible alternatives (e.g., office/warehouse or office/laboratory for industrial property) are stated. Although a great deal of judgment is involved, the appraiser provides a conclusion as to the highest and best use. This use need not be one that can be implemented immediately, but may be something to consider for the future.

HIGHEST AND BEST USE OF THE PROPERTY AS IMPROVED

When the property is already improved with a substantial building, there are only two practical alternatives for the subject: razing the improvements or continued operation as improved. When the improvements have lost much of their utility because of their effective age, obsolescence, and condition, demolition could be considered. However, it is often not economically feasible to demolish when there is sufficient income and utility to justify continued operation of the building for an interim period.

IX. Appraisal Mathematics and Statistics

Math concepts in appraisal fall into two categories:
1. The arithmetic of real estate finance, which is covered in Chapter 17.
2. Statistical concepts of mean, median, mode, range, and standard deviation, which follow.
- *Mean*—the average of a set of numbers. It is found by adding the amounts and dividing by the number of items.
- *Median*—the middle item in a ranking.
- *Mode*—the most popular amount, that is, the one that occurs most frequently in a list.
- *Range*—the difference between the largest and the smallest numbers in a list.

For example, consider seven homes that sold for the following amounts:

Number	Price
1	$300,000
2	340,000
3	400,000
4	420,000
5	480,000
6	480,000
7	540,000
Total	$2,960,000

The *mean*, or average, is found by totaling all the prices and then dividing by the number of sales (seven). In this example, the mean is $422,857. The *median* is $420,000, as three houses sold for more and three for less. The *mode* is the most popular price—in this case, $480,000, as two houses sold for that price and only one for every other price. The *range* is from $300,000 to $540,000, or $240,000.
- *Standard deviation*—a term used to describe the variance of the observations from the mean. It is important to remember that 66 percent of observations fall within one standard deviation from the mean, and 95 percent fall within two standard deviations.

X. Sales Comparison Approach

The sales comparison approach is based primarily on the principle of substitution, which holds that a prudent individual will pay no more for a property than it would cost to purchase a comparable substitute property. The approach recognizes that a typical buyer will compare asking prices and seek to purchase the property that meets his or her wants and needs for the lowest cost. In developing the sales comparison approach, the appraiser attempts to interpret and measure the actions of parties involved in the marketplace, including buyers, sellers, and investors.

COLLECTION OF DATA

Data are collected on recent sales of properties similar to the subject, called *comparables* (*comps*). Sources of comparable data include Realtor publications, public records, buyers and sellers, brokers and salespersons, and other appraisers. Salient details for each comp are described in the appraisal report. Because comps will not be identical to the subject, some price adjustment is necessary. The idea is to simulate the price that would have been paid if the comp were actually identical to the subject. Differences that do not affect value are not adjusted for. If the comp is *superior* to the subject, an amount is *subtracted* from the known sales price of the comp. *Inferior* features of the comp require that an amount be *added* to the comp's known sales price. From the group of adjusted sales prices, the appraiser selects an indicator of value that is representative of the subject.

SELECTION OF COMPARABLES

No set number of comparables is required, but the greater the number, the more reliable the result. How are comps selected? To minimize the amount of adjustment required, comps should be closely similar to the subject. How current and how similar the comps are depends on the availability of data. Comps should be verified by calling a party to the transaction. The appraiser must ascertain that comps were sold in an *arm's length* market transaction; that is, that the sales price or terms were not distorted by, for example, the fact that buyer and seller were relatives.

The following are common shortcomings in the selection process:
- The sale occurred too long ago. (The market may have changed since the sale took place.)
- The location is too different. (Location and surroundings have important effects on value.)
- Special financing was used in a comparable sale. (The price may have been based in part on favorable financing terms.)
- Too few comparables can be found. (One or two sales may not represent the market.)
- The comparable was not an open market transaction. (A sale to a relative or an intracompany sale, foreclosure, or the like is not considered an open market or arm's length transaction.)

When the subject is unusual or when market activity is slow, one or more of these problems may be unavoidable. However, if this is the case, the problem(s) should be acknowledged and taken into consideration when the final value opinion is rendered.

STEPS IN APPROACH

The steps involved in developing the sales comparison approach are as follows:
1. Research the market to obtain information pertaining to sales, listings, and sometimes offerings of properties similar to the property being appraised.
2. Investigate the market data to determine whether they are factually accurate and whether each sale represents an arm's length transaction.
3. Determine relevant units of comparison (e.g., sales price per square foot), and develop a comparative analysis for each.
4. Compare the subject and comparable sales according to the elements of comparison, and then adjust each sale as appropriate.
5. Reconcile the multiple value indications that result from the adjustment of the comparables into a single value indication.

UNITS OF COMPARISON

Units of comparison (see step 3 above) are defined as "the components into which a property may be divided for purposes of comparison."* For example, apartment complexes are typically analyzed on the basis of one or more of the following three units of comparison: sales price per square foot of rentable area, sales price per apartment unit, and gross income multiplier. Land is sold by the acre, front foot (along a road or street), square foot, and developable unit. All appropriate units of comparison should be analyzed for the property type being appraised, and the resulting value indications reconciled to a single indicated value or value range. The best unit of comparison for any property is the unit that is considered important in the market for that property type.

Adjustments are usually required to compare the comparable properties selected to the subject property. The adjustments may be applied either to the total sales price or to the unit or units of comparison. Income multipliers are not normally adjusted, however. The comparable sales are adjusted for differences in *elements of comparison*, which are defined as "the characteristics or attributes of properties and transactions that cause the prices paid for real estate to vary."† The adjustment process is an effort to isolate the amount paid for different features or sizes; thus it rests on the principle of contribution.

USE OF UNITS OF COMPARISON IN APPRAISALS

Real estate is more easily appraised using units of comparison. Just as meat is sold by the pound, fabric by the yard, precious metals by the troy ounce, and liquids by the fluid ounce, quart, or gallon, real properties are compared by a unit of comparison after adjustments are made to comparables to obtain a uniform quality level. The unit of comparison used may vary depending on the property type or use. Units of comparison may be used in all approaches to value.

LAND

Farm land and large vacant tracts are normally sold by the *acre* (1 acre equals 43,560 square feet). Valuable tracts are sold by the *square foot*, although land along a highway suitable for commercial development or waterfront property may be sold by the number of *front feet* (length along the highway or shoreline). A certain minimum or typical depth is associated with the frontage. Another way that land may be sold is per unit of allowable development. For example, when zoning permits 12 apartment units per acre, the price may be $120,000 per acre (or stated as $10,000 per developable unit).

IMPROVED PROPERTY

Improved properties may be sold by varying units of measurement, depending on their use. For example, office or retail space may be sold on a per-square-foot, motels on a per-room, and theaters on a per-seat basis. However, quality, condition, and other elements are also considered, and an adjusted price is estimated before the units are compared so that the units of comparison are truly comparable.

ELEMENTS OF COMPARISON

The following *elements of comparison* should be considered in the sales comparison approach:
1. Real property rights conveyed
2. Financing terms
3. Conditions of sale
4. Market conditions on date of sale
5. Location
6. Physical characteristics

Adjustments for these are made to the actual selling price of the comparable property.

---

*Ibid., p. 301.
†Ibid., p. 94.

Real Property Rights Conveyed

In most situations, fee simple title will be conveyed. However, when the comparables differ from the subject in the extent of rights conveyed, adjustment is required. The appraiser must also be aware of the effects of easements and leaseholds on the price and must apply adjustments accordingly.

Financing Terms

Generally the seller will receive cash from the sale, even when the buyer arranges a loan from a third party. When the property is sold with special financing, however, the price will be affected. Therefore, when the seller provides financing or pays points or excessive fees for the buyer's loan, the price received should be adjusted to a cash equivalent to result in the market value. Terms of financing, whether good or poor, affect the price but not the value.

Conditions of Sale

In some transactions, sellers or buyers may be unusually motivated, so that the price agreed upon does not necessarily reflect market value. This is true in cases of foreclosure and bankruptcy, as well as transactions in which a buyer requires a certain adjacent parcel for business expansion. A parent may sell property to a child at a bargain price, or a stockholder may sell to his wholly owned corporation at a high price, both in relation to the market. An appraiser must adjust these non-arm's-length transactions to the market, or not use them as comparables.

Maket Conditions on Date of Sale

Especially during periods of inflation or local economy changes, it is possible to determine shifts in price levels over time. In a rising market, a comparable property sold just a few months ago would fetch a higher price if sold now. For this reason it is important to identify the date of sale of each comparable. Unless a comparable sale is very recent, an adjustment may be needed for market conditions.

Location

Since real estate prices are greatly affected by location, an adjustment is warranted for this characteristic when a comparable's location differs significantly from the subject's. Because each location is unique, the adjustment is often subjective. For retail properties, traffic count is often a key variable.

Physical Characteristics

Physical characteristics of the property warrant adjustment. These characteristics include age, condition, construction, quality, maintenance, access, visibility, and utility.

THE ADJUSTMENT PROCESS

Adjustments may be made in terms of percentages or in dollar amounts. Either the total sales price may be adjusted, or the adjustments can be applied to one or more units of comparison. The adjustments should be made in sequential order, with the adjustment for real property rights always made first, the adjustment for financing terms then made to the sales price adjusted for real property rights conveyed, and so on. Adjustments for location and physical characteristics can be grouped together as a single cumulative amount or percentage. If characteristics are interrelated or interdependent, then cumulative percentage adjustments may be used. If they are independent, however, each should be applied to the actual price of the comparable property.

The *paired sale* technique is useful in adjusting for just one feature. If other sales are found for properties that are similar except for just one feature, the value of that feature can be captured. It is then applied to the comparable properties.

After adjustment, the sales will indicate a range in total value or unit value for the property being appraised. If the sales data are highly comparable, and the sales occurred in a reasonably efficient market, the range in indicated values should be tight. When market conditions are imperfect and comparable sales data are limited, however, the range in indicated values may be wider.

In reconciling the value indications provided by the comparable sales, the appraiser should consider the amount of adjustment required for each sale. Sales requiring lesser degrees of adjustment are typically more comparable and are given greater weight than sales requiring greater adjustment. Other factors must be considered, however, including the reliability of the sales data and the degree of support of the required adjustments. After consideration of these factors, a final point value or value range is set forth.

XI. Site Value

A *site* is land that has been cleared, graded, and improved with utility connections so that it is ready to be built upon. In a real estate appraisal, the site value is typically estimated even though the purpose of the appraisal is to estimate the value of the entire property, the improved real estate. The site value is estimated as part of the cost approach.

Site value may also give information about the entire property. For example, suppose that the site value is almost equal to the improved property value; this fact may provide a clue about the highest and best use of the property. It may help also in analyzing the possibility of replacing the existing building, or give information on the useful life of the present improvements.

There are several ways to estimate site value; sales comparison, land residual, allocation, extraction, and plottage and assemblage are discussed below.

SALES COMPARISON

The sales comparison technique for land is similar to that described above for improved properties, but it is easier to apply to land because there are fewer factors to consider. It is the most commonly used technique for land valuation.

LAND RESIDUAL

Improved properties may generate annual income. If the building value is known, the income attributable to the building may be subtracted from the total income; the difference is the income to the land. That amount may be converted to a land value by dividing by a capitalization rate (rate of return).

ALLOCATION

Allocation is a method of estimating land value as a fraction of total value. Suppose that, for the type of property in question, data from numerous comparables indicate that land is typically 25 percent of total value. The land value for the subject property is then estimated at 25 percent of total value unless there is some reason not to apply this technique (such as the presence of excess land on the subject).

EXTRACTION

The *extraction* method of estimating land value involves subtracting the depreciated cost of improvements from the total value of the property. It is used to best advantage when the improvements have little value.

PLOTTAGE AND ASSEMBLAGE

These terms relate to combining two or more parcels of land. The combination is called *assemblage*. When the combined parcel is worth more, because of increased utility, than the parcels would be if sold separately, the increment of value added is called *plottage*.

XII. Cost Approach

The cost approach to appraising is predicated on the assumption that the value of a structure does not exceed the current cost of producing a replica of it. This tends to hold true when a site is improved with a new structure that represents the highest and best use of the site.

Typically, an appraiser estimates the reproduction cost of the subject property, then subtracts for depreciation. The market value of the site (land prepared for use) is then added to the depreciated reproduction cost to arrive at a final estimate of value.

Steps in the cost approach, also called the *summation approach*, follow:
1. Estimate the value of the site as if vacant and available to be put to its highest and best use as of the date of the appraisal.
2. Estimate the reproduction or replacement cost new of the improvements.
3. Estimate all elements of accrued depreciation, including physical, functional, and economic obsolescence.
4. Subtract the total accrued depreciation from the replacement cost new of the improvements to determine the present worth of the improvements.
5. Add the estimated depreciated worth of all site improvements.
6. Add the total present worth of all improvements to the estimated site value to arrive at the value of the property as indicated by the cost approach.

The procedure for estimating land value is described in Chapter 14.

REPRODUCTION COST VERSUS REPLACEMENT COST

Reproduction cost is the cost of building a replica; *replacement cost* is the cost of replacing the subject with one that has equivalent utility but is built with modern materials and to current standards of design and function. Replacement cost new tends to set the upper limit on current value.

MEASURING REPRODUCTION COST OR REPLACEMENT COST

Four methods of measuring reproduction or replacement cost are as follows:
1. *Quantity survey*, whereby each type of material in a structure is itemized and costed out (the price of each nail, brick, etc., is reflected). Overhead, insurance, and profit are added as a lump sum.
2. *Unit-in-place*, whereby the installed unit cost of each component is measured (e.g., exterior walls, including gypsum board, plaster, paint, wallpaper, and labor). Equipment and fixtures are added as a lump sum.
3. *Segregated cost* or *trade breakdown*, which is similar to the unit-in-place method except that the units considered are major functional parts of the structure, such as foundation, floor, ceiling, roof, and heating system. Fixtures and equipment are added as a lump sum.
4. *Comparative unit*, whereby all components of a structure are lumped together on a unit basis to obtain the total cost per square foot or cubic foot. Costs include materials, installation, and builder's overhead and profit.

COST SERVICES

Companies that provide cost data, either through online computer services or as hard copy, include Marshall & Swift/Boeckh, R. S. Means, and Dow/Dodge (McGraw-Hill).

COST INDEXES

Cost indexes are prepared, using a construction inflation index, to update costs from the latest price schedules to the present time. Another index, a local multiplier, is printed for selected cities to show the variation from the benchmark region or city.

DEPRECIATION

Depreciation is a reduction in value, due to all sources, from cost new. *Accrued depreciation* is the total loss of value from all causes, measured from reproduction cost new. Depreciation is broken down into three elements—physical, functional, and external or economic—and each is further classified as curable or incurable.

PHYSICAL DETERIORATION

Physical deterioration is a reduction in the utility of improvements resulting from an impairment of physical condition and is commonly divided into curable and incurable components. *Curable physical deterioration* considers items (referred to as "deferred maintenance") that a prudent purchaser would anticipate correcting immediately upon acquisition of the property. It is assumed that the cost of effecting the correction will not be greater than the anticipated gain in value accrued by virtue of correcting the problem. This estimate is usually computed as a cost to cure. *Incurable physical deterioration* refers to items that cannot be physically or economically corrected.

FUNCTIONAL OBSOLESCENCE

Functional obsolescence is a loss of value due to characteristics inherent in the structures themselves. It results in a decreased capacity of the improvements to perform the functions for which they were intended, in accordance with current market tastes and standards of acceptability. Something becomes outmoded. As mentioned above, functional obsolescence consists of curable and incurable items.

Curable Functional Obsolescence

Curable functional obsolescence may be the result of either a deficiency or an excess. The measure of a deficiency is the excess cost to cure, whereas the measure of an excess is the reproduction cost of the superadequacy, less physical deterioration already charged, plus the cost to cure. As noted, in order for an item to be considered curable, the necessary cost to cure must not exceed the anticipated increase in value due to the cure.

Incurable Functional Obsolescence

Incurable functional obsolescence is caused by either a deficiency or an excess that, if cured, would not warrant the expenditure. In other words, the owner/purchaser would not be justified in replacing items whose cost would exceed the anticipated increase in value. If caused by a deficiency, obsolescence is estimated as the capitalized value of the rent loss due to the condition. An excess is measured by the reproduction cost of the item, less physical deterioration already charged, plus the present worth of the added cost of ownership due to the subject property and other factors relating to this property.

EXTERNAL OR ECONOMIC OBSOLESCENCE

External or economic obsolescence is a diminished utility of the structure due to negative influences from outside the site. It is almost always *incurable* on the part of the owner, landlord, or tenant. External obsolescence can be caused by a variety of factors, such as neighborhood decline; the property's location in a community, state, or region; market conditions; or government regulations.

DEPRECIATION CALCULATIONS

There are a number of ways to calculate the value loss from depreciation. These include the economic age-life method, the breakdown method, and market extraction. Definitions of two important terms are offered below as an aid to understanding depreciation calculations.

Economic life is the period over which improvements to real estate contribute to the value of the property. Economic life establishes the capital recovery period for improvements in the traditional residual techniques of income capitalization. It is also used in the estimation of accrued depreciation (diminished utility) in the cost approach to value estimation.

Effective age, as applied to a structure, is the age of a similar structure of equivalent utility, condition, and remaining life expectancy, as distinct from *chronological age*; that is, effective age is the age indicated by the condition and utility of the structure. If a building has had better than average maintenance, its effective age may be less than the actual age; if there has been inadequate maintenance, it may be greater. A 40-year-old building, for example, may have an effective age of 20 years because of rehabilitation and modernization.

Economic Age-Life Method

The ratio between the effective age of a building and its total economic life is its *economic age-life*. To estimate the building's incurable physical depreciation, this ratio is applied to the cost of the building or components after deferred maintenance has been subtracted.

Breakdown Method

With this method, the loss in value is separated into physical, functional, and external causes.

Cost Approach Example
Replacement Cost New

Office/warehouse building:		
(24,208 SF @ $41.56/SF)		$1,006,084
Site improvements and equipment:		
Parking lot	$150,000	
Signage, landscaping, misc.	10,000	
Subtotal, site improvements		160,000
Subtotal, hard costs		1,166,084
Developer/contractor profit:		
Building cost new @ 15%		174,912
Ad valorem taxes at 2.6% × $140,000		3,600
Marketing, misc.		2,000
Replacement cost new		1,346,596
Less: Accrued depreciation:		
Physical depreciation (based on direct cost)		
Curable	$120,000	
Incurable	802,686	
Subtotal	$922,686	
Obsolescence		
Functional	100,000	
External	220,000	
Subtotal	$320,000	
Total accrued depreciation		(1,242,686)
Estimated present value of improvements		103,910
Add: Estimated land value		140,000
Indicated value via cost approach		$243,910
Rounded to:		$240,000

Cost Approach Estimate of Value $240,000

XIII. Income Approach _____

Most of the income approach methodology will be found in the general certification section of Chapter 15. All appraisal candidates, however, are expected to understand gross rent multipliers (or gross income multipliers) and to be able to estimate income and expense.

GROSS INCOME MULTIPLIER

The *gross income multiplier* is simply the sales price divided by the rental income, generally on an annual basis. For example, if a building sold for $1,200,000 and earns $200,000 a year in rent, the multiplier is 6 ($1,200,000/$200,000 = 6). This multiplier is often used on a monthly rent basis, especially for houses. If a home sold for $120,000 and rents for $1,000 per month, the monthly multiplier is 120. The multiplier is applied to the subject's rent to estimate its value.

Generally, the gross rent multiplier is used as a sales comparison measure for income property. It may be used as the income approach for single-family housing.

ESTIMATE OF INCOME AND EXPENSES

The income most commonly used is called *net operating income (NOI)*, which is found for rental properties as follows:

1. Estimate *potential gross income* (the rental collected if all units are rented for an entire year).
2. Subtract a vacancy and collection allowance.
3. Subtract *operating expenses*. These include insurance, maintenance and repairs, real estate taxes, utilities, and other expenses essential to the operation of the property.

   Operating expenses are categorized as fixed or variable. *Fixed expenses* remain constant regardless of occupancy, whereas *variable expenses* go up and down depending on occupancy.

   Another category of operating expenses consists of reserves for the replacement of appliances, carpets, and other short-lived assets. Since these may last only 5–10 years, an amount is set aside annually as a provision to prevent distorting the income in the year these assets are replaced.

   Interest and principal payments and depreciation are *not* operating expenses.

The result—(1) minus (2) and (3)—is net operating income. NOI is then divided by a capitalization rate, which is the rate used to convert an income stream into a lump sum capital value. The capitalization rate must be adequate to provide for a return on the entire investment, as well as a recovery of the portion of the property that is subject to depreciation.

The rate of return on the entire investment can be estimated as in the following example:

> **Basic Rate:**
> *Safe, liquid rate of return on investment*
>   *(U.S. government bonds, insured savings)*   3%
> *Provision for illiquidity*   1%
> *Provision for investment management*   1%
> *Provision for risk*   2%
> *Rate of return on investment*   7%
> *Plus capital recovery: 80% of cost represented by improvements,*
>   *which are subject to a 40-year life = 80% × 2½% (straight-line*
>   *annual depreciation)*   2%
> *Capitalization rate*   9%

If net operating income is estimated at $100,000, the resulting value is $100,000 ÷ 0.09 = $1,111,111, rounded to $1,110,000. The formula employed is as follows:

$$\text{Value} = \frac{\text{Income}}{\text{Capitalization Rate}}$$

XIV. Partial Interests

The residential appraiser is expected to know the effects of certain partial interests, namely:
- Leaseholds and leased fees
- Life estates
- Easements
- Timeshares
- Cooperatives
- Undivided interests in common areas

LEASEHOLDS AND LEASED FEES

When property is leased, the tenant has a *leasehold*. This may be a valuable interest, particularly when the lease rent (called the *contract rent*) is below market rent and the lease is for a long term. The landlord's position is called *leased fee*. An appraiser should determine the effect of a lease on the market value of the fee simple and ascertain the definition of value being sought. Is it a leased fee value, or fee simple unencumbered?

LIFE ESTATES

A *life estate* allows a person to use property for his or her own lifetime or for the life of another person (*pur autre vie*). Upon death, the remainderman becomes the sole owner. Thus, the market value of the property is divided between two persons: one with the right of use for life and another whose use commences upon the life tenant's death.

EASEMENTS

An *easement* is the right to use property owned by another for a specific purpose. For example, billboards may be erected on easements, and power company transmission line paths and other land needed for utilities are often provided by the use of easements. Easements may enhance the value of real estate when they generate adequate revenue (billboard rent), attract desired services (utilities to the property), or provide access to other properties. They may detract from value when they represent nuisances (unsightly utility wires), indicate flood plains, or prevent alternative profitable property uses. Unless easements are specifically excluded by the appraisal report, an appraiser should ascertain the effect of easements on property being considered as well as easements on others' properties that the subject property owner can enjoy.

TIMESHARES

A *timeshare* is the right to use property for a given period of time each year. Often used for resort property, a timeshare may be ownership of a specific apartment unit for a specific period, such as the first week in April of each year, or it may represent the right to use any of a number of identical units in a condominium development for any week during a certain period (with prices varying for peak and off-season periods). The price of a weekly timeshare, when multiplied by 52 weeks, may exceed two to three times the value of the unit if sold in its entirety, but timeshare ownership often includes amenities (such as utilities, laundry service, and periodic redecoration) that would not be included in ownership of the unit itself.

COOPERATIVES

Some apartment buildings, especially in New York, are owned as cooperatives (co-ops). A corporation owns the building and can mortgage it. Stockholders own certain shares, which give each stockholder the right to occupy a certain unit. Stockholders are generally tenants and must pay their pro rata shares of maintenance expenses. Special tax laws allow the tenants to deduct interest on the mortgage and real estate taxes. An appraiser must recognize the valuation process for this type of property and understand how the stock is valued.

UNDIVIDED INTERESTS IN COMMON AREAS

Condominiums provide for separate ownership of individual units with the right to mortgage each unit. Common areas such as walkways, recreational facilities, and exterior walls are owned jointly. Each condo owner owns a share of the common area and may use it, as may all other condo owners.

XV. *Appraisal Standards and Ethics*

The Uniform Standards of Professional Appraisal Practice (USPAP) have been developed by the Appraisal Foundation. Appraisers belonging to an organization that is a member of the Appraisal Foundation adhere to these standards. The following are highlights of certain parts of the USPAP.

PREAMBLE

- The appraisal must be meaningful to the client and not misleading in the marketplace.
- The appraiser is to observe all the ethical standards set forth below.
- Certain competency provisions are to be observed.
- If departure provisions are utilized, the rules concerning their use must be observed. A departure provision is a "loophole," or provision for the appraiser to depart from the standards. For example, a departure provision allows an approach to be waived provided that the appraiser explains why that approach was not used.
- Users of an appraiser's services are encouraged to demand work in conformance with the standards.

ETHICS

To promote and preserve the public trust inherent in professional appraisal practice, an appraiser must observe the highest standards of professional ethics. The ETHICS RULE of USPAP is divided into four sections: Conduct, Management, Confidentiality, and Record Keeping.*

Conduct

- An appraiser must perform assignments ethically and competently in accordance with USPAP and any supplemental standards agreed to by the appraiser in accepting the assignment. An appraiser may not engage in criminal conduct. An appraiser must perform assignments with impartiality, objectivity, and independence, and without accommodation of personal interests.
- In appraisal practice, an appraiser must not perform as an advocate for any party or issue.
- An appraiser must not accept an assignment that includes the reporting of predetermined opinions and conclusions.
- An appraiser must not communicate assignment results in a misleading or fraudulent manner. An appraiser must not use or communicate a misleading or fraudulent report or knowingly permit an employee or other person to communicate a misleading or fraudulent report.
- An appraiser must not use or rely on unsupported conclusions relating to characteristics such as race, color, religion, national origin, gender, marital status, familial status, age, receipt of public assistance income, handicap, or an unsupported conclusion that homogeneity of such characteristics is necessary to maximize value.

---

*The sections that follow are taken from Appraisal Standards Board, *Uniform Standards of Professional Appraisal Practice,* 2005 edition (Washington, DC: Appraisal Foundation, 2004), pp. 7–9. Comments and footnotes have been omitted.

Management

The payment of undisclosed fees, commissions, or things of value in connection with the procurement of an assignment is unethical.

It is unethical for an appraiser to accept an assignment, or to have a compensation arrangement for an assignment, that is contingent on any of the following:

1. the reporting of a predetermined result (e.g., opinion of value);
2. a direction in assignment results that favors the cause of the client;
3. the amount of a value opinion;
4. the attainment of a stipulated result; or
5. the occurrence of a subsequent event directly related to the appraiser's opinions and specific to the assignment's purpose.

Advertising for or soliciting assignments in a manner that is false, misleading, or exaggerated is unethical.

Confidentiality

- An appraiser must protect the confidential nature of the appraiser-client relationship.
- An appraiser must act in good faith with regard to the legitimate interests of the client in the use of confidential information and in the communication of assignment results.
- An appraiser must be aware of, and comply with, all confidentiality and privacy laws and regulations applicable in an assignment.
- An appraiser must not disclose confidential information or assignment results prepared for a client to anyone other than the client and persons specifically authorized by the client; state enforcement agencies and such third parties as may be authorized by due process of law; and a duly authorized professional peer review committee except when such disclosure to a committee would violate applicable law or regulation. It is unethical for a member of a duly authorized professional peer review committee to disclose confidential information presented to the committee.

Record Keeping

- An appraiser must prepare a workfile for each appraisal, appraisal review, or appraisal consulting assignment. The workfile must include:
  - the name of the client and the identity, by name or type, of any other intended users;
  - true copies of any written reports, documented on any type of media;
  - summaries of any oral reports or testimony, or a transcript of testimony, including the appraiser's signed and dated certification; and
  - all other data, information, and documentation necessary to support the appraiser's opinions and conclusions and to show compliance with this Rule and all other applicable Standards, or references to the location(s) of such other documentation.
- An appraiser must retain the workfile for a period of at least five (5) years after preparation or at least two (2) years after final disposition of any legal proceeding in which the appraiser provided testimony related to the assignment, whichever period expires last.
- An appraiser must have custody of his or her workfile, or make appropriate workfile retention, access, and retrieval arrangements with the party having custody of the workfile.

COMPETENCY

The appraiser must properly identify the problem to be addressed and have the knowledge and experience to complete the assignment competently. If the appraiser does not have the required knowledge or experience, she must:

1. Disclose this fact to the client before accepting the engagement.
2. If engaged, take all steps necessary to complete the assignment competently.
3. Describe the deficiency and the steps taken to complete the assignment competently.

STANDARDS

The following are some standards to be followed in appraising real estate.

- *Standard 1.* In developing a real property appraisal, an appraiser must identify the problem to be solved and the scope of work necessary to solve the problem, and correctly complete research and analysis necessary to produce a credible appraisal. An appraiser must be aware of, understand, and correctly employ the recognized methods and techniques necessary to produce a credible appraisal.
- *Standard 2.* In reporting the results of a real property appraisal, an appraiser must communicate each analysis, opinion, and conclusion in a manner that is not misleading.
- *Standard 3.* In reviewing an appraisal and reporting the results of that review, an appraiser must form an opinion as to the adequacy and appropriateness of the report being reviewed and must clearly disclose the nature of the review process undertaken.
- *Standard 4.* In performing real estate or real property consulting services, an appraiser must be aware of, understand, and correctly employ the recognized methods and techniques necessary to produce a credible result.
- *Standard 5.* In reporting the results of a real estate or real property consulting service, an appraiser must communicate each analysis, opinion, and conclusion in a manner that is not misleading.

Questions on Chapter 14

1. All of the following types of broad forces affect value *except*
   (A) physical
   (B) intellectual
   (C) political
   (D) social
   (E) economic

2. Social, economic, governmental, and environmental influences that affect property value are called
   (A) laws
   (B) forces
   (C) factors
   (D) consequences
   (E) impacts

3. Compared with other assets, real estate is
   (A) immobile
   (B) expensive
   (C) long-lived
   (D) mortgageable
   (E) all of the above

4. The truly distinguishing characteristic of real estate as compared with other assets is
   (A) large size
   (B) long life
   (C) high price
   (D) uniqueness
   (E) fixed location

5. The primary economic distinguishing characteristic of land is
   (A) homogeneity
   (B) high cost
   (C) immobility
   (D) slow depreciation
   (E) no depreciation

6. Urban land derives its value primarily from its
   (A) size
   (B) natural beauty
   (C) concentration of population
   (D) location
   (E) buildings

7. Which of the following is a basic component of value?
   (A) Utility
   (B) Scarcity
   (C) Demand coupled with purchasing power
   (D) Transferability
   (E) All of the above

8. The value of real estate is determined in the market mainly by its
   (A) price
   (B) productivity
   (C) mortgage
   (D) size
   (E) height

9. Which of the following is an important governmental influence on neighborhood values?
   (A) Zoning code
   (B) Income level
   (C) Owner occupancy
   (D) Flood plain mapping
   (E) Ethnic concentration

10. *Realty* is best defined as rights in
    (A) land
    (B) improvements on and to land
    (C) buildings
    (D) fixtures
    (E) real estate

11. Built-in appliances are legally classified as
    (A) real estate
    (B) trade fixtures
    (C) chattels
    (D) personal property
    (E) amenities

12. The term *improvements to real estate* refers to
    (A) buildings only
    (B) buildings, fences, walkways, etc.
    (C) trees and buildings
    (D) all of the above
    (E) none of the above

13. Rights of condemnation are held by a
    (A) state government agency
    (B) local agency or authority representing a federal government agency
    (C) utility company
    (D) small municipality
    (E) all of the above

14. Eminent domain requires
    (A) appraisal processes for the estimation of real property value
    (B) just compensation for specific types of financial loss
    (C) due process for the taking of property through condemnation
    (D) both A and B
    (E) both B and C

15. Zoning and environmental protection regulations represent the exercise of
    (A) land use politics
    (B) public use
    (C) escheat
    (D) eminent domain
    (E) police power

16. All of the following are considered legal encumbrances *except*
    (A) leases
    (B) utilities
    (C) zoning
    (D) mortgages
    (E) liens

17. *Real property* is defined as
    (A) leased and unleased space
    (B) rights in realty
    (C) land and all improvements
    (D) the right to use or occupy real estate
    (E) realty

18. Which of the following expires upon the owner's death?
    (A) Fee tail
    (B) Remainder interest
    (C) Simple interest
    (D) Life estate
    (E) Estate for years

19. The most complete interest in real property is
    (A) fee tail
    (B) joint tenancy
    (C) tenancy in common
    (D) fee simple
    (E) life estate *pur autre vie*

20. A deed should be recorded in order to
    (A) give constructive notice of the transaction
    (B) comply with federal and state law
    (C) pass title
    (D) make the deed a legal document
    (E) establish the priority of claim of the purchaser

21. Property description is necessary to
    (A) identify and locate the subject property
    (B) identify the property rights being appraised
    (C) find the appropriate section in the report
    (D) find the official map coding of the subject property
    (E) tell where the property deed is recorded

Life estate b/c you have the estate for life.

22. One way in which land may be legally described is by
    (A) highest and best use
    (B) acreage
    (C) mailing address
    (D) metes and bounds
    (E) front footage

23. "Block 17, lot 5 of the Woodcreek Subdivision" is an example of a land description using which of the following systems?
    (A) Lot and block
    (B) Rectangular method
    (C) Metes and bounds
    (D) Government survey
    (E) Monuments survey

24. A value estimate is a
    (A) estimate of a selling price
    (B) prediction that property will sell for exactly the amount named
    (C) projection or extrapolation of historic price to future price
    (D) sophisticated guess by expert
    (E) promise or option to buy

25. *Loan value* is the same as
    (A) investment value
    (B) market price
    (C) replacement value
    (D) book value
    (E) market value

26. *Mortgage value* is synonymous with
    (A) market price
    (B) liquidation value
    (C) market value
    (D) assessed value
    (E) insurable value

27. An objective kind of value that can be estimated for property bought and sold in the market is called
    (A) value in use
    (B) value in exchange
    (C) economic value
    (D) potential value
    (E) insurable value

28. In appraisal, "market value" is most commonly identified with
    (A) value in use
    (B) value in exchange
    (C) assessed value
    (D) listing value
    (E) none of the above

29. Price and value are
    (A) not necessarily the same
    (B) synonymous
    (C) different, depending on financing terms
    (D) close together in an inactive market
    (E) used interchangeably in a report

30. Market price is the amount for which a property
    (A) should sell
    (B) was sold
    (C) will sell
    (D) could sell
    (E) would be appraised

31. All of the following statements are true *except:*
    (A) *Real property* refers to items that are not permanently fixed to a part of the real estate.
    (B) Appraising is the art and science of estimating the value of an asset.
    (C) Assets typically requiring appraisal include real and personal property.
    (D) Asset values change with time.
    (E) Markets change with supply and demand.

32. *Investment value* is best described as
    (A) market price
    (B) market value
    (C) the cost of acquiring a competitive substitute property with the same utility
    (D) the present worth of anticipated future benefits to a certain individual or institutional investor
    (E) value in exchange

33. Assessed value is usually based on
    (A) cost value
    (B) book value
    (C) market value
    (D) insurable value
    (E) replacement cost

34. The principle of anticipation
    (A) is future oriented
    (B) is past oriented
    (C) involves the "as of" date for an appraisal
    (D) predicts the loan-to-value ratio for the subject property
    (E) is substitution oriented

35. Which principle of value best affirms that value is the present worth of expected future benefits?
    (A) Supply and demand
    (B) Balance
    (C) Substitution
    (D) Anticipation
    (E) Conformity

36. What principle states that value levels are sustained when the various elements in an economic or environmental mix are in equilibrium?
    (A) Anticipation
    (B) Equivalence
    (C) Substitution
    (D) Balance
    (E) Highest and best use

37. The fundamental valuation principle underlying the sales comparison process is
    (A) contribution
    (B) substitution
    (C) conformity
    (D) change
    (E) anticipation

38. Which principle of value best affirms that the maximum value of a property generally cannot exceed the cost of its replacement?
    (A) Increasing and decreasing returns
    (B) Supply and demand
    (C) Substitution
    (D) Balance
    (E) Anticipation

39. The fact that the value of a property tends to equal the cost of an equally desirable substitute is an example of the principle of
    (A) balance
    (B) substitution
    (C) contribution
    (D) diminishing returns
    (E) supply and demand

40. The principle of substitution holds that a purchaser will pay no more for a property than
    (A) the maximum he can afford
    (B) the cost of acquiring an equally desirable substitute
    (C) the price of a previously owned property
    (D) the price of a property with greater utility
    (E) none of the above

41. The function(s) of a real estate market is (are) to
    (A) facilitate exchanges
    (B) set prices
    (C) allocate resources
    (D) adjust supply to demand
    (E) all of the above

42. In estimating current market value, an appraiser assumes all of the following *except that:*
    (A) The buyer is typically motivated.
    (B) The parties are knowledgeable.
    (C) A reasonable time will be allowed for market exposure.
    (D) The property will be marketed by a professional expert.
    (E) The property will be sold for cash or equivalent terms.

43. In which market are there many potential buyers but few properties available?
    (A) Demand
    (B) Buyer's
    (C) Seller's
    (D) Low-priced
    (E) Normal

44. A perfect market occurs when
    (A) there are numerous buyers and sellers who are knowledgeable and free to trade
    (B) all products are interchangeable and can be transported to better markets
    (C) the government allocates supply and demand perfectly
    (D) all of the above are true
    (E) A and B only are true

45. The identification and study of a pertinent market is called
    (A) market analysis
    (B) neighborhood review
    (C) property research
    (D) market segmentation
    (E) market interaction

46. If the typical occupancy rate in an area is 95 percent, what conclusion would you most likely draw about a subject property that has 100 percent occupancy?
    (A) Advertising is average.
    (B) The rents are high.
    (C) The rents are low.
    (D) Management is incompetent.
    (E) New construction will occur soon.

47. Which type of studies test the ability of various proposed improvements to meet investment objectives?
    (A) Market
    (B) Feasibility
    (C) Marketability
    (D) Cost-benefit
    (E) Prospectus

48. A decrease in land value is the result of
    (A) functional obsolescence
    (B) physical deterioration
    (C) market forces
    (D) wear and tear
    (E) obsolescence

49. To estimate market value, an appraiser follows the
    (A) appraisal report
    (B) valuation process
    (C) evaluation methodology
    (D) appraisal guidelines
    (E) report evolution technique

50. In appraising, the most important judgment is probably called for in
    (A) projecting selling rates
    (B) reconciling value indications
    (C) selecting good comparable data
    (D) performing neighborhood analysis
    (E) making rental market estimates

51. An "as of" date is specified in appraisals to
    (A) show when the appraiser inspected the property
    (B) indicate the prevailing price level
    (C) indicate the market conditions on which the value is estimated
    (D) indicate when the buyer agreed to purchase the property
    (E) indicate the value as of the closing date

52. An appraisal of real estate
    (A) guarantees its value
    (B) assures its value
    (C) determines its value
    (D) estimates its value
    (E) segments its value

53. Residential appraisers generally provide an estimate of
    (A) market price
    (B) mortgage loan value
    (C) cash value
    (D) assessed value
    (E) market value

54. Commercial real estate appraisers are most frequently asked to estimate
    (A) assessed value
    (B) liquidation value
    (C) insurable value
    (D) market value
    (E) intrinsic value

55. Legal transactions that frequently require appraisals are
    (A) income-tax-deductible charitable contribution of property, estate tax, and property settlement upon divorce
    (B) damage lawsuits, loan foreclosures, and security for bail bonds
    (C) company merger, tax basis, and loan assumptions
    (D) all of the above
    (E) none of the above

56. Knowledge of land value is required for all of the following *except*
    (A) condemnation actions
    (B) fire insurance
    (C) property taxation
    (D) a ground lease
    (E) a grazing lease

57. A market value estimate provided in an appraisal
    (A) changes with the use to which it is put
    (B) changes with the function of the appraisal
    (C) remains the same regardless of whom the appraisal is prepared for
    (D) depends upon the use or function of the appraisal
    (E) always reflects market value

58. In preparing an appraisal, definition of the problem identifies all of the following *except*
    (A) the real estate being appraised
    (B) the highest and best use for the property
    (C) the real property rights
    (D) the date of the value estimate
    (E) the use to which the appraisal will be put

59. In appraising, the data requirements are set by the
    (A) client
    (B) lender
    (C) seller
    (D) appraisal problem
    (E) appraiser

60. The requirement to verify data in an appraisal report varies according to
    (A) the appraiser's "gut feelings" about the reliability of the data
    (B) the purpose and intended use of the appraisal report
    (C) legal restrictions on the property
    (D) the type of value being sought
    (E) the use to which the property has been put

61. A property's immediate environment is
    (A) its pivotal point
    (B) a "comp" grid
    (C) a neighborhood
    (D) the adjacent uses
    (E) a natural boundary

62. The life cycle of a neighborhood illustrates the principle of
    (A) substitution
    (B) highest and best use
    (C) change
    (D) conformity
    (E) anticipation

63. The data required for an appraisal assignment are established by the
    (A) lending association
    (B) appraiser
    (C) buyer
    (D) Office of Thrift Supervision
    (E) nature of the appraisal problem

64. Which of the following exhibits is *least* frequently used in an appraisal?
    (A) A photograph of the subject property
    (B) An aerial photograph of the surrounding area
    (C) A plot plan
    (D) A floor plan
    (E) A photograph of a comparable property

65. In which market is the direct sales comparison approach most applicable?
    (A) Seller's
    (B) Buyer's
    (C) Reasonable
    (D) Active
    (E) Calm

66. The criteria for determining highest and best use include all of the following *except*
    (A) physical possibility
    (B) financial feasibility
    (C) legal permissibility
    (D) maximal productivity
    (E) effect on community welfare

67. The three approaches to estimating value are
    (A) cost, income, and replacement
    (B) replacement, income, and reproduction
    (C) cost, direct sales comparison, and income capitalization
    (D) reproduction, cost, and income
    (E) market, building residual, and multiplier

68. In appraising a dwelling built 50 years ago, the appraiser usually relies on the
    (A) current reproduction cost
    (B) original construction cost
    (C) current replacement cost
    (D) direct sales comparison approach
    (E) superior construction technique

69. Which approach would be best when appraising a 15- to 20-year-old house?
    (A) Cost
    (B) Feasibility study
    (C) Sales comparison
    (D) Income capitalization
    (E) Replacement cost new less accrued depreciation

70. The appraiser's final value estimate should be based on
    (A) an average of the three value indications given by the three approaches to value
    (B) a weighing of the reliability of the information analyzed in each of the three approaches to value
    (C) an average of the values in the three closest comparable sales
    (D) the correlation technique
    (E) adjustments for the most recent indicators in the local market

71. Before reconciliation the appraiser should
    (A) reinspect the subject property
    (B) evaluate the reliability of each approach to value
    (C) review the overall appraisal process and check for technical accuracy
    (D) seek the property owner's opinion
    (E) average the results from the approaches used

72. Since each value approach has its own strengths and weaknesses, an appraiser should
    (A) choose the approach that is the most popular with lenders
    (B) choose the approach that is the most popular with buyers
    (C) weigh the strengths and weaknesses of each approach and decide which is the most reliable for the subject property
    (D) weight each approach equally
    (E) use the approach that the client feels is most appropriate

73. The cost approach is often given more weight in the appraisal of
    (A) old or obsolete buildings
    (B) single-family houses more than 10 years old
    (C) new buildings or special-use buildings
    (D) commercial and industrial properties
    (E) vacant land

74. In reconciliation and conclusion of value, the appraiser should
    (A) describe the relevance of each value approach explored
    (B) discuss the reliability of the data used
    (C) provide arguments to justify his or her final conclusion of value
    (D) explain his or her judgments and reasoning
    (E) do all of the above

75. Value indications are reconciled into a final value estimate
    (A) throughout the appraisal
    (B) after the report of defined value
    (C) after each approach is completed
    (D) at the preliminary stage to let the client know what result to expect
    (E) after all three approaches have been completed

76. During the reconciliation process, an appraiser should ask:
    (A) How appropriate is each approach?
    (B) How adequate are the data?
    (C) What range of values do the approaches suggest?
    (D) all of the above
    (E) A and C only

77. Which of the following is the longest and most detailed type of appraisal report?
    (A) Restricted use
    (B) Summary
    (C) Self-contained
    (D) Oral
    (E) Detailed

78. All of the following are main sections in the typical narrative appraisal report *except*
    (A) introduction
    (B) engagement letter
    (C) description, analyses, and conclusion
    (D) addenda
    (E) valuation

79. An oral appraisal report
    (A) is not worth the paper it is written on
    (B) must be supported by a workfile
    (C) is unethical
    (D) is impossible
    (E) is a legitimate substitute for a written report

80. Standardized residential form reports
    (A) are adequate for all appraisals
    (B) may not be as detailed or complete as written reports
    (C) are seldom adequate for appraisals
    (D) allow little space for neighborhood analysis
    (E) are difficult to computerize

81. The highest and best use of a site is its
    (A) existing use
    (B) most probable use that is legally and physically possible and provides the highest financial return
    (C) immediate next use
    (D) synonymous with ordinary and necessary use
    (E) least expensive use

82. The important reason(s) for inspecting and analyzing the subject site is (are) to
    (A) ascertain its highest and best use
    (B) note any unusual characteristics
    (C) find comparable sales
    (D) be certain the property exists
    (E) all of the above

83. The length of a tract of land along a street is called the land's
    (A) depth
    (B) width
    (C) frontage
    (D) abutment
    (E) lineage

84. The number of square feet in 1 acre is
    (A) 64,000
    (B) 460
    (C) 440
    (D) 43,560
    (E) 34,560

85. The livable square footage of a single-family residence is usually measured from the
    (A) total interior (including interior walls)
    (B) inside room dimensions
    (C) interior plus basement
    (D) exterior
    (E) exterior, with adjustment for wall width

86. The most important item an appraiser needs for recording data during a building inspection is a
   (A) plat map
   (B) tape measure
   (C) checklist
   (D) clipboard
   (E) pencil or pen

87. A large home built in an area of small cottages is an example of
   (A) overimprovement
   (B) underimprovement
   (C) land regression
   (D) functional obsolescence
   (E) environmental aesthetics

88. The period over which a building may be profitably used is its
   (A) actual life
   (B) physical life
   (C) useful life
   (D) normal life
   (E) effective age

89. An improvement's remaining economic life is
   (A) its chronological age
   (B) its effective age
   (C) the future time span over which the improvement is expected to generate benefits
   (D) its effective age minus its chronological age
   (E) its effective age plus its chronological age

90. To be considered as a possible alternative for highest and best use, a use must be
   (A) physically and legally possible and financially feasible
   (B) physically and legally possible
   (C) already in existence and legal
   (D) physically possible and appropriate
   (E) legal and profitable

91. When applying the concept of highest and best use of land as if vacant, the assumption is made that
   (A) any existing building can be demolished
   (B) zoning cannot be changed
   (C) the basic characteristics of a site can be changed
   (D) vacant land produces maximum income
   (E) land is not subject to erosion

92. The highest and best use of land as if vacant forms part of the basis for
   (A) mortgage equity analysis
   (B) a property rights adjustment
   (C) an operating expense estimate
   (D) the cost approach
   (E) the square footage approach

93. The best assurance of appraisal accuracy results from the use of
   (A) the greatest number of adjustments
   (B) a gross dollar amount of adjustments
   (C) a large number of truly comparable properties
   (D) a net dollar amount of adjustments
   (E) market segmentation

94. The direct sales comparison approach to appraising derives an estimate of value from
    (A) sales of comparable properties
    (B) comparison of the architecture of properties
    (C) comparison of loans made on properties
    (D) original costs of comparable properties
    (E) checking prices in the *Wall Street Journal* stock market report

95. A gross rent multiplier is often used in the
    (A) direct sales comparison approach for single-family housing
    (B) income approach for income property
    (C) income approach for single-family property
    (D) cost approach
    (E) back-door approach to valuation

96. Gross rent multiplier analysis is
    (A) required in almost every residential appraisal
    (B) applicable to every residential appraisal
    (C) applicable to residential property valuation only
    (D) part of the direct sales comparison approach to valuation of commercial properties
    (E) seldom used for houses

97. In estimating site value, the direct sales comparison approach
    (A) does not apply to older residences
    (B) is the most reliable method available
    (C) is considered inferior to other methods·
    (D) is used only when the subject property is unimproved
    (E) is used for real estate but not for personal property appraisals

98. In an open market transaction, the subject property sold would not be
    (A) listed for at least 30 days
    (B) listed on a multiple listing service
    (C) advertised in local newspapers
    (D) sold to a relative
    (E) closed by a title company

99. The minimum number of comparable sales needed to apply direct sales comparison is
    (A) 3
    (B) 4
    (C) 10
    (D) 30
    (E) no set number

100. Physical units of comparison include
    (A) seats in a theater
    (B) rooms in a hotel
    (C) square feet of a house
    (D) cubic feet of a warehouse
    (E) all of the above

101. In GRM analysis an estimate of market value is derived by
    (A) dividing market rental by GRM
    (B) multiplying market rental by GRM
    (C) dividing GRM by market rental
    (D) multiplying net income by GRM
    (E) multiplying comparable sales by GRM

102. A limitation to using the direct sales comparison approach is the need for
    (A) an active market
    (B) many comparable properties
    (C) property representing the highest and best use
    (D) a long trend of historical data
    (E) informed buyers and sellers

103. Comparable sales that require little or no adjustment to the subject are usually sales
    (A) made within 2 years
    (B) of properties equal in square footage to the subject
    (C) of houses in the same neighborhood as the subject
    (D) of contiguous properties
    (E) in new developments with homes nearly identical to the subject

104. The date of sale of a comparable identifies
    (A) the motivation for the sale
    (B) the point in time when adjustments take place
    (C) the terms of sale
    (D) the market conditions when the sale was made
    (E) the functional utility of the property

105. A sale between relatives is suspected to be
    (A) a bona fide sale
    (B) a sale made at a distorted price
    (C) an arm's length sale
    (D) a seller-financed sale
    (E) a cash equivalence sale

106. Any recent previous sale of the subject property
    (A) should be considered confidential
    (B) may not under any circumstances be considered in estimating the current market value of the property
    (C) should be discussed in the appraisal report
    (D) is not an arm's length sale
    (E) should be used as a comparable sale, but adjusted for time and terms of sale

Questions 107–112 are based on the following information:

Factor	Subject	Comparable #1	Comparable #2	Comparable #3
Price		$270,000	$265,500	$261,000
Living area (square feet)	1,500	1,600	1,450	1,400
Condition	Good	Fair	Excellent	Good
Garage	One-car	Two-car	One-car	Two-car
Time of sale	Now	Last year	Last year	This year

Adjusted Sales Price: Prices have been rising by 5 percent per year in the area for this type of property.
Other Adjustments: Each square foot of livable area is judged to be worth $90; condition grades are fair, good, and excellent, with each difference in condition grade worth 5 percent; a two-car garage is judged to be worth $4,500 more than a one-car garage.

107. What is the size adjustment for Comparable #1?
     (A) +$4,500
     (B) −$4,500
     (C)   0
     (D) +$9,000
     (E) −$9,000

108. What is the size adjustment for Comparable #2?
     (A) +$4,500
     (B) −$4,500
     (C)   0
     (D) +$9,000
     (E) −$9,000

109. What is the condition adjustment for Comparable #1?
     (A)   0
     (B) +$13,500
     (C) −$13,500
     (D) +$27,000
     (E) −$27,000

110. What is the condition adjustment for Comparable #2?
     (A)   0
     (B) +$13,275
     (C) −$13,275
     (D) +$26,550
     (E) −$26,550

111. What is the garage adjustment for Comparable #2?
     (A)   0
     (B) +$4,500
     (C) −$4,500
     (D) +$9,000
     (E) −$9,000

112. What is the garage adjustment for Comparable #3?
     (A)   0
     (B) +$4,500
     (C) −$4,500
     (D) +$9,000
     (E) −$9,000

113. What would be the indicated value of a property that rented for $2,250 per month, using a monthly gross rent multiplier of 110, if the expenses attributable to the property were $375 per month?
     (A) $227,010
     (B) $247,500
     (C) $206,250
     (D) $183,375
     (E) $41,250

114. A 7-year-old residence is currently valued at $216,000. What was its original value if it has appreciated by 60 percent since it was built?
    (A) $81,000
    (B) $113,400
    (C) $135,000
    (D) $345,600
    (E) none of the above

115. An adjustment for market conditions would be made to reflect
    (A) a loan assumption
    (B) a sale between relatives
    (C) financing differences
    (D) a decrease in demand
    (E) differences in government regulation

116. For residential property, market value appraisals assume that
    (A) the purchaser pays all cash; no money is borrowed
    (B) an FHA or VA mortgage is used
    (C) a purchase money mortgage is considered
    (D) the value estimate is based on no special financing
    (E) the seller pays no more than 5 points

117. In considering comparable sales in a direct sales comparison appraisal,
    (A) the seller's motivation is significant
    (B) the date of sale is significant
    (C) the proximity of the comps to the subject property is most important
    (D) both A and B
    (E) none of the above

118. In estimating the market value of a comparable sale, an appraiser must consider all of the following *except*
    (A) whether the transaction was made in cash, terms equivalent to cash, or other precisely revealed terms
    (B) whether the property had reasonable exposure in a competitive market
    (C) whether a fair sale was transacted, with neither the seller nor the buyer acting under duress
    (D) whether the replacement cost of the property corresponds to its market value
    (E) whether the seller was related to the buyer

119. The terms of financing, whether good or bad,
    (A) have no effect on the market price
    (B) have no effect on the market value
    (C) have no effect on affordability
    (D) depend on the fiscal and monetary policy of the government
    (E) should be ignored when adjusting comparables

120. A tract home builder offers new houses for sale with different financing plans offered. The price is $300,000 if the builder pays no discount points, and $2,800 more for each point paid on the buyer's loan. Numerous recent sales have been made on these terms. You are appraising a house that sold with 2½ points. If you found no adjustments to make compared to other sales, the market value of the house would be
    (A) $300,000
    (B) $305,600
    (C) $307,000
    (D) $308,400
    (E) $308,000

121. In a 100-unit apartment building, rentals vary as follows:

Number of Units	Monthly Rental
15	$980
25	$1,020
30	$1,060
20	$1,100
10	$1,140

What is the modal rent for this building?
(A) $1,054
(B) $1,060
(C) $1,038
(D) $1,100
(E) $1,076

Questions 122–126 are based on the following information:
In a subdivision with 160 homes, the houses have varying numbers of bedrooms, as shown below:

Number of Bedrooms	Number of Homes
2	18
3	77
4	53
5	12

122. What is the mean number of bedrooms?
(A) 3.37
(B) 3.00
(C) 4.00
(D) 3.50
(E) not shown

123. What is the median number of bedrooms?
(A) 3.37
(B) 3.00
(C) 4.00
(D) 3.50
(E) not shown

124. What is the modal number of bedrooms?
(A) 3.37
(B) 3.00
(C) 4.00
(D) 3.50
(E) not shown

125. What is the average number of bedrooms?
(A) 3.37
(B) 3.00
(C) 4.00
(D) 3.50
(E) not shown

126. What is the range for the number of bedrooms?
    (A) 3.37
    (B) 3.00
    (C) 4.00
    (D) 3.50
    (E) not shown

127. The adjustment process in the direct sales comparison approach relies on the principle of
    (A) contribution
    (B) substitution
    (C) complexity
    (D) supply and demand
    (E) conformity

128. In selecting properties for a paired-sale comparison,
    (A) one of the pair should be next door or on the same street as the subject
    (B) the pair should offer different financing
    (C) the pair should be nearly identical to each other except for one important feature being considered
    (D) the pair should be virtually identical to each other, as is a pair of shoes or earrings
    (E) the pair should be selected to be quite different and to embody as many different features as possible

129. In the direct sales comparison approach, dollar adjustments for elements of comparison are made to the
    (A) sales prices of subject properties
    (B) listing prices of subject properties
    (C) sales prices of comparable properties
    (D) listing prices of comparable properties
    (E) appraised values of comparables

130. In the cost approach, land valuation is based on the principle of
    (A) variable proportions
    (B) highest and best use
    (C) diminishing returns
    (D) contribution
    (E) conformity

131. To be used as comparables, land sales must be
    (A) competitive with the subject
    (B) relatively recent
    (C) open-market transactions
    (D) adjusted to cash equivalent prices
    (E) all of the above

132. Price per front foot is
    (A) a physical unit of comparison
    (B) not as accurate as price per square foot
    (C) rarely used in commercial site analysis
    (D) an accurate guide to site marketability
    (E) useful when there are major physical differences between sites

133. Plottage is
    (A) the value of land between the subject property and another property
    (B) the bonus that is sometimes obtained by combining parcels
    (C) the price of land per plot
    (D) the value estimated while slowly walking on the land
    (E) the age of a piece of land since it was mapped

134. When two or more sites are assembled or created to produce greater utility, the value increase is called
    (A) capital gain
    (B) plottage
    (C) enclosure
    (D) physical adaptation
    (E) assembly

135. The act of combining two or more sites in an effort to develop one site with a greater value than the two sites have separately is called
    (A) assemblage
    (B) plottage
    (C) surplus land
    (D) excess land
    (E) a land contract

136. All of the following are cost estimation methods *except*
    (A) unit-in-place
    (B) unit-breakdown
    (C) quantity survey
    (D) comparative-unit
    (E) segregated cost

137. Which of the following tends to set the upper limits of value?
    (A) Replacement cost new
    (B) Market data approach
    (C) Income approach
    (D) Gross rent multiplier
    (E) Double declining balance method

138. A building that is too large for the neighborhood is an example of functional obsolescence in the form of overimprovement. Another example of functional obsolescence is
    (A) a sound building with a worn-out heating system
    (B) an awkwardly shaped floor plan in an office building
    (C) a residence abutting a new freeway
    (D) a building that will probably cost more to repair than the value added to the structure
    (E) an older building with modernized elevators

139. An inefficient floor plan would generally be classified as
    (A) physical depreciation
    (B) economic obsolescence
    (C) functional obsolescence
    (D) environmental obsolescence
    (E) none of the above

140. *Effective age* refers to
    (A) chronological age
    (B) average age
    (C) apparent age, considering the physical condition and marketability of a structure
    (D) warranty expiration
    (E) the ageless depreciation method

141. The effective age of a building will probably exceed its actual age when
    (A) a normal maintenance program has been carried out and the property experiences typical economic obsolescence
    (B) an inadequate maintenance program has been used
    (C) an above-average maintenance program has been used
    (D) the property is in a moderate climate
    (E) there is a full-time maintenance crew

142. Functional obsolescence in a house can be caused by
    (A) deterioration of the foundation
    (B) factors inherent in the house
    (C) factors external to the property
    (D) failure to paint when needed
    (E) worn-out carpeting

143. All other things being equal, when the building being appraised is much larger than the benchmark building described in the cost manual, the subject building's unit cost is probably
    (A) higher
    (B) lower
    (C) the same
    (D) adjustable by a local multiplier
    (E) none of the above

144. Reproduction cost is
    (A) original cost adjusted for inflation
    (B) the cost new of an exact replica of the subject
    (C) the cost of acquiring an equally desirable substitute
    (D) the current cost of constructing a functionally equivalent structure
    (E) available from brokerage offices

145. Determinants of building cost include
    (A) design
    (B) construction type
    (C) quality rating
    (D) local costs
    (E) all of the above

146. Subtracting an improvement's current market value from its reproduction cost new indicates
    (A) its sale price
    (B) the owner's profit
    (C) its replacement cost
    (D) accrued depreciation
    (E) replacement cost new

147. *Replacement cost new* refers to the cost of
    (A) constructing an exact replica of the subject building
    (B) constructing a building that would have similar or equivalent utility
    (C) reproducing the subject building on a different site
    (D) buying another property
    (E) an investment yielding similar returns

148. Examples of functional obsolescence do *not* include
    (A) poor room layout
    (B) peeling paint on exterior trim
    (C) a relatively short or narrow garage
    (D) inconveniently placed building support columns
    (E) uneconomical high ceilings

149. Which of the following best illustrates curable functional obsolescence?
    (A) Poor room layout with immovable load-bearing walls
    (B) Poorly located building support columns on an office floor
    (C) Inadequate electrical wiring in an older single-family house
    (D) A narrow, short carport that can be enlarged at low cost
    (E) Stains on the ceiling due to water penetration

150. What appraisal approach can be used for a public building?
    (A) Direct sales comparison
    (B) Income
    (C) Cost
    (D) Insurance
    (E) None of the above

151. Functional obsolescence that cannot be economically remedied is known as
    (A) physical depreciation
    (B) incurable depreciation
    (C) physical deterioration
    (D) locational deterioration
    (E) a curable loss

Questions 152–155 are based on the following information:
A residence is 12 years old but has been so well cared for that it is in as good condition as a typical 8-year-old property. Residences in this area typically last 60 years, and even that life span may be extended with extensive renovation.

152. The effective age of the residence is
    (A) 100 years
    (B) 60 years
    (C) 12 years
    (D) 8 years
    (E) none of the above

153. The chronological age of the residence is
    (A) 100 years
    (B) 60 years
    (C) 12 years
    (D) 8 years
    (E) none of the above

154. The remaining economic life of the residence is
    (A) 100 years
    (B) 60 years
    (C) 52 years
    (D) 48 years
    (E) none of the above

155. Normal life expectancy of the residence is
    (A) 100 years
    (B) 60 years
    (C) 12 years
    (D) 8 years
    (E) none of the above

156. The construction of a luxury home in a neighborhood almost completely developed with one- and two-bedroom apartments would
    (A) produce functional inadequacies
    (B) be called an underimprovement
    (C) result in plottage value
    (D) result in neighborhood amenities
    (E) be reasonable and appropriate

157. In the cost approach, a site is valued
    (A) as raw land
    (B) as if vacant
    (C) via the leased fee method
    (D) less accrued depreciation
    (E) as if unzoned

158. Functional obsolescence attributed to a property may result from
    (A) factors outside the property
    (B) physical deterioration
    (C) economic factors
    (D) changes in popular taste
    (E) functional area analysis

Questions 159–167 are based on the following information:

You are appraising a 20-year-old, single-family residence. It is typical of other houses in the neighborhood, and its estimated effective age is the same as its chronological age. Items needing immediate work at the time of the appraisal include exterior painting, with an estimated cost of $3,600, interior paint and decorating at $2,700, and storm door replacement at $450.

You have noted the following short-lived items and have estimated for each the cost new, effective age, and normal life expectancy.

Component	Cost	Effective Age (years)	Normal Life (years)
Roof	$4,500	5	20
Heating equipment	4,800	20	25
Light fixtures	2,400	20	25
Plumbing fixtures	6,000	20	40

The total estimated reproduction cost new of the house is $240,000. After completion of the work above, you estimate the house will have an effective age of only 15 years. Similar houses in the neighborhood are estimated to have an economic life new of 50 years. The subject has only one bathroom in a neighborhood of two-bathroom houses. It is rented for $1,800 per month, and this is its maximum rent. Several similar houses in the area with two bathrooms are rented for $1,950 per month. A number of sales of rented houses were analyzed, and a gross rent multiplier of 125 was indicated. A contractor has given you an estimate of $25,500 for adding another bathroom to the house.

159. Estimate curable physical deterioration.
    (A) $6,300
    (B) $3,600
    (C) $6,750
    (D) $450
    (E) None of the above

160. Estimate the dollar amount of *deferred* curable physical deterioration of the roof.
    (A) $4,500
    (B) 0
    (C) $2,250
    (D) $1,125
    (E) None of the above

161. Estimate the dollar amount of *deferred* curable physical deterioration of the heating equipment.
    (A) $3,840
    (B) $2,400
    (C) $3,600
    (D) 0
    (E) None of the above

162. Estimate the dollar amount of *deferred* curable physical deterioration of the light fixtures.
    (A) $1,800
    (B) $2,400
    (C) $1,536
    (D) $1,920
    (E) None of the above

163. What is your estimate of the dollar amount of *deferred* curable physical deterioration of the plumbing fixtures?
    (A) $4,800
    (B) $1,200
    (C) $2,400
    (D) $6,000
    (E) $3,000

164. For determination of incurable physical deterioration, what dollar amount is assigned to the remaining portion of the main structure?
    (A) $222,300
    (B) $240,000
    (C) $233,250
    (D) $215,550
    (E) none of the above

165. The functional obsolescence experienced by this property is
    (A) curable
    (B) deferred curable
    (C) incurable
    (D) deferred incurable
    (E) partially curable

166. What is your estimate of the dollar amount of functional obsolescence?
    (A) $15,000
    (B) $18,750
    (C) $22,500
    (D) $45,000
    (E) $48,000

167. What is your estimate (rounded) of the depreciated reproduction cost of the improvement?
    (A) $132,000
    (B) $168,000
    (C) $192,000
    (D) $204,000
    (E) $240,000

168. In appraisal, accrued depreciation is normally subtracted from
    (A) historic cost
    (B) actual cost new as of the date of the appraisal
    (C) reproduction cost new as of the date of the value estimate
    (D) depreciated cost as of the date of the value estimate
    (E) balance sheet assets

169. The cost of plumbing, heating, elevators, and similar building components may represent a smaller proportion of total costs when these components are installed in a large building than in a smaller one. This may be reflected in the
    (A) unit-in-place method
    (B) land-to-building ratio
    (C) quantity survey method
    (D) comparative-unit method
    (E) segregated cost method

170. The anticipated income that remains after deducting all operating expenses from effective gross income but before subtracting mortgage debt service is
    (A) cash flow
    (B) net operating income
    (C) potential gross income
    (D) after-tax cash flow
    (E) net income before debt service

171. The cost of painting and redecorating an apartment is
    (A) an operating expense
    (B) a fixed expense
    (C) an unnecessary expense if you have 100% occupancy
    (D) set aside in an owner's bank account as a reserve for redecoration
    (E) always justified for aesthetic reasons

172. Which of the following might be classified as a tangible rather than an intangible amenity?
    (A) Pride of ownership
    (B) A sense of security
    (C) Free utilities
    (D) Work satisfaction
    (E) Clean air

173. The lessor's interest in leased property is referred to as the
    (A) leasehold estate
    (B) leased fee estate
    (C) fee simple estate
    (D) remainder estate
    (E) residual estate

174. An ownership right retained by a landlord is
    (A) apparent authority
    (B) leased fee estate
    (C) leasehold estate
    (D) ingress and egress
    (E) fee tail

175. The monthly rental being paid under a lease for a comparable rental property is called the
    (A) market rental
    (B) net rental
    (C) effective rental
    (D) economic rent
    (E) contract rent

176. Timeshare units are most often used by
    (A) commuters
    (B) gardeners
    (C) attorneys
    (D) salespersons
    (E) vacationers

177. Which of the following is (are) important for good appraisal communication?
    (A) Word choice
    (B) Reading level
    (C) Sentence structure
    (D) Clarity
    (E) All of the above

178. Valuation estimates for which of the following purposes are normally outside the scope of a real estate appraiser's function?
    (A) Divorce (home valuation)
    (B) Mortgage financing
    (C) Condemnation
    (D) Personal injury
    (E) Insurance

179. An appraiser's workload should determine
    (A) the length and context of the appraisal report
    (B) the approaches included
    (C) the inspection detail
    (D) clerical responsibilities
    (E) none of the above

180. The purpose of which of the following is to analyze a property's potential for success?
    (A) Feasibility study
    (B) Marketability study
    (C) Market segmentation study
    (D) Appraisal report
    (E) Need study

181. The objective of the appraisal should be stated in the report because
    (A) it identifies the function of the report
    (B) it defines the problem and identifies the value sought
    (C) it absolves the appraiser of liability
    (D) the market needs this information
    (E) there are too many definitions of market price

182. It is ___ for an appraiser to receive or pay finder's or referral fees.
     (A) reasonable
     (B) unethical
     (C) necessary
     (D) customary
     (E) honest

183. Professional appraisal services are rendered
     (A) for professional attorneys
     (B) in a courtroom setting
     (C) on a fee basis only
     (D) generally on a retainer
     (E) contingent on the value estimate

184. For an appraiser to use the assistance of another appraiser is
     (A) inconsiderate
     (B) unethical
     (C) illegal
     (D) ethical
     (E) questionable

185. To provide a value range to a client who requests it and understands its meaning and use is
     (A) foolish
     (B) appropriate
     (C) unethical
     (D) impossible
     (E) improper but not unethical

186. Which item would an appraiser use to arrive at a net income for capitalization purposes?
     (A) Cost of loans against the property
     (B) Allowance for rent loss and vacancies
     (C) Federal income tax
     (D) Reserve for appreciation of buildings
     (E) Property manager's income from sale of cosmetics to tenants.

187. An apartment complex cost $450,000. It brings in a net income of $3,000 per month. The owner is making what percentage of return on the investment?
     (A) 7%
     (B) 8%
     (C) 11%
     (D) None of the above
     (E) Cannot be determined

188. Appraisals of single-family dwellings are usually based on
     (A) capitalization of rental value
     (B) asking prices of comparable houses
     (G) sales prices of comparable properties
     (D) the assessed valuation
     (E) REALTOR opinions of value

189. A "loss in value from any cause" is a common definition of
     (A) economic obsolescence
     (B) depreciation
     (C) principal of contribution
     (D) adverse leverage
     (E) external issues

190. If an appraiser finds that the fair rent for a vacant parcel of land is $1,400 per month and the interest rate is 11%, what is the approximate indicated land value?
    (A) $109,090
    (B) $138,560
    (C) $152,730
    (D) $210,000
    (E) None of the above

191. Economic obsolescence could result from each of the following *except*
    (A) new zoning laws
    (B) a city's leading industry moving out
    (C) misplacement of improvements
    (D) an outdated kitchen
    (E) re-routing of a highway

192. Which of the following is an appraiser's primary concern in the analysis of residential property?
    (A) marketability and acceptability
    (B) square foot area
    (C) functional utility
    (D) fixed and operating expenses
    (E) external obsolescence

193. To evaluate a vacant commercial site, an appraiser decides to use the land residual technique. Here is the information the appraiser gathered:

    Cost new of a proper building: $250,000
    Estimated net income before recapture: $32,800 per year
    Interest rate: 8.5%
    Estimated remaining economic life of building: 40 years

    What is the approximate estimated value of the land using this technique?
    (A) $31,000
    (B) $47,000
    (C) $48,182
    (D) $62,353
    (E) None of the above

194. Which of the following types of appraisal report would be the most comprehensive and detailed?
    (A) Self-contained
    (B) Summary
    (C) Restricted use
    (D) Oral
    (E) Complete

195. To estimate the value of a parcel of real property, an appraiser concentrated only on the cost to the buyer of acquiring a comparable substitute parcel. This estimate is most similar to which of the following appraisal approaches?
    (A) Cost
    (B) Income
    (C) Market
    (D) Depreciated value
    (E) None of the above

196. *Capitalization* is a process whereby an appraiser
    (A) converts income into capital value
    (B) determines depreciation reserves
    (C) establishes cost of capital investment
    (D) finds gross income of equity capital
    (E) adds the asset to the balance sheet

197. Appraisers estimate depreciation as a
    (A) loss in value from any cause
    (B) loss in purchasing power
    (C) loss in book value
    (D) tax write-off
    (E) adjustment to net operating income

198. Accountants measure depreciation as a
    (A) loss in value from any cause
    (B) loss in purchasing power
    (C) loss in book value
    (D) tax write-off
    (E) economic value decline

199. Which of the following is *not* a form of economic depreciation?
    (A) Physical deterioration
    (B) Original cost allocation
    (C) Functional obsolescence
    (D) Economic obsolescence
    (E) Loss in value

200. An appraisal may be
    (A) oral
    (B) written
    (C) an opinion of value
    (D) all of the above
    (E) none of the above

201. A fee appraiser is
    (A) an independent contractor
    (B) a bank fiduciary
    (C) a mortgage broker
    (D) a real estate salesperson
    (E) fee simple evaluator

202. A main goal of an appraiser is
    (A) measuring obsolescence
    (B) rendering a market value opinion
    (C) narrative reporting
    (D) meeting the sales contract amount
    (E) measuring the condition of appliances

203. A major factor in appraising a business opportunity is the
    (A) net income
    (B) number of employees
    (C) number of customers
    (D) owner's expertise
    (E) replacement cost of machinery

204. Prices of comparable sales are adjusted
    (A) to the subject property
    (B) upward if the comparable is inferior to the subject
    (C) downward if the comparable is superior to the subject
    (D) all of the above
    (E) none of the above

205. All other things being equal, the cost per square foot of a two-story house compared to a one-story house having the same square footage
    (A) is less
    (B) is more
    (C) is the same
    (D) depends on height
    (E) depends on market conditions

ANSWERS

1. **B**	36. **D**	71. **C**	106. **C**	141. **B**	176. **E**
2. **B**	37. **B**	72. **C**	107. **E**	142. **B**	177. **E**
3. **E**	38. **C**	73. **C**	108. **A**	143. **B**	178. **D**
4. **E**	39. **B**	74. **E**	109. **B**	144. **B**	179. **E**
5. **C**	40. **B**	75. **E**	110. **C**	145. **E**	180. **A**
6. **D**	41. **E**	76. **D**	111. **A**	146. **D**	181. **B**
7. **E**	42. **D**	77. **C**	112. **C**	147. **B**	182. **B**
8. **B**	43. **C**	78. **B**	113. **B**	148. **B**	183. **C**
9. **A**	44. **E**	79. **B**	114. **C**	149. **D**	184. **D**
10. **E**	45. **A**	80. **B**	115. **D**	150. **C**	185. **B**
11. **A**	46. **C**	81. **B**	116. **D**	151. **B**	186. **B**
12. **B**	47. **B**	82. **E**	117. **D**	152. **D**	187. **B**
13. **E**	48. **C**	83. **C**	118. **D**	153. **C**	188. **C**
14. **E**	49. **B**	84. **D**	119. **B**	154. **C**	189. **B**
15. **E**	50. **B**	85. **D**	120. **A**	155. **B**	190. **C**
16. **B**	51. **C**	86. **C**	121. **B**	156. **A**	191. **D**
17. **B**	52. **D**	87. **A**	122. **A**	157. **B**	192. **A**
18. **D**	53. **E**	88. **C**	123. **B**	158. **D**	193. **D**
19. **D**	54. **D**	89. **C**	124. **B**	159. **C**	194. **A**
20. **A**	55. **A**	90. **A**	125. **A**	160. **D**	195. **C**
21. **A**	56. **B**	91. **A**	126. **B**	161. **A**	196. **A**
22. **D**	57. **C**	92. **D**	127. **A**	162. **D**	197. **A**
23. **A**	58. **B**	93. **C**	128. **C**	163. **E**	198. **C**
24. **A**	59. **D**	94. **A**	129. **C**	164. **D**	199. **B**
25. **E**	60. **B**	95. **C**	130. **B**	165. **C**	200. **D**
26. **C**	61. **C**	96. **D**	131. **E**	166. **B**	201. **A**
27. **B**	62. **C**	97. **B**	132. **A**	167. **A**	202. **B**
28. **B**	63. **E**	98. **D**	133. **B**	168. **C**	203. **A**
29. **A**	64. **B**	99. **E**	134. **B**	169. **D**	204. **D**
30. **B**	65. **D**	100. **E**	135. **A**	170. **B**	205. **A**
31. **A**	66. **E**	101. **B**	136. **B**	171. **A**	
32. **D**	67. **C**	102. **D**	137. **A**	172. **C**	
33. **C**	68. **D**	103. **E**	138. **B**	173. **B**	
34. **A**	69. **C**	104. **D**	139. **C**	174. **B**	
35. **D**	70. **B**	105. **B**	140. **C**	175. **E**	

Chapter 15 / *Certified General Appraiser*

This chapter is of primary interest to a person who wishes to be licensed as a certified general appraiser. Much of the material will be of interest also to brokers, salespersons, and other appraisers but is not presently required by licensing examinations for those groups.

Items indicated by a dagger (†) in the Examination Content Outline in Chapter 14 are specifically covered here.

Legal Considerations in Appraisal

Property is generally classified as either real or personal. Whatever is more or less permanently affixed to land or buildings is *real property*; all other property is *personal property*. Questions frequently arise as to whether or not fixtures are part of the real estate in question; if they *are* part, they are included in the appraised value.

TRADE FIXTURES

A *trade fixture* is attached to a rented facility by a tenant who uses that fixture in conducting a business. No matter how trade fixtures are attached to real estate, they are personal property. Some examples are booths, counters, and bar stools in a restaurant, tanks and pumps in a service station, and shelves in a retail store. The tenant may remove these at the expiration of the lease.

In determining whether an item is a trade fixture, courts will consider:
1. *The manner of attachment.* Personal property can generally be removed without damage.
2. *The adaptation of the article to the real estate.* Items that are built specifically to be installed in a particular building and are unlikely to be used in another are probably real estate.
3. *The intent of the parties when the property was attached.*

MACHINERY AND EQUIPMENT

An appraiser needs to know whether or not to include these items in the real estate value estimate. For example, in a hotel there may be equipment in laundry facilities, guest exercise rooms, or restaurants that could be considered either real or personal property. In the office section of a warehouse, there could be heating, ventilation, and air conditioning equipment, lighting, and plumbing facilities for office workers. Depending on the same criteria described for fixtures, the appraiser has to classify the machinery and equipment as real or personal property.

Types of Value

All types of value were covered in Chapter 14 except *going-concern value*. This is the difference between the market value of a business and the market value of its assets. For example, a restaurant may be worth $1 million as a business even though its building, land, furniture, fixtures, and equipment have an aggregate market value of only $600,000. The $400,000 excess is the going-concern value.

When appraising business real estate, such as a hotel or motel, retail store, or storage service facility, an appraiser needs to recognize the difference between the business value and the real estate value. The value conclusion will, of course, depend on what is being appraised.

Economic Principles

All of these principles were discussed in Chapter 14 except *opportunity cost*, that is, the cost of an opportunity forgone by not choosing it. For example, suppose an investor buys mortgages on real estate that yield 10 percent rather than corporate bonds yielding 9 percent. The opportunity cost is the 9 percent yield on the bonds that were not bought.

Similarly, if an appraiser accepts an assignment for $8,000 that requires his full-time effort for a month, requiring him to turn down another assignment at $6,000 because of a time conflict, the $6,000 is the opportunity cost.

Real Estate Market Analysis

The three items of the Examination Content Outline that were not covered in Chapter 14 are *existing space inventory*, *current and projected space surplus*, and *new space*.

EXISTING SPACE INVENTORY

Existing space may be inventoried and categorized for a market or market segment. For example, for each office building in a city, a database may be used that includes, at a minimum, the following information:

Building name　　　　　　*Year built*
Building location　　　　*Class (A, B, C)*
Square feet retail　　　　*Occupancy rate*
Square feet office　　　　*Effective rent rate*
Rent rate asked　　　　　*Typical lease terms*

The database can then be sorted in various ways: by amount of space in each section of the city or by class, rent range, vacancy rate, and so on.

CURRENT AND PROJECTED SPACE SURPLUS

Using the database model described above, one can estimate an occupancy ratio for each part of the city and class of building, for example, and can then compare historical absorption rates with existing surplus space to estimate future occupancy. This comparison must be tempered by knowledge of specific important changes to come, such as the impending relocation of a corporate headquarters to another city. The analysis will provide insights as to the likelihood of a tightening of supply or a surplus of space.

NEW SPACE

The planning or engineering department of the city can provide information on the issuance of permits authorizing new construction. Since these permits will be for specific buildings, they will provide locations and sizes that may be added to the database. Construction and leasing activity will be recognized for new space; together these can offer a picture of the supply of space for the next 2 to 3 years in an office market, for example.

Appraisal Math and Statistics

All compound interest functions are reserved for the appraiser general certification examination. There are six of these functions; each is described below. All six functions are variations on the compound interest formula, which holds that interest in each period is based on the initial principal plus accrued but unpaid interest earned in prior periods. The six functions (and their column locations in standard six-function tables) are as follows:

- Future value of $1 (Column 1)
- Future value of an annuity of $1 per period (Column 2)
- Sinking fund factor (Column 3)
- Present value of $1 (Column 4)
- Present value of an annuity of $1 per period (Column 5)
- Installment to amortize $1 (Column 6)

FUTURE VALUE OF $1

This function is compound interest. Interest that has been earned and left on deposit becomes principal. In the next period, that principal will earn interest along with the initial principal. The formula for compound interest is as follows:

$$S^n = (1 + i)^n$$

where S^n = sum after n periods; i = periodic rate of interest; n = number of periods.

Table 15-1 indicates the growth of a $1.00 deposit that earns 10 percent compound interest for 5 years. Figure 15-1 illustrates the growth of $1.00 at compound interest.

Although Table 15-1 illustrates a compounding interval of 1 year, compounding may occur daily, monthly, quarterly, or semiannually. Interest rates are usually stated at a nominal annual

Table 15-1.
FUTURE VALUE OF $1
$1.00 Deposit at 10% Interest Rate for 5 Years

Year		Compound Interest and Balance
0	Deposit	$1.00
1	Interest earned	0.10
1	Balance, end of year	1.10
2	Interest earned	0.11
2	Balance, end of year	1.21
3	Interest earned	0.121
3	Balance, end of year	1.331
4	Interest earned	0.1331
4	Balance, end of year	1.4641
5	Interest earned	0.1464
5	Balance, end of year	$1.6105

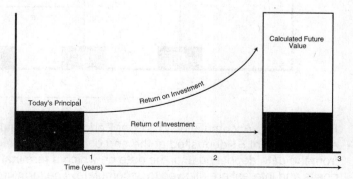

Figure 15-1.   Growth of Principal at Compound Interest

figure, such as 10 percent, but more frequent compounding increases the effective rate. The general formula is the same: $S^n = (1 + i)^n$.

FUTURE VALUE OF AN ANNUITY OF $1 PER PERIOD

This function offers the future value of a series of equal amounts deposited at the ends of periodic intervals. It is the sum of all these individual amounts, each deposited at the end of an interval, (period), plus appropriate interest. Note that this differs from the future value of $1 factor in two ways. First, the future annuity factor is based on a series of deposits, whereas the future value of $1 involves a single deposit. Second, the accumulation is based on a deposit at the end of each interval, whereas compound interest is based on a deposit made at the beginning of the total period.

The formula for the future value of $1 per period is as follows:

$$S_n = \frac{S^n - 1}{i} \quad \text{or} \quad \frac{(1 + i)^n - 1}{i}$$

where S_n = future value of annuity of $1 per period; i = periodic interest rate; n = number of periods considered. S^n is the future value of $1.

Table 15-2 shows the annual interest earned and end-of-period balances of the future value

Table 15-2.
FUTURE VALUE OF AN ANNUITY OF $1 PER PERIOD
Illustrated at 10% Interest Rate for Four Periods

End of period 1, initial deposit	$1.00
Interest, period 1	0.00
Balance, end of period 1	1.00
Interest, end of period 2	0.10
Deposit, end of period 2	1.00
Balance, end of period 2	2.10
Interest, end of period 3	0.21
Deposit, end of period 3	1.00
Balance, end of period 3	3.31
Interest, end of period 4	0.331
Deposit, end of period 4	1.00
Balance, end of period 4	$4.641

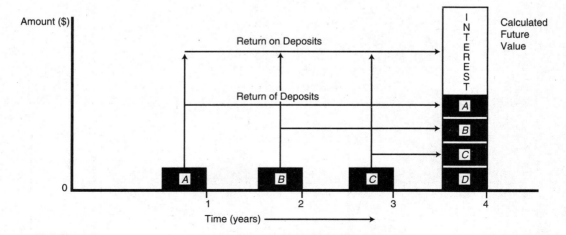

Figure 15-2.   Accumulation of $1 per Period (Future Value of an Annuity). *A, B, C,* and *D* each represent $1 deposited at the end of a year. Each deposit earns compound interest from the date deposited until the date on which a terminal amount is sought. Thus, all deposits and interest are allowed to accumulate. The terminal value is the sum of all deposits plus compound interest.

of an annuity of $1 per period at 10 percent interest. Figure 15-2 is an illustration of the function for four periods.

SINKING FUND FACTOR

This factor shows the deposit that is required at the end of each period to reach $1.00 after a certain number of periods, considering interest to be earned on the deposits. It is the reciprocal of the future value of an annuity of $1 per period.

For example, at a 0 percent rate of interest, $0.25 must be deposited at the end of each year for 4 years to accumulate $1.00 at the end of 4 years. If, however, the deposits earn compound interest at 10 percent, only $0.215471 need be deposited at the end of each of the 4 years.

Table 15-3 indicates how four periodic deposits grow to $1.00 with interest. Figure 15-3 offers a graphic presentation of the same data.

Table 15-3.
SINKING FUND FACTOR
Illustrated to Reach $1.00 in Four Periods at 10% Interest Rate

Deposit, end of period 1	$0.215471
Interest for period 1	0.000000
Balance, end of period 1	0.215471
Interest for period 2	0.021547
Deposit, end of period 2	0.215471
Balance, end of period 2	0.452489
Interest for period 3	0.045249
Deposit, end of period 3	0.215471
Balance, end of period 3	0.713209
Interest for period 4	0.071321
Deposit, end of period 4	0.215471
Balance, end of period 4	$1.000000

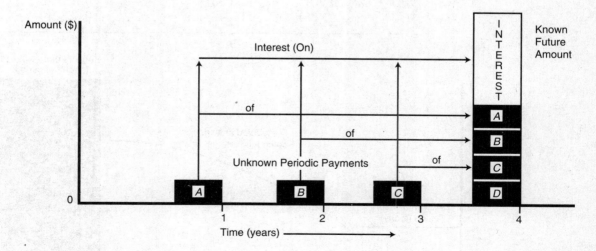

Figure 15-3. Sinking Fund Factor. *A*, *B*, *C*, and *D* are equal amounts deposited at the end of each year. Each deposit earns compound interest for the period of time it remains on deposit. At the end of the time period considered, the depositor can withdraw the terminal value. The sinking fund factor is computed in such a way that the terminal value will always equal $1.

PRESENT VALUE OF $1

This factor offers the value now of $1 to be received in the future. Money has a time value; a dollar to be received in the future is worth less than a dollar now. The amount of discount depends on the time between the cash outflow and inflow and the necessary rate of interest or discount rate.

Since the purpose of investing is to receive returns in the future, applying the present value of $1 factor to anticipated future income is a crucial step in valuing an investment. When applying a present value factor, the terms *discounting* and *discount rate* are used, as contrasted with *compounding* and *interest rate*, which are used in computing future values. Mathematically, the present value of a reversion is the reciprocal of the future value of $1.

For example, at a 10 percent discount rate, $100.00 that is expected 1 year from now has a present value of $90.91. As an arithmetic check, consider that, if an investor has $90.91 now and earns 10 percent during the year, the interest will amount to $9.09, making the principal in 1 year $100.00 ($90.91 original principal + $9.09 interest).

An investor who will get $100.00 in 2 years and pays $82.64 now receives a 10 percent annual rate of interest. As a check, consider that, after 1 year, $82.64 will grow to $90.91 with 10 percent interest, then to $100.00 in 2 years.

The formula for the present value of $1 is as follows:

$$V^n = \frac{1}{(1 + i)^n} \quad \text{or} \quad \frac{1}{S^n}$$

where V = present value of $1; i = periodic discount rate; n = number of periods.

Table 15-4 shows the present value of a reversion at 10 percent interest for 4 years. Figure 15-4 illustrates the present value of $1.

Table 15-4.
PRESENT VALUE OF $1
Illustrated at 10% Interest Rate for 4 Years

Year	Compound Amount	Reciprocal		Present Value of $1.00 Reversion
1	1.1	1/1.1	=	$0.909091
2	1.21	1/1.21	=	0.826446
3	1.331	1/1.331	=	0.751315
4	1.4641	1/1.4641	=	0.683013

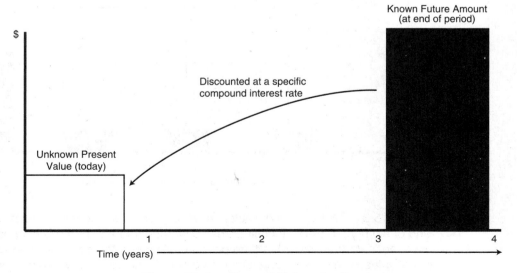

Figure 15-4.   Present Value of a Reversion

PRESENT VALUE OF AN ANNUITY OF $1 PER PERIOD

An ordinary annuity is a series of equal payments beginning one period from the present. It is also defined as a series of receipts. For example, the right to receive $1.00 at the end of each year for the next 4 years creates an ordinary annuity.

Table 15-5 shows the present value of an annuity of $1 each year for 4 years at a 10 percent interest rate. Figure 15-5 provides an illustration.

Table 15-5.
PRESENT VALUE OF AN ANNUITY OF $1 PER PERIOD
Illustrated for 4 Years at 10% Interest Rate

Year	Present Value of Reversion	Present Value of Annuity
1	$0.9091	$0.9091
2	0.8264	1.7355
3	0.7513	2.4868
4	0.6830	3.1698

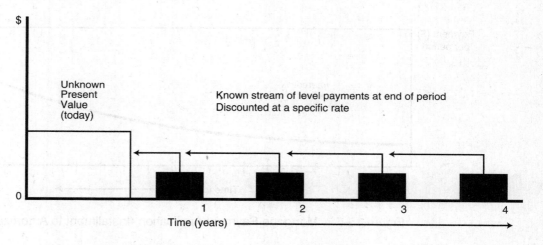

Figure 15-5.   Present Value of an Ordinary Annuity

INSTALLMENT TO AMORTIZE $1 (LOAN CONSTANT OR MORTGAGE CONSTANT)

This function shows the periodic payment required to retire a loan, with interest. It is the sum of the interest (or discount) rate and the sinking fund factor. It is the reciprocal of the present value of an annuity of $1 per period. This factor, which shows the constant payment necessary to amortize a loan in equal periodic installments, considers the term, interest rate, and principal of the loan.

As the interest rate increases or the amortization term shortens, the required periodic payment is increased. Conversely, lower interest rates and longer repayment periods reduce the required periodic payment. Each level payment in the installment to amortize $1 factor is a blend of interest and a reduction of the original principal.

The formula for the installment to amortize $1 is as follows:

$$\frac{1}{a_n} = \frac{i}{1 - V^n} \quad \text{or} \quad \frac{1}{a_n} = \frac{i}{1 - \dfrac{1}{(1 + i)^n}}$$

where a_n = present value of annuity of \$1 per period; i = interest rate; n = number of periods; V^n = present value of \$1.

Table 15-6 shows that the installment to amortize \$1 is the reciprocal of the present value of an annuity of \$1 factor. Figure 15-6 illustrates the distribution of periodic payments to interest and principal retirement.

Table 15-6.
INSTALLMENTS TO AMORTIZE $1 AS RECIPROCAL
OF PRESENT VALUE OF ANNUITY
Illustrated for 4 Years at 10% Interest Rate

Year	Present Value of Annuity	Installment to Amortize $1
1	$0.9091	$1.10
2	1.7355	0.5762
3	2.4868	0.4021
4	3.1698	0.3155

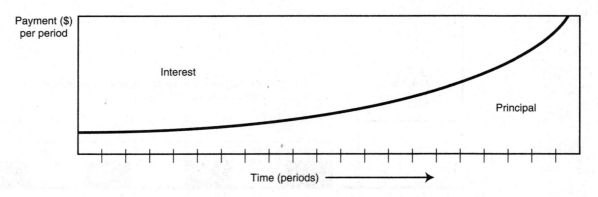

Figure 15-6. Mortgage Payment Application (Installment to Amortize $1)

As an example of use, suppose that a \$100 loan requires four equal annual payments at 10 percent interest. The required payment will be \$31.55. As a check, one can construct an amortization schedule as shown in Table 15-7.

Table 15-7.
AMORTIZATION SCHEDULE FOR A $100 LOAN
Level Payments at 10% for 4 Years

Year	Loan Balance at Beginning of Year	Add Interest at 10%	Less Interest and Principal Payment	Balance at End of Year
1	$100.00	$10.00	$31.55	$78.45
2	78.45	7.85	31.55	54.75
3	54.75	5.48	31.55	28.68
4	28.68	2.87	31.55	-0-

Sales Comparison Approach

Chapter 14 covers most of the details associated with sales comparisons. Here, gross income multipliers and overall rates are discussed, along with certain units of comparison, mineral rights and other vertical interests, and tenant improvements.

GROSS INCOME MULTIPLIERS

Gross income multipliers can be used to compare comparable properties to the subject property. The *gross income multiplier (GIM)* indicates the relationship between the annual revenues from a property and its selling price or value. In nearly all situations, the sales price is several times greater than the revenues and therefore is the numerator, with the revenues the denominator. The resulting factor is expected to be greater than 1, most frequently between 4 and 20.

POTENTIAL GROSS INCOME MULTIPLIER

Potential gross income (PGI) is the amount that would be received from rental properties if all units were fully occupied all year. For example, if a building contained 100 apartments, each renting for $1,000 per month, the PGI would be 100 × $1,000 × 12 months, or $1,200,000. If this building were to sell for $10 million, the *potential gross income multiplier (PGIM)* would be 8.333 ($10,000,000 ÷ $1,200,000).

EFFECTIVE GROSS INCOME MULTIPLIER

Effective gross income (EGI) is determined by subtracting an allowance for vacancy and collection losses from potential gross income. In the example above, if the appropriate allowance percentage rate is 5 percent of the $1,200,000 potential gross income, the allowance is $60,000. The EGI is therefore $1,200,000 minus $60,000, or $1,140,000. The *effective gross income multiplier (EGIM)* is the selling price divided by the EGIM, that is, $10,000,000 ÷ $1,140,000, or 8.772.

OVERALL RATE OF RETURN

The *overall rate of return* is the percentage relationship between the *net operating income (NOI)* and the sales price. Since NOI is a revenue amount, this ratio is almost always less than 1, typically 0.05 to 0.30.

NOI is EGI minus operating expenses (OE). Operating expenses are payments that must be made to run the property, but not financing expenses, such as interest, nor depreciation. Operating expenses include maintenance and repairs, payroll and payroll taxes, real estate property taxes, advertising, utilities, management fees, grounds maintenance, and replacement reserve.

Suppose, in the preceding example, that annual operating expenses are $440,000. Then NOI is $1,140,000 (EGI) minus $440,000 (OE), or $700,000. The overall rate of return is

$$\frac{\text{NOI}}{\text{Sales Price}} = \frac{\$700,000}{\$10,000,000} = 7 \text{ percent}$$

UNITS OF COMPARISON

The certified general appraiser is expected to be knowledgeable about some less obvious units of comparison, including those for specialized properties, such as motels and theaters. Units of comparison for these include the price per room for a motel and the price per seat for a theater. The computation is straightforward: after appraisal adjustments are made for the elements of comparison described below, the adjusted price is divided by the number of units.

An appraisal should emulate market conditions; for example, in the case of multiscreen theaters, the number of screens may become a unit of comparison.

MINERAL RIGHTS AND OTHER VERTICAL INTERESTS

A real estate appraiser is not expected to be a geologist or to be able to value subsurface rights (*mineral rights*), but she must recognize that in certain regions the minerals may have value. When some comparables sell with mineral rights and some without, the appraiser must take care to make the appropriate adjustments from the comparables to the subject property. The paired-sale technique (see Chapter 14) may be useful for this purpose.

An appraiser may need also to value other *vertical interests*, such as *air rights* (the right to build above property, starting from a certain height) and tunneling.

TENANT IMPROVEMENTS

Tenant improvements, known in the trade as TIs, are allowances given to a tenant to adapt the property for his use. For example, a retail tenant agrees to a 5-year lease at a rent of $25 per square foot per year. The landlord offers bare walls and will advance $15 per square foot, before occupancy, for the tenant to adapt the property to his use. If costs exceed the allowance, the tenant will be responsible.

When comparing rents, an appraiser must also consider TIs. One building may offer a low rent but contribute no TIs, whereas another has higher rents and a generous TI allowance. The appraiser must understand the market so as to properly estimate the market rent for the subject property.

Site Value

Two methods of estimating site value, in addition to those given in Chapter 14, are *ground rent capitalization* and *subdivision analysis*. These methods apply only in certain situations.

GROUND RENT CAPITALIZATION

In a few places, notably Hawaii, Baltimore, and Manhattan, there is a high concentration of ground lease ownership; that is, the building owner does not own the land but, as a tenant, leases it from the landowner. An appraiser can estimate land value by *capitalization*, that is, by dividing the annual rent by an appropriate capitalization rate. As a simple example, suppose that the rent on a lot in Baltimore is $120 per year, renewable forever. The appropriate rate of return on investment is 6 percent. Then the land value is $120 \div 0.06 = \$2,000$.

SUBDIVISION ANALYSIS

Subdivision analysis is a method of estimating the maximum that a subdivider can pay for a tract of land. This method involves a sales estimate (usually monthly or quarterly) and a cost estimate over time. Cash flows are then discounted to a present value.

The example shown in Table 15-8 was prepared on an annual basis. As can be seen from the table, $137,285 is the maximum that can be paid for land, and still allow the subdivision to be developed, under the assumptions shown.

Table 15-8.
SUBDIVISION DEVELOPMENT ANALYSIS

	Year			
	1	**2**	**3**	**4**
Lost sales units	0	10	15	20
Price per lot		$ 20,000	$ 22,000	$ 25,000
Total sales	-0-	200,000	330,000	500,000
Costs:				
Engineering	$ 40,000			
Utility installation	70,000	100,000		
Clearing and grading	50,000			
Advertising	25,000	25,000	25,000	25,000
Streets and sidewalks	50,000	50,000	60,000	-0-
Permits	10,000			
Contractor's overhead and profit	10,000	10,000	10,000	10,000
Legal and accounting	15,000			
Interest	20,000	15,000	15,000	15,000
Entrepreneurial profit			50,000	50,000
Total costs	$290,000	$200,000	$160,000	$100,000
Cash flow (total sales less Total costs)	(290,000)	-0-	170,000	$400,000
Discount rate @ 10%	× .90909	× .8264	× .7513	× .683
Present value	(263,636)	-0-	$127,721	$273,200
Sum of present value		$137,285		

Income Approach

A certified general appraiser is expected to know how to appraise income-producing property on the basis of the revenue it is expected to generate. A number of techniques used for this purpose are described below.

ESTIMATION OF INCOME AND EXPENSES

Income property valuation begins with an estimate of income and expenses, which was described, to a limited extent, under the sales comparison approach. The levels of income generated by a given property range from a top level, potential gross income, to a bottom level, owner's cash flow. Table 15-9 on the next page is a chart of income levels.

In addition to income, operating expenses must be considered, and an operating statement derived.

POTENTIAL GROSS INCOME

Potential gross income is the rent collectible if all units are fully occupied.

Types of Rent

In estimating potential gross income, the appraiser distinguishes between *market rent* (economic rent) and *contract rent*. Market rent is the rate prevailing in the market for comparable properties and is used in calculating market value by the income approach. Contract rent is the actual amount agreed to by landlord and tenant. If the leases are long-term, contract rent is important in calculating investment value.

Table 15-9.
LEVELS OF REAL ESTATE INCOME

	Potential gross income
Less:	Vacancy and collection allowance
Plus:	Miscellaneous income
Equals:	**Effective gross income**
Less:	Allowable expenses
	Maintenance and operating
	Administrative
	Utilities
	Real estate taxes
	Replacement reserves
	Etc.
Equals:	**Net operating income**
Less:	Debt service
	Mortgage principal
	Mortgage interest
Equals:	**Before-tax cash flow**
	(Cash throw-off or equity dividend)

Market rents represent what a given property should be renting for, based on analysis of recently negotiated contract rents for comparable space—but only those that are considered bona fide "market" rents. The market rent should be the amount that would result from a lease negotiated between a willing lessor and a willing lessee, both free from influence from outside sources.

Rental Units of Comparison

Rents must be compared in terms of a common denominator. Typical units of comparison are square foot, room, apartment, space, and percentage of gross business income of the tenant, as shown in Table 15-10.

Table 15-10.
RENTAL UNITS OF COMPARISON
FOR TYPES OF INCOME-PRODUCING PROPERTY

Rental Unit of Comparison	Type of Income-Producing Property
Square foot	Shopping centers, retail stores, office buildings, warehouses, apartments, leased land
Room	Motels, hotels, apartment buildings
Apartment	Apartment buildings
Space	Mobile home parks, travel trailer parks, parking garages
Percentages of gross business income	Retail stores, shopping centers, restaurants, gas stations

When the square foot unit is used for an office building or shopping center, the appraiser should note that some leases are based on *net leasable area (NLA)* and others on *gross leasable area (GLA)*. NLA is the floor area occupied by the tenant. GLA includes NLA plus common areas such as halls, restrooms, and vestibules. An office building with 100,000 square feet of GLA may have only 80,000 square feet of NLA, a difference of 20 percent. When leases are compared, it must be known whether rent is based on GLA or NLA.

EFFECTIVE GROSS INCOME

Effective gross income is the amount remaining after the vacancy rate and collection (bad debt) allowances are subtracted from potential gross income and miscellaneous income is added. Calculating effective gross income is an intermediate step in deriving the cash flow.

Vacancy and Collection Allowance

The losses expected from vacancies and bad debts must be subtracted from potential gross income. These losses are calculated at the rate expected of local ownership and management.

Miscellaneous Income

Miscellaneous income is received from concessions, laundry rooms, parking space or storage bin rentals, and other associated services integral to operating the project.

OPERATING EXPENSES

The potential list of operating expenses for gross leased real estate includes:
- Property taxes: city, county, school district, special assessments
- Insurance: hazard, liability
- Utilities: telephone, water, sewer or sewage disposal, electricity, gas
- Administrative costs: management fees, clerical staff, maintenance staff, payroll taxes, legal and accounting expenses
- Repairs and maintenance: paint, decoration, carpet replacement, appliance repairs and replacement, supplies, gardening/landscaping, paving, roofing
- Advertising and promotion: media, business organizations

Fixed versus Variable Expenses

Operating expenses may be divided into two categories. *Fixed expenses* do not change as the rate of occupancy changes. *Variable expenses,* on the other hand, are directly related to the occupancy rate: as more people occupy and use a building, variable expenses increase.

Fixed expenses include property taxes, license and permit fees, and property insurance. Variable expenses generally include utilities (such as heat, water, sewer), management fees, payroll and payroll taxes, security, landscaping, advertising, and supplies and fees for various services provided by local government or private contractors. There may be a fixed component in expenses normally classified as variable—for example, a basic fixed payroll cost regardless of the occupancy rate.

Replacement Reserve

Provision must be made for the replacement of short-lived items (e.g., carpeting, appliances, and some mechanical equipment) that wear out. Such expenditures usually occur in large lump sums; a portion of the expected cost can be set aside every year to stabilize the expenses. A replacement reserve is necessary because the wearing out of short-lived assets causes a hidden loss of income. If this economic fact is not reflected in financial statements, the net operating income will be overstated. An appraiser should provide for a replacement reserve even though most owners do not set aside money for this purpose.

NET OPERATING INCOME

Net operating income (NOI) is estimated by subtracting operating expenses and the replacement reserve from effective gross income. Any interest or principal payments are not considered in computing NOI.

NOI for each comparable sale should be estimated in the same way that the subject property's NOI is considered. All relevant income and operating expenses are included in consistent amounts or rates to uniformly apply a capitalization rate. Each dollar of error in stating NOI will be multiplied, perhaps by 10 or more, in the resulting value estimate.

OPERATING STATEMENT RATIOS

Operating statement ratios are informative comparisons of expenses to income. The *operating expense ratio* is the percentage relationship of operating expenses to potential or effective gross income. There are typical ratios for each type of property in a market area, and much higher or lower ratios may be a clue to the effectiveness of management policies, efficient or inefficient.

The *net income ratio* is the reciprocal of the operating expense ratio. It tells what the fraction of property net operating income is compared to potential gross income. The *break-even ratio* is the occupancy rate needed to have zero cash flow. It is the sum of operating expenses plus debt service, divided by potential gross income.

INCOME CAPITALIZATION

Income capitalization is a process whereby a stream of future income receipts is translated into a single present-value sum. It considers:
1. Amount of future income (cash flow).
2. Time when the income (cash flow) is to be received.
3. Duration of the income (cash flow) stream.

A *capitalization rate* is used to convert an income stream into a lump-sum value. The formula used is as follows:

$$V = \frac{I}{R}$$

where V = present value; I = periodic income; R = capitalization rate.

Direct Capitalization

Direct capitalization involves simple arithmetic division of two components to result in a capitalized value, as shown below:

$$\text{Property Value} = \frac{\text{Net Operating Income}}{\text{Overall Rate of Return}}$$

The appraiser considers other properties that have been sold and the net operating income generated by each to derive an *overall rate of return (OAR)*. A market-derived OAR is then divided into the subject's NOI to estimate the latter's value.

Overall Capitalization Rate

To derive an overall capitalization rate from market data, the appraiser must select similar properties that have sold recently and are characterized by income streams of risk and duration similar to those of the subject property. If sufficient comparables are available, an OAR can be derived directly from the market and the appraiser can use direct capitalization to convert forecast NOI into a market value estimate.

To illustrate, suppose an appraiser has found the following data:

Comparable	NOI	Sales Price	Indicated OAR
#1	$240,000	$2,000,000	0.120
#2	176,000	1,600,000	0.110
#3	210,000	2,000,000	0.105

If adequate data of this nature were consistently available, appropriate overall rates could be developed for all types of properties, and other methods of capitalization would be of little importance. Unfortunately, reliable, verified sales data are not plentiful, and caution should be exercised in using this capitalization method. The comparability of the sale properties to the subject property must be analyzed carefully. Appropriate application requires that the comparables considered be consistent in these respects:

- Income and expense ratios
- NOI calculations
- Improvement ratio
- Remaining economic life
- Date and terms of sale

The simplicity of direct capitalization makes it attractive, even though complex relationships of income, expenses, and rates of return may underlie the computation. Various ways to derive rates are described in this chapter.

The *overall capitalization rate* must include a return on and a return of investment. Return *on* investment is the compensation necessary to pay an investor for the time value of the money, risk, and other factors associated with a particular investment. It is the interest paid for the use of money, also referred to as *yield*. Return *of* investment deals with repayment of the original principal, referred to as *capital recovery*. The capitalization rate taken from the market presumably incorporates other factors, such as expected inflation, income tax effect on the property, and interest rates and loan terms. However, this is a presumption, without actual numbers being tested to validate the expectation.

The yield rate is a rate of return on investment. Since real estate tends to wear out over time, though its economic useful life may be 50 years or longer, an investor must receive a recovery *of* the investment in addition to a return on it. There are three ways to provide a return of investment:

1. Straight line
2. Annuity
3. Sinking fund at safe rate

Straight Line. The straight-line technique is useful when building income is forecast to decline. Under a straight-line method, an annual depreciation rate is computed as an equal percentage for each year of the asset's life. When the life is 50 years, the rate is 2 percent per year, totaling 100 percent over 50 years. Thus, 2 percent would be added to the 10 percent return on investment to provide a 12 percent capitalization rate. That rate is divided into the estimated building income to derive an estimate of building value.

Annuity. An annuity method is useful when the income is projected to be level annually for a finite life. The appraiser determines the capital recovery rate at the sinking fund factor at the investment's rate of return. At 10 percent return on investment for 50 years, this factor is 0.000859, offering a total capitalization rate of 0.100859 (0.10 + 0.000859).

Sinking Fund at Safe Rate. The sinking fund factor at a safe rate is used when reinvestment assumptions are conservative. The 5 percent sinking fund factor for 50 years is 0.004777. This provides a capitalization rate of 0.104777 (0.10 + 0.004777) when given a 10 percent rate of return on investment.

BAND OF INVESTMENT

Net operating income from real estate is typically divided between mortgage lenders and equity investors. Rates of return can be weighted by the portions of purchase capital contributed, to result in a rate of return applicable to the entire property. This method is called the *band of investment*. The yield or interest or discount rate is then used to capitalize all of the NOI into one lump-sum property value. This value would assume that a capital recovery provision is unnecessary since neither amortization nor recovery of equity invested is considered.

For example, suppose that lenders typically contribute 75 percent of the required purchase capital and seek an 8 percent rate of return on investment. Equity investors want a 12 percent rate of return on investment. The yield or discount rate for the entire property would be 9 percent, as shown in Table 15-11 on the next page. This rate consists purely of interest and as-

Table 15-11.
RATES OF RETURN FOR A MORTGAGED PROPERTY

Source of Funds	Portion of Purchase Capital		Rate of Return on Investment		Weighted Rate
Mortgage	0.75	×	0.08	=	0.06
Equity	0.25	×	0.12	=	0.03
Yield or discount rate for entire property					0.09

sumes no principal retirement of the loan and no capital appreciation or depreciation of the equity investment. Further, all of the NOI is paid each year to each investor, mortgage and equity. Repayment of all purchase capital will be made upon a resale of the property at an indefinite time in the future.

GROSS INCOME MULTIPLIERS

In the case of multipliers, gross rent (income) estimates are frequently used by investors. The estimated annual gross income is multiplied by a factor that has been derived as an accurate representation of market behavior for that type of property. A monthly gross income multiplier is typically used for residential housing, whereas annual multipliers are used for other types of property.

Ease of computation makes a rent multiplier a deceptively attractive technique. For appropriate application, however, everything about the subject being appraised and the comparables used must be alike, including the lease terms, tenant strength, operating expenses, and physical setting. The rent multiplier is, at best, a crude measuring device.

RESIDUAL TECHNIQUES

Residual techniques can be applied to income-producing property. The term *residual* implies that, after income requirements are satisfied for the known parts of the property, the residual, or remaining, income is processed into an indication of value for the unknown part. The three most commonly used types are (1) land, (2) building, and (3) equity residual techniques.

Land Residual Technique

The land residual technique is useful when improvements are relatively new or have not yet been built. Their values (or proposed costs) can be closely approximated, as can their estimated useful lives. For example, suppose recently constructed real estate improvements cost $1 million and have a 50-year economic useful life. The appropriate rate of return on investment is 10 percent because that rate is competitive with other investment opportunities perceived to have equal risk. Straight-line capital recovery is considered appropriate for the improvements. The annual recovery rate is 2 percent (100 percent ÷ 50 years = 2 percent per year), so the total required rate of return for the improvements is 12 percent. Annual net operating income for the first year is estimated to be $150,000. The improvements require a 12 percent return on $1 million of cost, which equals $120,000 of income. Subtracting this amount from the $150,000 net operating income leaves a $30,000 residual for the land. This amount, capitalized in perpetuity at 10 percent, offers a land value of $300,000. Capitalization of land income in perpetuity is appropriate because land is thought to last forever. This technique is summarized in Table 15-12.

The land residual technique is used also in estimating the highest and best use of land. Costs of different proposed improvements can be estimated, as can the net operating income for each type of improvement. A capitalization rate is multiplied by the estimated improvement cost, and the result subtracted from forecast net operating income. The result is forecast land income. Whichever type or level of improvement offers the highest

Table 15-12.
LAND RESIDUAL TECHNIQUE—STRAIGHT-LINE CAPITAL RECOVERY FOR BUILDINGS

Net operating income (first year)	$150,000
Less: Income attributable to improvements:	
10% (on) + 2% (of) = 12%; 0.12 × $1,000,000	− 120,000
Residual income to land	$30,000
Capitalized at 10% return on investment in perpetuity	$300,000

The total property value is then estimated at $1.3 million
($1 million for improvements plus $300,000 for land).

residual income to land is the highest and best use of the land, subject to legal and physical constraints.

Building Residual Technique

The building residual technique works in reverse of the land residual technique. When the land value can be estimated with a high degree of confidence (as when there are many recent sales of comparables), income attributable to the land is subtracted from net operating income. The residual income is attributable to the improvements and can be capitalized to estimate their value. Then the capitalized value of the improvements is added to the land value to obtain a total property value estimate.

As an example of the building residual technique, suppose that the land value is estimated at $200,000 through a careful analysis of several recent sales of comparable vacant tracts of land. A 10% discount rate is considered appropriate. Of the estimated $150,000 of annual NOI, $20,000 is attributable to the land. Capital recovery for land income is unnecessary since the land will last forever. The $130,000 balance of NOI is attributable to the improvements, which would be worth $1,083,333 using a straight-line capital recovery rate and 50-year life. The building residual technique is summarized in Table 15-13.

Table 15-13.
BUILDING RESIDUAL TECHNIQUE

Net operating income	$150,000
Less: Income to land: 10% of $200,000	− 20,000
Income to improvements	$130,000
Improvement value at straight-line capital	
recovery: (over 50 years) $130,000 ÷ 0.12	$1,083,333

Equity Residual Technique

The equity residual technique is an effort to estimate the value of the property when the mortgage amount and terms are known. Net operating income is calculated as in other techniques, and debt service is subtracted to result in cash flow. The cash flow is capitalized at an appropriate equity dividend rate to obtain equity value, which is added to the mortgage principal to provide a value estimate.

OWNER'S CASH FLOW FROM OPERATIONS

In this technique, net operating income is forecast for a number of years to some period in the future when a property sale is expected to occur. The cash flows from operations and resale are discounted by an appropriate discount rate, then totaled to offer a property value estimate.

ADJUSTMENTS TO CAPITALIZATION RATES

Depending on lease and market information, net operating income may be forecast to be level, to grow, or to decline. An appraiser must use known information and provide market evidence for the projections.

Financial results from real estate depend on lease terms and economic conditions. If the tenant's credit is triple A and the lease is long term at a fixed net rental rate, income should be assured. If the tenant's credit rating is not high, or the lease is not net or its term is short, value will depend on such factors as inflation, competition, interest rates, and economic conditions.

Current values may be strongly affected by expectations of future resale prices. An appraiser must therefore consider resale expectations when selecting a capitalization rate. This "cap rate" is raised when value decline is expected in the future, lowered when appreciation is anticipated.

ESTIMATING RESALE PRICE

Reversion

It is sometimes helpful to estimate a resale price based on expectations for the future. The resale price, less selling costs and outstanding debts, has a present value that, added to the present value of net operating income for each year, may be used to estimate today's value. The estimated resale price is diminished by selling expenses, including commissions and legal expenses, to result in proceeds from sale. Table 15-14 shows how a $1,000,000 resale price is diminished by transaction costs.

Table 15-14.
RESALE PRICE DIMINISHED BY TRANSACTION COSTS

Resale price		**$1,000,000**
Less seller's estimated expenses of sale:		
Title insurance policy	$ 3,000	
Attorney's fees	4,500	
Release of lien	200	
Survey of property	600	
Escrow fees	500	
Recording fees	200	
Broker's professional service fee (commission)	40,000	
Subtotal		− 49,000
Estimated receipts to seller		**$951,000**

Other Methods of Resale Price Estimation

The resale price can be estimated in several other ways. First, today's market value with a percentage annual growth or depreciation rate is applied. This method assumes that future values are related to today's value, often adjusted by expected inflation. Second, income forecast for the year after the sale is capitalized to obtain a resale price. Third, the sales price of encumbered property may be the cash flow after debt service, capitalized at an equity dividend rate, and added to the mortgage balance.

MEASURING RATE OF CASH FLOW

Cash flow is usually defined as the amount left after debt service. The rate of cash flow can be derived in two ways: dividend and yield.

EQUITY DIVIDEND RATE

The *equity dividend rate* (also called *cash-on-cash return*) is cash flow divided by the equity paid for the property. The result is a measure of cash return on investment. When cash flow can be measured accurately, it may be divided by a market-derived equity dividend rate to obtain the equity value. Equity value, plus mortgage balance, offers a property value estimate.

DEBT COVERAGE RATIO

The *debt coverage ratio* indicates a lender's margin of safety. It is computed by dividing net operating income by debt service. Lenders typically want a ratio ranging from at least 1.1 for the safest property, secured by a net lease from a tenant with triple A credit, up to 1.2 to 1.5 for apartments or office buildings and a minimum of 2.0 for recreational property.

DISCOUNTED CASH FLOW (YIELD) CAPITALIZATION

By contrast to first-year capitalization techniques, yield capitalization rates employ compound interest/present value factors. These rates are typically found in six-function compound interest tables, described on page 257, which offer a precise value for periodic cash flow and reversion based on a specific rate of return on investment.

DISCOUNTED CASH FLOW APPLICATION

Discounted cash flow capitalization is best applied when income from the property and a resale price can be forecast with reasonable certainty. This requires income forecasts of rents, operating expenses, and tenant improvements, as previously discussed.

The key to discounted cash flow is the *discounting process*, which is based on the fact that money to be received at some time in the future is worth *less* than money received today. The value that we assign to such *future incomes* is called *present value*, or *present discounted value*. Exactly what the present value of a future income is will depend on the answers to two questions: (1) when will the income accrue and (2) what is the *discount rate*? The discount rate is a rate of return, similar to an interest rate, that measures the risk and time value of the income to be received. How a discount rate is arrived at is discussed below, but there are a couple of basic rules that are useful: (1) the longer we have to wait for a future income, the less it is worth to us *today* (i.e., the lower is its present value), and (2) the higher the discount rate applied to a future income, the lower its present value (and vice-versa).

Appraisers value an income property by examining the net income that the property can be expected to provide in the future, and then finding a present value for that income. This can be done fairly easily using six-function tables or a financial calculator. However, most states don't allow applicants for licenses to use financial calculators (not yet, anyway), so we will take a brief look at the math involved.

Essentially, we derive a present value for each part of the future income stream, and then add all the values. For example, suppose we are appraising a property that will produce a net income of $10,000 per year for 5 years; at the end of 5 years it can be sold for $50,000. (This one-time income at the end of the holding period, either sale price or salvage value, is called a *reversion* by real estate appraisers.) Let's assume that we're using a discount rate of 12 percent. This means that we need a return of 12 percent a year (compounded) for this investment. To simplify, let's assume also that the incomes accrue at the *end* of each year. Then our income stream will be $10,000 a year for 4 years, with a fifth-year income of $10,000 *plus* the sale proceeds of $50,000, for a total fifth-year income of $60,000. Our income stream looks like the column below headed "Income."

Time	Income	Factor		Present Value
Year 1	$10,000	$1/1.12$	$= 0.892857$	$ 8,928.57
Year 2	$10,000	$1/(1.12)^2$	$= 0.797194$	7,971.94
Year 3	$10,000	$1/(1.12)^3$	$= 0.711780$	7,117.80
Year 4	$10,000	$1/(1.12)^4$	$= 0.635518$	6,355.18
Year 5	$60,000	$1/(1.12)^5$	$= 0.567427$	34,045.61
	Present value total			**$64,419.10**

We arrived at a present value of about $64,400. What we're saying, with this number, is that a future income of $10,000 a year for 5 years, plus a reversion of $50,000 at the end of 5 years, when discounted at 12 percent a year, is worth about $64,400 *today*. In other words, $64,400 invested today, at 12 percent annual return, will yield the income we project for the property.

How exactly did we do this? Let's look at the first year's income of $10,000. We don't get it for a year, but we have to pay for it *now*. Basically, we ask, "How much money, invested today, will grow to $10,000 in 1 year, given a 12 percent annual return?" This first year's income, then, will have a present value of $10,000/1.12 because we are looking for an amount that, once it has earned a 12 percent return, will *become* $10,000. What we did in the table was to figure out the *factor* for 12 percent for 1 year, which is the decimal equivalent of 1/1.12, and then multiply it by $10,000. The advantage of this method is that, once we figure out what 1/1.12 is, we can use that number to get the present value of *any* amount to be received 1 year from now at a rate of 12 percent.

For the 12 percent *factors* for periods beyond 1 year, we just divide by 1.12 *again* for *each* year longer that we have to wait for the income. For the present value of the second year's income, we multiply $10,000 by 1/1.12 *twice* (once for each year): $10,000 × 1/1.12 × 1/1.12, which is the same as $10,000 × 1/(1.12)^2. For the third year we use 1/(1.12)^3, and so on. Once we've figured out the present value of each of the five annual incomes, we just add them. You can check these numbers out yourself. For each year's income, start with the present value. Multiply it by 1.12; do this for each year that you have to wait, and you should end up with $10,000 for each of the first 4 years, and $60,000 for the fifth year.

Yield Rate Selection

An appraiser can attempt to construct a yield rate using the *buildup method,* by identifying the components of a required rate of return. Although there is general agreement in identifying the components (see below), the proportion of each component in the overall rate is arbitrary. Furthermore, the buildup is unnecessary because an investor acquires the entire property, which provides one rate. Although the buildup method is theoretical, it helps us to understand capitalization rates and to compare them with non-real estate investments.

To construct a built-up rate, begin with a liquid, risk-free rate, such as the rate on passbook accounts offered by financial institutions whose depositors' accounts are insured by a U.S. government agency. The rate is the minimum that must be paid as compensation for the time value of money.

Add to this risk-free rate a provision for the risk associated with the specific type of real estate being appraised. For example, risk is low where there is a strong tenant with captive customers, but high for property leased to weak tenants who have fickle customers.

Provisions must be made for illiquidity. *Liquidity* is a measure of how quickly an asset can be converted into cash. Compared to stocks and bonds, real estate is illiquid, particularly in a weak market or tight-money economy.

The burden of investment management must also be included. This is the decision making required of the investor and is distinguished from the everyday process of property management.

The components of the build-up method and their proportions in the overall built-up rate are summarized as follows:

Risk-free rate	5%
Risk of subject property	3%
Illiquidity of subject property	2%
Investment management	1%
Rate of return on investment	11%

Selecting the appropriate yield rate depends on numerous factors, especially the availability of accurate market data. An appraiser must consider the duration, quality, and amount of income from the property forecast for each future year. Other relevant factors include the earnings or yield rate required by the market and the portion of investment that is subject to capital recovery.

Ratio capitalization requires a realistic estimate of net operating income, which is divided by a supportable capitalization rate. The mathematical composition of the cap rate is derived from the market, tempered by property performance expectations.

Valuation of Partial Interests

The certified general appraiser is expected to have an extensive knowledge of partial interests in real estate. These include interests in a lease, lease provisions, and the identification of the various ownership positions within a property having different risk features.

LEASE INTERESTS

A *subleasehold* may be carved out of a lease interest. A subleasehold is the interest of the tenant's tenant; that is, a tenant may sublease his property, becoming a landlord to another tenant. The subtenant's interest may be valuable.

Renewal options in a lease give the tenant the right, but not the obligation, to extend the lease at whatever rent and terms are described in the option. This encumbrance can affect the value of the property either positively or negatively.

Tenant improvements must be analyzed to determine how they affect the property value. Are they to remain after the lease expires? Would a substitute tenant find them useful and pay a premium for them, or would they be expensive to demolish on demand?

Concessions granted in the market or by the property to attract tenants must be assessed. For example, suppose an office building rents for $25 per square foot on a 5-year lease, with the first year free. The property is appraised in the second year of the lease. Is the correct rent $25/per square foot or much less? How much rent can be capitalized? The appraiser needs to understand the market.

LEASE PROVISIONS

Net versus Gross Leases

A lease is typically referred to as *net* or *gross,* although most leases are neither absolutely net nor absolutely gross. In an absolute net lease the tenant (lessee) pays taxes, insurance, and operating expenses: maintenance, including repairs, alterations, replacements, and improvements, ordinary or extraordinary repairs whether interior or exterior, and so on. A net lease is the most straightforward approach for a single-tenant structure. The terms *triple-net* and *net-net-net* lease are often used to indicate a greater degree of net-ness than that for other leases. As to specific taxes, tenants pay taxes, special assessments, and the like; however, tenants do not pay obligations of the landlord (lessor), such as gift, income, inheritance, franchise, or corporate taxes, or a tax on the rental receipts of the landlord.

The real estate owner is a passive investor when a net lease is used, relying on net rent to provide a return on investment. The property is the owner's investment, not a business.

With a gross lease the landlord pays all operating expenses. The owner must become a businessperson, keeping firm control over operating expenses and assuring that money spent to comply with the lease is spent prudently.

With a *stop* (or *escalation*) clause in a gross lease, the landlord pays a base-year amount for the expense and the tenant pays the increase in expense each year. A net lease or stop clauses reduce the need for frequent rent adjustments, cost of living indexes, or short-term leases.

Operating Expenses

A properly written lease should specify whether landlord or tenant pays for each operating expense. It should also specify that the responsible party must present proof of payment, such as a paid property tax bill or insurance policy in conformity with requirements of the lease, to provide assurance of protection from risks covered by the lease. If the lessee in a net lease does not supply the information, the lessor should request it.

PERCENTAGE LEASES

A *percentage lease,* commonly used for a retail tenant, provides incentive to the landlord to make the property attractive and thus encourage retail sales. The landlord must be prepared to audit the tenant's retail sales records and to enforce provisions of the lease that protect the lessor's rights to a percentage of sales.

Most percentage leases require a fixed *minimum base rent* plus a percentage rent based on gross sales in excess of a certain amount. The base rent is often set as an anticipated average amount of sales per square foot for the particular type of business. For example, suppose industry norms for a ladies' fashion shop indicate that sales of $200 per square foot (SF) are typical. Rent for a 10,000-SF shop could be $100,000 per year plus 5 percent of sales above $2 million (10,000 SF × $200 typical sales = $2,000,000). Percentage rents would be imposed only when sales exceed the norm of $200/SF of floor area.

Different types of businesses have different typical percentage rents. For example, a jewelry store or other retailer selling luxury items tends to be relatively small, and has a high markup and low inventory turnover in comparison to a grocery or discount store. The percentage rental rate thus tends to be higher for the luxury or specialty store.

Certain lease provisions are necessary to assure fairness to both parties in administering a percentage lease. Monthly or annual sales reports may be required; and the landlord may have the right to hire an auditor, whose fee will be paid by the tenant if sales are understated or by the landlord if no discrepancies are found.

COST OF LIVING INDEX

Leases for multiple years without rent adjustments result in hardships to landlord or tenant during highly inflationary or deflationary periods. A long-term lease may have a *cost of living adjustment* that calls for changes in rent based on the change in some published index.

The index used and the frequency and amount of adjustment are negotiable. The Consumer Price Index (CPI), published by the Bureau of Labor Statistics of the U. S. Department of Labor, is usually chosen because of its frequency of computation and publication. A lesser known local index tied to rental rates, operating expenses, or real estate values may be satisfactory but can introduce elements of instability or potential manipulation, possibly resulting in litigation.

The adjustment period may be a single year or a multiple of years. This period should be short for a gross lease but may be longer for a net lease. With a net lease the landlord has less financial exposure to the risk of inflation because the tenant pays operating expenses.

The degree of adjustment may be only part of the full change in the index selected. For example, if 50 percent of the index was selected as the multiplier and the index rose by 20 percent, rent would increase by 10 percent. This provides some protection to the landlord (who perhaps bought the property with preinflation dollars) but does not inflict the full effect of inflation on the tenant.

EXCESS RENT

Excess rent is the difference between contract and market rents; the term implies that the tenant is paying more than would be paid for comparable property. If a property has several leases, the appraiser should prepare a schedule with the expiration date of each lease to assist in estimating the quality and duration of the income stream.

VALUATION CONSIDERATIONS

A property may have been fractionated, that is, split into different interests. For example, there may be two mortgages and/or a land lease. The appraiser needs to determine the volatility of income, the priorities of cash distributions, and the risks and rewards for each interest. In doing so, the value to each party having a fractional interest can be estimated by the appraiser.

Summary

The certified general appraiser is expected to have knowledge of income property valuation techniques and an understanding of their applications to specialized properties and interests that are beyond the expectations for a residential appraiser, broker, or salesperson.

Questions on Chapter 15

1. The fact that rents tend to be set by the market for equally desirable space reflects the principle of
    (A) balance
    (B) substitution
    (C) externalities
    (D) supply and demand
    (E) conformity

2. The net income that remains after the proper costs of labor, capital, and entrepreneurship have been paid is
    (A) surplus rent
    (B) opportunity cost
    (C) effective income
    (D) land rent
    (E) contract rent

3. All of the following are essential to the viability of an industrial district *except*
    (A) labor
    (B) materials
    (C) transportation
    (D) high technology
    (E) entrepreneurship

4. The present and future demand for a property and its absorption rate are considered in a
    (A) valuation report
    (B) market feasibility study
    (C) market segmentation study
    (D) highest and best use analysis
    (E) narrative appraisal

5. Real estate markets
    (A) are national in scope
    (B) do not meet the criteria for a perfect market
    (C) are centralized in nature
    (D) consist of used property only
    (E) are prevalent in former Communist countries

6. The federal discount rate, which is the interest rate that banks pay on the funds they borrow from the Federal Reserve, is most closely linked to
    (A) the inflation rate
    (B) the prime rate
    (C) long-term yield rates
    (D) interest rates on 30-year bonds
    (E) municipal bond rates

7. Credit-regulating devices used by the Federal Reserve include
   (A) moral suasion
   (B) reserve requirements
   (C) the federal discount rate
   (D) the Federal Open Market Committee
   (E) all of the above

8. Monetary policy helps control inflation by
   (A) regulating the money supply
   (B) encouraging rent control
   (C) reducing taxes
   (D) refusing to balance the budget
   (E) using a noncalendar year

9. The secondary mortgage market is where
   (A) mortgage bankers originate mortgage loans
   (B) second mortgages are originated
   (C) existing mortgages are bought and sold
   (D) the FNMA and GNMA make mortgage loans
   (E) the RTC searches for buyers of savings and loan associations

10. When inflation is expected to be high, investors tend to avoid
    (A) equity investments
    (B) long-term fixed-income investments
    (C) short-term investments
    (D) money market instruments
    (E) tangibles

11. Mortgage financing affects
    (A) equity dividends from real estate
    (B) equity yields from real estate
    (C) monetary policy
    (D) fiscal policy
    (E) both A and B

Questions 12–14 are based on the following information:
A $1,500,000 loan is issued with 5 discount points. The loan bears an 8% interest rate and has a 9% mortgage constant, with annual payments.

12. The original annual payment was
    (A) less than $120,000
    (B) $120,000
    (C) $135,000
    (D) more than $150,000
    (E) none of the above

13. The annual mortgage constant is
    (A) 8%
    (B) 8.25%
    (C) 9%
    (D) 9.75%
    (E) above 9.75%

14. What is the amount of the loan discount?
    (A) Less than $75,000
    (B) $75,000
    (C) $100,000
    (D) $150,000
    (E) More than $150,000

15. Which of the following is a valuation study?
    (A) Market value appraisal
    (B) Market and marketability study
    (C) Absorption analysis
    (D) Feasibility study
    (E) Technical impact study

16. Generally, the *least* reliable sources of sales data are
    (A) bankers
    (B) appraisers
    (C) newspaper articles
    (D) brokers
    (E) sellers

17. Operating income data do *not* include
    (A) vacancy rate
    (B) reproduction cost
    (C) operating expenses
    (D) utilities provided by the owner
    (E) lease terms

18. Industrial buildings are typically measured in terms of
    (A) gross living area
    (B) gross building area
    (C) net leasable area
    (D) gross rentable area
    (E) interior area

19. The appropriate time adjustment for a property is concluded to be an increase of 7% per year compounded. The time adjustment for a comparable sales property that sold for $40,000 two years ago is
    (A) −$5,796
    (B) −$5,600
    (C) −$2,800
    (D) +$5,600
    (E) +$5,796

20. How much must be deposited today, in a bank that pays 10% rate of interest with annual compounding, in order to realize $10,000 in 4 years?
    (A) $40,000
    (B) $9,077
    (C) $6,830
    (D) $4,000
    (E) $2,500

21. Ms. Brown has just paid $5 for a purchase option on some land. The option gives her the right to buy the property for $10,000 at the end of 2 years. The $5 paid for the option will not be applied to the purchase price. How much must Ms. Brown put aside today, in a bank that pays a 10% rate of interest with monthly compounding, to achieve a balance of $10,000 in 2 years?
    - (A) $12,100
    - (B) $10,000
    - (C) $8,194
    - (D) $6,720
    - (E) $5,000

22. A sample of 100 residences had an average square footage of 1500 with a standard deviation of 120 and normal distribution. This means that
    - (A) about 2 out of 3 have between 1380 and 1620 sq. ft.
    - (B) about 9 out of 10 have between 1380 and 1620 sq. ft.
    - (C) almost every home has between 1140 and 1560 sq. ft.
    - (D) almost every home has between 1380 and 1620 sq. ft.
    - (E) none of the 100 homes has any standard construction defect

23. In problem 22, two standard deviations would be
    - (A) 50 homes
    - (B) 1500 sq. ft.
    - (C) 240 sq. ft.
    - (D) 67% of all homes
    - (E) none of the above

Questions 24–28 are based on the following information:
Eleven recent sales of rental income property provided the following data:

Sale Number	Sales Price	Gross Monthly Rent
1	$162,000	$1,500
2	$184,000	$1,600
3	$152,000	$1,440
4	$160,000	$1,470
5	$183,000	$1,590
6	$134,000	$1,400
7	$144,000	$1,350
8	$176,000	$1,560
9	$132,000	$1,350
10	$183,800	$1,650
11	$153,000	$1,380

24. The range of gross rent multipliers is
    - (A) 675 to 825
    - (B) 66,000 to 92,000
    - (C) 95.7 to 115.8
    - (D) 150
    - (E) none of the above

25. The mean monthly rental is
    - (A) $1,350
    - (B) $1,400
    - (C) $1,470
    - (D) $1,480
    - (E) none of the above

26. The median monthly rental is
    (A) $1,350
    (B) $1,400
    (C) $1,470
    (D) $1,480
    (E) none of the above

27. The mode of the monthly rentals is
    (A) $1,350
    (B) $1,400
    (C) $1,470
    (D) $1,480
    (E) none of the above

28. The best estimate of the gross rent multiplier is
    (A) 92
    (B) 100
    (C) 108
    (D) 116
    (E) none of the above

29. In the sequence of adjustments in the sales adjustment process, the item adjusted for first should usually be
    (A) location
    (B) terms of financing
    (C) size
    (D) time
    (E) It makes no difference which is first.

30. The land development method in appraisal is used to estimate the value of vacant acreage that is ready to be subdivided. This method requires
    (A) study of current sales of subdivided lots
    (B) projection of land development costs
    (C) RTC approval
    (D) both A and B
    (E) none of the above

Questions 31–36 are based on the following information:
You are appraising a 20-acre tract of unimproved land. The site is zoned for single-family residential use. All utilities are available along the street on which the land fronts. From the engineers who will plat the proposed subdivision, your learn that 20% of the land area will be used for streets and sidewalks. You find that zoning will permit four lots per acre of net developable land after deducting streets. Research indicates that lots similar to those that will be available on the subject land sell for $18,000 and that the entire tract can be developed and sold in 1 year. You find that 40% of the sale price of each lot must be allocated to selling costs, overhead, contingencies, carrying cost, and developer's profit. Finally, your research discloses that 2,000 feet of streets (including water, storm sewer, and sanitary sewer lines) must be installed at a cost of $80 per foot.

31. How many lots can be developed?
    (A) 20
    (B) 64
    (C) 80
    (D) 88
    (E) 16

32. What is the gross sales price from the sale of all lots?
    (A) $288,000
    (B) $360,000
    (C) $1,152,000
    (D) $1,440,000
    (E) $1,584,000

33. What is the cost of installing streets and water and sewer lines?
    (A) $16,000
    (B) $32,000
    (C) $64,000
    (D) $160,000
    (E) none of the above

34. What is the total of selling cost, overhead, contingencies, carrying costs, and developer's profit?
    (A) $144,000
    (B) $460,800
    (C) $576,000
    (D) $633,600
    (E) none of the above

35. What is the total cost of development and overhead, including developer's profit?
    (A) $304,000
    (B) $320,000
    (C) $620,800
    (D) $733,600
    (E) none of the above

36. What is the developer's potential profit on the 20-acre tract?
    (A) less than $160,000
    (B) $160,000
    (C) $531,200
    (D) $1,152,000
    (E) $1,440,000

37. When there is a dearth of recent land sales data, which technique may the appraiser use to estimate land value?
    (A) Land residual
    (B) Property residual
    (C) Building residual
    (D) Mortgage residual
    (E) Property reversion

38. The annual net operating income from an apartment house is $22,000. With a capitalization rate of 11%, the indicated market value is
    (A) $2,420
    (B) $126,000
    (C) $176,000
    (D) $200,000
    (E) $242,000

39. A small office building sold for $1,200,000. The monthly net operating income is $13,000 per month. What was the overall capitalization rate?
    (A) 1.08%
    (B) 9.2%
    (C) 10.8%
    (D) 12%
    (E) 13%

40. For which of the following would the lowest ratio of operating expenses to gross income be incurred by the landlord?
    (A) Resort hotel
    (B) Net-leased retail store
    (C) Office building
    (D) Apartment building
    (E) Nursing home for the elderly

41. The band-of-investment technique is most useful when equity investors are primarily concerned with
    (A) land appreciation rates
    (B) building tax shelters
    (C) gross rent multipliers
    (D) equity capitalization rates
    (E) noise abatement

42. Which of the following is the preferred method of deriving a capitalization rate?
    (A) Summation
    (B) Band of investment
    (C) Direct comparison
    (D) Bank of investment
    (E) Monetary policy

43. Capitalization is employed in the
    (A) cost approach
    (B) direct sales comparison approach
    (C) income approach for income properties
    (D) income approach for residential properties
    (E) none of the above

44. Capitalization is the process whereby
    (A) income is converted to an indication of value
    (B) syndicates are formed
    (C) an asset is removed from accounting records
    (D) both A and B
    (E) none of the above

45. The operating expense ratio for income property is typically
    (A) between 4 and 10
    (B) under 100%
    (C) under 10%
    (D) under 2%
    (E) more than 10

46. In determining income and expenses, the first step is
    (A) a lease and rent analysis
    (B) an effective gross income estimate
    (C) an operating expense estimate
    (D) a reconstructed operating statement
    (E) a market analysis

47. A forecast using discounted cash flow analysis would include
    (A) income, vacancy, and operating expenses
    (B) an economic analysis
    (C) reversion at the end of the holding period
    (D) discounting expected future cash flows to a present value
    (E) all of the above

48. If the overall capitalization rate for income property were to increase while estimated net operating income remained the same, the resulting value estimate would
    (A) increase
    (B) decrease
    (C) remain the same
    (D) any of the above could occur
    (E) none of the above would occur

49. Estimated income property values will decline as a result of
    (A) increased net cash flows
    (B) lower capitalization rates
    (C) lower vacancy rates
    (D) increased discount rates
    (E) higher standard of living

50. *Income capitalization* is the term used to describe the process of estimating the value of income property by studying expected future income. This process
    (A) converts the net operating income of a property into its equivalent capital value
    (B) reflects the time value of money by reducing or discounting future income to its present worth
    (C) focuses on the present worth of future benefits
    (D) uses market interest rates
    (E) all of the above

51. When estimating the value of an income-producing property, the appraiser will *not* consider
    (A) income taxes attributable to the property
    (B) the remaining economic life of the property
    (C) potential future income
    (D) net operating income
    (E) expected future income patterns

52. In income capitalization, value is measured as the present worth of the
    (A) forecast reversion with a growth factor
    (B) forecast cash flow capitalized in perpetuity
    (C) forecast effective gross income (EGI) plus the reversion
    (D) forecast net operating income plus the reversion
    (E) cost of production

53. Income capitalization techniques are typically *not* used in valuing
    (A) retail properties
    (B) apartment buildings
    (C) office buildings
    (D) motels
    (E) single-family residences

54. The lump sum that an investor receives upon resale of an investment is called
    (A) net income
    (B) gross income
    (C) equity dividend
    (D) reversion
    (E) residual

55. The most commonly used capitalization rate is the
    (A) income rate
    (B) composite capitalization rate
    (C) interest rate
    (D) overall rate
    (E) underall rate

56. An ordinary annuity is
    (A) level in amount and timing
    (B) different from a variable annuity
    (C) received at the end of each period
    (D) a stream of income
    (E) all of the above

57. The procedure used to convert expected future benefits into present value is
    (A) residual analysis
    (B) capitalization
    (C) market capitalization
    (D) equity capitalization
    (E) compounding

58. A reconstructed operating statement for an owner-operated property should include
    (A) income tax
    (B) book depreciation
    (C) management charges
    (D) wages earned outside the property
    (E) imputed interest

59. *Yield* is defined as
    (A) overall capitalization
    (B) stopping to review work
    (C) letting another speak first
    (D) rate of return on investment
    (E) rate of return of investment

60. Which of the following is a specific expense item rather than a category?
    (A) Replacement reserve
    (B) Property taxes
    (C) Operating expenses
    (D) Fixed charges or expenses
    (E) Variable expenses

61. In yield capitalization, investor assumptions are
    (A) accrued
    (B) critiqued
    (C) regulated
    (D) questioned
    (E) simulated

62. The basic formula for property valuation via income capitalization is
    (A) $V = IR$
    (B) $V = I/R$
    (C) $V = R/I$
    (D) $V = SP/GR$
    (E) $V = I/F$

63. All of the following consider the time value of money *except*
    (A) net present value
    (B) discounted cash flow
    (C) internal rate of return
    (D) payback period
    (E) compound interest

64. A rent survey of apartment buildings reveals that one-bedroom units have a considerably higher occupancy factor than two-bedroom units. If the subject property contains only two-bedroom units, the appraisal should probably project
    (A) an average of the vacancy factors for all units surveyed
    (B) a higher vacancy factor than was found for one-bedroom units
    (C) a lower vacancy factor than was found for one-bedroom units
    (D) the same vacancy factor as was found for one-bedroom units
    (E) Projection from the information provided is impossible.

65. The quality of a forecast future income stream is indicated by its
    (A) amount
    (B) length
    (C) timing
    (D) mortgage
    (E) risk

66. The total anticipated revenue from income property operations after vacancy and collection losses are deducted is
    (A) net operating income
    (B) before-tax cash flow
    (C) effective gross income
    (D) potential gross income
    (E) property residual income

67. Which of the following is used in direct capitalization?
    (A) Internal rate of return
    (B) Overall capitalization rate
    (C) Building capitalization rate
    (D) Mortgage capitalization rate
    (E) Equity yield rate

68. Which of the following statements is true?
    (A) If the overall yield on the property is less than the mortgage rate, favorable leverage occurs.
    (B) When negative leverage occurs, the owner receives a cash yield on the property that is greater than if the property were not financed.
    (C) If the overall property yield equals the mortgage rate, the owner receives an additional yield on his investment by trading on the equity.
    (D) Financing the property at higher rates of interest than the overall rate may not be beneficial to the owner in terms of yield on the equity investment.
    (E) When a property generates cash flow, its owner pays tax on the money received.

69. Which of the following statements is true?
    (A) An investor usually considers the return from a property in the light of the risk being assumed.
    (B) An investor who assumes higher risk usually expects lower investment yield.
    (C) Higher-risk investments are generally associated with lower investment returns.
    (D) To maximize the overall risk position, the investor may wish to diversify real and/or personal property investments.
    (E) The lowest-risk investment is real estate.

70. *Capitalization rate* is
    (A) the annual rent divided by the purchase price
    (B) annual income and all gains or losses prorated to an effective annual amount—an internal rate of return
    (C) the percentage or decimal rate that, when divided into a periodic income amount, offers a lump-sum capital value for the income
    (D) unchanging with time
    (E) none of the above

Questions 71–75 are based on the following information:
    A $12 million office building is purchased with an 80% loan-to-value ratio mortgage, payable over 30 years at 11% interest with monthly payments of $91,423. At 100% occupancy, rents would be $2 million. The vacancy trend in the area is 2.5%. Operating expenses amount to $650,000, including $50,000 placed in a replacement reserve. The land is considered to be worth $2 million.

71. What ratio, expressed as a percentage, is between 80 and 85?
    (A) Improvement
    (B) Overall rate
    (C) Mortgage constant
    (D) Vacancy
    (E) Operating expense

72. What ratio, expressed as a percentage, is between 10 and 11?
    (A) Improvement
    (B) Overall rate
    (C) Mortgage constant
    (D) Vacancy
    (E) Operating expense

73. What ratio, expressed as a percentage, is between 11 and 12?
    (A) Improvement
    (B) Overall rate
    (C) Mortgage constant
    (D) Vacancy
    (E) Operating expense

74. What ratio, expressed as a percentage, is between 30 and 40?
    (A) Improvement
    (B) Overall rate
    (C) Mortgage constant
    (D) Vacancy
    (E) Operating expense

75. What ratio, expressed as a percentage, is between 0 and 5?
    (A) Improvement
    (B) Overall rate
    (C) Mortgage constant
    (D) Vacancy
    (E) Operating expense

76. Investors for apartments are seeking a 10% cash-on-cash return in the current market. The current interest rate on a 30-year mortgage for this type of property is 12% with monthly payments. Lenders will fund up to a 75% loan-to-value ratio. What is the overall rate of return using the band of investment technique?
    (A) 10–10.5%
    (B) 10.51–11%
    (C) 11.01–11.25%
    (D) 11.26–12%
    (E) None of the above

Questions 77–81 are based on the following information:
    A certain older office building in the heart of a downtown metropolitan area currently generates $40,000 net operating income. Income is expected to decline systematically over the estimated 10 remaining years of the building's useful life. Therefore, straight-line capital recovery (declining income to the building) is considered appropriate. The land is currently valued at $250,000, based on numerous recent sales of comparable properties. For this type of property, investors want a 10% interest (yield to maturity) rate.

77. How much of the first year's $40,000 net operating income is attributable to the land?
    (A) $15,000
    (B) $20,000
    (C) $25,000
    (D) $30,000
    (E) $40,000

78. How much of the net operating income is attributable to the building?
    (A) $15,000
    (B) $20,000
    (C) $25,000
    (D) $30,000
    (E) $40,000

79. What is the building capitalization rate, assuming straight-line capital recovery?
    (A) 5%
    (B) 10%
    (C) 15%
    (D) 20%
    (E) 25%

80. What is the value of the building, using the building residual technique?
    (A) $75,000
    (B) $100,000
    (C) $125,000
    (D) $130,000
    (E) $140,000

81. What is the combined value of the building and land?
    (A) $275,000
    (B) $300,000
    (C) $325,000
    (D) $330,000
    (E) $340,000

Questions 82–86 are based on the following information:
   A freestanding retail store is under a triple net lease for the next 25 years, with $20,000 rent payable at the end of each year. The tenant has a purchase option to buy the property at the end of the lease term for $150,000. The property is free and clear of debt. For this situation, investors seek a 12% rate of return on investment.

82. What is the present value of the rental income?
    (A) less than $100,000
    (B) $100,000 to $150,000
    (C) $150,000 to $175,000
    (D) $175,000 to $200,000
    (E) $200,000 to $250,000

83. On the assumption that the tenant will exercise her purchase option, what is the present value of the reversion?
    (A) less than $10,000
    (B) $10,000 to $20,000
    (C) $20,000 to $100,000
    (D) $100,000 to $150,000
    (E) more than $150,000

84. What is the present value of the property?
    (A) less than $100,000
    (B) $100,000 to $150,000
    (C) $150,000 to $175,000
    (D) $175,000 to $200,000
    (E) $200,000 to $250,000

85. What is the overall rate of return?
    (A) 10–10.5%
    (B) 10.5–11%
    (C) 11–11.25%
    (D) 11.25–11.5%
    (E) More than 11.5%

86. What is the equity dividend rate?
    (A) 10–10.5%
    (B) 10.5–11%
    (C) 11–11.25%
    (D) 11.25–12%
    (E) None of the above

87. The most common type of partial-interest appraisal involves
    (A) a leased property
    (B) a timeshare residence
    (C) a condominium
    (D) rezoning
    (E) condemnation

88. When contract rent exceeds market rent, the leasehold interest
    (A) is subleased
    (B) must be appraised
    (C) has no positive value
    (D) should be mortgaged
    (E) is the same as the leased fee

89. Lease provisions may describe all of the following *except*
    (A) rental payments and the term of use and occupancy
    (B) whether landlord or tenant pays operating expenses
    (C) rent escalations and renewal or purchase options
    (D) the credit rating of the tenant
    (E) assignment or subletting rights

90. *Overage rent* is the
    (A) actual rent over the entire lease term
    (B) percentage rent above guaranteed minimum rent
    (C) amount by which contract rent exceeds market rent
    (D) rent that is past due
    (E) rent the property could command in the open market if not subject to its lease

91. A lease normally states all of the following *except*
    (A) agreed terms of occupancy
    (B) rental payments
    (C) tenant's responsibilities and obligations
    (D) financing of the property
    (E) actions causing default

92. All of the following lease provisions are advantageous to the lessee *except*
    (A) an escape clause
    (B) a renewal option
    (C) a purchase option
    (D) an escalation clause
    (E) All of the above are advantageous.

93. Homeowners' associations are usually found in
    (A) planned unit developments (PUD)
    (B) condominiums
    (C) timeshares
    (D) both A and B
    (E) none of the above

94. If a $54,000 investment in real estate generates gross earnings of 15 percent, the gross monthly return most nearly is
    (A) $819
    (B) $705
    (C) $685
    (D) $637
    (E) $8,100

95. In arriving at an effective gross income figure, an appraiser of rental property makes a deduction for
    (A) real property taxes
    (B) repairs
    (C) vacancy
    (D) depreciation
    (E) replacement reserves

ANSWERS

1. **B**	17. **B**	33. **D**	49. **D**	65. **E**	81. **C**
2. **D**	18. **B**	34. **B**	50. **E**	66. **C**	82. **C**
3. **D**	19. **E**	35. **C**	51. **A**	67. **B**	83. **A**
4. **B**	20. **C**	36. **C**	52. **D**	68. **D**	84. **C**
5. **B**	21. **C**	37. **A**	53. **E**	69. **A**	85. **A**
6. **B**	22. **A**	38. **D**	54. **D**	70. **C**	86. **E**
7. **E**	23. **C**	39. **E**	55. **D**	71. **A**	87. **A**
8. **A**	24. **C**	40. **B**	56. **E**	72. **B**	88. **C**
9. **C**	25. **D**	41. **D**	57. **B**	73. **C**	89. **D**
10. **B**	26. **C**	42. **C**	58. **C**	74. **E**	90. **B**
11. **E**	27. **A**	43. **C**	59. **D**	75. **D**	91. **D**
12. **C**	28. **C**	44. **A**	60. **B**	76. **D**	92. **D**
13. **C**	29. **B**	45. **B**	61. **E**	77. **C**	93. **D**
14. **B**	30. **D**	46. **A**	62. **B**	78. **A**	94. **C**
15. **A**	31. **B**	47. **E**	63. **D**	79. **D**	95. **C**
16. **C**	32. **C**	48. **B**	64. **B**	80. **A**	

Chapter 16/*Taxation and Assessment of Property*

Real estate, because it is valuable and also hard to hide, has been subject to tax for nearly all of human history. Consequently, it is easy for officials to assess taxes on real estate. The property tax is an *ad valorem* tax; that is, it is based on the *value* of the thing being taxed. In effect, then, the tax bill on a large, valuable property should be more than the bill on a small, relatively low-valued one.

The property tax usually is the major source of income for city and county governments. In a sense, this may be just, because the real estate that provides the bulk of the taxes collected also benefits greatly from many of the services local government pays for with the property taxes it collects. Most important of these is fire protection, which accrues almost exclusively to real estate. Police protection and the provision and maintenance of local streets and roads also provide obvious benefits. Nearby, locally provided public amenities such as schools and parks make many kinds of real estate more valuable. The control of real estate development through zoning and building codes also tends to preserve the values of existing real estate improvements, as does the provision of planning services. In addition, local courthouses store the records that are necessary for the documentation of title to real estate.

Proposition 13

California's property tax system was entirely overhauled by Proposition 13, a measure that was passed overwhelmingly by voters on June 6, 1978. Key provisions of Prop 13 are:

1. Limits property tax to 1 percent of taxable value, plus the amount needed for payments on voter-approved indebtedness.
2. Requires that the base value of properties be figured as of their value on February 28, 1975. It allows annual increases for inflation on the base value, but increases may not exceed 2 percent each year.

    When a property is sold, the base amount rises to the sale amount, then it can increase by up to 2 percent per year. When property is improved with new construction, the value of the new portion is subject to tax at market value when built, plus 2 percent annual inflation, while the original structure maintains its 1975 base value, plus 2 percent annual inflation.
3. It prohibits state and local governments from imposing new ad valorem taxes on real estate, and from imposing transaction taxes on the sale of real estate.
4. Requires a two-thirds vote in each house of the Legislature to increase or impose state taxes, and approval of two-thirds of the electorate to increase or impose special taxes.

Several recent propositions have been added to Prop 13, which include:

*   A purchase by a spouse, or a transfer of a principal residence, plus up to $1 million of other real estate between parents and children, is not a purchase and change of ownership that triggers a tax increase.
*   Homeowners over age 55 and those who are severely disabled may transfer their ad valorem basis to another home in the same county, or possibly to a home in a different county.
*   Home improvements that enhance the usability of a home for a severely disabled person are not subject to reassessment.

Most taxable property is subject to Proposition 13, but not personal property, property owned by local government outside their borders, open-space lands, and utilities and railroads that are taxed by the State Board of Equalization.

County Tax Assessor

Each county in California has an elected county assessor who is governed by the state constitution, laws of the state, and rules of the State Board of Equalization. This person assesses all taxable property in the county (except state assessed property such as public utilities). The assessor should discover all assessable property, inventory and list it, appraise the property, and put it all on the tax roll. The assessor's responsibility is to assure that the full value of all taxable property is placed on the tax roll, so that the appropriate amount of tax is collected from each owner and in total countywide.

Taxable Property

All property is taxable in California, except that which is specifically exempt. This includes real property and personal property.

Real property includes land, mines, standing timber, and all improvements including buildings, fences, fixtures, and structures erected or affixed to the land.

Personal property includes whatever is not real property. Taxable tangible personal property includes portable machinery and equipment, office equipment, and tools. Nontaxable property includes household goods and business inventory. Intangible property is also exempt, including notes, shares of stock, insurance policies, and copyrights.

Equalization Board

The California Board of Equalization was established in 1879. Its current duties are to promote uniformity of taxation, within and among counties throughout the state to:
- Be certain that each county is taxing properly so that no county can gain an unfair share of state revenue guaranteed for funding public schools.
- Be certain that each county is taxing property at market value to gain the fullest revenues possible.
- Keep exemptions for veterans and homeowners at the amounts allowed.
- Assess public utilities and intercounty properties to provide uniformity.
- Maintain uniformity for taxing entities that operate in more than one county.

Exemptions

Certain exemptions are provided in California. Exempt property includes:
- Property owned by welfare organizations, colleges, churches, public schools, free libraries, free museums, and religious, hospital, charitable, and scientific organizations.
- $7,000 homeowner's tax exemption.
- Business inventory.
- $4,000 on veteran's property not already subject to a homeowner exemption; an exemption of up to $100,000 is allowed for a totally disabled veteran.

Assessment Process

The tax year for county-assessed property begins July 1. The lien date is March 1, four months earlier (See Table 16-1, Important California Property Tax Dates). Anyone who owns property on that date is liable for a tax up to 1 percent of the market value, plus an amount to pay for debt service on voter-approved projects. Most property will be taxed at 1 percent of its base, which could increase from 1975 by up to 2 percent per year. If there had been a change in ownership or newly constructed property, that property will be assessed at its market value. A supplemental tax roll allows newly constructed property to be added to the tax roll immediately, rather than waiting until the next March 1.

Tax Lien

On March 1, a lien is automatically placed on all assessed property for the amount of the tax. A state tax lien takes priority over all other liens except for holders of a security interest, mechanic's lien, someone who bought the property without knowledge of the lien, and a judgment lien creditor with a prior interest to the recording of the tax lien.

Tax Collection

The county tax assessor sends out bills on November 1, for payment in two installments. The first payment is due immediately and becomes delinquent on December 10. The second half is due February 1, and becomes delinquent April 10. If taxes are not paid by the delinquent date, a 10 percent penalty is added. A notice of default is published, and a penalty of 1.5 percent per month is added. The property owner can redeem the property within 5 years of the date the property became tax defaulted by paying the back taxes plus interest and penalties. After 5 years of default, the property may be sold to a taxing agency or a nonprofit agency, or sold at public auction.

The *unsecured* tax roll consists of things such as tenant-owned personal property and fixtures, office equipment and machinery. Payment is due March 1, and becomes delinquent August 31.

Taxes on the *supplemental roll* (which is used to add property constructed during the year) are due on various dates depending on when the bill is mailed. A bill is mailed between July 1 and October 31 that is payable in two equal installments and becomes delinquent on December 10 and April 10, respectively, the same dates as the regular tax roll.

Appeals Process

Property is reassessed when there is a change in ownership or new construction has been completed. The assessor may change the assessed value to recognize a reduction in value, correct an error, or to add a property that had escaped assessment. Except for changes due to annual adjustments for inflation, the assessor must notify the taxpayer of any other changes, generally on or before July 1. The property owners may appeal, generally between July 2 and September 15.

Table 16-1.
IMPORTANT CALIFORNIA PROPERTY TAX DATES

January 1.	Lien date for state-assessed properties, including public utilities, railroads, and other properties that cross county lines.
February 15.	State Board of Equalization advises county assessors on CPI percentage to be used.
March 1.	Lien date for county-assessed property.
March 15.	Legal deadline for filing most exemption claims except homeowners, veterans, disabled veterans, churches, and religious associations.
March 31.	Legal deadline for filing church and religious exemption claims.
April 15.	Legal deadline for filing homeowners', veterans', and disabled veterans' exemption claims, to get the full amount of exemption.
July 1.	Tax year begins. County assessor delivers completed assessment roll to the county auditor.
July 2 - September 15.	Taxpayers may file applications for reduction in assessed value with the clerk of the County Board of Supervisors.
August 31.	Last day to pay taxes without penalty on unsecured property.
December 1.	Last day to file veterans' and disabled veterans' exemption to receive 80% of the exemption.
December 10.	Last day to pay first installment of taxes on secured property without penalty. Also, last day to file homeowner's exemption to receive 80% of exemption.
April 10.	Last day to pay second installment of secured taxes without penalty.

In seeking relief, a taxpayer's first step is to visit with the assessor, then appeal to a county level board and then, having exhausted administrative remedies, go to court.

Property Tax Postponement

The Property Tax Postponement Law allows persons 62 and older, and those who are blind or disabled, to postpone taxes on a personal residence. To qualify, the individual must own at least a 20 percent interest in the property and have a total household income of not more than $24,000. This deferral creates a state tax lien on the property of the amount, plus interest. The past amount is declared due upon a property sale, termination of occupancy, or ending the disability.

Homeowner Assistance Program

Taxpayers over age 62 (and the blind or disabled of any age) with a household income of up to $12,000 may qualify for a refund of property taxes previously paid. An application is filed with the Franchise Tax Board, which reviews it and possibly grants a rebate.

Taxpayer Bill of Rights

The Property Taxpayer's Bill of Rights (Chapter 387, Stats. 1993) was enacted by the 1993 California Legislature. It establishes a position, *Property Taxpayers' Advocate*, to review the point of view of a taxpayer and help resolve various problems in tax issues.

Tax Computation

To figure the taxes in California, first determine the tax rate, which is generally 1 percent plus an amount for voter-approved indebtedness. The next step is to determine the assessed valuation and taxable value. In California, the assessment is the same as for the previous year, plus an increase of up to two percent if warranted by inflation. The assessed value may be increased to the property's market value for newly constructed improvements or if and when the property is sold.

In California, the homestead tax exemption is $7,000, which means that amount can reduce the tax assessment for those who claim it. Every homeowner should claim the homestead exemption for their principal place of residence. Veterans and disabled veterans may be able to enjoy further exemptions.

To demonstrate the effect of Prop 13, let's consider two examples: Eric and Judy Kohn and their new next-door neighbors, Scott and Susan Muldavin. Eric and Judy have been living in the same home since 1984. The house was assessed at $50,000 in 1985, the effective date of value for Prop 13. Twenty years of 2 percent annual increases have brought the assessment to $74,297. Subtracting a $7,000 homeowners' exemption gives $67,297 that is currently taxable. The tax at 1 percent is $672.97. One-half of that is due December 10, the other half by April 10.

This year, the Muldavins bought a similar house next door. They paid $400,000, and may subtract a $7,000 exemption, giving $393,000 as the taxable amount. One percent is $3,930, half due December 10, the other half by April 10.

The Muldavins will pay nearly six times the tax paid by the Kohns for an equivalent house. Subsequent increases for the Muldavins will be limited to 2 percent of their recent purchase price, whereas for the Kohns it is 2 percent above their present assessment. Consequently, the Muldavins will incur six times the increase of their neighbor.

Income Taxation

Income tax laws are numerous and complex. Some highlights affecting real estate are indicated below, distinguished between those that affect personal residences and those that apply to income-property.

Personal Residence Income Taxation

It is important to maintain records permanently concerning the acquisition of a personal residence. The initial cost serves as the basis for determining gain or loss, and that can stay with the owner through sales and purchases of subsequent homes.

HOME ACQUISITION DEDUCTIONS

The acquisition of a home gives rise to a tax deduction for discount points on a mortgage loan. Provided the discount points are for interest (not for services) and are customary in the area, they may be taken as an interest deduction. In 1994, the Internal Revenue Service announced that they will allow the deduction for discount points to a buyer, even when the points have been paid by the seller. If one bought a home in the three years prior to this ruling and paid points but did not claim a tax deduction, he or she may amend their tax return for that year to get a tax refund, provided the return is still open according to the statute of limitations. Points incurred to refinance a personal residence are treated differently from original debt. Points in a refinancing must be amortized (spread out equally each period over the life of the loan).

HOME OWNERSHIP TAX DEDUCTIONS

The two principal tax deductions allowed a homeowner (including a condominium or cooperative apartment owner) are for property taxes and interest expense. One can deduct interest on up to two residences for their cost, plus up to an additional $100,000 of debt. The maximum federal income tax rate at this writing is approximately 35 percent, so the tax deduction reduces the largest homeownership expense by up to that percentage.

HOME SALE

A married couple may exclude up to $500,000 of gain on the sale of a principal residence. A single individual may exclude up to $250,000 of gain. There are limits as to the frequency of exclusion and requirements for a principal residence.

Income-Property Income Taxation

The purchase of income-producing real estate ordinarily does not generate immediate income tax deductions. A buyer, however, should indicate how much was paid for land, how much for real estate improvements, and how much for personal property. Except for land that is not depreciable, depreciation for real estate improvements and personal property generate tax deductions.

OPERATIONS OF INCOME PROPERTY

Rental income is included as business income on one's tax return, Schedule C. Expenses of business operations are tax deductible. These include not only interest and ad valorem taxes, but also maintenance and repairs, management, insurance, and all other reasonable and necessary expenses to operate the property. Depreciation is a noncash expense that serves to reduce taxable income. Because depreciation provides a deduction without a cash payment, it is considered very favorable for owners. Under present tax law, apartment owners may depreciate their property (not land) over a 27½-year term. Owners of other property types, such as office buildings, warehouses, shopping centers, and so on, must use a 39-year depreciable life. Depreciation reduces the tax basis for property, which could cause a taxable gain upon resale.

RESALE

From the resale price of real estate, the adjusted tax basis is subtracted to derive the taxable gain. The adjusted tax basis is original cost less depreciation plus capital improvements. This gain is generally taxable as a capital gain. However, certain types of depreciation tax deductions may be taxable as ordinary income upon a sale.

EXCHANGE

Under Section 1031 of the Internal Revenue Code, there are opportunities to postpone the tax on a gain. One must identify potential replacement property within 45 days of the sale date of the previously owned property, and close within 180 days of sale. The old and the new property must be held for use in a trade or business, or held as an investment. The realized gain will be taxable to the extent the seller receives unlike property, including cash, which is called *boot*.

Questions on Chapter 16

1. An ad valorem tax is based on
   (A) income earned
   (B) the value of the thing being taxed
   (C) the size of the thing being taxed
   (D) something other than A, B, or C

2. The property tax is a form of
   (A) sales tax   (C) income tax
   (B) ad valorem tax   (D) excise tax

3. The major source of income for local government usually is
   (A) income taxes   (C) property taxes
   (B) licenses and fees (D) parking meters

4. Which of the following is (are) always exempt from real property taxes?
   (A) Income-producing property owned by a church
   (B) Government-owned property
   (C) Most restaurants
   (D) A hotel

5. A tax rate of 1.05 percent is the same as
   (A) $10.50 per $1,000 of value
   (B) $1.05 per $100 of value
   (C) both A and B
   (D) none of the above

6. If a property is assessed at $60,000 and the tax rate is 1.025%, the tax is
   (A) $61.50   (C) $615
   (B) $75.00   (D) $750

7. The appraised valuation of a property is $85,000. The property tax is based on 1 percent of appraised valuation.
   (A) The city tax is $850.
   (B) The county tax is $850.
   (C) The property taxes combined add up to $850.
   (D) The city and county taxes combined add up to $8,500.

8. Property subject to a lien for unpaid property taxes in California
   (A) can be sold at auction after 5 years
   (B) takes priority over all other liens
   (C) cannot exist unless taxes are at least 36 months overdue
   (D) is a form of adverse possession

9. Which of the following is *not* a good reason why real property taxes are so popular?
   (A) Real estate ownership is easy to hide.
   (B) Real estate is valuable.
   (C) Real estate is easy to find.
   (D) Real estate can be foreclosed to provide payment of unpaid tax levies.

10. Real property taxes are justifiable because
   (A) real property benefits from many services provided by property taxes
   (B) real property owners are wealthy and can afford to pay taxes
   (C) real property taxes are legal everywhere, whereas many other kinds of taxes are not
   (D) none of the above

11. California's law that limits the annual tax valuation increases for an existing property owner to two percent is called
   (A) the Property Tax Proposition
   (B) the California Tax Abatement Initiative of 1978
   (C) Proposition 13
   (D) the law has no specific name

12. A tax-deductible front-end interest cost on a mortgage loan or deed of trust for a newly purchased home is called
   (A) interest abatement
   (B) discount points
   (C) interest in advance
   (D) prepaid mortgage insurance

13. A tax deduction for business property that requires no cash outlay is
   (A) interest expense
   (B) vacancy loss expense
   (C) depreciation expense
   (D) management expense

14. The title of the official position in each county that is responsible for preparing tax rolls is the
   (A) County Tax Assessor
   (B) Taxpayer Gouging Division
   (C) State Tax Valuation Branch
   (D) Tax Valuator

15. In California the Homestead Exemption is
   (A) $10,000
   (B) $9,000 for married homeowners, $5,000 for single homeowners
   (C) $2,500
   (D) $7,000

16. A homeowner over age 55 who meets certain conditions may, once in a lifetime, exclude up to _____ of gain on the sale of his/her personal residence.
    (A) $75,000
    (B) $100,000
    (C) $125,000
    (D) $175,000 for married couples, $100,000 for single persons

17. In California, property taxes are limited to _____ percent of value, plus an amount for voter-approved indebtedness.
    (A) 1
    (B) 2
    (C) 2½
    (D) 2.8

18. The state government entity charged with assuring that counties assess properties uniformly and fairly is the
    (A) California State Tax Equity Council
    (B) California State Board of Equalization
    (C) California State Property Tax Board
    (D) California State Real Estate Tax Fairness Council

19. The two most important income tax deductions for homeowners are for _____ and _____.
    (A) repairs, maintenance
    (B) mortgage interest, repairs
    (C) mortgage interest, property taxes
    (D) mortgage payments, sales taxes

20. The initial cost of an asset, increased by capital expenditures and reduced by depreciation expense, from which gain or loss is measured, is
    (A) basic adjustment
    (B) basal metabolism
    (C) adjustment of base
    (D) adjusted basis

21. The federal income tax exemption on the gain from the sale of a house held long enough by a married couple is up to
    (A) $25,000
    (B) $125,000
    (C) $250,000
    (D) $500,000

22. The federal income tax exemption on the gain from the sale of a house held long enough by a single individual is up to
    (A) $25,000
    (B) $125,000
    (C) $250,000
    (D) $500,000

23. Cash or other unlike property included to equalize values in an exchange is called
    (A) slipper
    (B) equity
    (C) parity
    (D) boot

24. A Real Estate Investment Trust (REIT) must
    (A) be closely held (five or fewer owners)
    (B) distribute nearly all of its taxable income
    (C) own stocks or bonds
    (D) be the same as a limited partnership

25. Federal income tax rates are generally
    (A) regressive
    (B) neutral
    (C) progressive
    (D) none of the above

26. By California statute, an owner has _____ year(s) within which to redeem tax-delinquent property.
    (A) one
    (C) five
    (B) three
    (D) ten

27. Tax-delinquent real property not redeemed by the owner during the statutory redemption period is deeded to the
    (A) city
    (C) state
    (B) county
    (D) school district
    X B

ANSWERS

1. **B**	7. **C**	13. **C**	19. **C**	25. **C**
2. **B**	8. **A**	14. **A**	20. **D**	26. **C**
3. **C**	9. **A**	15. **D**	21. **D**	27. **B**
4. **B**	10. **A**	16. **C**	22. **C**	
5. **C**	11. **C**	17. **A**	23. **D**	
6. **C**	12. **B**	18. **B**	24. **B**	

Chapter 17/*Real Estate Arithmetic*

Real Estate Arithmetic Is Familiar

Many applicants for real estate license examinations worry about the part of the examination that features "mathematics." Actually, the science of mathematics encompasses such things as algebra, calculus, and a variety of exotic fields of study, NONE of which appears on real estate license examinations. It would be better, and less frightening, to refer to the real estate "mathematics" as real estate *arithmetic*, because that is actually what it is.

You have been through all the necessary arithmetic before! Every state requires applicants for real estate licenses to have a high school education or the equivalent. The "mathematics" you will encounter on the licensing examination is the kind of arithmetic taught in the sixth and seventh grades, so you should have been exposed to it at least that one time if you are eligible to take the licensing examination in your state. Of course, the arithmetic problems in elementary and junior high school probably didn't deal with real estate situations, but the arithmetic used (the manipulation of numbers) is similar to that required on the licensing examination.

To pass the licensing examination, you should know:

> *Basic manipulations:*
> addition
> subtraction
> multiplication
> division
> *How to work with:*
> fractions
> decimals
> percentages
> *How to figure areas of simple figures:*
> quadrilaterals (four-sided figures, including squares and rectangles)
> triangles
> circles

Every day you may work with many of the necessary arithmetic concepts, even though you may not realize it:

- You work with *decimals* whenever you deal with money. Decimals show numbers in tenths, hundredths, thousandths, and so on. The sum $17.62 is seventeen dollars and sixty-two cents. It is also 17.62 dollars, or seventeen and sixty-two one-hundredths dollars. You add and subtract decimals whenever you check a restaurant bill, balance your checkbook, or count a pocket full of loose change. You multiply with decimals when you figure the cost of four paperback books, each costing $4.99. You divide with decimals when the store is selling mousetraps at three for $1.99 and you want to buy only one.

- You work with *percentages* when you try to figure out sales taxes on purchases you make, when you figure out your income tax, and when you try to determine what an item will cost if the store sign says that everything is 40 percent off the price marked. If you work on a commission basis, you almost certainly work with percentages, since commission payments (including those in the real estate business) are nearly always expressed as percentages of sales. Finally, if you ever try to compute the interest on a loan, once again you will be manipulating percentages.

- You work with *fractions* when you follow a recipe that calls for 1⅓ cups of this and 2½ teaspoons of that, and you want to make three times as much because you're having a lot of people over for a party. Often when you're dealing with percentages and decimals, you are also dealing with fractions, because fractions, decimals, and percents are just three different ways of saying basically the same thing. Don't forget that in your pocket you may have a *half*-dollar or a *quarter*.
- You may even work with *areas* more than you think. Wrapping paper, paper towels, tissue paper, and the like all are measured in square feet or square inches. Wallpaper, carpeting, and the size of your house are all measured in terms of area, as is any land you may own.

A review of basic arithmetic isn't a function of this book; we assume that you can handle the arithmetic concepts described above. If you feel, however, that your arithmetic skills are *really* rusty, go to your local bookstore and buy Barron's *Arithmetic Made Easy*. It will give you all the help you'll need. You should find it in or near that same section where this book is sold (usually called "Study Aids," or something similar).

Calculators

What really helps with the arithmetic on the examination is that you *will be allowed to take a calculator in with you*. There may be some restrictions on the kind of calculator: usually, they don't allow "programmable" ones (so you can't "set up" problems in advance) or the kind that beep or make other disturbing noises.

You certainly don't need a fancy one. All you'll be doing is adding, subtracting, multiplying, and dividing. The cheapest calculators (in the blister packs at the checkout stand) perform these functions, of course, and most of them have some sort of memory, figure percents, and maybe even handle square roots. So big bucks are not going to be a problem. However, there are two things you should avoid.

Don't get a solar calculator. These don't have batteries; they use energy from a nearby light source such as a lamp. What happens if you take the exam in a big room and the nearest light is a fluorescent fixture 20 feet above your head? Get a calculator that runs on batteries, and make sure the batteries are *fresh*.

Also, don't buy one of those credit-card-sized things. You don't want to waste your time trying to find and hit tiny keys, and squinting to make out a small, dim display. Get a standard sized calculator, with a large, clear, easy-to-read display.

Once you have your calculator, work with it and get used to it. Read the instruction book. Learn how the memory works and how the percent (%) key is used.

Measurements

Make sure that you know certain measurements, because you can be certain that the exam questions will assume a familiarity with them.

Linear measures:

12 inches	=	1 foot
3 feet	=	1 yard
5280 feet	=	1 mile

Area measures:

144 square inches	=	1 square foot
9 square feet	=	1 square yard
640 acres	=	1 square mile

and here is one that *you absolutely must remember:*

1 acre = 43,560 square feet

Burn this into your memory! You can bet the farm (and all of its acreage) that you'll be asked questions that *require* you to know the number of square feet in an acre.

Special Terms You Should Know

You should know the following special *terms* used in real estate measurement; these are illustrated in Figure 17-1.

Depth refers to the straight-line distance from the front-lot line to the rear-lot line. If these lot lines aren't parallel, the term *depth* will refer to the *longest* straight-line distance between them. The lot shown in Figure 17-1 has a depth of 272 feet.

Frontage is the *lineal distance* (see *lineal foot* below) of the lot line that is also a part of a public street or other right-of-way. Frontage of corner lots usually is expressed as separate figures for the distance fronting on each of the streets the lot bounds. This would also apply to very deep lots that border streets at both ends, and so on. The frontage of the lot in Figure 17-1 is 133 feet.

Front foot refers to the distance that a lot borders on a street. For the lot illustrated in Figure 17-1, we can say that it has *133 feet of frontage* or that it has *133 front feet*. (To say that the lot has 133 front feet of frontage is redundant.)

Lineal foot refers to the distance between two particular spots. Note that lineal feet need not be a *straight* measure; rather, the term refers to the number of feet traveled while following a *particular path connecting the particular points involved*. In real estate, this term is used normally to describe irregular lot sides (such as the east side of the lot in Figure 17-1, which is 363 lineal feet on a lot that has only 272 feet of depth), irregular paths along roads, and so on.

Right-of-way (*R.O.W.*) refers to the area owned by the government within which a road is located. On maps, plats, and so on, the term R.O.W. usually refers to the width of the right-of-way area (which usually exceeds *pavement* width).

The mathematics problems you will encounter on the licensing examination are most likely to be in the form of *word problems*, that is, problems that describe a situation for which you have to find a mathematical answer.

The process to solve a math problem is:
1. *Read* the question.
2. Determine *what* is being asked for.
3. Determine *how* to arrive at the answer.
4. *Calculate* the answer.
5. *Check* the answer.

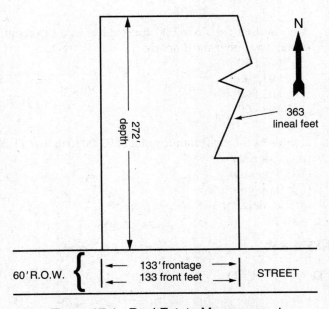

Figure 17-1. Real Estate Measurement

The last step is particularly important, especially when the problem is a complicated one; you have to make sure that you did all the calculations correctly, or your answer will be wrong. On most examinations, knowing *how* to do a problem will get you no credit; you must provide the *correct answer* as evidence that you know how to do that particular problem. You should be aware of one more fact: on mathematics questions offered in a multiple-choice format you have both an advantage and a possible disadvantage.

The advantage, which is always present, is that *you are given the correct answer to the problem*! Obviously, it *must* be among the ones you are to choose from; all you have to do is to figure out *which* one it is.

A possible disadvantage is that some of the *incorrect* answers may be answers you would arrive at by making common mistakes. You may be lulled into choosing the incorrect answer by assuming that, since your calculations gave you an answer that appears among the ones you must choose from, it *must* be correct. You should especially be on your guard if one of the choices given is something like "none of the above" or "none of the other answers is correct." This kind of choice *may* mean that none of the answers is correct, but it may also be included as a red herring.

Mistakes on mathematics problems may result from:

1. Incorrect reading of the problem. *Solution*: Read carefully!
2. Misunderstanding what is being asked for. *Solution*: Read carefully and slowly; you have plenty of time, so don't rush!
3. Not knowing how to do the problem correctly. *Solution*: Study this chapter carefully, so that you know how to approach all kinds of problems.
4. Incorrect calculation of the answer. *Solution*: Study the methods of calculation for all kinds of real estate problems, as outlined in this chapter.
5. Mistakes in arithmetic. *Solution*: Check your work, to make sure that you did your arithmetic correctly.

Note that these five common sources of errors can be controlled by applying the five steps in problem solving described previously.

Questions on Chapter 17 _____

1. A house sold for $113,900, which was 11 percent more than the cost of the house. The cost of the house was most nearly
    (A) $99,960
    (B) $100,400
    (C) $101,370
    (D) $102,610

2. A house that costs $75,000 appreciates by 11 percent, compounded annually. After two years, its value is most nearly
    (A) $97,000
    (B) $91,500
    (C) $90,000
    (D) $92,400

3. If interest for eight months of a $20,000 loan was $1,200, what is the rate of interest?
    (A) 7 percent
    (B) 8 percent
    (C) 9 percent
    (D) 10 percent

ANSWERS

1. **D**   2. **D**   3. **C**

Chapter 18/**Real Estate** ...

In discussing the various kinds of real esta...
this chapter that you have an adequate know...
ready before you tackle the sample problems; use...
calculator, if you aren't already. You must get used to...
culator because you'll be using one for the exam.

You are also assumed to be familiar with the basic metho...
volume; here we will confine ourselves to particular kinds of r...
encounter. Most of them can be characterized as specific *forms*...
recognize.

Before showing how to deal with them, however, we should pass on o...
solving these kinds of problems:

Draw a picture of the problem, if you possibly can. Then, with the picture a...
through the problem step by step.

We cannot stress this process too much. By drawing a picture of the problem, you...
at it. A picture really is valuable, especially if it helps you to visualize a problem. (Some...
of course, the problem on the exam will include a picture or diagram. But if it doesn't, supp...
your own!) Then when you do the problem, work it very carefully, step by step. Even if you feel
you can take some shortcuts, or do part of it in your head, DON'T! Solving problems this way
may be boring or tedious, but it helps to eliminate mistakes.

Sample math problems are below.

Problem Set A

The following problems deal with lengths, areas, and measures. The answers, along with the
methods of solution, are given at the end of the chapter. Use the space below each question to
work it out.

1. Brown's home measures 55 ft. long and 30 ft. wide. The outside walls are 8½ ft. high.
   Brown is going to paint these walls and wants to know how much the paint will cost
   him. There are two doors, each 3 ft. × 7½ ft., one picture window 12 ft. × 5 ft., and 6
   windows 2½ ft. × 4 ft. The doors and windows will not be painted. Each gallon can of
   paint will cover 320 sq. ft. and will cost $9.98.

Orsini wishes to subdivide her 76-acre tract into building lots. She will have to use 5,000 sq. ft. of land for streets, roads, parks, and so on. If the zoning code requires that each lot have at least 7500 sq. ft., what is the *maximum* number of lots that she can develop out of this land?

3. Steinfeld has a building that measures 65 ft. long × 35 ft. deep. One of the 65-ft. sides fronts directly on the sidewalk; he wants to build a sidewalk 8 ft. wide to surround the building on the other three sides. If the sidewalk costs $1.15 per square foot to build, what will be the total cost?

4. Johnson's lot is rectangular and contains 313 sq. yd. If the frontage is 41 ft., how deep is the lot?

5. A triangular plot of land is 500 ft. wide at the base and 650 ft. deep to the point of the triangle. What is the value of this lot, at $600 per acre?

6. Huang purchased the NW¼ of the SE¼ of a section of land. A road 66 ft. wide goes due north-south through the parcel, splitting it into two pieces. Huang did *not* acquire title to the road. How much land did he get?

Percent Problems

A great many real estate problems involve percents; these include commissions, interest, mortgage payments, loan discounts (points), depreciation, profit and loss, and return on investment. We will discuss each of these, but it should be remembered that the mathematics involved is the same for all of them: you will be looking for one of three things—a base, a rate, or a result.

Every percent problem can be stated as one of three variations of the following statement:

A is B percent of C.

Numerical examples of such a statement are "14 is 50 percent of 28" and "63 is 90 percent of 70." Of course, if you know all three numbers, you don't have a problem.

All percent problems are like the statement above, except that one of the numbers is missing: the problem is to find that missing number.

Type 1:	*A is B percent of ?*	*(C is missing.)*
Type 2:	*A is ? percent of C*	*(B is missing.)*
Type 3:	*? is B percent of C*	*(A is missing.)*

The solutions to these problems are as follows:

$$A = B \times C$$
$$B = A \div C$$
$$C = A \div B$$

An easy way to remember these is that A is B multiplied by C. To find either B or C, you divide A by the other. Here are some examples illustrating the three variations of the percent problem:

1. What is 88.5 percent of 326? ($\underline{?}$ is B percent of C.)
2. 16 is what percent of 440? (A is $\underline{?}$ percent of C.)
3. 43 is 86 percent of what? (A is B percent of $\underline{?}$.)

The solutions are as follows:

1. The missing item is A. $A = B \times C$. $A = 0.885 \times 326$. $A = 288.51$.
2. The missing item is B. $B = A \div C$. $B = 16 \div 440$. $B = 0.0363636 = 3.63\%$
3. The missing item is C. $C = A \div B$. $C = 43 \div 0.86$. $C = 50$.

COMMISSION PROBLEMS

Commission problems naturally are very popular on real estate examinations because most licensees are paid in commissions. A real estate commission is simply what the employer pays the agent for performing his function. Most often, the commission is a portion of the sale price received by a seller because of the efforts of the agent to secure a buyer. Typical commission rates vary from as low as 1 percent or less to over 10 percent, depending on the kind of property, the prevailing custom in the area, and the success of the agent, or the employer, in negotiating the listing contract.

The simplest commission problems are like this one:

Jones sells Smith's house for $327,000. Jones's commission is 6 percent of the sale price. What is her commission, in dollars?

Here the solution is to find 6 percent of $327,000; 0.06 × $327,000 = $19,620.

This *same* problem, which is the type 1 described above, can also be stated as a type 2 or type 3 problem:

Type 2: Jones sells Smith's house for $327,000 and receives a commission of $19,620. What is her commission rate?

Type 3: Jones sells Smith's house and receives a commission of $19,620, which is 6 percent of the sale price. What was the sale price?

These problems are simple. To make them more "interesting," they are often expanded in one of two ways. The first way is to make them more complicated, and there are two methods of doing that. The second way is to develop the question *backwards*; this often traps many unwary examinees, but if you pay attention it won't fool you.

First, let's look at the more elaborate kinds of commission problems. The two methods used are (a) to have you calculate the salesperson's share of a total commission and (b) to make the means of determining the commission more complicated.

Here (a) is illustrated:

O'Reilly sells Marino's house for $197,000. The commission is 6½ percent of the sale price. O'Reilly's broker receives 45 percent of this amount from the listing broker as the selling broker's share. O'Reilly herself is entitled to 60 percent of all commissions that she is responsible for bringing in. How much does O'Reilly get?

This may look complicated, but it is just three consecutive simple percent problems.

(1) How much was the total commission? A is 6½ percent of $197,000.00; A = $12,805.
(2) O'Reilly's broker received 45 percent of this amount. A is 45 percent of $12,805 = $5,762.25.
(3) O'Reilly gets 60 percent of that amount. A is 60 percent of $5,762.25 = $3,457.35.

This is the second kind (b):

> *Albertson sold Harding's house for $115,000. The commission rate is 7 percent of the first $50,000 of the sale price, 4 percent of the next $50,000, and 1.5 percent of everything over that. What was Albertson's total commission?*

Once again, we have several simple percentages to calculate: 7 percent of the first $50,000 is $3500; 4 percent of the next $50,000 is $2000; adding $2000 to $3500 yields a commission of $5500 on the first $100,000 (or $50,000 + $50,000). This leaves a balance of $15,000, to which we apply the commission rate of 1½ percent to get another $225, for a total commission of $5725.

This question could have been complicated further by going an additional step and asking, What was the effective commission rate on the sale? Here the question is, "What percent of the sale price is the actual commission?" First we say, $5725 is ? percent of $115,000. Then we take the additional step: $B = 5725 \div 115,000 = 0.0498$, so the percentage = 4.98 percent.

Now let's turn to the other general category of complicated commission problems—those in which the question is developed *backwards*. Here the question is phrased like this:

> *Baker sold her house; after paying a 7 percent commission she had $371,535 left. What was the sale price of the house?*

Many people will find 7 percent of $371,535, add it on, and GET THE WRONG ANSWER!! Their mistake is that the commission should be figured on the *sale price*, and they are figuring it on what the seller had left *after* the commission was paid. The way to solve these problems is simple: If Baker paid a 7 percent commission, then *what she had left* was 93 percent (or 100 percent − 7 percent) of the sale price. Now the problem becomes a familiar variation: $371,535 is 93 percent of ? $C = \$371,535 \div 0.93 = \$399,500$.

As you can see, this question is "backwards" in that you don't actually have to figure the dollar amount of the commission. On your examination be sure to look out for these kinds of problems; the best way to spot them is to follow the rule of *reading* the question and *then* trying to determine what you are asked to do.

You should be aware of the terminology used in commission figuring. The *commission* is the dollar amount arrived at by applying the *commission rate* to the *sale price*. If you are asked for the "commission," you are being asked to tell *how many dollars and cents* the commission payment was. If you are asked for the "commission rate" or the "rate," you are being asked to provide the *percent rate* of the commission.

INTEREST PROBLEMS

Interest is money paid to "rent" money from others. It is typically expressed as an annual percentage rate; that is, for each year that the money is borrowed, a certain percentage of the loan amount is charged as interest. Interest will most often be stated in annual percentage terms even for loans that have a duration of much less than 1 year. As an example, the "interest rate" on charge accounts, credit card accounts, and the like may be charged monthly, and the bill may be due within a month, but the interest rate still is expressed as an annual rate. This practice is becoming even more prevalent as a result of federal truth-in-lending laws, which *require* that the annual percentage rate (APR) be stated.

Usually, for short-term arrangements a monthly or quarterly rate will also be specified. If you are given only an annual rate and are required to calculate based on a monthly or quarterly rate, simply divide the annual rate by 12 to get the monthly rate, and by 4 to get the quarterly rate. If a problem gives a monthly or quarterly rate, multiply a monthly rate by 12 or a quarterly rate by 4 to get the annual rate. For example:

> *A rate of 12 percent annually is 1 percent monthly and 3 percent quarterly.*
> *A rate of 9½ percent annually is 2.375 percent quarterly or 0.791666 . . . percent monthly.*
> *A rate of 0.6 percent monthly is 1.8 percent quarterly or 7.2 percent annually.*

Interest is calculated in two ways, *simple* and *compound*.

Simple interest is calculated quite straightforwardly. To determine the interest charge for any period of time, we calculate the proportional interest, based on the annual rate. If the annual rate is 6 percent, interest for 2 years is 12 percent, interest for 6 months is 3 percent, and so on.

When *compound interest* is used, interest is charged on unpaid interest, as well as on the unpaid debt. This adds a complicating element to the calculation, since some sort of adjustment may be necessary to allow for the fact that interest is not being paid periodically, but is being allowed to accumulate over all or part of the term of the debt. Since in real life most debts are paid in monthly installments, one does not frequently encounter interest compounding in the payment of debts. One *does* encounter it in savings accounts, where a well-advertised feature is that, if a depositor does not withdraw the interest his principal earns, it is added to his balance and begins to earn interest too.

Before compound interest can be calculated, the compounding frequency must be given. This is expressed in units of time. Compounding can be daily, quarterly, semiannually, annually—indeed it can be over any period of time, even "continuously." Given a compounding term, interest is figured by first deriving an interest rate for the term involved. Then interest is calculated for *each* term, taking into account the fact that some or all of the interest earned so far may not have been paid out. Here is an example:

> *Berger borrows $1000 at 8 percent annual interest. The interest is compounded quarterly. How much interest will Berger owe after 9 months?*

First we must change the annual rate to a quarterly rate: 8 ÷ 4 = 2, so the quarterly interest rate is 2 percent.

For the first quarter, interest is 2 percent of $1000, or $20.

To calculate interest for the second quarter, we add the first quarter's interest to the balance to get $1020, upon which interest for the second quarter is due. Therefore, the second quarter's interest is 2 percent of $1020.00, or $20.40. In effect, for the second quarter there is $20 interest, again, on the initial balance of $1000, plus another 40¢ interest on the unpaid $20 of interest earned in the first quarter.

Interest for the third quarter of the 9-month period will be based on a balance of $1040.40, which is the original balance plus the interest accumulated in the first two quarters. Therefore, interest for the third quarter is 2 percent of $1040.40, or $20.81. The total interest for the 9 months (three quarters) will be $20.00 + $20.40 + $20.81, or $61.21.

Notice that compound interest will amount to *more* than simple interest, if the interest period extends over more than one compounding term. We can show this with the same problem, this time assuming that simple interest is paid. In this case, the interest is $20 each quarter, for a total of only $60, compared to the $61.21 charged under compound interest. The reason is that, with simple interest, interest is calculated only on the original loan balance. Compound interest includes interest on earned but unpaid interest as well as on the original principal, so a larger amount becomes subject to interest once the first compounding term has passed.

In real estate problems, interest questions usually involve *mortgage loans* and *loan discounts*, or *points*.

Mortgage Loans

Mortgage loans are like any other loans in that interest is charged for the use of someone else's money. Usually these loans require monthly payments, with part of the payment used to pay the interest due since the last payment and the remainder used to reduce the amount of the loan (the *principal*). Eventually, in this manner the loan will be fully paid off.

A very common question on this type of loan concerns the interest payable in any given month. This requires you to calculate the loan balance for that month before you can find the interest payment due. Here is an example:

> *Smith borrows $300,000 on a 30-year mortgage loan, payable at 9 percent interest per year. Payments are $2,413.87 per month. How much interest is to be charged in each of the first 3 months?*

The first step in the solution is to determine the *monthly* interest rate, since mortgage interest payments are made monthly. Therefore, we divide the annual rate of 9 percent by 12 and get an interest rate of ¾ percent or 0.75 percent per month.

Now we can find the interest payable in the first month, which is 0.0075 × $300,000 = $2,250.00. The total monthly payment is $2,413.87, so after the $2,250.00 interest is paid, there remains $2,413.87 − $2,250.00 = $163.87 to be used to reduce the loan. This means that the loan balance for the second month is $300,000.00 − $163.87 = $299,836.13.

Now we calculate interest for the second month: 0.0075 × $299,836.13 = $2,248.77. This means that in the second month $2,413.87 − $2,248.77 = $165.10 is used to reduce the loan, leaving a balance of $299,836.13 − $165.10 = $299,671.03 for the third month.

The third month's interest, then, will be 0.0075 × $299,671.03=$2,247.53. We can tabulate these results as follows:

Month	Loan Balance (Beginning of Month)	Loan Payment	Interest	Loan Payoff
1	$300,000.00	$2,413.87	2,250.00	$163.87
2	299,836.13	2,413.87	2,248.77	165.10
3	299,671.03	2,413.87	2,247.53	166.34
4	299,504.69	. . . .	. . . .	. . . . . .

There is a whole family of questions that would be answered using this same method, *making these same calculations*. Here are some examples, using the same information in the question we just solved ($300,000 30-year loan, monthly payments, 9% a year interest). Note that all of them can be answered using the information in the table above— information we've *already* calculated.:

(a) *What is the total amount of interest to be paid in the first three months?*
(b) *How much interest will be paid in the third month?*
(c) *How much will the loan be paid down in the first three months?*
(d) *What will the loan balance be after three months?*
(e) *What will the loan balance be at the beginning of the fourth month?*
(f) *What will the loan balance be after the third payment is made?*

Here are the answers:

(a) just add up the three interest amounts for months 1, 2, and 3:
$2,250.00 + $2,248.77 + $2,247.53 = **$6,746.30**.
(b) the interest amount for month 3: **$2,247.53**.
(c) add up the three loan payoff amounts: $163.87 + $165.10 + $166.34 = **$495.31**.
another way: subtract the balance at the end of 3 months from the original balance:
$300,000 − $299,504.69 = **$495.31**.
(d), (e), and (f) are all different ways of asking *exactly the same question*. The answer is, of course, **$299,504.69**.

This kind of loan is called *self-amortizing, equal payment*. The monthly payments are equal. However, as the loan balance is reduced a little each month, the portion of the payment representing interest decreases monthly, while the portion going to reduce the loan increases.

In some loans, called *level principal payment loans*, the loan amount is reduced the *same* amount with each payment. This means that the payments themselves get smaller each time, as the interest due decreases because the loan balance is decreasing. Here is an example:

> *Smith borrows $24,000 for 10 years at an annual rate of interest of 12 percent. He pays it back in the level principal payment manner each month. What will be his payments for the first, fourth, and tenth months?*

The first thing we must do here is to calculate the amount of the monthly level principal payment. Since 10 years is 120 months, the monthly principal payment is $24,000 ÷ 120 = $200. The monthly interest rate is 12% ÷ 12 = 1%.

In the first month, the entire $24,000 is on loan, so the payment is the level $200 payment plus 1 percent of $24,000, which is another $240. Therefore, the first month's total payment is $200 + $240 = $440.

For the fourth month, Smith will owe the original balance of $24,000 *less* the $200 payments that were made for each of the first 3 months. That amount totals $600, so for the fourth month he owes $24,000 − $600 = $23,400. Then, 1 percent of $23,400 is $234; this added to the level payment of $200 gives a payment of $434 for the fourth month.

The payment for the tenth month is calculated in the same way. At that time, nine payments will have been made, so the loan will have been reduced by 9 × $200 = $1,800, leaving a loan amount of $22,200. Since 1 percent of that amount is $222, the full payment for the tenth month will be $422.

Loan Discounts

The purpose of loan discounts is briefly explained in Chapter 13 ("Mortgages and Finance"). A loan discount is very simple to calculate, since it is merely a given percentage of the loan amount. You should be aware of the terminology, though, since these discounts often are referred to as *points*. One discount point is the same as a charge of 1 percent of the loan amount. Therefore, a discount of three points (often just referred to as "three points") is 3 percent of the loan amount. Frequently, a problem involving discounts will require you first to determine the loan amount; this can trap the unwary examinee, who makes the mistake of calculating the discount based on the purchase price instead of the *loan amount*. Here is an example:

> *Marilyn bought a home costing $195,000. She got a 95 percent loan, on which there was a charge of 3¾ points. What was the discount in dollars and cents?*

First we calculate the loan amount, which is 95 percent of $195,000: 0.95 × $195,000 = $185,250.

Now we can calculate the discount, which is 3¾ points, or 3¾ percent of the loan amount: 0.0375 × $185,250 = $6,946.88.

DEPRECIATION

Although the tax laws allow all sorts of complicated ways to calculate depreciation, the only one you have to worry about on licensing examinations is the simplest one, which is called *straight-line depreciation*. Straight-line depreciation assumes that the property depreciates an *equal* amount each year.

We will not argue here whether real estate does or does not, in fact, depreciate. Some does and some does not seem to. However, there are many reasons why one should be aware of the possibility of depreciation, not the least of which is that in the long run a real estate asset *will* wear out. The 50-year-old house that is being offered for ten times the original cost of construction also has a new roof, modernized heating and air-conditioning, new wiring, carpeting, kitchen installations, and plumbing. Nearly every visible surface has been repainted and remodeled.

When calculating depreciation, you must know the *useful life* of the property (sometimes referred to as *economic life*, or just plain *life*). Once you know this, you can easily calculate an annual *depreciation rate*: divide the useful life, in years, *into* 100 percent to get the percent rate of depreciation per year. For example:

> *10-year life: 100% ÷ 10 = 10% depreciation per year*
> *50-year life: 100% ÷ 50 = 2% depreciation per year*
> *35-year life: 100% ÷ 35 = 2.857% depreciation per year*

Once this has been done, most depreciation problems become only slightly elaborated versions of the standard three types of percentage *problems*. For example:

(a) *Madison owns a building for which he paid $550,000. If it has a total useful life of 30 years, what is its value after 5 years?*

(b) *Madison owns a building for which he paid $550,000. If it has a 40-year life, in how many years will it be worth $426,250?*

(c) *Madison owns a building worth $550,000. If it depreciates to $440,000 in 9 years, what is the total useful life?*

(d) *If a building depreciates at a 2½ percent per year, in how many years will it be worth 85 percent of its original value?*

Here is how the answer to each of these is found:

(a) Here you are asked to determine the value after 5 years, so you must determine how much the building depreciates each year. A 30-year life yields 3⅓ percent depreciation per year. Five years' depreciation, then, is 16⅔ percent. Therefore, in 5 years the building will be worth 83⅓% (100% − 16⅔%) of its original value: 0.8333 × $550,000 = $458,333.33, its value after 5 years.

(b) Here you want to know how long it takes for a certain depreciation to take place. A 40-year life is depreciation at 2½ percent per year. $426,250 is 77½ percent of $550,000 (426,250 ÷ 550,000). 100% − 77½% = 22½% total depreciation. At 2½ percent per year, that would take 9 years to accumulate (22.5 ÷ 2.5 = 9).

(c) Here you have to determine the useful life. $440,000 is 80 percent of $550,000 (440,000 ÷ 550,000 = 0.80). Therefore, the building depreciates 20 percent in 9 years, or 2.2222 . . . percent per year. Divide this figure into 100 percent to get the total number of years required for the building to depreciate fully: 100 ÷ 2.2222 = 45. Thus, the useful life is 45 years.

(d) In this problem you don't have to calculate the depreciation rate, since it is given to you (2½ percent per year). If the building depreciates to 85 percent of its original value, it will have depreciated 15 percent. 15% ÷ 2½% = 6 years' worth of depreciation.

PROFIT AND LOSS

Calculation of profit and loss is another slightly different version of the three types of percentage problems. The important thing to remember is that profit and loss are always expressed as percentages of *cost*. Cost is the original price that the seller paid for the property when he acquired it. If *his* selling price is higher than cost, he has a profit. If it is lower, he has a loss.

The *dollar value* of profit or loss is the difference between purchase price and sale price.

The *rate* of profit or loss is the percentage relationship between the purchase price and the dollar value of profit or loss.

Here are some examples:

(a) *Martina bought her house for $224,750 and sold it later for $279,500. What was her rate of profit?*

(b) *Samson Wrecking Company mistakenly tore down part of Habib's home. Before the home was damaged, it was worth $300,000. Afterward, it had sustained 28 percent loss. What was its value after the wrecking?*

(c) *Harrison sold his home for $210,250 and made a 45 percent profit. What had he paid for the home?*

Here are the solutions:

(a) First, determine the dollar value of the profit: $279,500 − $224,750 = $54,750. Then determine what percentage proportion the dollar value is of the *purchase price* ($54,750 is ? percent of $224,750). 54,750 ÷ 224,750 = 24.36 percent.

(b) The loss was 28 percent of the original value of $300,000: 0.28 × $300,000 = $84,000. $300,000 − $84,000 = $216,000 value afterward.

(c) The original price of the house, plus 45 percent, is now equal to $210,250. Therefore, $210,250 is 145 percent of the original price of the home ($210,250 is 145 percent of ?). 210,250 ÷ 1.45 = $145,000. As a check, Harrison's profit is $62,250 ($210,250 less $145,000), which is 45 percent of $145,000 ($ 62,250 ÷ $145,000 = 0.45).

RETURN ON INVESTMENT

The concept of return on investment is very similar to the concept of interest payments on loans. In the investment case, an investor spends money to buy an income-producing asset. She wants to make money from it; otherwise there is no point to the investment. She calculates her return and expresses it as a *percentage* of her investment being paid back to her each year. In a sense, she can be thought of as "lending" her money to the investment and having it "pay" her "interest" on her money.

It is possible to make deceptively simple-sounding investment questions so complicated that they can best be answered with the aid of a computer or a very sophisticated calculator. This fact needn't concern you, though. On licensing examinations the questions are kept simple enough that they can be calculated quickly by hand or, in states that allow their use, with simple, hand-held calculators that do no more than add, subtract, multiply, and divide.

If you think of return on investment problems as similar to interest problems, you should have no trouble with them. Here are some examples:

(a) *Bennett owns a building that cost him $650,000. How much income should the building produce annually to give Bennett a 15 percent return on his money?*

(b) *Maximilian paid $217,500 for a triplex apartment building. All units are identical. He lives in one unit and rents the other two. The total net income per month from rental is $1,775. What annual rate of return is he getting on his investment in the rental units?*

(c) *What monthly income should a building costing $385,000 produce if the annual return is to be 15 percent?*

Here are the solutions:

(a) The building should produce an income each year of 15 percent of $650,000: $0.15 \times \$650,000 = \$97,500$.

(b) This problem involves a lot of steps, but they are simple ones. First we must determine how much of the purchase price should be allocated to the two rental units. Since all three are the same, one-third of the purchase price ought to be allocated to each. This means that two-thirds of the price should be allocated to the two rental units: $\frac{2}{3} \times \$217,500 = \$145,000$. Next we must determine the annual dollar amount of income received. The monthly income is $1,775, so the annual income is $\$1,775 \times 12 = \$21,300$. Now we must find out what percent $21,300 is of $145,000 ($21,300 is ? percent of $145,000). $\$21,300 \div \$145,000 = 14.69$ percent, the annual rate of return.

(c) Here we must calculate a monthly dollar income. The annual income must be 15 percent of $385,000, or $57,750. The monthly income is one-twelfth of that amount, or $4,812.50.

Problem Set B

Here are some practice problems involving percents. The questions cover all of the kinds we have just discussed, including common variations. Answers are given at the end of the chapter.

1. Peters sold her home for $497,000 and made a 42 percent profit. How much did she pay for the home?

2. Rodriguez's home cost $249,500. He financed the purchase with a 90 percent loan. The discount was three points. How much was the dollar amount of discount?

3. Going back to problem 2, assume that the interest rate on Rodriguez's loan was 8½ percent per year and that the loan was for a 25-year period. How much interest would be payable with the first payment?

4. Talbot sold her building for $242,218.75. She had owned it for 7 years and had originally paid $287,500 for it. What was the annual rate of depreciation?

5. Sam Zealous, the real estate agent, sold I. M. Sellar's home for him. After paying Zealous a commission of 7½ percent of the sale price, Sellar ended up with $184,907.50. What was the sale price?

6. Winken, Blinken, and Nod are partners in the ownership of a certain property worth $440,000. The property produces a 21 percent return per year, in income collected monthly. Winken owns a 37 percent share of the building. How much is Winken's monthly income from the property?

7. In problem 6, Blinken owns a 22 percent share and Nod owns the rest. If $198,000 originally was paid for the property, what would be the dollar value of Nod's share of the profit if the partners were to sell the property today for its current value? What rate of profit does this represent?

8. Bernie, a real estate salesman for Gettum Realty, Inc., gets 52½ percent of all real estate commissions he brings into the firm. Bernie just sold Fred's home for $223,750. Fred had listed the home with a different broker in the same Multilist group as Bernie's broker. According to the Multilist rules, the listing broker received 40 percent of the commission, and the selling broker received the rest after a fee of 3 percent of the commission was paid to the Multilist group to cover its expenses. How much (dollar amount) of the 6½ percent commission on this sale was paid to Bernie?

9. Mr. Selkirk borrowed $5,000 to update the kitchen in his home. The loan was for 1 year, with no payments to principal to be made until the loan term was past. The interest rate was 10½ percent per year, with the interest payable quarterly. How much was the quarterly interest payment? If the interest had been allowed to compound quarterly, how much *extra* interest would Mr. Selkirk have had to pay in excess of simple quarterly interest?

10. Ms. Jessup just sold for $625,000 a building she bought 8 years earlier for $930,000. What was the percentage rate of her loss? What was the annual rate of depreciation she sustained?

11. Brown purchased a $1,400 note secured by a second mortgage for investment purposes. The seller allowed a 15 percent discount. The note provided for monthly payments of $122, including interest at 9 percent per annum over a one-year term. Brown received full payment on the above terms. What is the yield on Brown's investment, expressed as a percentage?

12. An office building provides $168,000 of annual net operating income. If it is purchased for $2,000,000, what is the overall rate of return?

13. An office building provides monthly rent of $12,400. It cost $2,000,000. What is the annual gross rent multiplier?

14. What is the annual potential gross income of an apartment complex with 20 one-bedroom units at $900 per month and 18 two-bedroom units at $1,050?

Proration

Proration, which is a necessary input into the calculation of closing statements, normally will come up only on examinations for broker's licenses. If you are seeking a brokerage license, you should cover the material in this section. Appraisal or salesperson candidates can skip it.

Two kinds of prorating methods are in common use. The most widely used one employs the *statutory year*; the other, the *actual year*.

The function of proration is to distribute equitably the costs of a particular charge that two or more people must share. In real estate, these costs usually are created by transactions associated with a title closing, in which allocations are made for charges that apply over the period in which both buyer and seller own the property. The most commonly prorated items are these:

- Real property taxes
- Property insurance
- Interest on assumed mortgage loans
- Prepaid or later-paid rentals

Property taxes are usually paid by the year; when a transaction occurs in the middle of a year, part of that year's property tax usually will be deemed, by the parties to the sale, to be payable by each one. Note that the government that collects the taxes does *not* prorate them; it collects the *full* amount of the taxes from whoever owns the property at the time the taxes are due. If, when the sale occurs, the year's property taxes have *already* been paid, the seller will have paid them and the buyer must recompense the seller for the portion of the taxes that apply to the part of the year when the buyer will own the property. On the other hand, if the taxes are due *after* the close of the sale, the buyer will have to pay them in full, for the entire year, when they come due. At the closing the seller pays the buyer for the share that applies during the period of the tax year when the seller owned the property.

Insurance usually is paid in advance. Often insurance policies are multiyear policies, although the premiums generally are payable annually. On licensing examinations, however, problems that involve closing often assume that the entire multiyear premium was paid at once when the policy was purchased; this is a device to see whether examinees read the questions completely. Since insurance usually is paid in advance, the buyer, if he assumes the existing insurance policy, recompenses the seller for the prepaid unused portion of the policy that the buyer gets from her.

When the buyer assumes the seller's mortgage loan, and the closing date is not the day after the loan payment is due and paid, the month's interest must be prorated between buyer and seller. Loan payments are due at the end of the monthly payment periods. When the next payment is due, the buyer will have to pay it in full, including the interest for an entire month during which he actually owned the property only part of the time. Therefore, the seller will have to pay the buyer for her share of the mortgage interest.

Rents work the other way, since they are payments *to* the owner rather than *by* the owner. Rent usually is paid in advance, but it is possible to have a situation where rent is paid at the *end* of the month or lease period. If rent is paid in advance, the seller will have been paid a full month's rent for the month in which the closing occurs; she must pay the buyer his prorated share of that month's rent already received. If the rent is paid at the end of the month, the buyer will get a full month's rent covering the month of sale, and he must recompense the seller for the period during which she owned the property. Because of these two types of situations examinees must read rent questions carefully.

COMPUTING PRORATIONS

To compute prorations an examinee must know three things:
1. How much—in money—is the item to be prorated?
2. To whom is payment to be made?
3. How much time is involved?

The discussion above covers the question of who pays whom what charges, but in summary we can state two easily remembered rules:
1. If the item was paid *before* closing, the buyer recompenses the seller.
2. If the item will be paid *after* closing, the seller recompenses the buyer.

These rules are fair because the seller had to pay all items due before closing, and the buyer will have to pay everything that comes due after closing.

Calculation of the amount of money due in the payment will vary, depending on the complexity of the problem. Sometimes the amount is specified exactly; other times it will have to be calculated. It is quite popular in licensing examinations to require the examinee to calculate the property tax bill before he can begin to prorate it (see Chapter 16). Usually the insurance premium and rentals will be given, since it is difficult to incorporate a sensible calculation method for them into a problem. Proration of the interest on assumed mortgages is another favorite candidate for calculation.

Calculation of the proration itself includes apportioning the time involved among the parties. Rent and interest usually are apportioned over 1 month, taxes over 1 year, and insurance over 1 or more years.

To prorate correctly, you must have two important pieces of information:
1. Who (buyer or seller) is supposed to "have" the day of closing?
2. Which calculation year (statutory or calendar) is being used?

You must be given this information somewhere in the examination. If you can't find it, ask one of the examination supervisors.

The Closing Day

The day of closing can be counted either as the buyer's first day or as the seller's last day. Which it is to be usually reflects local custom, so we can't state a general rule (although in the East and the South, the closing day most often is considered the seller's, while it tends to be the buyer's in the West).

The Statutory Year

Prorating items over a full year can involve very messy calculations, since everything has to be divided by 365 (or 366), the number of days in a year. Many banks and other financial institutions therefore have substituted the 360-day "statutory year" as a means of simplifying calculation. This system assumes the year to be made up of twelve 30-day months. Numbers such as 360 and 30, while large, can be divided easily by many other numbers, so that calculations involving them are less cumbersome.

For items paid monthly, such as interest and rent, the statutory year rarely is used, since its application can create visible distortion in 31-day months and, especially, in February. However, spread over a year or more, the error introduced with the statutory year becomes very small, so it is sometimes used for calculation of prorated taxes and insurance.

To prorate an item using the statutory year, first find the payment for the full period. Next, divide this payment by the number of months in the period to get the monthly cost, and divide the monthly cost by 30 to find the daily cost. After determining who pays whom, and for what length of time, you can calculate the prorated payment.

Using the statutory year was helpful when calculations were made by hand or with adding machines; now that calculators and computers are in common use, dividing by 365 (or 366) instead of 360 isn't such a big deal. As a result, the recent trend has been to use the actual year instead of the statutory year.

The Actual Year

If using the statutory year is forbidden, the actual year must be used. In this case, you need to calculate how many days of the period must be paid for. You then multiply this sum by the *daily* cost of the item to get the prorated payment. The difficulty comes in the fact that to get the daily rate you must divide the annual rate by 365, or 366 in leap years. Further, it often is confusing to try to count days elapsed in a significant part of a year, especially when dealing with odd beginning and ending dates. To try to figure how many days elapse between January 1 and July 26 of a given year is bad enough; to calculate the number of days that elapsed from, say, October 23 of one year to March 14 of the following year is even worse. If you must use the actual year, you have no alternative; you need to remember the number of days in each month and whether or not you're dealing with a leap year. Be sure to keep your calculator in good working order, and to be familiar with its use, to help you make actual-year computations.

Calculating Time with the Statutory Year

The statutory year lends itself well to calculation of elapsed time. In this type of calculation you want to find out how many days have elapsed between two dates, one of which is usually the closing date. To do this, write each date *numerically* as follows: YEAR—MONTH—DATE. June 17, 2006, would be 6—6—17. July 4, 2006, would be 6—7—4. To find the elapsed time, "subtract" the earlier date from the later one. Remember that you can "borrow" from adjacent left-hand columns just as you do in normal arithmetic subtraction. Also remember that you're borrowing months and years, not digits. Each month has 30 days, and each year has 12 months.

In the following example, we want to find the elapsed time between December 28, 2006, and March 19, 2007:

$$
\begin{array}{ccc}
7 - & 3 - & 19 \\
-\,6 - & 12 - & 28 \\
\hline
? & ? & ? \\
\end{array}
$$

First, we find the number of days; here we would have to subtract 28 from 19, and we can't do that. We must borrow a month (30 days) from the month column, to change the 19 to 49. $49 - 28 = 21$, so we have:

$$
\begin{array}{ccc}
& \overset{2}{3} - & \overset{49}{19} \\
7 - & 3 - & 19 \\
-\,6 - & 12 - & 28 \\
\hline
? & ? & 21 \\
\end{array}
$$

Now we look to the months; we must subtract 12 from 2. We can't do that, so we borrow a year, or 12 months, from the year column, and subtract 12 from 14:

$$
\begin{array}{ccc}
\overset{6}{7} - & \overset{\overset{14}{\cancel{2}}}{\cancel{3}} - & \overset{49}{\cancel{19}} \\
-\,6 - & 12 - & 28 \\
\hline
? & ? & 21 \\
\end{array}
$$

Since 6 subtracted from 6 leaves 0, the elapsed time between December 28, 2006, and March 19, 2007, is 2 months and 21 days.

Rounding in Proration

One very important warning must be given here. When you are calculating prorations, always carry your intermediate results (i.e., daily and monthly charges) to *at least two decimal places beyond the pennies*. Do *not* round to even cents until you have arrived at your *final* answer, because when you round you introduce a tiny error. This is acceptable with respect to your final answer, but intermediate answers will later be operated on, including multiplication by fairly large numbers. Each time a rounded number is multiplied, the rounding error is multiplied also! To prevent such errors from affecting your final result, always carry intermediate steps to at least two extra decimal places beyond what your final answer will have.

PRORATION EXAMPLES

Here is an example of proration for each of the four commonly prorated items: rent, interest, taxes, insurance.

Rent

Rent usually is paid in advance.

> *The closing date is May 19, 2006, and rent is payable for the calendar month on the first of each month. Who pays whom what in the proration of rent of $1,325 per month?*

Since the seller received the May rent payment on May 1, he should pay the buyer the portion of rent covering the part of the month *after* the closing date. May has 31 days; the closing date is May 19. Therefore, the buyer will own the property for $31 - 19 = 12$ days during May. The daily rent for May is $\frac{1}{31}$ of the monthly rent, since there are 31 days: $\$1,325 \div 31 = \$42.7419$. (Remember to carry to two extra decimal places.) The buyer's share of the rent, then, is $12 \times \$42.7419 = \$512.9032$, which rounds to $512.90. (Note that, if we had rounded the daily rental to $42.74 and then multiplied by the 12 days, the result would have been $512.88, or 2¢ off.)

Interest

Interest is paid after it has accrued. Normally, the interest period ends the day *before* a payment is due—that is, a payment due on the first of the month covers the preceding month; one due on the 18th of the month covers the period from the 18th of the preceding month through the 17th of the current one.

> *The closing date is September 22, 2006. Interest is payable, with the payment on the 16th of the month. The loan amount as of September 16, 2006, is $448,111. The interest rate is 6¼ percent per year. If the loan is assumed, who pays whom what for prorated interest?*

We have to calculate the monthly interest due and determine how much of that amount is paid by whom. First, the dollar amount of interest—this is $\frac{1}{12}$ of 6¼ percent of the loan balance of $448,111: $\frac{1}{12} \times 0.0625 \times \$448,111 = \$2,333.91$. Note that we have rounded off the monthly interest because the lender does that, too, each month.

The period involved here is 30 days, since September has that length. The seller will have to pay the buyer for all of the interest between September 16 and September 22, since on October 16 the buyer is going to have to pay the full month's interest. The seller will own the property for 7 days of that time. (At a glance, this appears incorrect since $22 - 16 = 6$. However, the seller owns the property on both the 16th and the 22nd, so we must add a day. Another way is to count the days on our fingers, starting with the 16th and ending with the 22nd.)

Now we must determine the daily interest charge, which is $2,333.85 ÷ 30 = $77.7950. We multiply this by 7 to get the seller's share for 7 days: $77.7950 × 7 = $544.565, which rounds to $544.57.

Taxes

Taxes are usually assessed for a full year, so we would use the statutory year for calculation, if permitted.

> *The closing date is April 27, 2006. Taxes are $1,188.54 per year. The tax year is March 1 to February 28 (or 29) of the following year. Who pays whom how much in prorated taxes? Use both the statutory and the actual year, assuming (a) that taxes are paid on June 1 and (b) that taxes are paid on March 15 of the tax year.*

This sample problem is probably more complex than any you will encounter on a licensing examination, but it demonstrates all the possibilities.

In situation (a) the seller pays his share to the buyer, since the taxes are due after the closing date and so must be paid by the buyer. In situation (b) the buyer pays the seller her share, because the taxes for the full tax year were paid by the seller before the closing date.

Statutory Year Calculations. The closing date is April 27, 2006, and the tax year begins March 1, 2006. Therefore the seller owns the property for 1 month and 27 days:

$$
\begin{array}{rrr}
6 & 4 & 28 \\
-\ 6 & 3 & 1 \\
\hline
 & 1 & 27
\end{array}
$$

Note that we did not use April 27, the closing date, in this calculation, because we consider the closing date as belonging to the seller. April 28, then, is the first day that the seller does *not* own the property, and so we must count from that day.

The seller's share is for 1 month and 27 days. The total tax payment is $1188.54 per year. Dividing by 12 yields a monthly tax charge of $99.0450. Dividing this amount by 30 yields a daily tax charge of $3.3015.

$$
\begin{array}{lll}
1 \text{ month @ } \$99.0450 & = & \$99.0450 \\
+\ 27 \text{ days @ } \$3.3015 & = & +\ \ 89.1405 \\
\hline
\text{Total seller's charge} & & \$188.1855 = \$188.19
\end{array}
$$

The seller's share is $188.19, so the buyer's share is the rest, or $1188.54 − $188.19 = $1000.35.

In situation (a), then, the seller pays the buyer $188.19.

In situation (b) the buyer pays the seller $1000.35.

Actual Year Calculations. When calculating using the actual year, we reduce everything to days. The year has 365 days, so, using the same problem, the daily tax charge is $1188.54 ÷ 365 = $3.25627. The seller owns the property for a total of 58 days: 31 days of March and 27 days of April of the tax year. Therefore the seller's share is 58 × $3.25627 = $188.8654 = $188.87. The buyer's share would be $1188.54 − $188.87 = $999.67.

In situation (a), taxes are paid on June 1 and the seller pays the buyer $188.87.

In situation (b), taxes are paid on March 15 and the buyer pays the seller $999.67.

Note two things about this calculation. First, the results are 68¢ different from those obtained with the statutory year method; this discrepancy occurs because of the different calculation technique. Second, when the daily charge was calculated, it was carried to *three* extra decimal places. In the actual year calculation, we might have to multiply by a number as large as 365, and the rounding error would be multiplied by that much. Carrying to three extra decimal places reduces this error.

Insurance

> *A 3-year insurance policy, dated October 22, 2004, is assumed on the closing date of August 11, 2006. The full 3-year premium of $559.75 was paid at the time the policy was bought. Who pays whom what if this policy is prorated?*

First we calculate the monthly insurance charge, which is $\frac{1}{36}$ (3 years, remember) of the premium of $559.75: $559.75 ÷ 36 = $15.5486. The daily charge is $\frac{1}{30}$ of that amount: $15.5486 ÷ 30 = $0.5183.

Now we must calculate how long the buyer will use the policy. If the policy is dated October 22, 2004, then it expires on October 21 (at midnight) of 2007.

$$
\begin{array}{rrr}
7 & 10 & 21 \\
-\ 6 & 8 & 11 \\
\hline
1 & 2 & 10
\end{array}
$$

The buyer will own the policy for 1 year, 2 months, and 10 days. He will pay the seller the prorated share, since the seller paid for the full 3 years when she bought the policy. (Now we just go ahead and figure 1 year and 2 months to be 14 months, to save the problem of calculating the annual premium.)

$$
\begin{array}{lll}
14 \text{ months @ } \$15.5486 & = & \$217.6804 \\
10 \text{ days @ } \$0.5183 & = & +\ \ \ 5.1830 \\
\text{Total payable to seller} & & \$222.8634 = \$222.86
\end{array}
$$

Calculating insurance according to the actual year can be cumbersome. To do this we ought to calculate first the annual premium, which is $\frac{1}{3}$ of $559.75 = $186.58333. The daily premium charge is this amount divided by 365: $186.58333 ÷ 365 = $0.51119. Note that once again we are carrying actual year calculations to an extra *three* decimal places.

Problem Set C

Here are some proration problems for you to practice with. Answers are given at the end of the chapter.

1. The closing date is June 26, 2006. Taxes are collected on a calendar-year basis and are payable on June 1 of each year. Taxes for the year are $3,899.50. A one-year insurance policy, dated May 2, 2006, is to be assumed by the buyer. A full one-year premium of $1,444.85 was paid when the policy was issued. A mortgage loan with a balance of $288,230.11, as of June 1, 2006, will be assumed. It has an interest rate of 5¼ percent per year; payments are made on the first of the month. Part of the property is rented, with rent of $550 per month payable in advance on the first of the month. Use the statutory year. Who pays whom what at closing?

2. The closing date is December 15, 2006. Taxes are $982, and cover the period from May 1, 2006, to April 30, 2007; they are not due and payable until the last day of the tax year. An insurance policy of 1 year, dated March 19, 2006, and costing $360, is to be assumed. The property is not rented, and the loan is not to be assumed. Use the *actual* year. Who pays whom what?

3. Use the statutory year for insurance and taxes. The closing date is April 20, 2006. Taxes are $1188 per year and are payable in four quarterly installments due March 31, June 30, September 30, and December 31 of each year. Quarterly tax payments are equal. An insurance policy costing $1046.55 for 5 years, dated July 16, 2003, is to be assumed. The property is not rented. Who pays whom what?

4. The closing date is September 25; use the statutory year. In this area, two property taxes are paid. A $555.10 *city* tax must be paid by August 15, while a $303.25 *county* tax must be paid by October 15. Taxes cover the calendar year in which they are paid. What is the *net* amount payable? Who pays it to whom?

Hints on Handling Mathematical Problems on Examinations _____

Now that the different kinds of mathematics problems that appear on licensing examinations have been discussed, a few remarks dealing with the proper ways to approach them are in order.

You should remember that your objective on the examination is to get a passing grade. It is *not* necessary that you get 100 percent—only enough to pass. Mathematical problems can be terrible time-consumers; therefore you should devote your time at the outset to the problems that do not take a lot of time. Save the complicated ones for later, when you have had the chance to answer all the "easy" questions. Many examinees determinedly tackle the mathematics first or spend tremendous amounts of time on a very few problems, only to find later that they have to rush just to have a chance of getting to every question on the examination.

Try to determine just how long a problem will take *before* you tackle it. If it's going to take a lot of time, postpone it. Then when you get back to the time-consuming questions, do first those that are worth the most points. This may mean that you will turn in your examination without finishing one or two of the really long arithmetic problems. That doesn't mean you're stupid—it means you're smart. Instead of slaving away over the few points these unfinished problems represented, you used your time to build up a good score on the other parts of the examination that could be answered quickly. However, before turning in your test paper, try to mark an answer for *every* question, even math problems not attempted. You might just guess the right answer!

Another point to remember concerning arithmetic questions is that you may not need all the information given. After you read the question and determine just what you are being asked to do, begin to search for the information you need to provide the answer. Do not assume that just because some information is included you must find some way of using it in your solution. Fairly often extra information has been included just to sidetrack or confuse examinees whose arithmetic skills make them unsure of themselves.

Problem Set A

1. **$39.92** total cost
The house is 55 ft. × 30 ft., or 170 ft. around. Since it is 8½ ft. high, the total wall area is
170 ft. × 8.5 ft. = 1445 sq. ft.
Now we must subtract for doors, the picture window, and other windows:
Doors: 3 ft. × 7.5 ft. = 22.5 sq. ft. each
Picture window: 12 ft. × 5 ft. = 60 sq. ft.
Windows: 2.5 ft. × 4 ft. = 10 sq. ft. each
Unpainted area includes:
2 doors @ 2.5 sq. ft.   ·45 sq. ft.
Picture window   60 sq. ft.
6 windows @ 10 sq. ft.   60 sq. ft.
Total unpainted area   165 sq. ft.
If 165 sq. ft. are unpainted, then 1280 sq. ft. (1445 − 165) must be painted. A gallon of paint covers 320 sq. ft. Therefore, we will need:
1280 sq. ft. ÷ 320 sq. ft. = 4 gal. of paint @ $9.98 = **$39.92** total cost

2. **352** lots
76 acres is 3,310,560 sq. ft. (76 × 43,560). Subtracting 665,000 sq. ft. for roads, parks, etc., leaves 2,645,560 sq. ft. to be devoted to lots. Each lot must be 7500 sq. ft.
2,645,560 sq. ft. ÷ 7500 sq. ft. = 352.74
Therefore, Orsini can get no more than **352** lots out of the land.

3. **$1389.20** total cost
The following diagram shows that the walk can be divided into two parts, each 43 ft. × 8 ft., and one part 65 ft. × 8 ft. These contain 344 + 344 + 520 = 1208 sq. ft. If 1 sq. ft. costs $1.15, then 1208 sq. ft. cost 1208 × $1.15 = **$1389.20**.

4. **68.707** ft.
There are 9 sq. ft. in 1 sq. yd., so the lot contains 313 × 9 = 2817 sq. ft. If the plot is rectangular, with frontage of 41 ft., the depth must be
2817 sq. ft. ÷ 41 ft. = **68.707** ft.

5. **$2238.29** total value
The formula for the area of a triangle is $A = ½ × B × H$. The base (B) is 500 ft.; the height, or depth (H), is 650 ft.
500 ft. × 650 ft. = 325,000 sq. ft.
325,000 sq. ft. × ½ = 162,500 sq. ft.
162,500 sq. ft. ÷ 43,560 sq. ft. = 3.73049 acres
The land is valued at $600 per acre, so the total value is
$600 × 3.73049 acres = **$2238.29**

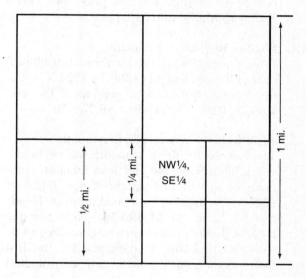

6. **38** acres
One section (1 square mile) contains 640 acres. (You have to know that fact.) The NW¼ of the SE¼ of a section, then, contains
¼ × ¼ × 640 = 40 acres

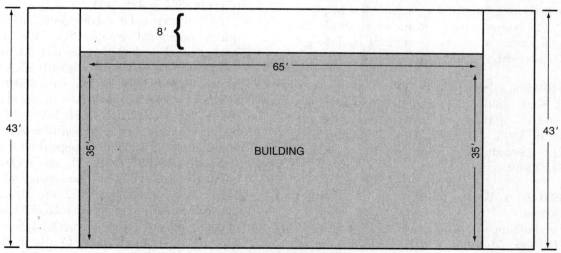

EXISTING SIDEWALK

Now we must determine how much of that 40-acre tract is taken up by the road. The road is 66 ft. wide. The 40-acre tract is ¼ mi. on a side (draw a diagram, if necessary, as shown); ¼ mi. is 1320 ft. (or 5280 ft. ÷ 4). Therefore, the road is 66 ft. × 1320 ft., since it crosses the entire tract.

1320 ft. × 66 ft. = 87,120 sq. ft.
87,120 sq. ft. ÷ 43,560 sq. ft. = 2 acres

If the road contains 2 acres, then Huang ended up with the rest of the 40 acres, or **38** acres.

Problem Set B

1. **$350,000** purchase price.
   If Peters sold her home for $497,000 and made a 42 percent profit, then $497,000 is 142 percent of her original purchase price: $497,000 ÷ 1.42 = **$350,000** purchase price.

2. **$6,736.50** discount on loan.
   First, the amount of the loan, which is 90 percent of the price of $249,500, or $224,550. The three-point discount is 3 percent of the loan amount: 0.03 × $224,550 = **$6,736.50**.

3. **$1,590.56** interest for the first month.
   The interest for the first month will be ¹⁄₁₂ of a year's interest on the full loan amount, since none of it will be paid back yet. 0.085 × $224,550 = $19,086.75 annual interest. Divide that by 12 to get **$1,590.56**. (Note that the term of the loan—25 years—has nothing to do with this problem. The interest for the first month is the same no matter how long or short the loan term is.)

4. **2¼ percent** depreciation per year.
   The building had depreciated a total of $45,281.25, which is $287,500 − $242,218.75. Next we determine what percent $45,281.25 is of $287,500: $45,281.25 ÷ $287,500 = 15¾%.
   This occurred over 7 years, so we divide the total depreciation of 15¾ percent by 7 to get **2¼ percent**.

5. **$199,900** sale price.
   If Sellar paid a 7½ percent commission, his $184,907.50 represents 92½ percent of the sale price (100% − 92½% = 7½%). $184,907.50 is 92.5 percent of ?. $184,907.50 ÷ .925 = **$199,900** sale price.

6. **$2,849** is Winken's share of the monthly income.
   The building's annual return is 21 percent of $440,000: $440,000 × .21 = $92,400 annual income. Divide by 12 to get the monthly building

income of $7,700. Winken gets 37 percent of that amount: $7,700 × .37 = **$2,849**.

7. **$99,220** Nod's share; **122.22 percent** rate of profit.
   Since Winken owns 37 percent and Blinken owns 22 percent, that leaves 41 percent for Nod (100 − 37 − 22 = 41). The total profit is $242,000 ($440,000 − $198,000). Nod's share is 41 percent of this: $242,000 × .41 = **$99,220**. Nod started with $81,180 (41 percent of $198,000) and his profit of $99,220 would be 122.22 percent of that amount ($99,220 ÷ $81,180 = 1.2222). Note that the rate of profit for the entire building is the same as it is for each of the three investors. This just means that all three of them experienced the same growth in wealth as did the entire investment. If you're skeptical about this, work it out for each of the other two investors and for the building as a whole.

8. **$4,352.22** paid to Bernie.
   This problem is cumbersome and time consuming, but not difficult. First we determine what percentage of the total commission goes to Bernie's broker: the other broker gets 40 percent; 3 percent goes to the Multilist group, so 57 percent is left for Bernie's broker (100 − 40 − 3 = 57). Now we figure the dollar amount of the 6½ percent commission: $223,750 × .065 = $14,543.75 total commission. Bernie's broker gets 57 percent of that: $14,543.75 × .57 = $8,289.94 to Bernie's broker. Bernie gets 52½ percent of that: $8,289.94 × .525 = **$4,352.22**.

9. **$131.25** quarterly payment; **$21.04** more per year for compounding
   The simple interest due quarterly is ¼ of the annual interest, which is 10½ percent of $5000, or 0.105 × $5000 = $525. The quarterly simple interest is $525 ÷ 4 = $131.25.
   To find accumulated compound interest requires additional computation. We already know, from the calculations we just did, that the interest for the first quarter is $131.25. For the second quarter, then, we will have $5000.00 + $131.25 = $5131.25 on which to calculate interest. Thus, ¼ × 0.105 × $5131.25 = $134.70, the interest due for the *second* quarter. At this point, a total of $265.95 of unpaid interest has accrued ($131.25 + $134.70), so for the third quarter interest must be calculated on $5265.95: ¼ × 0.105 × $5265.95 = $138.23. At the end of the third quarter a total of $404.18 in unpaid interest has accrued ($265.95 + $138.23); therefore, for the fourth quarter interest will be calculated on $5404.18. The inter-

est for the fourth quarter is ¼ × 0.105 × $5404.18 = $141.86, giving a total interest for the year of $546.04 ($404.18 + $141.86).

Simple interest would have been 4 × **$131.25** = $525.00, so with compound interest a total of **$21.04** more is paid ($546.04 − $525).

10. **32.8%** loss; **4.1%** annual depreciation rate
The total amount of the loss is $930,000 − $625,000 = $305,000. This is 32.8 percent of $930,000 ($305,000 ÷ $930,000 = 0.328). Profit and loss are calculated based on the *purchase* price originally paid. Since this depreciation occurred over an 8-year period, the annual depreciation rate is **32.8%** ÷ 8 = **4.1%**.

11. Financial calculator:

$1,400 × .85	= 1,190	PV
$122 payment	=	PMT
12 months	=	N
Calculate		i 3.34
Multiply i × 12 months	=	40.1

12. $168,000 ÷ $2,000,000 = 8.4%

13. $2,000,000 ÷ $12,400 monthly rent = 161.29 monthly GRM
161.29 ÷ 12 months = 13.44

14.

20 units × $900 × 12 months	=	$216,000
18 units × $1,050 × 12 months	=	226,800
Potential gross income	=	$442,800

Problem Set C

1. Taxes: **$1,993.08** payable to seller
Insurance: **$1,224.11** payable to seller
Interest: **$1,092.87** payable to buyer
Rent: **$73.33** payable to buyer
Taxes: June 26 represents 5 months and 26 days that the seller will own the property during the year. He has already paid the taxes, since they were due June 1. Therefore, the buyer must pay the seller for the 6 months and 4 days that she will own the property. One month's taxes is $3,899.50 ÷ 12 = $324.9583. One day's taxes is $324.9583 ÷ 30 = $10.8319.

6 months @ $324.9583	=	$1,949.7498
4 days @ $10.8319	=	+ 43.3276
Total taxes payable to seller:		$1,993.0774

= **$1,993.08** rounded
Insurance: The policy expires May 1, 2007, so the buyer will own it for 10 months and 5 days. The monthly charge is $1,444.85 ÷ 12 =

$120.4042. The daily charge is $120.4042 ÷ 30 = $4.0135.

10 months @ $120.4042	=	$1,204.0420
5 days @ $4.0135	=	+ 20.0675
Total insurance payable to seller:		$1,224.1095

= **$1,224.11** rounded
Interest: The next payment is due July 1; it includes all the interest for June and will be paid by the buyer. The seller must therefore pay the buyer his share (26 days) of the June interest. One year's interest is $288,230.11 × 0.0525 = $15,132.0808. One month's interest is $15,132.0808 ÷ 12 = $1,261.0067. One day's interest is $1,261.0067 ÷ 30 = $42.0336. The seller owes the buyer 26 days of interest: 26 × $42.0336 = $1,092.8736, or **$1,092.87** rounded.
Rent: The seller has been paid the $550 rent for the entire month of June; the buyer will own the property for 4 days in June, so the seller owes the buyer 4 days' worth of June rent. One day's rent proration is $550.00 ÷ 30 = $18.3333. Four days' worth of rent is 4 × $18.3333 = $73.3332, or **$73.33** rounded.

2. Taxes: **$616.10** payable to buyer
Insurance: **$91.73** payable to seller
Taxes: The taxes due cover from May 1 to December 15 for the seller, who has to pay his share to the buyer at closing, since the buyer will be liable for the entire year's tax bill at the end of the tax year. One day's tax charge is $982.00 ÷ 365 = $2.69041. The seller owns the property for 229 days (31 days each in May, July, August, and October; 30 days each in June, September, and November; and 15 days in December): 229 × $2.69041 = $616.10389 = **$616.10** payable to the buyer.
Insurance: One day's insurance is $360 ÷ 365 = $0.98630. The buyer must pay the seller, since the seller paid the full premium when the policy was bought. The buyer will own the property from December 16 (the day after closing, for prorating purposes!) through the expiration of the policy on March 18. She will own it for 93 days (16 in December, 31 in January, 28 in February, 18 in March): 93 × $0.98630 = $91.7259 = **$91.73** payable to the seller.

3. Taxes: **$66** due to buyer
Insurance: **$468.04** due to seller
Taxes: Taxes here are paid quarterly and not annually. The closing date is April 20, so the March 31 payment already has been made. The only payment that must be prorated is the June 30 payment, since it covers a period in which both buyer and seller will own the property. Quarterly taxes are $1188.00 ÷ 4 = $297.00.

Monthly taxes are $297.00 ÷ 3 = $99.00. Daily taxes are $99.00 ÷ 30 = $3.30. These numbers all come out even, and no rounding will be necessary, so no extra decimal places are required.

The seller will own the property for the 20 days of April during the second quarter. Therefore, he must pay the buyer 20 × $3.30 = **$66** for his share of the second quarter's taxes.

Insurance: The 5-year policy cost $1046.55; 1 year's insurance charge is $1046.55 ÷ 5 = $209.31. One month's charge is $209.31 ÷ 12 = $17.4425. One day's charge is $17.4425 ÷ 30 = $0.5814. The policy expires July 15, 2008.

$$
\begin{array}{ccc}
\scriptstyle 7 & \scriptstyle 6 & \scriptstyle 45 \\
8 - \not{7} - \not{15} \\
\underline{-\,6 - 4 - 20} \\
2 \quad\; 2 \quad\;\; 25
\end{array}
$$

The buyer will own the policy for 2 years, 2 months, and 25 days.

2 years @ $209.31	=	$418.62
2 months @ $17.4425	=	34.885
25 days @ $0.5814	= +	14.535
Total due seller for insurance		**$468.04**

4. Seller owes **$76.75** to buyer.
    In this problem, part of the tax is payable before the closing (by the seller) and part is payable after the closing (by the buyer). The seller owns the property for 8 months and 25 days of the year; the buyer owns it for 3 months and 5 days.

    City tax: This is payable by the buyer to the seller, since it was paid August 15. One month's tax is $555.10 ÷ 12 = $46.2583; one day's tax is $46.2583 ÷ 30 = $1.5419. The seller receives payment for 3 months and 5 days, or $146.48 from the buyer.

    County tax: This is payable by the seller to the buyer, since it is due *after* closing. The tax is $303.25 ÷ 12 = $25.2708 monthly; daily it is $25.2708 ÷ 30 = $0.8424. The seller owes a total of $223.23 to the buyer. Therefore, the seller owes a net of $223.23 − $146.48 = **$76.75** to the buyer.

Chapter 19/*Escrow and Closing Statements*

The *closing* of a transaction, also called *settlement*, is when money and property change hands. Picture this scene which is the case in many states but not California: the buyer and seller sit in a small room on opposite sides of a conference table, each next to their own attorney. The seller signs and hands over a deed to the property to the buyer while simultaneously, the buyer signs and hands over a certified check to the seller. Neither party releases a grip on the document they are about to give up until the document to be received is firmly in hand. If mortgage loans are involved, for example an old one to be paid off and a new one borrowed, a representative of each lender is present to secure their documents and legal positions. When the parties leave the room, money and title have changed hands. At that point, with rare exceptions, the transaction is irreversible.

In California, the above-described scene does not occur. Instead, an *escrow agent* is used. The buyer and seller, with the assistance of their broker, attorney and lender, give instructions to this escrow agent. When all the conditions for the sale are met, including the receipt of money, the escrow agent closes the sale. The escrow agent issues a check to the seller and records the title for the buyer, keeping a fee for this service.

Escrow Agents

An escrow agent is a third party (controlled by neither the buyer nor the seller) who receives money or documents from one party for transfer to the other party. The escrow agent is an obedient and trusted agent (with limited responsibilities as spelled out in the escrow instructions) of both buyer and seller. The escrow agent serves as a focal point for the transaction. Instead of sitting on opposite sides of a table in a closing room, the buyer and seller give instructions to the escrow agent. The escrow agent carefully examines the instructions, the documents, and performs an accounting of money. If everything fits and there are no conflicts, the sale is closed by the escrow agent, a process called *closing in escrow*. The buyer and seller can rest assured that nothing will occur unless all conditions of the sale have been met.

The escrow agent must:
1. Prepare required reports.
2. Calculate all amounts of expenses, including prorations of taxes.
3. Determine that all money and documents are together before closing the transaction.

The escrow agent's job is to make sure that all parties fulfill their obligations before closing. It is not the escrow agent's job to force either party to do anything, nor to urge or recommend anything to either party. The agent's responsibility is simply to determine that everything is in order, and not to close the transaction until it is. Upon closing, the escrow agent provides a settlement statement to both parties, which is a detailed accounting of all money and property.

The escrow agent should be fair and impartial to all parties, and disclose material facts concerning the transaction to all parties. The escrow agent must keep accurate and complete records. However, an escrow agent is not to comment on the viability or expected benefits of the transaction.

When there is a dispute between a prospective buyer and seller, the escrow agent should not interfere. Instead, the escrow agent may file an *interpleader* that forces the parties to go to court.

Who May Be an Escrow Agent

An escrow agent, also called an *escrow holder*, may be a bank, savings and loan association, title insurance company (see Chapter 9), attorney, real estate broker, or another party which or who must be incorporated. An escrow agent's license is not required of any of those parties. If not one of those parties, a company that wishes to be an escrow agent must be a corporation and obtain a license from the state of California for this purpose. Such an escrow company must provide a $25,000 surety bond.

The escrow agent typically employs individuals to do the actual work, and these employees are called *escrow officers*.

In southern California, escrow companies and financial institutions perform most transactions. Title insurance companies are typically used as escrow agents in northern California.

Real Estate Brokers as Escrow Agents

When a California real estate broker acts as an escrow agent, the state's Department of Corporations governs the broker's activities. The purpose of these regulations is to confine brokers to being escrow agents only to facilitate transactions that they broker. Some requirements are:

1. The broker must be a party to the transaction or the seller or the listing broker.
2. Agents of the broker, such as sales associates, may not act as escrow agents.
3. Escrows must not be the broker's main business, just incidental to the brokerage business, and the broker may not advertise services as an escrow agent outside the context of the brokerage business.
4. A broker must not form a network of escrow agents with other brokers.
5. All escrow funds must be kept in a separate trust account, subject to inspection by the California Commissioner of the Department of Corporations.

Creating an Escrow

Two requirements to create a valid escrow are:

1. A binding purchase agreement, and
2. A conditional delivery of the instruments of transfer, such as money, deeds, and loan documents. Delivery is conditional (not unconditional) in that the documents are returned intact if the contract fails to close.

Escrow Agent Duties

Duties that an escrow agent customarily performs include:

1. **Instructions**. The escrow agent is given specific instructions to carry out the terms of the contract. When parties separately give instructions to the escrow agent, the escrow instructions are called *unilateral*. In northern California, the practice is to give instructions unilaterally. In southern California, the practice is for the parties to give escrow instructions *bilaterally*, that is the buyer and seller provide one combined set of instructions to the escrow agent.

   Buyer and seller must sign instructions and give them to the escrow agent stating what they will do. These include the agreed purchase price, financing requirements, closing date, required inspections, insurance, possession date, expense prorations, and so on. The escrow agent thus gains statements from both parties indicating what conditions are required in order to close.

   After these instructions are given, one party cannot change them unilaterally, that is without written agreement of both parties.
2. **Title report.** The escrow agent orders a title report from a title company. A preliminary title report will indicate insurability of the title. If any problem appears, the escrow officer should inform all parties.

3. **Inspections.** Receives reports from inspectors (on wood destroying insects, physical house condition) and verifies the approval of the situation, or repairs, by the principals.

4. **Loan payoff.** Contacts existing lender for exact amount of loan payoff or amount to be assumed. Retires old loan at closing.

5. **Loan funding.** Be certain that all conditions are met for the new loan to be funded, and receive the check from the lender for the funds.

6. **Hazard insurance.** Be certain that hazard insurance coverage is secured. This will be a precondition to the loan. If the prior insurance policy will be cancelled, the unused premium will be refunded. If the prior policy continues, the amount will be prorated. Separate flood insurance is required in flood-prone areas.

7. **Prorations.** Charges to be divided between buyer and seller are done so, based on the cost and amounts remaining. These include taxes and special assessments, insurance, utilities and, for rental property, rents and security deposits.

8. **Final review.** Be certain that all problems have been cleared.

9. **Prepare Closing Statements.** Closing statements, in accordance with the Real Estate Settlements Procedures Act (RESPA) are prepared. They indicate amounts required from each party for each category of expense.

10. **Money transfers.** Accepts buyer's certified or cashier's check; write seller's check for the amount due.

11. **After closing.** Record deed, mortgage, and mail documents to appropriate party.

Responsibilities of Other Parties

For the escrow to work properly, buyers, sellers, and brokers need to be cooperative. Expectations of each are:

Buyer

1. Sign escrow instructions and give to escrow agent.
2. Provide copies of all contracts related to the transaction.
3. Review all documents: inspection reports, title reports, mortgage documents, etc.
4. Provide a check for the amount due.

Seller

1. Sign escrow instructions and give to escrow agent.
2. Provide copies of all contracts related to the transaction.
3. Provide all information related to the transaction, including documents related to any existing mortgage loan and/or other liens, and insurance policies.
4. If rental property, turn over leases, tenant security deposits, rent rolls, etc.

Real Estate Broker

1. Open escrow by bringing copies of the purchase agreement to the escrow agent.
2. Facilitate the actions of buyer and seller by providing coordination, explanations, and reminders.
3. Help arrange inspections, assure completion of contract provisions, and assist with both paperwork and physical checks.

Purpose of Closing Statements

Closing statements provide an accounting of all funds involved in a real estate transaction. These statements show the amount that the buyer must pay and that the seller will receive from the transaction. Buyer and seller each are given an accounting of all items they must pay for or are credited with in the transaction. Escrow agents should prepare a reconciliation for each sale as well, to "button up" the statements.

Debits and Credits

You need not be a bookkeeper to understand closing statements. Two columns are shown for the buyer and two for the seller. The two columns for each party are a debit column and credit column. Totals of debit and credit columns must agree with each other.

Listed in the debit column are amounts that the party being considered, buyer or seller, is charged for. Listed in the credit column are those that the party will receive credit for. Cash is needed to balance.

As a simple example, assume the sale of a $520,000 house on July 30, 2006. Assume that the seller has already paid taxes of $6,859.24 for the entire 2006–07 fiscal year. The seller should be credited with the payment of $520,000 for the house, and $6,306.68 of prepaid taxes for the remainder of the 2006 year (July 31, 2006 to June 30, 2007, during which time the buyer will own the house). Cash will be the offsetting debit.

The buyer will be debited for the house and paid-up taxes; cash is the offsetting credit. The closing statements will appear as follows:

	Seller Debit	Seller Credit	Buyer Debit	Buyer Credit
Real property		$520,000.00	$520,000.00	
Prepaid taxes		6,306.68	6,306.68	
Cash due from buyer				$526,306.68
Cash due to seller	$526,306.68			
Totals	$526,306.68	$526,306.68	$526,306.68	$526,306.68

(NOTE: If you cannot easily tell how the $6,306.68 of prorated property tax was calculated, you should review the section entitled "Proration" in Chapter 18.)

Now let us consider the same transaction, except that we will add two more items: A broker was involved, who earned a commission of $31,200 for making the sale; also, the buyer must pay $300 for a survey. The seller is to pay the commission, so the seller's statement will show a debit of the $31,200 broker's commission. The buyer's statement will show a debit of $300 for the survey. The new closing statement will appear as follows:

	Seller Debit	Seller Credit	Buyer Debit	Buyer Credit
Real property		$520,000.00	$520,000.00	
Prepaid taxes		6,306.68	6,306.68	
Sales commission	$31,200.00			
Survey fee			300.00	
Cash due from buyer				$526,606.68
Cash due to seller	$495,106.68			
Totals	$526,306.68	$526,306.68	$526,606.68	$526,606.68

An item that affects only one party is shown as a debit or a credit *only on the statement of the party affected.* For example, if the sales commission is paid by the seller, the amount appears only on the seller's closing statement. If the buyer pays for a survey, it appears only as a debit to him.

Items of value that are sold, exchanged, or transferred between buyer and seller are shown in *opposite* columns of *both* parties. For example, the transferred property is shown as a credit to the seller *and* as a debit to the buyer. *Never should an item transferred, exchanged, or taken over be shown as a credit to both parties or as a debit to both.* If an item is transferred, sold, or exchanged, it is a debit to one party and a credit to the other.

Items usually *debited* (charged) to the buyer that are likely to be encountered include the following:

1. Purchase price of the real property
2. Purchase price of personal property
3. Deed-recording fees
4. Title examination

5. Title insurance
6. Hazard insurance
7. Survey
8. Appraisal fee (sometimes charged to seller)
9. Prepaid taxes
10. Loan assumption fees

Items that are likely to be *credited* to the buyer are:
1. Earnest money deposits
2. Proceeds of a loan he borrows
3. Assumption of a loan
4. Trust deed to the seller (purchase money mortgage)
5. Current taxes unpaid to closing
6. Tenant rents paid in advance (the seller collected these)
7. Balance due to close (paid by buyer to close)

Items likely to be *debited* to a seller are:
1. Sales commission
2. Current but unpaid taxes
3. Existing debt, whether assumed or to be paid off
4. Loan prepayment penalties
5. Discount points for buyer's VA or FHA loan. Discount points on *conventional* loans may be charged to buyer or to seller depending on contractual arrangements, custom in the area, local law, and so on
6. Rent received in advance
7. Deed preparation

Items usually *credited* to a seller are:
1. Sales price of real property
2. Sales price of personal property
3. Prepaid taxes
4. Prepaid insurance (only if policy is assumed by buyer)
5. Escrow balance held by lender

COMPREHENSIVE SAMPLE PROBLEM

Abe Seller and Will Buyer are to close on Seller's house on January 30, 2007. The purchase price is $520,000. In addition, Buyer will pay $2,600 for appliances. Seller is to pay a commission of 6 percent of the sale price to XYZ Realty, Inc. County property taxes for calendar 2007 were $6,859.24, and were due on January 15, 2007. They were paid in full on that date by Mr. Seller. Since the house is in an unincorporated area, there is no city property tax.

The property was occupied by Ms. Happy Tenant, whose lease survives the sale. Her monthly rental is $3,100, paid on the first of each month. Rent is to be prorated to the date of closing.

Abe Seller owes $353,108.48 on a mortgage loan carrying an interest rate of 11¾ percent, which must be paid off at closing, plus interest for the entire month of January. He also will incur a 1 percent mortgage prepayment penalty. In addition, he has agreed to pay two discount points on Mr. Buyer's $490,000 VA mortgage loan.

Mr. Buyer will take over Mr. Seller's hazard insurance policy. The policy anniversary date is January 26, 2007. Mr. Seller has not yet paid the $2,920 annual premium, so Mr. Buyer will have to pay it at a later date.

At closing, Mr. Seller will be charged $500 for a termite inspection. Mr. Buyer will pay $300 for a survey, $500 for an appraisal and credit report, $264 for trust deed recording fees, and $48 to record the warranty deed. He also will be charged $2,680 for title insurance. Mr. Buyer will execute a trust deed in favor of Mr. Seller to secure a purchase money mortgage loan of $30,000 from Mr. Seller to Mr. Buyer. An $8,000 earnest money deposit from Mr. Buyer is being held in escrow by XYZ Realty, Inc., to be applied to the purchase price at closing.

Using Figure 19-1 and the information given above, complete the closing statement.

Figure 19-2 is a completed worksheet for this problem, Completed Statement Worksheet.

SETTLEMENT DATE:	BUYER'S STATEMENT		SELLER'S STATEMENT	
	DEBIT	CREDIT	DEBIT	CREDIT

Figure 19-1.   Settlement Statement Worksheet

Broker's Reconciliation

A cash reconciliation worksheet is used to assure that all cash receipts and disbursements are accounted for properly. Like a closing statement, it has two columns, which can be described as "cash receipts" and "cash disbursements," respectively. The totals of the two columns must agree.

The reconciliation can be prepared using the following steps:

1. Go down the debit column of the purchaser's closing statement.
   A. List the items that the broker will pay from the purchaser's account in the "disbursements" column of the reconciliation.
   B. On a separate worksheet called "Loan Proceeds" (page 337), list the items that the new mortgage lender will receive directly from the buyer or will withhold from the loan amount.
2. Go down the credit column of the buyer's closing statement.
   A. List on the broker's reconciliation, as a receipt, all cash paid by the buyer. Be sure to include the earnest money and cash paid at closing.
   B. On the top of the loan proceeds worksheet, list the amounts of mortgage money supplied at closing. Do not include assumed trust deeds or those taken by the seller in partial payment.
3. Go down the debit column of the seller's closing statement.
   A. List any amounts to be paid by the broker on behalf of the seller as a "disbursement" on the broker's reconciliation.
   B. List the sales commission as a disbursement on the broker's reconciliation.
   C. On the loan proceeds worksheet, list the balance of loans to be paid off, accrued interest, prepayment penalties, and discount points charged to the seller.

SETTLEMENT STATEMENT WORKSHEET

SETTLEMENT DATE: 1/30/07	BUYER'S STATEMENT		SELLER'S STATEMENT	
	DEBIT	CREDIT	DEBIT	CREDIT
PURCHASE PRICE	$520,000.00			$520,000.00
EARNEST MONEY		$8,000.00		
TRUST DEED		$490,000.00		
SECOND TRUST DEED		$30,000.00	$30,000.00	
PRORATED TAXES	$6,306.68			$6,306.68
PRORATED INSURANCE		$32.00	$32.00	
PRORATED RENT		$100.00	$100.00	
PERS. PROPERTY PURCH.	$2,600.00			$2,600.00
TRUST DEED PAYOFF			$353,108.48	
ACCRUED MORTGAGE INT.			$3,310.40	
PREPAYMENT PENALTY			$3,531.08	
BROKERAGE COMMISSION			$31,200.00	
DISCOUNT POINTS			$9,800.00	
TERMITE INSPECTION			$500.00	
DEED RECORDING	$48.00			
TRUST DEED RECORDING	$264.00			
SURVEY	$300.00			
APPRAISAL AND CREDIT REPORT	$500.00			
TITLE INSURANCE	$2,680.00			
DUE FROM BUYER/TO SELLER		$4,566.68	$97,324.72	
	$532,698.68	$532,698.68	$528,906.68	$528,906.68

Figure 19-2. Completed Settlement Statement Worksheet

4. Go down the credit column of the seller's closing statement. If the seller has paid cash and not received something from the buyer in return, it must be reconciled.

Items not selected in steps 1–4 include the property being sold and prorated charges. These items will not appear on the broker's reconciliation.

5. On the loan proceeds worksheet, sum all items, excluding the principal of the new loan, which was written on top of the page. Subtract the sum from the new loan principal to get the loan proceeds, and insert that amount as a receipt on the broker's reconciliation.

6. Total the receipts and the disbursements columns of the reconciliation. They should agree to complete the reconciliation.

Amounts shown in each column should be received/disbursed by the broker who has earned a commission.

LOAN PROCEEDS WORKSHEET

Amount borrowed on new loan		$490,000.00
Less: Discount points	$ 9,800.00	
Existing mortgage loan payoff	353,108.48	
Prepayment penalty	3,531.08	
Accrued interest payable	3,310.40	
. . . .	$369,749.96	− 369,749.96
Loan proceeds		$120,250.04

Figure 19-3 shows a broker's cash reconciliation statement for the sample problem described in the preceding section.

Address : **1999 Somewhere Parkway**   Closing Date : **January 30, 2007**

Mr. Abe Seller   **Mr. Will Buyer**
(Seller)   (Buyer)

	Receipts	Disbursements
From Buyer		
Earnest Money Deposited	8,000.00	
Check for Balance	4,566.68	
To Seller		
Check for Balance		97,324.72
Expenses		
Real Estate Commission		31,200.00
Preparation of Warranty Deed		
Preparation of Security Deed and Promissory Notes		
Title Fees		
Recording Trust Deed Security Deed xxxx		264.00
Recording Warranty Deed		48.00
Survey		300.00
Special Assessments		
First Trust Deed Proceeds	120,250.04*	
Appraisal and Credit Report		500.00
Termite Inspection		500.00
Title Insurance		2,680.00
	132,816.72	132,816.72

*See worksheet attached

Figure 19-3.   Cash Reconciliation Statement

Real Estate Settlement Procedures Act

The *Real Estate Settlement Procedures Act* (RESPA) covers most residential mortgage loans used to finance the purchase of one- to four-family properties. Included are a house, a condominium or cooperative apartment unit, a lot with a mobile home, and a lot on which a house will be built or a mobile home placed using the proceeds of a loan.

PURPOSE OF RESPA

The purpose of RESPA is to provide potential borrowers with information concerning the settlement (closing) process so that they can shop intelligently for settlement services and make informed decisions. RESPA does not set the prices for services; its purpose is merely to provide information about settlement (closing) and costs.

MATERIALS TO BE RECEIVED UNDER RESPA

Under RESPA, a person who files a loan application for property covered must receive from the lending agency a pamphlet titled *Settlement Costs and You* and a good-faith estimate of the costs of settlement services. The lender has 3 business days after receiving a loan application to mail these materials. From that time until settlement, the loan applicant has an opportunity to shop for loan settlement services. One business day before settlement, if the loan applicant requests, he has the right to inspect a Uniform Settlement Statement (page 340), which shows whatever figures are available at that time for settlement charges. At settlement the completed Uniform Settlement Statement is given to the borrower or his agent. When there is no actual settlement meeting, the Uniform Settlement Statement is mailed.

UNIFORM SETTLEMENT STATEMENT (HUD-1 FORM)

As discussed, the Uniform Settlement Statement (usually called the *HUD-1 Form*) is used in all RESPA-affected transactions (which include practically all residential transactions). The form is shown in Figure 19-4; it has been filled in using the same information as in the comprehensive sample problem described on page 335. Note that one item not mentioned in the sample problem is flood insurance, and no dollar figure is given on the form. Instead the notation "POC" ("paid outside closing") is used to show an item that may be important to the deal at hand, but was paid for or otherwise settled by the parties before closing.

SETTLEMENT COSTS AND YOU

The pamphlet *Settlement Costs and You* contains information concerning shopping for services, homebuyer's rights, and homebuyer's obligations. It also includes a sample Uniform Settlement Statement (HUD-1 Form) and describes specific settlement services. In addition, it provides information concerning a comparison of lender costs and describes reserve accounts and adjustments between buyer and seller.

Requirement to Report to the Internal Revenue Service

The Federal Tax Reform Act of 1986 created a requirement that brokers and/or settlement agents report the details of some real estate transactions to the U.S. Internal Revenue Service. The primary responsibility lies with the settlement agent, the person who actually handles the closing.

If there is no settlement agent, the responsibility rests with the buyer's broker and the seller's broker, in that order. Not all transactions need be reported.

A. Settlement Statement

U.S. Department of Housing
and Urban Development

OMB Approval No. 2502-0265
(expires 9/30/2006)

B. Type of Loan

1. ☐ FHA	2. ☐ FmHA	3. ☐ Conv. Unins.	6. File Number:	7. Loan Number:	8. Mortgage Insurance Case Number:
4. ☒ VA	5. ☐ Conv. Ins.				

C. Note: This form is furnished to give you a statement of actual settlement costs. Amounts paid to and by the settlement agent are shown. Items marked "(p.o.c.)" were paid outside the closing; they are shown here for informational purposes and are not included in the totals.

D. Name & Address of Borrower:	E. Name & Address of Seller:	F. Name & Address of Lender:
WILL BUYER 404 W. MAIN SOMEWHERE	ABE SELLER 915 OAK ST. SOMEWHERE ELSE	W.E. GOTCHA 4821 BIGG BLDG. ANYPLACE

G. Property Location:	H. Settlement Agent:	
915 OAK ST.	DUE ITRIGHT & CO.	
	Place of Settlement:	I. Settlement Date:
	4372 BIGG BLDG. ANYPLACE	1-30-07

J. Summary of Borrower's Transaction		**K. Summary of Seller's Transaction**	
100. Gross Amount Due From Borrower		**400. Gross Amount Due To Seller**	
101. Contract sales price	520,000.00	401. Contract sales price	520,000.00
102. Personal property (APPLIANCES)	2,600.00	402. Personal property (APPLIANCES)	2,600.00
103. Settlement charges to borrower (line 1400)	3,792.00	403.	
104.		404.	
105.		405.	
Adjustments for items paid by seller in advance		**Adjustments for items paid by seller in advance**	
106. City/town taxes to		406. City/town taxes to	
107. County taxes to	6,306.68	407. County taxes to	6,306.68
108. Assessments to		408. Assessments to	
109.		409.	
110.		410.	
111.		411.	
112.		412.	
120. Gross Amount Due From Borrower	532,698.68	**420. Gross Amount Due To Seller**	528,906.68
200. Amounts Paid By Or In Behalf Of Borrower		**500. Reductions In Amount Due To Seller**	
201. Deposit or earnest money	8,000.00	501. Excess deposit (see instructions)	
202. Principal amount of new loan(s)	490,000.00	502. Settlement charges to seller (line 1400)	41,500.00
203. Existing loan(s) taken subject to		503. Existing loan(s) taken subject to	
204. PURCHASE MONEY MORTGAGE	30,000.00	504. Payoff of first mortgage loan	353,108.48
205.		505. Payoff of second mortgage loan	
206.		506. 1ST MORTGAGE INTEREST	3,310.40
207.		507. 1ST MORTGAGE PREPAY PENALTY	3,531.08
208.		508. PURCHASE MONEY MORTGAGE	30,000.00
209.		509.	
Adjustments for items unpaid by seller		**Adjustments for items unpaid by seller**	
210. City/town taxes to		510. City/town taxes to	
211. County taxes to		511. County taxes to	
212. Assessments to		512. Assessments to	
213. PRORATED INSURANCE	32.00	513. PRORATED INSURANCE	32.00
214. PRORATED RENT	100.00	514. PRORATED RENT	100.00
215.		515.	
216.		516.	
217.		517.	
218.		518.	
219.		519.	
220. Total Paid By/For Borrower	528,132.00	**520. Total Reduction Amount Due Seller**	431,581.96
300. Cash At Settlement From/To Borrower		**600. Cash At Settlement To/From Seller**	
301. Gross Amount due from borrower (line 120)	532,698.68	601. Gross amount due to seller (line 420)	528,906.68
302. Less amounts paid by/for borrower (line 220)	(528,132.00)	602. Less reductions in amt. due seller (line 520)	(431,581.96)
303. Cash ☒ From ☐ To Borrower	4,566.68	603. Cash ☒ To ☐ From Seller	97,324.72

Section 5 of the Real Estate Settlement Procedures Act (RESPA) requires the following: • HUD must develop a Special Information Booklet to help persons borrowing money to finance the purchase of residential real estate to better understand the nature and costs of real estate settlement services; • Each lender must provide the booklet to all applicants from whom it receives or for whom it prepares a written application to borrow money to finance the purchase of residential real estate; • Lenders must prepare and distribute with the Booklet a Good Faith Estimate of the settlement costs that the borrower is likely to incur in connection with the settlement. These disclosures are manadatory.

Section 4(a) of RESPA mandates that HUD develop and prescribe this standard form to be used at the time of loan settlement to provide full disclosure of all charges imposed upon the borrower and seller. These are third party disclosures that are designed to provide the borrower with pertinent information during the settlement process in order to be a better shopper.

The Public Reporting Burden for this collection of information is estimated to average one hour per response, including the time for reviewing instructions, searching existing data sources, gathering and maintaining the data needed, and completing and reviewing the collection of information.

This agency may not collect this information, and you are not required to complete this form, unless it displays a currently valid OMB control number.

The information requested does not lend itself to confidentiality.

Figure 19-4.   HUD-1 Form

L. Settlement Charges

			Paid From Borrowers Funds at Settlement	Paid From Seller's Funds at Settlement
700.	**Total Sales/Broker's Commission based on price $ 520,000 @ 6 % = 31,200**			
	Division of Commission (line 700) as follows:			
701.	$ 31,200 to XYZ REALTY			
702.	$ to			
703.	Commission paid at Settlement			31,200.00
704.				
800.	**Items Payable In Connection With Loan**			
801.	Loan Origination Fee %			
802.	Loan Discount 2 %			9,800.00
803.	Appraisal Fee to			
804.	Credit Report 500 to MESSUP, INC.		500.00	
805.	Lender's Inspection Fee			
806.	Mortgage Insurance Application Fee to			
807.	Assumption Fee			
808.	HAZARD INSURANCE TO MILFORD INS. AGENCY			P.O.C.
809.	FLOOD INSURANCE TO MILFORD INS. AGENCY			P.O.C.
810.				
811.				
900.	**Items Required By Lender To Be Paid In Advance**			
901.	Interest from to @$ /day			
902.	Mortgage Insurance Premium for months to			
903.	Hazard Insurance Premium for years to			
904.	years to			
905.				
1000.	**Reserves Deposited With Lender**			
1001.	Hazard insurance months@$ per month			
1002.	Mortgage insurance months@$ per month			
1003.	City property taxes months@$ per month			
1004.	County property taxes months@$ per month			
1005.	Annual assessments months@$ per month			
1006.	months@$ per month			
1007.	months@$ per month			
1008.	months@$ per month			
1100.	**Title Charges**			
1101.	Settlement or closing fee to			
1102.	Abstract or title search to			
1103.	Title examination to			
1104.	Title insurance binder to			
1105.	Document preparation to			
1106.	Notary fees to			
1107.	Attorney's fees to			
	(includes above items numbers:)			
1108.	Title insurance 2,680.00 to RJL TITLE CO.		2,680.00	
	(includes above items numbers:)			
1109.	Lender's coverage $			
1110.	Owner's coverage $			
1111.				
1112.				
1113.				
1200.	**Government Recording and Transfer Charges**			
1201.	Recording fees: Deed $ 48.00 ; Mortgage $ 264.00 ; Releases $		312.00	
1202.	City/county tax/stamps: Deed $; Mortgage $			
1203.	State tax/stamps: Deed $; Mortgage $			
1204.				
1205.				
1300.	**Additional Settlement Charges**			
1301.	Survey $300 to JONES LAND SURVEY		300.00	
1302.	Pest inspection to ABC TERMITE CO.			500.00
1303.				
1304.				
1305.				
1400.	**Total Settlement Charges (enter on lines 103, Section J and 502, Section K)**		3,792.00	41,500.00

Figure 19-4.   HUD-1 Form (*continued*)

Questions on Chapter 19

1. To create an escrow in California there must be
   (A) a binding purchase agreement
   (B) a conditional delivery of documents
   (C) a real estate broker
   (D) A and B above

2. The escrow agent is an agent for
   (A) the buyer
   (B) the seller
   (C) the broker
   (D) both A and B

3. After escrow instructions have been given to the escrow agent, they may be changed orally by
   (A) the buyer
   (B) the seller
   (C) the real estate broker
   (D) none of the above

4. In northern California, most escrow instructions are
   (A) unilateral
   (B) unconditional
   (C) bilateral
   (D) semi-conditional

5. In northern California, most escrows are held by
   (A) escrow companies
   (B) financial institutions
   (C) title insurance companies
   (D) corporations

6. When there is a dispute between buyer and seller, the escrow agent may
   (A) take the seller's side
   (B) take the buyer's side
   (C) ask the real estate broker to decide the winner
   (D) file an interpleader to send the dispute to court

7. A real estate broker who wishes to be an escrow agent may
   (A) advertise aggressively of offering that service
   (B) assist other brokers who lack the expertise
   (C) offer the service only in connection with transactions they broker
   (D) pay a fee to a title insurance company

8. Which of the following is not exempt from escrow license laws
   (A) a savings and loan association
   (B) a mortgage banker
   (C) a title insurance company
   (D) a real estate broker

9. Providing information on tenant leases and security deposits to the escrow agent is the responsibility of the
   (A) seller
   (B) buyer
   (C) broker
   (D) lender

10. Written instructions to change an escrow agreement require permission from the
    (A) buyer
    (B) seller
    (C) both buyer and seller
    (D) broker

11. The purchase price is shown on the purchaser's closing statement as
    (A) a debit
    (B) a credit
    (C) both A and B
    (D) neither A nor B

12. The purchaser's earnest money held by a broker until closing is shown as
    (A) a debit to the purchaser
    (B) a credit to the seller
    (C) both A and B
    (D) neither A nor B

13. If property taxes for the current year have not yet been paid, they should be shown as
    (A) a credit to the buyer
    (B) a debit to the seller
    (C) both A and B
    (D) neither A nor B

14. A tenant paid rent at the beginning of the month. The sale of the property takes place during the middle of the month. The rent is prorated by
    (A) crediting the seller
    (B) debiting the buyer
    (C) both A and B
    (D) neither A nor B ← *X D* *since it is a renter.*

15. The buyer has arranged new financing for property. Closing statements, with respect to the mortgage principal, should show
    (A) a credit to the buyer
    (B) a debit to the seller
    (C) both A and B
    (D) neither A nor B   *X A*

16. The seller will pay a broker's commission. The commission is shown as
    (A) a credit to the seller
    (B) a debit to the seller
    (C) a debit to the buyer
    (D) A and C only

17. The buyer will take over the seller's insurance policy. The premium has been paid by the seller. The unexpired premium should be shown as
    (A) a credit to the seller
    (B) a debit to the buyer
    (C) both A and B
    (D) neither A nor B

18. The seller will accept a second trust deed from the buyer. The amount owed is shown as
    (A) a credit to the buyer
    (B) a debit to the seller
    (C) both A and B
    (D) neither A nor B   *X C*

19. The sale price of personal property to be paid for at closing is shown as
    (A) a credit to the buyer
    (B) a debit to the seller
    (C) both A and B
    (D) neither A nor B

20. An existing trust deed on the property is to be assumed by the buyer. The closing statements show the mortgage principal as
    (A) a credit to the buyer
    (B) a debit to the seller
    (C) both A and B
    (D) neither A nor B   *X C*

21. The buyer must pay $100 for a survey and credit report at closing. The settlement statements show
    (A) a debit to the buyer
    (B) a credit to the seller
    (C) both A and B
    (D) neither A nor B

22. The buyer has arranged a 10½ percent VA mortgage loan with two discount points that the seller will pay. The discount points are shown as
    (A) a debit to the seller
    (B) a debit to the buyer
    (C) both A and B
    (D) neither A nor B

23. The buyer is to assume the seller's mortgage loan and must also maintain the tax and insurance escrow account held by the mortgage lender. The escrow account balance is shown as a
    (A) debit to the buyer
    (B) credit to the seller
    (C) both A and B
    (D) neither A nor B

24. The tenant has a $250 security deposit in an account to be taken over by the buyer. At closing, the security deposit should be shown as a
    (A) credit to the buyer
    (B) credit to the seller
    (C) debit to the buyer
    (D) B and C only   *X A*

25. The seller incurs a prepayment penalty to pay off his mortgage loan. The penalty is shown as
    - (A) a credit to the seller
    - (B) a debit to the seller
    - (C) a credit to the buyer
    - (D) B and C only

26. The buyer, in connection with her new financing, must establish, at closing, a $500 escrow account for taxes and insurance. The escrow deposit is shown as
    - (A) a debit to the buyer
    - (B) a credit to the buyer
    - (C) a credit to the seller
    - (D) A and C only

27. The buyer will pay for warranty deed recording and title insurance at closing. These items are shown as
    - (A) a credit to the buyer
    - (B) a debit to the buyer
    - (C) a credit to the seller
    - (D) A and C only

28. RESPA is intended to
    - (A) regulate charges for settlement services
    - (B) provide information about settlement services to home loan applicants
    - (C) both A and B
    - (D) neither A nor B

29. After a home loan application is filed, how many business days does a lender have to provide a good faith estimate of settlement charges?
    - (A) 1
    - (B) 2
    - (C) 3
    - (D) 15

30. Upon the loan applicant's request, he has the right to inspect
    - (A) the seller's credit report
    - (B) a final Uniform Settlement Statement
    - (C) the broker's financial statement
    - (D) a Uniform Settlement Statement with whatever figures are available

31. Prepaid taxes on a closing statement are
    - (A) credited to the buyer
    - (B) credited to the seller
    - (C) debited to the seller
    - (D) paid at closing to the tax collector

32. During escrow, if an unresolved dispute should arise between the seller and buyer preventing the close of escrow, the escrow holder may legally
    - (A) arbitrate the dispute as a neutral party
    - (B) rescind the escrow and return all documents and monies to the respective parties
    - (C) file an interpleader action in court
    - (D) do any of the above

ANSWERS

1. **D**	9. **A**	17. **C**	25. **B**
2. **D**	10. **C**	18. **C**	26. **A**
3. **D**	11. **A**	19. **D**	27. **B**
4. **A**	12. **D**	20. **C**	28. **B**
5. **C**	13. **C**	21. **A**	29. **C**
6. **D**	14. **D**	22. **A**	30. **D**
7. **C**	15. **A**	23. **C**	31. **B**
8. **B**	16. **B**	24. **A**	32. **B**

PART V: OTHER LAWS AFFECTING REAL ESTATE

Chapter 20/*Fair Housing Law*

The Federal Fair Housing Act, Public Law 90–284, was enacted into law on April 11, 1968, as Title VIII of the Civil Rights Act of 1968.

Purpose

The purpose of the Fair Housing Act is expressed by Section 801 of the law, which states:

> *It is the policy of the United States to provide, within constitutional limitations, for fair housing throughout the United States.*

The following explanation of the need for fair housing is quoted directly from *Understanding Fair Housing*, U.S. Commission on Civil Rights.[*]

> *Housing is a key to improvement in a family's economic condition. Homeownership is one of the important ways in which Americans have traditionally acquired financial capital. Tax advantages, the accumulation of equity, and the increased value of real estate property enable homeowners to build economic assets. These assets can be used to educate one's children, to take advantage of business opportunities, to meet financial emergencies, and to provide for retirement. Nearly two of every three majority group families are homeowners, but less than two of every five nonwhite families own their homes. Consequently, the majority of nonwhite families are deprived of this advantage.*
>
> *Housing is essential to securing civil rights in other areas. Segregated residential patterns in metropolitan areas undermine efforts to assure equal opportunity in employment and education. While centers of employment have moved from the central cities to suburbs and outlying parts of metropolitan areas, minority group families remain confined to the central cities, and because they are confined, they are separated from employment opportunities. Despite a variety of laws against job discrimination, lack of access to housing in close proximity to available jobs is an effective barrier to equal employment.*
>
> *In addition, lack of equal housing opportunity decreases prospects for equal educational opportunity. The controversy over school busing is closely tied to the residential patterns of our cities and metropolitan areas. If schools in large urban centers are to be desegregated, transportation must be provided to convey children from segregated neighborhoods to integrated schools.*
>
> *Finally, if racial divisions are to be bridged, equal housing is an essential element. Our cities and metropolitan areas consist of separate societies increasingly hostile and distrustful of one another. Because minority and majority group families live apart, they are strangers to each other. By living as neighbors they would have an opportunity to learn to understand each other and to redeem the promise of America: that of "one Nation indivisible."*

---

[*]From *Understanding Fair Housing*, U.S. Commission on Civil Rights, Clearinghouse Publication 42, February 1973, p. 1.

Property Covered

The federal Fair Housing Act of 1988 extended the property covered to all single or multifamily dwelling units, with the few exceptions noted below. A *dwelling* is defined as any building or structure designed as a residence to be occupied by one or more families; included are mobile-home parks, trailer courts, condominiums, cooperatives, and time-sharing units. Community associations and "adult-only" communities are clearly included unless they qualify under an exception.

Housing-for-the-elderly communities are built and operated for older persons: specifically, 100 percent of the units must be occupied by residents 62 years of age or older, or 80 percent of the units must be occupied by at least one person age 55 or older, *and* significant facilities and services designed for use by elderly persons must be in place. Special facilities include an accessible physical environment, communal dining facilities, social and recreational programs, the availability of emergency and other health care facilities, and other amenities intended for the elderly. The apartments must publish and adhere to policies that demonstrate an intent to serve persons aged 55 and over.

Apartment complexes with four or fewer units are exempt from the federal Fair Housing Act when the owner occupies at least one unit, and single-family homes sold or rented by an owner are exempt. However, the exemption applies only to persons owning no more than three properties at one time and is subject to other restrictions. In selling, the owner may not use a real estate salesperson or broker and may not print, publish, or otherwise make any reference to preference, limitation, or discrimination on the basis of race, color, religion, sex, national origin, familial status, or handicap.

Discrimination in Sale or Rental

Section 804 of the Fair Housing Act makes it unlawful to do any of the following:

(a) *To refuse to sell or rent after the making of a bona fide offer, or to refuse to negotiate for the sale or rental of, or otherwise make unavailable or deny, a dwelling to any person because of race, color, religion, sex, national origin, familial status, or handicap.*

(b) *To discriminate against any person in the terms, conditions, or privileges of sale or rental of a dwelling, or in the provision of services or facilities in connection therewith, because of race, color, religion, sex, national origin, familial status, or handicap.*

(c) *To make, print, or publish, or cause to be made, printed, or published any notice, statement, or advertisement, with respect to the sale or rental of a dwelling that indicates any preference, limitation, or discrimination based on race, color, religion, sex, national origin, familial status, or handicap, or an intention to make any such preference, limitation, or discrimination.*

(d) *To represent to any person because of race, color, religion, sex, national origin, familial status, or handicap that any dwelling is not available for inspection, sale, or rental when such dwelling is in fact so available.*

(e) *For profit, to induce or attempt to induce any person to sell or rent any dwelling by representations regarding the entry or prospective entry into the neighborhood of a person or persons of a particular race, color, religion, sex, national origin, familial status, or handicap.*

1988 Amendments

Amendments to the federal Fair Housing Act that became law in 1988 extended protection to familial status and handicap. Familial status refers to members of a family. The amendment prohibits discrimination against people with children, adults living with or in the process of acquiring legal custody, of anyone under age 18, and pregnant women.

The physically and mentally handicapped are also covered. *Handicap* is defined as a mental or physical impairment that substantially limits a person's major life activities; included are persons with records of impairment. Current drug addicts, persons convicted of drug-related felonies, and transvestites are not protected as handicapped under the law, but alcoholics are covered.

The law also appears to prohibit restrictions that would prevent the handicapped from using necessary aids. For example, a person who requires a seeing-eye dog should be allowed to have one even if pets are otherwise prohibited in an apartment building. Similarly, that person would be allowed to take the dog through the hallway, even if dogs are generally prohibited in public parts of the building.

Today, nearly all dwelling units are subject to the Fair Housing Law.

Discrimination in New Construction

Under the 1988 amendments, newly constructed multifamily facilities (four or more units) must be accessible to the handicapped. In buildings with elevators, the handicapped must have access to 100 percent of the units, but only ground-floor units of garden-type apartments are required to be accessible.

Common areas in buildings must be accessible to all handicapped persons, and doors and hallways must be wide enough to allow passage of wheelchairs.

New living units must be constructed in a way that allows access for the handicapped, including the appropriate location of light switches, plugs, and environmental controls. Bathroom walls must be reinforced to allow future installation of grab rails, and the occupant must be allowed to install them. Requirements for removal, when the handicapped person vacates, are uncertain.

Discrimination in Financing

Section 805 of the Fair Housing Act applies to transactions after December 31, 1968. It states that it is unlawful for

> *any bank, building and loan association, insurance company or other corporation, association, firm or enterprise whose business consists in whole or in part in the making of commercial real estate loans, to deny a loan or other financial assistance to a person applying therefore for the purpose of purchasing, constructing, improving, repairing, or maintaining a dwelling, or to discriminate against him in the fixing of the amount, interest rate, duration, or other terms or conditions of such loan or other financial assistance, because of the race, color, religion, sex, or national origin of such person or of any person associated with him in connection with such loan or other financial assistance or the purposes of such loan or other financial assistance, or of the present or prospective owners, lessees, tenants, or occupants of the dwelling or dwellings in relation to which such loan or other financial assistance is to be made or given: Provided, that nothing contained in this section shall impair the scope or effectiveness of the exception contained in Section 803(b).*

Section 803(b) exempts a single-family house sale or lease by owner, if certain provisions are met. This exemption was described on page 346.

Federal law also prohibits lending institutions from *redlining*. Redlining is a practice whereby lenders designate certain areas as "too risky" and refuse to make loans on property in those areas. (The term *redlining* refers to outlining those areas in red on a map.) Before it was outlawed, redlining by lenders usually affected low-income areas and, particularly, areas whose populations were composed largely of minorities.

Discrimination in Brokerage Services

Section 806 of the Fair Housing Act states:

After December 31, 1968, it shall be unlawful to deny any person access to or membership or participation in any multiple-listing service, real estate brokers' organization or other service, organization, or facility relating to the business of selling or renting dwellings, or to discriminate against him in the terms or conditions of such access, membership, or participation, on account of race, color, religion, sex, national origin, familial status, or handicap.

Blockbusting

Blockbusting, that is, the soliciting of homeowners by unscrupulous real estate agents, brokers, or speculators who feed upon fears of homeowners, is prohibited by the Fair Housing Act. Blockbusters attempt to buy properties at very low prices from whites in racially transitional neighborhoods and then broker or sell them to blacks at high prices. Some blockbusters deliberately incite panic and white flight to achieve their greedy, unlawful goal.

Two Specific Exemptions

There are two specific, limited exemptions to the Fair Housing Laws. One exemption allows a religious organization to discriminate with respect to its noncommercial property. It does not, however, allow this exemption if the religion discriminates on the basis of race, color, sex, national origin, familial status, or handicap with respect to its membership. The other exemption allows private clubs that provide lodging as an incident to their main purpose to give preferential treatment to club members.

Enforcement by the Federal Government

Any person who claims to have been injured by a discriminatory housing practice or who believes that he will be irrevocably injured by a discriminatory housing practice that is about to occur (hereafter "person aggrieved") may file a complaint with the Secretary of the Department of Housing and Urban Development (HUD). Complaints must be in writing, must state the facts, and must be filed within 1 year after the alleged discriminatory housing practice occurred. The Attorney General conducts all litigation in which the Secretary of HUD participates as a party pursuant to the Fair Housing Act.

Enforcement by Private Persons

The rights granted to private persons by the Fair Housing Act may be enforced by civil action in appropriate U.S. district courts without regard to the amount in controversy, and in appropriate state or local courts of general jurisdiction. A civil action must be commenced within 1 year after the alleged discriminatory housing practice occurred.

Upon application by the plaintiff and in such circumstances as the court may deem just, a court of the United States in which a civil action under this section has been brought may appoint an attorney for the plaintiff and may, upon proper showing, authorize the commencement of a civil action without the payment of fees, costs, or security. A court of a state or subdivision thereof may do likewise to an extent not inconsistent with the law or procedures of the state or subdivision.

The court may grant as relief, as it deems appropriate, any permanent or temporary injunction, temporary restraining order, or other order, and may award to the plaintiff actual damages, injunctive or other equitable relief, and civil penalties up to $50,000 ($100,000 for repeating violators), together with court costs and reasonable attorney fees in the case of a prevailing plaintiff, provided that said plaintiff, in the opinion of the court, is not financially able to assume said attorney's fees.

Penalty for Injury, Intimidation, Discouragement

Under Section 901 of the Civil Rights Act of 1968 (Title IX) whoever

A. injures or threatens to injure or interfere with any person because of his race, religion, color, sex, national origin, familial status, or handicap, and who is selling, leasing, occupying, financing, etc., dwelling, or

B. intimidates persons who deal with others in housing on account of race, religion, color, sex, national origin, familial status, or handicap, or

C. discourages others from dealing with others in housing on account of race, religion, color, sex, national origin, familial status, or handicap

shall be fined up to $1000 or imprisoned for up to 1 year, or both. If bodily injury results, the penalty is a fine of $10,000 maximum or up to 10 years in prison, or both. If death results, the wrongdoer shall be imprisoned for any term of years or for life.

Other Fair Housing Laws

The Fair Housing Act was not the first law intended to prevent discriminatory practice in housing. The Supreme Court of the United States, in the 1917 *Buchanan* case, prohibited, on constitutional grounds, local governments from requiring residential segregation. This ruling is noteworthy because in 1896 the Supreme Court had established the doctrine that legally compelled segregation in such areas as public transportation and public education was constitutionally permissible. The Buchanan decision destroyed the doctrine as it applied to housing. In 1948, in *Shelley* v. *Kraemer*, the Supreme Court struck down as unconstitutional the legal enforcement of racially restrictive covenants.

The executive branch of the government took fair housing action for the first time in 1962, when President Kennedy issued an executive order on equal opportunity in housing. Although it represented a significant legal step forward, this executive order was limited. Its guarantee of nondiscrimination was restricted largely to housing provided through the insurance and guaranty programs administered by FHA and its sister agency, the Veterans Administration (VA), after the date of the order's issuance (November 20, 1962). Housing financed through conventional loans was not covered by the President's order, which also left hundreds of thousands of existing housing units receiving FHA and VA assistance immune from the nondiscrimination mandate. In fact, barely 1 percent of the nation's housing was covered by President Kennedy's executive order.

In 1964, Congress enacted Title VI of the Civil Rights Act of 1964, prohibiting discrimination in any program or activity receiving federal financial assistance. Among the principal programs affected by this law were low-rent public housing, a program directed to providing housing for the poor, and urban renewal. Like President Kennedy's executive order, Title VI excluded conventionally financed housing. It also excluded most FHA and VA housing that the executive order covered. Less than half of 1 percent of the nation's housing inventory was subject to the nondiscrimination requirement through Title VI.

In 1968, Congress enacted Title VIII of the Civil Rights Act of 1968, the federal Fair Housing Law. This law, which is the one described at the beginning of the chapter, prohibits discriminatory practices by all real estate brokers, builders, and mortgage lenders.

In June 1968, two months after enactment of Title VIII, the Supreme Court of the United States, in the landmark case of *Jones* v. *Mayer*, ruled that an 1866 civil rights law passed under the authority of the Eighteenth Amendment (which outlawed slavery) bars all racial discrimination in housing, private as well as public.

Today, over 90 percent of all U.S. housing is subject to the Fair Housing Law.

The Americans with Disabilities Act

The Americans with Disabilities Act (ADA), passed in 1992, considerably broadens the scope to which society in general must accommodate persons with disabilities. Many provisions of the act address discrimination in employment and access to public services. However, some of the most pervasive problems facing disabled persons have necessarily been involved with real estate: buildings are the most "barrier-prone" part of the physical environment. Narrow doors and hallways, variations in floor levels that require the negotiation of stairs, built-in facilities too high for the wheelchair-bound—the list of problems goes on and on.

Most new construction that may serve the public in general (almost anything except single-family housing) must meet barrier-free standards. Also, existing businesses with 15 or more employees must eliminate physical barriers that prevent disabled workers or customers from "functioning in the marketplace"; this *requirement* obviously requires considerable "retro-fitting" of existing real estate.

California Fair Housing Laws

THE RUMFORD ACT

The Rumford Act was passed in California in 1963. It prohibited discrimination based on race, color, creed, national origin, or ancestry in housing accommodation of three or more units, in public and redevelopment housing, and in owner-occupied single-family homes with public financing. The activities of real estate brokers, salespersons, and mortgage lenders were also covered.

In 1964, the voters enacted Proposition 14, which nullified the majority of the Rumford Act. In 1965, the California Supreme Court held Proposition 14 unconstitutional in violation of the equal protection clause of the federal Constitution. The Rumford Act was returned to its original full force and effect.

California's current Fair Employment and Housing Act (FEHA), California Government Code sections 12900–12996, prohibits housing discrimination based on marital status as well as race, color, religion, sex, national origin, or ancestry. The Department of Fair Employment and Housing enforces the law, which is based on the former Rumford Fair Housing Act.

CALIFORNIA HOUSING FINANCIAL DISCRIMINATION ACT OF 1977

This act, called the Holden Act, applies to owner-occupied residences of one to four families. The act prevents a lender from denying a loan or changing its terms for reasons unrelated to the credit of the borrower. Thus, *redlining* is prohibited under this act, as it is by the 1968 Civil Rights Act.

THE UNRUH CIVIL RIGHTS ACT

The *Unruh Civil Rights Act,* California Civil Code sections 51–51.3, provides protection from discrimination by all business establishments in California, including housing and public accommodations. Civil Code section 51(b) describes these protections:

> *All persons within the jurisdiction of this state are free and equal, and no matter what their sex, race, color, religion, ancestry, national origin, disability, or medical condition are entitled to the full and equal accommodations, advantages, facilities, privileges, or services in all business establishments of every kind whatsoever.*

Even though the language of the Act specifically outlaws discrimination in housing and public accommodations based on "sex, race, color, religion, ancestry, national origin, disability, or medical condition," the California Supreme Court has held that protections under the Unruh Act are not necessarily *restricted* to these characteristics. The Act is meant to cover all arbitrary and intentional discrimination by a business establishment on the basis of personal characteristics *similar* to those listed above.

Remedies under the Unruh Act include reimbursement of out-of-pocket expenses, cease-and-desist orders, damages for emotional distress, and exemplary damages. Court-ordered damages may include a maximum of three times the amount of the victim's actual damages. More information on this and other fair housing laws is available at the California Department of Fair Employment & Housing Web site at www.dfeh.ca.gov.

Questions on Chapter 20

1. The 1968 Fair Housing Act prohibits housing discrimination on the basis of
   (A) race and color
   (B) race, color, and religion
   (C) race, color, religion, and national origin
   (D) race, color, religion, national origin, sex, familial status, or handicap

2. The prohibitions of the 1968 Fair Housing Act apply to privately owned housing when
   (A) a broker or other person engaged in selling or renting dwellings is used
   (B) discriminatory advertising is used
   (C) both A and B
   (D) neither A nor B

3. The prohibitions of the 1968 Fair Housing Act apply to
   (A) multifamily dwellings of five or more units
   (B) multifamily dwellings of four or fewer units if the owner occupies one of the units
   (C) both A and B
   (D) neither A nor B

4. A single-family house privately owned by an individual owning fewer than three such houses may be sold or rented without being subject to the provisions of the Fair Housing Act unless
   (A) a broker is used
   (B) discriminatory advertising is used
   (C) both A and B
   (D) neither A nor B

5. The limiting of sale, rental, or occupancy of dwellings owned or operated by a religious organization for noncommercial purposes, provided that membership in said religion is not based on race, color, or national origin
   (A) is prohibited by the Fair Housing Act
   (B) is prohibited by the Civil Rights Act
   (C) both A and B
   (D) neither A nor B

6. A single-family house privately owned by an individual owning fewer than three such houses may be sold or rented without being subject to the provisions of the Fair Housing Act if
   (A) no more than one such house is sold in any 2-year period
   (B) a broker is employed to sell the house
   (C) both A and B
   (D) neither A nor B

7. What are the broker's responsibilities under the 1968 Fair Housing Act?
   (A) To show all houses to all prospects
   (B) To treat all prospects equally
   (C) Both A and B
   (D) Neither A nor B

8. Complaints about discrimination may be brought
   - (A) to the Secretary of Housing and Urban Development
   - (B) directly to court
   - (C) both A and B
   - (D) neither A nor B

9. If a minority prospect asks to be shown homes in white neighborhoods, the broker
   - (A) obliges and shows homes in white neighborhoods
   - (B) responds and shows homes as requested
   - (C) both A and B
   - (D) neither A nor B

10. The 1968 federal Fair Housing Law states that it is illegal to discriminate against any person because of race, color, religion, national origin, sex, familial status, or handicap
    - (A) in the sale, rental, or financing of housing or residential lots
    - (B) in advertising the sale or rental of housing
    - (C) both A and B
    - (D) neither A nor B

11. The broker's obligation in complying with the requirements for equal opportunity in housing is
    - (A) to replace white residents with minority homeowners
    - (B) to avoid any acts that would make housing unavailable to someone on account of color
    - (C) both A and B
    - (D) neither A nor B

12. The Civil Rights Act of 1968
    - (A) makes it illegal to intimidate, threaten, or interfere with a person buying, renting, or selling housing
    - (B) provides criminal penalties and criminal prosecution if violence is threatened or used
    - (C) both A and B
    - (D) neither A nor B

13. Court action may be taken by an individual under the Fair Housing Act
    - (A) only if a complaint is filed with HUD
    - (B) if action is taken within 1 year of the alleged discriminatory act
    - (C) if the alleged discriminatory act occurred on public property
    - (D) if the alleged discriminatory act caused damage of at least $500

14. Complaints under the California Fair Housing Act (Rumford Act) may be filed with the
    - (A) Secretary of State
    - (B) California Department of Fair Employment and Housing
    - (C) Department of Real Estate (DRE)
    - (D) California Association of Realtors (CAR)

15. The Unruh Civil Rights Act provides for
    - (A) actual damages
    - (B) punitive damages
    - (C) both A and B
    - (D) neither A nor B

16. An advertisement of an apartment for rent only to single women
    (A) is acceptable because they are better tenants
    (B) violates fair housing laws
    (C) is conditionally allowed
    (D) is altruistic

17. How can a real estate agent answer questions about a prospective buyer's race?
    (A) Such questions must be answered completely and accurately.
    (B) The agent is prohibited by law from answering such questions.
    (C) It is okay to lie.
    (D) The agent should use his or her best judgment about answering such questions.

18. The Rumford Act is principally concerned with
    (A) fair housing
    (B) fair employment
    (C) fair educational opportunities
    (D) fair discrimination

19. The Unruh Civil Rights Act
    (A) prohibits discrimination by individuals
    (B) prohibits discrimination by public schools
    (C) prohibits discrimination by businesses
    (D) prohibits discrimination by minorities

ANSWERS

1. **D**	6. **A**	11. **B**	16. **B**
2. **C**	7. **B**	12. **C**	17. **B**
3. **A**	8. **C**	13. **B**	18. **A**
4. **C**	9. **C**	14. **B**	19. **C**
5. **D**	10. **C**	15. **C**	

Chapter 21/*Truth-in-Lending Law*

Regulation Z of the Federal Reserve System, known as the Truth-in-Lending Act, became effective on July 1, 1969. Amendments established on April 1, 1981, became mandatory on April 1, 1982. The provisions affecting credit transactions in real estate are emphasized here, although the act covers other types of credit.

The purpose of Regulation Z is to let borrowers and consumers know the prevailing cost of credit so that they can compare costs among various credit sources and thus avoid the uninformed use of credit. Regulation Z also regulates the issuance of credit cards and sets maximum liability for their unauthorized use. In addition, it provides a procedure for resolving billing errors that occur in open end credit accounts. Regulation Z does not set maximum or minimum interest rates or require any charge for credit.

Coverage

Generally, Regulation Z applies to each individual or business that offers or extends credit when four conditions are met:
1. The credit is offered or extended to consumers.
2. The offering or extension of credit is done regularly (see definition of *creditor* below).
3. The credit is subject to a finance charge or is payable, pursuant to a written agreement, in more than four installments.
4. The credit is primarily for personal, family, or household purposes.

Definition of Creditors

Creditors are those who must comply with Regulation Z. A *creditor* is defined for this purpose as a person who arranges or extends credit more than 25 times a year (or more than 5 times in a year in the case of transactions secured by a dwelling).

The term *creditor* does not include a person (such as a real estate broker) who arranges seller financing of a dwelling or real property. However, a real estate broker may be a creditor in the following situations:
1. The broker acts as a loan broker to arrange for someone other than the seller to extend credit, provided that the extender of credit (the person to whom the obligation is initially payable) does not meet the *creditor* definition.
2. The broker extends credit, provided that the broker otherwise meets the *creditor* definition.

Penalties for Violation of Regulation Z

A lender who fails to make disclosures as required under the Truth-in-Lending Act may be sued for actual damages plus twice the amount of the finance charge, as well as court costs and attorneys' fees. The finance charge portion of damages is subject to a minimum of $100 and a maximum of $1000. If lenders are convicted in a criminal action for willfully or knowingly disobeying the act or the regulation, they may be fined up to $5,000, imprisoned for up to 1 year, or both.

Exempt Transactions

The following transactions are exempt from the Truth-in-Lending Law:
1. Business, commercial, agricultural, or organizational credit.
2. Extension of credit to other than a natural person, including credit to government agencies.
3. Credit over $25,000 not secured by real property or a dwelling.
4. Extension of credit that involves public utility service.
5. Securities or commodities accounts.
6. Home-fuel budget plans.

Annual Percentage Rate

Regulation Z takes ten printed pages to define *annual percentage rate (APR)*. Briefly summarized, APR means the true interest rate charged for the use of money.

Finance Charge

DEFINITION

The *finance charge* is the cost of consumer credit as a dollar amount. It includes any charge payable directly or indirectly by the consumer, and imposed (directly or indirectly) by the creditor, as part of or a condition of the extension of credit. It does not include any charge of a type payable in a comparable cash transaction.

EXAMPLES

1. Interest, time-price differential, and any amount payable under an add-on or a discount system of additional charges.
2. Service, transaction, activity, and carrying charges, including any charge imposed on a checking or other transaction account to the extent that the charge exceeds the charge for a similar account without a credit feature.
3. Points, loan fees, assumption fees, finder's fees, and similar charges.
4. Appraisal, investigation, and credit report fees.
5. Premiums or other charges for any guarantee or insurance that protects the creditor against the consumer's default or other credit loss.
6. Charges imposed on a creditor by another person for purchasing or accepting a consumer's obligation, if the consumer is required to pay the charges in cash, as an addition to the obligation, or as a deduction from the proceeds of the obligation.
7. Premiums or other charges for credit life, accident, health, or loss-of-income insurance, written in connection with a credit transaction.
8. Premiums or other charges for insurance against loss of or damage to property, or against liability arising out of the ownership or use of property, written in connection with a credit transaction.
9. Discounts for the purpose of inducing payment by a means other than the use of credit.

The following charges are not finance charges:
1. Application fees charged to all applicants for credit, whether or not credit is actually extended.
2. Charges for actual unanticipated late payment, for exceeding a credit limit, or for delinquency, default, or a similar occurrence.

3. Charges imposed by a financial institution for paying items that overdraw an account, unless the payment of such items and the imposition of the charge were previously agreed upon in writing.
4. Fees charged for participation in a credit plan, whether assessed on an annual or other periodic basis.
5. Seller's points.
6. Interest forfeited as a result of an interest reduction required by law on a time deposit used as security for an extension of credit.
7. The following fees in a transaction secured by real property or in a residential mortgage transaction, if the fees are bona fide and reasonable in amount:
   a. Fees for title examination, abstract of title, title insurance, property survey, and similar purposes.
   b. Fees for preparing deeds, mortgages, and reconveyance, settlement, and similar documents.
   c. Notary, appraisal, and credit report fees.
   d. Amounts required to be paid into escrow or trustee accounts if the amounts would not otherwise be included in the finance charge.
8. Discounts offered to induce payment for a purchase by cash, check, or certain other means.

Premiums for certain types of insurance are also excludable if certain conditions are met, and certain taxes and fees prescribed by law are excludable.

Content of Disclosures

The following are disclosure requirements for closed-end loans. Most real estate mortgages are considered closed-end because there are no subsequent credit advances. For each transaction, the creditor shall disclose the following information as applicable:
1. Creditor. The identity of the creditor making the disclosures.
2. Amount financed. The "amount financed," using that term, and a brief description such as "the amount of credit provided to you or on your behalf." The amount financed is calculated by:
   a. determining the principal loan amount or the cash price (subtracting any down payment);
   b. adding any other amounts that are financed by the creditor and are not part of the finance charge; and
   c. subtracting any prepaid finance charge.
3. Itemization of amount financed.
   a. A separate written itemization of the amount financed. (Good faith estimates of settlement costs for transactions subject to the Real Estate Settlement Procedures Act [RESPA] are acceptable substitutes.) These items include:
      i. The amount of any proceeds distributed directly to the consumer.
      ii. The amount credited to the consumer's account with the creditor.
      iii. Any amounts paid to other persons by the creditor on the consumer's behalf. The creditor shall identify those persons. (Generic names or general terms are acceptable for certain persons such as public officials, credit reporting agencies, appraisers, and insurance companies.)
      iv. The prepaid finance charge.
   b. The creditor need not comply with paragraph 3-a above if the creditor provides a statement that the consumer has the right to receive a written itemization of the amount financed, together with a space for the consumer to indicate whether it is desired, and the consumer does not request it.
4. Finance charge. The "finance charge" using that term, and a brief description such as "the dollar amount the credit will cost you."
5. Annual percentage rate. The "annual percentage rate," using that term, and a brief description such as "the cost of your credit as a yearly rate."

6.   Variable rate. If the annual percentage rate may increase after consummation, the following disclosures must be included:
   a.   The circumstances under which the rate may increase.
   b.   Any limitations on the increase.
   c.   The effect of an increase.
   d.   An example of the payment terms that would result from an increase.
7.   Payment schedule. The number, amounts, and timing of payments scheduled to repay the obligation.
   a.   In a demand obligation with no alternative maturity date, the creditor may comply with this paragraph by disclosing the due dates or payment periods of any scheduled interest payments for the first year.
   b.   In a transaction in which a series of payments varies because a finance charge is applied to the unpaid principal balance, the creditor may comply with this paragraph by disclosing the following information:
      i.   The dollar amounts of the largest and smallest payments in the series.
      ii.   A reference to the variations in the other payments in the series.
8.   Total of payments. The "total of payments," using that term, and a descriptive explanation such as "the amount you will have paid when you have made all scheduled payments."
9.   Demand feature. If the obligation has a demand feature, that fact shall be disclosed. When the disclosures are based on an assumed maturity of one year, that fact shall also be disclosed.
10.   Total sale price. In a credit sale, the "total sale price," using that term, and a descriptive explanation (including the amount of any down payment) such as "the total price of your purchase on credit, including your down payment of $_____ ." The total sale price is the sum of the cash price, the items described in paragraph 2-b, and the finance charge disclosed under paragraph 4 above.
11.   Prepayment.
   a.   When an obligation includes a finance charge computed from time to time by application of a rate to the unpaid principal balance, a statement indicating whether or not a penalty may be imposed if the obligation is prepaid in full.
   b.   When an obligation includes a finance charge other than the finance charge described in paragraph 11-a above, a statement indicating whether or not the consumer is entitled to a rebate of any finance charge if the obligation is prepaid in full.
12.   Late payment. Any dollar or percentage charge that may be imposed before maturity due to a late payment, other than a deferral or extension charge.
13.   Security interest. The fact that the creditor has or will acquire a security interest in the property purchased as part of the transaction, or in other property identified by item or type.
14.   Insurance. The items required by law in order to exclude certain insurance premiums from the finance charge.
15.   Certain security interest charges. The disclosures required by law in order to exclude from the finance charge certain fees prescribed by law or certain premiums for insurance in lieu of perfecting a security interest.
16.   Contract reference. A statement that the consumer should refer to the appropriate contract document for information about nonpayment, default, the right to accelerate the maturity of the obligation, and prepayment rebates and penalties. At the creditor's option, the statement may also include a reference to the contract for further information about security interests and, in a residential mortgage transaction, about the creditor's policy regarding assumption of the obligation.
17.   Assumption policy. In a residential mortgage transaction, a statement as to whether or not a subsequent purchaser of the dwelling from the consumer may be permitted to assume the remaining obligation on its original terms.
18.   Required deposit. If the creditor requires the consumer to maintain a deposit as a condition of the specific transaction, a statement that the annual percentage rate does not reflect the effect of the required deposit.

```
┌─────────────────────────────────────────────────────────────────────────────┐
│ Mortgage Savings and Loan Assoc.                                              │
│ Date:                                                                         │
│                                                                               │
│ ┌──────────────┬──────────────┬──────────────┬──────────────┐                │
│ │ ANNUAL       │ FINANCE      │ Amount       │ Total of     │                │
│ │ PERCENTAGE   │ CHARGE       │ Financed     │ Payments     │                │
│ │ RATE         │ The dollar   │ The amount   │ The amount   │                │
│ │ The cost of  │ amount the   │ of credit    │ you will     │                │
│ │ your credit  │ credit will  │ provided to  │ have paid    │                │
│ │ as a yearly  │ cost you.    │ you or on    │ after you    │                │
│ │ rate.        │              │ your behalf. │ have made    │                │
│ │              │              │              │ all payments │                │
│ │              │              │              │ as scheduled.│                │
│ │  10.85  %    │ $106,500.74  │ $44,605.66   │ $151,106.40  │                │
│ └──────────────┴──────────────┴──────────────┴──────────────┘                │
└─────────────────────────────────────────────────────────────────────────────┘
```

Your payment schedule will be:

Number of Payments	Amount of Payments	When Payments Are Due
360	$419.74	Monthly beginning 6/1/2006

This obligation has a demand feature.

You may obtain property insurance from anyone you want that is acceptable to Mortgage Savings and Loan Assoc. If you get the insurance from Mortgage Savings and Loan Assoc. you will pay $___ $150.00/year

Security: You are giving a security interest in:
☒ the goods or property being purchased.
☐ _____

Late Charge: If a payment is late, you will be charged $_____ **5** _____% of the payment.

Prepayment: If you pay off early, you may have to pay a penalty.

Assumption: Someone buying your house may, subject to conditions, be allowed to assume the remainder of the mortgage on the original terms.

See your contract documents for any additional information about nonpayment, default, any required repayment in full before the scheduled date, and prepayment refunds and penalties.

_____
e means an estimate

Figure 21-1. Sample of Mortgage with Demand Feature

DISCLOSURE FOR CERTAIN RESIDENTIAL MORTGAGE TRANSACTIONS

1. Time of disclosure. In a residential mortgage transaction subject to the Real Estate Settlement Procedures Act the creditor shall make good faith estimates of the disclosures described above before consummation, or shall deliver or place them in the mail not later than three business days after the creditor receives the consumer's written application, whichever is earlier. (See Figures 21-1, 21-2, and 21-3.)

2. Redisclosure required. If the annual percentage rate in the consummated transaction varies from the annual percentage rate disclosed by more than ⅛ of 1 percentage point in a regular transaction or more than ¼ of 1 percentage point in an irregular transaction, the creditor shall disclose the changed terms no later than consummation or settlement.

SUBSEQUENT DISCLOSURE REQUIREMENTS

1. Refinancings. A refinancing occurs when an existing obligation that was subject to this part of Regulation Z is satisfied and replaced by a new obligation undertaken by the same consumer. A refinancing is a new transaction requiring new disclosures to the consumer. The new finance charge shall include any unearned portion of the old finance charge that is not credited to the existing obligation. The following shall not be treated as a refinancing:

ANNUAL PERCENTAGE RATE	FINANCE CHARGE	Amount Financed	Total of Payments
State Savings and Loan Assoc.			Account number
The cost of your credit as a yearly rate.	The dollar amount the credit will cost you.	The amount of credit provided to you or on your behalf.	The amount you will have paid after you have made all payments as scheduled.
9.00 %	$83,452.22	$44,000.00	$127,452.22

Your payment schedule will be:

Number of Payments	Amount of Payments	When Payments Are Due
360	$354.03	Monthly beginning 6-1-2006

Variable Rate

The annual percentage rate may increase during the term of this transaction if the prime rate of State Savings and Loan Assoc. increases. The rate may not increase more often than once a year, and may not increase by more than 1% annually.

The interest rate will not increase above __15.00__ %. Any increase will take the form of higher payment amounts. If the interest rate increases by __1__ % in __one year__, your regular payment would increase to $ __$385.64__.

Security: You are giving a security interest in the property being purchased.

Late Charge: If a payment is late, you will be charged 5% of the payment.

Prepayment: If you pay off early, you ☐ may ☐ will not have to pay a penalty.

Assumption: Someone buying your house may, subject to conditions, be allowed to assume the remainder of the mortgage on the original terms.

See your contract documents for any additional information about nonpayment, default, any required repayment in full before the scheduled date, and prepayment refunds and penalties.

_____
e means an estimate

Figure 21-2.   Sample of Variable-Rate Mortgage

    a.   A renewal of a single payment obligation with no change in the original terms.

    b.   A reduction in the annual percentage rate with a corresponding change in the payment schedule.

    c.   An agreement involving a court proceeding.

    d.   A change in the payment schedule or a change in collateral requirements as a result of the consumer's default or delinquency, unless the rate is increased, or the new amount financed exceeds the unpaid balance plus earned finance charge and premiums for continuation of insurance of certain types.

    e.   The renewal of optional insurance purchased by the consumer and added to an existing transaction, if disclosures relating to the initial purchase were provided as required by this subpart.

2.   Assumptions. An assumption occurs when a creditor expressly agrees in writing with a subsequent consumer to accept that consumer as a primary obligor on an existing residential mortgage transaction. Before the assumption occurs, the creditor shall make new disclosures to the subsequent consumer, based on the remaining obligation. If the finance charge originally imposed on the existing obligation was an add-on or a discount finance charge, the creditor need only disclose:

    a.   The unpaid balance of the obligation assumed.

    b.   The total charges imposed by the creditor in connection with the assumption.

    c.   The information required to be disclosed under section 226.18(k), (l), (m), and (n) of Regulation Z.

    d.   The annual percentage rate originally imposed on the obligation.

    e.   The payment schedule under section 226.18(g) and the total of payments under section 226.18(h), based on the remaining obligation.

	Convenient Savings and Loan			Account number:

ANNUAL PERCENTAGE RATE The cost of your credit as a yearly rate.	FINANCE CHARGE The dollar amount the credit will cost you.	Amount Financed The amount of credit provided to you or on your behalf.	Total of Payments The amount you will have paid after you have made all payments as scheduled.
15.37 %	$177,970.44	$43,777	$221,548.44

Your payment schedule will be:

Number of Payments	Amount of Payments	When Payments Are Due
12	$446.62	Monthly beginning 6/1/2006
12	$479.67	" " 6/1/2007
12	$515.11	" " 6/1/2008
12	$553.13	" " 6/1/2009
12	$593.91	" " 6/1/2010
300	Varying from $637.68 to $627.37	" " 6/1/2011

Security: You are giving a security interest in the property being purchased.

Late Charge: If a payment is late, you will be charged 5% of the payment.

Prepayment: If you pay off early, you
    [X] may   ☐ will not   have to pay a penalty.
    [X] may   ☐ will not   be entitled to a refund of part of the finance charge.

Assumption: Someone buying your home cannot assume the remainder of the mortgage on the original terms.

See your contract documents for any additional information about nonpayment, default, any required repayment in full before the scheduled date, and prepayment refunds and penalties.

e means an estimate

Figure 21-3.   Sample of Graduated-Payment Mortgage

Rescission

The right to rescind (cancel) a transaction is called *recission*. Most lending contracts have a 3-day right of recission period; in other words, anytime during the first 3 *business days* after the transaction is agreed to, the borrower can decide to cancel the transaction without penalty. The practice of many lenders is not to advance funds until this 3-day period has expired. One significant exception to the right of recission concerns real estate loans that are part of a contract of sale (i.e., they represent seller financing that is agreed to in the sale contract).

To rescind a credit transaction, the borrower may notify the creditor of the rescission by mail, telegram, or other written means of communication. Generally, the right to rescind expires on midnight of the third business day following the loan transaction, delivery by the creditor of the notice of the right to rescind, or delivery of all material disclosures, whichever occurs last.

EFFECT OF RESCISSION

A consumer who exercises his right to rescind is not liable for any finance or other charge, and any security interest becomes void upon rescission. Within 20 days after receipt of a notice of rescission, the creditor shall return to the consumer any money or property given as earnest money, down payment, or otherwise, and shall take any action necessary or appropriate to reflect the termination of any security interest created under the transaction. If the creditor has delivered any money or property to the consumer, the consumer may retain possession of it until the performance of the creditor's obligations under this section. Then the consumer shall tender the property to the creditor, except that, if return of the property in kind would be impracticable or inequitable, the consumer shall tender its reasonable value. Tender of property shall be made at the location of the property or at the residence of the consumer, at the option of the consumer. Tender of money shall be at the creditor's place of business. If the creditor does not take possession of the property within 20 days after tender by the consumer, ownership of the property vests in the consumer without obligation on his part to pay for it.

Residential Mortgage Transactions: Summary of Distinctions

There are five parts of Regulation Z that provide different treatment for residential mortgage loans as compared to other types of credit. These are as follows:

1. Certain fees in connection with a residential mortgage can be excluded from finance charges. These are fees for title examination, title insurance, title abstract, survey, preparing deeds and mortgage documents, notary, appraisal and credit report, and amounts paid into an escrow account if such amounts are not otherwise included in a finance charge.

2. In a residential mortgage transaction, the creditor must include a statement as to whether a subsequent purchaser of the dwelling may assume the remaining obligation on its original terms.

3. The timing of disclosure under Regulation Z for residential mortgage transactions, which are also covered by the Real Estate Settlement Procedures Act (RESPA), coincides with RESPA's requirements.

4. When a mortgage loan is assumed, the creditor must look at the intentions of the party assuming it to determine the required disclosures. If this party will use the property as a principal dwelling, disclosures applicable for such use are necessary, even if the original borrower did not use the property for that purpose.

5. A transaction to construct or acquire a principal dwelling is not eligible for the right of rescission. The lien status (first or junior mortgage) does not matter. However, a transaction that is separate from the purchase, such as one to improve a residence, is covered by this right of rescission.

Questions on Chapter 21

1. The purpose of Regulation Z is to
   (A) set the maximum interest rates that may be charged
   (B) let borrowers know the cost of credit
   (C) both A and B
   (D) neither A nor B

2. Regulation Z applies to
   (A) all real estate salespersons and brokers
   (B) all retail stores
   (C) wholesale establishments only
   (D) none of the above → banks.

3. Regulation Z covers
   (A) borrowing from relatives
   (B) borrowing by a business
   (C) real estate credit transactions
   (D) inheritances

4. Under Regulation Z, borrowers must be told in writing of
   (A) the annual percentage rate for credit
   (B) the total dollar amount of the finance charge
   (C) both A and B
   (D) neither A nor B

5. Which of the following must be included as a "finance charge" for real property credit transactions?
   (A) fee for title insurance
   (B) fee for deed preparation
   (C) monthly payment, in dollars
   (D) none of the above

6. The annual percentage rate (APR) means the
   (A) true interest rate charged
   (B) total dollar amount of finance charges
   (C) monthly payment, in dollars
   (D) percentage of loan paid off each year

7. Under Regulation Z, a borrower may have the right to cancel, within 3 days, a
   (A) second mortgage used to improve his dwelling
   (B) first mortgage loan used to purchase his dwelling
   (C) home-improvement loan more than 1 year old
   (D) none of the above

8. To cancel a credit transaction, the borrower must inform the lender, within 3 days,
   (A) by phone
   (B) in writing
   (C) both A and B
   (D) neither A nor B

9. If a borrower cancels the contract within the 3-day period, she is responsible for
   (A) a 10 percent finance charge
   (B) a 1 percent finance charge
   (C) 3 days' interest
   (D) none of the above

10. The maximum penalty for conviction, in a criminal action, for willfully disobeying Regulation Z is up to
    (A) a $5000 fine
    (B) 1 year's imprisonment
    (C) both A and B
    (D) neither A nor B

11. Under the federal Truth-in-Lending Law, two of the most critical facts that must be disclosed to buyers or borrowers are
    (A) duration of the contract and discount rate
    (B) finance charge and annual percentage rate
    (C) carrying charges and advertising expense
    (D) installment payments and cancellation rights

ANSWERS

1. **B**	4. **C**	7. **A**	10. **C**
2. **D**	5. **D**	8. **B**	11. **B**
3. **C**	6. **A**	9. **D**	

Chapter 22 /*California Land Use Restriction and Regulation*

Numerous California state agencies, commissions, and the like regulate land use, building, development, contracting, etc. Also, local jusridictions can add on their own codes and standards so long as they don't violate state law.

Contractor Licensing

California has a *Contractors' License Law*, under which the *Contractors' State License Board* licenses building contractors. The law covers anyone doing building, contracting, remodeling, alteration, etc. of structures, except: (1) Owners doing their own work, provided it is not to prepare the property for sale, (2) jobs valued at less than $200, (3) oil and gas operations, (4) some work by public utilities and public entities and, (5) some kinds of agricultural construction. Contractors have to meet experience and knowledge qualifications and pass a licensing examination. They also must post a bond.

Housing Law

California's *Housing Law* is administered by the *Codes and Standards Division* of the *California Department of Housing and Community Development*. The housing law mandates minimum standards for construction and occupancy, applying to all dwellings, including hotels, apartment buildings, etc., as well as homes.

The building codes are very elaborate, and comply with *uniform codes* that have been promulgated nationwide by industry and government. They regulate construction standards for nearly all aspects of real estate construction. They apply statewide and are enforced by local government (municipal or county). The approval process begins with a *building permit*, applied for with the local building inspector, who must be furnished with the plans, specifications, materials lists, etc. The building permit must be obtained before any construction begins. As construction proceeds, the building inspector can require inspection from time to time to assure that code standards are being met. The finished construction must await a *certificate of occupancy* before it can be occupied and used. If there are only minor problems, a conditional certificate of occupancy can be issued, which provides a time limit for remedying the problems, during which use of the structure is allowed.

Administration of occupancy standards is the responsibility of local health officers. They also may halt or require modifications to construction that may contaminate water supplies, interfere with proper drainage, or present sewage disposal problems.

Mobile Homes

California regulates the construction and siting of mobile homes, the standards of mobile home subdivisions, and dealership in mobile homes. Mobile homes must be registered and licensed with the *Department of Housing and Community Development*. Federal regulation requires mobile homes to be constructed in compliance with the National Manufactured Home

Construction and Safety Standards, and also requires that buyers of manufactured homes receive a homeowner's manual. California's *Mobilehome Accommodation Structures Law* regulates the construction of buildings used with mobile homes. The *Mobilehome Parks Act* regulates mobile home park standards, and standards for recreational vehicle (RV) parks.

Mobile-home dealers who sell lots for mobile homes must have a mobile home dealer's license. Real estate licensees, however, may sell mobile homes singly, if they have been registered and licensed, or if they are part of real estate being sold.

City Planning and Zoning

Cities and counties are required by state law to have a general plan (sometimes called master plan) in effect. The plan should provide for and integrate varying land uses, transportation, housing, safety, sanitation, noise regulation, open space preservation, conservation, public utilities, etc. A local planning commission is supposed to formulate the plan.

A major aspect of city planning is *zoning*. The function of zoning is (a) to keep conflicting land uses from impinging on one another and (b) to control growth and development so that it is orderly and does not create problems with public services, traffic, etc. Zoning establishes a number of categories of land use, each of which has limitations and specifications regarding (a) *permitted uses*, (b) *lot coverage*: how much of the area of the lot may be covered by buildings? (c) *setback requirements*: how far from the lot lines must buildings be? (d) limitations on *building height* and *gross building area*, and (e) *density limitations*: how many units, buildings, square feet of construction are allowed on the lot?

Each jurisdiction's general plan must specify the zoning categories for all lands in the jurisdiction. However, there isn't any state standard or definition of zoning categories, so the nomenclature and limitation details vary widely throughout the state. Typically, however, zoning uses will be categorized as *agricultural*, *industrial*, *residential*, and *commercial*. The latter two categories may have many different density and use categories within them. Residential, for example, can range from large to small lot single family zoning (attached or unattached); multi-family use from duplex to high-rise apartments.

As time passes, it is very likely that changes will have to be made in the plans, and in zoning of some land, because no one and no plan can perfectly predict what will happen in the future. Sometimes zoning classifications will be changed over a large area; this is called *rezoning*. More often, individual landowners will ask for a *zoning variance*, allowing them to deviate from the limitations imposed by the zoning category applying to their land. Also, zoning administration often allows for *nonconforming uses* (such as churches and schools in an area zoned residential).

Subdivisions

Under California law, almost any time a parcel of land is divided into two or more smaller parcels it is called a *subdivision* and is regulated in some way. *The Subdivision Map Act* allows local jurisdictions to require filing of a subdivision plan whenever any parcel of land is divided into two or more smaller ones. This law does not apply throughout the state, but only where local governments have decided to apply it. The *Subdivided Lands Law* applies statewide. It is operated by the real estate commissioner and DRE. This law defines forms of ownership allowed in smaller subdivided lands (160 acres or less), and regulates their sale.

Subdivision Map Act

Localities will apply this law in order to assure that subdivisions fit into the local general plan (see above). It involves several steps and procedures. First is the filing of a *tentative map*, which does not have to be based on surveys or other intensive engineering work. It must, however, address certain concerns: boundaries of all subdivision parcels, names and sizes of new streets, water and sewage service, drainage, existing and proposed roadways, utility easements, drainage and water supply, storm sewerage and drainage. If the subdivision will have significant effects upon nearby land users, the local government holds hearings on the proposal. Within two years (three years if the local government grants a twelve-month grace period as allowed in the law) the *final map* must be submitted. It must be the result of engineering and survey. It must include any alterations from the tentative map required by the local government, must show lot and block number for every parcel, distance and direction of all boundary lines sufficient for legal description of all parcels. Other documents such as soil reports (drainage, percolation, and so forth), dedications (where land for streets, roads, schools, and rights-of-way are given to local government and, sometimes, public utilities), and various other approvals are also required as part of the final map.

Subdivided Lands Law

This law has two important parts: (1) the definition of subdivision types and (2) the requirement of a *Subdivision Public Report* for every subdivision under the law's purview.

The law defines four types of subdivision:

1. *Standard subdivision.* Lot owners own their land separately, and there is no common-interest ownership involved. These subdivisions are typically subdivisions of ordinary building lots that can be sold unimproved (but with streets and utilities installed) or improved (such as new homes for sale). Sellers may or may not arrange or provide financing for buyers.

2. *Undivided interest subdivision.* No owner owns by himself/herself. Rather, all owners are tenants in common with one another as co-owners of the entire subdivision. Each owner has nonexclusive ownership rights. An example would be a club property owned by club members, a campground or vacation area with shared facilities.

3. *Land project.* This is a subdivision of 50 or more lots in a "sparsely populated" area. Sparsely populated is defined as fewer than 1,500 registered voters inside an area including the subdivision and all property within two miles of the subdivision's boundaries. Land projects are basically unimproved land; usually lots are sold as "investments" for future use, often sold on land sales contract. The law allows buyers in a land project up to two weeks to rescind their purchase contract without penalty. Land projects are regulated by the Real Estate Commissioner and DRE.

4. *Common interest subdivision.* These are subdivisions in which owners may have a separate ownership or leasehold interest combined with a shared interest in certain portions of the subdivision that are called *common property* or *common areas*. There are several types of common interest subdivisions; the most familiar would be *condominium* projects or *planned unit developments (PUD's):*

   (a) CONDOMINIUM PROJECT: owners have exclusive ownership of a dwelling or other unit (there are condominium office and shopping developments), and common ownership with the other owners of such areas as parking areas, driveways and streets, amenities (pool, tennis, clubhouse), park and recreation areas, and the like. Condominium interests can be bought, sold, and financed like any other real property.

   (b) PLANNED UNIT DEVELOPMENT: A large subdivision containing a variety of land uses; includes exclusive ownership, condominium ownership.

   (c) STOCK COOPERATIVE PROJECT: Usually apartment buildings; residents own stock in the cooperative corporation that owns the building. The individual shareholders have rights of exclusive occupancy of part of the real estate (their "own" apartment) and share with the other shareholders the rights to use common property. Note that there is *not* individual ownership of one's unit (as in condominium), but rather one owns a share of the corporation which, itself, owns, and finances, the entire project. A *limited equity housing cooperative* is a stock cooperative financed by the *California Housing Finance Agency*.

   (d) TIME-SHARE PROJECT: These are relatively new and are confined almost exclusively to vacation properties. Owners have rights of occupancy to particular units for *particular periods of time* during the year, typically weekly time units.

A *time-share estate* is an estate interest in the property, and would be perpetual. A *time-share use* is not perpetual, and usually is a share in a leasehold of the property. The law allows buyers of time-share units a three-day period after purchase during which they can rescind without penalty.

The Subdivision Public Report

Before parcels in a subdivision may be sold, the real estate commissioner must issue a *subdivision public report* for the subdivision in question. Prospective purchasers of parcels in the subdivision must be given a copy of the report and allowed to read it. The report describes the subdivision and the subdivider; the nature of the interest(s) being sold; unusual expenses to be expected at closing or later (sewage and water connection fees are examples); the manner in which taxes, assessments and other payments are to be handled; restrictions and conditions affecting buyers' use of the property; environmental hazards and concerns; unusual easements and rights-of-way; building permits; and development requirements. These would be included in the report for a standard subdivision; common interest subdivision reports must be more detailed because they must spell out everything having to do with common ownership property, restrictions on use, agreements affecting common use property, management of common use property, etc.

Obviously, it can take quite a while to put together a public report. Therefore, subdividers are allowed to begin sales once they have compiled and obtained approval of a preliminary public report. However, the sales they make cannot be closed until the final public report becomes available and only then after buyers have received and read a copy of it. All original buyers of subdivided lands must provide a written statement that they have received and read the final property report.

Sales practices of subdivided lands are regulated by, and guidelines provided by, the Real Estate Commissioner. The public report is good for five years, but upon payment of additional filing fees can be renewed for another five years.

Other Land Use Regulation and Requirements

The *California Environmental Quality Act of 1970* requires any government body empowered to approve subdivisions (local governments and the Real Estate Commissioner) to have prepared an *environmental impact report* in any case where a project will have a significant impact on the environment. No subdivision may be approved if it, or the improvements expected to be built in it, will cause "substantial damage" to the environment, or do "substantial injury" to wildlife, fish, their habitat, etc.

The prevalence of earthquake zones in California led to the *Alquist-Priolo Special Studies Zone Act* (1975). *Special studies zones* are areas close to (within ¼ mile or so) active faults. Any project in such a zone must have a geologist's report to determine if there is any hazard from fault rupture. Oddly, this law is not concerned with the shaking effects of earthquake zones, but only with direct, sudden movement of land. Maps of these zones are available from the California Division of Mines and Geology. Note that sellers (*and their agents!*) of property within a special studies zone must disclose that fact to any prospective buyer.

The *Coastal Zone Conservation Act* is concerned with the entire Pacific coastline of California, up to 1,000 yards or so inland (in some places the *coastal zone* will go much further inland because of geology or terrain). Local governments are authorized to institute policies, including development regulation and zoning, designed to encourage coastal preservation.

Questions on Chapter 22

1. The law regulating construction and development of recreational vehicle parks is the
   (A) R/V Regulation Act
   (B) California Parking Lot Authority Act
   (C) Mobilehome Parks Act
   (D) Subdivision Map Act

2. Which of the following is not specified by zoning regulations?
   (A) Permissible building materials
   (B) Lot coverage
   (C) Setback
   (D) Density

3. Once a tentative subdivision map is filed, the subdivider has _____ to file the final map.
   (A) six months
   (B) one year
   (C) eighteen months
   (D) two years

4. The Smiths want to build an addition to their home. However, the planned construction will be two feet closer to the lot line than zoning regulations allow. To be allowed to build their addition, they would apply for
   (A) rezoning to a higher density
   (B) nonconforming use
   (C) a reevaluated zone allowance
   (D) a zoning variance

5. Which of the following would not be a zoning classification?
   (A) Agricultural zone
   (B) Special studies zone
   (C) Commercial zone
   (D) Residential zone

6. The Bennetts live in a detached home on a 65 by 120 foot lot in a neighborhood of similar homes on similar lots. Neither they nor their neighbors share rights to any land other than the lot their home is on, which they own. They live in
   (A) a land project
   (B) a standard subdivision
   (C) an undivided interest subdivision
   (D) a condominium

7. James is planning a subdivision of some land he owns. His land is one of the few known habitats of the smarmy mealworm (*grubbus disgustus*), which is the prime source of nourishment for the rare western vampire bat (*sangrislurpus lugosi*). The local government requires James to prepare
   (A) an environmental impact report
   (B) a special zoo to house the worms and the bats
   (C) a plan to transport the worms and bats to other known habitats in Utah
   (D) a worm and bat extermination plan

8. What is the state law that allows local government to regulate the development and building in a 1,000-yard strip along the Pacific coast of California?
   (A) California Pacific Conservation Act
   (B) Big Sur and Coastal Lands Act
   (C) Coastal Zone Conservation Act
   (D) Pacific Coast Regulation and Preservation Act

9. A large subdivision containing a variety of land uses including common-interest uses is a
   (A) land project
   (B) planned unit development
   (C) stock cooperative project
   (D) standard subdivision

10. Who issues the subdivision public report?
    (A) The Real Estate Commissioner
    (B) The Land Report Division of DRE
    (C) The Subdivided Lands Regulation Board
    (D) None of the above

11. Which does not have to appear on or be filed with the final subdivision map?
    (A) Boundary lines
    (B) Lot and block number for all parcels
    (C) Construction materials list
    (D) Name of subdivider

12. Which of the following is not a common-interest subdivision?
    (A) Planned unit development
    (B) Condominium project
    (C) Time-share project
    (D) Land project

13. What is the law that mandates minimum construction and occupancy standards for dwellings, hotels, apartments, etc., in California?
    (A) The Housing Law
    (B) The Occupancy and Building Standards Act
    (C) The Subdivided Lands Law
    (D) The Uniform Law

14. Which of the following must have a contractor's license?
    (A) Owner making improvements (but not to prepare for sale)
    (B) One being paid $1,500 by homeowner to do roof repairs
    (C) Oil field operator
    (D) Electric company employee repairing power lines

15. Under the Contractors' License Law, who licenses building contractors?
    (A) The Department of Real Estate
    (B) The Department of Housing and Community Development
    (C) The Department of Contractors' Standards and Licensing
    (D) The Contractors' State Licensing Board

16. Who issues building permits?
    (A) The Department of Real Estate
    (B) The local zoning board
    (C) The Building and Development Board
    (D) The local building inspector

17. A church in a residential area would be classified as _____ for zoning purposes.
    (A) a zoning variance
    (B) a nonconforming use
    (C) a rezoned requisite
    (D) a permitted residential use

18. Which of the following statements is not true?
    (A) Lot boundaries in a final subdivision map must have been surveyed.
    (B) A condominium project is not a common-interest subdivision.
    (C) A real estate broker may sell single mobile homes that have been licensed and registered, or are part of real estate.
    (D) Special studies zones are earthquake hazard areas.

19. A subdivision in a *sparsely populated area* (no more than 1,500 registered voters in or within two miles of the subdivision) is called a
(A) rural development project
(B) planned unit project
(C) land project
(D) unregulated subdivided project

20. Which of the following regulates the distance from a main structure to the boundaries of the lot it occupies?
(A) Setback requirement
(B) Density requirement
(C) Lot coverage requirement
(D) Occupancy requirement

21. A nonconforming use
(A) is allowed to continue unless the building is damaged
(B) is grandfathered
(C) was conforming before a zoning change
(D) all of the above

22. Private restrictions on the use of land may be created by
(A) private land use controls
(B) written agreement
(C) general plan restrictions in subdivisions
(D) all of the above

23. Covenants, conditions, and restrictions (CCRs) are usually recorded by a document called
(A) a plat
(B) subdivision rules
(C) Declaration of Restrictions
(D) common area designations

24. If CCRs and zoning conflict with each other,
(A) the more stringent rules apply
(B) either can be followed
(C) courts or mediation will be needed to settle the matter
(D) the developer will decide what to do

25. In California, the maximum for which one can sell a general liquor license five years old is
(A) $0
(B) $1,000
(C) $6,000
(D) There is no limit.

ANSWERS

1. **C**	6. **B**	11. **C**	16. **D**	21. **D**
2. **A**	7. **A**	12. **D**	17. **B**	22. **D**
3. **D**	8. **C**	13. **A**	18. **B**	23. **C**
4. **D**	9. **B**	14. **B**	19. **C**	24. **A**
5. **B**	10. **A**	15. **D**	20. **A**	25. **C**

PART VI: REAL ESTATE EXAMINATIONS

Chapter 23 / *Exam Preparation and Strategy*

Studying for the Exam

You can't expect to walk into the examination room cold and pass with flying colors. You have to be ready for the exam. This means more than just doing a lot of reading and trying to cram your head full of facts. You have to be psychologically ready and properly prepared to take the examination so that you can *do your best* on it. To do this you have to acquire the following things:

1. Knowledge
2. A positive attitude
3. Information about exam taking
4. Confidence
5. Rest

Let's take these things one by one:

1. Knowledge. Of course you have to have the knowledge to get through the examination; this means knowing the subject matter well. Begin by studying this book and your state's license laws. Also, if your state provides special examination preparation materials, study those, too. You can't expect to acquire all the requisite knowledge if you start just a short while before the examination. You should follow a *reasonable* study schedule so that you will be at maximum readiness the day of the examination (see Chapter 1).

2. A positive attitude. Your attitude should be one of confidence; after all, if you have worked hard to learn all the real estate concepts, then you DO know the required material. The exam simply is the place where you get your chance to demonstrate that you are qualified for a real estate license.

3. Information about exam taking. Some people panic at the prospect of taking an exam and end up doing badly as a result. This sort of thing does happen; but if you look at the examination in the proper perspective, it won't happen to you. If you are concerned about taking an examination after having been out of school for such a long time, the thing to do is to practice: take the model examinations in Chapter 24. Set up actual "examination conditions." Give yourself a time limit, and go right through each practice exam just as if it were the real thing. Use all the examination-taking techniques you'll read about in this chapter. Each model exam has a key at the end of the book so that you can grade your own performance. To guide your future study, note the areas where you did well and those where you did badly. Do this for *each* practice examination: first take the exam and grade it, then do more studying in your weaker areas before you take the next one.

In this way you'll accomplish three important objectives. First, you'll get used to the examination situation. Second, you'll gain practice in answering the kinds of questions featured on most real estate license examinations. Third, you'll be able to keep track of the subject areas where you need more study and practice.

4. Confidence. Here are the areas of subject matter that examinees worry most about: (a) arithmetic, (b) contracts, and (c) for broker examinees, closing statements. We have included detailed sections on all of these, as well as on all other real estate subjects. The arithmetic you need to know is exactly the same sort you had to do for homework in the sixth and seventh grades. Contracts inspire awe because they're supposed to be the province of lawyers. By now you know that a contract is just a piece of paper on which people put down facts concerning an agreement they've made. In regard to a contract, all you have to be sure of is to write what you are supposed to and to be clear in what you say. Even property description doesn't have to look like mumbo-jumbo. Metes and bounds descriptions just need to tell where the boundaries of a property lie; rectangular government survey descriptions use a peculiar but very high-powered shorthand that's easy to learn; lot and block number descriptions are great because they're simple and explicit.

Closing statements worry broker examinees because they look so mysterious. Actually, they're nothing but a record of where people's money goes in a real estate transaction. Once again, the important thing is accuracy. Also, if you think a bit about most of the items involved, it is easy to see if they should be paid by (or to) the seller or the buyer. All that's left is to line up all the numbers neatly so that they can be added easily. The tricky part about closing statements usually is the prorating of various items. As Chapter 18 explains, there is nothing mysterious about prorating; however, the calculations are long and clumsy, so there's room for error to sneak in if you're not careful.

Throughout this book an important aim has been to explain everything thoroughly. If you understand the subjects discussed, you should have no confidence problem: you *know* the basic principles of real estate.

5. Rest. Don't stay up studying the night before the exam! People are not at their best when tired or short of sleep. The day before the exam should be one of rest and relaxation.

You can, however, design a little last-minute study session that actually will help you, without disturbing your relaxation. Prepare a brief outline of the *important* points on which you know you need special effort. If contracts bug you, make a list of all the contracts and a brief description of each. Study this material for one-half hour in the morning, one-half hour in the afternoon, and one-half hour in the evening, but finish your studying *at least* two hours before bedtime. In that way you'll be strengthening your weaknesses, but you won't be spending so much time on studying that it interferes with the really important task at hand: getting yourself relaxed. The morning of the examination, if you have time, you can spend another half hour going over those notes one last time.

Two Important Rules

Your objective when you take any examination is to get as high a score as possible. The way to do that is to provide as many right answers as you can. This leads us directly to the most important rule of all in taking examinations.

ALWAYS ANSWER EVERY QUESTION. Even if you have to guess, write down an answer. If you leave the question blank, you can be certain that it will be counted as wrong because a blank answer is a wrong answer. If you guess, there is always the chance that the guess will be correct. Boiled down, the situation is as simple as this: you know you will get the question wrong if you leave it blank, but if you guess at an answer you may guess the right one.

The second rule is SKIP THE HARD QUESTIONS AT FIRST AND SAVE THEM FOR LAST. Many people start at the beginning of an examination and work their way through, one question at a time, until they run out of time. If they encounter a hard question, they battle with it for a long time and won't go on until they've licked it (or it has licked them). These people are lucky to get to the end of the exam before they run out of time; if they don't get to the end, they never even see some of the questions—and they might have been able to answer enough of those questions to earn a passing grade on the exam. On California's standardized examinations, all questions are worth the same. So what sense is there in spending 15 minutes, half an hour, or more on a single question, when you can use that same time to read and answer a couple of *dozen* questions correctly?

When you take the exam, start at the beginning. Read the instructions, then read the first question. Answer it if you can, and then go on to number 2. Answer that one if you can, and then go on to the next and the next and the next. When you come across a hard question that you have to think about, or that will take a lot of time to answer even if you know exactly how to get the answer (some arithmetic problems can be like that), skip it for the time being. Come back to it later, after you have gone all the way through the exam and answered all the questions that you can do fairly quickly.

Strategies for Handling Common Types of Questions _____

In order to know how to attack your state's particular examination, you have to be familiar with the special strategies for handling specific kinds of questions.

MULTIPLE-CHOICE QUESTIONS

This is a multiple-choice question:

The title of this chapter is

(A) How to Hammer a Nail
(B) Exam Preparation and Strategy
(C) I Was an Elephant for the FBI
(D) None of the above

The examinations are composed entirely of multiple-choice questions.

Always remember that with a multiple-choice question you are looking at the right answer! You just have to pick it out. Your strategy for answering such questions is as follows:

1. Read the question *completely* and *carefully*. Many people miss little key words such as *if*, *not*, *but*, and *except* that can completely change or limit the meaning of a sentence.

2. If the answer is obvious to you, mark it properly and go on to the next question. Then forget about the question you have just answered. Almost always, the answer you pick first is the right one, and you will very rarely improve an answer by coming back and stewing over it later.

3. If the answer is not obvious, begin the guesswork strategy. First look for all the choices that you know are wrong. You may not be sure of the right answer, but that doesn't mean you can't find some answers you know are wrong. Then guess an answer from the ones that are left.

   Remember to make your guesses educated. Usually you will be able to guide your guesswork by using some of your knowledge. You may be able to decide that a certain answer is much more likely to be right than the others. Always be sure to eliminate answers you *know* are wrong in order to limit your choices and thus improve your chances of guessing the right one. However, if it looks as though a long time will be needed to reach even a guesswork answer, skip the question and come back to it later if you have the time.

Using Computer Answer Forms _____

Figure 23-1 is an example of a computer examination form.° The big advantage to these forms is that they are graded by a machine that can evaluate and grade thousands of examinations a day, thereby saving an enormous amount of time and labor.

At the examination, you will be given the form and a *test booklet*. The examination questions and instructions will be written in the test booklet; you will "code" your answers onto the answer sheet. Usually you will be asked to make no marks at all on the test booklet; you should put your name and any other identification asked for in the appropriate spaces on the answer sheet. Remember one critical rule: *Do not make any marks at all on either the test or the answer sheet unless and until you are instructed to*. Normally the test booklet will contain very detailed and specific instructions on how to enter the necessary information on the answer sheet; in addition, the people administering the examination will give an oral and visual presentation on the same subject.

Using these answer sheets is really quite simple. Below is an example of a set of answer spaces for three different questions:

```
1 ::A:  ::B:  ::C:  ::D:
2 ::A:  ::B:  ::C:  ::D:
3 ::A:  ::B:  ::C:  ::D:
```

_____

° Do not expect the form you use for the exam to be *identical* to Figure 23-1.

NAME _____ SESSION ____ AM ☐ ____ PM ☐
LAST ____ FIRST ____ MIDDLE
SOC. SEC. # _____/_____/_____ Enter your IDENT. NUMBER EXAM CODE # _____

DATE _____ BOOK# _____
PLACE
OF EXAM _____ SALESMAN ☐ BROKER ☐
TITLE
OF EXAM _____
IMPORTANT: IN MARKING YOUR ANSWERS
FILL IN ANSWER BOX COMPLETELY

	4 :A: :B: :C: :D:	8 :A: :B: :C: :D:	12 :A: :B: :C: :D:
1 :A: :B: :C: :D:	5 :A: :B: :C: :D:	9 :A: :B: :C: :D:	13 :A: :B: :C: :D:
2 :A: :B: :C: :D:	6 :A: :B: :C: :D:	10 :A: :B: :C: :D:	14 :A: :B: :C: :D:
3 :A: :B: :C: :D:	7 :A: :B: :C: :D:	11 :A: :B: :C: :D:	15 :A: :B: :C: :D:
	19 :A: :B: :C: :D:	23 :A: :B: :C: :D:	27 :A: :B: :C: :D:
16 :A: :B: :C: :D:	20 :A: :B: :C: :D:	24 :A: :B: :C: :D:	28 :A: :B: :C: :D:
17 :A: :B: :C: :D:	21 :A: :B: :C: :D:	25 :A: :B: :C: :D:	29 :A: :B: :C: :D:
18 :A: :B: :C: :D:	22 :A: :B: :C: :D:	26 :A: :B: :C: :D:	30 :A: :B: :C: :D:
	34 :A: :B: :C: :D:	38 :A: :B: :C: :D:	42 :A: :B: :C: :D:
31 :A: :B: :C: :D:	35 :A: :B: :C: :D:	39 :A: :B: :C: :D:	43 :A: :B: :C: :D:
32 :A: :B: :C: :D:	36 :A: :B: :C: :D:	40 :A: :B: :C: :D:	44 :A: :B: :C: :D:
33 :A: :B: :C: :D:	37 :A: :B: :C: :D:	41 :A: :B: :C: :D:	45 :A: :B: :C: :D:
	49 :A: :B: :C: :D:	53 :A: :B: :C: :D:	57 :A: :B: :C: :D:
46 :A: :B: :C: :D:	50 :A: :B: :C: :D:	54 :A: :B: :C: :D:	58 :A: :B: :C: :D:
47 :A: :B: :C: :D:	51 :A: :B: :C: :D:	55 :A: :B: :C: :D:	59 :A: :B: :C: :D:
48 :A: :B: :C: :D:	52 :A: :B: :C: :D:	56 :A: :B: :C: :D:	60 :A: :B: :C: :D:
	64 :A: :B: :C: :D:	68 :A: :B: :C: :D:	72 :A: :B: :C: :D:
61 :A: :B: :C: :D:	65 :A: :B: :C: :D:	69 :A: :B: :C: :D:	73 :A: :B: :C: :D:
62 :A: :B: :C: :D:	66 :A: :B: :C: :D:	70 :A: :B: :C: :D:	74 :A: :B: :C: :D:
63 :A: :B: :C: :D:	67 :A: :B: :C: :D:	71 :A: :B: :C: :D:	75 :A: :B: :C: :D:
	79 :A: :B: :C: :D:	83 :A: :B: :C: :D:	87 :A: :B: :C: :D:
76 :A: :B: :C: :D:	80 :A: :B: :C: :D:	84 :A: :B: :C: :D:	88 :A: :B: :C: :D:
77 :A: :B: :C: :D:	81 :A: :B: :C: :D:	85 :A: :B: :C: :D:	89 :A: :B: :C: :D:
78 :A: :B: :C: :D:	82 :A: :B: :C: :D:	86 :A: :B: :C: :D:	90 :A: :B: :C: :D:
	94 :A: :B: :C: :D:	98 :A: :B: :C: :D:	
91 :A: :B: :C: :D:	95 :A: :B: :C: :D:	99 :A: :B: :C: :D:	
92 :A: :B: :C: :D:	96 :A: :B: :C: :D:	100 :A: :B: :C: :D:	
93 :A: :B: :C: :D:	97 :A: :B: :C: :D:		
	104 :A: :B: :C: :D:	108 :A: :B: :C: :D:	112 :A: :B: :C: :D:
101 :A: :B: :C: :D:	105 :A: :B: :C: :D:	109 :A: :B: :C: :D:	113 :A: :B: :C: :D:
102 :A: :B: :C: :D:	106 :A: :B: :C: :D:	110 :A: :B: :C: :D:	114 :A: :B: :C: :D:
103 :A: :B: :C: :D:	107 :A: :B: :C: :D:	111 :A: :B: :C: :D:	115 :A: :B: :C: :D:
	119 :A: :B: :C: :D:	123 :A: :B: :C: :D:	127 :A: :B: :C: :D:
116 :A: :B: :C: :D:	120 :A: :B: :C: :D:	124 :A: :B: :C: :D:	128 :A: :B: :C: :D:
117 :A: :B: :C: :D:	121 :A: :B: :C: :D:	125 :A: :B: :C: :D:	129 :A: :B: :C: :D:
118 :A: :B: :C: :D:	122 :A: :B: :C: :D:	126 :A: :B: :C: :D:	130 :A: :B: :C: :D:
	134 :A: :B: :C: :D:	138 :A: :B: :C: :D:	142 :A: :B: :C: :D:
131 :A: :B: :C: :D:	135 :A: :B: :C: :D:	139 :A: :B: :C: :D:	143 :A: :B: :C: :D:
132 :A: :B: :C: :D:	136 :A: :B: :C: :D:	140 :A: :B: :C: :D:	144 :A: :B: :C: :D:
133 :A: :B: :C: :D:	137 :A: :B: :C: :D:	141 :A: :B: :C: :D:	145 :A: :B: :C: :D:
	149 :A: :B: :C: :D:		
146 :A: :B: :C: :D:	150 :A: :B: :C: :D:		
147 :A: :B: :C: :D:			
148 :A: :B: :C: :D:			

Figure 23-1.   Computer Examination Form

For each question you have four answers to choose from: A, B, C, and D. When you have picked your answer, enter it on the examination form by *shading* the appropriate space with your pencil. Suppose, for example, you choose C:

:▬C▬:

Here are three easy sample questions. Answer them by shading the appropriate space in the answer set that follows.

1. If John has two apples and I have three, together we have
    (A) 4   (C) 6
    (B) 5   (D) 7

2. The capital of France is
   (A) London
   (B) Washington
   (C) Paris
   (D) Des Moines, Iowa

3. Those things in the middle of your face that you see with are
   (A) eyes
   (B) ears
   (C) nose
   (D) fingernails

```
1  ::A::  ::B::  ::C::  ::D::
2  ::A::  ::B::  ::C::  ::D::
3  ::A::  ::B::  ::C::  ::D::
```

The answers are obvious: 1 is B, 2 is C, 3 is A. The properly marked answer form is as follows:

```
1  ::A::  ■■■■  ::C::  ::D::
2  ::A::  ::B::  ■■■■  ::D::
3  ■■■■  ::B::  ::C::  ::D::
```

Model Examinations 1 and 2 in the next chapter can be applied to computer answer forms, and sample forms are included for your use. Chapter 26 provides the properly filled out computer answer forms for these two model examinations, as well as an answer key for each.

There are two things you must be careful of with respect to using computer answer forms. First, make sure you have enough pencils. Be certain that you are or are not required to bring your own pencils; if you are, get ordinary #2 pencils—the kind you can buy at any stationery store. And bring a little hand pencil sharpener along, too. After you sharpen a pencil, be sure to blunt the point by scribbling on some scratch paper before marking the answer form. You don't want to poke holes in it.

Second, our strategy of skipping the hard questions and saving them to the last means that you have to *make absolutely certain that you are putting the answer in the right space for that question!* Be especially careful here. The computer is very stupid! If you put answer marks in the wrong spaces, it will count them wrong.

By the way, the computer form used on the exam you take may be slightly different from the sample form shown here. However, it will be used in just the same way we use ours.

Onsite Scoring Systems (Keypad Answering and Scoring)

Pencil-and-paper examinations are slowly being replaced by various kinds of computerized exams. Some appraisal exams use a keyboard attached to a small terminal (screen) that displays the questions and the answer choices. You enter your choice of answer on the keypad, which also has keys allowing you to erase an answer, scroll back and forth in the exam, skip a question, and so on. Other forms use what appears to be a typical desktop personal computer, complete with a normal keyboard. If such a system is used, you usually can get some literature ahead of time that explains how to use the system. Naturally, it is important to know as much about it as you can in advance. Also, before you take the exam, the administrators will provide a detailed explanation and demonstration of how to use the equipment. Whatever the system, usually the instructions for using it (entering answers, erasing, scrolling, etc.) either appear on the screen (usually at the bottom or top) or can be accessed easily.

These devices have advantages and disadvantages. There are two major advantages. First, the machines make it easier to skip around within the exam without losing track of where you are and without any risk that you will put your answers in the wrong spaces. Second, most of the machines allow for instant scoring of your exam. When you are done, you "lock" the machine by pressing a special key. After that time, you no longer can enter or change answers. At that point, the administrators of the exam can instantly provide your score, since your answers are entered into the computer already. Usually you will be given a sheet that will tell you which questions you answered correctly and which you missed. In some examining centers, if the exam isn't over yet, you may be allowed to check your answers against the exam you just took and so tell exactly where you went wrong on the questions you missed.

The disadvantage of the examination machine is that it is unfamiliar to most people. However, it is no more complicated to use than an ordinary calculator. Rest assured that, if your examining center uses such a machine, it will be thoroughly explained before the exam starts, and there will be a brief practice session so that you can get familiar with it.

Chapter 24/**Model Examinations**

Salesperson License Examination 1 _____

Directions: Select the choice, marked A, B, C, or D, that best answers the question or completes the thought. Mark your answers clearly on the answer sheet. You have 3 hours and 15 minutes to complete this examination. Answers are on page 497, math solutions on page 502.

1. *Adverse possession* may establish
   - (A) use of property
   - (B) a claim to title
   - (C) who owes back taxes
   - (D) homestead rights

2. An *easement by prescription* may establish
   - (A) use of property
   - (B) a claim to title
   - (C) who owes back taxes
   - (D) homestead rights

3. Fifty feet of land was added to Apple's farm because a river changed its course. This is an example of
   - (A) accretion
   - (B) avulsion
   - (C) riparian rights
   - (D) usufructory

4. Fifty feet of beachfront land was removed by a flood. This is an example of
   - (A) riparian rights
   - (B) estovers
   - (C) avulsion
   - (D) emblements

5. If someone dies without a will, a(n) _____ is appointed to settle the estate.
   - (A) executor
   - (B) administrator
   - (C) notary public
   - (D) attorney-in-fact

6. If someone dies leaving a will, he or she died in this legal state.
   - (A) Testate
   - (B) Intestate
   - (C) Executory
   - (D) *Pur autre vie*

7. As used in real estate practices, the land of a *riparian* owner borders on
   - (A) a river
   - (B) a stream
   - (C) a watercourse
   - (D) any of the above

8. *Community property* is property owned by
   - (A) churches
   - (B) husband and wife
   - (C) the municipality
   - (D) the community

9. A person holding title to real property in severalty would most likely have
   - (A) a life estate
   - (B) an estate for years
   - (C) ownership in common with others
   - (D) sole ownership

10. Joint ownership of real property by two or more persons, each of whom has an undivided interest (not necessarily equal) without right of survivorship, is
    (A) a tenancy in partnership   (C) a tenancy in common
    (B) a tenancy by the entireties   (D) a leasehold tenancy

11. Generally, the taking of private land by governmental bodies for public use is governed by due process of law and is accomplished through
    (A) exercise of the police power   (C) reverter
    (B) eminent domain   (D) escheat

12. Governmental land use planning and zoning are important examples of
    (A) exercise of eminent domain   (C) deed restrictions
    (B) use of police power   (D) encumbrance

13. The covenant of *quiet enjoyment* most directly relates to
    (A) nuisances maintained on adjoining property
    (B) possession of real property
    (C) title to real property
    (D) all of the above

14. An interest in real property may be acquired either by prescription or by adverse possession. The interest resulting from prescription is
    (A) the right to use another's land   (C) an equitable interest
    (B) a possessory title   (D) a private grant

15. An unlicensed employee of a broker who prepares an advertisement to sell a house
    (A) is free to do so
    (B) must have the broker's prior written approval
    (C) must become licensed
    (D) must accurately describe the house

16. Copies of all listings, deposit receipts, canceled checks, and trust records must be retained by a licensed real estate broker for
    (A) one year   (C) three years
    (B) two years   (D) five years

17. If the broker, while acting as agent in a sale of real property, misrepresents the principal's property to a buyer, the broker may cause the principal to be subjected to
    (A) rescission of the sale by the buyer
    (B) a court action for damages by the buyer
    (C) tort liability
    (D) any of the above

18. A broker selling a property on which he holds an option should notify the purchaser that he is acting as
    (A) an optionor   (C) a beneficiary
    (B) a mortgagor   (D) a principal

19. The maximum commission a broker may charge a seller for the sale of residential income property is
    (A) set forth in the Real Estate Law
    (B) negotiable
    (C) no more than 10 percent of the total sales price
    (D) determined by local custom

20. The position of trust assumed by the broker as an agent for a principal is described most accurately as
   (A) a gratuitous relationship
   (B) a trustor relationship
   (C) a fiduciary relationship
   (D) an employment relationship

21. The Agency Relationship Disclosure Law became effective in
   (A) 1960
   (B) 1975
   (C) 1988
   (D) 1998

22. A qualified license applicant's name appears on a delinquent child support list. The applicant
   (A) cannot be licensed at all
   (B) must clear up the deficiency before licensing
   (C) may receive a temporary 150-day license
   (D) must be granted a license based on meeting educational and testing requirements

23. Of the following, which is the most important reason for a broker to maintain a trust fund account in addition to a regular business account?
   (A) It provides a means of control over the destiny of transactions being negotiated.
   (B) It is easier from an accounting point of view.
   (C) The bank is responsible for any loss to the trust fund account resulting from embezzlement.
   (D) It protects against possible consequences should a legal action be taken against the broker.

24. A California real estate license is good only in
   (A) the city where it was obtained
   (B) the county where it was obtained
   (C) the state of California
   (D) the 50 U.S. states

25. When a salesperson transfers a license, the new broker must advise the DRE within
   (A) three days
   (B) five days
   (C) ten days
   (D) thirty days

26. If the California Real Estate Commissioner needs legal advice, he would go to the
   (A) Real Estate Board
   (B) California Association of REALTORS®
   (C) state attorney general
   (D) in-house counsel

27. After one becomes a broker, the most appropriate term for that person is
   (A) REALTOR®
   (B) Realtist®
   (C) associate
   (D) broker

28. After one's real estate license expires, there is grace period of _____ to renew, upon paying fees, without a reexamination requirement.
   (A) one year
   (B) two years
   (C) five years
   (D) There is no grace period.

29. A broker must keep records for _____ year(s).
   (A) one
   (B) two
   (C) three
   (D) four

30. An unlicensed person who practices real estate may be
    (A) required to return to the state all commissions earned
    (B) fined up to $10,000 and subject to other possible legal action
    (C) prohibited from ever becoming licensed
    (D) all of the above

31. The maximum the DRE will pay to a victim from the recovery fund for one transaction is
    (A) $10,000   (C) $50,000
    (B) $20,000   (D) $100,000

32. The maximum DRE recovery fund disbursement on behalf of one real estate licensee is
    (A) $10,000   (C) $50,000
    (B) $20,000   (D) $100,000

33. Two offers are received by the broker at the same time. The broker must
    (A) present both offers
    (B) present only the higher offer
    (C) present only the offer that provides a greater commission
    (D) use his or her best judgment as to which offer to present

34. In a legal purchase contract, the seller is often referred to as the
    (A) trustor   (C) donor
    (B) divisor   (D) vendor

35. A contract based on an illegal consideration is
    (A) valid   (C) legal
    (B) void   (D) enforceable

36. A parcel of land is square, ½ mile by ½ mile. How many acres does it contain?
    (A) 40   (C) 320
    (B) 160   (D) 640

37. The instrument used to test for radon gas is a
    (A) micrometer   (C) spectrometer
    (B) radonometer   (D) metronome

38. The principal health problem with lead-based paint is
    (A) headaches   (C) asbestosis
    (B) lung cancer   (D) ingestion of paint chips by children

39. A *bill of sale* is used to transfer
    (A) assumed mortgage   (C) trust deed
    (B) subject to mortgage (D) personal property

40. If title and possession do not occur simultaneously, there should be an interim
    (A) lease (interim occupancy agreement)
    (B) option
    (C) exchange
    (D) novation

41. _____ means something is left to be done to a contract.
    (A) Executed   (C) Unfulfilled
    (B) Executory   (D) Unlisted

42. The date that a mechanic's lien takes is the date
    (A) the project began
    (B) the project was finished
    (C) the bill was presented
    (D) the bill was past due

43. A notary public
    (A) makes the statement
    (B) requires a graduate-level education
    (C) provides acknowledgment
    (D) assures a genuine deed

44. In real estate parlance, *alienation* means
    (A) walking away from a transaction
    (B) offending the seller
    (C) breaking a lease
    (D) transferring title

45. The booklet *A Homeowner's Guide to Earthquake Safety* must be given to buyers of dwellings of one to four units in
    (A) wood-frame buildings built before 1960
    (B) masonry buildings with wood-frame floors or roofs built before 1975
    (C) both A and B
    (D) neither A nor B

46. Lead-based paint disclosure is required for residential properties having one to four units that were built before
    (A) 1960
    (B) 1975
    (C) 1978
    (D) 1992

47. An "as is" sale of one to four dwelling units
    (A) requires a Real Property Transfer Disclosure statement
    (B) does not require a Real Property Transfer Disclosure statement
    (C) exempts the seller from mentioning undisclosed defects
    (D) reduces buyer risk

48. An injured party has _____ year(s) to file legal action on the Real Property Transfer Disclosure statement
    (A) one
    (B) two
    (C) three
    (D) five

49. The *Easton v. Strassburger* case makes it clear that when a seller and agent are in a transaction, material facts about the property must be disclosed to a potential buyer by the
    (A) seller
    (B) agent
    (C) seller and agent
    (D) neither seller nor agent except in response to a direct question from the buyer

50. If the agent or seller personally delivers the Real Property Transfer Disclosure Statement to the buyer after the offer is accepted, the buyer has _____ day(s) to rescind the contract.
    (A) one
    (B) three
    (C) twelve
    (D) The buyer cannot rescind the contract.

51. Under the Mello-Roos Community Facilities Act of 1982, disclosure of tax liens should be given to the
    (A) agent
    (B) buyer
    (C) seller
    (D) none of the above

52. The Mello-Roos Community Facilities Act of 1982 may be used to finance part of
    - (A) houses
    - (B) subdivisions
    - (C) shopping centers
    - (D) industrial developments

53. *Escheat* is a way for
    - (A) the State to receive title upon the death of an owner who leaves no will
    - (B) partnerships to get along
    - (C) individuals to pass title
    - (D) a spouse to receive title by divorce

54. The county recorder maintains
    - (A) tax rate data
    - (B) index of recordings
    - (C) broker license information
    - (D) all of the above

55. A quitclaim deed conveys only the present right, title, and interest of the
    - (A) grantor
    - (B) servient tenement
    - (C) grantee
    - (D) property

56. For a grant deed to be valid, the land description must be
    - (A) perfect
    - (B) approximate
    - (C) adequate
    - (D) within one acre of land

57. A *trust deed* is a
    - (A) security device
    - (B) exculpation matter
    - (C) novation
    - (D) all of the above

58. A *grant deed* is used
    - (A) as a security device
    - (B) to transfer title
    - (C) to transfer Civil War relics
    - (D) for the same purpose as a quitclaim deed

59. A grant deed must be signed by
    - (A) grantee
    - (B) grantor
    - (C) both grantee and grantor
    - (D) neither grantee nor grantor

60. The California "standard form" policy of title insurance on real property insures against loss occasioned by
    - (A) a forgery in the chain of recorded title
    - (B) liens or encumbrances not disclosed by official records
    - (C) rights of parties in possession of the property
    - (D) actions of governmental agencies regulating the use or occupancy of the property

61. A CLTA standard title insurance policy
    - (A) is commonly obtained by homeowners
    - (B) protects against forgery
    - (C) does not require an onsite property inspection
    - (D) all of the above

62. The maximum term of an agricultural lease in California is _____ years.
    - (A) 10
    - (B) 20
    - (C) 40
    - (D) 51

63. If a landlord files an unlawful detainer action, a tenant has _____ day(s) to appear.
    - (A) one
    - (B) three
    - (C) five
    - (D) thirty

64. The legal action to remove a defaulting tenant is a(n)
    (A) unlawful detainer action   (C) assignment
    (B) sublease   (D) recapture

65. A triple-net lease is one where the tenant pays
    (A) property taxes   (C) maintenance
    (B) insurance   (D) all of the above

66. A *strip shopping center* is a
    (A) regional mall   (C) nonconforming use
    (B) neighborhood center   (D) string of neighborhood stores

67. A commercial property investor is typically most interested in
    (A) land value   (C) tax shelter
    (B) current net income   (D) appreciation

68. Parallel wooden members used to support floor and ceiling loads are called
    (A) rafters   (C) headers
    (B) joists   (D) studs

69. *HVAC* refers to
    (A) high vacancy and collection
    (B) high volume and commissions
    (C) he vacates as convenient
    (D) heating, ventilation, and air conditioning

70. In a typical percentage lease, rent is calculated as a percentage of
    (A) assets of the lessee's business
    (B) net sales of the lessee's business
    (C) gross sales of the lessee's business
    (D) net taxable income of the lessee's business

71. In-house sales could result in an undisclosed
    (A) listing   (C) double commission
    (B) conflict of brokers   (D) dual agency

72. Failure to disclose a dual agency can lead to
    (A) loss of commission
    (B) license suspension or revocation
    (C) civil action by the injured party
    (D) all of the above

73. To be enforceable, a listing agreement for the sale of real estate must be
    (A) written on a special form
    (B) in written form
    (C) oral or in writing
    (D) for a term of at least 12 days

74. To be enforceable, a listing to sell personal property or a business opportunity must be
    (A) written on a special form   (C) oral or in writing
    (B) in written form   (D) for a term of at least 12 days

75. In order to plant a FOR SALE sign in the front yard, a broker must
    (A) be licensed
    (B) get the owner's permission
    (C) place the property in the multiple listing system
    (D) pay rent to the owner

76. A like-kind exchange or deferred like-kind exchange is allowed under Section _____ of the Internal Revenue Code.
    (A) 8
    (B) 1031
    (C) 1231
    (D) 1250

77. A *land contract* is also known as a(n)
    (A) installment land sale contract
    (B) real property sales contract
    (C) contract for deed
    (D) all of the above

78. In a typical land contract, the seller transfers the deed
    (A) at closing
    (B) upon receipt of disclosures
    (C) after the rescission period expires
    (D) when final payment is made

79. Like-kind exchanges of mortgaged property are based on
    (A) appraised property value
    (B) equity value
    (C) book value
    (D) adjusted tax basis

80. Before the expiration of an option, the optionee may
    (A) buy the property
    (B) choose to do nothing
    (C) sell the option
    (D) do any of the above

81. The Federal Housing Administration's role in financing the purchase of real property is to
    (A) act as the lender of funds
    (B) insure loans made by approved lenders
    (C) purchase specific trust deeds
    (D) do all of the above

82. The instrument used to remove the lien of a trust deed from record is called a
    (A) satisfaction
    (B) release deed
    (C) deed of conveyance
    (D) certificate of redemption

83. The type of mortgage loan that permits borrowing additional funds at a later date is called
    (A) an equitable mortgage
    (B) a junior mortgage
    (C) an open-end mortgage
    (D) an extensible mortgage

84. A loan to be completely repaid, principal and interest, by a series of regular, equal installment payments is a
    (A) straight loan
    (B) balloon-payment loan
    (C) fully amortized loan
    (D) variable-rate mortgage loan

85. The instrument used to secure a loan on personal property is called a
    (A) bill of sale
    (B) trust deed
    (C) security agreement
    (D) bill of exchange

86. A secured real property loan usually consists of
    (A) financing statement and trust deed
    (B) the debt (note) and the lien (deed of trust)
    (C) FHA or PMI insurance
    (D) security agreement and financing statement

87. When a loan is fully amortized by equal monthly payments of principal and interest, the amount applied to principal
    (A) and interest remains constant
    (B) decreases while the interest payment increases
    (C) increases while the interest payment decreases
    (D) increases by a constant amount

88. A *subordination clause* in a trust deed may
    (A) permit the obligation to be paid off ahead of schedule
    (B) prohibit the trustor from making an additional loan against the property before the trust deed is paid off
    (C) allow for periodic renegotiation and adjustment in the terms of the obligation
    (D) give priority to liens subsequently recorded against the property

89. PMI stands for
    (A) public money interest
    (B) payments made on investments
    (C) principal and mortgage interest
    (D) private mortgage insurance

90. High loan-to-value ratio loans generally are accompanied by
    (A) FHA insurance
    (B) VA guarantees
    (C) PMI
    (D) any of the above

91. Low interest rates cause
    (A) higher inflation rates
    (B) housing to be more affordable
    (C) higher loan-to-value ratios
    (D) owner financing to be more readily available

92. Rental income received appears on
    (A) balance sheet
    (B) cash flow statement
    (C) both of the above
    (D) neither of the above

93. A prepayment penalty is allowed on
    (A) FHA loans
    (B) VA loans
    (C) CalVet loans
    (D) all of the above

94. CalVet loans are financed by the sale of
    (A) bonds
    (B) mortgages
    (C) deeds
    (D) tax liens

95. A trust deed will always have a(n)
    (A) acceleration clause
    (B) assumability clause
    (C) prepayment penalty
    (D) lis pendens

96. *Capital markets* refers to
    (A) mortgages
    (B) bonds
    (C) stocks
    (D) all of the above

97. Mortgage bankers typically
    (A) originate loans
    (B) sell loans
    (C) borrow from banks under a line of credit
    (D) all of the above

98. Fannie Mae
    (A) buys loans
    (B) acquires loans in the secondary market
    (C) is the largest owner of mortgages in the United States
    (D) all of the above

99. When a buyer takes property *subject to* a loan, the seller
(A) is relieved of debt
(B) remains liable on the loan
(C) both A and B
(D) is no longer obligated on the loan

100. Mortgage bankers sell the loans they originate on the
(A) bank market
(B) FHLB market
(C) secondary market
(D) capital market

101. A "due on sale clause"
(A) means the loan is due when the property is sold ✓
(B) benefits the lender
(C) is a form of acceleration
(D) all of the above

102. Virtually all deeds of trust will have a clause that states that the full principal is due upon certain default. This is called a(n)
(A) release clause
(B) acceleration clause
(C) novation clause
(D) assignability clause

103. A VA loan amount is based on
(A) Certificate of Reasonable Value
(B) term of military service
(C) secondary mortgage market
(D) FNMA loan limits

104. Which item would an appraiser use to arrive at a net income for capitalization purposes?
(A) Cost of loans against the property
(B) Allowance for rent loss and vacancies
(C) Federal income tax
(D) Reserve for appreciation of buildings

105. An apartment complex cost $450,000. It brings in a net income of $3,000 per month. The owner is making what percentage of return on the investment?
(A) 7%
(B) 8%
(C) 11%
(D) None of the above

106. Appraisals of single-family dwellings are usually based on
(A) capitalization of rental value
(B) asking prices of comparable houses
(C) sales prices of comparable properties
(D) the assessed valuation

107. A "loss in value from any cause" is a common definition of
(A) economic obsolescence
(B) depreciation
(C) principal of contribution
(D) adverse leverage

108. If an appraiser finds that the fair rent for a vacant parcel of land is $1,400 per month and the interest rate is 11%, what is the approximate indicated land value?
(A) $109,090
(B) $138,560
(C) $152,730
(D) $210,000

109. Economic obsolescence could result from each of the following *except*
(A) new zoning laws
(B) a city's leading industry moving out
(C) misplacement of improvements
(D) an outdated kitchen

110. Which of the following is an appraiser's primary concern in the analysis of residential property?
   (A) marketability and acceptability
   (B) square foot area
   (C) functional utility
   (D) fixed and operating expenses

111. In order to evaluate a vacant commercial site, an appraiser decides to use the land residual technique. Here is the information the appraiser gathered:

   Cost new of a proper building: $250,000
   Estimated net income before recapture: $32,800 per year
   Interest rate: 8.5%
   Estimated remaining economic life of building: 40 years

   What is the approximate estimated value of the land using this technique?
   (A) $31,000   (C) $48,182
   (B) $47,000   (D) $62,353

112. Which of the following types of appraisal report would be the most comprehensive and detailed?
   (A) Self-contained   (C) Restricted use
   (B) Summary   (D) Oral

113. To estimate the value of a parcel of real property, an appraiser concentrated only on the cost to the buyer of acquiring a comparable substitute parcel. This estimate is most similar to which of the following appraisal approaches?
   (A) Cost   (C) Market
   (B) Income   (D) None of the above

114. *Capitalization* is a process whereby an appraiser
   (A) converts income into capital value
   (B) determines depreciation reserves
   (C) establishes cost of capital investment
   (D) finds gross income of equity capital

115. Appraisers estimate depreciation as a
   (A) loss in value from any cause   (C) loss in book value
   (B) loss in purchasing power   (D) tax write-off

116. Accountants measure depreciation as a
   (A) loss in value from any cause   (C) loss in book value
   (B) loss in purchasing power   (D) tax write-off

117. Which of the following is *not* a form of economic depreciation?
   (A) Physical deterioration   (C) Functional obsolescence
   (B) Original cost allocation   (D) Economic obsolescence

118. An appraisal may be
   (A) oral   (C) an opinion of value
   (B) written   (D) all of the above

119. A fee appraiser is
   (A) an independent contractor   (C) a mortgage broker
   (B) a bank fiduciary   (D) a real estate salesperson

120. A main goal of an appraiser is
(A) measuring obsolescence
(B) rendering a market value opinion
(C) narrative reporting
(D) meeting sales contract amount

121. A major factor in appraising a business opportunity is the
(A) net income
(B) number of employees
(C) number of customers
(D) owner's expertise

122. Prices of comparable sales are adjusted
(A) to the subject property
(B) upward if the comparable is inferior to the subject
(C) downward if the comparable is superior to the subject
(D) all of the above

123. All other things being equal, the cost per square foot of a two-story house compared to a one-story house having the same square footage
(A) is less
(B) is more
(C) is the same
(D) depends on height

124. If a $54,600 investment in real estate generates gross annual earnings of 15 percent, the gross monthly return most nearly is
(A) $819
(B) $705
(C) $685
(D) $637

125. In arriving at an effective gross income figure, an appraiser of rental property makes a deduction for
(A) real property taxes
(B) repairs
(C) vacancy
(D) depreciation

126. The federal income tax exemption on the gain from the sale of a house held long enough by a married couple is up to
(A) $25,000
(B) $125,000
(C) $250,000
(D) $500,000

127. The federal income tax exemption on the gain from the sale of a house held long enough by a single individual is up to
(A) $25,000
(B) $125,000
(C) $250,000
(D) $500,000

128. Cash or other unlike property included to equalize values in an exchange is called
(A) slipper
(B) equity
(C) parity
(D) boot

129. A Real Estate Investment Trust (REIT) must
(A) be closely held (five or fewer owners)
(B) distribute nearly all of its taxable income
(C) own stocks or bonds
(D) be the same as a limited partnership

130. Federal income tax rates are generally
(A) regressive
(B) neutral
(C) progressive
(D) none of the above

131. By California statute, an owner has _____ year(s) within which to redeem tax-delinquent property.
    (A) one
    (B) three
    (C) five
    (D) ten

132. Tax-delinquent real property not redeemed by the owner during the statutory redemption period is deeded to the
    (A) city
    (B) county
    (C) state
    (D) school district

133. A house sold for $113,900, which was 11% more than the cost of the house. The cost of the house was most nearly
    (A) $99,960
    (B) $100,400
    (C) $101,370
    (D) $102,610

134. A house that costs $75,000 appreciates by 11%, compounded annually. After two years, its value is most nearly
    (A) $97,000
    (B) $91,500
    (C) $90,000
    (D) $92,400

135. If interest for eight months of a $20,000 loan was $1,200, what is the rate of interest?
    (A) 7%
    (B) 8%
    (C) 9%
    (D) 10%

136. Brown purchased a $1,400 note secured by a second mortgage for investment purposes. The seller allowed a 15% discount. The note provided for monthly payments of $122, including interest at 9% per annum over a one-year term. Brown received full payment on the above terms. The yield on Brown's investment, expressed as a percentage, is
    (A) 23%
    (B) 31%
    (C) 34%
    (D) 40%

137. An office building provides $168,000 of annual net operating income. If it is purchased for $2,000,000, what is the overall rate of return?
    (A) 16.8%
    (B) 11.9%
    (C) 8.5%
    (D) 8.4%

138. An office building provides monthly rent of $12,400. It cost $2,000,000. The annual gross rent multiplier is most nearly
    (A) 1.2
    (B) 12.0
    (C) 13.4
    (D) 62

139. What is the annual potential gross income of an apartment complex with 20 one-bedroom units at $900 per month and 18 two-bedroom units at $1,050?
    (A) $36,900
    (B) $442,800
    (C) $44,280
    (D) $18,900

140. Prepaid taxes on a closing statement are
    (A) credited to the buyer
    (B) credited to the seller
    (C) debited to the seller
    (D) paid at closing to the tax collector

141. During escrow, if an unresolved dispute should arise between the seller and buyer preventing the close of escrow, the escrow holder may legally
    (A) arbitrate the dispute as a neutral party
    (B) rescind the escrow and return all documents and monies to the respective parties
    (C) file an interpleader action in court
    (D) do any of the above

142. Complaints under the California Fair Housing Act (Rumford Act) may be filed with the
   (A) Secretary of State
   (B) California Department of Fair Employment and Housing
   (C) Department of Real Estate (DRE)
   (D) California Association of REALTORS® (CAR)

143. The Unruh Civil Rights Act provides for
   (A) actual damages
   (B) punitive damages
   (C) both A and B
   (D) neither A nor B

144. An advertisement of an apartment for rent only to single women
   (A) is acceptable because they are better tenants
   (B) violates fair housing laws
   (C) is conditionally allowed
   (D) is altruistic

145. How can a real estate agent answer questions about a prospective buyer's race?
   (A) Such questions must be answered completely and accurately.
   (B) The agent is prohibited by law from answering such questions.
   (C) It is okay to lie.
   (D) The agent should use his or her best judgment about answering such questions.

146. The Rumford Act is principally concerned with
   (A) fair housing
   (B) fair employment
   (C) fair educational opportunities
   (D) fair discrimination

147. The Unruh Civil Rights Act
   (A) prohibits discrimination by individuals
   (B) prohibits discrimination by public schools
   (C) prohibits discrimination by businesses
   (D) prohibits discrimination by minorities

148. Under the federal Truth-in-Lending Law, two of the most critical facts that must be disclosed to buyers or borrowers are
   (A) duration of the contract and discount rate
   (B) finance charge and annual percentage rate
   (C) carrying charges and advertising expense
   (D) installment payments and cancellation rights

149. A nonconforming use
   (A) is allowed to continue unless the building is damaged
   (B) is grandfathered
   (C) was conforming before a zoning change
   (D) all of the above

150. Private restrictions on the use of land may be created by
   (A) private land use controls
   (B) written agreement
   (C) general plan restrictions in subdivisions
   (D) all of the above

Salesperson License Examination 2 _____

Directions: Select the choice, marked A, B, C, or D, that best answers the question or completes the thought. Mark your answers clearly on the answer sheet. You have 3 hours and 15 minutes to complete this examination. Answers are on page 498, math solutions on page 502.

1. If, upon receipt of an offer to purchase under certain terms, the seller makes a counteroffer, the prospective purchaser is
   (A) bound by his original offer
   (B) bound to accept the counteroffer
   (C) bound by the agent's decision
   (D) relieved of his original offer

2. A broker who makes profitable investments with earnest money deposits
   (A) must share 50 percent of the profits with the owners of the money he used
   (B) has done something illegal
   (C) may keep all the profits
   (D) must turn over the profits to the state's licensing authorities

3. A real estate broker must comply with
   (A) agency law
   (B) her state's real estate licensing law
   (C) both A and B
   (D) neither A nor B

4. Smith makes an offer on Jones's property and states that the offer will remain open for 3 days. The day after Smith has made the offer, he decides to withdraw it since Jones has neither rejected nor accepted it.
   (A) Smith cannot do this.
   (B) Smith can do this only if Jones was planning to reject the offer anyway.
   (C) Smith must give Jones at least half the remaining time to make a decision.
   (D) Smith may withdraw the offer.

5. In order to sell property belonging to a trust for which she is trustee, the trustee must have
   (A) a broker's license   (C) a trustor's license
   (B) a salesperson's license (D) none of the above

6. Appraised valuation is $250,000. Tax is based on 1 percent of appraised valuation. Which of the following is true?
   (A) Tax is $2,500.
   (B) Tax is $25,000.
   (C) City and county tax add up to $6,000.
   (D) None of the above

7. Paretsky's building is 90 ft. by 60 ft. He wishes to build a sidewalk 5 ft. wide and 6 in. thick all around the outside of the building. How many cubic yards of concrete will be needed?
   (A) 27.10   (C) 87.78
   (B) 29.63   (D) 263.34

8. In the absence of an agreement to the contrary, the deed of trust normally having priority will be the one that
   (A) is for the greatest amount
   (B) is a permanent mortgage
   (C) was recorded first
   (D) is a construction loan mortgage

9. A development in which a person owns her dwelling unit and, in common with other owners in the same project, also owns common property is
   (A) a leased fee
   (B) a condominium
   (C) a homestead
   (D) none of the above

10. Which of the following is true?
   (A) A condominium owner need not pay condominium fees that he feels are too high.
   (B) Condominium units are attached housing units.
   (C) Condominium is an ownership form, not an architectural style. ✓
   (D) Condominiums cannot be rented.

11. The money for making CalVet loans is provided by
   (A) the sale of bonds
   (B) the Department of Housing and Urban Development
   (C) the Federal Housing Administration
   (D) the Federal Savings and Loan Insurance Corporation

12. License law forbids
   (A) soliciting for listings before one is licensed ✓
   (B) collecting a commission from more than one party to a transaction ✗
   (C) showing property to other licensees ✗
   (D) the purchase by a broker of property that she has listed

13. What is usury?
   (A) collecting more interest than that allowed by law
   (B) building a structure that extends over someone else's land
   (C) selling property for less than the asking price
   (D) selling real estate without a license

14. Complaints about housing discrimination may be brought
   (A) to the Secretary of Housing and Urban Development
   (B) directly to court
   (C) either A or B
   (D) neither A nor B

15. Which of the following is (are) ALWAYS exempt from real property taxes?
   (A) Income-producing property owned by a church
   (B) Government-owned property ✓
   (C) Most restaurants
   (D) A private, for-profit school

16. Community property refers to
   (A) ownership by one person
   (B) ownership by a married couple
   (C) ownership by people who are related, but not married
   (D) ownership by unrelated people

17. For every purchase agreement there must be
   (A) an offer and acceptance
   (B) a mortgage loan
   (C) a broker
   (D) good consideration

18. Real estate brokers can lose their licenses for which of the following?
   (A) Using moneys received as commissions to pay office help
   (B) Representing the buyer in a transaction
   (C) Refusing a listing
   (D) Paying a commission to a nonlicensed person

19. A broker must keep all earnest money deposits in
    (A) her office safe
    (B) her business checking account
    (C) an escrow or trust account
    (D) a savings account

20. Eminent domain is
    (A) the right of the government to take private property for public use
    (B) the extent to which state boundaries reach out to sea
    (C) an ancient form of ownership not common today
    (D) the right of the federal government to pass laws that supersede state law

21. An 8-year-old downtown office building was worth $19,000,000 after depreciating at a rate of 3 percent per year. What was its original value?
    (A) $19,570,000
    (B) $23,560,000
    (C) $25,000,000
    (D) $27,777,000

22. Flaherty's mortgage loan is for $200,000 and carries an annual interest rate of 6%. Monthly payments are $1,200. How much will the principal be reduced by the *second* monthly payment?
    (A) $200
    (B) $201
    (C) $1,499
    (D) $1,500

23. Bernard signs a listing that guarantees the listing broker a commission payment if the sale is effected by any licensed agent. This is
    (A) an open listing
    (B) an exclusive agency listing
    (C) an exclusive right to sell listing
    (D) a net listing

24. Macrae negotiates with Ortez to list Ortez's property once Macrae is issued his real estate license. When the license is issued, Ortez signs a listing with Macrae.
    (A) The listing is valid.
    (B) The listing is invalid.
    (C) The listing is valid only at the listing price.
    (D) Macrae can collect only half the normal commission.

25. A licensee can lose his license for
    (A) selling properties quickly, at low prices
    (B) buying property for his own use from his principal
    (C) splitting a commission with another participating broker
    (D) none of the above

26. The 1985 base tax value of a house was $50,000. If the base has been increasing by 2 percent per year, how much is the base in 2006?
    (A) $50,000
    (B) $71,000
    (C) $75,783
    (D) $74,297

27. A conventional mortgage is
    (A) amortizing
    (B) guaranteed by FHA
    (C) not guaranteed by a government agency
    (D) approved by the VA

28. Among other things, the principal is obligated to
    (A) compensate the agent for her services
    (B) reimburse the agent for expenses incurred on behalf of the principal
    (C) both A and B
    (D) neither A nor B

29. Which of the following is NOT required to have a real estate license?
    (A) the resident manager of an apartment project
    (B) the resident manager of an apartment project who, for a fee, sells a house across the street
    (C) a student who sells houses as part of a research project
    (D) all of the above

30. Recordation of a deed is the responsibility of the
    (A) grantor
    (B) grantee
    (C) both A and B
    (D) neither A nor B

Questions 31–34 refer to the Far Hills Estates diagram on page 394.

31. Which of following statements is (are) true?
    (A) Four lots in Block E have frontage on two streets.
    (B) Iron Road has more lots fronting on it than any of the other streets on the plat.
    (C) both A and B
    (D) neither A nor B

32. Which lot has the greatest footage on Wood Lane?
    (A) Lot 11, Block E
    (B) Lot 12, Block E
    (C) Lot 1, Block L
    (D) Lot 19, Block E

33. Which lot has the greatest depth?
    (A) Lot 4, Block L
    (B) Lot 7, Block E
    (C) Lot 5, Block E
    (D) Lot 16, Block E

34. Which of following statements is (are) true?
    (A) The lots on the westerly side of Dale Road should appear in Block F.
    (B) There is no indication of where to find a plat of the easterly side of Lambert Drive.
    (C) Both A and B
    (D) Neither A nor B

35. Most California closings are in
    (A) escrow
    (B) premises
    (C) equity
    (D) consideration

36. The Statute of Frauds
    (A) requires certain contracts to be in writing to be enforceable
    (B) requires a license to operate as broker or salesperson
    (C) regulates escrow accounts
    (D) regulates the estate owning real estate

37. A warranty deed protects the grantee against a loss by
    (A) casualty
    (B) defective title
    (C) both A and B
    (D) neither A nor B

38. Brown's building rents for $8,500 per month. The building's market value is $470,000. Taxes are one percent of market value. What percentage of the building's rental income must be paid out in tax?
    (A) 6.4%
    (B) 10.7%
    (C) 4.6%
    (D) 34.5%

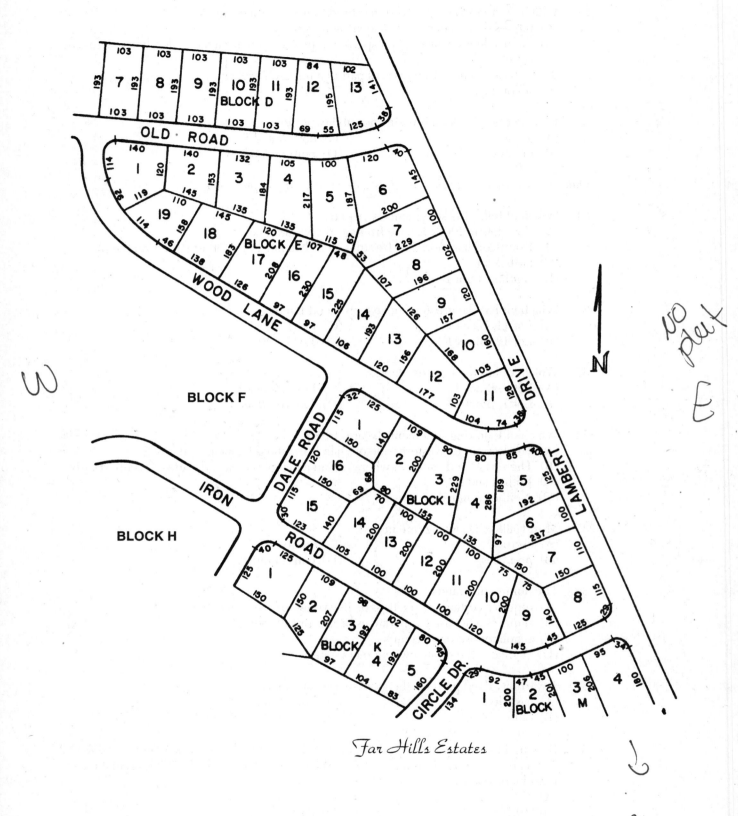

Far Hills Estates

39. Henderson bought a home for $420,000. Four years later he sold it for $599,000. What is the average annual rate of appreciation?
    (A) 9.92%   (C) 13.12%
    (B) 10.65%   (D) 42.62%

40. The income approach to appraisal would be most suitable for
    (A) a newly opened subdivision
    (B) commercial and investment property
    (C) property heavily mortgaged
    (D) property heavily insured

41. Real estate is defined as
    (A) land and buildings
    (B) land and all permanent attachments to it
    (C) land and everything growing on it
    (D) land only

42. A second deed of trust is
    (A) a lien on real estate that has a prior deed of trust on it
    (B) the first deed of trust recorded
    (C) always made by the seller
    (D) smaller in amount than a first deed of trust

43. Depreciation can be caused by
    (A) physical deterioration   (C) economic obsolescence
    (B) functional obsolescence   (D) all of the above

44. Income tax law exempts from taxation some of the gain on the sale of a principal residence. For a married couple, the exemption is a maximum of
    (A) $10,000   (C) $125,000
    (B) $25,000   (D) $500,000

45. Perkins bought 11 lots for $21,000 each. He keeps four and sells the remaining lots for a total of $28,000 more than he originally paid for all of them. What was the average sale price of each lot that he sold?
    (A) $21,000   (C) $37,000
    (B) $33,000   (D) $49,000

46. One discount point is equal to
    (A) 1% of the sales price   (C) 1% of the loan amount
    (B) 1% of the interest rate   (D) none of the above

47. Which of the following is NOT realty?
    (A) Fee simple estate   (C) Lumber
    (B) Leasehold for indefinite duration (D) Life estate

48. A minor is someone under the age of
    (A) 21   (C) 19
    (B) 20   (D) 18

49. A mortgaged property can be
    (A) sold without the consent of the mortgagee
    (B) conveyed by the grantor making a deed to the grantee
    (C) both A and B
    (D) neither A nor B

Questions 50 and 51 refer to the diagram below of a house and a lot.

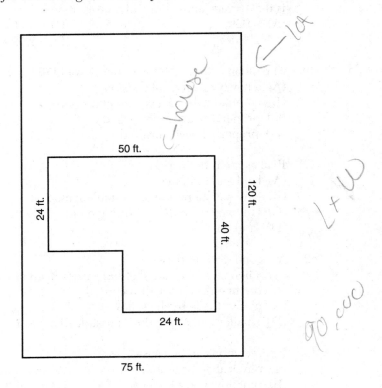

50. How many square feet are there in the house?
    (A) 384   (C) 1,584
    (B) 1,200   (D) 2,000

51. What percentage of the area of the lot is taken up by the house?
    (A) 13½%   (C) 22.2%
    (B) 17.6%   (D) 24.0%

52. Regulation Z covers
    (A) borrowing from relatives   (C) real estate credit transactions
    (B) borrowing by a business   (D) inheritances

53. A contract that gives someone the right but not the obligation to buy at a specified price within a specified time is
    (A) a contract of sale   (C) an agreement of sale
    (B) an option   (D) none of the above

54. The prohibitions of the 1968 Fair Housing Act apply to
    (A) multifamily dwellings of five or more units
    (B) multifamily dwellings of four or fewer units if the owner occupies one of the units
    (C) single-family dwellings
    (D) none of the above

55. Consideration that is of value only to the person who receives it is called
    (A) good consideration   (C) valuable consideration
    (B) near consideration   (D) no consideration

56. A potential mortgage lender seeks all but
    (A) good collateral   (C) adequate down payment
    (B) a buyer's need   (D) buyer's adequate income

57. A condominium homeowner's association may
    (A) require that certain owners sell their units and leave
    (B) assess fees for the upkeep of common property
    (C) practice discrimination, if it is done subtly
    (D) none of the above

58. If government takes private property it must
    (A) make just compensation for the property taken
    (B) require the property for a public use
    (C) both A and B
    (D) neither A nor B

59. The lot shown below sold for $78,300. What was the price per square foot?
    (A) $4.17   (C) $2.90
    (B) $3.56   (D) $2.45

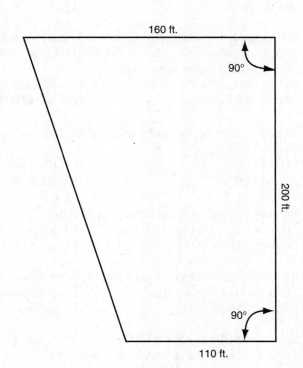

160 ft.

90°

200 ft.

90°

110 ft.

60. A salesperson receives 60 percent of the total commission on a sale for $315,000. The salesperson received $15,120. What was the rate of commission?
    (A) 4.8%   (C) 6¾%
    (B) 6%   (D) 8%

61. A tax rate of 1.06% is the same as
    (A) $10.60 per $1,000   (C) both A and B
    (B) .0106   (D) neither A nor B

62. A single-family house privately owned by an individual owning fewer than three such houses may be sold or rented without being subject to the provisions of the Fair Housing Act unless
    (A) a broker is used
    (B) discriminatory advertising is used
    (C) both A and B
    (D) neither A nor B

63. The transfer, by a tenant, of certain rights and obligations of an existing lease to another tenant is called
    (A) assignment of lease
    (B) a release
    (C) subletting
    (D) an eviction

64. A *contract for deed* is also known as
    (A) an installment land sales contract
    (B) a land contract
    (C) both A and B
    (D) neither A nor B

65. Nadel buys a new house costing $470,000. Land value is 15 percent of total price. The house contains 1,733 sq. ft. What is the cost per square foot of the house alone (not including the land)?
    (A) $411.50
    (B) $230.53
    (C) $271.20
    (D) $318.00

66. Salesman Jones works for a broker. Jones receives 42 percent of all commissions he brings in. Jones sells a home for $469,000, at a 6½ percent commission. What is the *broker's* share of the proceeds?
    (A) $12,803.70
    (B) $17,681.30
    (C) $30,485.00
    (D) $4,690.00

67. Rent for a 90 ft. by 60 ft. office is $6,300 per month. What is the annual rent per square foot?
    (A) $14.00
    (B) $11.00
    (C) $7.56
    (D) $140.00

68. An estoppel certificate is required when the
    (A) mortgage is sold to an investor
    (B) property is sold
    (C) property is being foreclosed
    (D) mortgage is assumed

69. An owner who seeks a loan and offers three properties as security will give
    (A) a blanket deed of trust
    (B) an FHA mortgage
    (C) a conventional deed of trust
    (D) a chattel mortgage

70. Ferraro bought a lot for $2,000 in 1963 and spent $130,000 to build a house on it in 1995. Today the house has increased 400 percent in value while the lot has increased 8,000 percent. What is the combined value of house and lot today?
    (A) $180,000
    (B) $182,000
    (C) $680,000
    (D) $812,000

71. A contract that has no force or effect is said to be
    (A) voidable
    (B) void
    (C) avoided
    (D) voidiated

72. Which of the following statements is (are) false?
    (A) FHA loans are insured loans.
    (B) VA loans are guaranteed loans.
    (C) both A and B
    (D) neither A nor B

73. To be enforceable, a purchase agreement must have
    (A) the signature of the wife of a married seller
    (B) an earnest money deposit
    (C) competent parties
    (D) witnesses

74. A broker listed a house for $350,000, at a 6 percent commission. The eventual sales price was $315,000. How much less was the broker's commission that it would have been if the house had sold at the listed price?
    (A) $210
    (B) $2,100
    (C) $18,900
    (D) $35,000

75. How many square feet are there in 1¼ acres?
    (A) 10,890
    (B) 44,649
    (C) 54,450
    (D) 152,460

76. Under Regulation Z, borrowers must be informed in writing of
    (A) the annual percentage rate
    (B) the total dollar amount of the finance charge
    (C) both A and B
    (D) neither A nor B

77. An item of personalty that is affixed to realty so as to be used as a part of it is
    (A) a fixture
    (B) a chattel
    (C) personal property
    (D) encumbered

78. The requirement that all parties to a contract have an understanding of the conditions and stipulations of the agreement is
    (A) consenting realty
    (B) a proper offer
    (C) good and valuable consideration
    (D) mutual agreement

79. A grant deed must be signed by
    (A) the grantee and the grantor
    (B) only by the grantor
    (C) both A and B
    (D) neither A nor B

80. In the application of the income approach to appraising, which of the following statements is true?
    (A) The higher the capitalization rate, the lower the appraised value.
    (B) The higher the capitalization rate, the higher the appraised value.
    (C) The present value is equal to future income.
    (D) none of the above

Questions 81–85 refer to the following listing contract narrative.

LISTING CONTRACT NARRATIVE

On June 16, 2006, you contact Mr. Sydney Purvis, whose two-story brick house has a "For Sale by Owner" sign in front. The house has 2,510 sq. feet of space, with four bedrooms (one downstairs) and three baths (one downstairs). It is federal colonial in style. The address is 8811 Quagmire Place, being Lot 18, Block G, Quagmire Estates Addition, Marin County, California. You have done some checking and know that Mr. Purvis has bought a new home. The house he is selling is 12 years old and has natural gas heat and hot water, central air conditioning, no basement, a breakfast area in the kitchen, a 98 ft. × 155 ft. lot, an entrance foyer and a center hall plan, and an attic with pull-down stairs. The tax rate is 1.04% of the assessed value. Mr. Purvis is moving in a week, so a prospective buyer can be offered immediate possession.

The next morning you call Mr. Purvis at his home (555-1116) and get no answer, so you call his office (555-2822) and he agrees to see you immediately to sign a listing agreement. At that time you find out that his current mortgage loan is not assumable, and that he will include all appliances (refrigerator, dishwasher, and dryer). He prefers to show the home only by appointment and will give you a key to keep handy at your office. Nearby schools are Dennis Elementary, DePalma Junior High, Moray High School, and St. Francis Parochial. You and Mr. Purvis agree on a 90-day listing at $337,500, with a 7½% commission, and your broker signs it.

81. If the property sells for the list price, the annual tax bill will be
    - (A) $3,375.00
    - (B) $3,510.00
    - (C) $25,312.50
    - (D) $6,750.00

82. The date of the listing is
    - (A) June 16, 2006
    - (B) June 17, 2006
    - (C) June 18, 2006
    - (D) September 15, 2006

83. Which of the following is *false*?
    - (A) The parochial school is St. Francis.
    - (B) The home has three bathrooms.
    - (C) The house has four bedrooms.
    - (D) The house is Spanish colonial in style.

84. Which of the following is *true*?
    - (A) The home will be shown only by appointment.
    - (B) The key to the home is under the doormat.
    - (C) both A and B
    - (D) neither A nor B

85. Which of the following is *true*?
    - (A) The home is now assessed for $337,500.
    - (B) The kitchen has a breakfast area.
    - (C) both A and B
    - (D) neither A nor B

86. Which of the following is correct?
    - (A) A section is 1 square mile.
    - (B) One square mile contains 840 acres.
    - (C) One acre contains 640 sections.
    - (D) A section is 2850 ft. on a side.

87. How many acres are in N½ NW¼ SE¼ of a given section?
    - (A) 20
    - (B) 40
    - (C) 160
    - (D) 180

88. Which of the following describes a section whose eastern boundary is 25 miles *west* of the principal meridian and whose northern boundary is 42 miles *north* of the base line?
    - (A) Section 35, T7N, R5W
    - (B) Section 35, T8N, R5W
    - (C) Section 2, T7N, R5W
    - (D) none of the above

89. How far must a rabbit hop in a straight line from the western boundary of NE¼, NW¼ to the eastern boundary of NE¼, NE¼ of the same section?
    - (A) 0.5 mi.
    - (B) 900 yd.
    - (C) 3960 ft.
    - (D) 14.667 acres

90. In a deed of trust, the lender is the
    - (A) beneficiary
    - (B) trustee
    - (C) trustor
    - (D) mortgagor

91. An ARM is
    - (A) a VA loan
    - (B) a CalVet loan for disabled veterans
    - (C) an FHA mortgage
    - (D) an adjustable rate loan

92. RESPA applies to the
    (A) Uniform Settlement Statement
    (B) Regulation Z
    (C) Proposition 13
    (D) Proposition 2½

93. A lender that discriminates on the basis of race has violated
    (A) RESPA
    (B) Truth in Lending
    (C) Proposition 13
    (D) Equal Credit Opportunity

94. The CalVet program
    (A) lends money to eligible veterans
    (B) insures private lenders against loss
    (C) guarantees loans
    (D) prevents foreclosures

95. CalVet loans are available for all but a
    (A) retail store building
    (B) single-family home
    (C) manufactured home in a park
    (D) farm

96. An installment land sales contract is also called a
    (A) purchase money mortgage
    (B) purchase agreement
    (C) land contract
    (D) Contract of Sale

97. The secondary mortgage market is not concerned with
    (A) adjustable rate mortgages
    (B) fixed rate mortgages
    (C) originating new mortgages
    (D) mortgage-backed securities

98. Escrow instructions can only be changed by
    (A) the buyer
    (B) the seller
    (C) both buyer and seller in writing
    (D) They are not changeable.

99. In northern California, escrows are most often held by
    (A) real estate brokers
    (B) title insurance companies
    (C) mortgage lenders
    (D) escrow companies

100. When can a real estate broker be an escrow agent?
    (A) Never
    (B) When ancillary to the brokerage transaction that he participates in
    (C) Anytime she pleases
    (D) When accompanied by a CPA

101. Igor has a 1-year lease that says the rent is $2,000 per month. However, the lease does not say when the rent shall be paid. Igor has to pay at the
    (A) end of each month
    (B) beginning of each month
    (C) end of the lease period
    (D) beginning of the lease period

102. Which of the following both originate mortgage loans and service them?
    (A) mortgage bankers
    (B) savings and loan associations
    (C) commercial banks
    (D) all of the above

103. Which of the following can be used as security for the payment of a debt?
    (A) mortgage
    (B) deed of trust
    (C) release of lien
    (D) A and B only

104. A lender may refuse to make a mortgage loan because of the
    (A) inability of the borrower to repay
    (B) location of the property
    (C) both A and B
    (D) neither A nor B

105. A trust deed held by the seller of the property is
    (A) a purchase money mortgage
    (B) a satisfaction piece
    (C) a lien dependent
    (D) a joint tenancy

106. A recorded instrument that concerns ownership rights to realty
    (A) gives constructive notice
    (B) notifies the public of the claims made in it
    (C) must be notarized or acknowledged
    (D) all of the above

107. Jones acquires a fee simple estate to land belonging to Green because Jones used and oc-
    cupied the land openly for a period of time, unmolested by Green. This is
    (A) an easement in gross
    (B) an adverse possession
    (C) an estoppel
    (D) a subrogation

108. A person who has another's power of attorney is called
    (A) an agent in place
    (B) a real estate broker
    (C) a lawyer
    (D) an attorney-in-fact

109. The right of California to take title to real estate for which no legal owner can be found
    is called
    (A) police power
    (B) tenancy
    (C) eminent domain
    (D) escheat

110. Zach dies without a will. According to the laws of California, Zelda receives title to Zach's
    real estate. Zelda has received
    (A) title by descent
    (B) clouded title
    (C) an easement
    (D) legacy title

111. A person may void a contract if it
    (A) was entered into under duress
    (B) was entered into with a minor
    (C) turned out to be a bad deal
    (D) all of the above

112. When instructions to the escrow agent are given separately by buyer and seller, they are
    (A) bilateral
    (B) literal
    (C) illiterate
    (D) unilateral

113. Which of the following has no warranty?
    (A) Executor's deed
    (B) Quitclaim deed
    (C) Grant deed
    (D) Trustee's deed

114. A worker who is not paid for work that improved real estate may file a
    (A) suit for quiet title
    (B) lis pendens
    (C) mechanic's lien
    (D) satisfaction piece

115. A parcel of land is 440 ft. by 817 ft. How many acres does it contain?
    (A) 17
    (B) 8.25
    (C) 11.67
    (D) More than 75

involuntary

116. Which of the following is a specific lien?
    (A) A judgment
    (B) A mechanic's lien
    (C) A lease
    (D) None of the above

117. Real estate is
    (A) land and buildings
    (B) land and all permanent attachments to it
    (C) land only
    (D) land and everything growing on it

118. In an agency relationship, the employer is called the
    (A) seller
    (B) buyer
    (C) principal
    (D) broker

119. Real estate licenses, once received, are
    (A) valid indefinitely
    (B) filed in the county record office
    (C) inheritable
    (D) valid for a limited period only ✓

120. In a lease contract, the tenant is the
    (A) lessee
    (B) lessor
    (C) leasee
    (D) leasor

121. Consideration that has value only to the person receiving it is
    (A) no consideration
    (B) good consideration
    (C) valuable consideration
    (D) good and valuable consideration

122. A general warranty deed protects the grantee against a loss by
    (A) casualty
    (B) defective title
    (C) defective materials
    (D) all of the above

123. A lease that requires the tenant to pay operating expenses of the property is a _____ lease.
    (A) gross
    (B) flat
    (C) net
    (D) step

124. Real estate licensing law in California is included in the
    (A) License Administration Code
    (B) Business and Professions Code
    (C) Real Estate Civil Code
    (D) Health and Public Safety Code

125. Licensed salesperson Jones wants to own a real estate brokerage business, but has failed the broker's examination many times. He forms a corporation, Jones Realty, Inc.; he owns 80 percent of the shares. The other 20 percent are owned by Broker Smith, who has agreed to be the broker-officer of the company.
    (A) They must have at least two more stockholders to satisfy the Corporations Code.
    (B) Smith and Jones both are in violation of the law.
    (C) Broker Smith can't be broker-officer and own shares at the same time.
    (D) All of the above are correct.

126. Which of the following statements is not true?
    (A) Lot boundaries in a final subdivision map must have been surveyed.
    (B) A condominium project is not a common interest subdivision.
    (C) A real estate broker may sell single mobile homes that have been licensed and registered, or are part of real estate.
    (D) Special studies zones are earthquake hazard areas.

127. A subdivision in a "sparsely populated" area (no more than 1,500 registered voters in or within two miles of the subdivision) is called a
    (A) rural development project
    (B) planned unit project
    (C) land project
    (D) unregulated subdivided project

128. Broker Johnson receives a cash deposit from Jones, who has signed a purchase contract to buy real estate from Smith. Which of the following may Broker Johnson do?
    (A) Invest the money, providing the proceeds and profits go to Smith at escrow closing.
    (B) Deposit the money with a neutral escrow depository.
    (C) Put the money in the brokerage office safe for safekeeping.
    (D) Deposit the money in his personal bank account.

129. The Kavanaughs want to build an addition to their home. However, the planned construction will be two feet closer to the lot line than zoning regulations allow. To be allowed to build their addition, they would apply for
    (A) rezoning to a higher density
    (B) nonconforming use
    (C) a reevaluated zone allowance
    (D) a zoning variance

130. Which of the following statements is false?
    (A) A state tax lien takes priority over all other liens.
    (B) In a closing statement, earnest money is an item likely to be credited to the buyer.
    (C) Joint tenants have the right of survivorship.
    (D) None of the above

131. If a borrower defaults on the payments to a mortgage loan, which clause allows the lender to demand immediate payment in full of the entire remaining loan balance?
    (A) Defeasance   (C) Acceleration
    (B) Subrogation   (D) Due-on-sale

132. Which of the following has the right of survivorship?
    (A) Joint tenant   (C) Tenant in common
    (B) Tenant in severalty   (D) Life tenant

133. In the covenant of seizin the
    (A) mortgagee states that he is foreclosing
    (B) lessor states that the lessee has not abided by the lease contract
    (C) grantor states that she owns the estate being transferred
    (D) lessee states that he is being evicted

134. Escheat is
    (A) the right to cross someone else's land to get to the road
    (B) a variety of fraud exclusive to real estate
    (C) the right to inherit if there is no will
    (D) none of the above

135. A lot is 75 ft. wide and contains 825 sq. yd. How deep is it?
    (A) 6 rods   (C) 32 yd.
    (B) 88 ft.   (D) ¹⁄₁₆ mi.

136. A broker's license is suspended for 6 months. The broker's two salespersons
    (A) also lose their licenses for 6 months
    (B) may continue to operate the broker's business
    (C) may, upon proper application, transfer their licenses to another broker
    (D) must place their licenses on inactive status for 6 months

137. One acre is equal to
    (A) 45,360 square feet
    (B) 54,630 square feet
    (C) 43,560 square feet
    (D) 17,810 square yards

138. The largest "bundle of rights" to real estate is a _____ estate.
    (A) leasehold
    (B) fee simple
    (C) life
    (D) homestead

139. In an exclusive right-to-sell listing,
    (A) only one broker is authorized to act as the seller's agent
    (B) if the seller finds the buyer, the seller still must pay the broker a commission
    (C) both A and B
    (D) neither A nor B

140. Salesperson Lois sold a house for $330,000. If her broker received 60 percent of the commission, and Lois's 45 percent share of that amount was $5,791.50, what was the commission rate charged on the sale?
    (A) 6 percent
    (B) 6.5 percent
    (C) 7 percent
    (D) 7.5 percent

141. A ¼-acre lot sold for $12,000. What was the price per square foot?
    (A) $1.10
    (B) 27.5 cents
    (C) $2.20
    (D) $1.82

142. To prove that he is entitled to a commission, a broker must show that
    (A) he was licensed throughout the transaction
    (B) the price was a fair one
    (C) all liens on the property have been settled
    (D) all of the above

143. A broker receives two offers on the same property at the same time. She should
    (A) submit both offers
    (B) submit the better offer while trying to improve the other one
    (C) submit the better offer and reject the other one
    (D) reject both offers

144. Since the broker is the seller's agent, he may
    (A) accept an offer on behalf of the seller
    (B) solicit offers for the seller's listed property
    (C) try to negotiate better terms before submitting an offer
    (D) work to get the buyer the best possible price

145. Which of the following is NOT an "improvement" to land?
    (A) Building
    (B) Driveway
    (C) Orchard
    (D) Tomato crop

146. Which of the following is (are) usually exempt from property taxes?
    (A) A post office
    (B) A hospital
    (C) A public school
    (D) All of the above

147. Real estate brokers advertise the most
    (A) on radio and TV
    (B) in newspapers
    (C) in magazines
    (D) on billboards

148. Which of the following is (are) evidence of involuntary alienation?
    (A) Deed in foreclosure
    (B) Quitclaim deed
    (C) Both A and B
    (D) Neither A nor B

149. Which of the following is a nonfreehold estate?
  (A) Fee simple estate
  (B) Leasehold estate
  (C) Life estate
  (D) None of the above

150. Sam's land has an easement to cross Karen's land to get to the lake. Sam subdivides his land into two parcels and sells one to George.
  (A) The easement no longer exists.
  (B) Sam's remaining land retains the easement, but George's does not.
  (C) Both Sam's remaining land and George's land have the easement rights.
  (D) Land benefiting from an easement cannot be subdivided.

Salesperson License Examination 3

Directions: Select the choice, marked A, B, C, or D, that best answers the question or completes the thought. Mark your answers clearly on the answer sheet. You have 3 hours and 15 minutes to complete this examination. Answers are on page 498, math solutions on page 504.

1. Jackson's will left to Mrs. Jackson the right to use, occupy, and enjoy Jackson's real estate until her death. At that time the real estate will become the property of their children. Mrs. Jackson is a
  (A) remainderman
  (B) life tenant
  (C) joint tenant
  (D) tenant in common

2. To prove his right to a commission, the broker must show
  (A) that he was licensed throughout the transaction
  (B) that he had a contract of employment
  (C) that he was the "efficient and procuring cause" of the sale
  (D) all of the above

3. Contracts made by a minor are
  (A) enforceable at all times
  (B) void
  (C) voidable by either party
  (D) voidable only by the minor

4. Mr. Beans owns land worth $50,000; Mr. Pork owns a house worth $300,000, subject to a $200,000 mortgage, which Beans will assume. For a fair trade,
  (A) Pork should pay $50,000 cash in addition
  (B) Beans should pay $50,000 cash in addition
  (C) they may trade properties evenly
  (D) none of the above

5. From the standpoint of the grantor, which of the following types of deed creates the least liability?
  (A) Grant
  (B) General warranty
  (C) Bargain and sale
  (D) Quitclaim

6. The lending of money at a rate of interest above the legal rate is
  (A) speculating
  (B) usury
  (C) both A and B
  (D) neither A nor B

7. A licensee's license must be
  (A) carried in her wallet at all times
  (B) posted in a public place in the broker's office
  (C) kept on the wall at the licensee's home
  (D) kept on the wall at the Real Estate Commission

8. The parties to a deed are the
   (A) vendor and vendee
   (B) grantor and grantee
   (C) offeror and offeree
   (D) acceptor and acceptee

9. A person must be licensed if he is to sell
   (A) his home
   (B) property belonging to an estate for which he is executor *admin of someone who died*
   (C) property belonging to other clients who pay him a commission
   (D) property that he has inherited

10. Which of the following is NOT an appraisal approach?
    (A) Cost
    (B) Sales comparison
    (C) Income
    (D) Trade

11. The most comprehensive ownership of land at law is known as
    (A) estate for years
    (B) life estate
    (C) fee simple
    (D) defeasible title

12. Each of the following pairs of words or phrases describes the same extent of land EXCEPT
    (A) 1 acre—43,560 square feet
    (B) 1 mile—5,280 feet
    (C) 1 square mile—460 acres
    (D) 1 section—640 acres

13. In order to sell property, one must
    (A) have a realtor's license
    (B) belong to a realtor's association
    (C) hire only realtors
    (D) none of the above

14. What are the broker's responsibilities under the 1968 Fair Housing Act?
    (A) To show all houses to all prospects
    (B) To treat all prospects equally
    (C) Both A and B
    (D) Neither A nor B

15. In order to be recorded, a deed must be in writing and must
    (A) be signed by the grantee
    (B) state the actual purchase price
    (C) be acknowledged — *recorded*
    (D) be free of all liens

16. When real estate is sold, the property tax base
    (A) is adjusted to the sales price
    (B) remains the same
    (C) is rolled back to 1975
    (D) raised by 2% per year

17. The purpose of the CalVet program is to
    (A) set the maximum interest rates that may be charged
    (B) assist veterans to buy homes and farms
    (C) both A and B
    (D) neither A nor B

18. Which of the following contractual arrangements would be unenforceable?
    (A) A agrees to buy B's house.
    (B) A agrees with B that B shall steal money from C.
    (C) A agrees to find a buyer for B's car.
    (D) A agrees with B that B shall make restitution to C for money stolen by B.

19. The two parties to a lease contract are the
    (A) landlord and the serf
    (B) rentor and the rentee
    (C) lessor and the lessee
    (D) grantor and the grantee

20. When a person deliberately lies in order to mislead a fellow party to a contract, this act is
    (A) fraud
    (B) misrepresentation
    (C) legal if no third parties are involved
    (D) all right if the lie is not written into the contract

21. A contract that transfers possession but not ownership of property is
    (A) a special warranty deed
    (B) an option
    (C) an easement
    (D) a lease

22. Egbert owns a building in life estate. Upon Egbert's death, ownership of the building will go to Ethel. Ethel is a
    (A) remainderman
    (B) life tenant
    (C) common tenant
    (D) reversionary interest

23. A person owning an undivided interest in land with at least one other, and having the right of survivorship, is said to be a
    (A) tenant in common
    (B) tenant at will
    (C) joint tenant
    (D) tenant at sufferance

24. A person who has some rights to use land, but not all possessory rights, is said to have
    (A) an interest in land
    (B) an estate in land
    (C) a life estate in land
    (D) a tenancy in common

25. Which of the following is NOT corporeal property?
    (A) Fee simple real estate
    (B) Leasehold
    (C) Easement
    (D) Fixture

26. A listing contract that says the broker will receive a commission no matter who sells the property is called
    (A) an open listing
    (B) a net listing
    (C) an exclusive agency listing
    (D) an exclusive right to sell listing

27. Which of the following best describes a land contract?
    (A) A contract to buy land only
    (B) A mortgage on land
    (C) A means of conveying title immediately while the purchaser pays for the property
    (D) A method of selling real estate whereby the purchaser pays for the property in regular installments while the seller retains title to the property

28. Ms. Maloney has a 3-month option on 20 acres at $20,000 per acre. She may
    (A) buy the property for $400,000
    (B) sell the option to another
    (C) not buy the land
    (D) all of the above

29. The mortgagor's right to reestablish ownership after delinquency before foreclosure is known as
    (A) reestablishment
    (B) satisfaction
    (C) equity of redemption
    (D) acceleration

30. A broker must place funds belonging to others in
    (A) his office safe, to which only he knows the combination
    (B) a safety deposit box
    (C) an account maintained by the Real Estate Commission
    (D) a trust, or escrow, account

31. A licensee's license can be revoked for
    (A) closing a deal
    (B) intentionally misleading someone into signing a contract that she ordinarily would not sign
    (C) submitting a ridiculous offer to a seller
    (D) all of the above

32. Capitalization is a process used to
    (A) convert income stream into a lump sum capital value ✓
    (B) determine cost
    (C) establish depreciation
    (D) determine potential future value

33. The number of square feet in 1 acre is
    (A) 45,630   (C) 46,530
    (B) 45,360   (D) 43,560

34. When changed surroundings cause an existing house to lose value, there is
    (A) physical deterioration   (C) functional obsolescence
    (B) economic obsolescence   (D) all of the above

35. An appraisal is
    (A) a forecast of value   (C) a prediction of value
    (B) an estimate of value   (D) a precise estimation of value

36. A state tax lien for unpaid property taxes
    (A) can be sold at auction within one year
    (B) takes priority over most other liens but not holders of a mechanic's lien of security interest, or judgment creditors established prior to the tax lien
    (C) cannot exist unless taxes are at least 36 months overdue
    (D) is a form of adverse possession

37. The prohibitions of the 1968 Fair Housing Act apply to privately owned housing when
    (A) a broker or other person engaged in selling or renting dwellings is used
    (B) discriminatory advertising is used
    (C) both A and B
    (D) neither A nor B

38. According to Regulation Z, to cancel a credit transaction the borrower must inform the lender, within 3 days,
    (A) by phone   (C) both A and B
    (B) in writing   (D) neither A nor B

39. A agrees to trade his car to B in exchange for a vacant lot that B owns.
    (A) This is a valid contractual agreement.
    (B) This is not a contract because no money changes hands.
    (C) This is not a contract because "unlike" items can't be traded.
    (D) This is not a valid contract because the car is titled in A's name.

40. A percentage lease requires the tenant to pay
    (A) a percentage of taxes and insurance
    (B) a percentage of net income as rent
    (C) a percentage of sales as rent
    (D) none of the above

41. A seller of real estate is also known as the
    (A) vendee   (C) vendor
    (B) grantor   (D) grantee

42. An estate at will is
    (A) a limited partnership   (C) an inheritance by will
    (B) a tenancy of uncertain duration (D) a life tenancy

43. A hands B a deed with the intent to pass title and orally requests B not to record the deed until A dies. When is the deed valid?
    (A) Immediately   (C) When A dies
    (B) When B records the deed   (D) Never

44. A quitclaim deed conveys only the interest of the
    (A) guaranteed   (C) claimant
    (B) property   (D) grantor

45. A gross lease requires the tenant to pay rent based on
    (A) gross sales   (C) gross profit
    (B) net sales   (D) none of the above

46. The recording of a deed
    (A) passes the title   (C) guarantees the title
    (B) insures the title   (D) gives constructive notice of ownership

47. The law that requires most real estate contracts to be written to be enforceable is the
    (A) Statute of Limitations
    (B) Statute of Frauds
    (C) Statute of Written Real Estate Agreements
    (D) Law of Property

48. In the absence of an agreement to the contrary, the deed of trust normally having priority will be the one that
    (A) is for the greatest amount   (C) was recorded first
    (B) is a permanent deed of trust (D) is a construction loan mortgage

49. A net listing is one
    (A) that requires the broker to seek a net price for the property
    (B) that is illegal in California
    (C) that most ethical brokers prefer to use
    (D) in which the broker's commission is the amount by which the sale price exceeds the agreed-upon net price the seller desires

50. Under Regulation Z, a borrower may have the right to cancel, within 3 days,
    (A) a second mortgage on his dwelling
    (B) a first mortgage loan used to purchase his dwelling
    (C) a home-improvement loan more than 1 year old
    (D) none of the above

51. Which of the following does not terminate an agency relationship?
    (A) Making an offer   (C) Resignation of agent
    (B) Death of either party   (D) Destruction of subject matter

52. The 1968 Fair Housing Act protects against housing discrimination on the basis of
    (A) race and color
    (B) race, color, and religion
    (C) race, color, religion, and national origin
    (D) race, color, religion, national origin, sex, familial status, and handicap

53. A person who dies leaving no will is said to have died
    (A) intestate   (C) unbequeathed
    (B) without heirs   (D) unwillingly

54. From the point of view of the grantee, the safest kind of deed that can be received is a
    (A) general warranty deed   (C) quitclaim or release deed
    (B) special warranty deed   (D) trustee's deed

55. What is NOT an essential element of a valid contract?
    (A) Offer and acceptance   (C) Lack of ambiguity
    (B) Capacity of participants   (D) Legal objective

56. In a grant deed, the seller transfers
    (A) a lien   (C) an easement
    (B) a lease   (D) a title

57. In order to do business, a licensee must
    (A) make proper application for a license
    (B) pass a licensing examination
    (C) have a license issued by the appropriate state agency
    (D) all of the above

58. When a loan is assumed on property that is sold,
    (A) the original borrower is relieved of further responsibility
    (B) the purchaser becomes liable for the debt
    (C) the purchaser must obtain a certificate of eligibility
    (D) all of the above

59. An estoppel certificate is often required when a
    (A) mortgage is sold to an investor   (C) property is being foreclosed
    (B) property is sold   (D) mortgage is assumed

60. Which of the following will not terminate a lease?
    (A) Performance   (C) Surrender
    (B) Breach   (D) Vacancy

61. The adjustment process in the direct sales comparison approach involves the principle of
    (A) contribution   (C) variable proportions
    (B) diminishing returns   (D) anticipation

62. A contract in which A agrees to allow B to use A's real estate in return for periodic payments of money by B is a
    (A) deed   (C) lease
    (B) contract of sale   (D) mortgage

63. Community property rights assure that
    (A) a husband receives a certain portion of his deceased wife's estate
    (B) wives and, in some states, children receive a certain portion of a deceased husband's or father's estate
    (C) husbands and wives share equally in property acquired during marriage
    (D) a homeowner cannot lose his entire investment in his home

64. When an individual holds property past the expiration of a lease without the landlord's consent, the leasehold estate she has is a
    (A) tenancy at sufferance   (C) common of pasturage
    (B) freehold estate   (D) holdover tenancy

65. A broker's unlicensed secretary
    (A) may sell property providing he does it under the broker's direct supervision
    (B) may sell or negotiate deals so long as he does not leave the office
    (C) may refer interested clients to the broker or her employed licensees
    (D) all of the above

66. In California, most purchases are closed
    (A) in toto   (C) in escrow
    (B) in time   (D) in rem

67. Which of the following is NOT required of an agent with respect to his principal?
    (A) To be loyal
    (B) To act in person
    (C) To account for the agent's own personal finances
    (D) To act in the principal's best interests

68. Community property refers to
    (A) a special form of joint ownership available only to married couples
    (B) ownership by two persons only
    (C) ownership by at least three persons
    (D) ownership by one person only

69. A person who has permission to use land, but has no other rights, has
    (A) tenancy at sufferance   (C) license
    (B) tenancy in common   (D) fee simple estate

70. When tastes and standards cause an existing house to lose value, there is
    (A) physical deterioration   (C) functional obsolescence
    (B) economic obsolescence   (D) all of the above

71. A rule-of-thumb method for determining the price a wage earner can afford to pay for a home is to multiply her annual income by
    (A) 1½   (C) 4
    (B) 2½   (D) 6

72. A real estate license, once received,
    (A) remains in effect indefinitely
    (B) is good for a limited period of time
    (C) must be filed in county records
    (D) may be inherited by the holder's spouse

73. Which of the following is most accurately described as personal property?
    (A) A fixture   (C) An improvement
    (B) A chattel   (D) Realty

74. A real estate broker is a
    (A) general agent   (C) secret agent
    (B) special agent   (D) travel agent

75. A broker may use escrow moneys held on behalf of others
    (A) for collateral for business loans
    (B) for collateral for personal loans
    (C) for salary advances to licensees in his employ
    (D) none of the above

76. Which of the following forms of deeds has one or more guarantees of title?
    (A) Quitclaim   (C) Warranty
    (B) Executor's   (D) Special form

77. The highest price a buyer is willing, but not compelled, to pay and the lowest price a seller is willing, but not compelled, to accept is
    (A) estimated value   (C) marginal value
    (B) economic value   (D) market value

78. To be valid, a deed need NOT necessarily be
    (A) signed   (C) sealed
    (B) written   (D) delivered

79. A person who receives title to land by virtue of having used and occupied it for a certain period of time, without actually paying the previous owner for it, receives title by
    (A) will   (C) alienation
    (B) descent   (D) adverse possession

80. A conventional mortgage is
    (A) amortizing
    (B) guaranteed by the FHA
    (C) not guaranteed by a government agency
    (D) approved by the VA

81. The party to whom a deed conveys real estate is the
    (A) grantee   (C) beneficiary
    (B) grantor   (D) recipient

82. Which is NOT considered a permanent attachment to land?
    (A) Anything growing on it   (C) Chattels
    (B) Fixtures   (D) Anything built on the land

83. The main appeal of VA mortgages to borrowers lies in
    (A) low interest rates   (C) unlimited mortgage ceiling
    (B) minimum down payments   (D) easy availability

84. For which reason is a deed recorded?
    (A) To insure certain title   (C) To meet a state requirement
    (B) To give notice to the world (D) To save title insurance cost

85. Ownership of real property is transferred
    (A) when the grantor signs the deed
    (B) when the grantor's signature has been notarized
    (C) when the deed is delivered
    (D) when the correct documentary stamps are put on the deed and canceled

86. A valid purchase agreement of real property must be signed by the
    (A) broker   (C) seller only
    (B) agent and seller   (D) buyer and seller

87. A sublease is a
    (A) lease made by a lessor
    (B) lease made by a lessee and a third party
    (C) lease for basement space
    (D) condition of property

88. "Hand money" paid upon the signing of an agreement of sale is called
    (A) an option   (C) earnest money
    (B) a recognizance   (D) a freehold estate

89. Market value appraisals assume that
    (A) the purchaser pays all cash (no mortgage financing)
    (B) FHA or VA financing is employed
    (C) the appraiser can determine the types of financing involved
    (D) the financing, if any, is on terms generally available in that area

90. A licensed salesperson
    (A) must work under the supervision of a broker
    (B) can collect commission payments only from his broker
    (C) must have his license held by his employing broker
    (D) all of the above

91. If the property is assessed at $600,000 and the tax rate is 1.1%, the tax is
    (A) $660   (C) $6,600
    (B) $66   (D) $66,000

92. Smith sold three lots for a total of $90,000. The first lot sold for 1½ times the price of the second lot. The second lot sold for twice the price of the third lot. How much did the first lot sell for?
    (A) $15,000   (C) $45,000
    (B) $30,000   (D) $90,000

93. Aaronson owns a 44-acre tract of land. In order to develop it, he must set aside 10 percent of the area for parks and must use 6.6 acres for streets, drainage, and other uses. If the minimum permissible lot size is 7,500 sq. ft., what is the maximum possible number of lots Aaronson can lay out?
    (A) 191   (C) 293
    (B) 180   (D) 81

94. Velez borrowed $7,500 for 4 years, paying interest every quarter. The total amount of interest she paid was $2,700. What was the annual interest rate?
    (A) 9%   (C) 27%
    (B) 10%   (D) 36%

95. Jim sold a parcel of land for $164,450. He made a profit of 43 percent. What was his purchase price?
    (A) $82,755.00   (C) $115,000.00
    (B) $93,736.50   (D) $164,450.00

96. Anne referred a customer to Connie, who sold the customer a house for $465,000. Connie paid Anne a referral fee of 12 percent of Connie's commission. If Anne received $3,906, what was the rate of the commission on Connie's sale?
    (A) 5%   (C) 6½%
    (B) 6%   (D) 7%

97. What monthly rent must Sam get on his land in order to earn an annual return of 11 percent on the $210,000 that he paid for the land? Assume that the tenant pays all property taxes.
   (A) $275
   (B) $1,552
   (C) $1,925
   (D) $23,100

98. Smith bought three lots for $100,000 each. If they increase in value by 25 percent each year *compounded*, in how many years will she be able to sell one of the lots for as much as she originally paid for all three?
   (A) 4
   (B) 5
   (C) 6
   (D) 7

99. How many acres are contained in a rectangular tract of land measuring 1,700 ft. by 2,100 ft.?
   (A) 81.96
   (B) 92.91
   (C) 112.01
   (D) 115.00

100. A backyard measures 100 ft. by 80 ft. The house is 40 ft. wide. A fence 4 ft. high is to be built around the yard, with the width of the house as part of the barrier. If fence fabric is $1.80 per square yard, how much will the necessary fence fabric cost?
   (A) $64
   (B) $256
   (C) $288
   (D) $2,304

101. The legal action that may be brought by a confused escrow agent is
   (A) contract law
   (B) agency law
   (C) interpleader
   (D) mediation

102. Proposition 13 limits the annual base value increases to
   (A) 1%
   (B) 2%
   (C) 5%
   (D) 10%

103. A reassessment of property value in California can occur
   (A) annually
   (B) every five years
   (C) every 10 years
   (D) upon title transfer, new construction, property assessment

104. When property with unpaid taxes is not redeemed by its owner for_____year(s), the state may claim ownership.
   (A) one
   (B) two
   (C) five
   (D) seven

105. A married homeowner who sells a principal residence at a gain, may exclude up to _____ of gain from taxable federal income.
   (A) $20,000
   (B) $50,000
   (C) $125,000
   (D) $500,000

106. To assure both a lender and a borrower of meeting payments, a home buyer may deposit each month ½ of the estimated annual taxes and insurance, in addition to principal and interest payments. The taxes and interest are placed by the lender in an account called an
   (A) impound account
   (B) earnest money account
   (C) interest accrual account
   (D) federal tax deposit account

107. A real estate license is required to be held by
(A) a trustee
(B) an attorney in the practice of law
(C) a mortgage loan broker
(D) a trust deed beneficiary

108. A person is not required to be licensed as a real estate broker
(A) to sell one's own home
(B) to sell a neighbor's home
(C) to sell a brother's home
(D) all of the above

109. Which of the following is (are) community property?
(A) A wife's inheritance from her parents received during marriage
(B) A husband's inheritance from his parents received during marriage
(C) A wife's salary from part-time job
(D) All of the above

110. For county assessed property, a tax lien is filed on
(A) January 1
(B) March 1
(C) July 1
(D) November 1

111. The state of California imposes
(A) state income tax
(B) inheritance tax
(C) gift tax
(D) both A and B

112. A lease that specifies certain increases in rent over the life of the lease is a _____ lease.
(A) reappraisal
(B) net
(C) step
(D) percentage

113. A lease in which the tenant's rent is based at least in part upon his gross business revenues is a _____ lease.
(A) reappraisal
(B) net
(C) step
(D) percentage

114. Which level of government does NOT usually enact zoning laws?
(A) federal
(B) state
(C) county
(D) city

115. A court will appoint _____ to settle and manage the estate of a person who dies intestate.
(A) a trustee
(B) an executor
(C) an administrator
(D) an attorney-in-fact

116. An unlicensed person who shares a real estate commission may be in violation of
(A) federal law
(B) license law
(C) zoning law
(D) common law

117. Millie wants to buy a house costing $367,500. For the loan she wants, she needs a 10 percent down payment and must pay a 1 percent origination fee, 2 points discount, and an 0.5 percent PMI fee. How much money does she need to obtain this loan?
(A) $36,750.00
(B) $48,326.25
(C) $49,612.50
(D) $63,210.00

118. The interest rate on a loan is 9 percent. The interest for the month of April was $468.75. What was the loan balance at the beginning of April?
    (A) $52,083
    (B) $55,799
    (C) $60,000
    (D) $62,500

119. Usury is defined as
    (A) collecting more interest than is allowed by law
    (B) building a structure that extends over someone else's land
    (C) selling property for less than the asking price
    (D) selling real estate without a license

120. Mortgage loans guaranteed or insured by the federal government include
    (A) conventional loans
    (B) all ARM loans
    (C) VA loans
    (D) all of the above

121. In a settlement statement, accrued interest on an assumed loan is treated as
    (A) credit to buyer, debit to seller
    (B) credit to both buyer and seller
    (C) credit to seller and doesn't appear on buyer's statement
    (D) debit to buyer, credit to seller

122. Sam wants to build a patio 60 feet by 20 feet and 4 inches thick. How many cubic yards of concrete will he need?
    (A) 12.4
    (B) 14.8
    (C) 120
    (D) 400

123. A real estate license may be revoked for
    (A) failing to account for money belonging to others
    (B) submitting an offer for much less than the asking price
    (C) representing both buyer and seller without the consent of both
    (D) either A or C

124. Will openly occupied Ward's land for a period of time, without interference from Ward, and then received fee simple title to the land. This was an example of
    (A) an easement in gross
    (B) adverse possession
    (C) estoppel
    (D) subrogation

125. Max has Beth's power of attorney. Beth is called
    (A) an agent in place
    (B) a real estate broker
    (C) a lawyer
    (D) an attorney-in-fact

126. The right by which the state takes title to real estate for which no legal owner can be found is
    (A) police power
    (B) tenancy
    (C) eminent domain
    (D) escheat

127. Which of the following types of deeds has no warranty?
    (A) Executor's
    (B) Quitclaim
    (C) General warranty
    (D) Trustee's

128. Louise does work on Joe's house, but is not paid. She may file a
    (A) mechanic's lien
    (B) satisfaction piece
    (C) notice of foreclosure
    (D) sheriff's auction

PURCHASE AGREEMENT NARRATIVE

On August 14, 2006, you show the home belonging to Sydney Purvis (refer to the listing contract narrative, page 428, for details) to a prospective purchaser, Ms. Miriam Stein.

Three days later Ms. Stein informs you that she wishes to offer $318,000 for the house, subject to getting a mortgage loan for at least 80 percent of the sale price, with a term of 30 years and at the currently prevailing rate of interest. Closing will be at the broker's office no later than September 18, 2006. Ms. Stein leaves her personal check for $6,000 as a deposit. Mr. Purvis will receive all cash at the closing, from the proceeds of Ms. Stein's loan, her deposit, and additional cash necessary to make up the purchase price.

The next day your broker draws up the contract and Mr. Purvis and Ms. Stein sign it.

Questions 129–133 refer to narrative above.

129. The broker's commission at 7 ½ percent will be
   (A) $16,200.00   (C) $23,850.00
   (B) $23,700.00   (D) $24,996.63

130. The purchaser requires a loan of at least
   (A) $260,400   (C) $240,000
   (B) $254,400   (D) $233,556.63

131. The contract allows how many days until closing?
   (A) 29   (C) 31
   (B) 30   (D) 32

132. After allowing for the deposit she has made and a mortgage loan of 80 percent of the purchase price, how much additional cash must the purchaser pay at closing?
   (A) $63,600   (C) $60,600
   (B) $57,600   (D) $54,600

133. The date of the contract is
   (A) August 14, 2006   (C) August 18, 2006
   (B) August 17, 2006   (D) August 20, 2006

Questions 134–135 refer to the diagram shown.

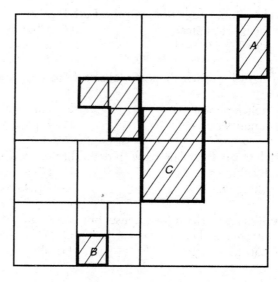

Section 20, T 14 S, R 16 W

134. Which of the following describes the shaded area marked *A*?
     (A) NE¼, NW¼, NE¼
     (B) E¼, NE¼
     (C) E½, NE¼
     (D) E½, NE¼, NE¼

135. How many acres are there in the shaded tract marked *A*?
     (A) 20
     (B) 40
     (C) 80
     (D) 160

136. A road is built through a section. It follows the line dividing E½, SE¼ from W½, SE¼ then follows the line dividing N½ from S½ until it reaches the western boundary of the section. How long is the part of the road inside the section?
     (A) 0.5 mi.
     (B) 0.75 mi.
     (C) 1 mi.
     (D) 1.25 mi.

137. A road is built along the northern boundary of SW¼, SE¼ of a given section. The road extends 66 ft. in width into the tract. How many acres in this tract are not covered by the road?
     (A) 27.81
     (B) 33
     (C) 38
     (D) 38.80

138. A properly done appraisal is
     (A) an authentication of value
     (B) an estimate of value
     (C) a prediction of value
     (D) a statement of exact value

139. If Murphy defaults on the payments to his deed of trust, under which clause may the lender demand immediate payment in full of the entire remaining loan balance?
     (A) Defeasance
     (B) Subrogation
     (C) Acceleration
     (D) Due-on-sale

140. Which of the following does NOT have the right of survivorship?
     (A) Joint tenant
     (B) Tenant in severalty
     (C) Tenant by the entirety
     (D) All of the above

141. An easement can be
     (A) the right to cross someone else's land to get to the road
     (B) a variety of fraud exclusive to real estate
     (C) the right to inherit if there is no will
     (D) none of the above

142. A broker's license is revoked. The broker's salespeople
     (A) also have their licenses revoked
     (B) may continue to operate the broker's business
     (C) may, upon proper application, transfer their licenses to another broker
     (D) must place their licenses on inactive status for a year

143. In an exclusive right-to-sell listing,
     (A) only one broker is authorized to act as the seller's agent
     (B) if the seller finds the buyer, the seller still must pay the broker a commission
     (C) the broker must use her best efforts to solicit offers
     (D) all of the above

144. Among the broker's functions, he may
     (A) accept an offer on behalf of the seller
     (B) solicit offers for the seller's listed property
     (C) try to negotiate better terms before submitting an offer
     (D) work to get the buyer the best possible price

145. Which of the following is an "improvement" to land?
    (A) Rezoning
    (B) Driveway
    (C) Orchard
    (D) All of the above

146. The required loan document, in addition to a deed of trust, is
    (A) a security deposit
    (B) a promissory note
    (C) a down payment
    (D) an escrow closing

147. The rent for Sam's store is based at least in part upon Sam's gross business revenues. Sam's lease is a _____ lease.
    (A) reappraisal
    (B) net
    (C) step
    (D) percentage

148. What is usury?
    (A) collecting more interest than that allowed by law
    (B) building a structure that extends over someone else's land
    (C) selling property for less than the asking price
    (D) selling real estate without a license

149. Joe wants to build a patio 20 yd. by 20 ft. and 6 in. thick. How many cubic yards of concrete will he need?
    (A) 22.2
    (B) 40.0
    (C) 20.0
    (D) 400

150. One township contains _____ sections.
    (A) 43,560
    (B) 5,280
    (C) 36
    (D) 640

Salesperson License Examination 4

Directions: Select the choice, marked A, B, C, or D, that best answers the question or completes the thought. Mark your answers clearly on the answer sheet. You have 3 hours and 15 minutes to complete this examination. Answers are on page 499, math solutions on page 505.

1. An appraisal is
    (A) a forecast of value
    (B) a prediction of value
    (C) an estimate of value
    (D) a statement of exact value

2. The number of square feet in 1 acre is
    (A) 640
    (B) 43,560
    (C) 45,360
    (D) 53,460

3. How is the *gross rent multiplier* calculated?
    (A) Market value/market rental
    (B) Monthly payment/market rental
    (C) Market rental/market price
    (D) Sales price/market price

4. A perfectly rectangular tract of land contains exactly 10.6 acres. The measurement on one side is 181 ft. To the nearest foot, how deep is the tract?
    (A) 255 ft.
    (B) 385 ft.
    (C) 1,817 ft.
    (D) 2,551 ft.

5. What is the maximum number of 8,000-sq.-ft. lots that can be platted from a 17.1-acre tract if 19 percent of the land must be used for streets and parks?
    (A) 17
    (B) 62
    (C) 75
    (D) 93

6. Laws that set minimum construction standards are
   (A) building codes
   (B) zoning codes
   (C) environmental laws
   (D) condemnation laws

7. Which of the following is NOT an appraisal approach?
   (A) Cost ✓
   (B) Trade
   (C) Sales comparison ✓
   (D) Income ✓

8. Value is determined by
   (A) supply and demand
   (B) asking prices
   (C) interest rates
   (D) active brokers

9. Permission for land use not normally permitted by the zoning classification of the property is
   (A) a differential
   (B) a zone change
   (C) a variance
   (D) an egregement

10. Smith sells a tract of land 400 ft. by 665 ft. for $171,000. To the nearest ten dollars, what is the price per acre?
    (A) $28,000
    (B) $29,500
    (C) $31,170
    (D) $32,280

11. In Green's city, the property tax rate is 1.05 percent of the market value of the property. Green just paid $425,000 for a home. What will the tax be?
    (A) $4,462.50
    (B) $446.25
    (C) $2,125
    (D) $4,250

12. When changes in taste cause a neighborhood to become less desirable, there is
    (A) physical deterioration
    (B) functional obsolescence
    (C) economic obsolescence
    (D) all of the above

13. The income approach is generally most suitable for appraising
    (A) commercial and investment property
    (B) single-family homes
    (C) heavily mortgaged property
    (D) heavily insured property

Questions 14–16 concern the following situation:

Mr. Jones died, leaving Mrs. Jones the right to use, occupy, and enjoy his real estate until her death, at which time their son Willis would receive a fee simple estate in the real estate.

14. Mrs. Jones is a
    (A) remainderman
    (B) life tenant
    (C) joint tenant
    (D) tenant in common

15. Willis is a
    (A) remainderman
    (B) life tenant
    (C) joint tenant
    (D) tenant in common

16. Mrs. Jones has a
    (A) fee simple estate in joint tenancy with Willis
    (B) fee simple estate as tenant in common with Willis
    (C) life estate
    (D) reversionary interest

17. A building 40 ft. by 22 ft. has exterior walls 10 ft. high. There are 13 windows, 4 sq. ft. each, and a door measuring 48 sq. ft. One gallon of paint covers 400 sq. ft. If the door and the windows are not to be painted, how many gallons of paint are needed to give the walls *two* full coats?
    (A) 2.85
    (B) 5.7
    (C) 3.1
    (D) 6.2

18. Bernini borrows $12,000. He pays $330 each quarter in interest. What is the annual interest rate on this loan?
    (A) 2¾%
    (B) 8%
    (C) 11%
    (D) 12%

19. In California, a person is no longer a minor at age
    (A) 16
    (B) 17
    (C) 18
    (D) 21

20. A person who appears to own a piece of real estate, but actually does not, has
    (A) good title
    (B) recorded title
    (C) constructive notice
    (D) color of title

21. A real estate broker is
    (A) a general agent
    (B) an attorney-in-fact
    (C) a special agent
    (D) an agent provocateur

22. Contracts made by a minor are
    (A) void
    (B) voidable by the minor
    (C) voidable by all parties
    (D) voidable by adult parties

23. The parties to a deed are
    (A) vendor and vendee
    (B) testator and testatee
    (C) grantor and grantee
    (D) offeror and offeree

24. Ms. Levy has the choice of renting a house for $2,250 per month, including utilities, or for $1,750 per month if she pays the utility bills. Average utility bills are $4,800 per year, but Ms. Levy feels she can reduce this by 35 percent. How much *per month* does she expect to save by paying the utility bills herself?
    (A) $0
    (B) $150
    (C) $180
    (D) $240

25. Salesman O'Hara gets 50 percent of the first $20,000 of commissions he brings in and 60 percent of all above that amount in 1 year. Last year he sold $1,100,000 of real estate, all at 7 percent commission. How much did O'Hara get to keep?
    (A) $77,000
    (B) $46,200
    (C) $44,200
    (D) $34,200

26. A quitclaim deed conveys only the interest of the
    (A) grantor
    (B) claimant
    (C) quittor
    (D) property

27. Which of the following will NOT terminate a lease?
    (A) Breach
    (B) Performance
    (C) Vacancy
    (D) Surrender

28. One discount point is equal to
    (A) 1% of the sale price
    (B) 1% of the loan amount
    (C) 1% of the interest rate
    (D) none of the above

29. Which of the following is NOT covered by title insurance?
    (A) Forged deed   (C) Tornado damage
    (B) Deed by incompetent   (D) Undisclosed heirs

30. Ownership of realty by one person is
    (A) tenancy in severalty   (C) tenancy by the entirety
    (B) conjoint tenancy   (D) tenancy sole

31. Green made an offer to purchase real estate from Blue. The offer gave Blue 7 days to
    consider it. Two days later, without hearing anything from Blue, Green found another
    property that he liked better. Green then wanted to withdraw his offer to Blue.
    (A) Green had to wait until the 7 days had passed.
    (B) Green was required to notify Blue of his desire to withdraw the offer, and to give
        Blue "reasonable time" to accept or reject it.
    (C) Green could withdraw the offer immediately.
    (D) none of the above

32. The secondary mortgage market is the market
    (A) for second mortgages
    (B) in which existing mortgages are bought and sold
    (C) in which junior mortgages are originated
    (D) for older, low-interest loan assumptions

33. A landowner leases her land to a lessee, who in turn leases the land to a sublessee. Who
    holds the *sandwich lease*?
    (A) Landowner   (C) Sublessee
    (B) Lessee   (D) None of the above

34. The deed used in California whereby a person warrants that he is the possessor and
    owner of property is
    (A) grant   (C) quitclaim
    (B) bargain   (D) trust

35. Title to land passes
    (A) on the date shown on the deed
    (B) upon recordation of the deed
    (C) when the deed is signed
    (D) upon delivery of the deed

36. Provisions for defeat of the trust deed are found in the _____ clause.
    (A) alienation   (C) foreclosure
    (B) acceleration   (D) defeasance

37. All trust deeds are
    (A) due on sale   (C) recorded
    (B) liens   (D) none of the above

38. A fixture is
    (A) anything that cannot be removed from the real estate without leaving a hole
    (B) anything the property owner says is a fixture
    (C) anything necessary to the proper and efficient use of the real estate
    (D) none of the above

39. Byrd lives in an apartment owned by Lyon. The lease has expired, but Byrd has stayed on
    and continues to pay rent to Lyon. This is an example of tenancy
    (A) by remainder   (C) at suffrance
    (B) at will   (D) in common

40. Which of the following is NOT real estate?
    (A) A flagpole affixed to a house
    (B) A tomato crop not ready for harvest
    (C) A greenhouse
    (D) All of the above *are* real estate.

41. The law that requires that all transfers of ownership rights to real estate be in writing is the
    (A) statute of frauds
    (B) statute of limitations
    (C) parol evidence rule
    (D) statute of liberties

42. After paying a 6½ percent commission, Jackson received net proceeds of $336,132.50 on the sale of his home. What was the sale price?
    (A) $21,848.60
    (B) $357,981.10
    (C) $359,500.00
    (D) $375,000.00

43. When a valid lease of real estate exists, and the rent is paid on time, which of the following is false?
    (A) The lessor cannot move in and use the property until the lease expires.
    (B) The lessee possesses the right of occupancy.
    (C) The lessee holds the fee to the real estate.
    (D) The lessor has a reversionary interest in the real estate.

44. The clause in a deed of trust that allows the lender to demand immediate payment in full of the remaining balance, if payment of the note is not made as contracted, is the _____ clause.
    (A) alienation
    (B) acceleration
    (C) foreclosure
    (D) amortization

45. All of the following should be recorded EXCEPT
    (A) an easement
    (B) a 20-year lease
    (C) a mortgage
    (D) a 6-month lease

46. In a typical deed of trust transaction, the trustor is the
    (A) borrower
    (B) third party
    (C) appraiser
    (D) closing agent

47. Which of the following has access to documents that have been recorded in the public records?
    (A) Prospective buyers
    (B) Prospective lenders
    (C) Appraisers
    (D) All of the above

48. Ms. Anderson sold a tract of land. After paying a 9 percent commission and paying 3 percent of the selling price in taxes, fees, and closing costs, she ended up with $176,000. What was the sale price of the land?
    (A) $181,280
    (B) $191,840
    (C) $197,120
    (D) $200,000

49. Farley's warehouse measures 52 ft. by 36 ft. The walls are 9 in. thick, and there are 13 support pillars inside the building, each 6 in. by 6 in. What is the area, in square feet, of the *net* interior floor space?
    (A) 1739
    (B) 1742¼
    (C) 1803⁵⁄₁₆
    (D) 1806⁹⁄₁₆

50. Title that establishes ownership of real estate in a reasonably clear manner upon examination of the public records is _____ title.
    (A) owner's
    (B) marketable
    (C) equitable
    (D) quiet

51. A certain property has no road frontage; however, there exists a recorded right of access across a neighboring parcel of land. This right is
    (A) a conditional title   (C) an easement
    (B) an entroversion   (D) a defeasance

52. An estate that may be terminated by any party at any time is an estate
    (A) for years   (C) in possession
    (B) at will   (D) in termination

53. If the commission in a listing contract is arranged so that the broker receives all of the purchase price in excess of a certain figure, the listing is a(an) _____ listing.
    (A) open   (C) gross
    (B) net   (D) multiple

54. Which of the following does NOT have the right of survivorship?
    (A) tenant in common   (C) tenant by the entirety
    (B) joint tenant   (D) All *have* the right of survivorship.

55. In a CalVet loan transaction, to whom is the discount (if any) paid?
    (A) CalVet   (C) The broker
    (B) No discount   (D) The buyer

56. In a VA loan transaction, who usually pays the discount (if any)?
    (A) The VA   (C) The seller
    (B) The lender   (D) The closing agent

57. A building that Montez leases is destroyed by an earthquake. Under common law,
    (A) the lease is no longer enforceable
    (B) Montez needn't pay rent until the building is rebuilt
    (C) Montez must rebuild the building, but may deduct the cost from the rent
    (D) Montez must continue to pay rent until the lease expires

58. Which of the following is neither real estate nor a fixture?
    (A) Ceiling   (C) Light bulb in chandelier
    (B) Chandelier on ceiling   (D) Light switch

59. Real estate brokers and salespeople should be familiar with
    (A) common law   (C) license law
    (B) agency law   (D) all of the above

60. Which of the following is NOT always a right possessed by an owner of a fee simple estate?
    (A) possession   (C) occupancy
    (B) easement   (D) disposition

61. Which of the following would NOT be considered commercial real estate?
    (A) office building   (C) shopping center
    (B) condominium home   (D) doctors' office complex

62. Smith wishes to develop a subdivision containing 55 lots averaging 10,500 sq. ft. each. An average of 1380 sq. ft. of street, sidewalk, and other space must be provided for each lot. What is the minimum number of acres that Smith will need?
    (A) 12   (C) 15
    (B) 14   (D) 17

63. Which of the following instructions from a seller may NOT be complied with by a real estate broker?
    (A) Don't put up a for sale sign in the yard.
    (B) Don't present offers for less than the listing price.
    (C) Don't show the property to persons who do not speak English.
    (D) Don't show the property on religious holidays observed by seller.

64. Real estate brokers' commissions usually are set by
    (A) the local board of realtors
    (B) the laws of California
    (C) agreement with other brokerage firms
    (D) agreement between property owner and broker

65. When a licensed salesperson advertises property for sale,
    (A) the name of the broker must be mentioned
    (B) only the salesperson's name must be mentioned
    (C) the name of the property owner must be revealed
    (D) the price must not be mentioned

66. Which form of listing does NOT allow the seller to sell her listed property by herself without paying the listing broker a commission?
    (A) Open listing   (C) Multiple listing
    (B) Exclusive right-to-sell listing   (D) Exclusive agency listing

67. A broker has a listing the terms of which allow him to earn a commission only if he finds a buyer before the seller or another broker does. This is an example of
    (A) an open listing   (C) a net listing
    (B) an exclusive right-to-sell listing   (D) an exclusive agency listing

68. Part of an addition that Sam builds to his home turns out to be on land belonging to June. This is an example of
    (A) accretion   (C) easement
    (B) riparian rights   (D) encroachment

69. Tina has the legal right to use Fred's driveway for her lifetime. Tina has
    (A) a life estate   (C) a license to use
    (B) an easement in gross   (D) a riparian right

70. Simpson wishes to install wall-to-wall carpeting in his home, which measures 42 × 28 ft. The outside walls are 6 in. thick, and the interior walls are 4 in. thick. There are 135 linear ft. of wall inside the home. The two bathrooms (each with interior measurements of 9 ft. × 6 ft.) and the kitchen (12 ft. × 12 ft.) are not to be carpeted. If installed carpeting costs $27.90 per square yard, how much will the job cost?
    (A) $2,511.00   (C) $3,013.20
    (B) $2,445.90   (D) $3,431.70

71. Ms. Farrell contracts to buy a house for $550,000. She pays $15,000 in earnest money and applies for a 75 percent loan. How much more money will she need to make up the purchase price of the home?
    (A) $133,750   (C) $107,500
    (B) $122,500   (D) $48,750

72. Leo allows Lemmie to stay in Leo's house while Leo is on vacation, but Lemmie must leave when Leo returns. Lemmie has
    (A) a short-term lease   (C) a license
    (B) a proprietary right   (D) an easement

73. An estate that has an indefinite duration is
    (A) a freehold estate
    (B) a renewable leasehold
    (C) an estate at suffrance
    (D) a nonfreehold estate

74. How many 100 ft. × 100 ft. lots can be made out of a 3-acre plot of land?
    (A) 6
    (B) 11
    (C) 13
    (D) 43

75. A lot sold for $225 a front foot. If the lot was 96 ft. deep and had an area of 6,336 sq. ft., how much did the lot sell for?
    (A) $11,770
    (B) $14,256
    (C) $14,850
    (D) $21,600

76. A "legal description" of land must
    (A) be sufficient to identify the property
    (B) carry measurements to the nearest inch
    (C) show the area of the land being described
    (D) all of the above

77. Increase in the size of a plot of land because of soil deposited by the flow of a stream is called
    (A) accretion
    (B) riparian right
    (C) depletion
    (D) amortization

78. If an offer is *rescinded*, it is
    (A) revised
    (B) altered
    (C) terminated
    (D) accepted

79. Which of the following is NOT necessarily required in a deed?
    (A) Acknowledgment
    (B) Grantee's signature
    (C) Date
    (D) Description of real estate

80. Government's right to regulate land use derives from
    (A) escheat
    (B) just compensation
    (C) police power
    (D) eminent domain

81. In a grant deed, the grantor assures that
    (A) there are no liens on the property
    (B) the estate granted is free of encumbrances placed on the property by the grantor
    (C) the grantor has not previously granted the property to another
    (D) B and C above

82. The term *security instrument* include(s)
    (A) a mortgage
    (B) a deed of trust
    (C) a lease
    (D) A and B only

83. In most situations in California, a _____ serves as trustee in a deed of trust.
    (A) lender
    (B) borrower
    (C) title company
    (D) real estate broker

84. When a trust deed is used in California, the redemption period following a trustee's fore-closure sale is
    (A) no period
    (B) three months
    (C) one year
    (D) five years

85. When a mortgage is foreclosed in California, the redemption period is
    (A) no period
    (B) three months under all situations
    (C) one year when the sale brings less than the debt
    (D) five years

86. The law that sets compensation limits for brokers on various types of loans is
    (A) Regulation Z
    (B) RESPA
    (C) Real Property Loan Law
    (D) Unruh Act

87. Which of the following is not a category of appraisal personnel in California?
    (A) Trainee license
    (B) Licensed
    (C) Certified residential
    (D) Generally trained

88. The agency in California that promotes tax uniformity within and among counties is
    (A) Uniformity Agency
    (B) Level Annuity Assessment Board
    (C) Equalization Board
    (D) State of California Appeals Board

89. An example of a private loan is one made by
    (A) Southern California Federal Savings
    (B) Northern California National Bank
    (C) California State Bank and Trust
    (D) California Stars and Stripes Corporation

90. To create an escrow, there must be
    (A) unconditional delivery of deeds
    (B) a binding contract
    (C) estoppels
    (D) all of the above

91. Property that is located in more than one county in California is assessed by
    (A) agreement of the counties
    (B) the larger county
    (C) both counties
    (D) the state of California

Questions 92–96 refer to the following listing contract narrative.

LISTING CONTRACT NARRATIVE

On June 16, 2006, you contact Mr. Sydney Purvis, whose two-story brick house has a "For Sale by Owner" sign in front. The house has 2510 sq. feet of space, with four bedrooms (one downstairs) and three baths (one downstairs). It is federal colonial in style. The address is 8811 Quagmire Place, being Lot 18, Block G, Quagmire Estates Addition, Marin County, California. You have done some checking and know that Mr. Purvis has bought a new home. The house he is selling is 12 years old and has natural gas heat and hot water, central air conditioning, no basement, a breakfast area in the kitchen, a 98 ft. × 155 ft. lot, an entrance foyer and a center hall plan, and an attic with pull-down stairs. The tax rate is 1.04% of the assessed value. Mr. Purvis is moving in a week, so a prospective buyer can be offered immediate possession.

The next morning you call Mr. Purvis at his home (555-1116) and get no answer, so you call his office (555-2822) and he agrees to see you immediately to sign a listing agreement. At that time you find out that his current mortgage loan is not assumable, and that he will include all appliances (refrigerator, dishwasher, and dryer). He prefers to show the home only by appointment and will give you a key to keep handy at your office. Nearby schools are Dennis Elementary, DePalma Junior High, Moray High School, and St. Francis Parochial. You and Mr. Purvis agree on a 90-day listing at $337,500, with a 7½ percent commission, and your broker signs it.

92. This contract is
   (A) an exclusive right to sell listing
   (B) an exclusive agency listing
   (C) an open listing
   (D) a net listing

93. If the property is sold at the listed price, the broker's commission will be
   (A) $9,810.00
   (B) $19,080.00
   (C) $25,312.50
   (D) $26,400.00

94. This listing will expire on
   (A) September 15, 2006
   (B) September 16, 2006
   (C) September 17, 2006
   (D) September 18, 2006

95. Which of the following telephone numbers can be used to contact the seller?
   (A) 555-1717
   (B) 555-2282
   (C) 555-1116
   (D) None of the above

96. Which of the following is *false*?
   (A) The lot size is 98 ft. × 155 ft.
   (B) The house is 21 years old.
   (C) The home has natural gas heat.
   (D) All of the above

Questions 97 and 98 refer to the diagram shown.

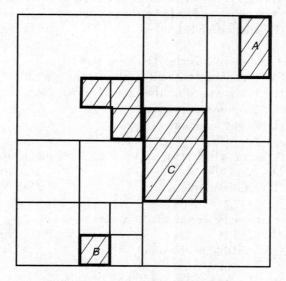

Section 20, T 14 S, R 16 W

97. Which of the following describes the shaded tract marked *B*?
   (A) SE¼, SW¼, SE¼
   (B) SW¼, SE¼, SW¼
   (C) SE¼, SW¼, NE¼
   (D) S¼, SE¼, S¼

98. What is the area of the shaded tract marked *B*?
    (A) 5 acres
    (C) 20 acres
    (B) 10 acres
    (D) 40 acres

99. A man owns SW¼, SW¼ of a section. He purchases the remainder of SW¼. By what percentage has he increased his holding of acreage?
    (A) 100%
    (C) 300%
    (B) 200%
    (D) 400%

100. Helen Smith purchases S½, NW¼, NE¼ of a section. What *percentage* of the total area of the section has she purchased?
    (A) 1⁷⁄₁₆%
    (C) 5%
    (B) 3⅛%
    (D) 31¼%

101. How is the *gross rent multiplier* calculated?
    (A) Market value/market rental
    (C) Market rental/market price
    (B) Monthly payment/market rental
    (D) Sales price/market price

102. Minimum allowable construction standards are established by
    (A) building codes
    (C) environmental laws
    (B) zoning codes
    (D) condemnation laws

103. An allowed land use that is NOT normally permitted by the property's zoning classification is
    (A) a dispensation
    (C) a variance
    (B) a zone change
    (D) a restrictive covenant

104. Peeling paint and loose floorboards are examples of
    (A) physical deterioration
    (C) economic obsolescence
    (B) functional obsolescence
    (D) both A and B

105. The sales comparison approach is generally most suitable for appraising
    (A) commercial and investment property
    (C) heavily mortgaged property
    (B) single-family homes
    (D) heavily insured property

106. A feature of a freehold estate is that it
    (A) is acquired without paying anything for it
    (B) is always acquired by adverse possession
    (C) has uncertain duration
    (D) is any leasehold estate

107. A person who has the appearance of owning land, but does not own it, has
    (A) good title
    (C) constructive notice
    (B) recorded title
    (D) color of title

108. A contract entered into by a minor can be
    (A) void
    (C) voidable by all parties
    (B) voidable by the minor
    (D) voidable by adult parties

109. Which of the following will NOT terminate a lease?
    (A) Surrender
    (C) Vacancy
    (B) Performance
    (D) Breech

110. In mortgage lending, one discount point is equal to
    (A) 1% of the sale price
    (C) 1% of the interest rate
    (B) 1% of the loan amount
    (D) 1% of the commission

111. Hooper's offer to purchase Looper's real estate stated that the offer would become void if not accepted within 5 days. The day after the offer was made, having heard nothing from Looper, Hooper wanted to withdraw his offer.
    (A) Hooper had to wait until the 5 days had passed.
    (B) Hooper was required to notify Looper of his desire to withdraw the offer, and to give Looper "reasonable time" to accept or reject it.
    (C) Hooper could withdraw the offer immediately.
    (D) None of the above

112. In a real estate transaction, title to land passes
    (A) on the date shown on the deed
    (B) upon recordation of the deed
    (C) upon notarization of the deed
    (D) upon delivery of the deed

113. A fixture is
    (A) anything that cannot be removed from the real estate without leaving a hole larger than 6 inches
    (B) anything the seller says is a fixture
    (C) anything needed for the proper use of the real estate
    (D) none of the above

114. The law that requires that all transfers of ownership rights to real estate be in writing is the
    (A) contract act
    (B) statute of limitations
    (C) statute of recordation
    (D) statute of frauds

115. All of the following should be recorded EXCEPT
    (A) a deed of trust
    (B) a 20-year lease
    (C) an executor's deed
    (D) a contract of sale

116. In a typical deed of trust transaction, the trustor is the
    (A) lender
    (B) borrower
    (C) appraiser
    (D) closing agent

117. A salesperson sold a property for $106,000. If the broker received 50 percent of the commission, and the salesperson's 60 percent share of that amount was $2,544, what was the commission rate charged on the sale?
    (A) 7%
    (B) 7.5%
    (C) 7.75%
    (D) 8%

118. An estate that any party can terminate at any time is an estate
    (A) for years
    (B) at will
    (C) in possession
    (D) leasehold entailed

119. A listing contract says that the seller receives $320,000, and the broker receives all of the purchase price over $320,000 as his commission. This is a(an) ____ listing.
    (A) open
    (B) net
    (C) multiple
    (D) exclusive

120. Jones leases a building that is damaged by a storm. Under common law,
    (A) the lease is no longer enforceable
    (B) Jones needn't pay rent until the building is repaired
    (C) Jones must repair the building, but may deduct the cost from rent
    (D) Jones must continue to pay rent until the lease expires

121. In each locality, real estate brokerage commissions are determined by
     (A) the local board of REALTORS®
     (B) the laws of the state
     (C) the board of estimate
     (D) agreement between property owner and broker

122. A lot sold for $980 a front foot. If the lot was 132 ft. deep and had an area of 6,468 sq. ft., how much did the lot sell for?
     (A) $64,680
     (B) $57,710
     (C) $48,000
     (D) $39,000

123. Which of the following is required for "mutual agreement" in a contract?
     (A) Offer and acceptance
     (B) Proper consideration
     (C) Description of the land
     (D) Legal form

124. In California, a 6-month lease
     (A) must be in writing
     (B) need not be written
     (C) may not be in writing
     (D) ought not to be written

125. The expenses of settlement are
     (A) paid by the broker
     (B) paid by the seller
     (C) negotiated between buyer and seller
     (D) paid by the buyer

126. In California a primary source of revenue for local government is
     (A) income taxes
     (B) sales taxes
     (C) property taxes
     (D) severance taxes

127. The purpose of real estate licensing laws is to protect
     (A) salespersons
     (B) lawyers and legislators
     (C) developers
     (D) the general public

128. In California, an unlicensed person who collects a real estate commission is
     (A) subject to duress
     (B) guilty of a misdemeanor
     (C) guilty of a felony
     (D) inactivated

129. Salesperson Jones pockets an earnest money deposit and is found out. Jones's broker must
     (A) report the incident to the state real estate authorities
     (B) repay the money if Jones cannot do so
     (C) pay to defend Jones in court, if necessary
     (D) both A and B

130. Listed real estate should be advertised in the name of the
     (A) owner
     (B) salesperson
     (C) broker
     (D) closing agent

131. A 2.6-acre lot sold for $188,000. What was the price per square foot?
     (A) $1.19
     (B) $1.55
     (C) $1.66
     (D) $1.82

132. Hamilton's broker license is revoked by the real estate commission. Hamilton may
     (A) apply for a salesperson's license
     (B) appeal the revocation to the courts
     (C) wait 6 months and apply for reinstatement
     (D) continue to operate his business until his existing listings are sold or have expired

133. Commissions from the sale of real estate
    (A) must be divided equally between broker and salesperson
    (B) must be divided equally among all participating brokers
    (C) are not taxable income
    (D) none of the above

134. Which is the superior lien?
    (A) Tax lien
    (B) First deed of trust
    (C) Junior deed of trust
    (D) Mechanic's lien that predates others above

135. A tenancy in severalty exists when
    (A) one person owns real estate
    (B) husband and wife own real estate together
    (C) any related persons own real estate together
    (D) none of the above

136. Which of the following is not a test of a fixture?
    (A) Manner of attachment
    (B) Intent of the person who put it there
    (C) Cost of the item
    (D) Custom in the community

137. During the life of the life tenant, the remainderman has
    (A) an easement in gross
    (B) a reversionary interest
    (C) a fee simple estate
    (D) a renewing leasehold estate

138. At settlement, taxes are
    (A) prorated
    (B) accrued
    (C) deficient
    (D) assessed

139. When parties to a contract agree to amend the contract, the document they prepare and sign is called a
    (A) deed amendment
    (B) satisfaction piece
    (C) novation
    (D) relinquishment

140. What kind of estate is received if the deed states that the grantor grants to the grantee "and his heirs and assigns forever"?
    (A) Fee simple
    (B) Leasehold
    (C) Life estate
    (D) Nonfreehold

141. A deed that conveys only the interest of the grantor is a
    (A) general warranty deed
    (B) bargain and sale deed
    (C) quitclaim deed
    (D) special warranty deed

142. A broker must keep the records of a transaction for _____ years after the transaction is concluded.
    (A) two
    (B) three
    (C) four
    (D) five

143. The zoning classification of a church in a residential area would be _____.
    (A) a zoning variance
    (B) a nonconforming use
    (C) a rezoned requisite
    (D) a permitted residential use

144. The _____ regulates how far from the boundaries of the lot a structure must be.
    (A) setback requirement
    (B) density requirement
    (C) lot coverage requirement
    (D) occupancy requirement

145. Which of the following is a common interest subdivision?
    (A) A standard subdivision
    (B) A study zone
    (C) A time-share project
    (D) A land project

146. What is the law that mandates minimum construction and occupancy standards for dwellings, hotels, apartments, etc. in California?
    (A) the Housing Law
    (B) the Occupancy and Building Standards Act
    (C) the Subdivided Lands Law
    (D) the Uniform Law

147. Total Recovery Account payment for one licensee (multiple transactions) is limited to
    (A) $10,000
    (B) $20,000
    (C) $50,000
    (D) $100,000

148. Which of the following must have a contractor's license?
    (A) An owner making improvements (but not to prepare for sale)
    (B) One being paid $1,500 by homeowner to do roof repairs
    (C) An oil field operator
    (D) An electric company employee repairing power lines

149. Under the Contractors' License Law, who licenses building contractors?
    (A) The Department of Real Estate
    (B) The Department of Housing and Community Development
    (C) The Department of Contractors' Standards and Licensing
    (D) The Contractors' State Licensing Board

150. Salesperson Sherry leaves the employ of Broker Bob and is employed by Broker Louise.
    (A) Sherry and Louise must notify DRE within 5 days of the change.
    (B) Sherry cannot do this without prior permission from DRE.
    (C) Sherry cannot do this unless Broker Bob agrees to it in writing.
    (D) Broker Louise must compensate Broker Bob, and register the compensation with DRE.

Broker License Examination, Part 1

Brokers should also take the salesperson exams, especially Examination 1.

Directions: Select the choice, marked A, B, C, or D, that best answers the question or completes the thought. Mark your answers clearly on the answer sheet. You have 2½ hours to complete Part 1, followed by a one-hour break. Answers are on page 499, math solutions on page 506.

1. The number of dollars remaining each year after cash expenses are deducted from cash rent receipts and other property income is
    (A) cash-on-cash
    (B) cash depletion
    (C) cash amortization
    (D) cash flow

2. A house recently sold for $350,000. If property is taxed at 1.2 percent, how much is the tax on this house?
    (A) $4,200
    (B) $2,140
    (C) $3,500
    (D) $5,600

3. Loss of value because a property is located in a rundown neighborhood is known as
    (A) physical deterioration
    (B) functional obsolescence
    (C) economic obsolescence
    (D) none of the above

4. Which of the following is NOT realty?
   - (A) A 50-year lease
   - (B) A fee simple estate
   - (C) An easement in gross
   - (D) A life estate

5. Which of the following is adequate recitation of consideration in a deed?
   - (A) "For ten dollars and other valuable consideration"
   - (B) "For natural love and affection"
   - (C) The actual amount of consideration paid
   - (D) All of the above

6. One type of depreciation generally is NOT curable. This type of depreciation is
   - (A) physical deterioration
   - (B) functional obsolescence
   - (C) economic obsolescence
   - (D) all of the above

7. Which of the following can enter into a listing agreement, in his own name, to sell real estate for a fee?
   - (A) A licensed salesperson
   - (B) A licensed broker
   - (C) A trustee
   - (D) None of the above

8. A licensed salesperson who wishes to sell her own property must
   - (A) list the property with her broker
   - (B) inform prospective purchasers that she is the owner
   - (C) not list the property with anyone because of possible conflict of interest
   - (D) not take the listing herself

Questions 9–13 refer to the following situation:

Robby buys a house from Juan. The price is $500,000. Robby gets a mortgage loan for 80% of the purchase price. The loan discount is three points paid by the seller. The broker's commission on the sale is 6%. The contract interest rate on the mortgage loan is 7%.

9. Assuming that there are no closing costs other than those cited above, how much does Juan end up with?
   - (A) $364,000
   - (B) $455,000
   - (C) $458,000
   - (D) $464,000

10. What is the dollar amount of the discount?
    - (A) $7,800
    - (B) $9,000
    - (C) $12,000
    - (D) $15,000

11. What is the lender's approximate effective rate of return on the loan?
    - (A) 10%
    - (B) 7⅜%
    - (C) 7%
    - (D) 6⅝%

12. Who pays the discount on the mortgage loan?
    - (A) Juan
    - (B) Robby
    - (C) The broker
    - (D) The lender

13. To whom is the discount paid?
    - (A) The broker
    - (B) The lender
    - (C) The VA
    - (D) The FHA

14. What is the cash-on-cash ratio for a property that has a cash flow of $16,900 and an initial investor's cash equity of $130,000?
    - (A) 7.69%
    - (B) 0.219
    - (C) 0.12
    - (D) 0.13

15. What percent of a square mile is 200 acres?
    (A) 27.5%
    (C) 31.25%
    (B) 43.478%
    (D) 10%

16. When a property is foreclosed, which claim takes last priority?
    (A) State tax lien
    (C) Second deed of trust
    (B) First deed of trust
    (D) Mechanic's lien for new roof

17. A house is valued at $355,560 for tax purposes. This is the
    (A) assessed value
    (C) market value
    (B) appraised value
    (D) replacement value

18. The fiscal year begins July 1. The first installment of taxes are due November 1. Tax rate is 1%. Assessed value is $184,300. If a sale of the property is closed on July 15, then at settlement
    (A) seller owes buyer 14 days
    (C) seller owes buyer 194 days
    (B) buyer owes seller 60 days
    (D) seller owes buyer 300 days

19. The mortgagor's right to reestablish ownership after default before foreclosure is called
    (A) acceleration
    (C) equity of redemption
    (B) resatisfaction right
    (D) redemption provenance

20. Regulation Z
    (A) sets maximum interest rates on mortgage loans
    (B) determines discounts on VA loans
    (C) allows borrowers to repay loans ahead of time without penalty
    (D) requires that borrowers be informed of the cost of credit

21. Which of the following statements is true?
    (A) A tenancy at will may be terminated at any time by either tenant or landlord.
    (B) GRM stands for gross reproduction method.
    (C) A tenancy in severalty involves a married couple.
    (D) All of the above

22. Which of the following represent(s) functional obsolescence?
    (A) No electrical outlets in some rooms
    (B) One bathroom in a 12-room house
    (C) Both A and B
    (D) Neither A nor B

23. An appraisal is
    (A) a forecast of value
    (C) a prediction of value
    (B) an estimate of value
    (D) a statement of exact value

24. At settlement, the buyer paid the seller $250.16 toward the annual tax bill of $763.20. If taxes are assessed for the calendar year and must be paid by July 15, what was the date of the settlement?
    (A) April 28
    (C) March 30
    (B) September 2
    (D) Can't be determined

25. What is the cash-on-cash ratio for a property having a cash flow of $8,360 and an initial investor's cash equity of $76,000?
    (A) 0.10%
    (C) 0.11
    (B) 0.105%
    (D) 0.12

26. What percent of 1 square mile is 96 acres?
    (A) 21%
    (C) 15%
    (B) 19.6%
    (D) 12%

27. Which claim is paid first at a foreclosure?
    (A) Tax lien
    (B) First mortgage
    (C) Second mortgage
    (D) Mechanic's lien

28. In an agency relationship, the principal is the
    (A) seller
    (B) buyer
    (C) broker
    (D) employer

29. In a lease contract, the landlord is the
    (A) leasee
    (B) leasor
    (C) lessee
    (D) lessor

30. If consideration has value only to the person receiving it, it is
    (A) personal consideration
    (B) good consideration
    (C) valuable consideration
    (D) good and valuable consideration

31. A lease that requires the landlord to pay operating expenses of the property is a _____ lease.
    (A) gross
    (B) flat
    (C) net
    (D) step

32. The first installment of taxes is due on November 1 of the year in which they are assessed. Tax rate is 1%. Assessed value is $53,250. If a sale of the property is closed on August 15, then at settlement,
    (A) taxes are not prorated
    (B) the seller's account is debited
    (C) the buyer's account is debited
    (D) taxes are deposited in the impound account

33. A real estate license should be
    (A) carried in the licensee's wallet
    (B) posted at the Real Estate Commission
    (C) posted in a public place in the broker's office
    (D) posted in the licensee's home

34. The usefulness of the cost approach in appraisal may be limited if the subject property is
    (A) a new structure
    (B) functionally obsolescent
    (C) in an inactive market
    (D) proposed construction

35. A tenant paid rent at the beginning of the month; the property sold in the middle of the month. To prorate rent at settlement, you would
    (A) credit the buyer
    (B) credit the seller
    (C) both A and B
    (D) neither A nor B

36. Which of the following is considered a "finance charge" for the purposes of Regulation Z?
    (A) Title insurance fee
    (B) Deed preparation fee
    (C) Monthly payment
    (D) None of the above

37. A person who is employed by a broker to rent property, but not to sell it,
    (A) must be licensed
    (B) need not be licensed
    (C) must have a special rent-only license
    (D) must be a licensed broker

38. The process whereby a person may have her real estate sold to pay a debt or claim is called
    (A) lien
    (B) foreclosure
    (C) covenant
    (D) defeasance

39. A person who owns an undivided interest in real estate with at least one other person, and has the right of survivorship, is called a
    (A) tenant in severalty
    (B) life tenant
    (C) tenant in common
    (D) joint tenant

40. Which is NOT considered real estate?
    (A) Fixtures
    (B) Trees
    (C) Chattels
    (D) Sidewalk

41. A person who dies and leaves no will is said to have died
    (A) without heirs
    (B) intestate
    (C) unbequeathed
    (D) unherited

42. A broker must keep funds entrusted to her, but belonging to others, in
    (A) an office safe to which only she has the combination
    (B) a savings account in the name of the person whose money it is
    (C) a trust or escrow account
    (D) a special account managed by the state

43. When a party to a contract has deliberately lied in order to mislead the other party(ies) into agreeing to the contract, this action is an example of
    (A) fraud
    (B) misrepresentation
    (C) duress
    (D) defeasance

44. If a party to a contract acts so as to make performance under the contract impossible, this action is an example of
    (A) discharge of contract
    (B) performance of contract
    (C) abandonment of contract
    (D) breach of contract

45. A minor may be bound by the courts to contracts for
    (A) personal property
    (B) realty only
    (C) necessaries
    (D) rent

46. Edgar purchases a house costing $387,500.00. The loan requires a 15% down payment, an origination fee of 0.75%, 2.25 points discount, and a 0.5% PMI fee. How much money does Edgar need for these expenses?
    (A) $38,750.00
    (B) $48,326.25
    (C) $69,653.13
    (D) $71,687.50

47. A makes an offer to buy B's real estate. B makes a counteroffer to A.
    (A) A is bound by his original offer.
    (B) A must accept the counteroffer.
    (C) A's original offer no longer exists.
    (D) A may not counteroffer back to B.

48. A purchase agreement for real estate must be signed by
    (A) buyer and seller
    (B) broker, buyer, and seller
    (C) buyer only
    (D) broker only

49. In a purchase agreement, the seller is the
    (A) grantor
    (B) vendee
    (C) grantee
    (D) vendor

50. Which of the following statements is true?
    (A) To be valid, a purchase agreement must be signed by the broker, if a broker assists in the transaction.
    (B) A corporation may be a party to a contract of sale.
    (C) A purchase agreement need not be written if it is closed within 1 year.
    (D) A person who is an attorney-in-fact must also be an attorney-at-law.

51. Which of the following must be included in a deed?
    (A) Proper description of the real estate
    (B) Street address, if the real estate is a house
    (C) Area of the land ("more or less")
    (D) All of the above

52. A deed is recorded
    (A) to give public notice
    (B) to insure title
    (C) to satisfy the law
    (D) to avoid extra taxes

53. The part of a deed that defines or limits the quantity of estate granted is the
    (A) habendum
    (B) premises
    (C) equity
    (D) consideration

54. A final payment larger than the intermediate payments to a note is called
    (A) an escalator
    (B) an amortization
    (C) a balloon
    (D) a reappraisal

55. The interest rate on a loan is 6%. The interest for the month of July was $456.41. What was the loan balance at the beginning of July?
    (A) $110,344
    (B) $102,788
    (C) $91,282
    (D) $95,250

56. A conventional mortgage loan is
    (A) self-amortizing
    (B) not government insured/guaranteed
    (C) approved by the FHA
    (D) uninsurable

57. The trust deed with the highest priority is usually the one
    (A) with the highest unpaid balance
    (B) with the highest original loan amount
    (C) with the highest interest rate
    (D) that was recorded first

58. The seller of real estate takes a note secured by a trust deed on the real estate as partial payment. The trust deed is
    (A) sale financed
    (B) a purchase money mortgage
    (C) a secondary mortgage
    (D) a first lien

59. An *ad valorem* tax is based on
    (A) the taxpayer's income
    (B) the sale price of the article taxed
    (C) the size and/or weight of the article
    (D) the value of the article taxed

60. A person who is too young to be held to a contract is called
    (A) minority-impaired
    (B) youthful
    (C) unavailable in law
    (D) incompetent

61. A contract in which rights to use and occupy real estate are transferred for a specified period of time is
    - (A) a deed
    - (B) an easement
    - (C) a life estate
    - (D) a lease

62. Whenever all parties agree to the terms of a contract, there has been
    - (A) mutual agreement
    - (B) legality of object
    - (C) consideration
    - (D) competency

63. Recording a deed
    - (A) passes title
    - (B) gives constructive notice
    - (C) insures title
    - (D) removes liens

64. Multiple listing
    - (A) causes lost commissions
    - (B) is a listing-sharing organization of brokers
    - (C) is illegal in some states
    - (D) is a violation of antitrust law

65. A contract that gives a person the right to buy during a specified time, but carries no obligation to do so, is
    - (A) a sale contract
    - (B) a land contract
    - (C) an option
    - (D) a bargain and sale

66. Jack wants to buy a house costing $334,500. The loan requires a down payment of $51,750, plus 1.5 percent origination fee, 2 points discount, and an 0.75% PMI fee. How much money does he need for these expenses?
    - (A) $51,750.00
    - (B) $58,995.75
    - (C) $65,966.25
    - (D) $63,766.88

67. The interest rate on a loan is 10.5%. The interest for the month of April was $496.56. What was the loan balance at the beginning of April?
    - (A) $49,656
    - (B) $56,750
    - (C) $60,000
    - (D) $62,500

68. Usury is defined as
    - (A) selling listed property for less than the seller's asking price
    - (B) selling real estate without a license
    - (C) collecting more interest than is allowed by law
    - (D) acquiring an easement by adverse possession

69. Ms. Simpson's broker license is revoked by the California Department of Real Estate. Ms. Simpson may
    - (A) apply for a salesperson's license
    - (B) appeal the revocation to the courts
    - (C) wait 6 months and apply for reinstatement
    - (D) continue to work her existing listings

70. Real estate commission payments
    - (A) must be divided equally among all participating brokers
    - (B) must be paid directly to the salesperson
    - (C) must be divided equally between broker and salesperson
    - (D) none of the above

Questions 71–80 are based on the following:

SETTLEMENT STATEMENT NARRATIVE

On September 18, 2006, you close a sale between Sydney Purvis (seller) and Miriam Stein (buyer). The sale price is $212,000, and your commission is 7½ percent of the sale price. Ms. Stein receives a mortgage loan for 80 percent of the sale price and has paid a deposit of $2,000.00. Ms. Stein will assume a 3-year fire insurance policy, which Mr. Purvis took out on October 22, 2004, paying the full 3-year premium of $888.75 at that time. Mr. Purvis's existing mortgage loan of $32,331.70 will be paid off at closing from the proceeds of the sale.

Mr. Purvis must pay attorney fees of $175.00, a deed preparation fee of $80.00, and miscellaneous fees of $356.55. Ms. Stein must pay attorney fees of $325.00, an appraisal fee of $100.00, a mortgage insurance premium of 2½ percent of the loan amount, and a title insurance premium of 0.425 percent of the purchase price. Taxes are $2,336.40 per year, and have been paid.

71. The buyer will owe what amount of cash at closing?
   (A) $53,642.42
   (B) $43,554.14
   (C) $13,797.96
   (D) $46,951.39

72. The seller will receive what amount of cash at closing?
   (A) $164,142.14
   (B) $116,465.55
   (C) $144,802.15
   (D) $68,907.11

73. With regard to the property taxes, which of the following is *true*?
   (A) The tax base will be increased to the selling price.
   (B) The seller pays $661.98 to the buyer.
   (C) The prorated amount is $2,336.40.
   (D) The prorated amount is $1,674.42 and is paid by buyer to seller.

74. The buyer's mortgage insurance premium is
   (A) $2,595
   (B) $1,775
   (C) $4,240
   (D) $5,300

75. The buyer's title insurance premium is
   (A) $397.80
   (B) $720.80
   (C) $801.00
   (D) $901.00

76. The buyer's loan will be
   (A) $176,800
   (B) $169,600
   (C) $88,400
   (D) $180,000

77. With regard to the prorated insurance policy, which of the following is *true*?
   (A) The prorated amount is $565.34.
   (B) The seller pays this amount to the buyer.
   (C) Both A and B
   (D) Neither A nor B

78. The seller will pay a broker's commission. The commission is shown as
   (A) a credit to the seller
   (B) a debit to the seller
   (C) a debit to the buyer
   (D) both A and C

79. The buyer will take over the unexpired portion of the seller's insurance policy, for which the seller has paid the full premium. The unexpired premium is a
    - (A) debit to the buyer
    - (B) credit to the seller
    - (C) both A and B
    - (D) neither A nor B

80. The payoff of the existing mortgage is
    - (A) a credit to the buyer
    - (B) a credit to the seller
    - (C) a debit to the seller
    - (D) none of the above

81. Which method of advertising do real estate brokers use the most?
    - (A) Radio and TV
    - (B) Magazines
    - (C) Newspapers
    - (D) Billboards

82. Which of the following is a nonfreehold estate?
    - (A) Fee simple estate
    - (B) Leasehold estate
    - (C) Life estate
    - (D) Qualified fee simple

83. A lease that spells out specific increases in rent during the term of the lease is a _____ lease.
    - (A) reappraisal
    - (B) net
    - (C) step
    - (D) percentage

84. A clause in a percentage lease that allows the lessor to cancel the lease if the lessee's revenues are not at least a minimum amount is a _____ clause.
    - (A) nonperformance
    - (B) net
    - (C) defeasance
    - (D) recapture

85. Zoning laws are usually NOT enacted by _____ government.
    - (A) federal
    - (B) state
    - (C) county
    - (D) city

86. A court appoints _____ to settle and manage the estate of a person who dies intestate.
    - (A) a trustee
    - (B) an executor
    - (C) an administrator
    - (D) an attorney-in-fact

87. A lot 59 ft. 6 in. wide contains 535.5 sq. yd. How deep is the lot?
    - (A) 5.33 rods
    - (B) 88 ft.
    - (C) 27 yd.
    - (D) 0.03 mi.

88. A broker's license is revoked. Salespersons whose licenses are held by this broker
    - (A) may apply to transfer their licenses to another broker
    - (B) must place their licenses on inactive status for 6 months
    - (C) also lose their licenses for 6 months
    - (D) may continue to operate the broker's business

89. The largest "bundle of rights" to real estate is a _____ estate.
    - (A) remainder
    - (B) fee simple
    - (C) life
    - (D) homestead

90. One of broker Mack's salespeople sold a house for $410,000. Mack received 48% of the commission and paid his salesperson 55% of that amount. How much did Mack keep, if the commission rate was 7%?
    - (A) $6,199.20
    - (B) $7,576.80
    - (C) $12,915.00
    - (D) $15,785.00

91. A 1.6-acre lot sold for $25,100. What was the price per square foot?
    (A) $3.61   (C) $1.88
    (B) $0.36   (D) $2.29

92. A broker who receives two offers on the same property at the same time should
    (A) reject both offers
    (B) submit both offers to the property owner
    (C) submit the better offer while trying to improve the other one
    (D) submit the better offer and reject the other one

93. As the seller's agent a broker may
    (A) reject an offer on behalf of the seller
    (B) work to get the buyer the best possible price
    (C) solicit offers for the seller's listed property
    (D) try to negotiate better terms before submitting an offer

94. Which of the following is not an "improvement" to land?
    (A) Building   (C) Corn crop
    (B) Sidewalk   (D) Flower bed

95. Unlicensed persons who receive shares of real estate commission payments may be in violation of
    (A) federal law   (C) zoning law
    (B) license law   (D) common law

96. A person who is employed by a broker to rent property, but not to sell it,
    (A) must be licensed   (C) must have a special rent-only license
    (B) need not be licensed   (D) must be a licensed broker

97. Which of the following statements is true?
    (A) A person who is an attorney-in-fact must also be an attorney-at-law.
    (B) To be valid, a purchase contract must be signed by the broker.
    (C) A corporation may be a party to a purchase contract.
    (D) A purchase contract need not be written if it is closed within 1 year.

98. Which of the following must be included in a deed?
    (A) Street address, if the real estate is a house
    (B) Area of the land ("more or less")
    (C) Proper description of land and improvements
    (D) Proper description of land

99. A deed is recorded
    (A) to give public notice   (C) to satisfy the law
    (B) to insure title   (D) to avoid extra taxes

100. The clause that defines or limits the quantity of estate granted in a deed is the
    (A) habendum   (C) addendum
    (B) premises   (D) consideration

END OF FIRST HALF OF EXAMINATION.
You may take a one-hour break at this point in the examination.

Broker License Examination, Part 2 _____

You have 2½ hours to complete Part 2.

101. In a mortgage, the contract specifies payments of $200 a month, and a final payment of $6,000 at the end of 30 years. The final payment is called
    (A) an escalator
    (B) an amortization
    (C) a balloon
    (D) a parachute

102. The process by which real estate is sold to pay debts or claims is known as
    (A) lien
    (B) foreclosure
    (C) covenant
    (D) defeasance

103. A person who owns an undivided interest in real estate with at least one other person, without the right of survivorship, is called a
    (A) tenant in severalty
    (B) life tenant
    (C) tenant in common
    (D) joint tenant

104. Brokers often hold funds belonging to others. They must keep these funds in
    (A) an office safe to which only the broker has the combination
    (B) a savings account in the name of the person whose money it is
    (C) a trust or escrow account
    (D) a special account managed by the state

105. When a party to a contract unintentionally misleads the other party(ies) into agreeing to the contract, this action is an example of
    (A) fraud
    (B) misrepresentation
    (C) duress
    (D) defeasance

106. If a party to a contract is responsible for making performance under it impossible, this action is an example of
    (A) specific performance
    (B) breach of contract
    (C) abandonment of contract
    (D) nonperformance of contract

107. At settlement, the buyer took over the seller's 1-year property insurance policy, which had been purchased on February 1 for $324.00. If the seller was credited for $63.00 at settlement, what was the settlement date?
    (A) May 10
    (B) November 20
    (C) July 19
    (D) Can't be determined

108. A minor may be bound by the courts to contracts for
    (A) personalty only
    (B) realty only
    (C) rent only
    (D) necessaries

109. Sally makes a counteroffer in response to Joe's offer to buy her lot.
    (A) Joe may not counteroffer back to Sally.
    (B) Joe is bound by his original offer.
    (C) Joe must accept the counteroffer as is, reject it, or let it expire.
    (D) If Joe makes a counteroffer, Sally may accept Joe's original offer.

110. A purchase agreement of real estate must be signed by
    (A) buyer only
    (B) broker, buyer, and seller
    (C) buyer and seller
    (D) broker only

111. In a quitclaim, the seller is the
    (A) grantor
    (B) vendee
    (C) grantee
    (D) vendor

112. If a property has more than one deed of trust on it, the one with the highest priority is usually the one that
    (A) has the highest interest rate
    (B) was recorded first
    (C) has the highest unpaid balance
    (D) has the highest original loan amount

113. The seller of real estate takes a note secured by a deed of trust on the real estate as partial payment. The deed of trust is
    (A) sale financed
    (B) a purchase-money mortgage
    (C) a secondary mortgage
    (D) a first lien

114. The market value of a house is $286,000. If property is taxed at 0.97 percent of market value, how much is the tax?
    (A) $2,774.20
    (B) $2,860.00
    (C) $8,580.00
    (D) $2,948.45

Questions 115–118 refer to the following situation:

May buys a house from Ray. The price is $400,000. May gets a mortgage loan for 90% of the purchase price. The loan discount is 2.5 points. The broker's commission on the sale is 6%. The contract interest rate on the mortgage loan is 7.5%.

115. What is the dollar amount of the discount?
    (A) $3,900
    (B) $10,000
    (C) $9,000
    (D) $11,000

116. What is the lender's effective rate of return on the loan?
    (A) 10.25%
    (B) 7.1875%
    (C) 7.8125%
    (D) 10.0%

117. Who pays the discount on the mortgage loan?
    (A) May
    (B) Ray or May
    (C) The broker
    (D) The lender

118. To whom is the discount paid?
    (A) The broker
    (B) The lender
    (C) Ray
    (D) May

119. An *ad valorem* tax is based on
    (A) size and/or weight of article taxed
    (B) value of article taxed
    (C) taxpayer's income
    (D) sale price of article taxed

120. Whenever all parties agree to the terms of a contract, there has been
    (A) reality of consent
    (B) legality of object
    (C) consideration
    (D) competency

121. A contract that gives someone the right to buy during a specified time, but carries no obligation to do so, is
    (A) a sale contract
    (B) a land contract
    (C) an option
    (D) a bargain and sale

122. The amount remaining each year after expenses have been deducted from rent receipts and other property income is
    - (A) cash-on-cash
    - (B) cash depletion
    - (C) cash amortization
    - (D) cash flow

123. A property in a rundown neighborhood may lose value because of
    - (A) physical deterioration
    - (B) functional obsolescence
    - (C) economic obsolescence
    - (D) red lining

124. Which of the following is an interest in real property?
    - (A) A l-year lease
    - (B) An equitable title
    - (C) A land contract
    - (D) A life estate

125. Which of the following can adequately describe the consideration in a deed?
    - (A) "For ten dollars and other valuable consideration"
    - (B) "For natural love and affection"
    - (C) The actual amount of consideration paid
    - (D) All of the above

126. Which type of depreciation generally is not curable?
    - (A) physical deterioration
    - (B) functional obsolescence
    - (C) economic obsolescence
    - (D) all of the above

127. What is the cash-on-cash ratio for a property that has a cash flow of $32,300 and an initial investor's cash equity of $222,750?
    - (A) 7.05%
    - (B) 0.0705
    - (C) 0.145
    - (D) 0.113

128. What percentage of a square mile is a lot 1,085 ft. by 900 ft.?
    - (A) 28.5%
    - (B) 18.494%
    - (C) 3.5%
    - (D) 1.57%

129. Max has a six-month lease that says the rent is $1,000 per week. The lease does not say when the rent shall be paid. When does Max have to pay?
    - (A) At the end of each month
    - (B) At the beginning of each month
    - (C) At the end of the lease period
    - (D) At the end of each week

130. Cortez got fee simple title to land that had belonged to Leone by using and occupying it openly for a certain time, unknown to and unmolested by Leone. This is an example of
    - (A) estoppel
    - (B) subrogation
    - (C) an easement in gross
    - (D) adverse possession

131. Baker gives Able his power of attorney. Able is called
    - (A) an agent in place
    - (B) a real estate broker
    - (C) a lawyer
    - (D) an attorney-in-fact

132. The right by which California can take title to real estate for which no legal owner can be found is called
    - (A) police power
    - (B) tenancy
    - (C) eminent domain
    - (D) escheat

133. Moe receives title to Zoe's real estate after Zoe dies without a will. Moe has received
    - (A) title by descent
    - (B) clouded title
    - (C) an easement
    - (D) legacy title

134. A parcel of land is 1,077 ft. by 607 ft. How many acres does it contain?
    (A) 14.9
    (B) 9.88
    (C) 13.22
    (D) More than 15

135. Of the following instruments, the one with no warranty is the
    (A) executor's deed
    (B) quitclaim deed
    (C) general warranty deed
    (D) trustee's deed

136. A worker who is not paid for work that improved real estate may file a
    (A) labor judgment
    (B) novation
    (C) mechanic's lien
    (D) lis pendens

137. When a property is foreclosed, which of the following claims takes first priority?
    (A) Mechanic's lien for original construction
    (B) Mortgage dated June 11, 2005
    (C) General lien
    (D) Mortgage dated July 22, 2006

138. In an agency relationship, the employer is called the
    (A) seller
    (B) agent
    (C) principal
    (D) broker

139. If consideration in a deed has value only to the person receiving it, it is
    (A) no consideration
    (B) good consideration
    (C) valuable consideration
    (D) good and valuable consideration

140. A lease that does not require the tenant to pay any of the operating expenses of the property is a _____ lease.
    (A) gross
    (B) flat
    (C) net
    (D) step

141. Sam's contractor quotes "per square foot" costs of $101.10 for the first 1,600 sq. ft. of house, $42.25 for square footage over 1,600, $22.50 for basements, $29.20 for attached garages. Sam wants a 2,100 sq. ft., two-story house, with a basement, and a 420-sq. ft. attached garage. What price (to nearest $1,000) will the contractor quote for the entire job?
    (A) $207,000
    (B) $219,000
    (C) $226,000
    (D) $242,000

142. A house is valued at $275,000 for tax purposes. This is the
    (A) assessed value
    (B) appraised value
    (C) market value
    (D) replacement value

143. Simmy buys a house and gets a mortgage loan for $128,000 to pay for it. Simmy becomes a
    (A) vendor
    (B) mortgagor
    (C) lessee
    (D) mortgagee

144. A function of Regulation Z is to
    (A) determine discounts on VA loans
    (B) set maximum interest rates on mortgage loans
    (C) allow borrowers to repay loans ahead of time without penalty
    (D) require that borrowers be informed of the cost of credit

145. An investor purchased three lots. Lot A cost $11,000, lot B cost 2.5 times the cost of A, and lot C cost half the cost of B. She then sold lots A and B for 25 percent more than the cost of all three lots. If she then sold lot C for twice its cost, what was her total profit (to the nearest $100)?
    (A) $19,100
    (B) $26,800
    (C) $33,800
    (D) none of the above

Questions 146–150 refer to the following listing contract narrative.

LISTING CONTRACT NARRATIVE

On June 16, 2006, you contact Mr. Sydney Purvis, whose two-story brick house has a "For Sale by Owner" sign in front. The house has 2510 sq. feet of space, with four bedrooms (one downstairs) and three baths (one downstairs). It is federal colonial in style. The address is 8811 Quagmire Place, being Lot 18, Block G, Quagmire Estates Addition, Marin County, California. You have done some checking and know that Mr. Purvis has bought a new home. The house he is selling is 12 years old and has natural gas heat and hot water, central air conditioning, no basement, a breakfast area in the kitchen, a 98 ft. × 155 ft. lot, an entrance foyer and a center hall plan, and an attic with pull-down stairs. The tax rate is 1.04% of the assessed value. Mr. Purvis is moving in a week, so a prospective buyer can be offered immediate possession.

The next morning you call Mr. Purvis at his home (555-1116) and get no answer, so you call his office (555-2822) and he agrees to see you immediately to sign a listing agreement. At that time you find out that his current mortgage loan is not assumable, and that he will include all appliances (refrigerator, dishwasher, and dryer). He prefers to show the home only by appointment and will give you a key to keep handy at your office. Nearby schools are Dennis Elementary, DePalma Junior High, Moray High School, and St. Francis Parochial. You and Mr. Purvis agree on a 90-day listing at $337,500, with a 7½ percent commission, and your broker signs it.

146. Which of the following is *false*?
    (A) Immediate possession is possible.
    (B) The listing price is $337,500.
    (C) The home has 2510 sq. ft.
    (D) The owner's home telephone number is 555-2822.

147. Which of the following is *true*?
    (A) The home is in Marin County.
    (B) The address is 8811 Quagmire Place.
    (C) The home telephone number is 555-1116.
    (D) All of the above

148. The home is Lot _____ of Block _____ of Quagmire Estates Subdivision.
    (A) 17, F
    (B) 18, G
    (C) 16, G
    (D) 18, F

149. Which features does the house have?
    (A) four bedrooms
    (B) central air conditioning
    (C) both A and B
    (D) neither A nor B

150. Which of the following is *true*?
    (A) The tax rate is 1.04%.
    (B) The home has four bedrooms on the second floor.
    (C) The house has 1½ baths on each floor.
    (D) The house is 15 years old.

PURCHASE AGREEMENT NARRATIVE

On August 14, 2006, you show a home belonging to Sydney Purvis to a prospective purchaser, Ms. Miriam Stein.

Three days later Ms. Stein informs you that she wishes to offer $318,000 for the house, subject to getting a mortgage loan for at least 80 percent of the sale price, with a term of 30 years and at the currently prevailing rate of interest. Closing will be at the broker's office no later than September 18, 2006. Ms. Stein leaves her personal check for $6,000 as a deposit. Mr. Purvis will receive all cash at the closing, from the proceeds of Ms. Stein's loan, her deposit, and additional cash necessary to make up the purchase price.

The next day your broker draws up the contract and Mr. Purvis and Ms. Stein sign it.

151. The deposit paid by the buyer is
    (A) $6,000, paid by check
    (B) $6,000, paid in cash
    (C) $7,500, paid by check
    (D) There is no deposit.

152. The parties to the contract are
    (A) Mr. Purvis (the seller) and your broker
    (B) Ms. Stein (the buyer) and you (the salesperson)
    (C) Mr. Purvis (the seller) and Ms. Stein (the buyer)
    (D) your broker and you (the salesperson)

153. The purchaser's loan must
    (A) be at an interest rate of 6 percent
    (B) be for a term of 30 years
    (C) be for 90 percent of the purchase price
    (D) The purchaser will pay all cash; there is no loan.

154. In this deal,
    (A) the purchase price is $318,000
    (B) the buyer will assume the seller's mortgage loan
    (C) closing will be on or before November 11, 2006
    (D) the buyer will make a down payment of $31,800

155. The closing
    (A) will be at the broker's office
    (B) will be no later than September 18, 2006
    (C) both A and B
    (D) neither A nor B

Questions 156–161 refer to the diagram shown.

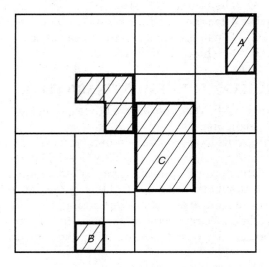

Section 20, T 14 S, R 16 W

156. Which of the following describes the irregular shaded area marked *C*?
   (A) NW¼, SE¼ and S½, SW¼, NE¼ and SE¼, SE¼, NW¼ and N½, SE¼, NW¼
   (B) NW¼, SE¼ and S½, SW¼, NE¼ and E½, SE¼, NW¼ and NW¼, SE¼, NW¼
   (C) both A and B
   (D) neither A nor B

157. What is the area of the irregular shaded area marked *C*?
   (A) 80 acres   (C) 0.25 sq. mi.
   (B) 0.125 sq. mi.   (D) 90 acres

158. What is the area of the portion of the irregular shaded tract marked *C* that is located in NW quarter of the section?
   (A) 20 acres   (C) 40 acres
   (B) 30 acres   (D) 80 acres

159. How far is the *center* of the illustrated section from the base line?
   (A) 86½ mi. north   (C) 24½ mi. south
   (B) 81½ mi. south   (D) 23½ mi. north

160. How far is the *center* of the illustrated section from the principal meridian?
   (A) 94½ mi. east   (C) 17½ mi. west
   (B) 94½ mi. west   (D) none of the above

161. If you travel exactly 4 miles due south from the center of the illustrated section, what section will you be in?
   (A) Section 5, T15S, R16W   (C) Section 8, T15S, R16W
   (B) Section 5, T14S, R17W   (D) Section 32, T14S, R16W

162. A $1 million investment property can be purchased with $200,000 down. This illustrates the principle of
   (A) highest and best use   (C) cash plow
   (B) leverage   (D) balance

163. California usury laws apply principally to
    (A) savings and loan associations
    (B) private lenders
    (C) commercial banks
    (D) loans arranged by a real estate broker

164. A reverse annuity mortgage is intended for
    (A) first-time home buyers
    (B) trade-up home buyer market
    (C) retired or elderly
    (D) a lending institution borrower

165. A large subdivision containing a variety of land uses including common-interest uses is a
    (A) land project
    (B) planned unit development
    (C) stock cooperative project
    (D) standard subdivision

166. Who issues the subdivision public report?
    (A) The Real Estate Commissioner
    (B) The Land Report Division of DRE
    (C) The Subdivided Lands Regulation Board
    (D) None of the above

167. Which must appear on or be filed with the final subdivision map?
    (A) Boundary lines
    (B) Cost of preparing the map
    (C) Construction materials list
    (D) State seal

168. One discount point will increase the yield-to-maturity on a 30-year loan by approximately
    (A) 1%
    (B) ½%
    (C) ¼%
    (D) ⅛%

169. An installment land sales contract is also called
    (A) purchase money mortgage
    (B) purchase agreement
    (C) land contract
    (D) contract of sale

170. The secondary mortgage market is concerned with
    (A) second mortgages
    (B) fixed rate mortgages
    (C) originating new mortgages
    (D) stocks in mortgage companies

171. Escrow instructions can only be changed by
    (A) buyer
    (B) seller
    (C) both buyer and seller in writing
    (D) They are not changeable.

172. An escrow agent is
    (A) an agent who represents both parties
    (B) an agent who represents the broker only
    (C) an agent of the state of California
    (D) an agent of the county courthouse

173. After filing a tentative subdivision map, a subdivider must file the final map within
    (A) six months
    (B) one year
    (C) eighteen months
    (D) two years

174. In northern California, escrows are most often held by
    (A) real estate brokers
    (B) title insurance companies
    (C) mortgage lenders
    (D) escrow companies

175. A real estate broker can be an escrow agent
    (A) never
    (B) when ancillary to the brokerage transaction that he participates in
    (C) anytime she pleases
    (D) when accompanied by a CPA

176. The legal action that may be brought by a confused escrow agent is
    (A) contract law
    (B) agency law
    (C) interpleader
    (D) mediation

177. Prorations of amounts other than interest are usually based on a
    (A) actual days in month
    (B) broker's count
    (C) 30-day month
    (D) 31-day month

178. Closing will take place on November 16 and the buyer is to be credited with ownership on the closing day. Rent of $1,200 was paid by the tenant on November 5 for the month. At closing, the buyer is credited for
    (A) $600
    (B) $630
    (C) $570
    (D) $330

179. The fiscal year for property tax purposes runs from
    (A) January 1 to December 31
    (B) July 1 to June 30
    (C) November 1 to October 31
    (D) none of the above

180. California property taxes are due in ____ installment(s).
    (A) one
    (B) two
    (C) four
    (D) twelve

181. Proposition 13 limits the annual base value increases to
    (A) 1%
    (B) 2%
    (C) 5%
    (D) 10%

182. Which of the following is specified by zoning regulations?
    (A) Permissible building materials
    (B) Street paving materials
    (C) Plant species permitted
    (D) Density

183. A reassessment of property value in California can occur
    (A) annually
    (B) every five years
    (C) every ten years
    (D) upon title transfer, new construction, property assessment

184. When property with unpaid taxes is not redeemed by its owner for____year(s), the state may claim ownership.
    (A) one
    (B) two
    (C) five
    (D) seven

185. A married homeowner who sells a principal residence at a gain may exclude up to_____ of gain from taxable federal income.
    (A) $20,000
    (B) $50,000
    (C) $100,000
    (D) $500,000

186. Which of the following is (are) community property?
     (A) A wife's inheritance from her parents received during marriage
     (B) A husband's inheritance from his parents received during marriage
     (C) A wife's salary from a part-time job
     (D) All of the above

187. A riparian owner
     (A) can do anything he or she pleases with the water
     (B) must have land ownership or rights to use that is adjacent to the stream and in the watershed of the stream
     (C) receives water ownership rights through a deed
     (D) may accelerate the speed of the water passing through, but not slow it

188. Most escrow proration instructions call for the use of a year based on
     (A) 360 days   (C) 366 days
     (B) 365 days   (D) actual days in the year

189. For county assessed property, a tax lien is filed on
     (A) January 1   (C) July 1
     (B) March 1   (D) November 1

190. Payment from the Recovery Account for any single transaction is limited to a total of
     (A) $10,000   (C) $50,000
     (B) $20,000   (D) $100,000

191. A California real estate license is good for negotiating
     (A) anywhere in the state of California
     (B) sale of any kind of real property
     (C) sale of property outside California, if negotiation occurs inside California
     (D) all of the above

192. A licensed salesperson may act independently (i.e., not in the employ of a broker)
     (A) in any transaction valued at less than $10,000
     (B) to sell her own house, provided all parties know she holds a license
     (C) if he owns at least 51percent of the stock in the brokerage firm that employs him
     (D) if all other parties involved in the transaction also are licensed

193. Property taxes are limited to _____ percent of the base value, plus special assessments that are voter approved.
     (A) 1   (C) 3
     (B) 2   (D) 4

194. In a grant deed, the grantor assures that
     (A) there are no liens on the property
     (B) the estate granted is free of encumbrances placed on the property by the grantor
     (C) the grantor has not previously granted the property to another
     (D) B and C above

195. A due-on-sale clause in a mortgage loan or deed of trust
     (A) was declared by the U.S. Supreme Court to be fully enforceable by all federally chartered lending institutions
     (B) is prohibited for all California loans
     (C) is an unfair trade practice
     (D) provides for the assumption of low interest loans

196. Proposition 2 in California
   (A) limits taxes to 2 percent of market value
   (B) limits tax increases to 2 percent per year
   (C) increases tax amounts from the 1 percent allowed by Proposition 13
   (D) exempts from usury any loan arranged by a real estate broker that is secured by real estate

197. An income tax deduction allowed to owners of rental real estate improvements (not land) that does not require a cash payment is
   (A) mortgage amortization
   (B) depreciation
   (C) interest
   (D) maintenance

198. Suppose that the fiscal tax year begins on July 1, and further suppose that one half of property taxes are due on November 1. The property tax assessment for the fiscal year is $720. At closing, using a 360 day year,
   (A) the seller is debited $240
   (B) the seller is debited $120
   (C) the seller is debited $600
   (D) the seller is credited $120

199. To create an escrow there must be
   (A) unconditional delivery of deeds
   (B) a binding contract
   (C) estoppels
   (D) all of the above

200. Providing information about a tenant is the responsibility of the
   (A) broker
   (B) seller
   (C) tenant
   (D) escrow agent

Appraiser License Examination

Directions: Select the choice, marked A, B, C, D, or E, that best answers the question or completes the thought. Mark your answers clearly on the answer sheet. You have 3 hours to complete this examination. Answers are on page 500, math solutions on page 509.

1. The present and future demand for a property and its absorption rate is considered in a
   (A) letter appraisal
   (B) market feasibility study
   (C) market segmentation
   (D) highest and best use analysis
   (E) transmittal letter

2. The appraiser's final value estimate should be based on
   (A) an average of three value indications obtained by the three approaches to value
   (B) a weighing of the reliability of the information analyzed in each of the three approaches to value
   (C) the average of the three closest comparable sales
   (D) the most sophisticated guess technique
   (E) adjustments for most recent indicators in the local market

3. The appropriate time adjustment is concluded to be an increase of 7 percent per year compounded. The time adjustment for a comparable sales property that sold for $240,000 two years ago is
    (A) −$34,776
    (B) −$33,600
    (C) −$16,800
    (D) +$33,600
    (E) +$34,776

4. The criteria for determining highest and best use include all of the following EXCEPT
    (A) physical possibility
    (B) financial feasibility
    (C) legal permissibility
    (D) probable use
    (E) effect on community welfare

5. The broad forces affecting value do NOT include
    (A) physical
    (B) life-style
    (C) political
    (D) social
    (E) economic

6. The certification of value section of an appraisal report states everything EXCEPT that
    (A) the appraiser has no interest in the property
    (B) the fee is not contingent upon any aspect of the report
    (C) the facts are correct to the best of the appraiser's knowledge
    (D) last year the property was appraised by another person
    (E) the property was personally inspected by the appraiser

7. One implication of competition and excess profit is that
    (A) there is a certain optimum combination of land, labor, capital, and entrepreneurship
    (B) an estimate of value should be based on future expectations
    (C) abnormally high profits cannot be expected to continue indefinitely
    (D) maximum value accrues to real estate when social and economic homogeneity are present in a neighborhood
    (E) the direct sales comparison approach becomes compelling

8. Cost indexes offered by standardized services are used to
    (A) derive units of comparison
    (B) catalog building components
    (C) estimate operating expenses
    (D) update past costs into current costs
    (E) estimate the local consumer price index

9. A demonstration narrative appraisal report
    (A) contains many items that are not considered in practice
    (B) is an appraisal report prepared for a client
    (C) contains all the items that might be used in practice
    (D) may be based on hypothetical or assumed data
    (E) should be prepared on a nontypical property to show appraisal expertise

10. In real estate a *submarket* is
    (A) a group of salespersons who deal mostly in the same type of property
    (B) a group of sales that occur at the same time
    (C) a group of similar properties in the same area
    (D) a small portion of the market of similar properties
    (E) an area where sandwiches on French bread are eaten

11. The fact that rents for equally desirable space tend to be set by the market reflects the principle of
    (A) balance
    (B) substitution
    (C) externalities
    (D) consistent use
    (E) conformity

12. The fee for an appraisal assignment is
    (A) based on a percentage of the final value estimate
    (B) agreed upon during the preliminary study stage
    (C) determined after the appraisal is completed
    (D) set by the fee schedule of the local board of REALTORS®
    (E) set by a fee scale from the Real Estate Commission

13. The last step in the appraisal process is to
    (A) write the report
    (B) reconcile all data
    (C) analyze the data
    (D) inspect the property
    (E) set the fee to be charged

14. The form in which a formal appraisal is presented is called
    (A) a presentation of value
    (B) an appraisal log
    (C) an appraisal report
    (D) a value certification
    (E) a narrative report

15. A formal appraisal report must include the
    (A) date of the value estimate
    (B) signature of the appraiser
    (C) identification of the property appraised
    (D) certification
    (E) all of the above

16. The highest and best use of land as if vacant forms part of the basis for
    (A) mortgage-equity analysis
    (B) a property rights adjustment
    (C) an operating expense estimate
    (D) the cost approach
    (E) the square footage approach

17. Identifying and studying submarkets of a larger market is called
    (A) market research
    (B) market survey
    (C) market agglomeration
    (D) market segmentation
    (E) market data

18. The identification and study of a pertinent market is called
    (A) market analysis
    (B) neighborhood review
    (C) property research
    (D) market reflection
    (E) market interaction

19. Which of the following is (are) important for good appraisal communication?
    (A) Word choice
    (B) Reading level
    (C) Grammatical correctness
    (D) Clarity
    (E) All of the above

20. All of the following are true EXCEPT
    (A) real property is a type of service
    (B) value is dependent on market conditions
    (C) a good or service has no value in exchange unless it possesses certain economic and legal characteristics
    (D) the price representing value is usually quoted in terms of money
    (E) real estate may be sold for all cash or financed

21. In estimating the market value of a comparable sale, an appraiser must consider all of the following EXCEPT
    (A) whether the transaction was made in cash, terms equivalent to cash, or other precisely revealed terms
    (B) whether the property had reasonable exposure in a competitive market
    (C) whether a fair sale was transacted, with neither the seller nor the buyer acting under duress
    (D) whether the replacement cost of the property corresponds to its market value
    (E) whether the seller was related to the buyer

22. In preparing an appraisal report, your analysis concludes that one of the approaches to value is not applicable to this particular case. You should
    (A) omit the approach altogether
    (B) base the approach on hypothetical data
    (C) state that the approach is not relevant
    (D) state that the approach is not applicable, explain the reasons for this contention, and provide supporting data
    (E) find another approach so as to include three approaches

23. In the cost approach the site is valued as if it were
    (A) vacant and available for development to its highest and best use
    (B) improved and suited for its intended use or development
    (C) developed and operating
    (D) attractively landscaped
    (E) without nearby utilities

24. *Investment value* is best described as
    (A) market price
    (B) market value
    (C) the cost of acquiring a competitive substitute property with the same utility
    (D) the present worth of anticipated future benefits to a certain entity
    (E) value in exchange

25. Location decisions involve analysis on which three levels?
    (A) General, specific, detailed
    (B) Country, state, community
    (C) Residential, commercial, industrial
    (D) Country, state, county
    (E) Region, neighborhood, site

26. The length of a tract of land along a street is called
    (A) depth
    (B) width
    (C) frontage
    (D) abutment
    (E) lineage

27. The most comprehensive type of appraisal report is
    (A) a form report
    (B) an oral report
    (C) a letter report
    (D) a narrative demonstration report
    (E) an unbiased report

28. The principle of _____ states that a buyer will not pay more for a site than for another equally desirable one.
    (A) anticipation
    (B) imbalance
    (C) substitution
    (D) balance
    (E) conformity

29. The principle of anticipation is
    (A) future oriented
    (B) past oriented
    (C) the "as of" date for an appraisal
    (D) the anticipated loan-to-value ratio for the subject property
    (E) similar to the principle of substitution

30. The principle of _____ states that value levels are sustained when the various elements in an economic or environmental mix are in equilibrium.
    (A) anticipation
    (B) equivalence
    (C) substitution
    (D) balance
    (E) highest and best use

31. Price and value are
    (A) not necessarily the same
    (B) synonymous
    (C) different, depending on financing terms
    (D) almost the same in an inactive market
    (E) interchangeable in a report

32. The purpose of a(n) _____ is to analyze a property's potential for success.
    (A) feasibility study
    (B) marketability study
    (C) market segmentation study
    (D) appraisal report
    (E) need study

33. A use must be _____ to be considered as a possible alternative for highest and best use.
    (A) physically and legally possible and financially feasible
    (B) physically and legally possible
    (C) already in existence and legal
    (D) physically possible and appropriate
    (E) legal and profitable

34. An appraiser
    (A) determines price
    (B) defends value
    (C) estimates price
    (D) estimates value
    (E) determines value

35. The objective of the appraisal should be stated in the report because
    (A) the market needs it
    (B) it defines the problem and identifies the value sought
    (C) it identifies the function of the report
    (D) it absolves the appraiser of liability
    (E) there are too many definitions of market price

36. The value estimate provided in an appraisal
    (A) changes with the use to which it is put
    (B) changes with the function of the appraisal
    (C) remains the same regardless of use
    (D) depends upon the use or function of the appraisal
    (E) always reflects market value

37. Population increases _____ demand for housing.
    (A) depress the
    (B) are incapable of stimulating the
    (C) have no effect on the
    (D) are likely to create a
    (E) are determined by the

38. Environmental hazards that an appraiser must be conscious of include all of the following EXCEPT
    (A) asbestos
    (B) radon
    (C) Drano
    (D) urea formaldehyde
    (E) PCBs

39. In analyzing the economic environment and market area, it is best to
    (A) start at the general level and work down to the specific
    (B) start at the specific and work up to the general level
    (C) limit the analysis to the national level
    (D) limit the analysis to the local level
    (E) generally consider traffic flow

40. The first step in the appraisal process is to
    (A) define the problem
    (B) gather data
    (C) analyze data
    (D) determine the approaches to the value
    (E) make a final value estimate

41. Combining two or more sites in order to develop one site with a greater value than the individual sites have separately is called
    (A) assemblage
    (B) plottage
    (C) surplus land
    (D) excess land
    (E) highest and best use of land

42. Assemblage is
    (A) always reflected in the market value
    (B) the act of bringing two or more smaller lots into common ownership for use
    (C) inappropriate for parcels containing 10 or more acres
    (D) uneconomical
    (E) illegal

43. Typically, land is appraised by the
    (A) square foot
    (B) front foot
    (C) acre
    (D) all of the above
    (E) none of the above

44. It is ____ for an appraiser to receive or pay finder's or referral fees.
    (A) reasonable
    (B) unethical
    (C) necessary
    (D) customary
    (E) convenient

45. A sale between relatives is considered
    (A) an arm's length transaction
    (B) a purely comparable sale
    (C) an open market sale
    (D) a distorted sale
    (E) a good deal

46. What of the following is true about zoning?
    (A) It reflects the expectation that government will preserve property values.
    (B) It is based on the right of government to regulate for health, morals, welfare, and safety.
    (C) It is inappropriate for parcels with mixed uses.
    (D) It represents an effort to establish the land's highest and best use.
    (E) It represents the right to reuse property.

47. For an appraiser to use the assistance of another appraiser is
    (A) inconsiderate
    (B) unethical
    (C) illegal
    (D) ethical
    (E) questionable

48. It is _____ to provide a value range to a client who requests it and understands its meaning and use.
    (A) foolish
    (B) appropriate
    (C) unethical
    (D) approximate
    (E) difficult

49. Any recent sale of a subject property being appraised
    (A) should be considered confidential
    (B) cannot, under any circumstances, be considered in estimating the current market value of the property
    (C) should be discussed in the appraisal report
    (D) was not an arm's length sale
    (E) should be used as a comparable sale, though adjusted for its time and terms

50. The dimensions of a warehouse are customarily measured from
    (A) the roof line
    (B) the midpoint of the exterior walls
    (C) the inside of finished walls
    (D) the outside of finished walls
    (E) the foundation slab

51. The construction of a luxury home in a neighborhood almost completely developed with one- and two-bedroom apartments would
    (A) produce external obsolescence
    (B) be called an underimprovement
    (C) result in plottage value
    (D) result in neighborhood amenities
    (E) be reasonable or appropriate

52. The most detailed, complex, costly and time-consuming method of cost estimation is the
    (A) quantity survey
    (B) trade breakdown
    (C) comparative unit
    (D) unit in place
    (E) comparable unit

53. An improvement's remaining economic life
    (A) is its chronological age
    (B) is its effective age
    (C) is the period over which the improvements are expected to generate benefits
    (D) is effective age minus chronological age
    (E) is effective age plus chronological age

54. The cost approach is most applicable when the property being appraised
    (A) has old improvements
    (B) has relatively new improvements that represent the highest and best use of the land
    (C) suffers substantial functional obsolescence
    (D) is more costly than the surroundings
    (E) has many older features that make interesting reading in a report

55. Price per front foot is
    (A) a physical unit of comparison
    (B) not as accurate as price per acre
    (C) rarely used in residential site analysis
    (D) an accurate guide to site marketability
    (E) useful when there are few physical differences between sites

56. Which is the last step in reconciliation?
    (A) Identify which of the three approaches to use.
    (B) Apply the three approaches to the data collected.
    (C) Apply judgment to the data collected.
    (D) Review previous work and analysis.
    (E) Select a final estimate of value.

57. The highest and best use of a site is its
    (A) existing use
    (B) most probable use
    (C) immediate next use
    (D) synonymous with ordinary and necessary use
    (E) different from most probable use

58. Markets in residential real estate are
    (A) equivalent to those for securities
    (B) related to physical boundaries
    (C) local
    (D) physically obscure
    (E) found by courthouse sales

59. Inflation tends to increase the value of
    (A) fixed-income securities
    (B) mortgages
    (C) deeds in lieu of foreclosure
    (D) real estate
    (E) debts

60. Real estate markets
    (A) are international in scope
    (B) meet none of the criteria of a perfect market
    (C) are centralized in nature
    (D) consist of used property only
    (E) are well developed in former Communist countries

61. The subject property has 85 percent occupancy. What conclusion would you most likely draw if the typical occupancy rate in the area was 95 percent?
    (A) Advertising is average.
    (B) The rents are high.
    (C) The rents are low.
    (D) Management is good.
    (E) New construction will occur soon.

62. The fact that the value of a property tends to equal the cost of an equally desirable substitute is an example of the principle of
    (A) balance
    (B) substitution
    (C) contribution
    (D) diminishing returns
    (E) supply and demand

63. Population flow to different regions of the United States will change primarily because of
    (A) changing economic opportunities
    (B) environmental control legislation
    (C) rezoning legislation
    (D) state tax policies
    (E) air conditioning in the Sunbelt

64. When each alternative use requires the same capital investment, the use that maximizes the investment's _____ on a long-term basis is the highest and best use.
    (A) diversified portfolio
    (B) operating expenses
    (C) net operating income
    (D) potential gross income
    (E) occupancy rate

65. What would be the indicated value of a property that rented for $750 per month, using a monthly gross rent multiplier of 100, if the expenses attributable to the property were $115 per month?
    (A) $75,670
    (B) $75,000
    (C) $68,750
    (D) $61,125
    (E) $13,750

66. Which of the following criteria most completely defines "highest and best use"?
    (A) Physically possible, legally acceptable, and generating a higher present land value than any other use
    (B) Legally authorized, politically viable, and socially acceptable
    (C) Physically possible, comparable to other uses in the neighborhood, and legally authorized
    (D) Comparable to other local uses, physically possible, and generating a higher present land value than any other use
    (E) The tallest and most beautiful structure that can be placed on the land

67. The total income anticipated from income property operations after vacancy and collection allowances and operating expenses are deducted is
    (A) net operating income
    (B) before-tax cash flow
    (C) effective gross income
    (D) potential gross income
    (E) property residual income

68. Which principle of value best affirms that value is the present worth of expected future benefits?
    (A) Supply and demand
    (B) Balance
    (C) Substitution
    (D) Anticipation
    (E) Conformity

69. Which principle of value best affirms that the maximum value of property generally cannot exceed the cost of its replacement?
    (A) Increasing and decreasing returns
    (B) Supply and demand
    (C) Substitution
    (D) Balance
    (E) Anticipation

70. Which of the following would be classified as a tangible rather than an intangible amenity?
    (A) Pride of ownership
    (B) A sense of security
    (C) A free dishwasher
    (D) Work satisfaction
    (E) Clean air

71. Which type of property is subject to ad valorem taxation?
    (A) Property owned by a religious organization and used for a religious purpose
    (B) New industrial plants that state and local governments have induced, with tax exemption as an incentive, to locate within their jurisdictions
    (C) Commercial property with more than 50 percent nonprofit tenants
    (D) State colleges and universities
    (E) A state capitol

72. Compared with other assets, real estate is
    (A) immobile
    (B) expensive
    (C) long-lived
    (D) mortgagable
    (E) all of the above

73. All of the following are sources of comparable sales EXCEPT
    (A) public records
    (B) brokers
    (C) buyers and sellers
    (D) mortgage servicers
    (E) appraisers

74. An allowance for vacancy and collection loss is estimated as a percentage of
    (A) net operating income
    (B) before-tax cash flow
    (C) effective gross income
    (D) potential gross income
    (E) after-tax cash flow

75. The annual net operating income from an apartment is $11,000. If a capitalization rate of 11% is used, the indicated market value is
    (A) $126,000
    (B) $176,000
    (C) $100,000
    (D) $242,000
    (E) $2,420

76. Which of the following statements is true of a *gross lease*?
    (A) The tenant pays all operating expenses.
    (B) The landlord pays all operating expenses.
    (C) This lease is used only for commercial properties.
    (D) Rent rises with the cost of living.
    (E) This lease must be drafted by an attorney.

77. Natural or manmade features that affect a neighborhood and its geographic location are _____ influences.
    (A) social
    (B) economic
    (C) government
    (D) environmental
    (E) legal

78. The four broad forces influencing value are
    (A) utility, transferability, demand, and supply (scarcity)
    (B) governmental, economic, social, and political
    (C) supply, demand, location, and popular taste
    (D) governmental, economic, social and physical
    (E) police power, eminent domain, taxation, and escheat

79. The federal government is active in which of the following areas?
    (A) Housing and urban development
    (B) Environmental protection
    (C) Monetary and fiscal policy
    (D) Secondary mortgage market encouragement
    (E) All of the above

80. Population increases _____ demand for housing.
    (A) depress the
    (B) are capable of diminishing the
    (C) have no effect on the
    (D) can create a
    (E) are determined by the

81. In eminent domain, "just compensation" means
    (A) the fair market value of the property
    (B) the current market value plus compensation for anticipated future benefits
    (C) the market value when the property was bought by the current owner
    (D) the insurable value
    (E) none of the above

82. The right of government or quasi-government units to take private property for public use upon the payment of just compensation is
    (A) escheat
    (B) condemnation
    (C) eminent domain
    (D) estoppel
    (E) an unconstitutional practice

83. _____ is the exercise of the right of government to take private property for public use.
    (A) Condemnation
    (B) Certified appraisal
    (C) Immediate justice
    (D) Land removal
    (E) Both A and B

84. The fullest and most common type of estate in realty is
    (A) fee tail
    (B) mortgage
    (C) supra leasehold
    (D) community property
    (E) fee simple

85. An estate in severalty is ownership by
    (A) more than two parties
    (B) two parties
    (C) one or two parties
    (D) one party
    (E) two or more parties with right of survivorship

86. Which of the following is evidence of real estate ownership?
    (A) Title
    (B) Defaulted mortgage
    (C) Estate
    (D) Fee simple
    (E) Tenancy

87. The concept of value in exchange assumes that
    (A) supply does not affect market value
    (B) a commodity is traded in a marketplace, and for that reason prices may be measured objectively
    (C) value can be determined without exposure in a marketplace
    (D) the real estate appraiser can be held liable if the property does not sell in a reasonable time for the appraised value
    (E) the property value will support a reasonable mortgage debt

88. The definition of market value in appraisal does NOT include
    (A) payment in cash or equivalent
    (B) exposure in the market
    (C) informed parties
    (D) topography of the property
    (E) probable price

89. "Value in exchange" is most closely related to
    (A) value in use
    (B) market value
    (C) investment value
    (D) sentimental value
    (E) none of the above

Questions 90–93 are based on the information below:

A 100-unit apartment complex includes 40 one-bedroom units that rent for $950 and 60 two-bedroom units that rent for $1,150 monthly. The vacancy rate is 5 percent; miscellaneous income is $5,000 annually. Operating expenses amount to $400,000. The mortgage loan requires payments of $630,000 annually.

90. Potential gross income is
    (A) $1,289,000
    (B) $112,000
    (C) $107,000
    (D) $1,284,000
    (E) $630,000

91. Effective gross income is
    (A) $1,224,800
    (B) $1,220,000
    (C) $824,800
    (D) $107,000
    (E) $400,000

92. Net operating income is
    (A) $1,224,800
    (B) $824,800
    (C) $424,800
    (D) none of the above
    (E) same as debt service

93. Before-tax cash flow is
    (A) $1,030,000
    (B) $824,800
    (C) $194,800
    (D) none of the above
    (E) same as potential gross income

94. Which statement is FALSE?
    (A) Value in use may be lower than value in exchange.
    (B) Market price is the amount actually paid for a good or service, a historical fact from a particular transaction.
    (C) Cost represents the amount paid for the construction of a building or the amount paid for its acquisition.
    (D) Value in use may be far higher than value in exchange.
    (E) The appraiser must be professionally designated for the value to be accurate.

95. The three common types of legal description are
    (A) metes and bounds; recorded lot, block, and tract; and government rectangular survey
    (B) government rectangular survey, private survey, and house number
    (C) metes and bounds, acreage blocks, and government rectangular survey
    (D) land survey, building survey, and depreciation
    (E) short legal, average legal, and long legal

96. Valuation of property for real estate tax purposes results in
    (A) assessed value
    (B) appraisal
    (C) a special assessment
    (D) a millage rate
    (E) none of the above

97. _____ can render existing supply obsolete and less valuable.
    (A) Inflation
    (B) Interest rates
    (C) Employment
    (D) Income levels
    (E) Changes in tastes and standards

98. One implication of competition and excess profit is that
    (A) a certain optimum combination of land, labor, capital, and entrepreneurship exists
    (B) an estimate of value should be based on future expectations
    (C) abnormally high profits cannot be expected to continue indefinitely
    (D) maximum value accrues to real estate when social and economic homogeneity is present in a neighborhood
    (E) the direct sales comparison approach becomes irrelevant

99. Because real estate markets deal with different desires and needs, they are said to be
    (A) fractionated
    (B) structured
    (C) segmented
    (D) submarketed
    (E) spacious

100. Demand for real estate clearly exists when
    (A) population and employment are on the rise
    (B) there is desire or need for space, plus available mortgage financing
    (C) there is desire or need for space, plus ability to pay
    (D) purchasing power increases
    (E) farm prices rise

Certified Residential Appraiser Examination

Directions: Select the choice, marked A, B, C, D, or E, that best answers the question or completes the thought. Mark your answers clearly on the answer sheet. You have 3 hours to complete this examination. Answers are on page 501, math solutions on page 509.

1. In economics, the four factors of production are
    (A) land, labor, capital, and improvements
    (B) land, labor, capital, and entrepreneurship
    (C) land, labor, capital, and money
    (D) land, improvements, labor, and materials
    (E) land, labor, site, and improvements

2. The law of supply and demand is
    (A) a basic economic principle
    (B) legislated by Congress
    (C) seldom used in the appraisal process
    (D) not applicable in the short term
    (E) all of the above

3. Which of the following is NOT an agent of production?
    (A) Land
    (B) Transportation
    (C) Labor
    (D) Capital
    (E) Entrepreneurship

4. Political forces affecting value may include
    (A) life-styles and living standards
    (B) topography
    (C) athletic levels and recreation facilities
    (D) government spending and taxation policy
    (E) primary registration and turnout

5. What are the two categories of tangible property?
    (A) Real property and personal property
    (B) Intangible property and real property
    (C) Real estate and intangible property
    (D) Legal and illegal investments
    (E) Open and shut transactions

6. Zoning is an exercise of the
   (A) equity courts
   (B) police powers
   (C) Environmental Protection Agency
   (D) right of condemnation
   (E) right of escheat

7. Which of the following types of property is subject to ad valorem taxation?
   (A) Property owned by a religious organization and used for a religious purpose
   (B) New industrial plants that state and local governments have induced, with tax exemption as an incentive, to locate within their jurisdictions
   (C) Commercial buildings leased in part by nonprofit foundations
   (D) State colleges and universities
   (E) A state capitol

8. A person owning less than the entire bundle of rights has
   (A) escheat
   (B) a fee simple title
   (C) a partial interest
   (D) personal property
   (E) a fee tail

9. A metes and bounds description begins and ends with the
   (A) street and house number
   (B) block number
   (C) point of beginning
   (D) grid coordinates
   (E) iron pin

10. A(n) _____ identifies a property in such a way that it CANNOT be confused with any other property.
    (A) coded map book
    (B) legal description
    (C) narrative appraisal
    (D) full city survey
    (E) engineering report

11. All of the following statements are true EXCEPT
    (A) real property is a type of service
    (B) value is dependent on market conditions
    (C) a good or service has no value in exchange unless it possesses certain economic and legal characteristics
    (D) the price representing value is usually quoted in terms of money
    (E) real estate may be sold for all cash or financing arranged

12. All of the following will affect the market value of a property EXCEPT
    (A) political factors
    (B) legal use restriction
    (C) acquisition cost to present owner
    (D) economic factors
    (E) social concerns

13. Market value is _____ the same as selling price.
    (A) always
    (B) never
    (C) sometimes
    (D) usually
    (E) none of the above

14. Price is
    (A) market value
    (B) most probable sales price
    (C) investment value
    (D) a historical fact
    (E) all of the above

15. Functional utility depends on
    (A) zoning
    (B) wear and tear on the structure
    (C) tastes and standards
    (D) age of the equipment
    (E) insurance requirements

16. *Value in use* is
    (A) subjective
    (B) objective
    (C) readily measurable
    (D) a market phenomenon
    (E) synonymous with market price

17. The value added to total property value by a particular component is an example of the principle of
    (A) substitution
    (B) anticipation
    (C) change
    (D) contribution
    (E) conformity

18. The concept that the value of a particular component is measured by the amount that its absence would detract from the value of the whole is
    (A) opportunity cost
    (B) substitution
    (C) competition
    (D) contribution
    (E) conformity

19. The market loss caused by depreciation in an older structure may be offset by all of the following EXCEPT
    (A) architectural interest
    (B) historical registration
    (C) strong demand relative to supply
    (D) strong supply relative to demand
    (E) renovation of the structure

20. Studying appraisal helps a person
    (A) to improve value estimation skills
    (B) to pass the real estate brokers' license examination
    (C) to understand other real estate courses
    (D) to communicate with appraisers
    (E) all of the above

21. A dramatic change in short-term demand for real estate in the local market is likely to immediately precipitate
    (A) construction
    (B) price changes
    (C) conversions
    (D) activity
    (E) no change in supply

22. The area and community analysis section of an appraisal report
    (A) should "sell" the community
    (B) should describe the community objectively
    (C) is a study by the state's industrial development commission
    (D) considers the negative aspects only
    (E) considers the positive aspects only

23. In analyzing the economic environment and market area, it is best to
    (A) start at the general level and work down to the specific
    (B) start at the specific and work up to the general level
    (C) limit the analysis to the national level
    (D) limit the analysis to the local level
    (E) generally consider traffic flow

24. Which of the following reports is usually NOT prepared by a real estate appraiser?
    (A) Marketability study
    (B) Economic study
    (C) Feasibility study
    (D) Transportation network study
    (E) Valuation study

25. An appraisal of a specific-purpose property for insurance purposes would depend most heavily on
    (A) book value
    (B) cost estimate
    (C) land value
    (D) highest and best use
    (E) specialty value

26. The first step in the appraisal process is to
    (A) define the problem to be solved
    (B) gather relevant data
    (C) analyze the data
    (D) inspect the property
    (E) set the fee to be charged

27. An appraisal is
    (A) an estimate of net realizable value
    (B) always concerned with the market value
    (C) a defensible estimate of market value
    (D) a precise statement of value
    (E) a broker's comparative sales analysis with further detail

28. The "as of" date in an appraisal report is
    (A) often the date of the last inspection
    (B) immaterial to the value estimate
    (C) the date on which the report is delivered
    (D) the date on which the property will be conveyed
    (E) the anticipated closing date

29. Sales data descriptions of an appraisal report contain
    (A) details about each comparable sale
    (B) an analysis of the data, using the value approaches
    (C) the investigation of market forces
    (D) analysis of the street each comparable property is on
    (E) zoning details

30. All of the following are ways to delineate a neighborhood EXCEPT
    (A) natural barriers
    (B) utility service
    (C) political boundaries
    (D) streets
    (E) income characteristics

31. All of the following are sources of comparable sales EXCEPT
    (A) public records
    (B) brokers
    (C) buyers and sellers
    (D) mortgage servicers
    (E) appraisers

32. Which of the following criteria most completely define "highest and best use"?
    (A) Legally authorized, politically viable, and socially acceptable
    (B) Physically possible, comparable to other uses in the neighborhood, and legally authorized
    (C) Physically possible, legally permissible, financially feasible, and generating a higher present land value than any other use
    (D) Comparable to other uses in the neighborhood, physically possible, and generating a higher present land value than any other use
    (E) The tallest and most beautiful structure that can be placed on land

33. The three basic approaches used to estimate value are
    (A) use, exclusion, and disposition
    (B) cost, sales comparison, and use
    (C) cost, sales comparison, and market data
    (D) cost, sales comparison, and production
    (E) cost, sales comparison, and income capitalization

34. Units of comparison are used in
    (A) only the sales comparison approach
    (B) only the cost approach
    (C) only the income capitalization approach
    (D) A, B, and C
    (E) the appraisal of special-purpose properties only

35. Final value estimates should be rounded to reflect the
    (A) absence of good data
    (B) property's location
    (C) fact that a selling price will probably be a round number
    (D) lack of precision associated with an opinion
    (E) high value of real estate

36. When reconciling the adjusted sales prices of comparables, the greatest emphasis should be given to
    (A) the average
    (B) the median
    (C) the mode
    (D) the mean of A, B, and C
    (E) none of the above

37. Which of the following forms of appraisal report is NOT recommended?
    (A) Completely filled-in institutional form
    (B) Telephone conversation
    (C) Letter report
    (D) Long narrative report
    (E) Demonstration

38. Which of the following approaches would probably be given the most weight in appraising a large office building?
    (A) Reproduction cost
    (B) Subdivision development
    (C) Replacement cost
    (D) Income capitalization
    (E) Market absorption

39. The form in which a formal appraisal is presented is called
    (A) a presentation of value
    (B) an appraisal log
    (C) an appraisal report
    (D) a value certification
    (E) a narrative report

40. The form of an appraisal report
    (A) has no influence on the appraisal process
    (B) is the same, regardless of the problem
    (C) is set by the amount of the fee
    (D) is determined by the appraiser
    (E) determines the appraisal framework

41. The effective age and the useful life of a building represent judgments made by the
    (A) appraiser
    (B) property owner
    (C) tax assessor
    (D) buyer
    (E) insurer

42. The period over which existing improvements are expected to continue to contribute to property value is their
    (A) effective age
    (B) remaining economic life
    (C) remaining physical life
    (D) period of diminishing returns
    (E) chronological age

43. For a building, *effective age* is best defined as
    (A) the average age of the roof
    (B) the actual age divided by the age-life
    (C) the age of other property in equivalent condition and utility
    (D) the chronological age of the building
    (E) the period over which the building may be effectively used

44. The *utility* of real estate is its
    (A) attractiveness to the trained observer
    (B) longevity
    (C) capacity to satisfy human needs and desires
    (D) effective demand
    (E) remaining economic life

45. In appraising a residence, adjustments are NOT made to the comparable property for
    (A) age
    (B) lot value
    (C) assessed valuation
    (D) terms of sale
    (E) size

46. When a site has improvements on it, the highest and best use
    (A) is not definable
    (B) is its existing use
    (C) is its potential use
    (D) depends on whether or not the existing use is changeable
    (E) may be different from its existing use

47. To be considered as a comparable, a property
    (A) must have been sold within the past 5 years
    (B) must be competitive with the subject
    (C) must have been sold by an open-market transaction
    (D) must be a similar color
    (E) Both B and C

48. The direct sales comparison approach is better than the income or cost approach because
    (A) fewer comparable properties are required, so it is easier to outline the results to clients
    (B) there are fewer mathematical calculations, so there is less chance of mathematical errors
    (C) the market for real estate is slow to change
    (D) it is always easier to obtain data for the direct sales comparison approach
    (E) none of the above is true

49. The appraisal of an established 20-year-old motel on a road with numerous competitive motels would most likely be based on the
    (A) square foot area of improvements
    (B) number of units
    (C) reproduction cost
    (D) gross rent multiplier
    (E) occupancy rate

50. In applying gross rent multiplier analysis to the subject property, the appraiser would use the
    (A) market rental
    (B) actual rent being paid
    (C) rent currently asked by the owner
    (D) rent offered by a potential tenant
    (E) rent listed in advertising the property

Questions 51–56 are based on the following information:

Factor	Subject	Comparable 1	Comparable 2	Comparable 3
Price		$270,000	$265,500	$261,000
Living area (sq. ft.)	1,500	1,600	1,450	1,400
Condition	Good	Fair	Excellent	Good
Garage	One-car	Two-car	One-car	Two-car
Time of sale	Now	Last year	Last year	This year

Adjusted Sales Price: Prices have been rising by 5 percent per year in the area for this type of property.

Other Adjustments: Each square foot of livable area is judged to be worth $90; condition grades are fair, good, and excellent, with each difference in condition grade worth 5 percent; a two-car garage is judged to be worth $4,500 more than a one-car garage.

51. What is the size adjustment for Comparable 1?
    (A) +$4,500
    (B) −$4,500
    (C)   0
    (D) +$9,000
    (E) −$9,000

52. What is the size adjustment for Comparable 2?
    (A) +$4,500
    (B) −$4,500
    (C)   0
    (D) +$9,000
    (E) −$9,000

53. What is the condition adjustment for Comparable 1?
    (A)   0
    (B) +$13,500
    (C) −$13,500
    (D) +$27,000
    (E) −$27,000

54. What is the condition adjustment for Comparable 2?
    (A)   0
    (B) +$13,275
    (C) −$13,275
    (D) +$26,550
    (E) −$26,550

55. What is the garage adjustment for Comparable 2?
    (A)   0
    (B) +$4,500
    (C) −$4,500
    (D) +$9,000
    (E) −$9,000

56. What is the garage adjustment for Comparable 3?
    (A)   0
    (B) +$4,500
    (C) −$4,500
    (D) +$9,000
    (E) −$9,000

57. In estimating the market value of a comparable sale, an appraiser must consider all of the following EXCEPT
    (A) whether the transaction was made in cash, terms equivalent to cash, or other precisely revealed terms
    (B) whether the property had reasonable exposure in a competitive market
    (C) whether a fair sale was transacted, with neither the seller nor the buyer acting under duress
    (D) whether the replacement cost of the property corresponds to its market value
    (E) whether the seller was related to the buyer

58. The terms of financing, whether good or bad,
    (A) have no effect on the market price
    (B) have no effect on the market value
    (C) have no effect on affordability
    (D) depend on fiscal and monetary policy
    (E) should be ignored when adjusting comparables

59. Adjustments for the property rights conveyed, financing, conditions of sale, date of sale, and location are often made to the _____ of the comparable property.
    (A) unit price
    (B) actual sales price
    (C) price per square foot
    (D) gross income multiplier
    (E) cash equivalent value

60. Cumulative percentage adjustments may be used
    (A) when the characteristics are interdependent
    (B) when the characteristics are independent
    (C) when dollar figures are available
    (D) when unimproved properties are being appraised
    (E) under no circumstances

61. The best unit of comparison for vacant land is
    (A) the square foot
    (B) the total lot
    (C) a combination of square foot and front foot units
    (D) the linear foot
    (E) the unit considered important by the market

62. You are asked to appraise a vacant building lot. The neighborhood is about 75% built up. Most lots in the area are from 55 to 65 ft. wide; the lot under appraisal is 60 ft. Comparable sales indicate that lots are selling at $120 to $150 per front foot. What is a good estimate of the price range for this lot?
    (A) $9,000–$11,000
    (B) $7,200–$9,000
    (C) $5,400–$6,750
    (D) $6,600–$7,600
    (E) $6,600–$11,250

63. In appraising a residential property by the cost approach, the appraiser considers the
    (A) sales prices of comparable properties
    (B) depreciation of the land
    (C) depreciation of improvements
    (D) potential for new competition
    (E) potential misuse of this approach

64. In the cost approach, _____ is deducted after estimating the cost to reproduce an existing structure.
    (A) land cost
    (B) cost to maturity
    (C) depreciation
    (D) cash equivalence
    (E) personal property value

65. External or economic obsolescence can be caused by all of the following EXCEPT
    (A) economic factors
    (B) political factors
    (C) social factors
    (D) factors within the property
    (E) legal factors

66. Economic obsolescence in a residence does NOT result from
    (A) an outdated kitchen
    (B) construction of a freeway near the property
    (C) the presence of an earthquake fault nearby
    (D) building restrictions in the community
    (E) factors external to the subject property itself

67. Reproduction or replacement cost includes all of the following EXCEPT
    (A) direct or hard costs
    (B) indirect or soft costs
    (C) entrepreneurial profit
    (D) fixed and variable expenses of operations
    (E) elevator shafts

68. In analyzing obsolescence, the test of curability of a component in a building is whether the cost to cure is no greater than the
    (A) expected increase in value
    (B) reproduction cost new
    (C) replacement cost
    (D) installation cost
    (E) economic life of the new component

69. Which of the following is NOT a type of depreciation?
    (A) Entrepreneurial loss
    (B) External obsolescence
    (C) Physical deterioration
    (D) Functional obsolescence
    (E) Economic obsolescence

70. Estimation of accrued depreciation and obsolescence does NOT involve
    (A) physical deterioration
    (B) economic obsolescence
    (C) financial structure
    (D) functional obsolescence
    (E) wear and tear

71. In appraisal, accrued depreciation is really an estimate of
    (A) physical deterioration
    (B) diminished utility
    (C) book depreciation
    (D) capital recovery
    (E) sinking fund factor

72. The cost approach is NOT useful for
    (A) checking value approaches
    (B) appraising institutional or special-use properties
    (C) estimating the value of new property
    (D) appraising older homes in an active market
    (E) insurance appraisals

Questions 73–75 are based on the following information:

An appraiser noted the following about a rental home:

needs exterior paint	$750 cost to cure
needs new water heater	$250 cost to cure
has one bath in market for two	$4,000 capitalized rent loss
has poor floor plan	$2,500 capitalized rent loss
is located next to a convenience store	$1,200 capitalized rent loss

73. How much is curable physical deterioration?
    (A) $250
    (B) $750
    (C) $4,000
    (D) $2,500
    (E) None of the above

74. How much is functional obsolescence?
    (A) $250
    (B) $1,000
    (C) $6,500
    (D) $7,700
    (E) None of the above

75. How much is environmental obsolescence?
    (A) $250
    (B) $750
    (C) $1,200
    (D) $2,500
    (E) $4,000

76. *Cash-on-cash return* is
    (A) the annual cash flow divided by the equity investment
    (B) an internal rate of return that represents annual income and all gains or losses pro-rated to an effective annual amount
    (C) a percentage or decimal rate that, when divided into a periodic income amount, offers a lump-sum capital value for income
    (D) a value that does not change with time
    (E) none of the above

77. Which report is usually NOT prepared by a real estate appraiser?
    (A) Marketability study
    (B) Economic study
    (C) Feasibility study
    (D) Mineral valuation study
    (E) Highest and best use

Questions 78–81 are based on the information below.

You are appraising a 40-acre tract of unimproved land. The size is zoned for single-family residential use. All utilities are available along the street on which the land fronts. The engineers who will plat the proposed subdivision told you that 20 percent of the land area will be used for streets and sidewalks. Zoning will permit four lots per acre of net developable land after deducting streets. Research indicates that lots similar to those that will be available on the subject land will sell for $18,000 each and that the entire tract can be developed and sold in 1 year. You find that 40 percent of the sale price of each lot must be allocated to selling cost, overhead, contingencies, carrying cost, and developer's profit, and that 2,000 feet of streets (including water, storm sewer, and sanitary sewer lines) must be installed at a cost of $80 per foot.

78. What is the number of lots to be developed?
  (A) 40
  (B) 128
  (C) 80
  (D) 88
  (E) 32

79. What is the gross amount that will be realized from the sale of all the lots?
  (A) $720,000
  (B) $2,304,000
  (C) $1,440,000
  (D) $1,584,000
  (E) $576,000

80. What is the cost of installing streets, water, and sewer lines?
  (A) $16,000
  (B) $32,000
  (C) $64,000
  (D) $160,000
  (E) None of the above

81. What is the amount of selling cost, overhead, contingencies, carrying cost and developer's profit?
  (A) $921,600
  (B) $576,000
  (C) $288,000
  (D) $633,600
  (E) None of the above

82. Which of the following forms of appraisal report is NOT recommended?
  (A) Completely filled-in institutional form
  (B) Telephone conversation
  (C) Letter report
  (D) Long narrative report
  (E) Demonstration

83. The term *vertical interests* does NOT refer to rights to
  (A) subsurface mineral extraction
  (B) the construction of railroad tunnels
  (C) the use and regulation of air space
  (D) subdivision and development
  (E) the construction of buildings over railroad yards

84. Inflation tends to increase the value of
    (A) fixed-income securities
    (B) mortgages
    (C) deeds in lieu of foreclosure
    (D) tangible long-lived investments
    (E) debts

85. With an amortized mortgage loan,
    (A) interest only is paid until maturity
    (B) some principal is repaid with each payment
    (C) the entire principal is repaid before maturity
    (D) equal amounts of principal are repaid each period
    (E) there is a balloon payment at maturity

Questions 86–89 are based on the following information:

A building contains 50 one-bedroom units and 150 two-bedroom units. The one-bedroom units rent for $550 monthly; two-bedroom are $675. The vacancy rate is 7 percent; operating expenses are estimated at 40 percent of effective gross income. There is $2,000 annual income from vending machines.

86. Potential gross income is
    (A) $64,375
    (B) $1,547,000
    (C) $1,545,000
    (D) $717,425
    (E) None of the above

87. Effective gross income is
    (A) $64,375
    (B) $1,547,000
    (C) $1,545,000
    (D) $1,438,850
    (E) None of the above

88. Net operating income is
    (A) $64,375
    (B) $268,970
    (C) $863,310
    (D) $719,425
    (E) None of the above

89. Operating expenses are
    (A) $1,545,000
    (B) $54,075
    (C) $2,000
    (D) $719,425
    (E) $575,540

90. In one step of the land residual technique, the building capitalization rate is applied to the known building value to estimate the
    (A) highest and best use of the site
    (B) cost of the building
    (C) income needed to support the land
    (D) net operating income needed to support the building
    (E) land value

91. The basic formula for property valuation via income capitalization is
    (A) $V = IR$
    (B) $V = I/R$
    (C) $V = R/I$
    (D) $V = SP/GR$
    (E) $V = I/F$

92. All of the following lease provisions are advantageous to the lessee EXCEPT
    (A) an escape clause
    (B) a renewal option
    (C) a purchase option
    (D) an escalation clause
    (E) none of the above

93. When each alternative use requires the same capital investment, the use that maximizes the investment's _____ on a long-term basis is the highest and best use.
    (A) diversified portfolio
    (B) operating expenses
    (C) net operating income
    (D) potential gross income
    (E) occupancy rate

94. Land purchased for $500,000 cash appreciates at the rate of 15 percent compounded annually. About how much is the land worth after 5 years? Disregard taxes, insurance, and selling expenses.
    (A) $1,000,000
    (B) $875,000
    (C) $575,000
    (D) $375,000
    (E) $75,000

95. A land speculator expects that a certain 100-acre tract can be sold to a subdivider 4 years from now for $10,000 per acre. If holding and selling costs are disregarded, what cash price today (rounded to the nearest $1,000) would allow the speculator to realize a 15 percent compounded annual rate of return on the entire tract?
    (A) $572,000
    (B) $5,000
    (C) $600,000
    (D) $6,000
    (E) None of the above

96. Gross income multipliers are generally considered part of
    (A) the cost approach
    (B) the direct sales comparison approach
    (C) the income capitalization approach
    (D) the insurance approach
    (E) none of the above

97. Use of a gross rent multiplier is valid when the subject and comparable properties have similar
    (A) potential gross incomes
    (B) effective gross incomes
    (C) net operating incomes
    (D) operating expense ratios
    (E) cash flows

98. Time-distance relationships between a site and all relevant origins and destinations are called
    (A) access roads
    (B) transit facilities
    (C) ingress and egress
    (D) linkages
    (E) synergies

99. The land on which a 10-year-old house is located is valued at $128,000, and the reproduction cost of the dwelling is $92,000. Straight-line depreciation is 2 percent per year, applied to the building only. If there is no other obsolescence, what is the indicated value of the property?
    (A) $196,000
    (B) $201,600
    (C) $217,000
    (D) $217,700
    (E) $220,000

100. An allowance for vacancy and collection loss is estimated as a percentage of
    (A) net operating income
    (B) before-tax cash flow
    (C) effective gross income
    (D) potential gross income
    (E) after-tax cash flow

Certified General Appraiser Examination

Directions: Select the choice, marked A, B, C, D, or E, that best answers the question or completes the thought. Mark your answers clearly on the answer sheet. You have 3 hours to complete this examination. Answers are on page 501, math solutions on page 510.

1. Effective gross income is income after an allowance for
    (A) depreciation
    (B) operating expenses
    (C) cash expenditures
    (D) both A and B
    (E) none of the above

2. In discounted cash flow analysis, the reversion to be received at the end of the holding period is
    (A) a separate cash flow
    (B) an annuity in arrears
    (C) an ordinary annuity
    (D) a percentage of annual income
    (E) an amount to be capitalized in perpetuity

3. To earn 12 percent annual cash return on a cash investment, what should you pay for a property that earns $4,000 per month and has operating expenses of $1,250 per month?
    (A) $150,000
    (B) $275,000
    (C) $229,166
    (D) $333,333
    (E) $400,000

4. In selecting an overall capitalization rate for an income-producing property, the appraiser will consider all of the following EXCEPT
   (A) return on invested capital
   (B) risk factors
   (C) return of invested capital
   (D) the interest rate on the existing loan, which was arranged last year
   (E) the interest rate prevailing in the market

Questions 5–8 are based on the following information:

A 200-unit apartment complex includes 80 one-bedroom units that rent for $475 and 120 two-bedroom units that rent for $575 monthly. The vacancy rate is 5%; miscellaneous income is $5,000 annually. Operating expenses amount to $400,000. The mortgage loan requires annual payments of $630,000.

5. Potential gross income is
   (A) $1,289,000
   (B) $1,284,000
   (C) $112,000
   (D) $107,000
   (E) None of the above

6. Effective gross income is
   (A) $1,224,800
   (B) $1,220,000
   (C) $824,800
   (D) $107,000
   (E) None of the above

7. Net operating income is
   (A) $1,224,800
   (B) $1,220,000
   (C) $824,800
   (D) $424,800
   (E) None of the above

8. Before-tax cash flow is
   (A) $1,030,000
   (B) $824,800
   (C) $424,800
   (D) $194,800
   (E) None of the above

9. To obtain the present value of a series of incomes, a(n) _____ rate is applied.
   (A) discount
   (B) income
   (C) overall capitalization
   (D) equity capitalization
   (E) stated

10. A fast-food chain could buy the building and land necessary for a new outlet for $200,000. Instead, an investor bought the property for this amount and leased it for $2,000 per month over a 20-year term. Rent is payable at the end of each month. What yield to maturity is implied by the lease, assuming that, at the end of 20 years, the property is still worth about $200,000?
    (A) 8%
    (B) 10%
    (C) 12%
    (D) 14%
    (E) 15%

11. When market rent is less than contract rent, the difference is known as
    (A) overage rent
    (B) excess rent
    (C) percentage rent
    (D) gross rent
    (E) slippage rent

12. If a particular buyer requires a recapture of the building portion of the purchase price in 25 years, what is the indicated recapture rate for the building, assuming straight-line recapture?
    (A) 0.25%
    (B) 2%
    (C) 4%
    (D) 20%
    (E) 25%

13. In a high-rise, 100-unit apartment building there is a basement laundry area that brings in $100 monthly from the concessionaire. The laundry income is
    (A) included, as miscellaneous income, in potential gross income
    (B) included, as other income, in effective gross income
    (C) deducted from effective gross income
    (D) added to before-tax cash flow
    (E) distributed to the maintenance workers

14. A forecast using discounted cash flow analysis would include
    (A) income, vacancy, and operating expenses
    (B) an economic analysis
    (C) reversion at the end of the holding period
    (D) discounting expected future cash flows to a present value
    (E) all of the above

15. In discounted cash flow analysis, the reversion to be received at the end of the holding period is
    (A) a separate cash flow
    (B) an annuity in arrears
    (C) an ordinary annuity
    (D) a percentage of annual income
    (E) an amount to be capitalized in perpetuity

16. A $1,000,000 property will have a 70% loan at a 10% annual mortgage constant. What must the net operating income be to produce a 15% cash-on-cash return?
    (A) $150,000
    (B) $90,000
    (C) $115,000
    (D) $75,000
    (E) $750,000

17. Income capitalization is the term used to describe the process of estimating the value of income property by studying expected future income. This process
    (A) converts the net income of a property into its equivalent capital value
    (B) reflects the time value of money by reducing or discounting future income to its present worth
    (C) focuses on the present worth of future benefits
    (D) uses market interest rates
    (E) all of the above

18. To earn 12% on your investment, what should you pay for a property that earns $6,000 per month and has operating expenses of $1,250 per month?
    (A) $475,000
    (B) $150,000
    (C) $229,166
    (D) $333,333
    (E) $400,000

19. The land development method is used to estimate the value of vacant acreage that is ready to be subdivided. This method requires
    (A) the study of current sales of subdivided lots
    (B) the projection of land development costs
    (C) RTC approval
    (D) both A and B
    (E) none of the above

20. A technique of income capitalization in which the analyst need not distinguish interest rates from capital recovery rates, but that is most useful for comparable income properties, is
    (A) direct capitalization
    (B) building residual
    (C) land residual
    (D) bank of investment
    (E) internal rate of return

21. A mortgage is
    (A) a gift from the mortgagee
    (B) a transfer of real estate to a financial institution
    (C) any loan
    (D) a pledge of real estate as collateral for a loan
    (E) a cloud on the title to real estate

22. The portion of the loan payment for recapture of the investment capital in a mortgage is
    (A) principal, interest, taxes, and insurance
    (B) principal reduction or amortization
    (C) interest and principal payment
    (D) negative amortization
    (E) mortgage banking

23. An appraisal is
    (A) an establishment of value
    (B) a prediction of sales price
    (C) a mathematically precise forecast of value
    (D) an estimate of rental levels
    (E) an estimate of value

24. An appraiser
    (A) determines value
    (B) determines price
    (C) estimates value
    (D) measures price
    (E) forecasts price

25. An appraiser
    (A) determines rent rates
    (B) sets value
    (C) suggests financing
    (D) estimates value
    (E) inspects electrical, mechanical, and plumbing for working condition

26. The _____ establishes the market conditions prevailing when the appraisal is made.
    (A) statement of limitations
    (B) statement of conclusions
    (C) introductory note
    (D) transmittal letter
    (E) date of the value estimate

27. Analysis of a location involves which three levels?
    (A) General, specific, detailed
    (B) Country, state, community
    (C) Residential, commercial, industrial
    (D) Country, state, county
    (E) Region, neighborhood, site

28. Market data are used
    (A) in the direct sales comparison approach
    (B) in the income approach
    (C) in the cost approach
    (D) in statistical analysis
    (E) all of the above

29. The cost approach is most applicable when the subject property
    (A) has new improvements that represent the highest and best use
    (B) is in an active local market for similar properties
    (C) produces a positive cash flow
    (D) is in an area where many comparable properties have recently been sold
    (E) exhibits a great deal of functional obsolescence

30. In preparing an appraisal report, your analysis concludes that one of the approaches to value is not applicable to this particular case. You should therefore
    (A) omit the approach altogether
    (B) base the approach on hypothetical data
    (C) state that the approach is not relevant
    (D) state that the approach is not applicable, explain the reasons for this contention, and provide supporting data
    (E) find another approach so as to include three approaches

31. Reconciliation involves
    (A) averaging the unadjusted sales prices of comparables
    (B) recalculating all data
    (C) averaging all estimates derived, weighting each according to its importance
    (D) placing primary emphasis on the estimate deemed most reliable
    (E) averaging estimates from the three approaches, giving each equal weight

32. Cost and market value are more likely to be almost the same when properties are
    (A) new
    (B) old
    (C) depreciated
    (D) syndicated
    (E) appraised

33. In appraisal, reconciliation is
    (A) an estimate of value
    (B) one of the three approaches used in estimating value
    (C) a process of reevaluation that leads to the final value estimate
    (D) an assurance of checkbook accuracy
    (E) a process that is similar to correlation in statistics

34. The essential elements of an appraisal report
    (A) usually follow the valuation or appraisal process
    (B) vary with the type of report
    (C) depend on the client's needs
    (D) depend on the fee charged
    (E) depend on the number of comparables located

35. A demonstration narrative appraisal report
    (A) contains many items that are not included in the usual report
    (B) is an appraisal report prepared for a fussy client
    (C) contains all the items that may be used in practice and is generally the most detailed report
    (D) may be based on hypothetical or assumed data
    (E) should be prepared on a nontypical property to show appraisal expertise

36. A parcel of land that is improved to the point of being ready to be built upon is called
    (A) realty
    (B) land
    (C) a site
    (D) terrain
    (E) a location

37. Before performing a site inspection, an appraiser should
    (A) gather basic information about the site
    (B) know the reasons for the site inspection
    (C) have a map or drawing of the site
    (D) have writing materials for taking notes
    (E) all of the above

38. Environmental hazards that an appraiser must be conscious of include all of the following EXCEPT
    (A) asbestos
    (B) radon
    (C) Drano
    (D) urea formaldehyde
    (E) dry cleaning chemicals

39. The term that denotes the attractiveness and usefulness of a property is
    (A) price estimate
    (B) highest and best use
    (C) location
    (D) functional utility
    (E) value in use

40. Combining two or more sites in order to develop one site with a greater value than the individual sites have separately is called
    (A) assemblage
    (B) plottage
    (C) surplus land
    (D) excess land
    (E) highest and best use of land

41. In the cost approach, the valuation of land involves the principle of
    (A) conformity
    (B) contribution
    (C) highest and best use
    (D) marginal productivity
    (E) variable proportions

42. The highest and best use of land is the reasonable use
    (A) to which land is currently being put
    (B) to which land can be put without adverse effect over the short term
    (C) to which land can most profitably be put over the short term
    (D) to which land can most profitably be put over the long term
    (E) whereby land will become agriculturally productive

43. The direct sales comparison approach should be used
    (A) without exception
    (B) on residential properties only
    (C) on residential and income properties
    (D) in all cases where comparable sales are available
    (E) on vacant land

44. The direct sales comparison approach involves
    (A) analyzing sales
    (B) comparing properties that have recently been sold to a subject property
    (C) analyzing market rentals
    (D) both A and B
    (E) none of the above

45. If the monthly rental for the subject property is $1,150 and the gross rent multiplier is 127, what estimate of value is indicated?
    (A) $149,500
    (B) $150,000
    (C) $145,850
    (D) $146,250
    (E) $146,000

46. The direct sales comparison approach
    (A) uses the replacement cost of improvements, added to a comparable vacant land value
    (B) uses data on recent sales of comparable properties
    (C) uses the income-producing capability of the property
    (D) involves multiple listing service data
    (E) requires at least three comparable sales for application

47. What is the indicated value of a property that rents for $1,500 per month, using a monthly gross rent multiplier of 110, if the expenses attributable to the property are $125 per month?
(A) $151,340
(B) $165,000
(C) $137,500
(D) $122,250
(E) $27,500

48. A 7-year-old residence is currently valued at $216,000. What was its original value if it has appreciated by 60% since it was built?
(A) $81,000
(B) $113,400
(C) $135,000
(D) $345,600
(E) None of the above

49. For residential property, market value appraisals assume that
(A) the purchaser pays all cash; no money is borrowed
(B) an FHA or VA mortgage is used
(C) a purchase money mortgage is considered
(D) the value estimate is based on no special financing
(E) the seller pays no more than five points

50. In considering comparable sales in direct sales comparison appraisal,
(A) the seller's motivation is significant
(B) the date of sale is significant
(C) the proximity of the properties is most important
(D) both A and B
(E) none of the above

Questions 51–53 are based on the following information:

Seven comparables have been found for a single-family dwelling being appraised and gross rent multipliers calculated from the sales prices as follows:

Comparable	GRM
1	125
2	125
3	127
4	127
5	127
6	128
7	130

51. What is the mean GRM?
(A) 125
(B) 126
(C) 127
(D) 128
(E) 130

52. What is the median GRM?
    - (A) 125
    - (B) 126
    - (C) 127
    - (D) 128
    - (E) 130

53. What is the mode for the GRMs?
    - (A) 125
    - (B) 126
    - (C) 127
    - (D) 128
    - (E) 130

54. Land prices are analyzed and adjusted in the sales comparison process. These adjustments may involve
    - (A) adding or subtracting lump-sum amounts
    - (B) adding or subtracting percentages
    - (C) accumulating percentages
    - (D) using several units of comparison
    - (E) any of the above

55. The adjustment process in the direct sales comparison technique involves
    - (A) identifying the similarities between properties and adjusting the sales prices
    - (B) analyzing the comparables and adjusting the prices for similarities
    - (C) identifying the significant differences between the subject and comparable properties and adjusting the sales prices of the comparables for differences
    - (D) locating competitive properties and ranking them in the order of desirability
    - (E) adjusting the subject to be like the comparables

56. In the cost approach, the site is valued as if it were
    - (A) vacant and available for development to its highest and best use
    - (B) improved and suited for its intended use or development
    - (C) developed and operating
    - (D) attractively landscaped
    - (E) lacking nearby utilities

57. The direct sales comparison approach is especially suitable for appraising land zoned for which of the following types of use?
    - (A) Single-family residential
    - (B) Commercial
    - (C) Industrial
    - (D) Multifamily residential
    - (E) Any of the above

58. All of the following are accepted classifications of accrued depreciation for appraisal purposes EXCEPT
    - (A) functional obsolescence
    - (B) economic obsolescence
    - (C) accounting allocation
    - (D) physical deterioration
    - (E) external obsolescence

59. Accrued depreciation can be defined in appraisal terms as
    (A) an increase in value from inflationary gains
    (B) a total loss in value from all causes
    (C) diminished utility from trade imbalance
    (D) competitive pressures
    (E) functional form changes

60. The cost estimates used in appraisal typically reflect
    (A) wholesale costs
    (B) current cost levels
    (C) typical costs to build a building like this subject
    (D) the actual historic cost of the building being appraised
    (E) both B and C

61. Cost indexes are used to
    (A) derive units of comparison
    (B) catalog building components
    (C) estimate operating expenses
    (D) update past costs into current costs
    (E) estimate the local consumer price index

62. The most detailed, time-consuming, and costly method of estimating cost new is
    (A) unit of comparison
    (B) quantity survey
    (C) trade breakdown
    (D) unit-in-place
    (E) segregated cost

63. In calculating depreciation, a limitation of the age-life method is that it
    (A) tends to ignore physical deterioration
    (B) cannot be used with estimates of cost new
    (C) is based on replacement cost rather than reproduction cost
    (D) tends to ignore functional and economic obsolescence
    (E) is difficult to compute

64. Two baths are required to serve a three-bedroom house if
    (A) the appraiser believes they are necessary
    (B) the selling price is more than $225,000
    (C) two baths are demanded by a typical purchaser of a three-bedroom house in the given market
    (D) four or more persons will live in the house
    (E) one of the bedrooms is at the opposite end of the house from the other two

65. Which is the most precise yet least used cost estimation method?
    (A) Index method
    (B) Quantity survey method
    (C) Comparative square foot method
    (D) Unit-in-place method
    (E) Segregated cost method

66. A defect is considered curable if
    (A) major structural alterations are not required
    (B) the cost of the cure represents more than 25% of the remaining utility
    (C) the cost to cure the condition is less than or equal to the anticipated addition to value
    (D) the cost to cure increases the remaining economic life of the improvement
    (E) the cure is in conformity with building codes

67. External or economic obsolescence is normally NOT
    (A) curable by the owner, the landlord, or the tenant
    (B) discovered during the neighborhood analysis portion of appraisal
    (C) evident in both land and buildings
    (D) caused by forces outside the property
    (E) also called environmental obsolescence

68. A house built in 1975 and appraised in 2004 would have
    (A) a useful life of 29 years
    (B) a chronological age of 29 years
    (C) an effective age of 29 years
    (D) an economic age of 29 years
    (E) a 29-year-old replacement cost

69. In one step of the land residual technique, the building capitalization rate is applied to the known building value to estimate the
    (A) highest and best use of the site
    (B) cost of the building
    (C) income needed to support the land
    (D) net operating income needed to support the building
    (E) land value

70. An example of partial interest is
    (A) a life estate
    (B) a leasehold estate
    (C) a lengthy attention span
    (D) a short attention span
    (E) both A and B

71. A condominium is
    (A) a type of mortgage on real estate
    (B) a building like a cooperative
    (C) a legal concept of ownership
    (D) a zero-lot-line house
    (E) a style of housing

72. Clarity and accuracy contribute to the
    (A) quality of an appraisal
    (B) quantity of evidence
    (C) appraisal fee
    (D) final value estimate
    (E) appearance of the report

73. If an appraiser is asked to undertake an assignment on a property type with which she has no previous experience and is otherwise unfamiliar, she should
    (A) refuse the assignment
    (B) accept the assignment, thereby expanding her abilities, but reduce the fee
    (C) ask the client to hire another appraiser to help her
    (D) associate herself with another appraiser experienced in this type of assignment and inform the client of this fact
    (E) get the necessary computer software to solve the problem

74. Real estate markets are composed of
    (A) buyers only
    (B) sellers only
    (C) types of property
    (D) buyers and sellers
    (E) appraisers and counselors

75. Real estate supply factors include
    (A) the current housing supply
    (B) new construction activity
    (C) tax depreciation allowances
    (D) both A and B
    (E) none of the above

76. The mortgage constant is a function of all of the following EXCEPT
    (A) the term of the loan
    (B) the borrower's income level
    (C) the interest rate
    (D) the term of amortization
    (E) It is a function of all of the above.

77. The benefit(s) forgone from a project that cannot be built is (are) called
    (A) anticipation
    (B) substitution
    (C) opportunity cost
    (D) surplus productivity
    (E) marginal cost

78. The debt coverage ratio
    (A) is federally approved for residential valuation
    (B) can be applied uniformly to all properties
    (C) is the most equitable method of determining a cap rate
    (D) indicates the safety of the loan
    (E) is generally less than 1.00

79. The _____ is a key safety factor for the lender.
    (A) maturity term
    (B) sales price
    (C) loan-to-value ratio
    (D) age of the improvements
    (E) land value

80. A parcel of land is sold for $115,000. If it appreciated at 12% per year, and the seller held it for four years, how much did the seller pay for it (disregard taxes, selling costs, etc.)?
    (A) $60,000
    (B) $101,000
    (C) $73,000
    (D) $62,500
    (E) $81,700

81. A 30-year-old building with an effective age of 20 years has a total life expectancy of 50 years. How much depreciation has occurred?
    (A) 10%
    (B) 20%
    (C) 40%
    (D) 60%
    (E) None of the above

82. A plot of land, 100 ft. × 200 ft., along an interstate freeway, is situated 12 miles north of the central business district of a city with a population approaching 1 million. Which of the following would be the highest and best use of the land?
    (A) Service station
    (B) Convenience store
    (C) Two-story office building
    (D) Medical office building
    (E) There is not enough information to make a determination.

83. A $2 million shopping center is purchased with a 75% loan-to-value ratio mortgage, payable monthly over 25 years at 12% interest. It generates $205,000 annual net operating income. The land is considered to be worth $500,000; the balance of cost is represented by land improvements. What is the improvement ratio?
    (A) 25%
    (B) 50%
    (C) 75%
    (D) 100%
    (E) None of the above

84. The adjustment for below-market-rate financing may provide an estimate of
    (A) market price
    (B) cash equivalence
    (C) property price
    (D) creative financing
    (E) replacement cost

85. Land or site appraisals assist in
    (A) the sale and purchase of land
    (B) land development
    (C) ad valorem and income tax situations
    (D) all of the above
    (E) none of the above

86. Overall rate of return is
    (A) the annual net operating income divided by the purchase price
    (B) annual income and all gains or losses prorated to an effective annual amount minus an internal rate of return
    (C) a percentage or decimal rate that, when divided into a periodic income amount, offers a lump-sum capital value for the income
    (D) an income that is unchanging with time
    (E) none of the above

87. All of the following are used in the valuation of income-producing property EXCEPT
    (A) rental rates
    (B) operating expenses
    (C) income taxes
    (D) net leasable area
    (E) vacancy and collection allowance

88. A $1 million property will have a 75% loan at a 12% annual mortgage constant. What must the net operating income be to produce a 15% cash-on-cash return?
    (A) $75,000
    (B) $90,000
    (C) $127,500
    (D) $150,000
    (E) $750,000

89. If a particular buyer requires a recapture of the building portion of the purchase price in 25 years, what is the indicated recapture rate for the building, assuming straight-line capture?
(A) 0.25%
(B) 2%
(C) 4%
(D) 20%
(E) 25%

90. In a high-rise 100-unit apartment building there is a basement laundry area that brings in $100 monthly from the concessionaire. The laundry income is
(A) included, as miscellaneous income, in potential gross income
(B) included, as other income, in effective gross income
(C) deducted from effective gross income
(D) added to before-tax cash flow
(E) distributed to the maintenance workers

91. In an appraisal of income property, which of the following items should be excluded from the expense statement?
(A) Mortgage loan interest payments
(B) Ordinary and necessary current expenses
(C) Projected replacement reserve
(D) Management fees
(E) Advertising expenses

Questions 92–95 are based on the following information:

A building contains 25 one-bedroom units and 75 two-bedroom units. The one-bedroom units rent for $550 monthly; two-bedrooms are $675. The vacancy rate is 7%; operating expenses are estimated at 40% of effective gross income. There is $1,000 annual income from vending machines.

92. Potential gross income is
(A) $773,500
(B) $772,500
(C) $719,425
(D) $64,375
(E) None of the above

93. Effective gross income is
(A) $773,500
(B) $772,500
(C) $719,425
(D) $64,375
(E) None of the above

94. Net operating income is
(A) $64,375
(B) $286,970
(C) $431,655
(D) $719,425
(E) None of the above

95. Operating expenses are
    (A) $1,000
    (B) $54,075
    (C) $287,770
    (D) $719,425
    (E) None of the above

96. Which approach involves an investigation of the rent schedules of the subject property and the comparables?
    (A) Cost approach
    (B) Just compensation evaluation
    (C) Income approach
    (D) Comparable rent approach
    (E) All of the above

97. Property free and clear of indebtedness is offered for sale. The property is net-net leased (the tenant pays all operating expenses) for $90,000 per year under a 30-year lease. Rent is payable annually at the end of each year. The building cost $850,000, including a developer's profit and risk allowance; the land cost $100,000, and its value is well established by comparable sales. It is estimated that the building will be worth only about half its current cost at the end of the lease term, and that the land will remain constant in value over that period. A 10% discount rate is considered appropriate. Using the building residual technique estimate the value of the building.
    (A) Between $250,000 and $300,000
    (B) Between $300,000 and $750,000
    (C) Between $750,000 and $1,000,000
    (D) Between $1,000,000 and $1,500,000
    (E) Not within any of the above ranges

98. Which of the following statements is true of a *gross lease*?
    (A) The tenant pays all operating expenses.
    (B) The landlord pays all operating expenses.
    (C) This lease is used only for commercial properties.
    (D) Rent rises with the cost of living.
    (E) This lease must be drafted by an attorney.

99. Land purchased for $100,000 cash appreciates at the rate of 15%, compounded annually. About how much is the land worth after 5 years? Disregard taxes, insurance, and selling expenses.
    (A) $200,000
    (B) $175,000
    (C) $115,000
    (D) $75,000
    (E) $15,000

100. An allowance for vacancy and collection loss is estimated as a percentage of
    (A) net operating income
    (B) before-tax cash flow
    (C) effective gross income
    (D) potential gross income
    (E) after-tax cash flow

Chapter 25/*Answer Keys and Explanations*

Following are answer keys to all the model examinations in Chapter 24.
A final section contains explanations of all the arithmetic questions in all the examinations.

Salesperson License Examination 1 _____

1. **B**	26. **C**	51. **B**	76. **B**	101. **D**	126. **D**
2. **A**	27. **D**	52. **B**	77. **D**	102. **B**	127. **C**
3. **A**	28. **B**	53. **A**	78. **D**	103. **A**	128. **D**
4. **C**	29. **C**	54. **B**	79. **B**	104. **B**	129. **B**
5. **B**	30. **B**	55. **A**	80. **D**	105. **B**	130. **C**
6. **A**	31. **B**	56. **C**	81. **B**	106. **C**	131. **C**
7. **D**	32. **D**	57. **A**	82. **B**	107. **B**	132. **B**
8. **B**	33. **A**	58. **B**	83. **C**	108. **C**	133. **D**
9. **D**	34. **D**	59. **B**	84. **C**	109. **D**	134. **D**
10. **C**	35. **B**	60. **A**	85. **C**	110. **A**	135. **C**
11. **B**	36. **B**	61. **D**	86. **B**	111. **D**	136. **D**
12. **B**	37. **C**	62. **D**	87. **C**	112. **A**	137. **D**
13. **B**	38. **D**	63. **C**	88. **D**	113. **C**	138. **C**
14. **A**	39. **D**	64. **A**	89. **D**	114. **A**	139. **B**
15. **B**	40. **A**	65. **D**	90. **D**	115. **A**	140. **B**
16. **C**	41. **B**	66. **D**	91. **B**	116. **C**	141. **B**
17. **D**	42. **A**	67. **B**	92. **B**	117. **B**	142. **B**
18. **D**	43. **C**	68. **B**	93. **C**	118. **D**	143. **C**
19. **B**	44. **D**	69. **D**	94. **A**	119. **A**	144. **B**
20. **C**	45. **C**	70. **C**	95. **A**	120. **B**	145. **B**
21. **C**	46. **C**	71. **D**	96. **D**	121. **A**	146. **A**
22. **C**	47. **A**	72. **D**	97. **D**	122. **D**	147. **C**
23. **D**	48. **B**	73. **B**	98. **D**	123. **A**	148. **B**
24. **C**	49. **C**	74. **C**	99. **B**	124. **C**	149. **D**
25. **B**	50. **B**	75. **B**	100. **C**	125. **C**	150. **D**

Salesperson License Examination 2

1. D	26. C	51. B	76. C	101. A	126. B
2. B	27. C	52. C	77. A	102. D	127. C
3. C	28. C	53. B	78. D	103. D	128. B
4. D	29. A	54. A	79. B	104. A	129. B
5. D	30. B	55. A	80. A	105. A	130. A
6. A	31. B	56. B	81. B	106. D	131. C
7. B	32. A	57. B	82. B	107. B	132. A
8. C	33. A	58. C	83. D	108. D	133. C
9. B	34. B	59. C	84. A	109. D	134. D
10. C	35. A	60. D	85. B	110. A	135. A
11. A	36. A	61. C	86. A	111. A	136. C
12. A	37. B	62. C	87. A	112. D	137. C
13. A	38. C	63. C	88. C	113. C	138. B
14. C	39. B	64. C	89. C	114. D	139. C
15. B	40. B	65. B	90. A	115. B	140. B
16. B	41. B	66. B	91. D	116. B	141. A
17. A	42. A	67. A	92. A	117. B	142. A
18. D	43. D	68. A	93. D	118. C	143. A
19. C	44. D	69. A	94. A	119. D	144. B
20. A	45. C	70. D	95. D	120. A	145. D
21. C	46. C	71. B	96. A	121. B	146. D
22. B	47. C	72. D	97. C	122. B	147. B
23. B	48. D	73. C	98. C	123. C	148. A
24. B	49. C	74. B	99. B	124. B	149. B
25. D	50. C	75. C	100. B	125. B	150. C

Salesperson License Examination 3

1. B	26. D	51. A	76. C	101. C	126. D
2. D	27. D	52. D	77. D	102. B	127. B
3. D	28. D	53. A	78. C	103. D	128. A
4. B	29. C	54. A	79. D	104. C	129. C
5. D	30. D	55. C	80. C	105. D	130. B
6. B	31. B	56. D	81. A	106. A	131. C
7. B	32. A	57. D	82. C	107. C	132. B
8. B	33. D	58. B	83. B	108. A	133. C
9. C	34. B	59. A	84. B	109. C	134. D
10. D	35. B	60. D	85. C	110. B	135. A
11. C	36. B	61. A	86. D	111. D	136. D
12. C	37. C	62. C	87. B	112. C	137. C
13. D	38. B	63. C	88. C	113. D	138. B
14. B	39. A	64. A	89. D	114. A	139. C
15. C	40. C	65. C	90. D	115. C	140. B
16. A	41. C	66. C	91. C	116. B	141. A
17. B	42. B	67. C	92. C	117. B	142. C
18. B	43. A	68. A	93. A	118. D	143. D
19. C	44. D	69. C	94. A	119. A	144. B
20. A	45. D	70. C	95. C	120. C	145. B
21. D	46. D	71. B	96. D	121. A	146. B
22. A	47. B	72. B	97. C	122. B	147. D
23. C	48. C	73. B	98. B	123. D	148. A
24. A	49. D	74. B	99. A	124. B	149. A
25. C	50. A	75. D	100. B	125. D	150. B

Salesperson License Examination 4

1. C	26. A	51. C	76. A	101. A	126. C
2. B	27. C	52. B	77. A	102. A	127. D
3. A	28. B	53. B	78. C	103. C	128. B
4. D	29. C	54. A	79. B	104. A	129. B
5. C	30. A	55. B	80. C	105. B	130. C
6. A	31. C	56. C	81. D	106. C	131. C
7. B	32. B	57. D	82. D	107. D	132. B
8. A	33. B	58. C	83. C	108. B	133. D
9. C	34. A	59. D	84. A	109. C	134. D
10. A	35. D	60. B	85. C	110. B	135. A
11. A	36. D	61. B	86. C	111. C	136. C
12. B	37. D	62. C	87. D	112. D	137. B
13. A	38. D	63. C	88. C	113. D	138. A
14. B	39. B	64. D	89. D	114. D	139. C
15. A	40. B	65. A	90. B	115. D	140. A
16. C	41. A	66. B	91. D	116. B	141. C
17. B	42. C	67. A	92. A	117. D	142. B
18. C	43. C	68. D	93. C	118. B	143. B
19. C	44. B	69. B	94. A	119. B	144. A
20. D	45. D	70. A	95. C	120. D	145. C
21. C	46. A	71. B	96. B	121. D	146. A
22. B	47. D	72. C	97. B	122. C	147. D
23. C	48. D	73. A	98. B	123. A	148. B
24. D	49. A	74. C	99. C	124. B	149. D
25. C	50. B	75. C	100. B	125. C	150. A

Broker License Examination

1. D	26. C	51. A	76. B	101. C
2. A	27. A	52. A	77. D	102. B
3. C	28. D	53. A	78. B	103. C
4. C	29. D	54. C	79. C	104. C
5. D	30. B	55. C	80. C	105. B
6. C	31. A	56. B	81. C	106. B
7. B	32. B	57. D	82. B	107. B
8. B	33. C	58. B	83. C	108. D
9. C	34. B	59. D	84. D	109. C
10. C	35. A	60. D	85. A	110. C
11. B	36. D	61. D	86. C	111. A
12. A	37. A	62. A	87. C	112. B
13. B	38. B	63. B	88. A	113. B
14. D	39. D	64. B	89. B	114. A
15. C	40. C	65. C	90. A	115. C
16. C	41. B	66. D	91. B	116. C
17. A	42. C	67. B	92. B	117. B
18. A	43. A	68. C	93. C	118. B
19. C	44. D	69. B	94. C	119. B
20. D	45. C	70. D	95. B	120. A
21. A	46. C	71. D	96. A	121. C
22. C	47. C	72. A	97. C	122. D
23. B	48. A	73. A	98. D	123. C
24. B	49. D	74. C	99. A	124. D
25. C	50. B	75. D	100. A	125. D

126. **C**	141. **B**	156. **C**	171. **C**	186. **C**
127. **C**	142. **A**	157. **D**	172. **A**	187. **B**
128. **C**	143. **B**	158. **B**	173. **D**	188. **A**
129. **D**	144. **D**	159. **B**	174. **B**	189. **B**
130. **D**	145. **B**	160. **D***	175. **B**	190. **B**
131. **D**	146. **D**	161. **C**	176. **C**	191. **D**
132. **D**	147. **D**	162. **B**	177. **C**	192. **B**
133. **A**	148. **B**	163. **B**	178. **A**	193. **A**
134. **D**	149. **C**	164. **C**	179. **B**	194. **D**
135. **B**	150. **A**	165. **B**	180. **B**	195. **A**
136. **C**	151. **A**	166. **A**	181. **B**	196. **D**
137. **A**	152. **C**	167. **A**	182. **D**	197. **B**
138. **C**	153. **B**	168. **D**	183. **D**	198. **A**
139. **B**	154. **A**	169. **C**	184. **C**	199. **B**
140. **A**	155. **C**	170. **B**	185. **D**	200. **B**

Appraiser License Examination

1. **B**	21. **D**	41. **B**	61. **B**	81. **A**
2. **B**	22. **D**	42. **B**	62. **B**	82. **C**
3. **E**	23. **A**	43. **D**	63. **A**	83. **A**
4. **E**	24. **D**	44. **B**	64. **C**	84. **E**
5. **B**	25. **E**	45. **D**	65. **B**	85. **D**
6. **D**	26. **C**	46. **B**	66. **A**	86. **A**
7. **C**	27. **D**	47. **D**	67. **A**	87. **B**
8. **D**	28. **C**	48. **B**	68. **D**	88. **D**
9. **C**	29. **A**	49. **C**	69. **C**	89. **B**
10. **C**	30. **D**	50. **D**	70. **C**	90. **D**
11. **B**	31. **A**	51. **A**	71. **C**	91. **A**
12. **B**	32. **A**	52. **A**	72. **E**	92. **B**
13. **A**	33. **A**	53. **C**	73. **D**	93. **C**
14. **C**	34. **D**	54. **B**	74. **D**	94. **E**
15. **E**	35. **B**	55. **A**	75. **C**	95. **A**
16. **D**	36. **C**	56. **E**	76. **B**	96. **A**
17. **D**	37. **D**	57. **B**	77. **D**	97. **E**
18. **A**	38. **C**	58. **C**	78. **D**	98. **C**
19. **E**	39. **A**	59. **D**	79. **E**	99. **C**
20. **A**	40. **A**	60. **B**	80. **D**	100. **C**

*the correct answer to #160 is 100½ miles *west*.

Certified Residential Appraiser Examination

1. **B**	21. **B**	41. **A**	61. **E**	81. **A**
2. **A**	22. **B**	42. **B**	62. **B**	82. **B**
3. **B**	23. **A**	43. **C**	63. **C**	83. **D**
4. **D**	24. **D**	44. **C**	64. **C**	84. **D**
5. **A**	25. **B**	45. **C**	65. **D**	85. **B**
6. **B**	26. **A**	46. **E**	66. **A**	86. **C**
7. **C**	27. **C**	47. **E**	67. **D**	87. **D**
8. **C**	28. **A**	48. **E**	68. **A**	88. **C**
9. **C**	29. **A**	49. **B**	69. **A**	89. **E**
10. **B**	30. **B**	50. **A**	70. **C**	90. **D**
11. **A**	31. **D**	51. **E**	71. **B**	91. **B**
12. **C**	32. **C**	52. **A**	72. **D**	92. **D**
13. **C**	33. **E**	53. **B**	73. **E**	93. **C**
14. **D**	34. **D**	54. **C**	74. **C**	94. **A**
15. **C**	35. **D**	55. **A**	75. **C**	95. **A**
16. **A**	36. **E**	56. **C**	76. **A**	96. **B**
17. **D**	37. **B**	57. **D**	77. **D**	97. **D**
18. **D**	38. **D**	58. **B**	78. **B**	98. **D**
19. **D**	39. **C**	59. **B**	79. **B**	99. **B**
20. **E**	40. **A**	60. **A**	80. **D**	100. **D**

Certified General Appraiser Examination

1. **E**	21. **D**	41. **C**	61. **D**	81. **C**
2. **A**	22. **B**	42. **D**	62. **B**	82. **E**
3. **B**	23. **E**	43. **D**	63. **D**	83. **C**
4. **D**	24. **C**	44. **D**	64. **C**	84. **B**
5. **B**	25. **D**	45. **E**	65. **B**	85. **D**
6. **A**	26. **E**	46. **B**	66. **C**	86. **A**
7. **C**	27. **E**	47. **B**	67. **A**	87. **C**
8. **D**	28. **E**	48. **C**	68. **B**	88. **C**
9. **A**	29. **A**	49. **D**	69. **D**	89. **C**
10. **C**	30. **D**	50. **D**	70. **E**	90. **B**
11. **B**	31. **D**	51. **C**	71. **C**	91. **A**
12. **C**	32. **A**	52. **C**	72. **A**	92. **B**
13. **B**	33. **C**	53. **C**	73. **D**	93. **C**
14. **E**	34. **A**	54. **E**	74. **D**	94. **C**
15. **A**	35. **C**	55. **C**	75. **D**	95. **C**
16. **C**	36. **C**	56. **A**	76. **B**	96. **C**
17. **E**	37. **E**	57. **E**	77. **C**	97. **C**
18. **A**	38. **C**	58. **C**	78. **D**	98. **B**
19. **D**	39. **D**	59. **B**	79. **C**	99. **A**
20. **A**	40. **B**	60. **E**	80. **C**	100. **D**

Answer Explanations—Arithmetic Questions

SALESPERSON LICENSE EXAMINATION 1

36. ½ mile × ½ mile = ¼ square mile
¼ square mile × 640 acres per square mile = 160 acres

105. $3,000 monthly income × 12 months = $36,000
$36,000 annual income ÷ $450,000 cost = 8%

108. $1,400 rent per month × 12 = $16,800 per year
$16,800 ÷ .11 = $152,727

111. $250,000 building cost × 11% = $27,500 income to building
11% is derived from 8.5% interest + 2.5% depreciation
$32,800 total income less $27,500 = $5,300 income to land
$5,300 ÷ .085 = $62,353

124. $54,600 × 15% = $8,190 annual earnings
$8,190 ÷ 12 months = $682.50

133. $113,900 ÷ 1.11 = $102,613
The 1.11 represents original cost plus 11%.
As a check: $102,613 × 1.11 = $113,900

134. $75,000 × 1.11 = $83,250 after one year
$83,250 × 1.11 = $92,407 after two years
The 1.11 equals 1 plus 11%.

135. $1,200 interest for 8 months would give 1.5 × $1,200 = $1,800 for 12 months
$1,800 ÷ $20,000 = 9%

136. Financial calculator:
$1,400 × 0.85   = 1,190   *PV*
$122 payment   =   *PMT*
12 months   =   *N*
Calculate   *i*   3.34
Multiply *i* × 12 months =   40.1

137. $168,000 ÷ $2,000,000 = 8.4%

138. $2,000,000 ÷ $12,400 monthly rent = 161.29 monthly GRM
161.29 ÷ 12 months = 13.44

139. 20 units × $900 × 12 months   = $216,000
18 units × $1,050 × 12 months =   226,800
Potential gross income   = $442,800

SALESPERSON LICENSE EXAMINATION 2

6. If the tax is 1 percent of the appraised value of $250,000, then the tax is
0.01 × $250,000 = $2,500

7. This is a sidewalk question; remember not to count the corners twice. The total sidewalk area is 320 ft. × 5 ft. = 1,600 sq. ft. Since the sidewalk is 6 in., or half a foot deep, the cubic measure is 800 cu. ft. Also, 1 cu. yd. contains 27 cu. ft. (3 ft. × 3 ft. × 3 ft.), so the total number of cubic yards is
800 cu. ft. ÷ 27 cu. ft. = 29.63 cu. yd.

21. After depreciating for 8 years at 3 percent per year, the building has lost 24 percent of original value (8 × 0.03 = 0.24). This means that it is now worth the remaining 76 percent of its original value. If that sum is $19,000,000 then the original value is
$19,000,000 ÷ 0.76 = $25,000,000

22. Six percent of $200,000 is 0.06 × $200,000 = $12,000. Interest for a single month would be $12,000 ÷ 12, or $1,000. Therefore, of the $1,200 *first* payment, $1,000 goes to interest, leaving $200 to reduce the principal. This means that Flaherty will pay interest on $199,800 the second month. Figuring the same way, we get a monthly interest charge of $999 for the second month on that amount; this will leave $201 by which the second monthly payment will reduce the principal.

26. Using a financial calculator:
$N = 20$
$i = 2$
$PV = 50,000$
Solve for FV
$50,000 × (1 + .02)^{20} = $74,297$

38. Annual rent is $8,500 × 12 = $102,000. Taxes are 1 percent of the value of $470,000:
.01 × $470,000 = $4,700
Taxes, then, are 4.6% of annual rent:
$4,700 ÷ $102,000 = .046 = 4.6%

39. Total appreciation is $590,000 − $420,000 = $179,000. Total percent appreciation is
$179,000 ÷ $420,000 = 42.619%. Average over 4 years is
42.619% ÷ 4 = 10.65%

45. The 11 lots originally cost a total of 11 × $21,000 = $231,000; Perkins sells 7 lots for a total of $28,000 more than that, or $231,000 + $28,000 = $259,000. The average sale price would be
$$\$259,000 \div 7 = \$37,000$$

50. The house is a combination of two rectangles: one is 50 ft. × 24 ft. (1,200 sq. ft.) and the other, smaller part jutting out to the bottom is 24 ft. × 16 ft. (384 sq. ft.). You get the 16 ft. measurement by subtracting the 24 ft. of the short side of the house from the 40 ft. of the long side.
$$1,200 \text{ sq. ft.} + 384 \text{ sq. ft.} = 1,584 \text{ sq. ft.}$$

51. The lot is 120 ft. × 75 ft. = 9,000 sq. ft. The area taken by the house is
$$1,584 \text{ sq. ft.} \div 9,000 \text{ sq. ft.} = 0.176 = 17.6\%$$

59. This figure is a trapezoid. The top (*T*) and bottom (*B*) are of unequal lengths, while the height (*H*) does not change. The formula for this figure is
$$\text{Area} = \frac{1}{2} \times (T + B) \times H$$
The area of the lot, then, is
$$\frac{1}{2} \times (110 \text{ ft.} + 160 \text{ ft.}) \times 200 \text{ ft.}$$
$$= \frac{1}{2} \times 270 \text{ ft.} \times 200 \text{ ft.} = 27,000 \text{ sq. ft.}$$
If the lot is sold for $78,300.00, the price per square foot is
$$\$78,300.00 \div 27,000.00 = \$2.90$$

60. The salesperson's $15,120 was 60 percent of total commission, so
$$\$15,120 \div 0.6 = \$25,200 \text{ total commission}$$
Since the sale price was $315,000, the *rate* of commission was
$$\$25,200 \div \$315,000 = 0.08 = 8\%$$

65. First find the value of the house alone. Land is 15% of the total value, which means that the house is 85% of the total (100% − 15% = 85%). Then the house is worth
$$0.85 \times \$470,000 = \$399,500$$
If the house has 1,733 sq. ft., the cost per square foot is
$$\$399,500 \div 1,733 \text{ sq. ft.}$$
$$= \$230.525, \text{ which rounds to } \$230.53.$$

66. First find the amount of the total commission:
$$0.065 \times \$469,000 = \$30,485$$
If Jones can keep 42 percent of this, then the broker must get to keep the remaining 58 percent. Therefore, the broker's share is:
$$0.58 \times \$30,485 = \$17,681.30$$

67. Area = 90 ft. × 60 ft. = 5,400 sq. ft., and $6,300 × 12 mo. = $75,600 per year. Annual rent per square foot is
$$\$75,600 \div 5,400 \text{ sq. ft.} = \$14$$

70. The lot value has increased by 8000 percent. Don't forget that the lot was worth 100 percent of its value in 1963, so if it has gone up by 8000 percent, then today it is worth 8100 percent, or 81 times, its original value.
$$81 \times \$2,000 = \$162,000 \text{ lot value today}$$
Similarly, since the house is worth 400 percent more, today it is worth 500 percent of its original value:
$$5 \times \$130,000 = \$650,000 \text{ house value today}$$
House and lot together are worth $162,000 + $650,000 = $812,000 today.

74. There are two ways of answering this question.
(A) You can figure the commissions on $350,000 and $315,000 and subtract.
$$0.06 \times \$350,000 = \$21,000$$
$$0.06 \times \$315,000 = \$18,900$$
$$\$21,000 - \$18,900 = \$2,100, \text{ the correct answer.}$$
(B) You can subtract $315,000 from $350,000 and get $35,000, which is the difference in price. The broker will lose the commission on that amount, so
$$0.06 \times \$35,000 = \$2,100, \text{ also the correct answer}$$

75. One acre contains 43,560 sq. ft., so
$$1.25 \times 43,560 \text{ sq. ft.} = 54,450 \text{ sq. ft.}$$

81. The tax rate is 1.04 percent on $337,500
$$0.0104 \times \$337,500 = \$3,510$$

115. One acre contains 43,500 sq. ft. The tract in this problem is 440 ft. × 817 ft. = 359,480 sq. ft. Then
$$359,480 \div 43,560 = 8.253 \text{ acres,}$$
$$\text{or } 8.25 \text{ rounded}$$

135. Since 1 sq. yd. is 3 ft. × 3 ft. = 9 sq. ft., 825 sq. yd. is 825 × 9 = 7,425 sq. ft.; 7,425 ÷ 75 = 99 ft. None of the answers is 99 ft., but three choices are expressed in measures other than feet; 1¹⁄₁₆ mi. is 5,280 ÷ 16 = 330 ft., which is *not* 99 ft.; 32 yd. is 32 × 3 = 96 ft., *not* 99; 6 rods is 16.5 × 6 = 99 ft., the correct answer.

140. First we find the amount of the total commission. Lois's share of $5,791.50 was 45 percent of the total her firm received. Then $5,791.50 ÷ 0.45 = $12,870. Lois's firm's share, which was 60 percent of the total; $12,870 ÷ 0.6 = $21,450 total commission.

The house sold for $330,000; $21,450 ÷ $330,000 = 0.065, or 6.5%

141. Because ¼ acre contains 43,560 ÷ 4 = 10,890 sq. ft.,

$12,000 ÷ 10,890 = $1.102, or $1.10 rounded

SALESPERSON LICENSE EXAMINATION 3

91. The tax is 1.1 percent of $600,000, so .011 × $600,000 = $6,600.

92. Let the price of the first lot be a, the second b, and the third c. The total of all the lots is $90,000.
$a = 1.5b$ and $b = 2c$, or $.5b = c$. Therefore,
$$1.5b + b + .5b = \$90,000$$
$$3b = \$90,000$$
$$b = \$30,000$$
$$c = \$15,000$$
$$a = \$45,000$$

93. If Aaronson uses 10 percent of the 44 acres for parks, he will use 4.4 acres. Add that to the 6.6 other acres that must be used for streets, etc., and you get a total of 11 acres not devoted to lots. This leaves 33 acres, or 33 × 43,560 sq. ft. = 1,437,480 sq. ft. for lots. If each lot must be at least 7,500 sq. ft., then the maximum number of lots is
$$1,437,480 \text{ sq. ft.} \div 7,500 \text{ sq. ft.}$$
$$= 191.664, \text{ or } 191 \text{ full lots}$$

94. Velez paid $2,700 interest over 4 years; this comes to $675 per year ($2,700 ÷ 4). The annual interest rate was
$$\$675 \div \$7,500 = 0.09 = 9\%$$

95. If Jim made a profit of 43 percent, then he sold the land for 143 percent of its purchase price. The purchase price was
$$\$164,450 \div 1.43 = \$115,000$$

96. Anne's $3,906 was 12 percent of Connie's commission, which must have been $3,906 ÷ 0.12 = $32,550. If the sale price was $465,000, the rate of commission was
$$\$32,550 \div \$465,000 = 0.07 = 7\%$$

97. 11% of $210,000 is $23,100.
$$\$23,100 \div 12 = \$1,925 \text{ monthly}$$

98. How many years will be required for $100,000 to compound to $300,000 at 25 percent per year?
One year: 1.25 × $100,000 = $125,000
Two years: 1.25 × $125,000 = $256,250
Three years: 1.25 × $156,250 = $195,313
Four years: 1.25 × $195,313 = $244,141
Five years: 1.25 × $244,141 = $305,176
It will take about 5 years.

99. Area = 1,700 ft. × 2,100 ft. = 3,570,000 sq. ft.
3,570,000 sq. ft. ÷ 43,560 sq. ft. = 81.96 acres

100. The backyard is 100 ft. + 80 ft. + 100 ft. + 80 ft. = 360 ft. around. From this we subtract the 40 ft. taken up by the house, to get 320 lineal ft. of fence needed. If the fence is 4 ft. high, it will have 320 ft. × 4 ft. = 1,280 sq. ft. of fence fabric; 1,280 sq. ft. is 142.222 sq. yd. (1,280 ÷ 9 = 142,222).
142.222 sq. yd. × $1.80 = $256.00 total cost

117. We have to calculate the down payment, the origination fee, the discount, and the PMI fee and then add all of these to get the answer.
Down payment is 10 percent. $367,500 × 0.10 = $36,750 down payment
Origination fee, discount, and PMI fee all are calculated as part of the *loan amount* (not the sales price). The loan will equal the sales price less the down payment, or $367,500 − $36,750 = $330,750 loan amount.
Origination fee (1%) is $330,750 × 0.01 = $3,307.50
Discount (2%) is $330,750 × 0.02 = $6,615
PMI fee (½%, or 0.5%) is $330,750 × 0.005 = $1,653.75
$36,750 + $3,307.50 + $6,615 + $1,653.75 = $48,326.25

118. We have to calculate the monthly interest rate, because we are given a monthly interest payment; 9% ÷ 12 = 0.75% = 0.0075. The interest payment of $468.75 is 0.75% of the loan amount.
$$468.75 \div 0.0075 = \$62,500$$

122. We have to determine the number of cubic yards in the patio. First we determine the number of cubic feet. The patio is 60 ft. × 20 ft. = 1,200 sq. ft. It is 4 in. thick = $^{4}/_{12}$ ft. or $^{1}/_{3}$ ft. So 1,200 ÷ 3 = 400 cu. ft. is the *volume* of the patio. Since 1 cu. yd. is 3 × 3 × 3 = 27 cu. ft.,
    400 ÷ 27 = 14.82 cu. yd., or 14.8 rounded

129. The commission is 7½ percent of $318,000.
    0.075 × $318,000 = $23,850

130. The mortgage loan is at least 80 percent of the price.
    0.8 × $318,000 = $254,400

132. Cash that the buyer must provide is $318,000 − $254,400 = $63,600. Since she already has paid $6,000 in earnest money, she must pay an additional $57,600 at closing.

137. The northern boundary of SW¼, SE¼ is ¼ mi., or 1,320 ft. Area is 1,320 ft. × 66 ft. = 87,120 sq. ft.; 87,120 sq. ft. ÷ 43,560 sq. ft. = 2 acres. Since SW¼, SE¼ contains 40 acres, the part uncovered by the road is 38 acres.

149. Because 20 yd. is 20 × 3 = 60 ft., the area of the patio is 60 × 20 = 1,200 sq. ft. The patio is 6 in., or ½ ft., thick. Then 1,200 × 0.5 = 600 cu. ft., the *volume* of the patio. One cubic yard is 3 × 3 × 3 = 27 cu. ft. Therefore, Joe will need
    600 ÷ 27 = 22.22, or (rounded)
    22.2 cu. yd. of concrete

SALESPERSON LICENSE EXAMINATION 4

4. The number of square feet in 10.6 acres is
    10.6 × 43,560 sq. ft. = 461,736 sq. ft.
    If one side of the tract is 181 ft., the other must be
    461,736 sq. ft. ÷ 181 ft. = 2,551.0276
    = 2,551 ft., rounded off

5. The number of square feet in 17.1 acres is
    17.1 acres × 43,560 sq. ft. = 744,876 sq. ft.
    If 19 percent must be set aside, 81 percent is left for lots, or
    0.81 × 744,876 sq. ft. = 603,349.56 sq. ft.
    If each lot must have at least 8,000 sq. ft., the maximum number of lots is
    603,399.56 sq. ft. ÷ 8,000 sq. ft. = 75.4, or a maximum of 75 full lots

10. Area = 400 ft. × 665 ft. = 266,000 sq. ft.
    266,000 sq. ft. ÷ 43,560 sq. ft. = 6.1065 acres
    $171,100 ÷ 6.1065 acres = $28,002.85, or $28,000 per acre

11. Tax is 1.05 percent of the property value of $425,000. Tax is:
    0.0105 × $425,000 = $4,462.50

17. A building that is 40 ft. × 22 ft. is 124 ft. around (40 + 22 + 40 + 22). The total wall area is 124 ft. × 10 ft., or 1,240 sq. ft. From this we subtract the 52 sq. ft. of windows (4 sq. ft. × 13) and the 48 sq. ft. of door to get 1,140 sq. ft. of wall area needing paint. One gallon of paint covers 400 sq. ft. For one coat of paint we need 1,140 sq. ft. ÷ 400 sq. ft. = 2.85 gal., so two coats will require twice as much, or 5.7 gal.

18. Annual interest = $330 per quarter × 4 = $1,320. The interest rate is
    $1,320 ÷ $12,000 = 0.11 = 11%

24. Ms. Levy will pay $500 less rent per month if she pays the utility bills herself. Average bills are $4,800 per year, which is $400 per month ($4,800 ÷ 12). Levy thinks she can reduce this by 35 percent, which means that she expects to pay only 65 percent of the $400 monthly average, or 0.65 × $400 = $260. She saves $500 on rent and expects to pay $260 of that for utilities, so she expects to save $240 per month.

25. Total commissions brought in by O'Hara = 7% × $1,100,000 = $77,000. He gets 50 percent of the first $20,000 (or $10,000) *plus* 60 percent of the rest. In his case, the rest is $57,000.
    0.6 × $57,000 = $34,200
    To this we add his $10,000 share of the first $20,000 to get a total income for him of $44,200.

42. If Jackson paid a 6½ percent commission, then the $336,132.50 he has left represents the remaining 93½ percent of the sale price. The sale price then must be
    $336,132.50 ÷ 0.935 = $359,500

48. Ms. Anderson paid out a total of 12 percent of the selling price in fees, so her $176,000 is the 88 percent of the sale price that she has left. Therefore, the sale price was
    $176,000 ÷ 0.88 = $200,000

49. The 9-in.-thick walls are ¾ ft. thick. Therefore, the interior dimensions of the floor are 50½ ft. × 34½ ft. (remember, the walls are at *both* ends):

    50.5 × 34.5 = 1,742.25 sq. ft. gross,

    from which we subtract the area taken up by the pillars. They are each ½ ft. × ½ ft., or ¼ sq. ft. Their total area is

    13 × ¼ sq. ft. = 3¼ sq. ft.

    Subtracting this amount from 1,742.25 leaves a net of 1,739 sq. ft.

62. The lots contain 10,500 sq. ft. each and must each have 1,380 sq. ft. additional amenity. Therefore, Smith will need a minimum of 11,880 sq. ft. for each lot (10,500 sq. ft. + 1,380 sq. ft.). Since he wants 55 lots, he will need at least 55 × 11,880 sq. ft. = 653,400 sq. ft.; 653,400 sq. ft. ÷ 43,560 sq. ft. = 15 acres exactly.

70. Interior gross dimensions are 41 ft. × 27 ft. = 1,107 sq. ft. (Remember to subtract 6 in. of outside wall from each end.) Interior wall area is ⅓ ft. × 135 ft. = 45 sq. ft. Each bathroom is 54 sq. ft. The kitchen is 144 sq. ft. This is a total area of 297 sq. ft. *not* to be carpeted, leaving 810 sq. ft. because 1 sq. yd. contains 9 sq. ft. (3 ft. × 3 ft.), the total number of square yards to be carpeted is 810 sq. ft. ÷ 9 sq. ft. = 90 sq. yd. At $27.90 per square yard, the total cost is $2,511 (90 sq. yd. × $27.90).

71. To determine how much Ms. Farrell still needs, we subtract from the $550,000 purchase price the $15,000 earnest money payment and the 75 percent loan. The loan is 75 percent of $550,000, or $550,000 × 0.75 = $412,500. $550,000 less $15,000 is $535,000. Subtracting the $412,500 loan leaves $122,500 still needed.

74. A lot 100 ft. × 100 ft. contains 100 × 100 = 10,000 sq. ft. The 3-acre plot contains 43,560 × 3 = 130,680 sq. ft.; 130,680 ÷ 10,000 = 13.068, or 13 full lots.

75. The width of the lot is 6,336 ÷ 96 = 66 ft. At $225 a front ft. the lot would sell for 66 × $225 = $14,850.

93. The commission is 7½ percent of $337,500.

    0.075 × $337,500 = $25,312.50

99. The man owns ¼ of the total, and he buys the rest, which is ¾ of the total, or 3 times more (300%) than he already had.

100. S½, NW¼, NE¼ contains 20 acres. A section contains 640 acres. Therefore, Ms. Smith has bought

    20 ÷ 640 = 0.03125 = 3.125% = 3⅛%

117. First we find the amount of the total commission. Salesperson's share of $2,544 was 60 percent of the total the firm received. $2,544 ÷ 0.6 = $4,240 for the firm's share, which was 50 percent of the total. $4,240 ÷ 0.5 = $8,480 total commission.

    Because the house sold for $106,000,

    $8,480 ÷ $106,000 = 0.08, or 8%

122. We have to determine the number of front feet in the lot, and multiply that number by $980 to determine the price the lot sold for.

    6,468 ÷ 132 = 49 front ft. 49 × 980 = $48,020, or $48,000 rounded

131. $188,000 ÷ 2.6 acres = $72,307.69 per acre

    $72,307.69 ÷ 43,560 = $1.65997, or $1.66 rounded

BROKER LICENSE EXAMINATION

2. The tax is 1.2 percent of $350,000:

    0.012 × $350,000 = $4,200

9. We must subtract the broker's commission and the loan discount from the $500,000 sale price, since seller (Juan) must pay both.

    6% of $500,000 is $500,000 × 0.06 = $30,000 commission.

    Loan is 80 percent of $500,000. $500,000 × 0.80 = $400,000 loan. Discount is 3 points, or 3 percent of $400,000. $400,000 × 0.03 = $12,000.

    Total payments by Juan are $30,000 commission + $12,000 loan discount, or $42,000.

    $500,000 − $42,000 = $458,000

10. In question 9, we found the loan discount to be $12,000.

11. We figure the *effective* rate to the lender of a mortgage loan by adding ⅛ *of 1 percent* to the *contract* interest rate for each *one* point of discount paid on the loan. The contract interest rate is 7 percent; there are 3 points discount. Thus, the effective rate is 7% + ⅜%, or 7⅜% (7.375%).

14. Cash-on-cash ratio is the annual cash return received, divided by the cash spent (original equity) to acquire the investment.
$$\$16,900 \div \$130,000 = 0.13$$

15. One square mile contains 640 acres.
$$200 \div 640 = 0.3125, \text{ or } 31.25\%$$

18. The sale occurs 14 days (July 15 − July 1 = 14 days) after the fiscal year begins, so seller owes buyer 14 days worth of taxes. The other information in the problem is irrelevant.

24. In this problem we have to determine how long the buyer owned the property. We know he owned it at the end of the year. We calculate time from his tax payment, and then figure backwards from December 31 to determine the date of settlement. Remember: the settlement date is considered a day that the *seller* owned the property. The total tax bill is $763.20; $763.20 ÷ 12 = $63.60 per month; $63.60 ÷ 30 = $2.12 per day.
First we determine how many *whole months* the buyer owned the property by dividing the buyer's share of taxes ($250.16) by the monthly tax share of $63.60; $250.16 ÷ $63.60 = 3.93333. Thus, the buyer owned the property for 3 whole months (October, November, and December) and then some. Now we know that the settlement occurred sometime in September.
We subtract the 3 whole months worth of taxes from the buyer's share; 3 × $63.60 = $190.80; $250.16 − $190.80 = $59.36. The buyer also owned the property for $59.35 "worth" of September.
$59.36 ÷ $2.12 = 28 of September's 30 days. Thus, the closing had to be on 30 − 28 = 2 of September.

25. Cash-on-cash ratio is annual cash return received, divided by the cash spent (original equity) to acquire the investment.
$$\$8,360 \div \$76,000 = 0.11$$

26. Because 1 sq. mi. contains 640 acres,
$$96 \div 640 = 0.15, \text{ or } 15\%$$

46. We have to calculate the down payment, the origination fee, the discount, and the PMI fee and then add all of these to determine the answer.
Down payment is 15 percent; $387,500 × 0.15 = $58,125 down payment
Origination fee, discount, and PMI fee all are calculated as part of the *loan amount* (not the sales price). The loan will be the sales price less the down payment, or $387,500 − $58,125 = $329,175 loan amount
Origination fee (0.75%) is $329,375 × 0.0075 = $2,470.31
Discount (2.25%) is $329,375 × 0.0225 = $7,410.94
PMI fee (0.5%, or ½%) is $329,375 × 0.005 = $1,646.88
$$\$58,125 + \$2,470.31 + \$7,410.94 + \$1,646.88 = \$69,653.13$$

55. We have to calculate the monthly interest rate, because we are given a monthly interest payment; 6% ÷ 12 = 0.5% = 0.005. The interest payment of $456.41 is 0.5 percent of the loan amount.
$$456.41 \div 0.005 = \$91,282 \text{ rounded}$$

66. We know the down payment and must calculate the origination fee, the discount, and the PMI fee and then add all of these to determine the answer.
Origination fee, discount, and PMI fee all are calculated as part of the *loan amount* (not the sales price). The loan will be the sales price less the down payment, or $334,500 − $52,750 = $282,250 loan amount
Origination fee (1.5%) is $282,750 × 0.015 = $4,241.25
Discount (2%) is $282,750 × 0.02 = $5,655
PMI fee (0.75%) is $282,750 × 0.0075 = $2,120.63
$$\$51,750 + \$4,241.25 + \$5,655 + \$2,120.63 = \$63,766.88$$

67. We have to calculate the monthly interest rate, because we are given a monthly interest payment; 10.5% ÷ 12 = 0.875% = 0.00875. The interest payment of $496.56 is 0.875% of the loan amount.
$$496.56 \div 0.00875 = \$56,750 \text{ rounded}$$

71, 72. See worksheet on page 512.

73. The annual property taxes are $2,336.40. The closing date is September 18, and the seller has already paid the full year's tax bill. The buyer will own the house for the remaining 12 days of September and the three months of October, November, and December.
$2,336.40 ÷ 12 = $194.70 taxes per month
$194.70 ÷ 30 = $6.49 taxes per day
3 months @ $194.70 = $584.10
12 days @ $6.49 =   77.88
Total tax proration $661.98, paid by buyer to seller

74. The mortgage insurance premium is 2½ percent of the mortgage amount. The mortgage is 80 percent of $212,000.00
$$0.8 \times \$212,000 = \$169,600$$
$$0.025 \times \$169,600 = \$4,240$$

75. The title insurance premium is 0.425 percent of the sale price.
$$0.00425 \times \$106,000 = \$901$$

76. The buyer's loan will be $0.8 \times \$212,000 = \$169,600$.

77. The 3-year premium is $888.75, which is $296.25 annually, $24.6875 monthly, and $0.8229 daily. The policy expires on October 21, 1997, leaving the buyer with 1 year, 1 month, and 3 days of insurance.

1 year	$296.25
1 month	24.6875
3 days @ 0.8229	2.4687
Total prorated amount paid by buyer to seller	$323.41

Neither answer is correct.

87. Because 59 ft. 6 in. = 59.5 ft. and 535.5 sq. yd. = $535.5 \times 9 = 4,819.5$ sq. ft., we have $4,819.5 \div 59.5 = 81$ ft. of depth. This answer is not one of the choices. However, three of the answers are expressed in measures other than feet: 0.03 mi. is $0.03 \times 5,280 = 158.4$ ft.; 5.33 rods is $5.33 \times 16.5 = 87.95$ ft. Both of these choices are incorrect. However, 27 yd. is $27 \times 3 = 81$ ft., which is correct.

90. The commission was 7 percent; $410,000 \times 0.07 = \$28,700$ total commission. Mack's 48 percent share is $28,700 \times 0.48 = \$13,776$; 55 percent of that was paid to the salesperson, leaving $1 - 0.55 = 0.45$ or 45 percent for Mack.
$$\$13,776 \times 0.45 = \$6,199.20$$

91. Because 1.6 acres is $1.6 \times 43,560 = 69,696$ sq. ft.,
$$\$25,100 \div 69,696 = 0.3601,$$
$$\text{or } \$0.36 \text{ rounded}$$

107. We have to determine how long the seller owned the property, and then figure from February 1 (the day the insurance policy was purchased) to determine the date of settlement. Remember, the settlement date is considered a day that the *seller* owned the property.
The total bill was $324; $324 \div 12 = \$27$ per month, and $27 \div 30 = \$0.90$ per day
First we determine how many *whole months* of the policy year the buyer owned the prop-

erty. We divide her share of the policy cost ($63) by the monthly share of $27; $63 \div \$27 = 2.33333$. Thus, the buyer owned the property for 2 whole months and part (0.3333) of a third; $0.3333 \times 30 = 10$ more days. The policy expires January 31, so the buyer's 2 full months are December and January. Since she had already owned the policy for 10 days at the beginning of December, the settlement must have occurred in November. $30 - 10 = 20$ of November.

114. Market value is $286,000 and tax is 0.97 percent:
$$.0097 \times \$286,000 = \$2,774.20$$

115. The discount is based on the *loan amount*. The loan is 90 percent of $400,000; $0.9 \times \$400,000 = \$360,000$. The discount is 2.5 points, or 2.5%.
$$0.025 \times \$360,000 = \$9,000.$$

116. For every 1 point discount paid, we increase the *effective* rate of return to the lender by ⅛ percent, or 0.125 percent. The contract interest rate is 7.5 percent, and there are 2.5 points; $2.5 \times 0.1255 = 0.3125$ percent, which we add to the contract rate.
$$7.5\% + 0.3125\% = 7.8125\%$$

127. Cash-on-cash ratio is the annual cash return received, divided by the cash spent (original equity) to acquire the investment.
$$\$32,300 \div \$222,750 = 0.145 \text{ rounded}$$

128. There are $1,085 \times 900 = 976,500$ sq. ft. in the lot. Because 1 sq. mi. contains $5,280 \times 5,280 = 27,878,400$ sq. ft.,
$$976,500 \div 27,878,400 = 0.035,$$
$$\text{or } 3.5\% \text{ rounded}$$

134. The area is $1,077 \times 607 = 653,739$ sq. ft., and $653,739 \times 43,560 = 15.0078$ acres. The only acceptable answer, therefore, is "more than 15."

141. This problem isn't difficult, but it requires several calculations. It is wise to leave time-consuming problems such as this one until after you have answered the simpler questions.
We have to calculate the cost of the house, basement, and garage and then add them together.
House: First 1,600 sq. ft. cost $101.10 \times 1,600 = \$161,760$. There are $2,100 - 1,600 = 500$ additional sq. ft. to pay for. $500 \times \$42.25 = \$21,225$ additional. $161,760 + \$21,225 = \$182,985$ for the house.

Basement: Note that this as a two-story house. Therefore, the basement will be only *half* the area of the house, or $2,100 \div 2 = 1,050$ sq. ft.; $1,050 \times \$22.50 = \$23,625$ for the basement.
Garage: $420 \times \$29.20 = \$12,264$
$$\$182,985 + \$23,625 + \$12,264$$
$$= \$218,894, \text{ or } \$219,000 \text{ to the nearest } \$1,000$$

145. First we calculate the cost of the lots. We know A costs $11,000. B costs 2.5 times that amount; $2.5 \times \$11,000 = \$27,500$. C costs half the price of B; $\$27,500 \div 2 = \$13,750$. So $\$11,000 + \$27,500 + \$13,750 = \$52,250$, the cost of all three lots.
A and B were sold for 25 percent more than this amount, or 125 percent of this amount, or $1.25 \times \$52,250 = \$65,312.50$. C was sold for twice its cost; $\$13,750 \times 2 = \$27,500$. Thus, $\$65,312.50 + \$27,500 = \$92,812.50$, the amount all three lots sold for. $\$92,812.50 - \$52,250 = \$40,562.50$. However, this is not one of the answer choices. Therefore, "none of the above" is correct.

178. Buyer will own property for 15 days (November 16–30), or half of the month, so buyer gets half the rent:
$$0.5 \times \$1,200 = \$600$$

APPRAISER LICENSE EXAMINATION

3. $1.07 \times 1.07 = 1.1449$, which is 14.49 percent increase. Then
$$0.1449 \times \$240,000 = \$34,776$$

65. The expenses don't matter, since GRM applies to gross rental, without regard for expenses.
Therefore, value = rent × GRM, or
$$\$750 \times 100 = \$75,000$$

75. Value = NOI / rate:
$$\$11,000 \div 0.11 = \$100,000$$

90. Monthly rents: $40 \times \$950 = \$38,000$; $60 \times \$1,150 = \$69,000$; $\$69,000 + \$38,000 = \$107,000$.
Potential annual gross income = $\$107,000 \times 12 = \$1,284,000$

91. Effective gross income is potential gross income plus miscellaneous income, less vacancy.
Vacancy is 5 percent of potential gross rent:
$$\$1,284,000 \times 0.05 = \$64,200 \text{ vacancy}$$
$$\$1,284,000 + \$5,000 - \$64,200$$
$$= \$1,224,800$$

92. NOI is effective gross less operating expenses:
NOI = $\$1,224,800 - \$400,000 = \$824,800$

93. Before-tax cash flow is NOI less mortgage servicing:
$$\$824,800 - \$630,000 = \$194,800$$

CERTIFIED RESIDENTIAL APPRAISER EXAMINATION

51. Comp 1 is 100 sq. ft. larger than subject, so adjustment will be negative. −100 sq. ft. at $90:
$$100 \times \$90 = -\$9,000$$

52. Comp 2 is 50 sq. ft. smaller than subject, so adjustment will be positive: +50 sq. ft. at $90:
$$+50 \times \$90 = +\$4,500$$

53. Comp 1 is one condition grade worse than subject, so adjustment (+5 percent) will be positive:
$$\$270,000 \times +0.05 = +\$13,500$$

54. Comp 2 is one condition grade better than subject, so adjustment (−5 percent) will be negative:
$$\$265,500 \times -0.05 = -\$13,275$$

55. Comp 2 and subject have same garage situation, so no adjustment is made.

56. Comp 3 has 2-car garage, subject has 1-car, so adjustment is negative: −$4,500.

62. Subject is 60 feet wide, front footage comps are $120 to $150 per front foot. $\$120 \times 60 = \$7,200$.
$$\$150 \times 60 = \$9,000, \text{ so } \$7,200 \text{ to } \$9,000$$
$$\text{is indicated range.}$$

73. Exterior paint ($750) and water heater ($250) are the items of curable physical deterioration; they add up to $1,000. No answer of $1,000 is given, so the correct answer is "None of the above."

74. Functional obsolescence items are one bath ($4,000) and poor floor plan ($2,500); these add up to $6,500.

75. Location next to convenience store ($1,200) is the only environmental item given.

78. 20 percent of the land can't be built upon which leaves 80 percent that can:
$$0.8 \times 40 = 32 \text{ developable acres.}$$
Zoning allows 4 lots per developable acre:
$$4 \times 32 = 128 \text{ lots allowed}$$

79. At an average price of $18,000, the 128 lots will gross $2,304,000.
$$\$18,000 \times 128 = \$2,304,000$$

80. Cost of installing 2,000 feet of streets, etc., at $80 per foot:
$$2,000 \times \$80 = \$160,000$$

81. These expenses amount to 40 percent of total sales; $2,304,000 \times 0.4 = $921,600

86. Monthly rents: $50 \times \$550 = \$27,500$; $150 \times \$675 = \$101,250$; $\$27,500 + \$101,250 = \$128,750$
Potential annual gross income = $128,750 \times 12 = $1,545,000

87. Effective gross income is potential gross income plus miscellaneous income, less vacancy.
Vacancy is 7 percent of potential gross rent: $\$1,545,000 \times 0.07 = \$108,150$ vacancy
$$\$1,545,000 + \$2,000 - \$108,150$$
$$= \$1,438,850$$

88. NOI is effective gross less operating expenses, which are 40 percent of effective gross, so NOI is 60 percent of effective gross:
$$\text{NOI} = \$1,438,850 \times 0.6 = \$863,310$$

89. Operating expenses are 40 percent of NOI:
$$\$1,438,850 \times 0.4 = \$575,540$$

94. $(1.15)^5 \times \$500,000 = 1.15 \times 1.15 \times 1.15 \times 1.15 \times 1.15 \times \$500,000 = 2.011 \times \$500,000$, or $1,000,000 rounded.

95. Expected sale price in 4 years: 100 acres $\times$ $10,000/acre = $1,000,000. Today's value would be $1,000,000/(1.15)^4$; $(1.15)^4 = 1.15 \times 1.15 \times 1.15 \times 1.15 = 1.749$.
$$\$1,000,000 \div 1.749 = \$571,753, \text{ or}$$
$$\$572,000 \text{ rounded}$$

99. Building has depreciated 2 percent a year for 10 years, or 20 percent total; thus it's worth 80 percent of reproduction cost: $92,000 \times 0.8 = $73,600. Add $128,000 land value to get answer of $201,600.

CERTIFIED GENERAL APPRAISER EXAMINATION

3. Cash return per month: $4,000 - $1,250 = $2,750; $2,750 \times 12 = $33,000 per year.
$$\$33,000 \div 0.12 = \$275,000$$

5. Monthly rents: $80 \times \$475 = \$38,000$; $120 \times \$575 = \$69,000$; $\$38,000 + \$69,000 = \$107,000$.
Potential annual gross income =
$$\$107,000 \times 12 = \$1,284,000$$

6. Effective gross income is potential gross income plus miscellaneous income, less vacancy.
Vacancy is 5 percent of potential gross rent: $\$1,284,000 \times 0.05 = \$64,200$ vacancy
$$\$1,284,000 + \$5,000 - \$64,200$$
$$= \$1,224,800$$

7. NOI is effective gross less operating expenses:
$$\text{NOI} = \$1,224,800 - \$400,000 = \$824,800$$

8. Before-tax cash flow is NOI less mortgage servicing:
$$\$824,800 - \$630,000 = \$194,800$$

10. Since it is assumed that the property will keep its value of $200,000 for the entire 20 years, use simple capitalization. Annual rent is $24,000; value is $200,000:
$$\$24,000 \div \$200,000 = 0.12, \text{ or } 12\%$$

12. Recapture rate is $100\%/25$ years = 4% per year.

16. Property is worth $1,000,000. A 70 percent loan is $700,000, which leaves $300,000 equity. A 10 percent constant applied to the loan is $700,000 \times 0.10 = $70,000. A 15 percent cash-on-cash return to the $300,000 equity is $300,000 \times 0.15 = $45,000. The mortgage constant payment + cash on cash return = NOI, so
$$\text{NOI} = \$70,000 + \$45,000 = \$115,000$$

18. Monthly NOI is $6,000 - $1,250 = $4,750. Annual NOI is $4,750 \times 12 = $57,000.
$$\$57,000 \div 0.12 = \$475,000 \text{ value}$$

45. Value = rent $\times$ GRM:
$1,150 \times 127 = $146,050, or $146,000 rounded

47. When using GRM, you ignore expenses, so don't pay any attention to the $125 monthly expenses. Just use the monthly rent of $1,500. Value = rent $\times$ GRM:
$$\$1,500 \times 110 = \$165,000$$

48. The residence is now worth 160 percent of what is was worth when it was built:
$$\$216,000 \div 1.6 = \$135,000$$

51. To find the mean, add the seven GRMs, divide by 7:
$$(125 + 125 + 127 + 127 + 127 + 128 + 130) \div 7 = 889 \div 7 = 127$$

52. The GRMs are already arranged in order; the median is the one in the middle (the fourth): 127.

53. The mode is the value that appears most often. Since 127 appears three times (more than any other GRM value), the mode is 127.

80. Purchase price will be $\$115,000/(1.12)^4$. $(1.12)^4 = 1.12 \times 1.12 \times 1.12 \times 1.12 = 1.574$.
$$\$115,000 \div 1.574 = \$73,084$$
$$= \$73,000 \text{ rounded}$$

81. Effective depreciation is figured for 20 out of a total of 50 years, or $20/50 = 0.4 = 40\%$

83. You are given more information than you need. Improvement ratio is value of improvements/total property value. Since total value is $2,000,000 and land is worth $500,000, improvements are worth $1,500,000.
$$\$1,500,000 \div \$2,000,000 = 0.75 = 75\%$$

88. Loan is 75 percent of value: $\$1,000,000 \times 0.75 = \$750,000$. 12 percent constant: $\$750,000 \times 0.12 = \$90,000$. There is $250,000 of equity, for which 15 percent cash-on-cash is desired: $\$250,000 \times 0.15 = \$37,500$.
NOI will have to be mortgage payment + desired cash return:
$$\$37,500 + \$90,000 = \$127,500$$

89. Recapture rate is 100% / 25 years = 4% per year.

92. Monthly rents: $25 \times \$550 = \$13,750$; $75 \times \$675 = \$50,625$; $\$13,750 + \$50,625 = \$64,375$.
Potential annual gross income =
$$\$64,375 \times 12 = \$772,500$$

93. Effective gross income is potential gross income plus miscellaneous income, less vacancy.
Vacancy is 7 percent of potential gross rent: $\$772,500 \times 0.07 = \$54,075$ vacancy
$$\$772,500 + \$1,000 - \$54,075 = \$719,425$$

94. NOI is effective gross less operating expenses, which are 40 percent of effective gross.
NOI is 60 percent of effective gross:
$$\$719,425 \times 0.6 = \$431,655$$

95. Operating expenses are 40 percent of NOI:
$$\$719,425 \times 0.4 = \$287,770$$

97. Land value is $100,000; 10 percent of that ($10,000) is return to land, so $\$90,000 - \$10,000 = \$80,000$ is the return to the building. This implies a value of a little less than $800,000 for the income over 30 years ($80,000/0.1), *plus* the present value of a reversion of about $400,000, which wouldn't be very much. The range $750,000 to $1,000,000 clearly is correct.

99. Value will be $(1.15)^5 \times \$100,000 = 2.011 \times \$100,000 = \$201,100 = \$200,000$ rounded.

SALESPERSON LICENSE EXAMINATIONS

NAME_____

LAST   FIRST   MIDDLE

SESSION   AM ☐   PM ☐

SOC. SEC. # _____ / _____ / _____

Enter your IDENT. NUMBER ↓

EXAM CODE # _____

DATE_____

PLACE OF EXAM_____ SALESMAN ☐ BROKER ☐ _____

BOOK# _____

TITLE OF EXAM_____

IMPORTANT: IN MARKING YOUR ANSWERS FILL IN ANSWER BOX COMPLETELY

1 :A: :B: :C: :D:	4 :A: :B: :C: :D:	8 :A: :B: :C: :D:	12 :A: :B: :C: :D:
2 :A: :B: :C: :D:	5 :A: :B: :C: :D:	9 :A: :B: :C: :D:	13 :A: :B: :C: :D:
3 :A: :B: :C: :D:	6 :A: :B: :C: :D:	10 :A: :B: :C: :D:	14 :A: :B: :C: :D:
	7 :A: :B: :C: :D:	11 :A: :B: :C: :D:	15 :A: :B: :C: :D:
16 :A: :B: :C: :D:	19 :A: :B: :C: :D:	23 :A: :B: :C: :D:	27 :A: :B: :C: :D:
17 :A: :B: :C: :D:	20 :A: :B: :C: :D:	24 :A: :B: :C: :D:	28 :A: :B: :C: :D:
18 :A: :B: :C: :D:	21 :A: :B: :C: :D:	25 :A: :B: :C: :D:	29 :A: :B: :C: :D:
	22 :A: :B: :C: :D:	26 :A: :B: :C: :D:	30 :A: :B: :C: :D:
31 :A: :B: :C: :D:	34 :A: :B: :C: :D:	38 :A: :B: :C: :D:	42 :A: :B: :C: :D:
32 :A: :B: :C: :D:	35 :A: :B: :C: :D:	39 :A: :B: :C: :D:	43 :A: :B: :C: :D:
33 :A: :B: :C: :D:	36 :A: :B: :C: :D:	40 :A: :B: :C: :D:	44 :A: :B: :C: :D:
	37 :A: :B: :C: :D:	41 :A: :B: :C: :D:	45 :A: :B: :C: :D:
46 :A: :B: :C: :D:	49 :A: :B: :C: :D:	53 :A: :B: :C: :D:	57 :A: :B: :C: :D:
47 :A: :B: :C: :D:	50 :A: :B: :C: :D:	54 :A: :B: :C: :D:	58 :A: :B: :C: :D:
48 :A: :B: :C: :D:	51 :A: :B: :C: :D:	55 :A: :B: :C: :D:	59 :A: :B: :C: :D:
	52 :A: :B: :C: :D:	56 :A: :B: :C: :D:	60 :A: :B: :C: :D:
61 :A: :B: :C: :D:	64 :A: :B: :C: :D:	68 :A: :B: :C: :D:	72 :A: :B: :C: :D:
62 :A: :B: :C: :D:	65 :A: :B: :C: :D:	69 :A: :B: :C: :D:	73 :A: :B: :C: :D:
63 :A: :B: :C: :D:	66 :A: :B: :C: :D:	70 :A: :B: :C: :D:	74 :A: :B: :C: :D:
	67 :A: :B: :C: :D:	71 :A: :B: :C: :D:	75 :A: :B: :C: :D:
76 :A: :B: :C: :D:	79 :A: :B: :C: :D:	83 :A: :B: :C: :D:	87 :A: :B: :C: :D:
77 :A: :B: :C: :D:	80 :A: :B: :C: :D:	84 :A: :B: :C: :D:	88 :A: :B: :C: :D:
78 :A: :B: :C: :D:	81 :A: :B: :C: :D:	85 :A: :B: :C: :D:	89 :A: :B: :C: :D:
	82 :A: :B: :C: :D:	86 :A: :B: :C: :D:	90 :A: :B: :C: :D:
91 :A: :B: :C: :D:	94 :A: :B: :C: :D:	98 :A: :B: :C: :D:	
92 :A: :B: :C: :D:	95 :A: :B: :C: :D:	99 :A: :B: :C: :D:	
93 :A: :B: :C: :D:	96 :A: :B: :C: :D:	100 :A: :B: :C: :D:	
	97 :A: :B: :C: :D:		
101 :A: :B: :C: :D:	104 :A: :B: :C: :D:	108 :A: :B: :C: :D:	112 :A: :B: :C: :D:
102 :A: :B: :C: :D:	105 :A: :B: :C: :D:	109 :A: :B: :C: :D:	113 :A: :B: :C: :D:
103 :A: :B: :C: :D:	106 :A: :B: :C: :D:	110 :A: :B: :C: :D:	114 :A: :B: :C: :D:
	107 :A: :B: :C: :D:	111 :A: :B: :C: :D:	115 :A: :B: :C: :D:
116 :A: :B: :C: :D:	119 :A: :B: :C: :D:	123 :A: :B: :C: :D:	127 :A: :B: :C: :D:
117 :A: :B: :C: :D:	120 :A: :B: :C: :D:	124 :A: :B: :C: :D:	128 :A: :B: :C: :D:
118 :A: :B: :C: :D:	121 :A: :B: :C: :D:	125 :A: :B: :C: :D:	129 :A: :B: :C: :D:
	122 :A: :B: :C: :D:	126 :A: :B: :C: :D:	130 :A: :B: :C: :D:
131 :A: :B: :C: :D:	134 :A: :B: :C: :D:	138 :A: :B: :C: :D:	142 :A: :B: :C: :D:
132 :A: :B: :C: :D:	135 :A: :B: :C: :D:	139 :A: :B: :C: :D:	143 :A: :B: :C: :D:
133 :A: :B: :C: :D:	136 :A: :B: :C: :D:	140 :A: :B: :C: :D:	144 :A: :B: :C: :D:
	137 :A: :B: :C: :D:	141 :A: :B: :C: :D:	145 :A: :B: :C: :D:
146 :A: :B: :C: :D:	149 :A: :B: :C: :D:		
147 :A: :B: :C: :D:	150 :A: :B: :C: :D:		
148 :A: :B: :C: :D:			

Photocopy this answers sheet for Salesperson License Examinations 1, 2, 3, and 4.

BROKER LICENSE EXAMINATION, PARTS 1 AND 2

1 :A: :B: :C: :D:	4 :A: :B: :C: :D:	8 :A: :B: :C: :D:	12 :A: :B: :C: :D:
2 :A: :B: :C: :D:	5 :A: :B: :C: :D:	9 :A: :B: :C: :D:	13 :A: :B: :C: :D:
3 :A: :B: :C: :D:	6 :A: :B: :C: :D:	10 :A: :B: :C: :D:	14 :A: :B: :C: :D:
	7 :A: :B: :C: :D:	11 :A: :B: :C: :D:	15 :A: :B: :C: :D:
16 :A: :B: :C: :D:	19 :A: :B: :C: :D:	23 :A: :B: :C: :D:	27 :A: :B: :C: :D:
17 :A: :B: :C: :D:	20 :A: :B: :C: :D:	24 :A: :B: :C: :D:	28 :A: :B: :C: :D:
18 :A: :B: :C: :D:	21 :A: :B: :C: :D:	25 :A: :B: :C: :D:	29 :A: :B: :C: :D:
	22 :A: :B: :C: :D:	26 :A: :B: :C: :D:	30 :A: :B: :C: :D:
31 :A: :B: :C: :D:	34 :A: :B: :C: :D:	38 :A: :B: :C: :D:	42 :A: :B: :C: :D:
32 :A: :B: :C: :D:	35 :A: :B: :C: :D:	39 :A: :B: :C: :D:	43 :A: :B: :C: :D:
33 :A: :B: :C: :D:	36 :A: :B: :C: :D:	40 :A: :B: :C: :D:	44 :A: :B: :C: :D:
	37 :A: :B: :C: :D:	41 :A: :B: :C: :D:	45 :A: :B: :C: :D:
46 :A: :B: :C: :D:	49 :A: :B: :C: :D:	53 :A: :B: :C: :D:	57 :A: :B: :C: :D:
47 :A: :B: :C: :D:	50 :A: :B: :C: :D:	54 :A: :B: :C: :D:	58 :A: :B: :C: :D:
48 :A: :B: :C: :D:	51 :A: :B: :C: :D:	55 :A: :B: :C: :D:	59 :A: :B: :C: :D:
	52 :A: :B: :C: :D:	56 :A: :B: :C: :D:	60 :A: :B: :C: :D:
61 :A: :B: :C: :D:	64 :A: :B: :C: :D:	68 :A: :B: :C: :D:	72 :A: :B: :C: :D:
62 :A: :B: :C: :D:	65 :A: :B: :C: :D:	69 :A: :B: :C: :D:	73 :A: :B: :C: :D:
63 :A: :B: :C: :D:	66 :A: :B: :C: :D:	70 :A: :B: :C: :D:	74 :A: :B: :C: :D:
	67 :A: :B: :C: :D:	71 :A: :B: :C: :D:	75 :A: :B: :C: :D:
76 :A: :B: :C: :D:	79 :A: :B: :C: :D:	83 :A: :B: :C: :D:	87 :A: :B: :C: :D:
77 :A: :B: :C: :D:	80 :A: :B: :C: :D:	84 :A: :B: :C: :D:	88 :A: :B: :C: :D:
78 :A: :B: :C: :D:	81 :A: :B: :C: :D:	85 :A: :B: :C: :D:	89 :A: :B: :C: :D:
	82 :A: :B: :C: :D:	86 :A: :B: :C: :D:	90 :A: :B: :C: :D:
91 :A: :B: :C: :D:	94 :A: :B: :C: :D:	98 :A: :B: :C: :D:	
92 :A: :B: :C: :D:	95 :A: :B: :C: :D:	99 :A: :B: :C: :D:	
	96 :A: :B: :C: :D:	100 :A: :B: :C: :D:	
101 :A: :B: :C: :D:	104 :A: :B: :C: :D:	108 :A: :B: :C: :D:	112 :A: :B: :C: :D:
102 :A: :B: :C: :D:	105 :A: :B: :C: :D:	109 :A: :B: :C: :D:	113 :A: :B: :C: :D:
103 :A: :B: :C: :D:	106 :A: :B: :C: :D:	110 :A: :B: :C: :D:	114 :A: :B: :C: :D:
	107 :A: :B: :C: :D:	111 :A: :B: :C: :D:	115 :A: :B: :C: :D:
116 :A: :B: :C: :D:	119 :A: :B: :C: :D:	123 :A: :B: :C: :D:	127 :A: :B: :C: :D:
117 :A: :B: :C: :D:	120 :A: :B: :C: :D:	124 :A: :B: :C: :D:	128 :A: :B: :C: :D:
118 :A: :B: :C: :D:	121 :A: :B: :C: :D:	125 :A: :B: :C: :D:	129 :A: :B: :C: :D:
	122 :A: :B: :C: :D:	126 :A: :B: :C: :D:	130 :A: :B: :C: :D:
131 :A: :B: :C: :D:	134 :A: :B: :C: :D:	138 :A: :B: :C: :D:	142 :A: :B: :C: :D:
132 :A: :B: :C: :D:	135 :A: :B: :C: :D:	139 :A: :B: :C: :D:	143 :A: :B: :C: :D:
133 :A: :B: :C: :D:	136 :A: :B: :C: :D:	140 :A: :B: :C: :D:	144 :A: :B: :C: :D:
	137 :A: :B: :C: :D:	141 :A: :B: :C: :D:	145 :A: :B: :C: :D:
146 :A: :B: :C: :D:	149 :A: :B: :C: :D:	153 :A: :B: :C: :D:	157 :A: :B: :C: :D:
147 :A: :B: :C: :D:	150 :A: :B: :C: :D:	154 :A: :B: :C: :D:	158 :A: :B: :C: :D:
148 :A: :B: :C: :D:	151 :A: :B: :C: :D:	155 :A: :B: :C: :D:	159 :A: :B: :C: :D:
	152 :A: :B: :C: :D:	156 :A: :B: :C: :D:	160 :A: :B: :C: :D:
161 :A: :B: :C: :D:	164 :A: :B: :C: :D:	168 :A: :B: :C: :D:	172 :A: :B: :C: :D:
162 :A: :B: :C: :D:	165 :A: :B: :C: :D:	169 :A: :B: :C: :D:	173 :A: :B: :C: :D:
163 :A: :B: :C: :D:	166 :A: :B: :C: :D:	170 :A: :B: :C: :D:	174 :A: :B: :C: :D:
	167 :A: :B: :C: :D:	171 :A: :B: :C: :D:	175 :A: :B: :C: :D:
176 :A: :B: :C: :D:	179 :A: :B: :C: :D:	183 :A: :B: :C: :D:	187 :A: :B: :C: :D:
177 :A: :B: :C: :D:	180 :A: :B: :C: :D:	184 :A: :B: :C: :D:	188 :A: :B: :C: :D:
178 :A: :B: :C: :D:	181 :A: :B: :C: :D:	185 :A: :B: :C: :D:	189 :A: :B: :C: :D:
	182 :A: :B: :C: :D:	186 :A: :B: :C: :D:	190 :A: :B: :C: :D:
191 :A: :B: :C: :D:	194 :A: :B: :C: :D:	198 :A: :B: :C: :D:	
192 :A: :B: :C: :D:	195 :A: :B: :C: :D:	199 :A: :B: :C: :D:	
193 :A: :B: :C: :D:	196 :A: :B: :C: :D:	200 :A: :B: :C: :D:	
	197 :A: :B: :C: :D:		

APPRAISER EXAMINATIONS

NAME_____   SESSION   AM ☐   PM ☐

LAST   FIRST   MIDDLE   Enter your
SOC. SEC. #_____ / _____ / _____   IDENT.   EXAM CODE #_____
NUMBER

DATE_____   BOOK#_____

PLACE
OF EXAM_____ SALESMAN ☐ BROKER ☐

TITLE
OF EXAM_____

IMPORTANT: IN MARKING YOUR ANSWERS
FILL IN ANSWER BOX COMPLETELY

	4 :A: :B: :C: :D: :E:	8 :A: :B: :C: :D: :E:	12 :A: :B: :C: :D: :E:
1 :A: :B: :C: :D: :E:	5 :A: :B: :C: :D: :E:	9 :A: :B: :C: :D: :E:	13 :A: :B: :C: :D: :E:
2 :A: :B: :C: :D: :E:	6 :A: :B: :C: :D: :E:	10 :A: :B: :C: :D: :E:	14 :A: :B: :C: :D: :E:
3 :A: :B: :C: :D: :E:	7 :A: :B: :C: :D: :E:	11 :A: :B: :C: :D: :E:	15 :A: :B: :C: :D: :E:
	19 :A: :B: :C: :D: :E:	23 :A: :B: :C: :D: :E:	27 :A: :B: :C: :D: :E:
16 :A: :B: :C: :D: :E:	20 :A: :B: :C: :D: :E:	24 :A: :B: :C: :D: :E:	28 :A: :B: :C: :D: :E:
17 :A: :B: :C: :D: :E:	21 :A: :B: :C: :D: :E:	25 :A: :B: :C: :D: :E:	29 :A: :B: :C: :D: :E:
18 :A: :B: :C: :D: :E:	22 :A: :B: :C: :D: :E:	26 :A: :B: :C: :D: :E:	30 :A: :B: :C: :D: :E:
	34 :A: :B: :C: :D: :E:	38 :A: :B: :C: :D: :E:	42 :A: :B: :C: :D: :E:
31 :A: :B: :C: :D: :E:	35 :A: :B: :C: :D: :E:	39 :A: :B: :C: :D: :E:	43 :A: :B: :C: :D: :E:
32 :A: :B: :C: :D: :E:	36 :A: :B: :C: :D: :E:	40 :A: :B: :C: :D: :E:	44 :A: :B: :C: :D: :E:
33 :A: :B: :C: :D: :E:	37 :A: :B: :C: :D: :E:	41 :A: :B: :C: :D: :E:	45 :A: :B: :C: :D: :E:
	49 :A: :B: :C: :D: :E:	53 :A: :B: :C: :D: :E:	57 :A: :B: :C: :D: :E:
46 :A: :B: :C: :D: :E:	50 :A: :B: :C: :D: :E:	54 :A: :B: :C: :D: :E:	58 :A: :B: :C: :D: :E:
47 :A: :B: :C: :D: :E:	51 :A: :B: :C: :D: :E:	55 :A: :B: :C: :D: :E:	59 :A: :B: :C: :D: :E:
48 :A: :B: :C: :D: :E:	52 :A: :B: :C: :D: :E:	56 :A: :B: :C: :D: :E:	60 :A: :B: :C: :D: :E:
	64 :A: :B: :C: :D: :E:	68 :A: :B: :C: :D: :E:	72 :A: :B: :C: :D: :E:
61 :A: :B: :C: :D: :E:	65 :A: :B: :C: :D: :E:	69 :A: :B: :C: :D: :E:	73 :A: :B: :C: :D: :E:
62 :A: :B: :C: :D: :E:	66 :A: :B: :C: :D: :E:	70 :A: :B: :C: :D: :E:	74 :A: :B: :C: :D: :E:
63 :A: :B: :C: :D: :E:	67 :A: :B: :C: :D: :E:	71 :A: :B: :C: :D: :E:	75 :A: :B: :C: :D: :E:
	79 :A: :B: :C: :D: :E:	83 :A: :B: :C: :D: :E:	87 :A: :B: :C: :D: :E:
76 :A: :B: :C: :D: :E:	80 :A: :B: :C: :D: :E:	84 :A: :B: :C: :D: :E:	88 :A: :B: :C: :D: :E:
77 :A: :B: :C: :D: :E:	81 :A: :B: :C: :D: :E:	85 :A: :B: :C: :D: :E:	89 :A: :B: :C: :D: :E:
78 :A: :B: :C: :D: :E:	82 :A: :B: :C: :D: :E:	86 :A: :B: :C: :D: :E:	90 :A: :B: :C: :D: :E:
	94 :A: :B: :C: :D: :E:	98 :A: :B: :C: :D: :E:	
91 :A: :B: :C: :D: :E:	95 :A: :B: :C: :D: :E:	99 :A: :B: :C: :D: :E:	
92 :A: :B: :C: :D: :E:	96 :A: :B: :C: :D: :E:	100 :A: :B: :C: :D: :E:	
93 :A: :B: :C: :D: :E:	97 :A: :B: :C: :D: :E:		

Photocopy this answers sheet for Appraiser License, Certified Residential Appraiser,
and Certified General Appraiser Examinations.

Index